Taxes and Business Strategy:
A Planning Approach

Myron S. Scholes
Mark A. Wolfson

Stanford University
Graduate School of Business

Prentice Hall
Englewood Cliffs, New Jersey 07632

Editorial/production supervision and interior design: Mia McCroskey
Acquisitions editor: Joseph Heider
Cover design: Bruce Kenselaar
Prepress buyer: Trudy Pisciotti
Manufacturing buyer: Robert Anderson

Printed in the United States of America

10 9 8 7 6 5 4 3 2 1

ISBN 0-13-885740-7

Prentice Hall International (UK) Limited, *London*
Prentice-Hall of Australia Pty. Limited, *Sydney*
Prentice-Hall Canada Inc., *Toronto*
Prentice-Hall Hispanoamericana, S.A., *Mexico*
Prentice-Hall of India Private Limited, *New Delhi*
Prentice-Hall of Japan, Inc., *Tokyo*
Simon & Schuster Asia Pte. Ltd., *Singapore*
Editora Prentice-Hall do Brasil, Ltda., *Rio de Janeiro*

To Anne, Sara, Laura, Charlie, and Sheila
with love and appreciation

Contents

xiv
Contents

Preface

The field of tax research is undergoing dramatic changes. This is partially attributable to the rapid changes in tax laws, most notably the 1986 Tax Act, that render traditional approaches to tax education (which rely heavily on imparting current tax rules) such a transitory learning experience. In addition, given the increasing reality of a global economy, restricting attention to U.S. tax rules is simply inadequate. Of more lasting relevance is a framework that provides a way to analyze how tax rules affect decision making. Managers must understand how changes in tax rules influence the behavior of their customers, their employees, their suppliers, and their competitors, to avoid operating at a competitive disadvantage. This, in turn, has consequences for how current tax rules affect taxpayers' economic balance sheets.

It is our experience that researchers, students, policy makers, and practitioners alike come to appreciate the value of learning a microeconomic theory of tax planning. They enjoy coming to understand the concepts that they can bring to bear in thinking about how tax rules affect decision making and how these concepts are brought to life in real-world situations. Our objective is to equip readers with the ability to adapt quickly to the ever-changing set of tax rules they confront, and to improve their accuracy in predicting how the economic environment will change under alternative tax regimes.

Throughout the book we build on a conceptual framework, bringing it to life by applying it to a multitude of practical problems. We use many institutional examples and incorporate tax rules to illustrate the concepts. The book covers many applied topics in an attempt to showcase the richness of the framework. Some of the illustrations we use are based deliberately on tax rules that have been changed, and others use current tax rules that are certain to change in the future. Our purpose here is two-fold: we wish to explain how tax rules affect observed institutional arrangements, but we also wish to illustrate how the conceptual framework can be used to predict the effects of changes in tax rules. And when current tax rules appear to create behavior that tax policy makers might find objectionable, we warn that changes in the rules might be on the horizon.

It is not our intention to write a "how to" book that practitioners can use to beat the tax system. Such a book is too short-lived for our tastes. Why, you might ask, if we didn't plan to make money by explaining to others how to beat the taxing authority, did we write this book? There are many reasons. First, we were able to combine our research and teaching in a way that was very meaningful to us. We have always felt that the best teaching from both the professors' and the students' viewpoints arises when research and teaching are complementary activities. Second, when we initially tried to teach this course, we couldn't find a book that came close to covering material in a manner or with the breadth that we sought.

The first time we taught some of the material covered in this book, we had no clear agenda or vision. We taught the course largely as a collection of topics. We attempted to bring a general set of microeconomic tools to bear on the analysis of particular tax planning problems. After the course was finished, we realized that we hadn't really provided a unifying framework that could be applied to all the problems that we covered.

The next time we taught the course, we concentrated on developing a conceptual framework. The topics then became applications to illustrate the basic framework. This proved to be far more satisfactory, and it greatly accelerated the rate at which we were able to solve various tax planning problems. We decided to write this book when we discovered that the framework we had developed allowed us to analyze a broad set of these problems in a systematic way that led to conclusions differing from those we read in the popular press, in journals, and in texts. We became enthusiastic about sharing the framework with others.

We completed 27 chapters for the first edition of this book. This includes 9 conceptual chapters and 18 applications chapters. We have plans to complete more applications chapters, but we first plan to write research papers on these topics before adapting them for the book. Chapters that we hope to add in the future include those on compliance and audit strategies; the political economy of tax laws; tax planning for closely-held business enterprises; and the many uses of partnerships. We have also contemplated additional chapters on financial service firms such as banks, insurance companies, and other financial institutions, as well as tax planning for firms facing financial distress. We have not, however, omitted these topics from the book. Rather, they are incorporated throughout.

You needn't be a tax expert to benefit from this book. Frankly, we aren't, at least compared to some of the "black belts" we know. But we also believe we have much to say to tax experts as well as novices. Knowledge of a little algebra will help, because we build algebraic models to illustrate and apply the concepts.

Each chapter of the book closes with a summary of the key points, discussion questions, and some more challenging questions and problems. An instructor's manual for teachers using the book is available, which includes supplementary materials to facilitate class presentations.

Acknowledgments

We are indebted to a long list of students, colleagues, and associates for helping us with this project. We would like to thank the Graduate School of Business at Stanford University and the foresight of its deans, Robert Jaedicke and Charles Holloway, for supporting our efforts to establish a new course at the business school on how taxes affect business decisions—a course founded on a research tradition. Prior to our developing a new course, the business school offered a popular rules-oriented tax course taught by a talented practitioner. We must thank our first few students who dared to sign up for that first class. Our greatest compliment from the students of that first class was how they enjoyed seeing us argue with one another about the right way to solve various tax-planning problems. In this respect, the material in this book is literally "battle-tested." These and later students provided invaluable feedback and constructive criticism. They know who they are and how important they were to the quality of the book. Numerous doctoral students were also of tremendous help. Special thanks go to Mark Mazur, Uri Ronnen, Mary Lea McEnally, Eric Terry, Eunsang Lee, Matthew Richardson, Richard Stanton, and Jamie Alexander.

We must also thank our colleagues at Stanford. In particular, Pete Wilson, now at the Harvard Business School, was extraordinarily helpful in pointing out aspects of the material that were unclear or misleading. He greatly improved the presentation of the material in most of the first 17 chapters. Other Stanford colleagues that deserve special thanks include Jim Patell, Paul Pfleiderer, and Jeremy Bulow at the Graduate School of Business, and Ronald Gilson of the Stanford Law School who gave us valuable comments on Chapters Twenty-Three through Twenty-Six.

Another scholar that we must thank is Patric Hendershott, for providing detailed and influential comments on Chapters Twenty-One and Twenty-Two. We are also indebted to our colleagues whose research, teachings, and advice influenced the development of the book. In particular we wish to thank Ray Sommerfeld, Merton Miller, Joe Stiglitz, Walter Blum, and Michael Brennan for their invaluable assistance.

We are grateful to Ernst and Young for generous research support, and we thank them for sponsoring several summer tax conferences that allowed us to bring together a group of talented professors each summer to discuss and refine the material in the text. In particular we thank Bill Duncan of Ernst and Young for his enthusiastic support. We would also like to thank the participants of these Stanford Summer Tax Conferences for their invaluable comments on the book. Special thanks go to John Elliott, Leonard Goodman, Amy Dunbar, Alan MacNaughton, Jeff Gramlich, Katherine Schipper, Richard Sansing, Dan Dhaliwal, Walter O'Connor, Wayne Shaw, Robert McDonald, Ed Outslay, and Dan Subotnik.

We would also like to thank the National Bureau of Economic Research, and Martin Feldstein and James Poterba, for encouraging us to present our material at a summer colloquium for National Bureau researchers. They also contributed significantly to the development of several chapters. We received many excellent suggestions from the discussants and the participants of the Bureau workshop. In particular, we would like to thank Alan Auerbach, Oliver Hart, Joel Slemrod, Larry Summers, and David Bradford for their insightful comments.

Nancy Banks deserves special recognition for pushing us to get the book out and for doing such a tremendous job in producing the book, from typing, to proofing, to editing, to interacting with the publisher, to being extremely helpful in the design of the book itself. We deeply appreciate her efforts on our behalf. Finally, our thanks to Mia McCroskey for her editorial assistance and to Joe Heider at Prentice Hall for his support and guidance.

Myron S. Scholes
Mark A. Wolfson

CHAPTER 1
Introduction

Our broadest objective in this book is to provide you with a framework that is useful for thinking about how taxes affect business activities. Although we will not stress it very often, we also hope that it becomes apparent that the framework is equally applicable to the analysis of how the conduct of business is affected by many other regulatory policies. Examples of such other regulatory policies include international trade agreements, monetary policy, rate regulation for public utilities, currency restrictions, regulation of the securities markets, the banking industry, and the pharmaceutical industry, and a host of other government programs not reflected in the tax law, such as agricultural subsidies.

The framework we develop is highly integrative: investment strategies and financing policies within firms are linked through taxes. That is, the investments that a firm undertakes depend on the ways in which they are financed. In addition, financing decisions depend on the investments that the firm undertakes. By investments we mean not only the actively-managed assets the firm uses to run its business but also passive assets such as bonds, stocks, and direct investments in other entities. Our approach differs from that of others in that much of our focus is on the evolving strategies applicable to existing firms. These firms make incremental investment and financing decisions that depend, in part, on past investment and financing decisions. New strategies depend on past strategies because it is costly to adjust investment and financing decisions once they have been made. From this brief introduction, it is obvious that we take a rather broad look at what we call the economic balance sheets of firms and the factors that affect firms' asset and financing positions.

1.1 Why Do Tax Rules Influence Investment Decisions?

Tax rules affect the before-tax rates of return on assets. We explain why some firms select investments with high before-tax rates of return while others select assets with low before-tax rates of return even when both types of investments are available to all firms. By before-tax rate of return, we mean the rate of return earned from investing in an asset before any taxes are paid to domestic and foreign federal, state, and local taxing authorities. On the assets side of the ledger, we make much of the fact that before-tax rates of return differ because (1) the returns to different types of assets are taxed differently, (2) the returns to similar assets are taxed differently if they are located in different tax jurisdictions, (3) the returns to similar assets located in the same tax jurisdiction are taxed differently if they are held through different legal organizational forms (such as a corporation versus a sole proprietorship), and (4) the returns to similar assets located in the same tax jurisdiction and held through the same legal organizational form are taxed differently depending upon such factors as: (i) the operating history of the organization, (ii) the returns to other assets held by the organization, and (iii) the particular characteristics of the individual owners of the organization.

Tax rules also influence the financing decisions of firms through their effect on the cost of financing the firms' activities. A firm is said to make a "capital structure decision" when it decides how it will finance its activities. The capital structure of a firm is composed of various types of ownership claims, some of which are called debt and others of which are called equity. We emphasize that the cost of issuing a capital structure instrument depends on the tax treatment it is accorded, which, in turn, depends on whether the instrument (1) is *debt*, *equity*, or a *hybrid*, (2) is issued to an *employee*, a *customer*, a *related party*, a *bank*, or any one of a number of other special classes of suppliers of capital, and (3) is issued by a corporation, a partnership, or some other legal organizational form. It also depends upon the tax jurisdiction in which the capital structure instrument is issued.

1.2 Structure and Themes of the Book

This book contains two parts. In the first part, we develop the fundamental concepts that represent the building blocks of our framework. Then we consider how this framework can be applied to specific decision settings.

Three key themes run throughout the building block chapters:

1. Effective tax planning requires the planner to consider the tax implications of a proposed transaction for all of the parties to the transaction.
2. Effective tax planning requires the planner, in making investment and financing decisions, to consider not only explicit taxes (tax dollars paid directly to taxing authorities) but also implicit taxes (taxes that are paid indirectly in the form of lower before-tax rates of return on tax-favored investments).
3. Effective tax planning requires the planner to recognize that taxes represent only one among many business costs, and all costs must be

considered in the planning process: to be implemented, some proposed tax plans may require exceedingly costly restructuring of the business.

Traditional approaches to tax planning fail to recognize that **effective tax planning** and **tax minimization** are very different things. The reason is that in a world of costly contracting, implementation of tax-minimizing strategies may introduce significant costs along *nontax* dimensions. Therefore, the tax-minimization strategy may be undesirable. After all, a particularly easy way to avoid paying taxes is to avoid investing in profitable ventures.

We view efficient tax planning as part of the larger problem of the efficient design of organizations. In developing this organizational design theme, we adopt a **contractual perspective**. Contracts specify the rights of various parties to make decisions and to receive cash flows in differing circumstances. We focus on how the tax-related cash flows specified by contracts affect the prices at which assets are traded. We further stress how these cash flows affect the ways in which production is organized by business units.

A Planning Approach

As the subtitle of the book suggests, we adopt a planning approach to taxes and business strategy. More precisely, we adopt a *global* planning approach. The key themes we have just described suggest that there are four ways in which we do this. First and most obvious is the geographical dimension: effective tax planning exploits differences in tax circumstances across different taxpayers, both domestically and internationally. Here we adopt a global perspective in a geographical sense.

The other three global hooks into our framework relate to each of the three themes that run throughout the book:

- multinational approach: *all* contracting parties must be taken into account in tax planning. This is a global, rather than a unilateral, approach.
- importance of hidden taxes: *all* taxes must be taken into account. We are interested in a global measure of taxes, not simply explicit taxes.
- importance of nontax costs: *all* costs of business must be considered, not just tax costs.

Taxing Authority as Investment Partner

All of the interesting problems in tax planning arise because, from the standpoint of individual taxpaying entities, the taxing authority is an uninvited party to all contracts. The taxing authority brings to each of its "forced" ventures with taxpayers a set of contractual terms (tax rules). Unlike other contracting parties, the taxing authority does not negotiate these terms separately for each venture. Such a policy would simply be too expensive. Instead, it announces a standard set of terms by which taxpayers must live. In addition, although the taxing authority claims a partnership interest in taxpayer profits, it exercises no voting rights. Nor does it engage in direct monitoring of taxpayer performance to determine whether taxpayers are violating the contractual terms. Of course, the taxing authority does conduct random audits. Moreover, being a partner in all firms enables the taxing authority to determine when taxpayers are reporting results far out of line with what other taxpayers are reporting in similar situations.

The specific contractual rules that the taxing authority imposes on its joint venturers (the Tax Code) results from a variety of socioeconomic forces. Among other things, taxes are designed to (1) finance public projects (such as national defense and a legal system that enforces property rights in most tax jurisdictions), (2) redistribute wealth (high income individuals pay tax at higher rates than do low income individuals), and (3) encourage a variety of economic activities that are deemed to be in the public interest.

From a social policy standpoint, tax rules are most controversial when they are designed to discriminate among different economic activities. Success is achieved when the rules subsidize those activities for which the benefits to society as a whole exceed the private benefits to the individuals engaging directly in the activities. But this desirable outcome is by no means guaranteed. It is possible that special tax favors are bestowed undeservedly on taxpayers that mount successful lobbying efforts. Indeed, one might view the Tax Reform Act of 1986 in the U.S. as a movement away from using tax rules to encourage particular activities.

For better or for worse, tax-favored treatment is granted to a variety of activities by taxing authorities around the world. Common examples include the favorable treatment accorded charitable organizations and educational institutions, energy-related investments, research and development activities, agricultural production, investments in productive equipment, foreign export activities, retirement-oriented savings vehicles, and entrepreneurial risk-taking activities.

Noble as the objectives listed earlier might be, any tax system designed to achieve a variety of social goals inevitably provides considerable private incentives to engage in tax planning. Any tax system that seeks both to redistribute wealth as well as subsidize certain economic activities gives rise to a system of marginal tax rates that may vary widely from one contracting party to the next, for a given contracting party over time, and for a given contracting party over different economic activities.

The vast majority of taxpayers around the world pay no more tax than they believe they must. And nontrivial resources are spent to arrange their affairs in a way that keeps the tax bite as painless as possible. It is precisely this fact that provides tax policy with so much potential as a means of achieving a variety of social goals.

To illustrate, consider the case of low-income housing that U.S. citizens, through their elected representatives, have chosen to subsidize for many years through various tax benefits. If taxpayers were not responsive to these tax incentives (and refused to build low-income housing to garner the tax benefits), subsidizing low-income housing through tax policy would be infeasible. Instead, the government would have to enter on the expenditure side, engaging directly in the construction and management of the low-income housing itself. Both tax subsidies and direct government expenditures to increase the supply of low-income housing generate deadweight costs. This suggests that we must be careful in criticizing tax loopholes and tax subsidies if we desire to achieve our social objectives. The direct government expenditure alternative may be far more costly than a tax system that favors private construction of the properties.

While the deadweight costs associated with time spent in tax planning may seem socially wasteful, the relevant question is how much waste would exist using alternative means to achieve the same social goals. In other words, how does the net benefit of the altered economic activity brought about by the tax system compare with the benefits of the next best alternative? Obviously, if we could implement social policy through a mechanism that would result in the absence of any waste, we would do so, but this is not a realistic goal.

Tax planning (or tax avoidance, as it is sometimes more pejoratively labelled) has long earned the blessing of the U.S. courts. For example, in a famous 1947 court opinion, Judge Learned Hand wrote (and similar statements appear in official documents of other countries as well):

> "Over and over again courts have said that there is nothing sinister in so arranging one's affairs as to keep taxes as low as possible. Everybody does so, rich or poor, and all do right, for nobody owes any public duty to pay more than the law demands: taxes are enforced exactions, not voluntary contributions. To demand more in the name of morals is mere cant."

(Commissioner v. Newman, 159 F.2d 848 (CA-2, 1947))

The Importance of a Contractual Perspective

Morality issues aside, let us now return to the first of the three key themes that run throughout the building block chapters: namely, that to organize production at minimum cost requires that the tax positions of all parties to the contract be considered, both at the time of contracting and in the future. Among other things, this observation exposes the naiveté of distinguishing between business tax planning and personal tax planning, or of tax planning for one type of business in isolation from tax planning for all other types of business.

For example, as we will see in later chapters, it is costly to prescribe an effective compensation policy for a firm without simultaneously conducting some sort of personal tax planning analysis for each of its employees. Similarly, it is costly to prescribe an effective capital structure policy for a firm (that is, determining whether operations should be financed with debt, preferred stock, common stock, or other financial instruments) without simultaneously considering how the returns to prospective lenders and shareholders of the firm will be taxed.

To be more concrete, consider the decision as to whether business equipment should be bought or leased. In the U.S., as in most countries around the world, the government encourages capital investment by permitting rapid depreciation on buildings, equipment, and machinery. That is, the business can deduct the cost of the investment from its taxable income using a schedule in which the write-off rate exceeds the rate of economic depreciation of the investment. Alternatively, if a business entity rented plant and equipment over its economic life, the rental payments could be deducted only as they are made during this period. The present value of rental deductions is often far less than the present value of depreciation deductions.

We cannot conclude, however, that owning assets minimizes the taxes of all firms using machinery and equipment in their businesses. Once we analyze the tax positions of both low tax-bracket and high tax-bracket taxpayers, we might find low tax-bracket taxpayers better off passing up tax savings and renting. The reason is that low tax-bracket and high tax-bracket businesses will find it desirable to enter into a contract that arranges property rights so that the low tax-bracket businesses effectively sell their tax benefits to high tax-bracket businesses. This is accomplished by reducing the rental rate to the low tax-bracket taxpayer in exchange for the right to take rapid depreciation, for tax purposes, on the equipment.

Implicit Taxes and Tax Clienteles

The leasing example illustrates two very important principles to which we will return time and time again throughout the text:

- implicit taxes and
- tax clienteles.

Implicit taxes arise because the before-tax investment returns available on tax-favored assets are less than those available on tax-disfavored assets. In the example above, a reduction in the rental rate is required to induce renters to forego the tax benefits of ownership, and this decreases the pre-tax investment return garnered by property lessors. Another common example is the reduced yield available on tax-exempt municipal bonds in the U.S. relative to taxable corporate bonds of equal risk. Here, the reduced yield represents a form of tax that is paid to the issuing municipalities rather than to the Federal government.

The concept of **tax clienteles** is closely related to that of implicit taxes. Tax clienteles arise because of cross-sectional differences in tax rates. Certain taxpayers are more likely than others to own various kinds of assets or to organize production in particular ways. Examples of tax clienteles are high tax-bracket taxpayers who are more likely to hold tax-exempt municipal bonds rather than taxable corporate bonds and who are more likely to be lessors and owners of depreciable equipment rather than lessees.

As we will discover throughout the book, implicit taxes and tax clienteles are pervasive. Every topic we cover will be an application of one or both of these principles.

1.3 Topics Covered in this Book

Having outlined some of the major themes of the book, let us provide some indication of how the book develops. In the next chapter, we cover some fundamentals on the structure and evolution of tax laws, including a discussion of the legislative process through which tax law changes are made in the U.S. This material is important if we are to acquire an appreciation for current and future tax rule uncertainty. Then in Chapters Three and Four, we illustrate how *identical production and investment strategies* can be undertaken through a variety of *different legal organizational forms*, each of which is taxed very differently. We go on to show how the after-tax returns from investing through some organizational forms dominate the returns from investing through other organizational forms.

In Chapter Five, we focus on *different investments* undertaken within a *given organization*. Differences in the tax treatment of investment returns give rise to implicit taxes that bring after-tax returns of these differentially-taxed assets into closer alignment with one another.

In Chapter Six, we demonstrate that when there are no costs to implementing certain tax-planning strategies, the availability of alternative legal organizational forms and investment projects that are taxed differently provides an opportunity to eliminate all income taxes through simple arbitrage techniques (generating positive after-tax returns by buying one asset while simultaneously selling another asset with neither investment cost nor risk). In addition, we show that when there are no costs to implementing certain tax-planning strategies, differentially-taxed assets force all taxpayers in the economy to pay taxes on their last dollar of income at identical tax rates, no matter how wealthy they are and no matter how progressive the legislated tax rate schedule is. Again, the availability of simple arbitrage techniques ensures this outcome. A corollary here is that there will be no distinct tax clienteles. At the margin, all taxpayers will be indifferent to whether they hold tax-favored or tax-disfavored investments.

But these results have miserable predictive power. Even the most casual of empiricists can confirm two counter-factual propositions: (1) the government does indeed collect substantial sums of tax revenues and (2) taxpayers do not all face the same marginal tax rate; tax clienteles not only exist, they are pervasive.

Obviously, some important economic forces have been omitted from the analysis in the first six chapters. In Chapter Seven we incorporate the importance of *frictions* and *restrictions*. By frictions we mean transaction costs incurred in the marketplace that make implementation of certain tax-planning strategies costly. By restrictions, we mean restraints imposed by the taxing authority that prevent taxpayers from using certain tax arbitrage techniques to reduce taxes in socially undesirable ways.

It is these frictions and restrictions that make the potential returns to tax planning so high. Once certain tax-planning strategies have been implemented, they may be very costly to reverse or change as economic circumstances, including the tax rules themselves, change.

We complete the development of the conceptual framework in Chapters Eight and Nine by exploring tax planning in the presence of (1) differentially taxed assets, (2) market frictions and tax rule restrictions, and (3) uncertainty concerning pre-tax investment returns and tax rules.

In the second part of the book, the concepts developed in the first nine chapters are applied to a variety of organizational settings. We begin in Chapters Ten, Eleven, and Twelve with compensation and pension planning, where we emphasize the importance of considering the tax consequences of compensation alternatives to both the employer *and* the employee. We also stress the importance of nontax factors in designing efficient compensation policies. Chapter Twelve, which is devoted to employee stock ownership plans (ESOPs), evaluates whether the recent proliferation of employee stock ownership plans in U.S. corporations can be attributed to their tax or incentive features. Our analysis suggests that a more likely explanation for the explosive growth of ESOPs is their effectiveness as a weapon against hostile takeovers.

We then add a crucial dimension to the tax-planning problem by introducing different tax jurisdictions, which leads us to the subject of multinational tax planning. Chapters Thirteen and Fourteen cover this important topic, and we augment this material in a number of later chapters.

In multinational businesses, a given taxpayer may face different tax rates in different tax jurisdictions. Such a taxpayer may have an incentive to enter into transactions that transfer income out of highly taxed pockets and into modestly taxed pockets in the same pair of trousers. But one needn't own pants with differentially taxed pockets to exploit differences in tax rates across taxpayers. Unrelated taxpayers facing different tax rates can also contract with one another to shift taxable income from those facing high tax rates to those facing low tax rates.

In Chapter Fifteen, we address these issues in the context of capital structure decisions. Here we see that taxes encourage two kinds of marriages between firms and capital suppliers: those between high-tax-rate firms and low-tax-rate capital suppliers and those between low-tax-rate firms and high-tax-rate capital suppliers. Moreover, the kinds of financial instruments issued in the two relationships are very different. This chapter also emphasizes that financing decisions cannot be made without simultaneously considering the tax characteristics of the assets' side of the firm's balance sheet.

Chapter Sixteen applies the discussion in Chapter Fifteen to a particular set of firms: commercial banks. Here we present empirical evidence of tax clienteles and of the importance of nontax factors in tax planning for a homogeneous set of firms.

Chapter Seventeen continues in the empirical vein by presenting evidence on the magnitude of implicit taxes for certain types of assets. It also considers the balance sheet structure of start-up companies and the restructuring behavior of seasoned firms that experience tax-loss carryforwards. Relative to the empirical evidence on commercial banks, the analysis here is based on more firm-specific considerations.

In Chapter Eighteen, we consider the degree to which debt financing can be used to eliminate corporate-level taxes so that corporate income will be subjected to only one level of taxation, that at the shareholder level. We also consider the degree to which debt financing of foreign operations can be used to avoid high levels of taxation on foreign income.

In Chapters Nineteen and Twenty, we turn to a discussion of how ownership rights in investments are repackaged through organizational arrangements to achieve both tax and nontax objectives. Chapter Nineteen focuses on tax-sheltered investments and Chapter Twenty considers financial assets. We describe a number of legal organizational forms that have arisen to effect a repackaging of claims to both tax deductions and different types of taxable (and nontaxable) income. The tax shelter chapter concentrates on implicit taxes and tax clienteles associated with tax-favored investments. It also emphasizes the inevitable incentive problems that arise when unrelated parties enter into contracts in which one party takes actions or makes decisions on behalf of others who have less information. The chapter on repackaging ownership rights to financial assets illustrates how dramatically the creation of new financial instruments can alter the set of effective tax-planning strategies. It also illustrates how difficult it can be to implement desired tax policy in a global capital market when tax rules vary across different tax jurisdictions.

Chapters Twenty-One and Twenty-Two consider how the repackaging of claims to various components of income and deductions can be effected for real estate, a particularly important category of assets. Here we emphasize how taxes affect not only the manner in which real estate is legally held and financed, but also how tax planning affects such aspects of real estate management as *when to sell* assets as well as the *manner* in which the sale should take place. The ideas developed here represent the core concepts required to evaluate the tax benefits of such corporate restructurings as mergers and acquisitions.

We then consider tax-planning strategies for *collections* of assets (firms or divisions). Chapters Twenty-Three through Twenty-Six are devoted to corporate reorganizations and restructurings. Among the distinctive features of these chapters is the analysis we conduct and the evidence we present on how changes in tax laws during the 1980s have affected merger and acquisition activity as well as divestitures. We also demonstrate how the tax rules pertaining to preservation of tax attributes (like net operating loss carryforwards) following corporate reorganizations can be used as defensive weapons to discourage hostile take-overs. We further model the value of such tax attributes to current owners and prospective buyers. Our analysis in these merger and acquisition chapters is enlivened by a description of relevant experiences of a number of corporations.

In Chapter Twenty-Seven, our final chapter, we emphasize the importance of integrating estate and gift tax-planning considerations into the income tax-planning problem. We consider the degree to which tax laws encourage both charitable and noncharitable gifts. Moreover, we assess the extent to which charitable transfers are encouraged relative to noncharitable transfers. We further analyze the trade-offs between lifetime transfers of wealth and bequests. We find interesting parallels between this problem and the repatriation problems faced by multinational corporations. As in most of the other applications chapters, we pay considerable attention to the nontax aspects of the tax planning problem.

1.4 Intended Audience for this Book

We can identify two broad categories of users for whom this book is appropriate:

1. tax planners (those who wish to avoid being beaten by other tax planners and by social planners) and
2. social planners (those who wish to participate in the design of effective social policies, while at the same time avoid being beaten by other social planners and by tax planners).

We believe that a course built around the ideas developed in this book differs fundamentally from those offered in other business schools, law schools, and economics programs. Such courses tend to be of two types: (1) tax policy-oriented, where the objective is to explore macroeconomic effects of existing or proposed tax systems or (2) tax law-oriented, where the concern is either with principles of tax laws and judicial doctrines or primarily with the details of the tax rules themselves and ways to minimize taxes for a given set of transactions, rather than planning which transactions ought to take place.

Our book falls into neither of these camps. We develop neither a macro-tax-policy approach nor a transactional-tax-law approach. Instead we adopt a *micro*economic perspective. Our interest is in the implications of tax rules for individual and firm behavior.

Similarly, our primary goals are neither to evaluate the welfare effects of various tax rules, nor to provide narrow training to exploit "tax loopholes." Unfortunately, many business-school tax courses are viewed by their customers as aspiring to achieve the latter of these objectives. For example, on December 23, 1985, the *Wall Street Journal* published an editorial written by two Harvard MBA students entitled "What They *Do* Teach You at Harvard Biz". It begins:

> We matriculated in Harvard Business School with the belief that our education was to prepare us to attain three goals: to become leaders in society, successful general business managers and wealthy individuals. In addition, however, we have discovered that a large portion of the school's curriculum is devoted to preparing us to both understand and 'beat' the U.S. tax system.

Later in the editorial, reflecting on a class in their Entrepreneurial Management course that covered the topic of "Tax Factors in Business Decisions," they write:

> It is clear that we had learned nothing that day that would make us better leaders. We might have learned how to be more successful businessmen and wealthy individuals, but certainly not through any creation of wealth. We had merely spent another day learning how to beat Uncle Sam. As we looked at our real-estate homework for the next day, with its tax shelters, sale-leasebacks, and depreciation recapture rules, we realized that tomorrow would be more of the same.

If after reading this book you come away with feelings similar to those expressed in the editorial, we will be quite disappointed. It is true that we will occasionally appear to take much pleasure in describing clever tax-planning techniques. And while our objective is certainly *not* to teach you how to "beat" the tax system, we will occasionally provide you with the tools necessary to build better organizational mousetraps wherein taxes play an important role. But this means that we are providing you with the tools to evaluate whether the tax system is meeting its various legislative objectives without giving rise to excessive distortions in economic activity. And perhaps most important, we hope that you will come away from reading this book recognizing that our framework applies to far broader issues than simply how one factors taxes into business decisions.

In light of the major tax law changes introduced by the Tax Reform Act of 1986, you may well ask, "What is the half-life of the knowledge gained by investing time to read and to understand this book?" To make matters worse, the Tax Reform Act of 1986 is unusual only in the *degree* of change it introduced into the U.S. Tax Code; Congressional bills that introduce major changes in tax rules are by no means unusual. In fact, they have been the rule rather than the exception over the past quarter of a century: Congress passed bills that changed the Tax Code in 20 of the 25 years preceding the 1986 restructuring. And we can assure you that the 1986 bill is *not* the bill to end all tax bills, as we have already seen in the years following this act. We will see many more legislative changes in the years to come. Moreover, it is naive to restrict attention to changes in tax laws in a given tax jurisdiction. For example, every time any country changes its tax regime, it changes the terms of trade faced by U.S. investors. Once we recognize this, we realize that many changes in tax rules take place every year both in the U.S. and abroad.

For these reasons, tax books and related tax courses that stress mastery of current tax rules become obsolete rather quickly. Absent a framework to determine the implications of the rules for business decisions, the knowledge gained in a rules-oriented course represents little more than accumulated trivia. This is precisely what led us to develop this book. We think that the basic tool-kit we will be sharing with you is appropriate to deal with virtually any tax regime we are likely to experience in the future. Moreover, we believe that these tools are as appropriately used to study non-U.S. taxes as they are to study U.S. taxes.

All changes in tax regimes involve turning two kinds of dials:

- levels of tax rates and
- relative tax rates:
  - across different tax paying units,
  - across different tax periods for the same taxpayer, and
  - across different economic activities for the same taxpayers and same time period.

Our framework is designed to deal with just such differences. And our intent is to make you leaders rather than followers in understanding how business activities inevitably become reorganized as the rules of the game evolve.

We should also emphasize that while this is not a rules-oriented book, you will still learn a good deal about current tax rules. This will be necessary for three reasons: (1) to breathe life into the basic framework by providing illustrations, (2) to test the basic framework's ability to explain economic activities that are going on around us, and (3) to help you to apply the basic framework to specific decision contexts that many of you now face or will be facing in short order.

Summary of Key Points

1. Tax rules are pervasive in their effect on the investment and financing decisions of businesses.

2. Since it is costly to recontract, investment and financing decisions that have been made in the past influence current and future investment and financing decisions.

3. Tax rules influence investment and financing decisions because they affect the before-tax rates of return on investment and financing alternatives. More highly explicitly taxed investments require higher before-tax rates of return compared to alternatives that bear low explicit taxes. Investment and financing alternatives that face low explicit taxes (due to favored treatment under the tax law) bear high implicit taxes.

4. Firms that find themselves with low marginal tax rates are encouraged by the tax system to contract with firms that face high marginal tax rates. For example, the firm with a higher marginal tax rate will find that by acquiring high implicitly taxed assets, it will be in its proper investment clientele. Similarly, the low-tax firm will find that by issuing assets that bear high implicit taxes, it will be in its proper financing clientele.

5. All of these tax-planning actions are tempered by the nontax costs of achieving tax savings.

6. Effective tax planning requires that consideration be given to (i) the tax implications of a proposed transaction to all parties of the contract, (ii) explicit taxes, implicit taxes, and tax clienteles, and (iii) the costs of implementing various tax-planning strategies.

Discussion Questions

1. Why is tax minimization different from efficient tax planning?

2. Under what circumstances should social planners encourage taxpayers to engage in costly tax planning?

3. Give five examples of investments that bear high implicit taxes. Who should undertake these investments? Do they?

4. Which of the following statements accurately describes an efficient tax plan?

    a. High-tax-bracket investors should invest in municipal bonds.

    b. It is rarely a good strategy to pay explicit taxes.

    c. Renting durable business assets is more efficient than owning for low-tax-rate investors.

    d. Employees prefer to defer receipt of their compensation (assuming this succeeds in postponing the recognition of taxable income) whenever they expect their tax rates to fall in the future.

CHAPTER 2
Tax Rule Uncertainty and Judicial Doctrines

In the introductory chapter, we discussed how the tax system seeks to achieve a variety of social goals and how this naturally gives rise to:

- tax rates varying across different economic activities,
- tax rates varying across different individual taxpaying units, and
- tax rates varying for a given taxpaying unit over time.

These differential tax rates, in turn, provide strong incentives for taxpayers to engage in tax planning. These incentives are the key ingredients that allow the tax system to be used to implement desired social policy.[1]

A problem with this approach, however, is that tax rules adopted for the purpose of achieving certain social goals are generally *overinclusive*; that is, the rules themselves encourage some taxpayers to exploit their ambiguity and, as a result, lead to some socially *un*desirable economic activity. The response to overinclusiveness is to fine-tune the tax system. In particular, when taxpayers have gone "too far" in their efforts to avoid taxes, the Congress or the Treasury (or both) fight back by establishing legislative restrictions (tax bills), judicial restrictions (court cases), or administrative guidelines on what taxpayers can do.[2]

---

[1] This is admittedly a rather rosy view of the tax system. We adopt this perspective at this stage more for pedagogical convenience than for descriptive validity. We acknowledge that private parties have incentives to seek legislation that is beneficial to them, even if it leads to reduced social welfare. We do not mean to deny the existence of legislative "capture" on the part of certain groups of taxpayers, even when the public debate takes on a "public interest" melody.

[2] Of course, legislative changes are designed to do much more than simply plug tax loopholes that have become technologically feasible. Congress also uses them to change the distribution of wealth in the economy or to change the degree to which certain economic activities are subsidized in light of changes in the economy.

To combat socially undesirable tax planning, Congress imposes two classes of restrictions. These include (1) very broad restrictions that apply to a great variety of transactions, and (2) very specific restrictions that respond to particular abuses of the tax system.

Of course, Congress must be careful not to impose *too* many restrictions or to make enforcement of the rules *too* uncertain. Tax rule and enforcement uncertainty may discourage precisely the transactions that Congress wishes to encourage. In other words, *restrictions* can be overinclusive as well.

Moreover, the costs associated with imposing many specific restrictions can be quite high. These include (1) legislative costs, such as the cost of elected representatives and their research and administrative staffs, the cost of lobbyists, and the cost to the general public of becoming informed so that they can participate in the legislative process, and (2) compliance costs that increase with the complexity of the tax system, and which in turn are increasing as the number of restrictions increase.

Life would be simple, indeed, if tax rules were unambiguous. But tax rules, like all other areas of the law, are far from clear. Even if you could claim to have committed to memory the entire Internal Revenue Code, you would be able to resolve only a small degree of ambiguity in how a tax return should be prepared. As technically detailed as the Tax Code may seem to be, it still contains rules that are far too general to indicate clearly how particular transactions are to be taxed.

As a result, the inherent ambiguity in the tax law gives rise to numerous disputes between taxpayers and the taxing authority, since these parties have opposing interests regarding the assessment of tax liabilities. This in turn gives rise to the active involvement of the judicial branch of government (the court system) to resolve disputes. And as disputes are resolved by the courts, the tax rules take on greater and greater detail; that is, the courts help to interpret the rules.

Contrary to the incessant calls for system overhaul that we commonly read about in the press, our current tax system is unlikely to change in *structure* very dramatically. Consider an alternative system in which rules exist for each and every type of transaction. The scope of the rule-writing problem becomes obvious when we consider that taxpayers may enter into an infinite variety of contracts. Determining how the tax laws apply to each possible contractual arrangement would be prohibitively expensive. Instead, we adopt a more sensible approach. We codify the general rules and allow the courts, or negotiation between taxpayers and the taxing authority, to resolve ambiguities on an *exception* basis.

We can make the tax system simple only if we abandon using it as a means of achieving desired social policies. In fact, the Tax Act of 1986 is a clear move in this direction. Many tax rule changes brought about by this major piece of legislation were designed to "level the playing field," so to speak; that is, they removed or reduced tax subsidies for certain economic activities. But as we mentioned earlier, it is not obvious that these changes are desirable, since the alternative means of implementing policy may well be both more costly and less effective.

In this chapter, we consider some of the difficulties associated with using the tax system to achieve social goals. In particular, we identify a few classes of tax-planning games that aggressive taxpayers might naturally be inclined to play, and we will provide examples of the *broad restrictions* that are imposed when such tax-planning games lead to socially undesirable outcomes.

Then, after introducing a few more concepts in the next several chapters, we elaborate on the importance of more specific tax-rule restrictions. In subsequent chapters, where we consider how transaction and information costs affect taxpayers' abilities to engage in socially unacceptable tax planning, we will see that the Congress need not impose as many tax rule restrictions where transaction costs are high.

2.1   Types of Tax Planning

Over the years, taxpayers have displayed considerable ingenuity in their attempts to have their income (1) converted from one *type* to another, (2) shifted from one *pocket* to another, and (3) shifted from one *time period* to another. Briefly, we will consider each of these types of tax planning activities.

Converting Income from One Type to Another

"Capital gains" are typically realized on the sale of capital assets such as common stock or a house. Wages, interest on bonds, and royalties are examples of items that typically give rise to "ordinary income." In most countries, capital gains are taxed very favorably relative to ordinary income. This was certainly true in the U.S. prior to the Tax Reform Act of 1986, and it remains true today in a variety of circumstances, although the differences in rates are less dramatic than they used to be. Attempts to convert ordinary income into capital gains have probably accounted for more tax-planning abuses than any other activity. Undoubtedly this was an important motivating force behind making capital gains less tax-favored under the 1986 Act.

Besides the capital gains/ordinary income distinction, tax liabilities are often affected by whether income is classified as:

- interest, dividend, or operating income,
- having been earned domestically or abroad,
- deriving from an actively-managed business or from a passive investment,
- deriving from a profit-seeking business or from an activity engaged in as a hobby.

For example, whether income is classified as interest or operating income may determine the amount of deductible interest expense. It may also determine whether so-called personal holding company rules apply. Whether income is deemed to be U.S.-sourced or foreign-sourced may affect not only the rate of tax that applies to the income, but also the portion of foreign taxes paid that the U.S. will permit as a credit against U.S. income tax liability. Whether income is deemed to come from an actively-managed business or a passive investment may affect whether losses from such activities are currently tax-deductible. Whether income is deemed to come from an activity engaged in for profit or an activity that is a hobby may affect whether losses from such activities will *ever* be deductible.

These examples are by no means exhaustive. Many other labelling distinctions are important to taxpayers, particularly in the foreign tax area.

Illustration #1: A number of years ago, a coin company sold silver coins to the public. The company guaranteed a generous rate of appreciation on the coins if held for at least one year, although the guaranteed rate was slightly below the going rate of interest. The coins, however, were sold to the public at a price so far above market value that any rational investor would fully expect to sell back the coins at the guaranteed appreciation rate at the end of the year (that is, the probability that the coins would finish "in the money" was effectively zero). By selling back the coins a year later, investors achieved long-term-capital-gains treatment, taxable at rates well below those applying to ordinary income, despite the absence of any real risk related to changes in silver prices. The only risk was that the coin company would go bankrupt. Moreover, the coin company took "losses" incurred on sales of silver as ordinary tax deductions rather than capital losses because as a coin dealer, the silver coins represented their inventory. The coin company was effectively borrowing money, and the "interest" it paid to customers was fully tax-deductible by the company and taxable to customers as a capital gain rather than as interest income. Customers were willing to accept a lower interest rate on the loan to achieve a capital gain rather than ordinary income. This enabled the coin company to capture some of the tax-related benefits of the arrangement.

Illustration #2: An example with an interesting history relates to the question of whether a security issued to raise money for a corporation is debt or equity. Interest paid on debt is tax-deductible to a corporation, whereas dividends paid on common and preferred stock are not. Suppose that there is a tax advantage to issuing debt. It may be rather arbitrary whether the corporation calls the instrument debt or equity. Some corporations have extremely high debt-to-equity ratios. This is quite common following so-called leveraged recapitalizations and leveraged buyouts. In these transactions a great deal of the equity is replaced with debt. But it is also true of a number of start-up corporations, particularly those that are closely held (that is, largely owned by just a few shareholders). To deal with situations in which some corporations called most of their capital "debt" in their legal documents, the IRS proposed some regulations specifying conditions under which legal instruments labelled as debt would be treated as equity in accordance with their economic substance. Because the IRS couldn't create regulations in this area that made any sense across a broad set of circumstances, the regulations were never issued in final form, despite years of effort. On the other hand, such regulations do exist in a number of other countries.

Shifting Income from One Pocket to Another

All other things being equal, high tax-bracket taxpayers would prefer to have their income earned through a tax-exempt pension fund rather than on personal account, where it is fully taxable. They also prefer to have their income earned by their low tax-bracket children, or by their low tax-bracket business (perhaps one located in a low-tax foreign jurisdiction), rather than earned by themselves.

> Illustration #3: Several years ago, banks advertised generous interest rates on Individual Retirement Accounts, on which the earnings are tax-exempt, only if the depositor also purchased a fully-taxable certificate of deposit at below-market rates of interest. If permitted by the taxing authority, this is clearly a smart idea: the tax-exempt pocket of the taxpayer obtains a return in excess of market rates while the taxable pocket obtains a below-market rate of return. Like most loopholes, the IRS eventually caught on and, using its broad powers, cracked down. However, it took several years of abuse before the IRS announced its policy to impose penalties on such tie-in arrangements.

Shifting Income from One Time Period to Another

If tax rates are constant or declining over time, taxpayers prefer to delay the recognition of income until it can be taxed at as low a rate as possible. It is also desirable to defer the payment of taxes as long as interest is not being charged on the tax liability. If tax rates are increasing over time, it pays to accelerate the recognition of income unless interest rates are very high.[3]

The U.S. tax system, as in most systems around the world, typically does not tax income until certain types of exchanges take place. For example, income from the appreciation of most assets is not taxed until the assets are sold, and even then, the income *may* not be taxed until cash is received from the sale. This relief feature of the tax law is motivated by a desire to avoid forcing taxpayers to liquidate assets or borrow money to pay their accrued tax liability. Such relief would be unnecessary if it were costless to liquidate assets or to borrow money, that is, if there were no market frictions. But in many circumstances, such frictions are very important, and without the relief provisions, taxpayers would be forced to engage in economically wasteful transactions to meet their tax liability. Alternatively, they might choose to forego socially desirable activities (such as the sale of an asset with a note) in anticipation of possible problems with making tax payments. On the other hand, the granting of tax relief of this sort has drawbacks as well. Such relief gives rise to tremendous potential for abuse, especially when the cost to liquidate certain assets is low. Although it may be socially inefficient for them to do so, taxpayers can and do incur real costs in timing their sales to shift income from one period to another.

---

[3] For example, if tax rates are 28% today and 33% in one year, it pays to accelerate the payment of the tax unless the taxpayer can invest 28¢ today to return more than 33¢ after tax in one year. Such an investment would have to yield nearly 18% *after tax* in one year to warrant postponing the payment of the tax. Of course, nontax factors might also figure importantly in the taxpayer's decision of whether to defer recognition of the income .

In this chapter, we illustrate some of the many ways in which income can be shifted across time periods. We will see that taxpayers could permanently defer the payment of all income taxes, if transaction costs were low enough and if tax rule restrictions were absent. This is a theme we revisit more fully in later chapters as well.

Illustration #4: As discussed below, the IRS is granted authority to adjust a taxpayer's method of accounting to ensure that it "clearly reflects income." Most abuses of accounting methods involve postponing taxable income. A related consideration comes under the label of "constructive receipt." This doctrine basically prevents taxpayers from turning their backs on income they have already earned and could collect easily. Examples include (1) interest credited on bank accounts where funds are available for withdrawal at any time, and (2) year-end paychecks that can be picked up at the payroll department.

Illustration #5: In the late 1970s, a commonly used tax-planning strategy involved commodity futures.[4] By buying a future on a commodity such as silver (that is, taking a "long" position) and simultaneously selling a future on silver (that is, taking a "short" position) with a different delivery month, risk could be reduced dramatically and taxable income could be shifted easily across time periods.[5] Risk is reduced because the gain (loss) on the long future is offset to a great extent by the loss (gain) on the short future. Taxable income could be shifted by selling the losing position in one tax year to postpone income and selling the winning position in a later tax year. Moreover, by becoming a partner in a broker-dealer organization (an organization that is in the business of buying and selling futures contracts to provide a liquid market to customers who wish to trade), it was possible for such diverse entities as doctors, lawyers, and real estate barons to convert ordinary income into untaxed long-term capital gains. Unlike other investors, the securities a broker-dealer holds to make a market for customers, who buy and sell securities, is considered inventory. Gains and losses on the sale of inventory give rise to ordinary income and loss. But dealers can secure capital gain treatment on the sale of their securities provided that the securities are clearly listed in the dealer's records as being held for investment rather than as inventory for resale.

Brokers used to have up to a month to decide whether to label their investment positions as inventory or capital assets. As a consequence,

---

[4] A long position in a commodity future is a contract in which the investor promises to accept delivery of the commodity and to purchase it at a specified price and at a specified date in the future. In a short position, the investor promises to deliver the commodity and sell it at the specified time and price. In most futures contracts the underlying commodity is not really delivered. Instead, the futures contract is cancelled prior to, or at, the delivery date by taking "offsetting positions" in the commodity future. That is, a long position is cancelled by selling a future in the same commodity for the same delivery date.

[5] Such investment positions are commonly referred to as commodity straddles.

losing positions could be classified as inventory and winning positions as investment. This allowed realized losses on commodity futures to offset ordinary income from other activities, and unrealized gains were held in the investment account and converted into long term gains, taxed at favorable rates. Congress largely closed down this tax avoidance device in 1981 by adding Section 1092 and Sections 1256(b) and (g) to the Code. The former prevents tax deductions from the loss part of a commodity straddle to be taken until the corresponding gains are recognized. The latter requires commodity futures positions to be marked to market value at tax year-end, and the resultant unrealized gains (losses) are taxed as income each year. In addition, the decision by a broker-dealer of whether to allocate investment positions to inventory or the investment account must now be made by the end of the acquisition day for each security.

Illustration #6: Another common technique used to shift income across time periods in the 1960s and 1970s was the use of leveraged tax shelter investments involving nonrecourse debt (that is, debt secured only by the assets purchased with the loan). The "sham" in these transactions involved investors purchasing an interest in a depreciable asset at a highly inflated price relative to its fair market value for a small cash down payment. A large nonrecourse loan would be arranged to finance the rest of the purchase. The investor would then receive substantial depreciation deductions, and perhaps investment tax credits, based on the inflated price of the asset. The investor could then default on the nonrecourse loan in a later period, recapturing as income the previous tax losses taken in excess of the cash lost. Depending on the length of the holding period, some or all of any investment tax credit previously taken might have to be recaptured. The present value of the early benefit exceeded the discounted cost of the later recapture, even when tax rates were constant over time. If the recapture were timed to coincide with a period of relatively low tax rates, the tax savings were even larger.

The IRS has long maintained a large audit inventory involving transactions of these types. And proving that the schemes are shams is not always easy. In 1976, so-called "at risk" rules were introduced into the Tax Code to prevent tax losses from being deducted unless the taxpayer was at risk with respect to such losses; that is, the taxpayer was obligated to make up any deficits with future payments. The Tax Reform Act of 1986 went a step further to prevent the deductibility of certain losses even where the taxpayer is fully at risk with respect to the losses.

2.2 Broad Restrictions on Taxpayer Behavior

Many of the illustrations described in Section 2.1 clarify why it is desirable to build restrictions into the law. The *broad legal restrictions* on taxpayer behavior essentially give the taxing authority the right to ask whether the transactions entered into by the taxpayer "pass the smell test." In other words, the tax collector can question whether there is a valid business purpose for the taxpayer's transactions other than tax minimization. If a taxpayer engages in a set of transactions that are deemed to have no valid business purpose other than tax avoidance, and if a similar economic outcome could have been achieved using simpler transactions, the taxing authority is allowed to recharacterize the transactions, producing a less favorable tax treatment. And if there *is* some business purpose to the transactions, is it sufficient? The courts play an important role in interpreting these elusive concepts and in allowing their definition to evolve over time as the socio-economic environment changes. Let's take a closer look at some of the broad restrictions that are involved.

Examples of Broad Restrictions on Taxpayer Behavior in the U.S. Substance-Over-Form and Business-Purpose Doctrines

Among the most powerful tools at the disposal of the Internal Revenue Service (IRS) to discipline aggressive tax planners are the closely related doctrines of substance-over-form and the business-purpose. We just alluded to the business-purpose doctrine in the previous paragraph.[6] The substance-over-form doctrine allows the IRS to look through the legal form of transactions to their economic substance.

The landmark case of Gregory (a taxpayer) v. Helvering (an IRS Commissioner) illustrates these doctrines well. In that case the aggressive taxpayer tried to transform a dividend into a capital gain as follows: Gregory (1) split the corporation in two in a tax-free reorganization, and (2) liquidated one of the two new corporations.

Prior to the 1986 Tax Act, the complete liquidation of a U.S. corporation (whose balance sheet included no inventories or depreciable assets) was a nontaxable event at the corporate level. The liquidation gave rise to a capital gain to shareholders, taxed at well below ordinary income tax rates; and much of the proceeds of the sale came back to shareholders as a nontaxable return of capital. Dividends, on the other hand, have always been taxed at ordinary rates to individual shareholders.

The court viewed the economic substance of Gregory's two transactions to be equivalent to a dividend. Moreover, because it saw no business purpose for the two transactions other than tax avoidance, it ruled that the less favorable dividend treatment be applied for tax purposes.[7]

---

[6] Revenue Canada, the Canadian counterpart to the IRS in the U.S., has access to a similar weapon, the "general anti-avoidance rule." As indicated by Ernst & Whinney (*Tax News International*, December 1988), "Revenue Canada can apply (the general anti-avoidance rule) to eliminate any form of tax advantage resulting from one transaction or a series of transactions, where any step in the series is undertaken primarily to obtain a tax benefit ... and it represents a misuse of any one provision of the Income Tax Act, or an abuse of the Act overall." (p. 5)

[7] Similarly, in the U.K., "the case of *Furniss v. Dawson* ... established that a pre-ordered series of transactions should be regarded as a single composite transaction for U.K. tax purposes where one or more steps were introduced with no business purpose other than U.K. tax avoidance." (Price Waterhouse, *International Tax Review*, January/February 1989, p.11)

Of course, there are ways to transfer property out of a corporation and into the hands of shareholders at capital gains rates, or as a nontaxable return of capital, without liquidating. The simplest way, which has become quite popular lately for many very large corporations, is to repurchase shares of stock in the open market.[8] If share repurchases are proportional to shareholder interests, however, the share repurchases will be considered to be an ordinary dividend. This is another example of the substance-over-form doctrine. The requirement that share repurchases be disproportionate to avoid being classified as dividend distributions can be much more of a problem in closely held firms than in widely held public corporations. In closely held firms, disproportionate share repurchases can have a substantial impact on the voting control of the firm. This nontax cost can greatly reduce the attractiveness of implementing the tax plan.

The IRS has also tried (often unsuccessfully) to use the substance-over-form argument when taxpayers essentially manufacture riskless assets from portfolios of risky assets. While the returns to risky assets are generally taxable at capital gains rates, the returns to riskless assets are taxable (or tax deductible) at ordinary income tax rates. Consider the possibilities when capital gains tax rates are below ordinary tax rates. Suppose that taxpayers could borrow at the riskless interest rate, take an ordinary tax deduction for the interest, and then use the proceeds to purchase a portfolio of risky assets that, together, are not risky. If the portfolio of risky assets earns the riskless interest rate before tax, but is taxed at favorable capital gains tax rates, such taxpayers could wipe out their tax bills. We will expand on this tax arbitrage notion in Chapter Six.

The substance-over-form and business-purpose doctrines have been codified in several parts of the Internal Revenue Code. By *codified*, we mean that Congress has passed tax bills transforming the judicial support for these doctrines into statutes or laws. The IRS's broadest ability to recharacterize transactions from their legal form into their economic substance is reflected in Internal Revenue Code Section 482. This section has been used most extensively by the IRS in cases involving international transfer pricing (e.g., interest rates on loans; or sales prices on transfers of goods or services between parent and subsidiary corporations operating in different countries). The motivation for playing games with transfer prices is that the parent and subsidiary may face very different tax rates. Section 482 has also been applied to a variety of transactions among related individuals who are taxed at different rates within the same tax jurisdiction (such as parents and children).

The motivation for allowing the IRS to invoke Section 482 and to recharacterize transactions is to prevent taxpayers from taking unreasonable advantage of situations where their left pocket and right pocket are taxed differently. Other Code sections that give the IRS broad powers include:

---

[8] The January 3, 1989 *Wall Street Journal* reported that during 1988 many large U.S. corporations repurchased their shares. UAL Corporation's repurchase of $2.84 billion of their own stock was the largest, followed by IBM with $2.00 billion, CSX $1.86 billion, Sears Roebuck $1.75 billion, RJR Nabisco $1.38 billion, Digital Equipment $1.26 billion, Gillette $1.19 billion, Schlumberger $1.11 billion, Dow Chemical $1.04 billion, and GTE $1.01 billion. For an analysis of share repurchase programs prior to 1988, see John B. Shoven and Laurie Simon Bagwell, "Cash Distributions to Shareholders," *Journal of Economic Perspectives* (Summer 1989), pp.129-140.

Section 446(b)   allows the IRS to adjust a taxpayer's method of accounting when the method chosen by the taxpayer "does not clearly reflect income."

Section 269   requires that there be a valid nontax business purpose for a merger with a company that carries tax losses forward before those losses can be used by the newly-merged entity to offset future taxable income.

Related-Party versus Arms-Length Contracts

It is worth noting that the IRS worries much less about form-over-substance problems in contracts between parties with opposing interests than it does between related parties. Why? Parties with opposing interests cannot always afford to write a contract in which the legal form differs much from the economic substance. Otherwise, if one party fails to perform as promised under the contract, the courts may not enforce the other party's property rights in the desired way.

For example, suppose a manufacturer buys steel from several suppliers to use in his manufacturing operations. For tax purposes, he determines that it would be very advantageous for him to reduce his taxable income this period and increase it next period. One possibility is to arrange for a supplier to ship some steel at a very high price this year with the understanding that the price will be correspondingly lower next year.

The problem with such an arrangement is that once the supplier has received above-market payment for this year's shipments, there is little incentive for her to keep the manufacturer happy for next year's shipment. Or the supplier might claim that the agreement was to deliver materials of inferior quality next period. If the contract is very explicit, so as to deter contractual breach by the supplier (since the breach of an explicit contract may be remedied by bringing legal action), the tax plan will fail if audited by the IRS. So it is not surprising that the IRS worries about related-party contracting more so than arms-length contracts.

Assignment-of-Income Doctrine

The courts have enabled the IRS to invoke another related doctrine, "assignment of income." Here the taxpayer instructs one party to pay income on the taxpayer's behalf to a third party, transferring the tax liability to the third party as well (the third party is presumably in a lower tax bracket). As an example, a taxpayer may wish to give a child an interest in partnership income (the fruit of the tree) but not an interest in partnership capital (the tree itself).[9] By the assignment of income doctrine, the taxpayer must give away the whole tree to be successful in shifting taxable income. Because taxpayers have devised numerous ways to skirt this doctrine, the 1986 Tax Act introduced some restrictions to attack these income-

---

[9] This is similar to the situation that arose in the court case of Helvering v. Horst, where a father sought to make a gift of detachable bond coupons to his sons and have the son be taxed on the interest income. The Supreme Court ruled that it was the father who was taxable on the interest income.

Chapter 2   Tax Rule Uncertainty and Judicial Doctrines

shifting plans between parents and children. As a result, the rules of family tax planning have undergone some dramatic changes. In particular, all but a small amount of passive income earned by children under 14 years of age is now taxed as if it were earned by the parent.

The landmark case in the "assignment of income" area is Lucas v. Earl. In this case, a husband and wife entered into a contract providing the wife with a claim to 50% of the husband's income. The taxpayer resided in a noncommunity property state. (In a community property state, the wife automatically is deemed to earn 50% of the husband's income.) The couple then filed separate tax returns, and given the progressive income tax schedule (tax rates increase with the level of taxable income), the total tax bill was less than it would have been had they filed a joint tax return. When the court agreed with the IRS Commissioner that this was unacceptable, the assignment-of-income doctrine was born.

Interestingly enough, a couple of Tax Court cases involving baseball players have clarified the assignment-of-income doctrine.[10] One involves Randy Hundley, a Chicago Cubs catcher (48 TC 339 (1967)).[11] His dad trained him as a youth, and Hundley agreed as a teen to give his dad half of any bonus he might receive later. The Tax Court blessed this arrangement, claiming that Hundley's father had earned his share of the bonus.

By contrast, we have the case of a Philadelphia Phillies ballplayer, Richie Allen (50 TC 466 (1969)). Although Allen arranged for his employer to pay his mother half of his bonus, the Tax Court ruled this to be an assignment of income and taxed the full bonus to Allen. In reaching their conclusion, the Tax Court emphasized that Allen's mother knew nothing about baseball.

An income-shifting strategy commonly used for years (but eliminated by the 1984 Tax Act) involved making an interest-free loan to a child, the exact equivalent of assignment of income. The Crown family popularized this idea by setting up a trust to control the investment of assets. The Crown family members are the major shareholders of General Dynamics, the world's largest private defense contractor. This family has effectively used tax planning at much more than just the family level. General Dynamics didn't pay a dime in taxes to the Federal government in more than ten years ending in 1984, despite having reported billions of dollars of net income on their financial statements sent to shareholders.[12] As we discuss in Chapter Five, however, General Dynamics may well have paid plenty of "implicit taxes" to other parties.

2.3   The Legislative Process and Sources of Tax Information[13]

Despite the many broad restrictions that exist, numerous opportunities for abuse remain. Moreover, they will always exist so long as the tax system encourages

---

[10] This example is an old favorite of Ray Sommerfeld's.

[11] This is the standard citation for the court case. For further information, see Pratt, Burns, and Kulsrud, *Federal Taxation* (Irwin), 1989 Edition, Chapter 2.

[12] For further discussion of this, see James Wheeler and Edmund Outslay, "The Phantom Federal Income Taxes of General Dynamics Corporation," *The Accounting Review* (October 1986), pp. 760-774.

[13] For a more extensive discussion see Ray M. Sommerfeld and G. Fred Streuling, *Tax Research Techniques*, American Institute of Certified Public Accountants (New York), Tax Study #5, 1976.

particular economic activities. But such restrictions also clearly make tax planning more difficult. As we mentioned in the introductory chapter, effective tax planning requires that the tax and nontax implications of proposed transactions be considered for all parties to the transaction. But as we just discussed, simply determining the tax implications of proposed transactions is not a trivial undertaking: it requires knowledge of tax rules that are inherently ambiguous.

A crucial step in minimizing the ambiguities of the tax implications of proposed transactions is seeking the proper authority for applying a particular tax rule. The remainder of this chapter will review how one does just this for U.S. tax rules. This should provide some idea of how the tax professionals you may hire spend their time. It will also help to make it feasible for you to research your own tax problems. And finally, it should give you a better idea of how the tax system is laid out.

Primary and Secondary Authorities

We can distinguish between primary and secondary types of authority for determining the appropriate tax treatment for a transaction. The most important primary authority is the Internal Revenue Code. The Code provides *statutory* authority. Gathering authoritative support for the proper tax treatment of a particular transaction should always begin here. Other primary authorities include treasury regulations, judicial decisions, administrative pronouncements (for example, by the IRS), and Congressional Committee Reports. Secondary authorities consist primarily of tax professionals (for example, accountants and lawyers), commercial tax services, and tax journals. In the discussion that follows, we introduce each of these authorities and how they are used.

To develop an understanding of how the primary authoritative sources can help clarify the way a transaction should be treated for tax purposes, we must understand the *legislative process*, the means by which tax bills are enacted. The passage of such legislation gives rise to the most dramatic changes in tax rules.

The Legislative Process

With minor exceptions, all tax bills originate in the House of Representatives, and then are forwarded to the House Ways and Means Committee. If the bill is a major one, the Ways and Means Committee will hold public hearings. Then the Ways and Means Committee prepares a report that it sends back to the floor of the House. This committee report, which may provide important authoritative support by indicating the legislative intent of the bill, is often considered in court cases to help resolve taxpayer and IRS disputes.

The bill is then debated on the floor of the House, typically under "closed rule," where debate is limited and no amendments are permitted.[14] If the House bill is passed, it is sent along to the Senate, where it is forwarded to the Senate Finance Committee. After public hearings, the Senate Finance Committee sends its report, along with proposed amendments to the House bill, back to the floor

---

[14] See Michael J. Graetz, "Reflections on the Tax Legislative Process: Prelude to Reform," *Virginia Law Review* (November 1972), pp. 1389-1450.

of the Senate. There it is debated under "open rule" with unlimited debate and amendment and under intensified lobbying pressure.[15] If passed, both House and Senate Committee Reports are forwarded to a Conference Committee.

The Conference Committee is composed of members of both the House and the Senate. Its task is to iron out House and Senate disagreements. The Conference Report, which concentrates on differences between the House and Senate bills, makes recommendations for the resolution of these differences. The report is sent back to the House and then the Senate for a vote on the Conference Committee's compromise bill. Upon approval, the bill is sent to the President for signature or veto. If the President vetos the bill, the veto can be overridden by a two-thirds override vote of the House and Senate members.[16]

Regulations and Revenue Rulings that Result from the Passage of a Tax Act

Once a bill is passed, the Treasury is generally the first to interpret it. They issue proposed Treasury Regulations that provide general interpretations. Interested parties can request public hearings of the proposed regulations. The Treasury Department also issues *Revenue Rulings*, which are specific interpretations. These result from a request for rules clarification from a taxpayer with a particular set of actual or proposed transactions.

Here are two situations in which a rulings request might be made:

1. Two corporations that plan to effect a tax-free reorganization may wish to obtain IRS assurance that their merger will not be taxable to the target company's shareholders; that is, the IRS will bless the merger, in advance of the transaction, as being a tax-free reorganization.

2. A dozen investors are contemplating a business venture. It is anticipated that the venture will incur losses in the first year of operations. To pass through the losses to the individual tax returns of the venture's investors, they wish to be taxed as a partnership rather than as a corporation. To avoid an unpleasant surprise, the investors may seek a private letter ruling to ensure that the venture won't be taxed as a corporation.

Revenue Rulings represent official IRS policy. The Treasury will publish a rulings request from a taxpayer as a Revenue Ruling if it is of sufficient general interest. Otherwise it issues a *private* letter ruling. Private rulings are available to the public under *The Freedom of Information Act*, but they cannot be cited as precedent in a court of law. Still, they may be valuable as an indication of IRS policy.

Revenue Rulings are published in the weekly *Internal Revenue Bulletins*. They are also published in the "Current Matters" section of the Commerce Clearing House and Maxwell Macmillan tax services (described more fully below). Because Revenue Rulings may be revoked or amended, their current

---

[15] *Ibid.*

[16] For an entertaining description of the high drama surrounding the passage of the Tax Reform Act of 1986, see Alan S. Murray and Jeffrey H. Birnbaum, *Showdown at Gucci Gulch* (Random House), 1987. The process for enacting legislation in many states is quite similar to that for passage of Federal bills.

status must be determined before relying upon them. Merten's *Law of Federal Income Taxation* has a convenient current status table, as do the Commerce Clearing House and Maxwell Macmillan tax services.

The Role of Judicial Decisions

Judicial decisions also play an extremely important role in the interpretation of the tax rules. There are two court levels: courts of original jurisdiction and courts of appeal. Courts of original jurisdiction include the U.S. Tax Court, U.S. District Courts, and the U.S. Claims Court. While only U.S. District Courts offer jury trials, the U.S. Tax Court hears only tax cases and the presiding judge is more familiar with the tax law than is the typical judge presiding in other courts.

Courts of appeal include the 13 circuit courts (numbered 1 through 11 plus the District of Columbia plus the Federal Circuit Court) and the Supreme Court. Legal precedent is circuit-specific; that is, different circuits can hand down different decisions based on identical facts. When this happens, the Supreme Court is often called upon to provide uniformity of treatment.

Regular decisions of the U.S. Tax Court (the more important cases) are published in the *Tax Court Reporter*. Memorandum decisions of the U.S. Tax Court (dealing primarily with questions of fact with only one judge writing the decision) are published in Commerce Clearing House's *Tax Court Memorandum Decisions* and in Maxwell Macmillan's *TC Memorandum Decisions*. All tax-related cases from all of the other courts (District Courts, Claims Court, Circuit Courts of Appeal, and the Supreme Court) are published in Commerce Clearing House's *U.S. Tax Cases* and Maxwell Macmillan's *American Federal Tax Reports*, among other places.

Secondary Authorities

To this point we have discussed almost exclusively sources of *primary* authority: statutory (Internal Revenue Code); administrative (Treasury Regulations, Treasury Rulings); and judicial (cases from the U.S. Tax Court, District Courts, Claims Court, Circuit Courts, and Supreme Court). For the nonexpert, secondary sources are probably more useful. Perhaps the most helpful of these are intermediaries and tax professionals (most notably accountants and lawyers). These intermediaries in turn rely on other secondary authorities, especially the commercial tax services. The two most popular tax services are Commerce Clearing House's *Standard Federal Tax Reporter* and Maxwell Macmillan's *Federal Taxes*. Each Section of these services begins with a layman's discussion of an area of the tax code, introducing the subject in general terms. This is followed in turn by (1) the text of the Internal Revenue Code Section (the statutes established by the passage of tax legislation), (2) the text of Treasury Regulations (Treasury's interpretation of the Code), (3) editorial explanations (sometimes including tax-planning tips), and finally (4) synopses of court decisions, Revenue Rulings, and other Treasury pronouncements that pertain to the Code section, along with citations to complete documents. Because the commercial tax services are very convenient, it is well worth taking the time to flip through one.

Chapter 2   Tax Rule Uncertainty and Judicial Doctrines

Another extremely useful reference is the Bureau of National Affairs *Tax Management Portfolios*, of which there are several hundred. The portfolios are 50-200 pages in length. Each portfolio deals with a specific tax topic (such as sale-and-leaseback transactions, and corporate acquisitions planning). The material is presented in a way that proceeds from the general to the specific. A useful feature of the portfolios is that they contain excellent bibliographies. Also useful is the frequent inclusion of excerpts from the congressional record that pertain to the enactment of relevant legislation. As well, the inclusion of sample contracts or wordings to be included in the corporate minutes that are likely to pass muster with the taxing authority to secure the desired tax treatment is also useful.

Another useful reference is Commerce Clearing House's *Tax Articles*, which lists articles and their abstracts, by Code section number, by topic, and by author. In addition, the Maxwell Macmillan tax service has had a tab entitled "Index to Tax Articles," which is organized by Code section numbers.

Summary of Key Points

1. Tax rules that are designed to motivate socially desirable activities often motivate transactions that reduce taxpayers' tax liabilities but serve no social purpose.

2. This gives rise to tax rule restrictions that serve to limit exceedingly aggressive tax-planning behavior.

3. Ambiguity in the tax law is pervasive. As a result, numerous disputes arise between taxpayers and the taxing authority, parties with opposing interests regarding the assessment of tax liabilities. The courts may be used to resolve these disputes.

4. Several classes of tax-planning strategies that are commonly employed include attempts to convert tax-disfavored types of income into a more favorably-taxed type, to shift income from a highly-taxed pocket to another lower-taxed pocket of the same taxpayer, and to shift income from a time period of high tax rates into one of lower tax rates.

5. The business-purpose doctrine and the substance-over-form doctrine are broad restrictions on taxpayer behavior. The taxing authority often has the right to recharacterize transactions in a way that affects the tax outcome if the transactions can be shown to have had no other purpose than tax avoidance and a simpler set of transactions could have been undertaken. The taxing authority can also look through a transaction's legal form to its economic substance.

6. As a result, the taxing authority can deny tax benefits or recharacterize a transaction in a way that is less favorable to the taxpayer.

7. The business-purpose and the substance-over-form doctrines have been codified in the tax code. That is, judicial support for these doctrines has been transformed into statutes or laws. For example, Section 482 allows the IRS to recharacterize transactions from their legal form into

their economic substance. It is used heavily in cases involving transfer pricing transactions among related parties.

8. Assignment of income is another important doctrine. The taxing authority uses this doctrine to prevent high-tax-bracket taxpayers from assigning their income to related low-tax-bracket taxpayers for the sole purpose of reducing their joint tax bill.

9. Taxpayers undertake many transactions on terms that do not reflect the underlying economic realities, whose sole purpose is to reduce taxes. The taxing authority pursues taxpayers who undertake these sham transactions.

10. The handling of sham transactions on an individual basis is expensive, so many tax rule restrictions are borne out of a desire to close down certain socially undesirable tax-planning avenues before taxpayers have a chance to use them. For example, the "at risk" rules require that taxpayers be exposed to risk of economic loss before any tax losses resulting from a transaction may be deducted.

11. Tax law ambiguity can frustrate legitimate tax planning.

12. Because tax rules are ambiguous, taxpayers must be aware of primary and secondary authorities for determining the appropriate tax treatment for a transaction. Understanding the legislative process by which tax laws are passed and determining the legislative intent of Congress provides additional guidance in interpreting the tax rules. The intent of Congress may play an important role in the court's interpretation of the tax rules.

13. Various sources of information can help to provide guidance in predicting how transactions will be treated for tax purposes. Some of these sources were introduced in this chapter. Others are listed in the appendix to this chapter.

Discussion Questions

1. True or False? Discuss.

    a. Congress drafts very tight and specific tax rules to prevent taxpayers from misinterpreting them.

    b. Most tax legislation is initiated in the Senate.

    c. The Treasury drafts regulations and issues revenue rulings to clarify the tax rules.

    d. Revenue Rulings issued by the Treasury can be relied upon by taxpayers, while private letter rulings are only valid for the taxpayer who requested the ruling.

    e. The courts cannot change the substance of tax laws through their judicial rulings.

2. Why might Congress and the Treasury avoid drafting tax rules that are very specific? What costs would such rules impose on the Internal Revenue Service? What benefits might they bestow on certain taxpayers?

3. How do such judicial doctrines as substance over form and business purpose affect taxpayer behavior? Is it socially beneficial to have such doctrines?

4. What incentives exist for taxpayers to shift income from one party to another? Are there costs associated with such income-shifting? Give examples of such costs in a family-planning situation. How would the elimination of the assignment-of-income doctrine affect the costs of shifting income? What could taxpayers do to mitigate these costs?

5. Why do the tax laws sometimes discriminate against related-party contracts? Is this always in society's best interest?

6. Should the taxing authority always agree to provide a revenue ruling requested by a taxpayer to clarify the tax treatment of a proposed transaction? Should taxpayers requesting rulings be assessed a fee to cover the taxing authority's cost of responding?

7. Suppose the U.S. were to convert its tax system from an income tax to a national sales tax on sales of goods and services. Certain necessities, like food, would be exempted from taxation, and low-income households would be granted tax refunds. Would such a tax system eliminate incentives to shift activities (a) from one period to the next, (b) from one type to another, and (c) from one pocket to another?

Exhibit 2.1

Sources of Information on Tax Legislation

Several excellent publications follow the evolution of proposed tax legislation and document the dates on which certain legislative events take place. These include:

- BNA (Bureau of National Affairs) *Daily Tax Report*
- BNA *Weekly Tax Report*
- *Tax Notes Today*: a daily electronic newsletter available on LEXIS, an electronic news retrieval service
- *Tax Notes*: a weekly tax service. Each issue contains
  - a summary of bills introduced
  - a description of change in the status of bills, by day
  - a description of public hearings on proposed legislation
  - a calendar of future congressional hearings
  - a summary of lobbying letters sent to Treasury, organized by IRC section number

- a complete reporting of developments, all organized by IRC section number, relating to
  - Treasury regulations
  - Judicial decisions
  - Administrative pronouncements
- a list of recently published tax articles by Code section number.

An especially interesting feature of *Tax Notes* is the document retrieval service: for a modest cost they will rush you complete texts of any documents to which they refer (they will even deliver within 24 hours if you pay Federal Express charges).

If it is important to track down copies of Committee Reports (House Ways and Means, Senate Finance, or Conference), they can be found in

- The government documents section of most law libraries
- *Weekly Internal Revenue Bulletin*, which is bound into *Cumulative Bulletins* every 6 months
- *U.S. Code Congressional and Administrative News*
- Parts of the major acts appear in the Maxwell Macmillan and Commerce Clearing House tax services under the titles *Federal Taxes* and *Standard Federal Tax Reporter*, respectively.

Sometimes it is important to know the date on which a particular rule that now appears in the Code first became effective. Two good sources for laws passed prior to 1954, are

- *Federal Tax Laws Correlated* (By Walter Barton and Carol Browning; Warren, Gorham, and Lamont; 1969)
- Seidman's *Legislative History of Federal Income Tax and Excess Profits Tax Law, 1939-1953* and Seidman's *Legislative History of Federal Income Tax Laws, 1861-1938*

Two additional sources that are useful for tracking down legislative histories of more recent changes in the Tax Code are

- Maxwell Macmillan's *Federal Taxes Cumulative Changes*
- BNA's *Primary Sources*

CHAPTER 3
Organizational Form: Savings Vehicles

In this chapter, we discuss alternative organizational forms through which to save for future consumption. Examples of organizational forms used as savings vehicles include money market mutual funds and pension fund accounts. In the next chapter we discuss alternative organizational forms, such as corporations and partnerships, through which goods and services are produced.

We begin by discussing a number of different legal organizational forms through which individuals save for the future. To facilitate comparisons, the same underlying investment will be held in each of the vehicles. As a result, the before-tax rates of return will be identical in each case. The investment returns will be taxed quite differently across the alternatives, however, so the after-tax rates of return will differ widely.

In the absence of transaction and information costs (or frictions) and/or explicit restrictions imposed by the taxing authority, different after-tax returns across the savings vehicles would allow investors to eliminate their taxes by employing tax-arbitrage strategies. By tax arbitrage, we mean earning a relatively high after-tax rate of return by investing through a tax-favored organizational form, financed at a relatively low after-tax cost by borrowing through a different organizational form. We'll defer a discussion of the nature of existing restrictions and frictions that keep the system in check until we cover some preliminaries. At this stage, our objective is simply to demonstrate the sensitivity of investment performance to differences in the tax treatment across alternative savings arrangements. This is why we assume that the before-tax rates of return are identical across the alternatives. It allows us to turn only one dial at a time. With differing underlying investments, after-tax returns would differ because of both risk and tax differences, and, as a result, it would be difficult to parse out the effects of the different tax treatments on after-tax returns.

We begin in Section 3.1 by comparing the relative attractiveness of six differentially-taxed savings vehicles when tax rates are constant year to year. In Section 3.2, we demonstrate how changes in tax rates over time can affect the relative attractiveness of the six savings arrangements. Finally, in Section 3.3, we demonstrate that if tax rates not only change over time but also differ across taxpayers, whole new classes of savings vehicles are created. An example is deferred compensation contracts, where employees, in effect, undertake savings through their employers. We refer to the savings vehicles in Sections 3.1 and 3.2 as those available through an **impersonal marketplace**, while those in Section 3.3 are arranged in **personal markets**, such as within firms or within families.

If the new class of personalized savings vehicles analyzed in Section 3.3 is to be compared meaningfully to those in Section 3.2, it is necessary to consider the tax consequences of a particular savings program to all its parties (for example, both the employee and the employer in the case of deferred compensation contracts). In appropriate circumstances, the personalized savings vehicles offer the highest after-tax return on investment.

3.1 Constant Tax Rates:
Saving through an Impersonal Marketplace

We assume in this section that tax rates are constant over time. We also assume that our investor cannot affect the before-tax rates of return on the investment by buying more or less of it. In other words, the market for investment is perfectly competitive. We begin by considering some relatively straightforward ways to save for future consumption. In particular, suppose that the only investment that can be held in each organizational form is an interest-bearing security such as a fully secured (virtually riskless) corporate bond.

Table 3.1 lists six categories of savings vehicles that are distinguished by their tax attributes. Tax treatments across the six savings vehicles differ along three dimensions: (1) whether deposits into the savings accounts give rise to an immediate tax deduction (only Vehicle VI does); (2) the frequency with which investment earnings are taxed (annually as in Vehicles I and III; only when the investment is liquidated as in Vehicles II, IV, and VI; or never as in Vehicle V); and (3) the rate at which the investment earnings are taxed (ordinary rates as in Vehicles I, II, and VI; capital gains rates as in Vehicles III and IV; or complete tax exemption as in Vehicle V).

Each of these different organizational forms have existed in the United States as well as in many foreign tax jurisdictions. Examples of Savings Vehicle I include corporate bonds and money market accounts offered by mutual funds, banks, and savings and loan associations. A common example of Savings Vehicle II in the U.S. is a single premium deferred annuity contract (SPDA) offered by insurance companies. Vehicle III includes certain mutual funds and Vehicle IV includes shares in certain corporations located in tax jurisdictions where the interest on investment is tax exempt. While Savings Vehicles III and IV are relatively rare, Savings Vehicles V and VI are used heavily. Examples of Savings Vehicle V include the savings portion of certain life insurance policies in the U.S.

Table 3.1 Six Different Legal Organizational Forms Through Which Investors Can Hold Riskless Bonds

Savings Vehicle (Example)	Is the Investment Tax Deductible?	Frequency that Earnings are Taxed	Rate at which Earnings are Taxed	After-tax Accumulation Per After-Tax Dollar Invested
I (Money market fund)	No	Annually	Ordinary	$[1 + R(1-t)]^n$
II (Single premium deferred annuity)	No	Deferred	Ordinary	$(1 + R)^n(1-t) + t$
III (Mutual fund)	No	Annually	Capital Gains	$[1 + R(1-gt)]^n$
IV (Foreign corporation)	No	Deferred	Capital Gains	$(1 + R)^n(1-gt) + gt$
V (Insurance policy)	No	Never	Exempt	$(1 + R)^n$
VI (Pension)	Yes	Deferred	Ordinary	$\dfrac{1}{1-t}(1 + R)^n(1-t)$ or $(1 + R)^n$

where:
R = before-tax rate of return
n = number of time periods
t = ordinary tax rate
g = percentage of capital gain taxed as ordinary income when the capital gain becomes taxable

and postal (so-called "maruyu") accounts in Japan, and an example of Vehicle VI is a pension account.

In the discussion below, we elaborate on these examples, but we avoid detailing many of the technical nuances that apply to each of them. Discussion of these nuances would simply cloud the general points and obscure the taxonomy that we are developing in this chapter. We discuss each of these investment alternatives more fully in subsequent chapters.

In Table 3.1, we show the after-tax accumulations per dollar of initial investment of six different legal organizational forms through which investors can hold our riskless asset.[1] The after-tax accumulations are a function of their respective tax treatments, the before-tax rate of return on the investment, the number of periods the investment is held, and the tax rates on ordinary income and capital gains. Examples of ordinary income include wages earned from employment and interest earned on bonds, while examples of capital gains income include the realized gain on the sale of common stock or on the sale of a home.

---

[1] Table 3.1 is reproduced on the inside back cover of this book.

3.1 Constant Tax Rates: Saving Though an Impersonal Marketplace

Review of Compound Interest

An understanding of the algebraic expressions in Table 3.1 requires an understanding of the simple principle of compound interest. If $1 is invested at rate r per period, and the principal plus interest is reinvested for n periods, the accumulation after n periods is

$$(1 + r) \times (1 + r) \times \cdots \times (1 + r) \text{ or } (1 + r)^n. \tag{3.1}$$

For example, if the rate of return on investment were 12% per year, the after-tax accumulation per dollar invested for 10 years would be given by $(1 + .12)^{10} = $3.11.[2]$

In the case of Savings Vehicle I, tax at rate t must be paid each period on the interest earned at before-tax rate R. The after-tax interest rate earned each period, then, is R - tR or R(1 - t). Substituting R(1 - t) for r in expression 3.1 above yields

$$[1 + R(1 - t)]^n,$$

which is the expression given in Table 3.1.

Investments in Savings Vehicles I and II

Savings Vehicle I: Deposits into a money market savings account are not tax deductible. Earnings on the investment are typically taxed fully each year at ordinary tax rates. Savings Vehicle I is the least tax advantageous of our savings vehicles in the sense that it produces the lowest after-tax accumulation when individual tax rates are assumed to be constant over time.

Savings Vehicle II: Deposits into a single premium deferred annuity contract (SPDA) through an insurance company in the U.S. are not tax deductible. The taxes on the investment earnings, however, are deferred and taxed at ordinary income tax rates only when the investor takes money out of the contract.

Although slightly oversimplified, the mechanics of an SPDA investment are as follows. The investor turns over cash to an insurance company, which in turn invests in interest-bearing securities. The insurance company pays no taxes on the interest it accumulates from holding the securities on behalf of its policyholders. In this way, the insurance company effectively acts as a conduit through which investors save for future consumption.

The value of deferral (and hence the attractiveness of Vehicle II over Vehicle I) can be considerable. In Savings Vehicle II, the investment earnings compound at the before-tax rate of return R rather than at the after-tax rate of return, R(1 - t), as in Vehicle I. Just prior to liquidation of the investment, then, each dollar invested in Vehicle II grows to $(1 + R)^n$. Tax at rate t is paid only on the earnings $[(1 + R)^n - 1]$ at the end of time period n when the account is liquidated. This leaves the investor with

$$(1 + R)^n - t [(1 + R)^n - 1] = (1 + R)^n (1 - t) + t. \tag{3.2}$$

---

[2] Alternatively, if we knew that a dollar invested today for n periods yields F dollars in the future, and we wish to know the annualized rate of return, r, we could determine this by noting that $F = (1 + r)^n$. Solving for r, we get $r = F^{1/n} - 1$. For example, if we know that a $1.00 investment today accumulates to $3.11 in 10 years, this implies a rate of return of 12% per year ($3.11^{(1/10)} - 1 = .12$ or 12%).

Chapter 3   Organizational Form: Savings Vehicles

Another way to look at this result is to note that investors pay tax on the entire accumulation except the initial investment of $1. This explains the derivation of the accumulation that is shown for Savings Vehicle II in Table 3.1.

In Table 3.2 we illustrate the after-tax accumulation and the after-tax annualized rate of return achieved by investing in Savings Vehicles I and II for different holding periods, assuming that R = 7% and t = 30%. The after-tax rate of return on Savings Vehicle I, a money market account, would be 7% × (1 - .3) = 4.9% per year after tax. This is true no matter how long the investment horizon is. In contrast, the after-tax rate of return on Savings Vehicle II, an SPDA, changes with its holding period. To calculate the after-tax rate of return per year on Savings Vehicle II, we must first find the after-tax accumulation for a given holding period. Let us suppose that an investor deposits one dollar in Savings Vehicle II for five years. This $1 accumulates to $1.28 after tax (as shown in Table 3.2, under a holding period of 5 years). To show how $1.28 was derived, note that an investment of $1 for 5 years at 7% grows to $1(1.07)^5 or $1.40 before tax. At the end of five years, on withdrawing the accumulated sum from the account, tax is owed on the amount withdrawn in excess of the initial investment. In this example, the excess is equal to $.40 and the tax on the excess is .3 × $.40 or $.12, leaving $1.28 after tax (or $1.40 - $.12). Alternatively, using equation 3.2, we can derive the same after-tax dollar amount directly:

$$\$1(1.07)^5(1 - .3) + \$.30 = \$1.40 \times .7 + \$.30 = \$1.28.$$

Notice that except for investment horizons of only one period (when an SPDA becomes equivalent to a money-market account), the after-tax accumulation in an SPDA (Vehicle II) always exceeds that in a money-market account (Vehicle I). Moreover, the longer the holding period, the greater the differential in the accumulation. After 40 years, for example, $1 accumulates to $10.78 after tax in an SPDA, or 59% more than the $6.78 in a money-market account.

The after-tax annual rates of return are shown in the bottom panel of Table 3.2. For example, after 5 years an investment of $1 in Vehicle I grows to $1.27. This translates to an annual rate of return of $(1.27)^{(1/5)} - 1$ or 4.9%. Notice that while all of the after-tax annualized rates of return are 4.9% in a money-market savings

Table 3.2 After-Tax Accumulation per Dollar Invested and Rates of Return for Different Holding Periods for Savings Vehicles I and II when R = 7% and t = 30%.

Holding Period (n):	1	5	10	20	40	100	1000
After-Tax Accumulation ($)							
Vehicle							
I	1.05	1.27	1.61	2.60	6.78	119.55	5.96×10^{20}
II	1.05	1.28	1.68	3.01	10.78	607.70	1.69×10^{29}
After-Tax Rates of Return per Period (%)							
I	4.90	4.90	4.90	4.90	4.90	4.90	4.90
II	4.90	5.09	5.31	5.66	6.12	6.62	6.96

3.1   Constant Tax Rates: Saving Though an Impersonal Marketplace

account, they increase in an SPDA with the number of holding periods. In fact, as the number of periods becomes large, the after-tax rate of return per period approaches the before-tax rate of 7%.

Although 7% is equal to the before-tax rate of return, one must be careful *not* to conclude that a long-term investment in an SPDA is nearly equivalent to achieving tax exemption on investment returns. To see this, one can show that as n grows very large, the accumulation from investing in an SPDA approaches a fraction of 1 - t (or 70% in our example) of the accumulation from investing tax-free at rate R per period. The reason is that as the investment horizon becomes very large, nearly all of the return to the SPDA is interest (the original dollar deposited becomes relatively unimportant over long investment periods); and when the SPDA is cashed out, the earnings (which represent almost the entire contract when n is very large) will be taxed fully at ordinary rates.[3]

Hybrid Savings Vehicles

Although not listed in Table 3.1, certain savings vehicles permit tax deferral on only a *part* of the earnings until the investment is liquidated. Previously untaxed earnings are then taxed at ordinary rates. This savings vehicle is taxed as a hybrid of Vehicles I and II. For example, earnings on investments in dollar-denominated bonds through certain foreign corporations located in a relatively low tax-rate country are taxed at local tax rates rather than at the higher domestic rates. With some important exceptions that we discuss in the chapters on multinational tax planning, such income is not taxable in the home country of the investor until it is repatriated. Since the interest earned is taxed at a lower rate than in the home country, it compounds faster than if the same investment were made at home. The after-tax return available through this hybrid vehicle will always be between that available in Vehicle I (no deferral) and Vehicle II (100% deferral). Certain trusts can also give rise to this hybrid tax treatment.[4] Still another example is a contingent interest bond, where part of the interest is paid at maturity as a function of some performance index.

Differences in After-Tax Accumulations in Savings Vehicles I and II as a Function of Pretax Rates of Return

The advantage of an SPDA over a money market account increases with the level of pretax rates of return. For example, if R were 12% rather than 7%, Vehicle I

---

[3] SPDAs have been very popular as investments for both individual investors and for corporations. In fact, they had become so popular as a means for corporations to fund the deferred compensation programs of their executives that the Tax Reform Act of 1986 eliminated the ability of corporations and partnerships to defer tax with SPDAs. Only individual investors can use SPDAs after the 1986 Act to defer the tax on interest income. Moreover, the 1986 Act imposes an additional excise tax of 10% if the SPDA is surrendered, in part or in whole, prior to age 59.5, unless withdrawals take the form of a life annuity.

[4] A trust is a legal entity through which property is managed by one party for the benefit of another. For U.S. income tax purposes, the undistributed earnings of a trust are often taxed to the trust rather than to the beneficiary. The hybrid tax treatment discussed in the text can be achieved in certain cases when the tax rate of the trust is below that of the beneficiary.

Chapter 3   Organizational Form: Savings Vehicles

would accumulate to $5.02 in 20 years, and Vehicle II would accumulate to $7.05 for each dollar invested. Vehicle II returns just over 40% more than does Vehicle I when R = 12%, whereas Table 3.2 indicates that Vehicle II beats Vehicle I by less than 16% ($3.01 versus $2.60) when R = 7%.

Investments in Savings Vehicle III

Deposits into Vehicle III are nondeductible, as in Vehicles I and II. Unlike Vehicles I and II, however, investment earnings are taxed periodically at capital gains tax rates (or more generally, at fraction g of ordinary rates). There is generally a distinction between the rates at which capital gains income and ordinary income are taxed. Most countries exclude a substantial portion of capital gains from taxation.[5] Capital gains and losses arise from the sale or exchange of capital assets, which includes such passive investments as common stocks, bonds, and real estate. Between 1921 and 1987, a distinction existed between capital gains and ordinary income rates in the U.S. Although the distinction in rates disappeared in many circumstances in 1988 and was reintroduced to a limited extent in 1991, the difference between capital gain and ordinary income treatment remains particularly important in the U.S. in several circumstances:

- if property is transferred by bequest, the capital gains rate remains zero;
- if property is transferred by gift to a lower tax-bracket taxpayer, the effective capital gains tax rate becomes the lower tax rate of the donee;
- if property is transferred as a charitable contribution, the capital gains tax rate may vary between 0% and 24% depending upon whether the donor is subject to the so-called alternative minimum tax;
- if a taxpayer has sold other capital assets at a loss, the capital gains tax rate could vary between 0% and the ordinary rate, depending upon how binding the so-called capital loss limitations are.

At this point you need not understand any of these specific sources of difference between ordinary income rates and capital gains rates. You should simply be aware that in many circumstances the distinction is important. You should also be aware that the difference between ordinary income and capital gains tax rates are likely to change numerous times in the future. We address some of the implications of this in Section 3.2.

Examples of Vehicle III include arrangements wherein capital gain is recognized annually through "mark-to-market" rules or annual "sale." Mark-to-market rules apply to futures contracts in the U.S., where they are classified as capital assets and where assets still held at year-end are taxed *as if* they are sold at that time. The annual-sale treatment would apply to certain mutual funds, investing exclusively in our fully-taxable bonds, that distribute annual income by repurchasing mutual fund shares from fundholders. The share repurchase

---

[5] For example, the maximum long term capital gains tax rate on stocks, bonds, and nondepreciable real estate in 1989 was 0% in West Germany and Switzerland and 20% in Canada, Japan (or 1% of the gross sales price of the asset, if less), and the Netherlands. Capital gains are adjusted for inflation in Australia and the U.K., among other places. For further discussion, see Ernst & Young, *Washington Tax Reporter* (August 1989).

triggers capital gains treatment equal to the income on the underlying bonds held in the fund.

Comparison of Savings Vehicles II and III

Savings Vehicle III may be more or less attractive than Savings Vehicle II depending on n, the length of time the investment is held, and g, the percentage of the investment return that is taxed at ordinary rates. For example, if $g = 0$, Vehicle III always dominates II even for $n = 1$. In this case, the returns on the investment are tax exempt. For $g > 0$, Vehicle III dominates Vehicle II for short investment horizons but Vehicle II dominates Vehicle III for long investment horizons.

Assume, for example, that $g = .5$: half of the gain is taxed as ordinary income. Then $1 grows to $1 + R(1 - .5t)$ at the end of 1 year. When $R = 7\%$, the after-tax return is 5.95% (or $7\%(1 - .5 \times 30\%)$) per year. This return exceeds the money market savings account return by 1.05% per year (or $5.95\% - 7\%(1 - 30\%)$). While the rate of tax on capital gains is 15%, it is 30% on ordinary income. The 15% tax rate reduction on capital gains, relative to ordinary income, multiplied by the 7% pretax return, yields the 1.05% after-tax return differential. Earning 5.95% per year after tax dominates the after-tax return from investing in SPDAs for holding periods of up to 31 years. Beyond 31 years, SPDAs provide the superior after-tax investment returns.

Investments in Savings Vehicle IV

In Savings Vehicle IV, as with the preceding ones, deposits are not tax deductible; however, the tax on the earnings is deferred and taxed at capital gains rates when the investment is liquidated. Examples of this vehicle include an investment in the common stock of an investment company located in a tax haven country (that is, one in which the tax rate is near 0%),[6] or bond investments held by corporations in tax haven countries.[7]

Note from the formula given in Table 3.1 that the accumulation in Vehicle IV is similar to that for Vehicle II, except that income is taxed at the more favorable rate gt rather than at ordinary rate t. Vehicle IV is superior to Vehicles II and III except for special cases: $g = 0$ (all capital gains are tax exempt, as they have been for many taxpayers in a number of countries) or $g = 1$ (all capital gains are taxed at ordinary rates as in the U.S. in many cases under the 1986 Tax Act).

---

[6] This opportunity was closed down for U.S. investors by the Tax Reform Act of 1986 for companies that invest only in passive investments such as stocks and bonds. These companies are classified under the Act as "passive foreign investment companies" and income is *de facto* taxed as earned at ordinary tax rates (as Savings Vehicle I). This opportunity still exists, however, for investors resident in a number of other countries.

[7] The corporation holding bonds in tax haven countries must be engaged in real economic activities, rather than just holding passive investments, if the U.S. shareholder is to qualify for Vehicle IV tax treatment. For the qualifying corporation, interest income is tax free to the tax haven corporation. For U.S. shareholders, income is subject to capital gains taxation when shares are sold or when the corporation is liquidated, as long as the corporation is not a so-called "controlled foreign corporation," that is, has no five U.S. shareholders that together own more than 50% of the common stock.

Chapter 3   Organizational Form: Savings Vehicles

Table 3.3 After-Tax Accumulation per Dollar Invested and Rates of Return for Different Holding Periods for Savings Vehicles I, II, and IV when R = 7%, g = .5, and t = 30%.

Holding Period (n):	5	10	20	40	100	1000
			After-Tax Accumulation ($)			
Vehicle						
I	1.27	1.61	2.60	6.78	119.55	5.96×10^{20}
II	1.28	1.68	3.01	10.78	607.70	1.69×10^{29}
IV	1.34	1.82	3.44	12.88	737.71	2.06×10^{29}
			After-Tax Rates of Return per Period (%)			
I	4.90	4.90	4.90	4.90	4.90	4.90
II	5.09	5.31	5.66	6.12	6.62	6.96
IV	6.06	6.18	6.37	6.60	6.83	6.98

When g = 0, Vehicles III and IV both yield after-tax returns equal to before-tax rates of return (of 7% in our example). When g = 1, Vehicle IV becomes equivalent to an SPDA (that is, Vehicle II). Table 3.3 illustrates the superiority of Vehicle IV over Vehicles I and II for the case in which capital gains are taxed at half the ordinary rates.

Investments in Savings Vehicle V

While deposits into Savings Vehicle V accounts are not tax deductible, the earnings on the investment are entirely tax exempt. An example of this investment vehicle is the savings portion of a whole life (or universal life) insurance contract. As we discuss more fully in later chapters, a whole life policy consists of term (or pure) insurance plus a savings account. Earnings on bonds held in the saving account are tax exempt, so the pretax return is also equal to the after-tax return. Insurance companies typically invest the savings portion of the portfolio in ordinary interest-bearing securities.[8]

Note that the after-tax accumulation in Savings Vehicle V dominates that for Savings Vehicles I through IV as long as the capital gains tax rate is not 0%. In the special case of tax exemption for capital gains income, Vehicles III and IV generate exactly the same after-tax accumulations as in Vehicle V.

Investments in Savings Vehicle VI

In Savings Vehicle VI, the investment is tax deductible, and investment earnings are tax-deferred. An example is a pension plan. While contributions to the plan

---

[8] If the insurance policy is surrendered prior to death, a portion of the interest may be taxable as ordinary income. In particular, if withdrawals from the policy exceed the premiums paid into the policy (including both the savings *and* the insurance components of the premiums), the excess is taxed as ordinary income. In this case, the insurance policy becomes an example of Savings Vehicle IV. Why? Because only a portion of the interest income is taxable (only that portion of the interest that exceeds the term insurance premiums), and even this is taxable only when and if the policy is surrendered for cash.

3.1   Constant Tax Rates: Saving Though an Impersonal Marketplace

are tax deductible and earnings on investments in the plan are not taxed, distributions from the plan are fully taxable to the pensioner.[9]

Each dollar deposited into the pension fund grows to $(1 + R)^n$ dollars in n periods before the pension assets are distributed to the taxpayer and to $(1 + R)^n(1 - t)$ dollars after tax if the entire accumulation is taxed at rate t at time n when it is withdrawn. Since each dollar invested in the pension fund costs only $1 - t$ dollars after tax, the after-tax return per after-tax dollar invested is

$$\frac{1}{(1 - t)} (1 + R)^n(1 - t) = (1 + R)^n.$$

When tax rates are constant over time, Vehicles V and VI are equivalent; that is, pension savings are equivalent to tax exemption. One can think of the pension fund as a tax-free partnership with the government. For every $1 - t$ dollars you invest in the partnership, your partner (the government) invests t dollars. Collectively, the partnership has one dollar invested. This dollar grows at rate R each period for n periods. Before liquidating, the partnership has accumulated $(1 + R)^n$ dollars. You are entitled to fraction $1 - t$ of the partnership assets and your partner takes the remaining fraction t. So you take home $(1 - t)(1 + R)^n$ dollars on an initial investment of $1 - t$ dollars. Your return per dollar invested is simply $(1 + R)^n$.

Dominance Relations and Empirical Anomalies

Up to this point, we have demonstrated that investors realize different after-tax rates of return on identical assets held through different legal organizational forms. We have shown several strict dominance relations among the savings vehicles; that is, investors would always prefer to avoid utilizing some of the savings vehicles. In the absence of frictions and restrictions, we would never observe such tax-disfavored savings vehicles as ordinary money market savings. And yet, in the real world, money market savings command a larger share of our savings than most tax-favored forms of savings. The reasons, as we have suggested earlier, relate largely to frictions and restrictions.

3.2 Changes in Tax Rates over Time in an Impersonal Market

In this section we relax the assumption of constant tax rates through time. Even without frictions and restrictions, the dominance relations derived in Section 3.1 disappear when we introduce intertemporal changes in tax rates. In such a setting, Vehicles V and VI are no longer equivalent; tax-exempt saving through an insurance account is no longer equivalent to saving through a pension account. In particular, when tax rates are rising over time, pensions (and single-premium deferred annuities) become less attractive, and when tax rates are falling over time, they become *more* attractive.

---

[9] We ignore here the penalties for early withdrawal from pension plans (i.e., a 10% nondeductible excise tax penalty on withdrawal before age 59.5) and the penalties for excess income from pension plans, but we consider their effects in subsequent chapters.

Chapter 3   Organizational Form: Savings Vehicles

Whereas Vehicle V returns $(1 + R)^n$, irrespective of tax rates, Vehicle VI returns:

$$\frac{(1 + R)^n (1 - t_n)}{(1 - t_o)} \tag{3.3}$$

where the subscript on each tax rate refers to the time at which taxes are saved or paid. When $t_n > t_o$ (that is, tax rates in retirement at time n are relatively high), Vehicle V is superior. On the other hand, if $t_n < t_o$ (that is, tax rates today are relatively high), Vehicle VI is superior.

A pension plan can be viewed as a tax-exempt partnership with the government in which the taxpayer puts up fraction $1 - t_o$ of the capital in exchange for fraction $1 - t_n$ of the liquidation proceeds from the partnership. The taxpayer does better than tax exemption when t_n is lower than t_o, and worse than tax exemption when t_n is higher.

For example, consider a situation faced by many high-income taxpayers following passage of the Tax Reform Act of 1986. Suppose the marginal tax rate in 1986 was 50%, but the rate was expected to fall to 28% in retirement. With this configuration of tax rates, a pension provides an after-tax accumulation of 44% more than complete tax exemption! Using equation 3.3:

$$\frac{1}{.5} (1 + R)^n (1 - .28) = 1.44 (1 + R)^n.$$

On the other hand, in 1988, many high-income taxpayers, facing extant tax rates of 28%, expected tax rates to increase by the time they retired. If they expected rates to increase to 40% at the time of retirement, then pensions would accumulate to $(1 + R)^n (.6)/(.72)$ or 16.7% *less* after tax than complete tax exemption. In this case, investing in the pension plan is exactly the same as investing in a tax-exempt insurance policy that imposes a back-end termination fee of 16.7% on all distributions!

In fact, when tax rates are increasing, the pension plan is even worse than investing in a money market savings account over short investment horizons. If current tax rates are 28% and will increase to 40% in 5 years (n = 5) and R = 7%, a pension investment accumulates at a rate of only 3.2% per year after tax or 1.7% less per year than ordinary money market savings.[10] By comparison, an SPDA contract would yield 4.4%, well above the pension return, but still below the 4.9% available on ordinary money market savings.

On the other hand, for n = 10, the after-tax return from investing in a pension plan is 5.1% per year, which is better than investing in money market savings. Moreover, it now beats the 4.7% return available through SPDAs. The best after-tax return among all of the alternatives when tax rates are expected to rise in the future is the 7% available through investing in universal life insurance policies.

The best alternative among the savings vehicles depends not only on how a particular organizational form is taxed but also on how tax rates in the future are expected to differ from current rates. While one particular organizational form may dominate another when tax rates remain constant, the ranking could

---

[10] After tax, the individual invests $1/(1 - .28)$ at a 7% rate of return for 5 years, and then pays tax on the accumulated amount at a 40% rate. At the end of 5 years, the after-tax accumulation is $1/(1 - .28) \times (1.07)^5 \times (1 - .4) = \$1.1688$. The annualized rate of return is $(1.1688)^{(1/5)} - 1 = .0317$ or 3.2%.

change if tax rates increase or decrease in the future. When we add frictions and restrictions, the rankings change further and in ways that differ across taxpayers, even when they face the same set of statutory tax rates over time.

3.3   Changes in Tax Rates in Personal Markets

Cross Sectional Differences in Tax Rates

Thus far, we have considered savings vehicles available through an **impersonal marketplace**. Taxpayers can invest in money market accounts or pension plans and hold fully-taxable bonds without worrying about the tax characteristics of the issuer of the bonds. When taxpayers possess different tax characteristics, however, they often find it desirable to contract with one another in a way that exploits these different tax characteristics. As a result, by contracting in these **personal markets**, taxpayers expand their savings opportunities.

As a simple illustration of the contracting process in personal markets, let us consider a deferred compensation contract between an employer and an employee. An employee can arrange to save for future consumption by agreeing to defer the receipt of current compensation until some future date. As we will see, whether this is desirable purely from a tax standpoint (we ignore incentive considerations for now), depends upon both the employee's and the employer's current and future tax rates as well as the opportunities each has to invest idle funds in the market-place.

The specific question we now wish to consider is whether to offer an employee a dollar of salary to be paid today or a deferred compensation contract that promises to pay a stipulated bonus at time period n. To see whether current or deferred compensation is preferred, we must again avoid comparing apples and oranges. A convenient way to proceed is to determine the deferred compensation amount (or bonus) that leaves either the employer or the employee indifferent between the two plans and then see which of the plans is preferred by the other party to the contract. This will identify the mutually-preferred contract. Through negotiations, both parties can be made better off by sharing the gains from tax planning.

For example, how much can an employer afford to provide to an employee in n periods as a deferred compensation payment in exchange for paying $1 of salary to the employee today? If compensation is deferred, so is the timing of the tax deduction to the employer and the timing of taxable income to the employee. Note that by not paying $1 of salary today, the employer saves only $1 - t_{co}$ dollars after tax, where t_{co} is the employer's tax rate today.[11] In n years, the after-tax savings to the employer from salary deferral would accumulate to

$$(1 - t_{co})(1 + r_{cn})^n,$$

where r_{cn} is the employer's annualized after-tax rate of investment return on marginal investments made for a period of n years. This is the rate of return that

---

[11] While t_{co} might be thought of as the current corporate tax rate, the employer certainly need not be a corporation for the following analysis to apply.

Chapter 3   Organizational Form: Savings Vehicles

the employer can achieve with the after-tax cash saved from deferring the salary payment to the employee.

When the deferred compensation payment is made at time n (in the amount of D_n), the employer receives a tax deduction, so the after-tax cost of the payment becomes $D_n(1 - t_{cn})$. To be indifferent between current salary and a deferred payment, the employer must be able to set aside $1 - t_{co}$ now to satisfy its future deferred compensation obligation. This occurs if the after-tax deferred compensation payment at time n is equal to what the $1 - t_{co}$ after-tax dollars saved by not paying current salary would accumulate to if invested for n periods. That is:

$$D_n(1 - t_{cn}) = (1 - t_{co})(1 + r_{cn})^n$$

or

$$D_n = (1 + r_{cn})^n \frac{(1 - t_{co})}{(1 - t_{cn})}.$$

Note that if the employer's tax rate is constant over time ($t_{co} = t_{cn}$), the employer can afford to pay its own after-tax rate of return on the $1 of salary as deferred compensation. If the tax rate is increasing, however, the employer can afford to pay an even larger amount of deferred compensation in the future because future deductions are more valuable. On the other hand, if the tax rate is decreasing, the employer can afford to pay less than the after-tax rate of return on the savings.

For example, suppose that the after-tax corporate rate of return on investment is 6%. The employer is contemplating a five-year (n = 5) deferred compensation contract. That is, rather than paying $1 of salary currently, the employer is considering a deferred compensation payment to be made in five years. If the employer's tax rate were constant, the employer could afford to offer a deferred payment of

$$(1 + .06)^5 = \$1.34.$$

How much more or less can the employer afford if its tax rates change over time? The answer appears in Table 3.4. The differences can be significant. For example, if the employer's current tax rate is 50%, and it will be 30% in 5 years, Table 3.4 indicates that the employer can only afford a deferred compensation

Table 3.4 Deferred Compensation Amounts for a Five-Year Deferral Period and an After-Tax Investment Return of 6% that Have the Same After-Tax Cost to the Employer as a Dollar of Immediate Salary: Sensitivity to Changes in Tax Rates Over Time

t_{cn}	t_{co} 30%	40%	50%
30%	1.34	1.15	.96
40%	1.56	1.34	1.12
50%	1.87	1.61	1.34

t_{co}, t_{cn} = employer's current and future marginal tax rates, respectively.

payment of 96 cents in 5 years for each dollar of current salary deferred. On the other hand, if the employer's tax rate increases from 30% to 40%, the employer can afford a deferred payment equal to $1.56 for each dollar of current salary that is postponed for 5 years.

Now that the employer has been made indifferent between a salary and a deferred compensation contract, let's turn next to the employee. What contract does the employee prefer? The employee must compare salary today versus a deferred compensation payment n periods from today. That is,

Salary: $(1 - t_{po})(1 + r_{pn})^n$

Deferred Compensation: $D_n (1 - t_{pn})$ or $(1 + r_{cn})^n \dfrac{(1 - t_{co})}{(1 - t_{cn})} (1 - t_{pn})$.

The employee will prefer whichever contract leaves more after tax in n years. A little algebra shows that salary will be preferred to deferred compensation if and only if:

$$\frac{(1 - t_{po})(1 + r_{pn})^n}{(1 - t_{pn})(1 + r_{cn})^n} > \frac{(1 - t_{co})}{(1 - t_{cn})}.$$

In this relation, three key factors combine to determine precisely whether salary or deferred compensation is preferable:

1. The employee's tax rate today versus n periods from today. If the employee's tax rate is declining, then deferred compensation tends to be preferable. The income is recognized when the employee's tax rate is low.
2. The employer's tax rate today versus n periods from today. If the employer's tax rate is increasing, then deferred compensation tends to be preferable. The employer prefers to take the deduction when tax rates are high.
3. The after-tax rate of return on investment for the employer versus that of the employee. If the employer can save at a higher after-tax rate of return than can the employee, then deferred compensation tends to be preferable. In effect, a deferred compensation contract allows the employee to save at the employer's higher rate of return on investment.

Since deferred compensation is favored if the employee's tax rate is expected to decrease in the future, it may be especially appropriate for employees who expect to face a lower tax rate in retirement or for employees on temporary assignment in a high-tax-rate foreign country.[12] Deferred compensation arrangements may also be desirable when tax rates are expected to decrease due to statutory changes in tax rates voted by the legislature. Here, however, one must be careful not to adopt a unilateral tax-planning perspective. A decline in tax rates for the employee need not favor deferred compensation if tax rates also decline

---

[12]Some tax jurisdictions do not permit the deferral of taxable income through the adoption of deferred compensation arrangements. This is an example of a tax rule restriction.

Chapter 3   Organizational Form: Savings Vehicles

for the employer. We will take a closer look at this common phenomenon in the chapter on employee compensation planning.

Since deferred compensation is favored if the employer's tax rate is expected to increase in the future, it may be especially appropriate when a firm in a net operating loss carryforward position cannot effectively use current tax deductions.[13] Deferring compensation increases current taxable income but reduces future taxable income. This smoothing of taxable income is tax advantageous for firms experiencing net operating loss carryforwards. Another example of changing tax brackets that favors deferred compensation relates to the so-called "alternative minimum tax." If the corporation finds itself subject to the alternative minimum tax (that taxes income at a marginal rate of 20%) and expects to be subject to the higher marginal tax rate under the "regular" tax in the future, deferring compensation increases current taxable income when marginal tax rates are lower.

For the employer with an opportunity to earn at a greater after-tax rate of return than its employees, saving through the corporation by way of a deferred compensation contract is tax advantageous. To see this, assume that $r_{pn} = 6\%$ and $r_{cn} = 8\%$. Then, after tax, deferred compensation beats salary by a factor of

$$(1.08/1.06)^n - 1 = 1.9\% \text{ for } n = 1; 9.8\% \text{ for } n = 5; \text{ and } 20.1\% \text{ for } n = 10.$$

While this may not be as striking as the difference brought about by changing tax brackets, it is still worth considering. But we don't want to overemphasize the importance of differences in after-tax earnings opportunities that are available to the employer and the employee. If there were a large difference, employers presumably would borrow money from employees and invest it until the difference largely disappears. In other words, deferred compensation arrangements do not represent a unique means of exploiting differences in after-tax investment opportunities of employers and employees. The same is true of changing tax brackets over time. There are many substitutes for deferred compensation contracts to shift taxable income across time periods.

In this section we have emphasized the effects of changes in tax rates and differences in investment opportunities on the desire of employers and employees to use current or deferred compensation contracts. Whether deferred compensation contracts are desirable also depends on incentive contracts between employees and employers, as well as on uncertainty regarding the employee's and employer's future tax rates and income levels.

---

[13] Firms in the U.S. and a number of other countries that experience net operating losses can carry them back as an offset to income earned in previous years. This results in a refund of past taxes paid. The carryback period is limited, however. If there is insufficient past income against which to offset current losses, the losses are carried forward to shelter income from taxation in future years. We discuss other tax-planning strategies for firms with net operating loss carryforwards in Chapter Eight.

Summary of Key Points

1. Numerous organizational forms are available to save for future consumption. We considered a number of alternative savings vehicles that were distinguished by the tax treatment of investment returns. While investments made in most savings vehicles do not give rise to immediate tax deductions, investments in pensions do. While the earnings on some investments are taxed annually, the earnings on others are partially or fully tax-deferred or may be tax exempt altogether. Earnings in some vehicles are taxed at ordinary rates while earnings in other vehicles attract tax at capital gains rates. Because of these differing tax treatments, the after-tax accumulation and rate of return from holding a fully-taxable bond in each of these savings vehicles varies dramatically across the alternatives.

2. With constant tax rates, pension savings and tax-exempt savings through insurance contracts dominate money market accounts and such other savings vehicles as single premium deferred annuities.

3. Without frictions and restrictions, the dominant returns available from some organizational forms would result in tax arbitrage opportunities. Investors would save only through the dominant organizational forms.

4. If tax brackets change through time, the dominance relations can disappear. For example, when tax rates are increasing over time, money market accounts (the least tax-advantageous organizational form when tax rates are constant) can provide higher after-tax rates of return than pension accounts (the most tax-advantageous organizational form when tax rates are constant).

5. The introduction of frictions and restrictions further alters the rankings of the alternatives. Empirically, we find that investors use all of the organizational forms that we analyzed to save for future consumption.

6. When we add cross-sectional differences in tax rates and investment opportunities, additional tax-planning opportunities arise that can be exploited through personalized contracting. For example, it may be advantageous to undertake savings through deferred compensation contracts. An important lesson here is that the tax positions of both the employee and employer must be considered to determine whether deferred compensation represents an effective organizational arrangement. For example, while falling employee tax rates over time favor deferred compensation arrangements, such contracts may be undesirable when employer tax rates are also falling through time.

7. When opportunities exist to contract in personal markets, effective tax planning requires that we consider the tax and investment opportunities of all parties to the contract. It is convenient to make all but one of the parties indifferent across the contract alternatives in deciding which tax-planning alternative is favored.

8. Nontax factors, such as motivational and risk-sharing considerations between employees and employers, might tip the choice in favor of current compensation even though deferred compensation is tax-favored, or *vice versa*.

Discussion Questions

1. Identify three tax characteristics that distinguish among alternative savings vehicles.

2. The interest income on bonds issued by tax-exempt organizations is often exempt from federal taxation in the U.S. In comparing savings vehicles, why is it inappropriate to view these bonds as perfect substitutes for such savings accounts as tax-exempt life insurance contracts?

3. With constant tax rates over time, why does a single premium deferred annuity contract (SPDA) provide greater after-tax rates of return than does a money market account? How is the difference in after-tax accumulations in these two vehicles affected by the level of interest rates? Why does the length of the holding period affect the after-tax rates of return per period on SPDAs and not on money market accounts?

4. Under what circumstances is an investment that is taxed each period at capital gains rates preferred to an SPDA contract (taxed at ordinary rates on investment income but only at the point of liquidation)? When is Vehicle IV (income deferred and taxed at capital gains rates at the point of liquidation) preferred to an SPDA?

5. Why do a pension account and the savings portion of a life insurance product provide the same after-tax rates of return if tax rates are constant over time? In comparing these two savings vehicles, is it appropriate to have the same number of dollars invested in both alternatives?

6. If tax rates are constant over time, why might a taxpayer prefer to save through a money market account rather than a pension account or a tax-exempt insurance policy?

7. If tax rates are changing over time, do pension accounts dominate tax-exempt savings accounts?

8. Why do rising tax rates make single premium deferred annuities and pension accounts less attractive relative to ordinary money market accounts than when tax rates are falling?

9. What do we mean by personal and impersonal markets? What are the important differences between a personal market and an impersonal market from a tax-planning standpoint?

10. In determining the tax advantage of a current salary contract versus a deferred compensation contract, why is it useful to set the contractual terms so as to hold one party indifferent to the choice of contract? Does

it matter whether the employee or the employer is made indifferent between the two choices?

11. Employees favor deferred compensation contracts if they expect their tax rates to fall in the future. Would it always be wise for employers to grant such contracts to employees in this case? Why?

Problems

1. Alternative Savings Vehicles

   Fully-taxable bonds yield 10% per year before tax, tax-exempt bonds yield 6.5%, and the pretax return on single premium deferred annuities (SPDAs) is 9.5%.

   a. What are the after-tax rates of return per period (for holding periods of 3, 5, 10, and 20 years) for an investment in (1) tax-exempt bonds; (2) taxable bonds; (3) SPDAs cashed out after age 59.5 (no excise tax); and (4) SPDAs cashed out *before* age 59.5 requiring a 10% nondeductible excise tax (in addition to the normal tax) on the accumulated interest, for an investor facing: (i) a 40% ordinary tax rate each period; and (ii) a 30% ordinary tax rate each period?

Holding Period	Tax-Exempt Bonds	Taxable Bonds	SPDAs (no penalty)	SPDAs (with penalty)
3 years				
30% taxpayer				
40% taxpayer				
5 years				
30% taxpayer				
40% taxpayer				
10 years				
30% taxpayer				
40% taxpayer				
20 years				
30% taxpayer				
40% taxpayer				

   b. How do optimal investment strategies change as a function of tax rates, lengths of investment horizon, and age?

   c. At age 34.5, you deposited $50,000 into an SPDA yielding 9.5%. Ten years later, to finance the purchase of a second home, you require a mortgage exceeding the cash-out value of your SPDA. As an alternative to liquidating your SPDA, you can borrow funds at an annual interest rate of 11%, tax deductible, for fifteen years. Your current tax rate is 30%, and you expect it to remain at that level. How much better or worse off, after tax, will you be at age 59.5 if you invade your SPDA today (and incur the 10% excise tax) to reduce the size of the required mortgage?

d. How does your answer to (c) change if the interest expense incurred on the debt used to finance the expenditure is not tax-deductible (for example, you purchased a flashy, expensive personal automobile)?

2. Personal Financial Planning: Choosing Among Alternative Savings Vehicles

This exercise is designed to introduce you to how differences in the legal organizational form through which savings are undertaken affect future consumption opportunities. In particular, we want you to deduce how to increase your wealth using Keogh accounts and deferred annuities to supplement money market accounts and municipal bond investments.

a. Assume that you find yourself in a relatively simple environment. Inflation is 4 percent per year, and the real rate of interest is 2 percent per year. Assume that the annual before-tax earnings rate on taxable bonds (whether held through money market accounts, Keoghs, or deferred annuities) is 6.08 percent [(1.04)(1.02) - 1]; that is, 6.08 percent is the nominal rate of interest. Municipal bonds are priced such that the implicit tax rate is always 28 percent; that is, municipal bonds yield 6.08% × (1 - .28). No borrowing is allowed. Although most deferred annuity contracts impose a declining schedule of surrender charges if liquidated within five to ten years from the date of deposit, you may ignore the penalty for purposes of this problem.

Tomorrow is your 51st birthday. You consumed liberally during your lost youth (exotic vacations and the like), and you haven't a dime in savings at the present time. Your thoughts now turn to accumulation of wealth for your twilight years. You currently earn $100,000 per year in self-employment income (paid once a year on your birthday, so tomorrow is your next "payday"). You will retire just after you receive your annual income on your 66th birthday. Your income will grow by the nominal rate of interest. You plan to consume 40 percent of your self-employment income each working year (e.g., $40,000 on your 51st birthday), saving whatever is left after consumption and payment of taxes on self-employment income and money market interest income. Your income tax liability will run at a flat rate of 33 percent of taxable income throughout your life.

Your task is to allocate annual savings among the alternative investment vehicles listed above (and elaborated upon below) so as to achieve the highest after-tax level of wealth at retirement. Although a more complete analysis would entail conditioning your investment allocations, in part, on your planned consumption behavior in retirement, your assignment in this problem is to act as though your objective function is particularly simple; namely to maximize the after-tax value (after "cashing out" your Keogh and deferred annuity contracts, if any) of your retirement "nest egg."

Investment Alternatives (in addition to municipal bonds and fully taxable money market savings accounts):

Keogh: The typical Keogh account is essentially a defined contribution pension plan. Funds invested in a Keogh account accumulate investment income tax-free, and each dollar removed from the account is taxed at ordinary income rates when withdrawn. Funds can be withdrawn after age 59.5 without penalty. Withdrawals made before age 59.5, however, require a 10 percent non-deductible excise tax in addition to the ordinary tax. Assume that the maximum annual Keogh contribution permitted is 20 percent of self-employment income (e.g., $20,000 on your 51st birthday). Assume that the special averaging options for lump-sum distributions are not available.

Deferred Annuity: These contracts are acquired with after-tax dollars; that is, deposits into the account are not tax-deductible. Income earned on the contract accumulates tax-free, and only the interest is taxed (at ordinary rates) on withdrawal from the fund. Partial withdrawals are treated as interest first. Assume that there are no load fees incurred to buy into the annuity contract, and no surrender charges are assessed upon liquidation of the account. Also ignore any excise taxes on withdrawals. As with money market and Keogh accounts, funds invested in the deferred annuity accumulate interest at the 6.08 percent rate that taxable bonds yield.

Required:

Generate a spreadsheet that shows how your income is allocated to consumption, taxes, and various savings vehicles over your working life so as to reach your goal of "cashing out" all savings to realize the maximum after-tax "nest egg" on your 66th birthday. Your analysis should include a brief description of and rationale for the savings strategy you chose to undertake. You should also calculate the after-tax cash-out value on your 66th birthday after consuming.

Note for *parts b, c, and d*: Your answer should include a brief summary of how your savings strategies differ from that chosen in *part a*.

b. Repeat the analysis conducted in *part a*, assuming that the funds invested in the deferred annuity accumulate interest at 25 basis points less than the rate on fully taxable bonds (i.e., 5.83 percent), because of administrative costs associated with this savings vehicle. All investments other than deferred annuities continue to accrue interest at 6.08 percent, as in *part a*.

c. Repeat the analysis conducted in *part a* (ignoring the change made in *part b*), assuming that in the year following your 57th birthday, you will take an unpaid sabbatical for one year to retool. Although you will not earn self-employment income during your sabbatical, you wish to consume $60,000 on your 58th birthday. This will require you to liquidate some of your retirement savings. Your retooling will enable you to increase your self-employment income by 20 percent relative to what it otherwise would have been during your remaining working years. You should assume that you anticipated taking this future sabbatical at the time you began to formulate your retirement savings strategy (that is, on the day before your 51st birthday).

d. Repeat the analysis in *part a* (ignoring the changes made in *parts b and c*), assuming that just after your 62nd birthday, your tax rate increases permanently to 40 percent from 33 percent. That is, any taxable income on your 62nd birthday is taxed at 33%, but any taxable income on your 63rd through 66th birthdays is taxed at 40%. To keep the problem tractable, assume that pretax rates of return on all savings vehicles are unaffected by the change in your tax rate. Moreover, assume that the change in tax rate from 33 percent to 40 percent is not a surprise. In particular, assume that you *know* of the forthcoming change in tax rate as early as your 51st birthday.

CHAPTER 4
Production Decisions and
Organizational Form

In Chapter Three, we considered how differences in the tax treatment of earnings across alternative savings vehicles affect after-tax investment returns. In this chapter, we focus on the taxation of the returns to businesses that produce goods and services. Sole proprietorships, partnerships, and corporations are a few examples of organizational forms in which such activities are undertaken. As we will see, significant differences in tax treatment can result from undertaking identical investment projects that generate the same before-tax cash flows through different legal organizational forms. Such tax treatment differences can have an important influence on the selection of the organizational forms used to conduct business activities.

To illustrate the nature of these tax differentials, let us consider a few important tax rules affecting corporations and partnerships in the U.S. Corporations are required to pay an entity-level tax on their taxable income. They file tax returns and pay tax on corporate taxable income in ways very similar to individuals. Shareholders pay additional tax (at their own statutory rates) on dividends that are paid out of corporate earnings and profits, and they pay tax on gains from the sale of their shares. This means that corporate stockholders are effectively taxed twice on income, once at the corporate level and again when profits are distributed by way of a dividend or the sale of shares.[1] In contrast, partners and sole proprietors are subject to only one level of taxation at their own

---

[1] In many countries, corporate and personal taxes are *integrated*, in that shareholders are granted a tax credit for the corporate taxes they pay indirectly as owners. In fully integrated systems, this arrangement results in single taxation of income earned through corporations. Note that double taxation can also be avoided if distributions of corporate income (dividendes and capital gains) are deductible at the corporate level or are exempted from taxation to owner-recipients. This situation is approximated in countries where capital gains are exempted from taxation and dividend yields are low.

personal rates. Rather than pay an entity-level tax, partnerships and proprietorships act as conduits through which income flows to their owners. For example, partners record their share of partnership profits and losses on their own tax returns, whether the profits are distributed or not.

It is worth emphasizing that only corporate income attributable to stockholders, the residual claimants, is subject to **double taxation**. Income distributed to creditors, employees, and suppliers, in the form of interest, compensation, and other costs to produce and sell goods and services, is *not* taxed at the corporate level. Instead, this income is taxed exclusively to its recipients, just like partnership income.

In this chapter, we begin by analyzing the effects of taxes on the returns from productive activities undertaken through corporations and partnerships. We employ a simplified model where there are no transaction or information costs (frictions). The model's primary implication is that an investor's choice between the corporate form of organization (two levels of taxation) and the partnership form (one level of taxation) depends on the length of the investment horizon as well as three tax parameters: (1) the investor's personal tax rates on ordinary income, (2) corporate-level tax rates, and (3) the shareholder-level tax rates on the returns to investing in corporate shares. The model provides insights into how a specific investor might choose an organizational form. It does not explain, however, how partnerships and corporations can compete successfully against each other in the marketplace. In fact, one implication of this model is that if all investors faced exactly the same three tax parameters, we would not expect to observe both partnerships and corporations producing the same goods and services.

Moreover, as we will discuss fully in Chapter Six, in the absence of frictions and restrictions, even if investors initially faced differences in these three tax parameters, leading some investors to produce goods and services through partnerships and others to produce identical goods and services in corporate form, tax-arbitrage opportunities would prevent this from being an equilibrium situation. As investors exploited the arbitrage possibilities, their tax positions would be altered, and the activity would continue until all investors faced the same three tax characteristics. As a result, once again we would not expect to observe both partnerships and corporations producing the same goods and services.

In the real world, partnerships and corporations *do* compete head to head. This can occur quite naturally in the presence of market frictions and tax-rule restrictions. As we have emphasized before, to maximize after-tax returns, investors must account for both tax and nontax factors. In this chapter, we consider special tax provisions for both partnerships and corporations that reduce the differences in after-tax rates of return that are otherwise predicted by the model. Similarly, we touch on market frictions that might prevent one organizational form from dominating another. That is, while one organizational form may enjoy less favorable tax treatment than another, the tax-disfavored entity may still be able to compete effectively against its rival if nontax factors cause its *before*-tax profitability to be greater. For example, if tax rules favor partnerships over corporations, the corporate form may still be preferable, because corporate owners enjoy limited liability, easy transferability of owner-ship, and a relatively active market for management control. In contrast, it is relatively expensive to limit liability, to trade partnership interests, and to change control of the organization.

A reduced rate of shareholder-level or corporate-level taxation makes corporations more competitive relative to partnerships. This is important to corporate strategists because reducing either corporate or shareholder tax rates lowers the corporate cost of capital, that is, the rate of return that the corporation must earn on investment projects of a designated risk if they expect to cover their costs of financing the projects. Moreover, as with the analysis of savings vehicles in Chapter Three, changes in tax rates across time might affect entrepreneurs' preference ranking over the corporate and partnership organizational forms.

We concentrate in this chapter on the standard partnership and corporate form, leaving for later chapters special considerations regarding the taxation of such institutions as universities and charities (i.e., tax-exempt organizations) and special types of corporations such as banks. Multinational corporations, as well, face unique tax considerations that we will address in later chapters.

4.1 Organizational Forms for Producing Goods and Services: Constant Tax Rates

We begin with a brief overview of the taxation of several organizational forms used to produce goods and services. The income statement of **sole proprietorships** in the U.S. is filed along with the owner's personal tax return. The profits of the business are taxed only once at the personal level. In this regard, the sole proprietorship serves as a conduit through which the income of the business is passed through to the tax return of its owner.

A U.S. **partnership** is another legal organizational form that serves as a tax conduit between the business and its partners. The partnership files its own information tax return, including an income statement, a balance sheet, and a schedule of specific allocations to each of the partners. These allocations are broken down by type of income and expense (for example, depreciation, interest, rent, and capital gains); partners report their designated share of income and expense on their own tax returns. The partnership entity does not pay any income tax. Partnerships may have two classes of partners: general partners and limited partners. As with a sole proprietor, general partners face personal liability limited only by their personal resources and the bankruptcy laws. A limited partner, on the other hand, like a stockholder of a corporation, faces a more limited liability: the investor usually is at risk for only the amount invested in the business. As with most shareholders in widely held corporations, a limited partner typically does not participate actively in the operations of the business.[2]

Unlike partnerships, U.S. **corporations** are taxed directly on their taxable income. In addition to corporate-level taxes, stockholders are also taxed on dividend income and realized capital gains at their own personal rates. If the

---

[2] Indeed, active participation in the management of the business may void the limited liability protection of "limited" partners.

taxable income of the corporation were $1 and the corporate marginal tax rate were 40%, corporate after-tax profits would be $.60 (or $1 × (1 - .4)). If the corporation then pays a cash dividend of $.60 (its entire after-tax profits), shareholders pay tax on this dividend at their own personal tax rates. Dividends, like wages or interest receipts, are typically taxed at ordinary rates.[3] For example, if shareholders face a 30% marginal tax rate, they retain only $.42 of the initial $1 of corporate before-tax earnings ($.6 × (1 - .3)), a 58% total rate of tax.

Shareholders also realize capital gains and losses on the sale of their stock. Such income is granted special treatment. It is taxed only when realized under the tax laws, which ordinarily occurs upon a sale. Capital gains (losses) on the sale of stock are computed as the difference between the sale price and the basis of the asset (usually the purchase price).[4] Although realized capital gains and dividends were typically taxed at the same rate in the U.S. from 1988 through 1990, capital gains are taxed at a lower rate than dividends in most tax systems. And in the U.S., prior to the 1986 Tax Act, 60% of long-term capital gains (gains from an asset held for more than six months under the 1986 rules) was excluded from taxation. Thus, an investor facing a 50% marginal tax rate on ordinary income faced a tax rate of only 20% on long-term gains (or .4 × .5). The 1986 Tax Act eliminated the 60% exclusion of capital gains. The 1990 Tax Act raised the top marginal tax rate on ordinary income to 31% but capped the capital gains tax rate at 28%.[5]

Although income earned by U.S. corporations is subjected to two levels of tax, the common reference to the corporation as a "**double tax**" system can be misleading. This is true for several reasons. First, shareholders are taxable only on the after-tax profits earned by the corporation. The taxes paid by the corporation are effectively deducted in determining the income taxed at the shareholder level. Second, the after-tax income earned at the corporate level is not taxed instantly to shareholders unless the corporation immediately pays out all of its after-tax earnings as a dividend or shareholders sell their shares each period. Other sources of reduction in the two-level tax include:

---

[3] For many years, U.S. investors excluded from taxable income the first $100 of dividends received from U.S. corporations ($200 if a married couple filed a joint return). Moreover, the shareholders of selected corporations received special tax treatment for dividends. For example, from 1982 through 1985, investors holding qualified public utility stock could reinvest $750 of cash dividends ($1500 for a joint return) without paying a current tax on these qualifying dividends. The reinvestment effectively converted dividends into unrealized capital gains, taxable only when shares are sold.

[4] The basis of the asset at the time of sale often differs from the initial purchase price because the company may have declared a stock dividend or a stock split. For example, a 10% stock dividend results in a 10% increase in the number of shares held and a corresponding reduction in the basis per share of 1/11 or 9.09%. If the initial purchase price and basis of a stock was $55, then after a 10% stock dividend, the new basis per share would be $50 (or $55/1.1).

Another common circumstance in which the basis of a share of stock falls below its purchase price is when dividends are distributed in excess of "accumulated earnings and profits." Such dividends are treated for tax purposes as a nontaxable return of capital, that is, as a refund of part of the purchase price.

[5] The top tax rates on both ordinary income and capital gains under the 1990 Tax Act can actually be higher once one factors in the effect of phasing out personal exemptions, itemized deductions, and other deductions at certain levels of income.

- an ability to distribute corporate profits in a tax-deductible way via interest, rent, royalty, compensation and other payments, rather than by way of nondeductible dividends to stockholders,
- reduced tax rates at the shareholder level (for example, as discussed earlier, capital gains in most countries are partially excluded from income),
- reduced corporate-level tax rates for certain entities (for example, U.S. savings and loan associations),
- deferral of corporate income taxes (for example, income earned abroad and not repatriated by way of dividend income, by certain majority-owned foreign subsidiaries), and
- lower corporate tax rates than personal tax rates (for example, prior to the 1986 Tax Act in the U.S. and currently in many other countries).

After-Tax Returns to Pass-Through (e.g., Partnership) and Non Pass-Through (e.g., Corporate) Forms of Organization

We develop a simple model to compare the after-tax returns from investing in partnership (or sole proprietorship) form to those from investing in corporate form. Let us assume initially that the before-tax rate of return on a project is constant at a rate of R per year whether the project is undertaken in corporate or partnership form. The project lasts for n years, at which point the organization is assumed to liquidate.

All after-tax income generated in the interim is reinvested in the business at rate R per period before tax. Distributions at rate $t_p R$ are made each period from the partnership to enable partners to pay their personal tax. If the project is undertaken in partnership form, partners pay tax at their marginal tax rates, t_p, each year, as income is earned. A partner's after-tax accumulation for an initial $1 investment is[6]

$$[1 + R(1 - t_p)]^n. \tag{4.1}$$

For example, assume that R = 20%, n = 5 years, and t_p = 40%. A partner's after-tax accumulation for a $1 investment is

$$\$1 \, [1 + .2(1 - .4)]^5 = \$1.76.$$

If, instead, the project is undertaken in corporate form, shareholders pay tax at their ordinary tax rate, t_p, on a fraction g of the corporate distributions in excess of their "basis" (unrecovered investment cost for tax purposes) when the firm liquidates or when shareholders sell their shares. So, the shareholder-level tax rate on liquidation (or sale) of their shares is gt_p.

For example, suppose that on either a liquidation or a sale, shareholder gains are taxed at capital gains rates and that shareholders can exclude 90% of these capital gains from their taxable income. In this case, the shareholder-level tax rate on capital gains is 4% (or gt_p = 10% × 40%).

---

[6] Note that this assumes there is no capital gain or loss on the liquidation of the partnership interest. At time n, partners receive a liquidating distribution of all after-tax partnership income generated over n periods, plus their initial dollar invested.

In addition to the shareholder-level tax, the corporation must pay taxes each year at rate t_c on the before-tax return, R. Combining the annual corporate-level tax and the shareholder-level tax, the after-tax accumulation to the owners in a corporation for an initial $1 investment is as follows:

$$= \quad [1 + R(1 - t_c)]^n - gt_p\{[1 + R(1 - t_c)]^n - 1\}$$

Proceeds from sale of corporate shares - Tax on the gain from sale

$$= \quad [1 + R(1 - t_c)]^n (1 - gt_p) + gt_p. \tag{4.2}$$

We have already seen a form of equation 4.2 in the last chapter. More specifically, the accumulation in 4.2 is exactly the same as that on a single premium deferred annuity for n periods in which the account grows at rate $R(1- t_c)$ each period, and all earnings are taxed at time n at rate gt_p.

Assuming that $t_c = 30\%$, the five-year after-tax accumulation in corporate form is

$$\$1[1 + .2(1 - .3)]^5 (1 - .1 \times .4) + \$1 \times .1 \times .4 = \$1.89.$$

This provides an annual after-tax rate of return of 13.56% (or $1.89^{1/5} - 1$) or 1.56% more than the partnership. Ignoring nontax considerations, a taxpayer will prefer to invest in a partnership (or proprietorship) rather than a corporation whenever the accumulation in equation 4.1 exceeds that of equation 4.2, or

$$\underbrace{[1 + R(1- t_p)]^n}_{} > \underbrace{[1 + R(1 - t_c)]^n(1 - gt_p) + gt_p.}_{} \tag{4.3}$$

Partnerships (P)   Corporations (C)

For what values of t_c, t_p, and g in relation 4.3 will investors prefer partnership to corporate form? Before considering the question at this level of generality, let us consider the case of n = 1. When n = 1, relation 4.3 simplifies to

$$\underbrace{(1 - t_p)}_{P} > \underbrace{(1 - t_c)(1 - gt_p)}_{C} \tag{4.4}$$

Thus, for a one-period investment, if $t_p = 40\%$, $t_c = 30\%$, and g = 10%, the corporate form is preferred to the partnership form because

$$1- .4 = .6 < (1 - .3)(1 - .1 \times .4) = .672.$$

Although there are two levels of taxation on corporate income, the product of one minus the corporate-level tax rate and one minus the shareholder-level tax rate happens to be higher than one minus the ordinary personal tax rate in this example. If policymakers had set the corporate-level tax rate at 35%, rather than 30%, and allowed investors to exclude 81% of their realized capital gain from taxation, rather than 90%, investors facing a 40% marginal tax rate would be about indifferent between investing in partnership and corporate form (as can be seen by substituting for g = .19, $t_c = .35$ and $t_p = .4$ in inequality 4.4).

If all projects lasted for only one period and there were only tax factors to consider, unless the configurations of t_p, t_c, and g were such that condition 4.4 was an equality, projects would be undertaken in either partnership or corporate form, but not both. Tax policymakers would have to be careful in establishing the relation between ordinary personal tax rates, t_p, and the two levels of corporate taxation, t_c and gt_p, if they wished to avoid having taxes affect the choice of organizational form.

Once we leave the world of one-period investments, whether the partnership is preferred to the corporation depends also on the value of deferring the payment of the shareholder-level capital-gains tax. The value of the **deferral** is greater the higher is the after-tax accumulation in the corporation, $R(1 - t_c)$. It is also increasing in the *length* of the deferral period, n.

For example, if n = 5 years, the accumulation in corporate form after both corporate and shareholder-level taxes for g = .19, t_c = .35, and t_p = .4 is

$$\$1[1 + .2(1 - .35)]^5 (1 - .19 \times .4) + \$1 \times .19 \times .4 = \$1.78.$$

This compares with an accumulation of \$1.76 in partnership form. The \$1.78 accumulation in corporate form provides an annual after-tax rate of return of 12.2% versus 12% in partnership form and 12% in a corporation in which the shareholder-level tax is paid each period rather than only once at the end of 5 years. So the value of the deferral of the shareholder-level tax is rather slight in this case.

From these examples, we see that shareholders accumulate more after tax if they can defer the payment of shareholder-level taxes. As a result, the firm's dividend policy also affects the after-tax accumulation. Shareholders who receive dividends pay tax earlier than shareholders who don't receive dividends. Moreover, if g is less than 1 for capital gains and equal to 1 for dividends, omitting dividends is an optimal policy, since paying tax at rate gt_p (g < 1) is superior to paying tax at rate t_p.[7]

The Choice of Partnership or Corporate Form in Special Cases

As indicated above, whether the partnership form provides greater after-tax rates of return than does the corporate form depends upon four factors: (1) the ordinary tax rate, t_p, (2) the corporate tax rate, t_c, (3) the taxes that are paid at the shareholder level, gt_p, and (4) the length of the investment horizon. Let us consider the following cases:

1. The corporate tax rate, t_c, is equal to the ordinary tax rate, t_p, and after-tax corporate income is tax exempt at the shareholder level (that is, g = 0). In this setting, investors are indifferent between producing in partnership or corporate form. Both provide investors the same after-tax rate of return. In effect, corporate income is taxed only once and at the same rate as if generated in partnership form.

---

[7] Suggesting that a non-dividend paying policy is optimal may sound counter-intuitive. After all, we usually think of announcements of an increase in the dividend as good news that increase the value of publicly traded shares of stock. Such increases in value, however, reflect the revelation of management's favorable information about the future profitability of the firm, and this is beyond the scope of the present model. The fact remains that declaring dividends is an expensive way to signal this private information in that it exacts a tax cost as we have illustrated.

4.1   Organizational Forms for Producing Goods and Services: Constant Tax Rates

2. The corporate tax rate, t_c, is equal to the ordinary tax rate, t_p, but $g > 0$. Because shareholders pay additional tax on the same level of after-tax profits as is earned in partnership form, a partnership is preferred to a corporation. To illustrate the advantage of the partnership form over the corporate form, assume that $t_c = t_p = .5$, $g = .2$, and $R = 10\%$. Partnership investments return $10\% \times (1 - .5) = 5\%$ after tax, while corporate investments return $10\% \times (1 - .5) \times (1 - .2 \times .5) = 4.5\%$ after tax for one-year investments. If shareholders can defer, but not eliminate, the payment of shareholder-level taxes, the advantage of the partnership over the corporation is reduced.

3. The corporate tax rate, t_c, is less than the personal tax rate, t_p, and after-tax corporate income is tax exempt at the shareholder level (that is, $g = 0$). In this case, investing through the corporation dominates investing through a partnership for any length of the investment horizon. For example, with a 10% before-tax rate of return on investment, a corporate tax rate, t_c, of 40%, and a personal tax rate, t_p, of 50%, investors earn a 6% after-tax rate of return on investment in corporate form but only 5% in partnership form.

4. The corporate tax rate, t_c, is less than the personal tax rate on partnership income, t_p, and the shareholder-level tax is positive (i.e., $gt_p > 0$). With this configuration of corporate and personal tax rates, the ranking of the organizational forms is ambiguous. Depending on shareholder-level taxes, either corporate form *or* partnership form could be preferred. For example, suppose that $t_c = 46\%$ (the maximum corporate tax rate in the U.S. prior to the 1986 Tax Act), $t_p = 50\%$ (the maximum personal tax rate in the U.S. prior to the 1986 Act), and $g = 16\%$. With $g = 16\%$, the shareholder-level tax rate on after-tax corporate income, gt_p, is 8% (or $.16 \times .5$). From relation 4.4, investors facing this special configuration of tax rates are essentially indifferent between corporate and partnership form for one-year investments. On the other hand, longer-term investments would favor the corporation.

As we suggested earlier, the effective shareholder-level tax rate on corporate distributions or dispositions of shares depends on the length of the deferral period, which in turn is affected by dividend policy. Reasonable arguments have been made that the choice between partnership and corporation was essentially tax-neutral for many investors in the U.S. during the 1980s prior to the 1986 Tax Act.[8] During this period of time, t_c and t_p were indeed 46% and 50%, respectively, for profitable businesses. So if the capital gains inclusion rate, g, was greater than 16%, partnerships were preferred, and if g was less than 16%, corporations were preferred.[9]

---

[8] See Merton H. Miller, "Debt and Taxes," *Journal of Finance* (May, 1977), pp. 261-275.

[9] While the statutory inclusion rate in the U.S. during this period of time was 40% on long-term capital gains in most circumstances, opportunities to defer the payment of the capital gains tax reduced the effective inclusion rate. We will explore this factor later in this chapter.

Prior to the 1980s, maximum personal tax rates, t_p, were far greater than the corporate tax rate (for example, 70% personal rates versus less than 50% corporate rates). This favored the corporate form unless for nontax reasons current corporate profits were distributed as dividends and shareholders were unable to convert dividends into capital gains by using arbitrage strategies.[10]

If there were no tax-rule restrictions or market frictions, investors faced with a diversity of marginal tax rates could earn arbitrage profits if corporations and partnerships produced the same goods and services. Partnerships and corporations could not be equally attractive to all taxpayers. And where the after-tax returns to the two organizational forms differ, investors could profit by short-selling (or borrowing claims to) investments that provide lower after-tax yields and investing the proceeds in investments providing higher after-tax yields. We will elaborate on this form of arbitrage in Chapter Six.

4.2 Determining the Corporate, the Personal, and the Shareholder-Level Tax Rates

The four cases above illustrate that tax rules can lead to a preference for producing goods and services through a particular type of legal entity. To compare investing in partnership and corporate forms, we used a very simple model in which the corporate tax rate, t_c, the personal tax rate, t_p, and the capital gains rate, gt_p, were given. We now relax some of the assumptions of this simple model. In this section, we recognize that the corporate tax rate is not constant across corporate organizations or over time. We also acknowledge that the shareholder-level tax varies across individual investors and is a function of both the holding period for shares and the after-corporate-tax return. We also show that the shareholder-level tax depends on the legal organizational forms through which stock is held. And with progressive income tax rates, the ordinary rate, t_p, also varies among investors.

While marginal tax rates are readily observable for many corporations and individuals, the shareholder-level tax rate depends on such idiosyncratic factors as the holding period of investors, the proportion of after-tax profits that the firm pays out as dividends, and the statutory fraction of capital gains income that is taxable at ordinary rates, g. In many of our examples and cases, we have assumed that g and the shareholder-level tax rate is far lower than would result from the complete payout of all after-tax corporate profits as taxable dividends each year. For example, although g has not been as low as 20% for most taxpayers in the U.S., the effective annual shareholder-level tax rate on shares could be quite low once deferral of the tax is considered.

Let us assume that R = 10% in either partnership or corporate form, and g = .2. Now suppose that t_p = 70% (as existed for high income taxpayers in the U.S. during the 1970s) and t_c = 48%. With this configuration of rates, the after-tax rate of return in partnership form would be 3.0% per year ($10\% \times (1 - .7)$) and the after-tax rate of return in corporate form would be 4.5% per year (or $10\% \times (1 - .48)(1 - .2 \times .7)$). During the early 1970s, the personal tax rate on

---

[10] We will investigate such arbitrage strategies in Chapter Six.

partnership income was high enough relative to the corporate rate to swamp the disadvantage of the double taxation of corporate income. During the early 1970s, many professional organizations were incorporated. Although they faced a shareholder-level tax when they liquidated their corporations, many doctors, lawyers, and consultants incorporated to escape the high personal tax rate and to shelter income at the lower corporate tax rate of less than 50%.[11] After the Economic Recovery Tax Act was passed in 1981, many of these corporations converted back to partnerships (or alternative organizational forms in which profits are taxed directly to owners rather than being taxed first at the entity level). This movement accelerated with the 1986 Tax Act as the corporate tax rate was set above the personal tax rate.

When personal tax rates are below corporate tax rates, the after-tax rate of return in partnership form is greater than the after-tax rate of return in corporate form. With the 1986 Tax Act, the partnership tax rate not only fell below the corporate tax rate, but in addition shareholders faced a further tax on dividends and capital gains. As a result of the 1986 Tax Act, partnerships became superior to corporations as a way to minimize taxes. But as we will explain in more detail in Chapter Six, the nontax advantages of the corporate form and the cost of converting from one form to another may have been enough to overcome the tax disadvantages of continuing to operate in corporate form. As we stress throughout the text, good tax-planning strategies don't always result in minimizing taxes: tax minimization may be sacrificed because of nontax costs and benefits that differ across the tax-planning alternatives.

Net Operating Losses and the Corporate Tax Rate

The corporate tax rate is not the same for all corporations. Start-up companies might generate net operating losses for many years before becoming profitable. With net operating losses, a corporation does not pay tax currently. Losses can be carried back for three years and carried forward for a period of fifteen years under current U.S. tax rules.[12] The loss in one tax year offsets profits in the third prior tax year first. The firm receives a rebate of the tax paid on the profits previously reported. For example, if the corporation experienced a net operating loss in 1988 when the statutory tax rate was 34%, and it paid taxes in 1985 at a 46% marginal tax rate, it would receive a rebate of $.46 on every dollar of net operating loss in 1988, up to the taxes it paid in 1985. Once the 1985 taxable income is exhausted, further net operating losses in 1988 would result in rebates of taxes paid in 1986 and then 1987. This opportunity did not go unnoticed by corporate America. A number of companies sold or closed plants at a loss following the drop in corporate tax rates to secure tax refunds at a 46% rate.

Because a start-up firm might take several years to generate taxable profits, if it ever turns profitable at all, the marginal tax rate of a start-up company is often

---

[11] Another important factor contributing to the decision to incorporate was the generous opportunities to postpone the payment of tax by making tax-deductible contributions to pension accounts on behalf of corporate owner-managers. We will explore this consideration further in Chapter Eleven.

[12] Most countries allow tax losses to be carried forward, but a number of countries do not allow losses to be carried back to offset previously taxed income. In addition, while many countries allow losses to be carried forward for only a few years, some allow indefinite carryforwards.

Chapter 4   Production Decisions and Organizational Form

far less than the statutory corporate tax rate. This might appear to make the corporate form relatively more attractive than a partnership. But if start-up losses can be deducted against other income earned by a partner, operating in partnership form might prove advantageous: a higher personal than corporate tax rate makes the deduction of losses more valuable for the partnership. When the partnership becomes profitable, it could convert to a corporation. As we discuss later, there are restrictions on the deductibility of losses generated from so-called passive partnership activities. A partner must be actively involved in the operations of the business to deduct its losses against other income.

Further Complications in Determining the Shareholder-Level Tax Rate

We have seen that ranking the tax costs of the corporate and partnership form is difficult when investors face different shareholder-level tax rates due to different investment horizons and different personal tax rates. The analysis becomes even more complicated if the returns on stock held in different organizational forms are taxed differently. Then the after-tax rates of return to stock depend not only on investor and project characteristics but also on the choice of organizational form in which it is held. For example, consider the following five investor groups that hold common stock:

1. **Fully Taxable Investors:** Wealthy investors hold a large fraction of the market value of common stock. Such high-income investors typically defer realization of capital gains. Their effective tax rate on shares depends partly on how long they defer capital gains and the proportion of the capital gain that is excluded from tax. As we will discuss in later chapters, it also depends on the characteristics of other investments they hold in their portfolio. For these investors, the shareholder-level tax could be very low (especially prior to the 1986 Tax Act).

2. **Tax-Exempt Organizations:** These include pension funds, universities, hospitals, charities, religious organizations, and other untaxed corporations. They escape tax on both dividend and capital gains income. For this group, the before-tax rate of return on shares is the same as the after-tax rate of return on shares (i.e., $gt = 0$).

   Tax-exempt organizations might appear to be natural candidates for investing in partnerships. But the earnings from active participation in such investments are classified as "unrelated business income" and are taxed at corporate rates. The corporate tax can be avoided if tax-exempt entities invest passively in limited partnership interests, but the presence of debt in the partnership's capital structure taints the passive income, subjecting it once again to corporate tax on unrelated business income. So in many circumstances, tax-exempt organizations face the same tax burden whether investing in corporate entities or partnerships. Tax-exempt organizations are more naturally suited to passive investment in assets like taxable bonds, for which the income they earn escapes taxation.

3. **Corporations:** When a corporation owns a partnership interest, the partnership income is subjected to double taxation, just as if the project

were undertaken directly by the corporation. When a corporation invests in the stock of other corporations, the income may be subjected to *triple* taxation, twice at the corporate level and once at the personal shareholder level, although some relief may be granted at the corporate level.[13]

4. **Foreign Investors:** Foreign nonresident investors do not pay U.S. taxes on realized capital gains on common stock of corporations they do not control. They may, however, face home-country tax on such gains. Depending on the jurisdiction of residency, the tax rate could be well above or well below the rate faced by U.S. investors. U.S. corporations are required to withhold a tax of from 0% to 30% of the dividends they pay to foreigners depending upon the foreigners' countries of residence and the treaties between the U.S. and the respective countries. As an aside, interest income earned by foreign investors on U.S. bonds issued after 1984 are exempt from U.S. withholding tax. Capital gains on real estate transactions are subject to U.S. withholding tax.

   Under certain circumstances, foreign investors can have a strong preference for undertaking passive investment in the U.S. through a U.S. corporation rather than a partnership, even though a U.S. investor may prefer the partnership form. This could occur if the foreign investor's home country assessed a high tax rate on partnership income earned in the U.S. but exempted capital gains.

5. **Broker-Dealers:** Broker-dealers make markets in common stock. As a result, they hold inventories of stock to facilitate their market-making activities. Like gains and losses on inventory holdings in other businesses, all broker-dealer income (both dividends and capital gains and losses) is taxable at ordinary rates. For broker-dealers, the shareholder-level tax rate is typically the corporate or personal marginal tax rate depending upon whether the business is organized as a corporation or a partnership. Note that a broker-dealer is indifferent between a dollar of capital gain and a dollar of dividend income. Although this is also true for tax-exempt entities, it is not true of all investors. For example,

---

[13] U.S. corporations are exempt on a fraction of dividend income received from other U.S. corporations. Although this fraction currently is 70% (80% exempt if the shareholder owns at least 20% of corporate stock and 100% exempt if the shareholder owns at least 80% of the corporate stock), it was 85% prior to the 1986 Tax Act. Canadian corporations receive a 100% exemption for dividends received from other Canadian corporations. If taxes were the only consideration, U.S. corporations should not invest in the stock of other U.S. corporations if they can undertake the same investments directly, even if the corporation they invested in had a policy of paying out 100% of its after-tax profits as dividends that are 70% tax exempt. An investment in the stock of another corporation would simply result in *triple*, rather than double, taxation of corporate income.

To see this, note that a direct investment in a project that yields R before tax, yields $R(1 - t_c)$ after corporate tax. An investment in the stock of a corporation that undertakes the same project and distributes a dividend yields only

$$R(1 - t_c)(1 - g_d t_c),$$

where g_d is the fraction of the dividend that is taxable to the corporate investor (e.g., 30% after 1987). As long as $g_d > 0$ (some dividend tax is paid), direct investments in the project dominate an investment in the same project through another corporation.

individual investors typically prefer capital gain income and those corporate investors eligible for a substantial tax exemption on dividend income typically prefer dividend income.

Corporate Taxation: Hybrid Forms

Although many corporate stockholders are subject to double taxation on corporate income, several corporate organizational forms enable shareholders to avoid some or all of the entity-level tax and still retain some of the nontax advantages of the corporate form. As a result, these corporate forms may be more competitive with the partnership form in appropriate circumstances. Examples include:

1. **S-Corporations:**[14] S-Corporations are limited-liability corporations that are taxed as pass-through entities. Stockholders report their pro-rata share of income (loss) on their own income tax return just as if they were taxed as partners. An S-Corporation must have 35 or fewer stockholders, only one class of stock, and no foreign or corporate shareholders.

   As we have discussed, the 1986 Tax Act favored organizational forms, like S-Corporations, that avoid an entity-level tax. In 1985, there were approximately 75,000 S-Corporation elections. In the 5 weeks spanning the end of 1986 and the beginning of 1987 there were approximately 225,000 S-Corporation elections, or 3 times as many (over this 5-week period) as occurred throughout all of calender 1985.[15] This suggests that the costs of operating as an S-Corporation relative to a regular corporation did not outweigh the advantages of avoiding an entity-level tax subsequent to the 1986 Tax Act for a large number of businesses.

2. **Small Business Corporations (Section 1244):** Original stockholders that collectively contribute up to $1,000,000 of equity in such an entity are permitted to deduct realized capital losses against their other income without regard to the usual annual limitation that applies to the sale of regular stock (currently $3,000). The annual Section 1244 deduction limit is $50,000 per taxpayer ($100,000 for a joint return). To qualify, the corporation must be primarily an operating company rather than engage primarily in passive investment.

3. **Foreign Subsidiaries:** Many U.S. corporations' foreign subsidiaries earn business income in countries where marginal tax rates are below those of the U.S. Only when the U.S. parent repatriates these profits are they taxable at the higher U.S. tax rates. At that time, the U.S. also provides a credit for the foreign taxes that have been paid. By initially paying lower taxes to a foreign government, the U.S. corporation defers the payment of the incremental tax due to the U.S. government relative to what would have been paid had the same activity been carried out in

---

[14] The name *S-Corporation* is derived from the subchapter of the tax code defining this structure, Subchapter S.

[15] *Tax Notes*, 2/1/88, p. 434, quoting Ronald Perlman.

4.2   Determining the Corporate, the Personal, and the Shareholder-Level Tax

the U.S. Such deferral reduces both the present value of the tax and the annualized corporate marginal tax rate.[16]

4. **Close Corporations:** Close corporations are corporations that are owned by just a few shareholders as is common in family or small business concerns. Relative to widely held firms, there tends to exist considerable trust among the owners and employees of closely held firms. In fact, closely held firms are typically owner-managed. By paying themselves generous salaries and bonuses, owner-managers can avoid part of the corporate-level tax. Unlike dividend payments and capital gains to owner-managers, compensation payments are a tax-deductible expense to the corporation. Many consulting firms that are incorporated pay out most of their before-tax profits as year-end bonuses to avoid the corporate-level tax. There are limits here, however. The taxing authority may seek to treat part of compensation as a disguised dividend.

   A special category of close corporations is **personal service corporations**. The principal activity of such an entity is personal services performed by owner-employees.

5. **Not-for-Profit Corporations:** A tax-exempt entity can produce certain goods and services and avoid the corporate tax on the earnings. Prominent examples include not-for-profit hospitals, universities, and religious organizations. In addition, prior to the 1960s, most savings and loan associations were effectively exempt from the corporate tax. The "owners" of all of these tax-exempt enterprises are effectively taxed as a special type of partnership. For example, doctors in not-for-profit hospitals may draw larger salaries as hospital income increases, and such income is taxed only at the personal level. Moreover, although the same opportunity exists in for-profit corporations, deferred salary in tax-exempt entities may be invested at rates of return that are not reduced by entity-level taxation.[17]

6. **Tax-Imputation Corporations:** A number of countries have a "tax imputation" system that converts part of the corporate-level tax into a partnership-level tax. For example, France, Italy, the U.K., Germany, and Canada allow partial or full imputation. By imputation we mean that if the corporation pays a dividend to its stockholders from its after-tax corporate income, stockholders (a) receive a credit (as compensation for the corporate taxes that are imputed to have been paid by them) equal to some fraction of the dividend they receive and (b) declare as dividend income (on which ordinary tax rates are levied) the dividend received plus the tax credit amount. For example, if the corporate tax rate were 40%, $1.00 of before-tax profits results in $.60 of profits after

---

[16] But investing in low-tax foreign jurisdictions may give rise to reduced before-tax rates of return on investment. This is the essence of implicit taxation that is the focus of the next chapter.

[17] The likelihood is great that before-tax rates of return are lower in activities that are tax exempt than in activities that are taxed at the corporate level. Once again, we will discuss this in the next chapter on implicit taxes.

Chapter 4   Production Decisions and Organizational Form

corporate tax. In a full imputation system, if the corporation pays a $.60 cash dividend, it issues to its stockholders $.40 in tax receipts along with a form instructing them to declare $1.00 of dividend income on their personal tax returns. The shareholder in a 30% tax bracket, for example, records $1.00 of income on which tax of $.30 is due. The $.40 tax receipt leaves a net credit of $.10 to be used to offset any tax due on other income. This converts the corporate form to the partnership form of taxation for those investors with sufficient taxable income to use the tax credit. The corporate income attracts only one level of taxation at personal tax rates. As a result of the imputation system, tax-exempt shareholders such as pension funds are forced to pay tax at high corporate marginal tax rates. For them, the $.40 tax receipt has no value unless they generate "unrelated business income" which is otherwise taxable. Despite this fact, a large portion of German stock is held by tax-exempt entities, although Germany is a high tax-rate country.

7. **Corporations Subject to a Progressive Tax Rate:** Many countries have a progressive corporate tax-rate system where the marginal tax rate of corporations with low levels of taxable income is below that of those with higher levels of taxable income. Because of a progressive corporate tax in the U.S., aggressive taxpayers have, in the past, established multiple small corporations. This enabled some entrepreneurs to earn substantially higher returns after paying both the U.S. corporate and shareholder-level tax than was possible by operating as a partnership. This "loophole" has been closed, and all commonly controlled corporate businesses are now integrated for tax purposes; the progressive corporate rate remains for only a very limited amount of corporate taxable income.[18]

8. **Real Estate Investment Trusts (REITs):** This entity is organized as a trust or corporation that receives most of its earnings from real estate activities. If all of the earnings are distributed each year to beneficiaries or shareholders, the REIT avoids an entity-level tax. To qualify for this pass-through treatment, the REIT must satisfy such constraints as having a minimum of one hundred shareholders, no significant concentration of ownership, and at least 70% of its assets and income in qualified real estate.

9. **Real Estate Mortgage Investment Conduits (REMICs):** This is another pass-through entity. Substantially all of the REMIC assets must consist of qualified mortgages and mortgage-related assets. REMICs have two classes of owners: owners of "regular" interests and owners of "residual" interests. The former are like bondholders and the latter are like stockholders, except that REMICs do not pay an entity-level tax.

To compare investing in partnership and corporate forms, we began our analysis with a very simple model in which the corporate tax rate, t_c, the personal

---

[18] As we will discuss at greater length in Chapter Eight, the fact that net operating losses can only yield tax savings if they offset other taxable income also gives rise to progression in corporate tax rates. But here the progressivity encourages corporate mergers to minimize the chance of generating losses.

4.2   Determining the Corporate, the Personal, and the Shareholder-Level Tax

tax rate, t_p, and the capital-gains inclusion rate, g, were given. In certain circumstances, even though there is double taxation of corporate income, investors achieve higher after-tax returns in corporate form than in partnership form. When we relaxed the assumptions of this simple model, we found many differences in tax treatment within the corporate form and among different shareholders. This expands the set of circumstances in which corporations may be tax-preferred. And as we discuss later, both frictions and tax rule restrictions allow the same activities to co-exist in both partnership and corporate form even when tax rates differ across the alternatives.

4.3 Changing Preferences for Organizational Forms Induced by Tax Rule Changes: The Case of the U.S. during 1986-88

Prior to the 1986 Tax Act, the corporate tax rate was lower than the personal tax rate. The shareholder-level tax rate was quite low for long-term investors. They could defer payment of the tax on long-term capital gains and exclude 60% of the realized gains from taxation. Dividends were taxed at ordinary rates. The 1986 Tax Act changed the rate structure. Corporate tax rates were set above the highest personal tax rate, and realized capital gains became fully taxable at ordinary rates. In this section, we compare the effects of the changes in the 1986 tax rules on the required before-tax rates of return to produce goods and services in corporate form and in partnership form. Our objective is to illustrate the degree to which the 1986 Tax Act appears to have bestowed a large tax advantage on the partnership form. In Table 4.1, we show representative U.S. maximum marginal tax rates for corporations and individuals on ordinary taxable income, dividends, and realized capital gains for the years 1986-1988.

Before turning to the effects of the 1986 Tax Act, let us be a bit more precise about how capital gains (losses) are taxed in the U.S. If investors sell stock held longer than some minimum holding period (6 months for sales of assets prior to 1977 and between 6/22/84 and 12/31/87, 9 months for sales of assets in 1978, and

Table 4.1 Maximum Marginal Tax Rates on Ordinary Income, Dividends, and Capital Gains In the U.S., 1986-1988

	1986	1987	1988
Individuals:			
Ordinary Income	50.0%	38.5%	28% (33%)
Dividends	50.0%	38.5%	28% (33%)
Long-Term Capital Gains	20.0%	28.0%	28% (33%)
Corporations (calendar-year taxpayer):			
Ordinary Income	46.0%	40.0%	34.0%
Dividends (from domestic corporations)	6.9%	8.0%	10.2%
Long-Term Capital Gains	28.0%	28.0%	34.0%

12 months for sales of assets between 1/1/78 and 6/22/84 and after 1/1/88), they realize long-term capital gain or loss. Long-term losses are netted against long-term gains to create what is called net long-term gain (loss).

Prior to the 1986 Tax Act, if the investor sold assets held for more than 6 months, a net long-term gain was taxed at 40% of the investor's marginal tax rate (i.e., $g = .4$). On a net long-term loss, a deduction from taxable income equal to 50% of up to $6,000 of net long-term loss (or $3,000) could be taken by couples filing joint returns. For example, if a couple generated $8,000 in net long-term losses, they were allowed to reduce taxable income by $3,000 and carry over $2,000 of the long-term loss to apply to future tax years. If the investor also had short-term gains and losses, all short-term losses were netted against short-term gains, and the net gain was added to the net long-term gain. The resulting gain, if net short-term, was taxable at full personal tax rates. A net short-term loss was fully deductible up to a maximum of $3,000 per year (on a joint return).

The Tax Reform Act of 1986 reduced the capital gains (loss) exclusion to 0% in many circumstances, although it remained 100% in some important cases as described in Chapter Three (such as death and charitable contributions). The 1986 Tax Act preserved all of the capital gain and loss netting rules.

For corporations, the marginal tax rate on ordinary income was below that of high-income individuals for tax year 1986. In 1987 and 1988, the corporate tax rate exceeded the top personal tax rate. Corporations faced a tax of 34% in 1988 (up from 28%) on net long-term gains. As with individuals, corporate short-term gains are taxed as ordinary income, and net capital losses are carried forward to offset future capital gains. Unlike individuals, corporations are permitted *no* current deduction for net capital losses.

U.S. corporations exclude a portion of the dividends they receive from other domestic corporations from taxation. In 1986, they could exclude 85% of such dividends. This resulted in a marginal tax rate of 6.9% on dividend income (or $46\% \times (1 - .85)$). The exclusion percentage was reduced to 80% in 1987 and to 70% in 1988. Thus, the marginal tax rate on dividend income for 1988 is 10.2% (or $34\%(1 - .7)$).

The Required Before-Tax Rates of Return on Corporate and Partnership Activities

Although we have argued that the tax rules now favor partnerships over corporations in the U.S., the corporate sector of the economy continues to dominate as the vehicle through which goods and services are produced. For this to persist, the cost of converting from corporate form to partnership form or the nontax advantages of corporate form must be considerable. In this section, we determine how large the before-tax return advantage of corporations must be (a reflection of the nontax advantages) to preserve indifference between the partnership and the fully taxable corporation. We use the actual tax rates in effect before and after the 1986 Tax Act (as given in Table 4.1). As you might expect from our previous discussions, the differentials depend on the shareholder-level tax rate and the relation between t_c and t_p.

Taxes at the Personal (Shareholder) Level:
The Required Rate of Return on Shares

Let us denote the before-tax rate of return in corporate form as R_c and in partnership form as R_p. Previously we assumed that the before-tax rate of return (R) was the same in corporate and partnership form. In this section, we allow for the possibility that for nontax reasons it might not be equally costly to produce identical goods and services in a partnership as in a corporation. For example, relative to corporate stockholders, partners might not enjoy as well-defined property rights (due to relatively sparse case law), might have poorer access to capital markets, and might face higher administrative costs.

After corporate taxes, *but before shareholder taxes*, the corporation realizes a return of r_c (where $r_c = R_c - t_c R_c$ or $R_c(1 - t_c)$). After personal taxes, the partnership realizes a return of r_p (where $r_p = R_p(1 - t_p)$). Let us assume that both R_p and R_c are constant across time, so we needn't employ a second subscript to denote time.

What level of corporate after-tax return, r_c, will make a tax planner indifferent between corporate and partnership form? We will denote this particular level of return as r_c^*. To find r_c^*, assume initially that the corporation pays no dividends,[19] and shareholders pay tax on realized capital gains at tax rates below the personal tax rate ($0 < gt_p < t_p$). Suppose the typical shareholder holds stock for n years. To be competitive, the after-tax rate of return on shares must be equal to the after-tax rate of return on undertaking the same investment in partnership form. Equating the after-tax returns from an initial investment of $1 in both corporate and partnership form, we find:

$$[(1 + r_c^*)^n (1 - gt_p) + gt_p]^{1/n} - 1 = r_p \qquad (4.5)$$

The left hand side of equation 4.5 has the following interpretation. A stock investment appreciates at rate r_c per year for n years. At time n, the firm buys back all of its shares and a shareholder-level tax is paid at rate gt_p on the entire value of the repurchased shares, except for the initial dollar invested, which is returned tax free to the investor. The after-tax accumulation at time n is $(1 + r_c)^n(1 - gt_p) + gt_p$. Accumulation in non-dividend-paying common stock is exactly the same as accumulation in a single premium deferred annuity that accrues interest at rate r_c and is taxed at rate gt_p upon surrender. The annual rate of return is determined by taking the nth root of the after-tax accumulation per dollar invested and then subtracting 1.

Even armed with equation 4.5, the tax planner has a difficult task to determine r_c^*. The tax planner must know the holding period and the personal tax rate of the firm's shareholders. And the task is complicated further by the fact that shareholders face different tax rates and investment horizons.

Still, equation 4.5 holds the key to determining before-tax required rates of return. Consider the tax rules that existed just prior to the 1986 Tax Act when shareholders could exclude 60% of long-term gains from taxation. Assume that

---

[19]With g < 1, paying no dividends maximizes the value of corporate shares. Paying dividends not only reduces the deferral period for stockholder taxes, but also subjects income to a tax at rate t_p rather than at a lower rate gt_p. Of course, we have ignored nontax factors here in suggesting that dividends should be omitted.

Chapter 4   Production Decisions and Organizational Form

Table 4.2 Required Annualized Pretax Return on Shares with a 60% Capital Gains Exclusion Rate on Gains from the Sale of Shares (g = .4) for Different Investor Marginal Tax Rates (t_p) and Holding Periods (n), with a Before-Tax Partnership Return (R_p) of 10%

		Required Before-Tax Rates of Return On Stocks (%), r_c^* (after corporate tax but before shareholder tax)					After-Tax Return[†]	R_p
t_p	n:	1	5	10	20	50		
50%		6.25	6.11	5.97	5.76	5.43	5.0	10.0
40%		7.14	7.00	6.86	6.65	6.35	6.0	10.0
30%		7.95	7.82	7.70	7.52	7.27	7.0	10.0

[†] This is the after-tax rate of return on both stocks and partnerships.

the typical shareholder has a personal tax rate, t_p, of 50% and holds shares for 5 years (n = 5). Assume that before tax, projects undertaken in partnerships return 10% (R_p = 10%). Then after-tax partnership returns are 5% (or 10% × (1-50%)). To be competitive, stocks must appreciate at a rate exceeding 5% but less than 10%, since shareholders face a tax on share appreciation but on favorable terms. The required return is given by solving for r_c^* in equation 4.5. The stock must appreciate at a rate of 6.11% per year (after corporate level tax but before shareholder-level tax).[20] A 6.11% appreciation rate on stock results in a 5% after-tax rate of return to shareholders. That is, if shareholders pay tax on their realized capital gains at the end of 5 years, they realize exactly the same after-tax rate of return as if they had invested in a partnership that yields 10% pretax and 5% after tax. At a before-tax return of 6.11% per year, each dollar invested in stock grows to $1.345 in 5 years. After paying tax at a capital gains rate of 20% on the $.345 of realized gain, shareholders retain $1.276. Accumulating $1.276 after tax in 5 years per dollar of initial investment is equivalent to an after-tax rate of return of 5% per year (($1.276)^{1/5} - 1 = .05$). Table 4.2 gives the required annual before-tax rate of return on corporate shares, r_c^*, for various holding periods and marginal tax rates.

Note that for any level of the personal tax rate, t_p, the required before-shareholder-tax rate of return, r_c^*, falls with increases in the holding period. As n increases without limit, r_c^* approaches the after-tax return on partnerships. Note that because of the capital gains exclusion on shares, the required before-shareholder-tax return to shares is below the before-tax rate of return to partnerships (of 10% in Table 4.2) even for short holding periods. Investors require higher before-tax rates of return on investments that are taxed less favorably. For example, if a bond were as risky an investment as the investment in the partnership, the bond would also require a 10% before-tax rate of return to provide the same after-tax return as partnership or corporate stock investments.

[20] Solving for r_c^* in equation 4.5, we find:

$$r_c^* = \{[(r_p + 1)^n - gt_p] / (1 - gt_p)\}^{1/n} - 1.$$

Plugging in values of 5% for r_p, 40% for g (or 1 - 60%), and 5 for n, yields r_c^* = .0611.

4.3 Changing Preferences for Organizational Forms Induced by Tax Rule Changes

The reason that the required before-shareholder-tax return on shares decreases as the investment horizon lengthens, is that holding onto the shares allows the capital gains tax to be deferred. This means that for any given rate of annual appreciation on shares, the after-tax return on shares increases with the length of the holding period, just as was true of a single premium deferred annuity contract. One can view this as a reduction in the shareholder-level tax rate as the holding period on shares (or the interest rate) increases. As this tax rate decreases, so does the level of the before-tax return on shares required to achieve a target level of after-tax return.

The Required Rate of Return on Stocks in the Presence of Dividends

In establishing the required rate of return on shares in equation 4.5, it was assumed that all returns were taxed as capital gains. If, instead, shares pay a dividend at rate d, and such dividends are taxed at rate t_p, the required return on shares over a *single* period, r_c^*, satisfies:[21]

$$(1 + r_c^* - d)(1 - gt_p) + gt_p + d(1 - t_p) = 1 + r_p \qquad (4.6)$$

That is, the after-tax capital gain on shares must be equal to the after-tax partnership return less the after-tax dividend return on the shares. Solving for r_c^*, we find that

$$r_c^* = [(1 + r_p - d(1 - t_p)) - gt_p]/(1 - gt_p) + d - 1.$$

If dividends are taxed less favorably than are capital gains to individual shareholders, as we assume here, the required return on shares is increasing in the dividend yield. For example, when total stock returns are taxed at capital gains rates, the 40% taxpayer requires a before-tax return on stocks of 7.14% over a 1-year horizon to yield the 6% after-tax return available in partnerships. (See the 40% row of Table 4.2.) That is, $7.14\% \times (1 - .4 \times .4) = 6\%$. But when the dividend yield is 3%, the after-tax dividend return is only $3\% \times (1 - 40\%)$ or 1.8%. This leaves a required after-tax capital gain of 6% - 1.8% or 4.2%. Since capital gains are taxed at a rate of 16% for the 40% taxpayer, the required before-tax capital gain is 4.2%/(1 - .16) or 5%. The total required return, then, is 8%, consisting of 5% in capital gains and 3% in dividends.

Table 4.3 reports the required before-tax rates of return, for various investor tax rates and holding periods, for a stock that pays a 3% dividend, given a capital gains exclusion rate of 60% as in Table 4.2. In calculating the values in Table 4.3, it is assumed that dividends distributed to shareholders are reinvested in the partnership sector at rate r_p.[22]

In comparing required returns in Tables 4.2 and 4.3, note that in addition to higher before-tax rates of return on stock when dividend yields are positive, the

---

[21] In Chapter Six, we will explore arbitrage strategies that may allow dividends to be taxed more favorably than at rate t_p.

[22] The table values for r_c^* satisfy:

$$(1 + r_c^* - d)^n (1 - gt_p) + gt_p + d(1 - t_p) \sum_{t=1}^{n} (1 + r_c^* - d)^{t-1} (1 + r_p)^{n-t} = (1 + r_p)^n$$

Chapter 4   Production Decisions and Organizational Form

Table 4.3 Required Annualized Pretax Return on Shares *Paying a 3% Dividend Rate* with a 60% Capital Gains Exclusion Rate on Gains from the Sale of Shares (g = .4) for Different Investor Marginal Tax Rates (t_p) and Holding Periods (n), with a Before-Tax Partnership Return (R_p) of 10%

		Required Before-Tax Rates of Return On Stocks (%), r_c^*					After-Tax Return[†]	R_p
t_p	n: 1	5	10	20	50			
50%	7.38	7.28	7.17	7.02	6.76		5.0	10.0
40%	8.00	7.90	7.80	7.64	7.40		6.0	10.0
30%	8.57	8.48	8.38	8.24	8.04		7.0	10.0

[†]This is the after-tax rate of return on both stocks and partnerships.

required returns fall off more slowly in Table 4.3 as the length of the investment horizon increases. The reason, of course, is that when dividends are paid, a smaller fraction of the total return on shares comes from capital gains, and it is only the tax on capital gains that is reduced as the investment horizon increases.

The Effective Annualized Tax Rate on Shares

Tables 4.2 and 4.3 show required before-tax rates of return on stocks if they are to compete with partnerships. These returns depend on the length of the investment horizon. We find it convenient to define a variable that captures the hypothetical annual rate of tax that shareholders could pay *each year* on their pretax stock returns that would be equivalent to paying the shareholder-level tax they actually pay when they sell their shares. Call this variable the **effective annualized tax rate on shares**, and denote it t_s. If shareholders paid tax at rate t_s each year on their total stock returns (dividends plus capital gains), they would end up with the same after-tax accumulation as they actually achieve. For example, in Table 4.2, we find that for a personal tax rate of 50% and a 10-year holding period, the annual required before-shareholder-level-tax rate of return is 5.97%. That is, if shares appreciate at an expected rate of return of 5.97% per year, their value will be just high enough in 10 years so that shareholders can sell their shares, pay capital gains taxes, and be left with an amount equivalent to the accumulation on a savings account that pays a tax-exempt return of 5% per year for 10 years. The effective annualized tax rate on shares is found from

$$r_c^*(1 - t_s) = r_p. \tag{4.7}$$

$$t_s = 1 - r_p/r_c^* \tag{4.8}$$

So t_s = 1 - .05/.0597 or 16.2%. If investors paid tax at a rate of 16.2% on accrued gains each year, this would be equivalent to paying tax at a 20% capital-gains rate (.4 × .5) on selling their shares in 10 years.[23]

---

[23] Because t_s varies with n, the investment horizon, we will sometimes use a time subscript for t_s to indicate the particular length of the deferral period.

4.3 Changing Preferences for Organizational Forms Induced by Tax Rule Changes

Required Before-Tax Rate of Return: Corporations Versus Partnerships

Having defined r_c^*, we can now express easily the required before-tax return on projects undertaken by corporations, R_c^*, since it must solve:

$$R_c^* (1 - t_c) = r_c^* \qquad (4.9)$$

Substituting 4.9 into 4.7 and noting that $r_p = R_p(1 - t_p)$, we can now determine the required before tax return on corporate projects relative to partnership projects:

$$\frac{R_c^*}{R_p} = \frac{(1 - t_p)}{(1 - t_c)(1 - t_s)} \qquad (4.10)$$

Note that if the effective annualized tax rate on shares, t_s, is low and the corporate tax rate is somewhat below the personal tax rate, the required rate of return on corporate projects could be approximately equal to that on partnership projects. For example, if the corporate tax rate is 46%, the personal tax rate is 50%, and the effective shareholder-level tax rate is 8%, the required return on corporate projects is barely higher than that on partnership projects.

If the personal tax rate is only 40% rather than 50%, however,

$$\frac{R_c^*}{R_p} = \frac{(1 - .4)}{(1 - .46)(1 - .08)} = 1.208 .$$

In other words, the pretax return on corporate projects must exceed that on partnership projects by 21%. If partnership projects yield 10% pretax, corporate projects must yield 12.08% (or $.10 \times 1.208$) to provide the same after-tax return. In the absence of a nontax advantage of corporations over partnerships of at least 2.08% pretax, corporations could not compete with partnerships for the same investments under these circumstances.

Post 1986 Tax Act Equilibrium

As indicated earlier, the 1986 Tax Act increased the capital gains inclusion rate from 40% to 100%. This caused a dramatic increase in the required before-shareholder-tax rate of return on shares, r_c^*, for every tax bracket and holding period. For illustrative purposes, we assume that the before-tax rate of return on partnership investments remains unchanged at 10%, as in Table 4.2. The required rates of return on non-dividend-paying shares (before shareholder-level taxes) on an annualized basis are given in Table 4.4 for various combinations of t_p and n. The table values are determined by solving for r_c^* from equation 4.5, using a value of 1.0 for g.

With capital gains fully taxable at ordinary rates (Table 4.4), investors demand a greater before-tax rate of return on shares than when capital gains were partially tax exempt (Table 4.2). For shorter holding periods, the required before-shareholder-tax rate of return is close to the required before-tax rate of return for partnerships. Stockholders retain the advantage only of the deferral of capital

Table 4.4 Required Annualized Pre-Tax Return on Non-Dividend-Paying Shares with a 0% Capital Gains Exclusion Rate (g = 1) for Different Investor Marginal Tax Rates (t_p) and Holding Periods (n), with a Before-Tax Partnership Return (R_p) of 10%

		Required Before-Tax Rates of Return on Stocks (%), r_c^*					After-Tax Return[†]	R_p
	n: 1	5	10	20	50		
t_p							
50%	10.0	9.20	8.48	7.57	6.37	5.0	10.0
40%	10.0	9.35	8.77	8.02	7.04	6.0	10.0
30%	10.0	9.51	9.07	8.48	7.74	7.0	10.0
28%	10.0	9.54	9.13	8.58	7.89	7.2	10.0

[†]This is the after-tax rate of return on both stocks and partnerships.

gains taxes for n periods.[24] On the other hand, with higher capital gains tax rates, the advantage of tax deferral becomes more significant.

Annualized Tax on Shares after the 1986 Tax Act

Assume that the typical investor is taxed at a marginal tax rate of 28% and holds shares for 5 years. From Table 4.4, we find that for this investor r_c^* is 9.54%. Since the shareholder realizes only 7.2% after shareholder taxes, the annualized equivalent tax rate on shares from equation 4.8 is 24.5% (or 1 - .072/.0954).

By contrast, from Table 4.2, for t_p = 50%, n = 5, and g = .4, t_s is equal to 18.2% (or 1 - .05/.0611). So t_s has increased by nearly one third despite the fall in t_p by nearly half. In fact, at 24.5%, the effective tax rate on shares is nearly as high as the 28% tax rate on partnership income, whereas prior to the Tax Reform Act, the tax rate on shares (at 18.2%) was substantially below the 50% rate on ordinary income.

It may be of interest, particularly to policymakers, to calculate from Table 4.4 the corporate tax rate that would equate the required before-tax return on corporate projects and partnership projects for different investment horizons. Given a 10% return on partnership projects, the rate, t_c^*, solves:

$$10\%(1 - t_c^*) = r_c^*$$

---

[24]Of course, tax law changes could result in a change in g at some future date (as the 1990 Act provides in some circumstances). By retaining their shares, investors have an option to realize capital gains when and if capital gains tax rates are reduced. This in turn reduces the required rate of return on shares. Moreover, as we have discussed before, the capital gains rate is zero if shares are held until death or, in many circumstances, if appreciated shares are donated to charity.

where the values for r_c^* are the values in Table 4.4. Given a personal tax rate of 28%, t_c^* is equal to:

0.0%	for	n= 1
4.6%	for	n= 5
8.7%	for	n=10
14.2%	for	n=20
21.1%	for	n=50
28.0%	as	$n \to \infty$

The longer the holding period, the greater the advantage of deferring the shareholder tax. This allows the corporate tax rate to be set at an increasingly higher level (approaching the tax rate on partnership income in the limit) if the objective is to equate the required returns on corporate and partnership projects.

Required Rate of Return at the Corporate Level after the 1986 Tax Act

For t_p = 28%, t_c = 34%, and t_s = 24%, the required return on corporate projects becomes quite a bit higher than that for partnerships:

$$\frac{R_c^*}{R_p} = \frac{(1 - .28)}{(1 - .34)(1 - .24)} = 1.44 .$$

If partnership projects earn 10% pretax, corporate projects must earn 14.4% to be competitive in the sense of providing the same after-tax return to investors.[25] Table 4.5 lists required annualized pre-tax rates of return on corporate projects before and after the 1986 Tax Act for different holding periods, given a before-tax partnership return of 10%. The calculations are for the case in which the return from shares comes entirely from capital gains (no dividends). The perspective adopted is that of a wealthy set of individuals choosing between corporate and partnership form to undertake investment.

The table indicates the substantial degree to which the 1986 Act increased the required nontax advantage of corporations over partnerships if they are to overcome the tax advantages of the latter. The table also indicates that if the capital gains inclusion rate were 70% rather than 100% (with a corporate rate of 34% and a personal tax rate on ordinary income of 28%), corporations would still be required to invest in projects that yield a *third* more, before tax, than partnership projects, assuming investors have a five-year investment horizon.

Unless there are substantial compensating nontax benefits, our analysis suggests that partnerships dominate corporations if new equity must be issued to finance investment projects after the 1986 Tax Act. By implication, for tax reasons alone, the dollar volume of new issues of common stock to finance

---

[25] The corporate projects must earn even *more* if the stock pays dividends that are taxed each period at ordinary rates. For example, with a 3% dividend yield, the required return on corporate projects increases to 14.8% versus 10% for partnership projects.

Chapter 4 Production Decisions and Organizational Form

Table 4.5 Required Annualized Pre-Tax Rates of Return (in %) on Corporate Projects (R_c) for Non-Dividend-Paying Shares in the U.S. Before and After the 1986 Tax Act for Different Holding Periods, Given a Before-Tax Partnership Return (R_p) of 10%.

Time Period	g	t_c	t_p	n: 1	5	10	20	50
Pre - 1987	0.4	.46	.50	11.57	11.32	11.05	10.67	10.05
Post - 1987	1.0	.34	.28	15.15	14.45	13.83	13.00	11.95
Post - 1987*	0.7	.34	.28	13.57	13.34	12.79	12.29	11.61

* This row indicates the post-1987 required before-tax returns on corporate projects if the capital gains inclusion rate is reduced from 100% to 70%.

investments should have fallen and the number of partnership and S-Corporation formations (to undertake new projects) should have increased.

4.4 Nontax Advantages of Operating in Corporate Form and the Costs of Converting from Corporate Form to Partnership

To be taxed as a partnership, the tax law requires that a partnership differ in economically significant ways from a corporation. Prior to the 1987 Tax Act, any association (including a partnership) was taxed as a corporation unless it failed to exhibit at least two of the following characteristics: (a) continuity of life, (b) centralization of management, (c) easy transferability of ownership, (d) limited liability, and (e) an economic purpose to the organization. With the 1987 Tax Act, easy transferability of partnership interests (e.g., interests traded on an organized exchange such as the New York Stock Exchange) results, with some exceptions, in the partnership being taxed as a corporation.

As we will indicate in subsequent chapters, corporations do enjoy significant nontax advantages over partnerships. Moreover, there can be significant tax and nontax costs to convert from one form to another.[26] These tax and nontax factors make it undesirable for many organizations to operate as partnerships, particularly if they are already "stuck" in corporate form. Some of the more important nontax factors include:

1. **Transaction costs of operating as a large partnership**: Reorganization costs, underdeveloped case law, uncertain property rights in various circumstances, lack of limited liability, and greater operating costs increase the costs to operating as a partnership.

---

[26] For example, Code Section 336 requires taxable income to be recognized on the termination of corporate life to the extent the fair market value of the assets exceeds the "basis" (cost for tax purposes) in the stock.

2. **Access to capital markets**: Large corporations that are traded on organized exchanges typically have easier access to markets for both debt and equity capital. Likewise, shareholders value the right to acquire or sell their assets in liquid markets, a right that is typically absent in the market for partnership interests.

3. **Control of management:** It is more difficult for limited partners to control the actions of managers (the general partners) than it is for stockholders to control managers of corporations.

Even with these corporate nontax benefits, the double taxation of corporate profits cannot be too onerous. Otherwise, costly changes in organizational form will result. On the other hand, tax rules change over time, and it is costly to switch back and forth between partnership and corporate form. Fewer corporations will convert to partnership form if the tax rules are expected to change in favor of the corporate form in the future. In fact, all of the capital gains rules were left intact in the Code despite the elimination in the 1986 Tax Act of favorable tax rates on long-term capital gains in most circumstances. This made it easier for Congress to vote an increase in the exclusion rate for long-term capital gains at a subsequent date, which reduces the corporate tax disadvantage.

Finally, we have not yet analyzed fully the investment and financing strategies that corporations may undertake to mitigate the effects of double taxation. We do so in the chapters on capital structure and corporate reorganization.

Summary of Key Points

1. Different organizational forms can be used to produce goods and services. Due to differences in tax treatment, conducting identical activities in different organizational forms can result in different after-tax rates of return.

2. Corporations are subject to double taxation in many countries, once at the corporate level and then again at the shareholder level. In contrast, partnerships are taxed only at the investor level.

3. With equal before-tax rates of return on investment, the partnership dominates the corporate form if the corporate and the ordinary tax rates are the same but there is a non-zero tax on corporate profits at the shareholder level.

4. With equal before-tax rates of return on investment, the corporate form dominates the partnership form if the corporate tax rate is below the ordinary tax rate and the tax at the shareholder level can be kept sufficiently low.

5. More generally, corporations dominate partnerships, from a tax stand-point, if one minus the corporate tax rate, multiplied by a factor of one minus the effective annualized tax rate on income from holding shares of corporate stock, exceeds one minus the tax rate on partnership income; that is:

$$(1 - t_c)(1 - t_s) > (1 - t_p).$$

6. If the partnership form dominates the corporate form along the tax dimension, and both forms undertake similar investments, some combination of market frictions, tax rule restrictions, and nontax benefits of operating in corporate form would be necessary to prevent arbitrage.

7. Cross-sectional differences in ordinary and shareholder tax rates create opportunities for tax arbitrage in the presence of both corporate and partnership forms of organization. Without frictions or restrictions, if some investors were indifferent between producing in either organizational form, other investors with different tax rates would strictly prefer to invest through one organizational form and finance the investment by borrowing claims against the returns to the other organizational form.

8. When personal tax rates exceed corporate rates, there exists a unique tax rate on shares, for a given holding period for stock investment, that makes it equally attractive to produce through partnerships as through corporations. Investors with longer investment horizons prefer corporate investments; investors with shorter horizons prefer partnerships.

9. Prior to the 1981 Tax Act, with maximum personal tax rates set well above the corporate tax rate and shareholder-level tax rates set well below personal rates on ordinary income, the corporate form was tax-favored relative to partnerships for many businesses. This was less true of service businesses due to the presence of a 50% maximum personal tax rate on earned income (versus a 70% top rate for unearned income). But in the decades preceding the 1970s, when earned income was not only taxed at the same high rate as unearned income, but was also taxed at rates as high as 90% (versus approximately 50% at the corporate level and a maximum 25% capital gains tax rate on shares, which could be reduced further through tax deferral privileges), corporations were especially tax-favored.

10. While the required before-tax rates of return at the corporate level might have been quite close to the required before-tax rates of return at the partnership level between the Economic Recovery Tax Act of 1981 and the Tax Reform Act of 1986, this is unlikely to be true subsequent to the Act. This is so because (1) the corporate tax rate exceeds the top personal tax rate for the first time and (2) the shareholder-level tax on after-tax corporate profits has increased dramatically.

11. When corporate-level tax rates exceed personal tax rates, and shareholder-level taxes on corporate income are also positive, unless there exist nontax benefits to operating through the corporate form, or unless there are nontrivial costs to corporate liquidation, the tax rules would lead corporations to dissolve.

12. Nontax benefits of corporate over partnership form include limited liability, better-established corporate case law, a more effective market for corporate control than for partnership control, superior corporate access to capital markets, and the ease of transferability of corporate ownership interests, which enhances investor liquidity.

Discussion Questions

1. Give five examples of organizational forms that are used to produce goods and services. What tax characteristics distinguish one from the other?

2. Suppose that the tax rate on personal income, t_p, is equal to 40%, the corporate tax rate, t_c, is equal to 32%, and that the capital-gains inclusion rate, g, is 40%. Also assume that the before-tax rate of return on investment to both the corporation and the partnership is 20% per year. These tax rates and investment returns are constant over time.

   True or False? (Support your answer with numerical examples.)

   a. The annualized after-tax rate of return to investing in corporate form increases with the length of the investor's holding period. Explain.

   b. The annualized after-tax rate of return to investing in partnership form increases with the length of the partner's holding period. Explain.

   c. If a corporation paid out its entire after-tax profits as fully taxable dividends each year, shareholders would realize a lower before-tax rate of return than if they retained the after-tax profits. Explain.

   d. Since the corporate tax rate is below the personal tax rate, corporate form is always preferred to partnership form.

   e. Since corporate income is subject to two levels of taxation, partnership form is always preferred to corporate form.

3. What are the major variables that affect the magnitude of the shareholder-level tax? Give examples to illustrate the importance of each variable. Is it possible to rank the importance of each variable?

4. Why might one group of investors prefer corporate form while another group of investors prefers partnership form?

5. What factors might lead to cross-sectional and time-series differences in corporate tax rates, personal tax rates, and shareholder-level tax rates? How do these differences affect tax planners? How do these differences affect tax policymakers?

6. Following the 1986 Tax Act, the corporate rate of 34% was set above the personal rate of 28% and 100% of realized capital gains became taxable at investors' ordinary rates. What are the required before-tax rates of return (that is, the cost of equity capital) to corporations and to partnerships if investors require that the after-tax rate of return on investments of similar risk be equal to 20% per year and the typical shareholder holds shares for eight years? Under what circumstances might we see both a corporation and a partnership producing the same goods and services in light of these required before-tax rates of return?

Chapter 4   Production Decisions and Organizational Form

Problems

1. With the Tax Reform Act of 1986, corporate tax rates fell from 46% in 1986 to 40% in 1987 and to 34% for income earned subsequent to 1987. Since there is a three-year carryback for net operating losses, would it be tax-advantageous for those firms that were profitable during 1984-1986 to generate net operating losses during 1987-1989 by: (1) selling certain assets at a loss; (2) postponing the recognition of income; and (3) accelerating certain tax-deductible expenditures? If the after-tax discount rate is 7%, how tax-advantageous is this strategy? What specific actions might a firm have undertaken to generate net operating losses in 1987-1989?

2. Because U.S. corporations are allowed to exclude from taxable income 70% (100% for Canadian corporations) of the dividends they receive from other U.S. (Canadian) corporations, it is sometimes suggested that they should invest in dividend-paying common or preferred stock. Is it tax-advantageous for a U.S. corporation to buy dividend-paying stock? Is it tax-advantageous for a U.S. corporation to buy adjustable-rate preferred stock (short-term dividend-paying preferred stock, with a dividend yield that floats in direct proportion to short-term treasury yields) instead? Is it tax-advantageous for a corporation to issue the preferred stock? Is it tax-advantageous for Canadian companies to buy common stock in other Canadian corporations?

3. Is it tax-advantageous for corporations to pay dividends to shareholders other than corporations? How did the 1986 Tax Act affect the calculus here?

4. Let us assume, as was true of wealthy individuals in the U.S. in the 1960s, that the personal tax rate is 70% and that 50% of realized capital gains can be excluded from taxation. Assume that the corporate rate is 48%. The before-tax rate of return on investments is 15%. You are asked to advise a doctor as to whether she should incorporate. What would be the tax-advantageous strategy for 5, 10, and 15-year investment horizons? Suppose that she did incorporate and that five years later the personal tax rate falls unexpectedly to 50%. Should she then liquidate her corporation and start a new partnership?

5. A U.S. corporation has a wholly owned foreign subsidiary in a low-taxed country. The subsidiary returns 20% a year before tax. The foreign-country tax rate is 25% and the U.S. corporate tax rate is 40%. Corporate tax in the U.S. is assessed only when profits are repatriated and the profits are taxed at a rate equal to the difference between U.S. and foreign rates, that is, 15%. Compare the after-tax rates of return of a U.S. corporation's strategy of repatriating profits each year versus deferring repatriation of after-foreign-tax profits for 10 years. Assume that funds invested in the U.S. *also* earn 20% a year before tax.

CHAPTER 5
Differentially Taxed Economic Activities and Implicit Taxes: Effects on Asset Prices

In Chapter Three, we discussed how different tax treatments of investment returns influenced the after-tax rates of return to alternative savings vehicles. To facilitate comparisons, we held the same investment in each savings vehicle. In Chapter Four, we discussed how different tax treatments of the returns to productive activities undertaken in different organizational forms affect their after-tax rates of return. To facilitate comparisons, we assumed that the same goods and services were produced in these alternative organizational forms.

In this chapter, we hold the organizational form constant, but we vary the tax treatments for different economic activities. We stress how taxing activities unequally influences the relative pricing and the before-tax rates of return on investments. For example, if we buy a building to rent space to others, we can deduct from rental income not only the costs of running the business but also part of the purchase price of the building each year ("depreciation") before paying taxes on any remaining net income. On the other hand, an investment in equipment that generates the same pretax cash flows as the rental building might give rise to more liberal depreciation allowances and, as a result, higher after-tax cash flows than the real-estate investment. Because the equipment's after-tax cash flows exceed those for the rental property, investors are willing to pay more for the equipment.

More generally, when two assets give rise to identical pretax cash flows, but the cash flows to one asset are taxed more favorably than those to the other asset, taxpayers will bid for the right to hold the tax-favored asset. As a result, the price of the tax-favored asset will increase relative to the price of the tax-disfavored asset and the before-tax rates of return on the tax-favored asset will decrease (relative to the before-tax return on the tax-disfavored asset). And since the before-tax cash flows for the two investments are identical, the pretax rate of return to the tax-favored asset will fall below that for the tax-disfavored asset. In important special cases, their prices will adjust such that their after-tax rates of return will be the same to all investors. In fact, as we explain in more detail below, without further tax rule restrictions or market frictions, the equalization of after-tax rates of return is a necessary condition for market equilibrium.

Given differences in tax treatment, if after-tax returns are to be equalized, then before-tax rates of return must differ across the assets. More lightly taxed investments require lower before-tax rates of return than do more heavily taxed investments. As a result, investors pay taxes **explicitly** on heavily taxed investments and they pay taxes **implicitly** on lightly taxed investments through lower before-tax rates of return. Moreover, taxing investments differentially gives rise to **tax clienteles**. That is, the natural investors ("clientele") for lightly taxed assets will often be a different set of investors than for the more heavily taxed investments.

Throughout most of the discussion that follows we assume that markets are perfect. In this setting, no transaction costs are incurred to undertake investments or to manage them. All investors are assumed to possess identical information regarding the future cash flows from investment alternatives. Moreover, investors act as though their behavior has no influence on the prices at which assets can be bought and sold. For example, renting a house or a car is assumed to provide the same service flows as owning a house or a car. A renter is assumed to manage property in exactly the same manner as would an owner. As a result, property owners incur no monitoring costs or other informational costs as a consequence of renting property to others. Moreover, if investments must be sold, it is easy and costless to establish their market value. The assumption of perfect markets is as convenient as it is nondescriptive of the world. In subsequent chapters, we will relax this assumption.

5.1   Implicit Taxes

Implicit taxes arise because the prices of investments that are tax-favored are bid up in the marketplace. As a result, the **before-tax** rates of return on tax-favored investments are lower than are those on tax-disfavored investments. Taxes are paid implicitly through lower before-tax rates of return on investment.[1] To calculate implicit taxes requires a benchmark asset against which to compare pretax returns. For example, suppose our benchmark asset is an asset whose returns are taxed fully each year at ordinary rates. That is, tax is not deferred on any part of the economic gain that accrues from holding the asset. A fully taxable bond that is default-free, the interest rate on which is set to market rates each period, is an example of such an asset. The interest earned on the bond is fully taxable each year. Moreover, there are no changes in the economic value of the bond over time with which to contend. We would then refer to investments that are taxed more lightly than fully taxable bonds as tax-favored investments and those that are taxed more heavily as tax-disfavored investments.

---

[1] In subsequent chapters, when we relax the assumption of perfect markets, we will broaden the definition of implicit taxes to include the effect of market imperfections on before-tax rates of return.

Investments may be granted one or more of several types of tax-favored status, including

- full tax exemption (e.g., municipal bonds in the U.S.),
- partial exemption (e.g., capital assets in most countries),
- tax credits (e.g., investment tax credit, targeted jobs credit, alcohol fuel credit, research and experimental credit, low-income housing credit, energy investment credit, payroll tax credit, and rehabilitation investment credit),
- tax deductions permitted at a rate faster than the decline in economic value of the asset (e.g., accelerated depreciation on business property and immediate expensing of research and experimental costs, advertising expenditures, and personnel costs incurred to expand to new markets), and
- taxable income permitted to be recognized at a rate slower than the increase in the economic value of the asset's cash flows (e.g., most assets that appreciate in value).

Similarly, there are many sources of tax-disfavored treatment. These include

- special tax assessments (e.g., Windfall Profits Tax on oil, import duties, and excise taxes),
- taxable income recognition at a rate faster than income is earned (e.g., risky bonds, where the high coupon rate received is fully taxable even though it includes a default premium that, economically, represents a return of capital rather than interest income), and
- tax deductions at a rate slower than the decline in economic value (e.g., non-amortizable goodwill or trademarks that have finite economic lives).

The low before-tax rates of return on municipal bonds, relative to fully taxable bonds of comparable risk, provide the most direct and vivid illustration of the concept of implicit taxes. Municipal bonds are issued by state and local authorities. The interest earned on most of these bonds is exempt from federal taxation in the U.S.[2] For this reason, they are called tax-exempt bonds. Investors bid up the prices of these municipal bonds such that their before-tax return is lower than the return on fully taxable bonds.

The residents of certain states are exempt not only at the federal level but also at the state level if they hold municipal revenue or general obligation bonds issued by authorities within their own state. These instruments are called doubly tax exempt. If residents of a given state hold municipal bonds of out-of-state issuers, however, they pay state income taxes on the interest earned on these out-of-state bonds.

---

[2] Bonds issued by local governments are not exempt from taxation at the national level in all countries. Provincial bonds in Canada, for example, are fully taxable at the federal level.

State taxation also affects the prices of municipal bonds. Certain states (for example, California and New York), tax their residents at high marginal tax rates and exempt their residents from paying tax on interest from state and local bonds issued within their own borders. Municipal bonds issued by such states are priced to yield a lower rate of return relative to municipal bonds issued by states with low marginal tax rates such as Texas (which has no state income tax) or states that tax the interest on bonds issued by municipalities within their own borders. For example, California residents bid up the prices of California municipal bonds relative to the prices of equally risky Texas municipal bonds. To understand why, assume that a California resident faces a 10% marginal state income tax rate and a 30% marginal federal tax rate. For those who itemize deductions, state income taxes are deductible at the federal level in the year paid. As a result, for a California resident, a 7% out-of-state municipal bond that is exempt from federal taxation but subject to California taxation is equivalent to a doubly tax-exempt California bond that yields 6.51% (or $7\% \times [1 - .10 \times (1 - .30)]$).

Interest derived from an investment in corporate bonds is fully taxable at both the federal and state level. Interest earned on obligations issued by the federal government (like treasury bills, bonds, and notes) and certain authorities (such as Banks for Cooperatives, Federal Farm Credit Banks, Federal Home Loan Banks, and Federal Land Banks) is fully taxable at the federal level but exempt from all state income taxes. Puerto Rico also issues bonds that are exempt at the federal level and in all fifty states. Even after controlling for differences in risk, the before-tax returns to treasury securities tend to be lower than the returns to non-treasury securities. A California resident facing a 10% state and a 30% federal marginal tax rate, would be indifferent between holding treasury securities yielding 9% and equally risky non-treasury securities yielding 10%. Both securities yield 6.3% after all relevant taxes.

5.2   The Implicit Tax Rate, the Explicit Tax Rate, and the Total Tax Rate

Adjusting for Risk

For the same amount of promised coupons and principal repayment, the prices of bonds with a high risk of default are lower than the prices of bonds with a low risk of default. Thus, holding taxes constant, the required rate of return on a risky bond exceeds that of a less risky bond. Since we wish to isolate the effects of differential tax treatments on required before-tax rates of return, it is convenient to adjust the before-tax rates of return on bonds for differences in risk and differences in nontax costs. We use the term **risk-adjusted** to indicate that we are comparing the returns on alternative investments after adjusting for risk differences (and for nontax cost differences). After isolating the effects of differential taxation on before-tax returns, we introduce risk and nontax-cost differences into the analysis.

Computing the Implicit Tax

The **implicit tax** on the returns to any asset is defined as the difference between the before-tax return on a fully taxable bond (our benchmark security) and the risk-adjusted before-tax return on an alternative asset (such as a tax-favored municipal bond). For example, assume that the pretax return on fully taxable bonds is 10% and that the risk-adjusted return on tax-exempt bonds is 7%. The implicit tax on tax-exempt bonds would then be 3% or simply 10% less 7%. The implicit tax on the fully taxable bond is zero.

What is the **implicit tax** *rate*? The implicit tax rate, t_{Ia}, on a particular investment, a, is that tax rate which, if applied explicitly to fully taxable bonds, would leave a return equal to the *before-tax* rate of return on the alternative investment. If we define R_b to denote the risk-adjusted before-tax return on fully taxable bonds and R_a to denote the risk-adjusted before-tax return on the alternative investment, the implicit tax rate is given by

$$R_b(1 - t_{Ia}) = R_a,$$

or

$$t_{Ia} = (R_b - R_a)/R_b. \tag{5.1}$$

What is the implicit tax rate on tax-exempt bonds? Substituting for $R_b = 10\%$ and $R_a = 7\%$ in equation 5.1, we find that the implicit tax rate on municipal bonds is 30% (or [10% - 7%]/10%).[3] Thus, paying tax at a rate of 30% on fully taxable bonds would result in a return of 7%, the same as the before-tax rate of return on tax-exempt bonds. Although investors do not pay any explicit tax on the interest earned from holding municipal bonds, they pay the tax implicitly at a tax rate of 30% through a lower before-tax rate of return. As shown in equation 5.1, the implicit tax rate is computed by subtracting the risk-adjusted before-tax return on the fully taxable investment from the risk-adjusted before-tax return on the alternative investment and dividing the difference by the risk-adjusted before-tax return on the fully taxable bond.

To whom is the implicit tax paid? In our tax-exempt municipal bond example, it is paid to the issuers of the tax-exempt securities. The issuing municipalities receive an implicit subsidy by way of a lower cost of capital. In the example, the subsidy is at the rate of 30% of normal (that is, fully taxable) borrowing costs. This taxing scheme, which uses implicit taxes to subsidize municipal spending programs, is similar to an alternative scheme in which all bonds (including municipal bonds) are fully taxable at the federal level and the federal government remits the tax collected on municipal bonds to each issuing authority. In this alternative setting, the before-tax returns on municipal and fully taxable bonds would be 10%. Whether the bond was labeled a municipal or a taxable bond would make no difference to investors.

---

[3] Although our discussion will concentrate on pretax return differences between fully taxable bonds and tax-favored assets, we could also calculate implicit taxes on assets whose returns are taxed less favorably than fully taxable bonds. These assets would yield a pretax premium. They would be priced to yield a *negative* implicit tax.

Total Tax Rates in a Competitive Market

The total taxes paid on any investment is the sum of implicit taxes plus explicit taxes, where implicit taxes are measured relative to some benchmark asset. In a competitive equilibrium, the risk-adjusted after-tax return on all assets must be equal. Otherwise, there will exist arbitrage profit opportunities. We denote this common after-tax return as r^*.

In the preceding section, we defined the implicit tax on any asset (say asset a) to be the difference between the pretax return on our benchmark asset (which we take here to be fully taxable riskless bonds), and the pretax return on the asset in question, that is, $R_b - R_a$. The explicit tax on any asset is the difference between its pretax and after-tax return; that is, $R_a - r_a$. In a competitive equilibrium, the explicit tax can be expressed as $R_a - r^*$. The total tax, then, is equal to:

$$\text{Implicit Tax} \ + \ \text{Explicit Tax}$$

$$= \ (R_b - R_a) \ + \ (R_a - r^*)$$

$$= \ R_b - r^*.$$

In other words, the total tax is the same for all assets.

Just as we defined the implicit tax rate as the implicit tax as a fraction of the pretax return on our benchmark asset (that is, $(R_b - R_a)/R_b$)), we define the **explicit tax rate** as the explicit tax as a fraction of the pretax return on our benchmark asset (that is, $(R_a - r^*)/R_b$)). This definition ensures that the *total tax rate* (that is, the implicit tax rate plus the explicit tax rate) is the same for all assets.[4]

To illustrate, suppose that fully taxable bonds yield 10% before tax, partially taxable bonds yield 8% before tax, and tax-exempt bonds yield 7%. Each security is riskless. As Table 5.1 shows, while the mix of implicit and explicit taxes differs across the three assets, the total tax rate is the same (30%) for each of them. This implies that the statutory tax rate on ordinary taxable income is 30%.[5]

To avoid confusion, we wish to reemphasize that our measure of the explicit tax rate for any asset requires that the pretax return of the *benchmark* asset appear in the denominator. So, for example, the explicit tax rate on the partially taxable asset is 1%/10% or 10% and *not* 1% divided by the pretax return on the partially taxable asset, which would be 12.5%. Our reason for using this definition is that it ensures that total tax rates will coincide for all assets.

5.3 The Implicit Tax Rate on Differentially Taxed Assets

Adjusting for risk is a bit trickier in comparing fully taxable bonds with an investment in, say, depreciable assets than it is for comparing taxable and tax-exempt bonds, but it is only a matter of degree. In either case, we require a model

---

[4] Once we introduce market imperfections, the total tax rate may vary among assets as we will see, for example, in our discussion of tax clienteles.

[5] The reader can verify that the fraction of income, g, from the partially taxable asset that is taxable at the statutory rate of 30% is 41.67%. This can be determined by noting that

$$.08(1 - .3g) = .07.$$

Table 5.1 Implicit, Explicit, and Total Tax Rates for Differentially Taxed Asset Returns

	Fully Taxable Bond	Partially Taxable Bond	Tax-Exempt Bond
Pretax Return[1]	10%	8%	7%
Implicit Tax[2]	0%	2%	3%
Implicit Tax Rate[3]	0%	20%	30%
Explicit Tax[4]	3%	1%	0%
Explicit Tax Rate[5]	30%	10%	0%
Total Tax[6]	3%	3%	3%
Total Tax Rate[7]	30%	30%	30%

[1]R_b, R_p, and R_e, respectively.

[2]$R_b - R_b = 10\% - 10\% = 0\%$.
$R_b - R_p = 10\% - 8\% = 2\%$.
$R_b - R_e = 10\% - 7\% = 3\%$.

[3]Implicit Tax/R_b.

[4]All after-tax returns are equal to $r_e = 7\%$:
$R_b - 7\% = 10\% - 7\% = 3\%$.
$R_p - 7\% = 8\% - 7\% = 1\%$.
$R_e - 7\% = 7\% - 7\% = 0\%$.

[5]Explicit Tax/R_b.

[6]Implicit Tax + Explicit Tax.

[7]Implicit Tax Rate + Explicit Tax Rate or
(Implicit Tax + Explicit Tax)/R_b.

to adjust for differences in risk. Such models as the *capital asset pricing model* or the *arbitrage pricing model*, for example, could be used to compute before-tax risk premiums. Investors require the same *expected* after-tax returns on investment with equally risky after-tax cash flows. As a result, the required before-tax risk premiums will differ across differentially taxed assets. To illustrate this, assume that two assets pay identical pretax cash flows. One asset is tax exempt and is priced so that its expected return is 10.5% each year in perpetuity. Assume that the riskless rate on tax-exempt assets is 7% and the riskless rate on fully taxable riskless assets is 10%. Then, the after-tax risk premium on this exempt asset is 3.5% (or 10.5% - 7%). Investors require this risk premium to compensate them for the risk that they will not receive some of the promised interest coupons or principal repayments. Without this premium, investors would prefer to own a riskless investment. Thus, if the asset's expected annual-dollar return was $10.50, its price would be $100 (or $10.50/.105).

Now suppose that our other investment gives rise to returns that are taxed at a statutory rate of 30% per year. Then the after-tax income to the taxable asset is only 70% of the pretax income. Assuming that the after-tax cash flows to this investment are of comparable risk to those of the 10.5% tax-exempt bond, each dollar of expected pretax cash flow from the taxable bond is valued at only 70% as much as the dollar of expected cash flow from the tax-exempt bond. So if the taxable bond is to trade at the same price as the tax-exempt bond, it must yield an expected before-tax rate,[6] $\widetilde{R}_b$, such that

$$\widetilde{R}_b (1 - 30\%) = 10.5\%$$

or

$$\widetilde{R}_b = 15\%$$

Recall that the riskless rate on taxable bonds is 10%. Since the risky taxable investment returns 15%, its before-tax risk premium is 5% (or 15% - 10%). Equivalently, the 5% risk premium on the taxable asset is equal to the risk premium on the tax-exempt asset grossed up by a factor of one minus the 30% tax rate, or 3.5%/.7.

We have been working with risk-adjusted before-tax returns. In an earlier example we computed the implicit tax rates on assets by comparing the risk-adjusted return of 10% on the taxable asset (or 15% - 5% risk adjustment on the taxable asset) with the risk-adjusted return of 7% on the tax-exempt asset (or 10.5% - 3.5% risk adjustment on the tax-exempt asset). We could just as well have compared the required rates of return on the risky assets to compute implicit taxes. A before-tax expected rate of return of 15% on the taxable risky asset is equivalent to a before-tax expected rate of return of 10.5% on the tax-exempt risky asset. From these returns, we find that the implicit tax rate to be 30% (or (.15 - .105)/.15). The greater the risk premium, the greater the before-tax rates of return on the taxable asset relative to the tax-exempt asset. To illustrate, we show the required before-tax rates of return on assets as a function of their risk for three different asset classes in Figure 5.1.

The required before-tax returns on municipal bonds, common stocks, and fully taxable bonds increase as risk increases (as measured by some asset pricing model such as the asset's *beta* in the *capital asset pricing model*). As risk increases, the required rates of return on fully taxable assets such as bonds increase faster than those for municipal bonds and common stocks. Indeed the slope of the line for fully taxable assets is $1/(1 - t_{Ie})$ times the slope of the line for tax-exempt assets. As we illustrated in the last chapter, the required rates of return on stock are less than the required rate of return on fully taxable bonds of similar risk either because part of the gain to investing in common stock is exempt from taxation or because the tax on stock appreciation can be deferred.

While it is obvious that tax-favored municipal bonds require lower before-tax rates of return than taxable bonds, it is less obvious that tax-favored direct investments yield lower before-tax rates of return than taxable bonds. Risk premiums on direct investments tend to mask the effects of tax differentials on asset returns. For example, consider the investments denoted by X on the lines for fully taxable and partially taxable assets in Figure 5.1. If the before-tax risk-adjusted return on an investment project is 8% when the after-tax risk-adjusted rate is 6%, the project's explicit tax, as a fraction of its own pretax return, is 25% (or (.08 - .06)/.08). If the after-tax risk premium on the investment project is 6%, and the risk premium is taxed at a 25% tax rate, the before-tax risk premium is 8%

---

[6] Here and elsewhere, we use a twiddle over a variable to denote a risky return.

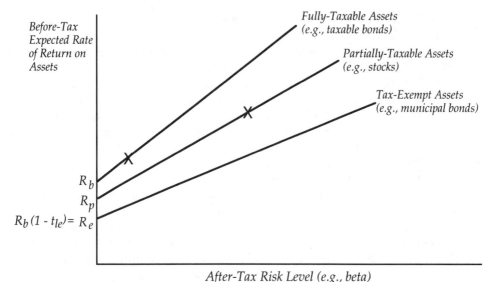

Before-Tax
Expected Rate
of Return on
Assets

Fully-Taxable Assets
(e.g., taxable bonds)

Partially-Taxable Assets
(e.g., stocks)

Tax-Exempt Assets
(e.g., municipal bonds)

R_b

R_p

$R_b(1 - t_{le}) = R_e$

After-Tax Risk Level (e.g., beta)

FIGURE 5.1   Expected Return versus Risk on Differentially Taxed Assets

(or 6%/(1 - .25)) for a total before-tax rate of return of 16%. Although the risky investment project yields 16% and the riskless bond yields 10% pretax, the risk premium on the project is *not* 6% but, rather, 8%. If the marginal tax rate on the bond investment is 40%, a bond with the same risk as the project would require a before-tax return of 20% (or 10% + 6%/(1-.4)), a 10% risk premium. Unless we adjust properly for risk differences in comparing investments, it might appear as though the tax-favored investment, if anything, bears a *negative* implicit tax rather than the 20% *positive* implicit tax rate it actually bears. Note that all three assets earn 12% after tax.

Stockholder Taxes

In Chapter Four, we developed the notion of implicit taxes indirectly in computing the required rate of return on common shares after corporate tax, but before shareholder tax. On a risk-adjusted basis, the required before-tax rate of return on shares would be equal to the after-tax bond rate if the explicit tax on shares were zero. But stockholders do pay explicit taxes on dividend income and realized capital gains income, so the risk-adjusted before-tax required rate of return to stock investment is greater than the after-tax bond rate. For an investor to be indifferent among investing in alternative assets in a competitive market, the total of explicit plus implicit taxes must be the same on every investment. Therefore, if the explicit tax on shares were at a rate equivalent to 1% of the stock *price* per year, the before-tax rate of return on shares would be 1% above the after-tax rate of return on bonds on a risk-adjusted basis. Stockholders would find that after paying this explicit tax, they earn the after-tax bond rate on a risk-adjusted basis.

Tax Credits and Accelerated Depreciation

Let us now consider how tax credits and accelerated depreciation deductions affect before-tax required rates of return on investments. Depreciation allowances on property, plant, and equipment reduce taxable income. Different schedules of allowable deductions apply to different classes of property. The more accelerated is the depreciation schedule, the closer the taxpayer comes to expensing the cost of the investment immediately. For example, if the cost of an investment is $100,000 and the taxpayer's marginal tax rate is 40%, an immediate deduction of the entire cost of the investment would reduce taxes by $40,000 (or $100,000 × .4). With a slower rate of depreciation, the present value of the deduction depends on the after-tax discount rate. For a given depreciation schedule, the higher the discount rate, the lower the present value of the depreciation tax shelter. For a given (positive) discount rate, the slower the rate of depreciation, the lower the present value of the tax shelter. For example, assume a straight-line depreciation schedule over two years and a 9% after-tax discount rate. That is, the taxpayer is allowed to deduct $50,000 in the first year and an additional $50,000 in the second year from taxable income. Assuming that the deductions can be used immediately to reduce taxes (in other words, the taxpayer reduces estimated tax payments when the equipment is acquired), the after-tax present value of the depreciation deductions is

$$\$38,349 = \$50,000 \times .4 + \frac{\$50,000 \times .4}{1.09} ,$$

$1,651 lower than with an immediate deduction.

In many countries, taxpayers have been granted investment tax credits on the purchase of certain types of equipment equal to a fraction of the asset's purchase price. A tax credit is like a tax receipt. For example, if equipment costs $20,000 and a 10% tax credit is available, the tax credit would be $2,000. If the taxpayer owed $15,000 in taxes on other income, the $2,000 tax credit reduces the required tax payment from $15,000 to $13,000. Generally, a tax credit is more valuable than a deduction. Whereas tax credits reduce taxes dollar for dollar, deductions reduce taxes by a fraction equal to the tax rate. With the 1986 Tax Act, investment tax credits were eliminated (at least temporarily) in the U.S., although a number of other types of tax credits were retained.

Implicit Tax Rate on Investment in Equipment

Liberal depreciation allowances and tax credits on equipment affect the required before-tax rates of return on investment. The more liberal the depreciation allowances or investment tax credits, the lower the required before-tax rate of return on investment and the higher the implicit tax. To illustrate the effects of liberal depreciation and investment tax credits on the implicit tax rate, assume that the taxing authority allows very fast write-offs of the cost of certain equipment. In fact, the deduction allowances (coupled with investment tax credits) are so liberal as to be equivalent, in present value, to an immediate expensing of the cost of the investment.[7] Research and development investments and advertising

---

[7] For example, under the 1981 Tax Act, automobiles were depreciable over a three-year period at the rates of 25%, 38%, and 37% of the purchase price, respectively. Beyond this, a 6% investment tax credit was available. Given an after-tax discount rate of 10% per year, a marginal tax rate of 40%, and assuming that the tax savings are realized, on average, half way through each tax year, the present

Chapter 5   Differentially Taxed Economic Activities and Implicit Taxes

expenditures are literally accorded this treatment.[8] Also assume that all of the returns resulting from the investment are fully taxable. We can define the investor's marginal tax rate as t_{po} today and t_{pn} in n years. For simplicity, suppose that our project generates no cash flows until time n, at which time it generates $(1 + R)^n$ dollars (so the before-tax rate of return on investment per period is R). The after-tax return per dollar of after-tax investment can be expressed this way:

$$\text{After-Tax Return} / \text{After-Tax Investment}$$

$$= \frac{(1 + R)^n(1 - t_{pn})}{(1 - t_{po})} \tag{5.2}$$

Since the taxpayer deducts the investment cost, a \$1 investment today has an after-tax cost of $\$1(1 - t_{po})$. For example, if the investor's marginal tax rate were 40%, the after-tax investment cost would be \$.60 per dollar invested. So an investment of $\$1/(1 - t_{po})$ dollars has an after-tax cost of only \$1. If the investment is held for n years and returns $\$1(1 + R)^n$ before tax per dollar invested, the taxpayer retains $\$1(1 + R)^n(1 - t_{pn})$ after tax, because tax at rate t_{pn} is paid on the entire dollar return. Thus, if the project returns 8% per year before tax for 5 years, and the taxpayer's marginal tax rate is still 40%, the taxpayer retains \$.882 after tax (or $(\$1.08)^5(1 - 40\%)$) per dollar invested. Because the taxpayer earned \$.882 after tax on an after-tax investment of \$.60, the 5-year return per dollar invested is \$1.469 or (\$.882/.6). The return per year is 8% (or $1.469^{.2} - 1$).

In the special case of constant tax rates ($t_{pn} = t_{po}$), the before-tax return and the after-tax return on investment are the same (i.e., 8% in the above illustration). We can see this from expression 5.2. With constant tax rates, 5.2 simplifies to $(1 + R)^n$. This means that the after-tax rate of return per period is R. But R is also the before-tax rate of return on investment, so the before-tax and the after-tax rates of return on investment coincide—the return is tax exempt.

If we assume that marginal tax rates are constant, then in equilibrium, the required before-tax rate of return, R, on this project must be equal to the after-tax bond rate, r_b, on a risk-adjusted basis. Note that this is exactly the required return on tax-exempt municipal bonds as well. If investors could earn rates of return higher than r_b, they could profit by borrowing at rate r_b after tax and investing at the higher rate. As a result, they would bid up the prices of the inputs necessary to undertake the tax-sheltered investment. In addition, with more investment, they might reduce the output prices of goods and services to consumers. This would continue until the expected after-tax rate of return on the last dollar of

value of the tax savings per dollar of initial investment in an automobile was approximately: $.4 \times [\$.25/1.05 + \$.38/(1.05 \times 1.1) + \$.37/(1.05 \times 1.1^2)] + \$.06 = \$.40$. This is equivalent to immediate expensing of each dollar of investment cost, which, in itself, would give rise to a tax rebate of \$.40 (or $.4 \times \$1$).

Slightly more generous investment incentives existed for so-called five-year property, which included most depreciable machinery and equipment. Here, the depreciation schedule was 15% in year 1, 22% in year 2, 21% in year 3, 21% in year 4, and 21% in year 5. In addition, a 10% investment tax credit was available. Calculations similar to those above for automobiles result in a present-value tax saving equal to \$.41 per dollar invested, or slightly *more* than if immediate expensing were allowed and no investment tax credits were available.

[8] In some countries, investors are permitted an immediate tax deduction for research and development expenditures equal to *more* than 100% of the expenditure.

5.3   The Implicit Tax Rate on Differentially Taxed Assets

investment is equal to that on the next best alternative, the after-tax bond rate or the municipal bond rate, on a risk-adjusted basis.

Expression 5.2 is familiar to us because we used the same algebra when describing the returns to investing in pension funds in Chapter Three. In both the investment here and pension fund investing, we deduct the cost of the investment and the returns are fully taxable. The major difference, however, is that while the pension fund can invest in fully taxable bonds to return the *before-tax* bond rate, competition causes the before-tax return on our tax-favored investment to be equal to the *after-tax* bond rate on a risk-adjusted basis. The difference between the pretax rate of return on fully taxable bonds and that on the tax-sheltered investment represents an implicit tax that is paid to customers (by way of reduced prices) and/or factor suppliers (by way of increased prices for inputs).

In expression 5.2, we allowed for the possibility of changes in marginal tax rates over time. If tax rates were expected to fall (i.e., $t_{pn} < t_{po}$), the required before-tax rate of return on investment would be less than the after-tax bond rate, r_b. If, on the other hand, tax rates were expected to increase (i.e., $t_{pn} > t_{po}$), the converse would be true. To illustrate the power of changes in tax rates, consider the following example. Assume that $t_{po} = 40\%$ and $t_{pn} = 30\%$; $n = 5$ years; and the after-tax bond rate, r_b, is equal to 7%. We know that on a risk-adjusted basis, in equilibrium, that the cumulative n-year after-tax return for this investment and a fully taxable bond must be the same:

$$\frac{(1 + R)^n (1 - t_{pn})}{(1 - t_{po})} = (1 + r_b)^n \qquad (5.3)$$

Solving for the required risk-adjusted before-tax rate of return per period, R, we find that

$$R = \left[\frac{(1 + r_b)^n (1 - t_{po})}{(1 - t_{pn})} \right]^{1/n} - 1.$$

Substituting the values for r_b, t_{po}, and t_{pn} from our example, we find that

$$R = \left[\frac{1.07^5 (1 - .4)}{(1 - .3)} \right]^{1/5} - 1 = 3.75\%.$$

A before-tax required rate of return of 3.75% is well below the after-tax rate of return on bonds of 7%. Because the government puts up 40% of every dollar invested but in return requires only 30% of the resultant returns, investors bid up the investment price of the project (or reduce prices for goods and services) such that the before-tax rate of return falls below the tax-exempt bond rate. By construction, the pretax return of 3.75% per year for five years provides exactly the same after-tax return per dollar of after-tax investment as investing in fully taxable (or tax-exempt) bonds, that is, 7%.

On the other hand, if tax rates are expected to increase in the future, the required before-tax rates of return on the project would exceed the after-tax bond rate, and the project would bear some explicit tax. An analogous result occurs when tax rates remain constant over time, but the depreciation and tax credit allowances are insufficient to amount to the equivalent of an immediate expensing of the cost of the investment. Explicit taxes will be paid on the project's returns and the before-tax required rate of return on the project will exceed the municipal bond rate.

Favorable tax treatment (such as liberal depreciation allowances or investment tax credits) stimulates demand for investments. Increased investment exerts upward pressure on factor prices (e.g., labor costs and equipment costs), unless the supply of such factors is perfectly elastic, and downward pressure on consumer prices unless consumer demand is perfectly elastic. For example, accelerating real-property depreciation rates encourages the production of more rental units. But the increase in supply of rental units puts downward pressure on rental rates. This, in turn, encourages people to rent the units from the increased supply.

Because of the anticipated increased supply of rental units and lower rental rates, the resale prices of existing rental units do not increase by the full value of the increase in present value of the depreciation-related tax savings. It takes time, however, for the capital stock and for the prices of goods and services (e.g., rental rates) to adjust to changes in depreciation allowances. If we had a capital stock that could be redeployed instantly to new uses, the capital stock and the prices of goods and services would adjust immediately to unanticipated changes in depreciation allowances and the prices of underlying assets would not change. With adjustment costs to change the capital stock, neither the supply of capital nor prices would adjust as quickly, and an unanticipated liberalization of tax allowances would generally create capital gains for the holders of capital assets. Conversely, the owners of the capital stock would experience capital losses on an unanticipated elimination of a tax shelter (e.g., less liberal depreciation allowances).

The Tax-Neutral Depreciation Schedule

If depreciation and tax credit allowances are equal to actual economic depreciation (in present value), the required before-tax rate of return on investment will equal the before-tax bond rate on a risk-adjusted basis. Such investments will bear no implicit taxes. If the rate of depreciation is slower in present value than economic depreciation, the before-tax rate of return on a risk-adjusted basis will exceed the before-tax bond rate.

To see this, define R to be the annualized before-tax rate of return on investment *in excess of the decline in market value of the investment due to economic depreciation*, E. Let D denote tax depreciation per dollar of investment and C denote investment tax credit per dollar of investment available at the time the investment is undertaken. Assume that C can be used fully to reduce taxes currently due. Then the after-tax return on investment in period 0 (the time of the investment) is C, and in period i is

$$(R + E_i)(1 - t) - E_i + D_i t. \tag{5.4}$$

In words, taxable income from the project, before depreciation deduction, is equal to $R + E_i$, the after-tax return for which is $(R + E_i)(1 - t)$. Economic depreciation is nondeductible, so the after-tax return is reduced by this full amount, but tax depreciation equal to D_i *is* tax deductible and yields an after-tax cash flow of $D_i t$. Expression 5.4 can be simplified to

$$R(1 - t) + (D_i - E_i)t.$$

In equilibrium, the present value of the after-tax return must be equal, on a risk-adjusted basis, to the after-tax return on bonds:[9]

$$C + \sum_{i=1}^{n} \frac{R(1 - t) + (D_i - E_i)t}{(1 + r_b)^i} = \sum_{i=1}^{n} \frac{R_b(1 - t)}{(1 + r_b)^i} \tag{5.5}$$

Note that if tax depreciation equals economic depreciation each period ($E_i = D_i$) and there are no investment tax credits available ($C = 0$), expression 5.5 simplifies to:

$$\sum_{i=1}^{n} \frac{R(1 - t)}{(1 + r_b)^i} = \sum_{i=1}^{n} \frac{R_b(1 - t)}{(1 + r_b)^i} \tag{5.6}$$

This implies that $R = R_b$: the before-tax rate of return on investment is equal to the before-tax bond rate and all taxes are explicit.

If investment tax credits are present and/or if tax depreciation is faster than economic depreciation, then additional tax savings must be added to the left-hand-side of equation 5.6. To maintain equality, R must be less than R_b, and the investment project would bear implicit tax. Alternatively, if tax depreciation is slower than economic depreciation and tax credits are small, then a negative adjustment would be required to the left-hand-side of 5.6. This would imply $R > R_b$, and this gives rise to a negative implicit tax to compensate for the tax-disfavored treatment.[10]

5.4 Clienteles

Taxpayers bear a total tax burden equal to the sum of explicit and implicit taxes. Taxpayers in a 30% statutory tax bracket would be indifferent between investing in taxable bonds yielding 10% before tax and municipal bonds yielding 7% (as well as any other investment in the economy that returns 7% after tax on a risk-adjusted basis). Such taxpayers are indifferent between paying all implicit, all explicit, or any combination of explicit and implicit taxes that totals 30%. Taxpayers who are indifferent between purchasing two equally risky assets, the returns to which are taxed differently, are called the **marginal investors**. Investors with statutory tax rates different from that of the marginal investors are *not*

---

[9] We assume that the investment is never sold, or if it is, that any gain or loss is taxed at rate t. Our basic conclusions are unaffected if gains and losses on sales are taxed at different rates, but the notation gets a bit more cumbersome.

[10] If an asset is sold for a price that exceeds its depreciated value, depreciation is recaptured up to the initial investment in the asset. That is, tax at ordinary rates is paid on the difference between the cost of the investment and the depreciated basis in the investment. A capital gains tax is paid on any excess of sale price over the initial cost of the investment. In addition, investment tax credits may be subject to recapture on an early sale of the investment. We focus on these issues in the chapter on property turnover.

indifferent to the choice of differentially taxed assets. We now turn to a consideration of investment strategies for these **inframarginal investors**.

Taxpayers in the same tax brackets are attracted to investments that are taxed similarly. Returning to our tax-exempt and taxable bond example, investors with high marginal tax rates prefer tax-exempt bonds, and investors with low marginal tax rates represent the natural **clientele** for fully taxable bonds. Unless investors correctly identify their natural tax clienteles, they will not maximize their after-tax rates of return.

For example, assume that the implicit tax rate on municipal bonds is 30% and that taxable bonds yield 10% before tax. The clientele for fully taxable bonds are taxpayers with marginal tax rates below 30%. A taxpayer with a 20% marginal tax rate will earn 8% after tax by investing in fully taxable bonds, 1% greater than in municipal bonds. The investor is better off paying explicit taxes of 20% by investing in taxable bonds than paying implicit taxes of 30% by investing in municipal bonds.

Analogously, an investor whose marginal tax rate is 40% is better off investing in municipal bonds. Paying an implicit tax rate of 30% is less expensive than an explicit tax rate of 40%. While the implicit tax rate is the same for all investors, explicit tax rates vary among investors. Taxpayers with high explicit tax rates are led to invest in assets that bear high implicit taxes. It is only the marginal investors who lack any "brand loyalty." In the absence of transaction costs, they would jump back and forth between taxable and municipal bonds as relative prices change.

Tax clienteles are pervasive, and they apply to organizations as well as individuals. For example, if a corporation faces a lower statutory tax rate than the implicit tax rate on tax-exempt assets, holding fully taxable bonds is a superior investment to holding municipal bonds.

With different clienteles, market frictions or tax rule restrictions are required to prevent arbitrage opportunities from existing. We will develop this theme in Chapter Six.

5.5   Implicit Taxes and Corporate Taxpayers

Over the years, many corporations have been nonpayers of explicit taxes. The primary reasons for this include the availability of generous depreciation deductions, tax credits, immediate write-off of certain investments (like advertising, research and development, and certain personnel costs), and interest expense deductions, along with myriad opportunities to postpone the recognition of taxable income.

Some industries enjoy special tax rules. The oil industry receives very rapid write-offs of the cost of drilling wells; timber companies are allowed to treat much of their profits as capital gains; and defense contractors used to be able to postpone substantial sums of income on long-term contracts by using the "completed contract method of accounting" to reduce explicit taxes.

Citizens for Tax Justice published a study in 1985 that is entitled "Corporate Taxpayers and Corporate Freeloaders." The study highlights those corporations that pay no explicit taxes. Their mission is to politicize corporations that use "loopholes" to avoid paying taxes. During the period of one of their studies, the federal corporate tax rate was 46% on pretax profits. The study claims that "129 of the companies—or almost half—managed to pay absolutely nothing in federal income taxes, or to receive outright tax rebates, in at least one of the four years from 1981 to 1984. ... The 129 companies earned $66.5 billion in pretax domestic profits in the years they did not pay federal income taxes ..." Nine companies paid no federal taxes in each of the four years: Boeing, ITT, General Dynamics, Transamerica, First Executive, Mitchell Energy and Development, Greyhound, Grumman, and Lockheed. It would appear that the nonpayment of explicit taxes by such well-known companies was a motivating force for many of the changes in the 1986 Tax Act.

The study also goes on to state, "One of the unfair aspects of our current tax system is the way it rewards some companies and penalizes others. While many companies get off scot-free, a few pay a great deal of tax." The study lauds those corporations that pay explicit taxes, claiming that it is inherently unfair that some corporations avoid paying their share.

While explicit taxes are one element in the "fairness" equation, we have already argued that the total tax burden includes not only explicit taxes but also implicit taxes. When we add in implicit taxes, the so-called corporate free-loaders might actually have paid taxes at a high rate.

Some business organizations publicize that implicit taxes are an important component of their total tax burden. For example, in the 1986 Annual Report of United Virginia Bankshares, we find very direct references to implicit taxes: "Banks have been criticized for paying too little in taxes. The fact is banks pay a lot of taxes. ... Banks pay the municipalities the tax that would have otherwise been paid to the federal government by accepting a lower interest rate on municipal securities." They go on to give other examples of implicit taxes such as the lost income on the idle balances that they are required to leave on deposit with the Federal Reserve Bank. They show that while their explicit tax rate was .7%, their total tax rate in 1986, including implicit taxes, was 49.7%.[11]

An interesting example of the non-payment of explicit taxes and its potential effect on prices is General Dynamics. By using the "completed contract method of accounting," General Dynamics was able to postpone the payment of all explicit federal taxes for many years. To the extent that General Dynamics must bid competitively against other firms for the right to supply goods to the Defense Department, however, it may pay substantial sums of implicit taxes. If the defense contract market were perfectly competitive, General Dynamics would pay a full implicit tax. The recipient of the implicit tax in this case would be the Defense Department. Because of this accounting method, the Defense Department is charged lower prices for goods and services through the competitive bidding process. However, some might argue that the defense market is not very competitive. As a result, General Dynamics might have been able to capture a large fraction of the explicit tax savings for itself.

As another example, the Federal Home Loan Bank Board auctioned off a number of troubled savings and loan associations (thrifts) at year-end 1988. Buyers were granted very favorable tax treatment, and this touched off a furor

---

[11] Of course, the bank fails to include any implicit *subsidies* in this total tax calculation, such as that due to a below-market cost of insurance on federally insured demand deposits.

among many in Congress and in the press. As in the defense procurement example, however, the granting of favorable tax treatment should in principle increase the prices submitted by bidders for the failed thrifts.[12] Here, however, empirical evidence suggests that bidders have been successful in capturing much of the tax benefits for themselves. It is interesting to note that the Federal Deposit Insurance Corporation has actively publicized its view that the tax savings available by acquiring a failed bank represent an asset that they expect bidders to pay for through higher bids. They have even held seminars for this purpose.[13]

Many in Congress believe that because of tax loopholes, corporations avoid paying taxes and, as a result, fail to pay their fair share of the tax. For this reason, Congress passed an Alternative Minimum Tax (AMT) provision to replace a weaker "add-on" corporate tax as part of the Tax Reform Act of 1986. The AMT has as its goal that every corporation should pay some explicit taxes.

Summary of Key Points

1. Different economic activities are taxed differently, even if undertaken in the same organizational form. The unequal taxation of returns affects the demand for investment and thereby affects the before-tax rates of return.

2. If two assets yield identical pretax cash flows, but one is more heavily taxed than the other, then the price of the more lightly taxed asset will be bid up relative to the price of the more heavily taxed asset.

3. Absent market frictions, asset prices adjust so that the after-tax rates of return are equalized across assets for all investors in the economy.

4. Differential tax treatment of asset returns gives rise to implicit taxes. For example, those investments that are tax-favored relative to fully taxable bonds earn lower before-tax rates of return than do fully taxable bonds. The difference in rates of return between fully taxable bonds and the tax-favored asset is an implicit tax. That is, a tax is paid implicitly through the lower before-tax rates of return.

5. Investments that are tax-*disfavored* relative to fully taxable bonds earn *higher* before-tax rates of return than do fully taxable bonds. Taking fully taxable bonds as the benchmark case, the implicit tax on the relatively tax-disfavored asset is negative.

6. In comparing the returns to different assets, it is important to distinguish between risk differences and taxation differences. Risky investments are priced to provide risk premiums. A risky investment that is lightly taxed (such as common stocks) can yield high before-tax rates of return and still bear substantial implicit tax relative to less risky assets that are fully taxed (such as taxable bonds).

7. The implicit tax rate is found by subtracting the before-tax required rate of return on the fully taxable bond from the risk-adjusted before-tax rate

---

[12] For further discussion, see *Crisis Resolution in the Thrift Industry: Beyond the December Deals* (Report of the Mid American Institute Task Force on the Thrift Crisis: Chicago), March 1989.

[13] See *Perspective* (KPMG Peat Marwick), May 1989.

of return on the alternative investment and dividing this difference by the before-tax required rate of return on the fully taxable bond. Tax is paid at this rate implicitly through a lower before-tax rate of return.

8. The implicit tax is typically not paid directly to the taxing authority. The taxpayer can be viewed as acting as a transfer agent for the government, with the taxpayer remitting a part of the tax to the beneficiary of a governmental subsidy or transfer payment. For example, municipal bond issuers receive the implicit tax as a subsidy. Customers of goods and services produced in capital-intensive industries with liberal depreciation allowances and tax credits pay lower prices. Renters face lower rental rates when depreciation allowances are very liberal.

9. If competition is imperfect and market frictions result in deadweight costs, not all benefits of the implicit tax go directly to the consumer. Some remain with the producers, and some go to no one (an economic loss to the system).

10. If the tax-deduction-equivalents of depreciation and tax credits on an investment have a present value equal to (greater than, less than) the present value of the period-by-period decline in the market value of the investment, the required before-tax rate of return on the investment will be equal to (less than, greater than) the before-tax rate of return on the fully taxable bond on a risk-adjusted basis.

11. Changing tax rates over time affect the required before-tax rates of return on long-term investments. If tax rates are expected to fall in the future, the availability of accelerated depreciation magnifies the reduction in the required before-tax rates of return on investment relative to fully taxable assets. Taking deductions when tax rates are high and recognizing income when tax rates are low is generally a good tax-planning strategy.

12. When tax rates are increasing over time, accelerated depreciation may be undesirable. We must be careful, however, to take account of interest rate effects. The present value of postponing deductions might be below the present value of an immediate deduction even if tax rates are expected to increase.

13. With unexpected changes in tax rates, investors might suffer capital gains and losses on long-term investments. Since capital cannot be redeployed or augmented instantaneously, favorable changes in tax rules will cause existing capital to appreciate in value and unfavorable changes in tax rules will cause existing capital to depreciate in value.

14. If, in addition to differentially taxed assets, we have differentially taxed investors, the proper clientele for investments depends upon the mix of implicit and explicit taxes levied on the investments. The marginal investor setting prices in the market is defined to be the one who is indifferent between investing in the differentially taxed assets. The proper clientele for high implicitly taxed investments are investors whose statutory tax rates exceed that of the marginal investor setting prices in the market. And the proper clientele for high explicitly taxed

investments are investors whose statutory tax rates are less than that of the marginal investor.

15. Investors with statutory tax rates different from the marginal investor setting prices in the market are "inframarginal" investors. It is the inframarginal investors who form clearly identifiable clienteles as a function of the level of implicit tax rates across investments.

16. Many policy makers appear to ignore implicit taxes in their public statements. If we measure the progressivity of our tax structure by focusing exclusively on explicit taxes, the U.S. tax structure does not appear very progressive. That is, the explicit tax as a percentage of the total income is about the same for wealthy and poor taxpayers. If, on the other hand, implicit taxes and subsidies are incorporated into the tax burden calculations, the tax schedule is much more progressive. The reason is that wealthy investors tend to own high implicitly taxed assets such as municipal bonds, common stock, and real estate.

Discussion Questions

1. True or False? Discuss.
   a. The implicit tax rate on an asset cannot be calculated without a benchmark asset against which to compare pretax returns.
   b. The implicit tax rate is always positive.
   c. The implicit tax rate is always less than the explicit tax rate.
   d. While explicit taxes are paid to taxing authorities, implicit taxes are subsidies paid to the issuers of securities, to consumers of goods and services, and to suppliers of factor inputs.

2. If the before-tax rate of return on a riskless fully taxable bond is 7%, and the before-tax rate of return on a riskless tax-favored asset is 5%, what is the implicit tax rate on the tax-favored asset? If a tax-exempt riskless asset earns a before-tax rate of return of 4%, what is the explicit tax rate for the marginal investor on the riskless tax-favored asset that returns 5%?

3. Risk differences among assets mask the effects of differential taxation on returns. If we know the required after-tax risk premiums on assets, how can we determine the effects of differential taxation on their expected before-tax rates of return?

4. Capital investment in many countries is tax-favored. For example, in 1989, Singapore allowed a 100% tax depreciation write-off in the year of purchase for certain automated production equipment. Similar tax treatment was allowed on a variety of capital expenditures in the United Kingdom during the early 1980s. How do investment tax credits and liberal depreciation allowances affect the required before-tax rates of return on investment? Could the risk-adjusted before-tax rates of return on investment be lower than the tax-exempt riskless bond rate in

equilibrium? Why? Could the risk-adjusted before-tax rate of return on investment be higher than the before-tax riskless bond rate?

5. Why do countries encourage investment by offering tax incentives such as investment tax credits or liberal depreciation allowances? What alternative methods exist to achieve the same goals? How would you judge whether tax incentives were superior to the alternatives?

6. What is an investment clientele? If the market sets implicit tax rates, why are we interested in determining the proper clientele for various investments? Why should a corporate strategist be interested in clienteles?

7. How does the concept of implicit taxes apply to investments undertaken in different tax jurisdictions?

Problems

1. Answer the following three parts.

   a. Suppose there exists three riskless assets. The first yields a fully taxable return of 7% before tax; the second yields a pretax return of 6%, only half of which is taxable; and the third yields a 5% fully tax-exempt return. Over what range of tax rates does each asset yield the highest after-tax return? How does this relate to tax clienteles?

   b. Suppose the tax rate schedule is as follows: 20% on the first $5,000 of investment income, 30% on the next $5,000 of investment income, and 40% on investment income exceeding $10,000. If you had $150,000 to invest and you had to invest in only one of the three assets, which one would maximize after-tax income?

   c. Can you beat the investment strategy in (b) by investing in a portfolio of assets? What is the optimal investment (the one that maximizes after-tax income) over investment ranges of $0 to $500,000.

2. The investments below all bear the same after-tax risk. Calculate the risk-adjusted pretax rates of return for assets II, III, and IV, as well as the expected pretax return (*unadjusted* for risk) for assets III and IV. Explain your answer, and give examples of each of these assets that are observed in the marketplace.

Asset	Expected Pretax Return	Tax Treatment of Risk-Adjusted Return	Risk-Adjusted Pretax Return	Tax Treatment of Risk Premium	Risk-Adjusted After-Tax Return
I	20%	Fully Taxable	10%	Fully Taxable	6%
II	12%	Tax Exempt	?	Tax Exempt	6%
III	?	Tax Exempt	?	Taxed at 25%	6%
IV	?	Fully Taxable	?	Taxed at 25%	6%

CHAPTER 6
Arbitrage and the Effects of Restrictions and Frictions on the Tax-Planning Equilibrium

In Chapter Three, after-tax returns from passive investment in a given asset were shown to vary across differentially taxed savings vehicles through which the asset is held. In Chapter Four, after-tax returns from investment in a given productive venture were shown to vary across differentially taxed organizational forms. Only frictions (that is, brokerage fees and other information-related costs that are required to buy or sell assets) and tax rule restrictions could have prevented one organizational form from dominating another.

In this chapter, we demonstrate that in the absence of such frictions and restrictions, if one savings vehicle or organizational form dominated another savings vehicle or organizational form, taxpayers could eliminate all of their taxes. They would accomplish this by holding negative quantities of wealth through the inferior vehicles (that is, borrow or promise to pay the after-tax rate earned on the inferior vehicle) and positive amounts of wealth through the superior vehicles. This is a form of tax arbitrage.

Implicit taxes and tax clienteles were the central focus of Chapter Five. Differential taxation of investment returns was shown to give rise to implicit taxes, a reduction in the before-tax rate of return on a tax-favored asset relative to a fully taxable asset of equal risk. The before-tax rates of return on tax-favored assets are lower because investors bid up their prices. Tax clienteles were also shown to be closely linked to implicit taxes. High marginal-tax-rate taxpayers concentrate their holdings in tax-favored assets, and low marginal-tax-rate taxpayers concentrate their holdings in tax-disfavored assets. In this chapter, we demonstrate that in the absence of frictions and restrictions, the existence of two differentially taxed assets requires that all rational taxpayers in the economy face identical marginal tax rates. This is so, no matter how disparate the wealth positions of taxpayers and no matter how progressive the statutory tax rate schedule might be.

We then move to a consideration of the forces that prevent tax arbitrage from being implemented effectively; namely, tax-rule restrictions and market frictions. We emphasize restrictions in this chapter, and we introduce the effect of frictions on the ability of taxpayers to conduct tax arbitrage. We then expand the analysis of frictions in Chapter Seven. Both forces play a central role in preventing arbitrage, and in some respects they are substitutes. In fact, as frictions are reduced or eliminated by the creation of new markets or transaction-enhancing technologies, the imposition of new restrictions may be required to prevent the forms of arbitrage that we discuss in this chapter. As will become clear shortly, in the absence of frictions, the tax rule restrictions that we observe are simply insufficient to eliminate arbitrage opportunities. This implies that the more costly it is to implement tax-planning strategies, the fewer are the number of explicit restrictions required to prevent the implementation of those strategies that are considered to be socially undesirable.

In Chapter Two, we discussed some of the broad tax law restrictions that prevent taxpayers from engaging in socially undesirable tax planning, such as the business-purpose doctrine and the substance-over-form doctrine. In this chapter, we consider some of the more specific restrictions in the tax law that are designed to prevent taxpayers from being too successful in reducing their taxes by exploiting differential taxation of organizational forms and by exploiting differences in tax rates across taxpayers and over time.

6.1 Tax Arbitrage: Introduction

As with any type of arbitrage, tax arbitrage involves the purchase of one asset (a "long" position) and the sale of another (a "short" position) to create a sure profit despite a zero level of net investment. We will distinguish between two types of tax arbitrage: (1) **organizational-form arbitrage** and (2) **clientele-based arbitrage**.

Organizational-form arbitrage involves taking a long position in an asset or a productive activity through a *favorably taxed* organizational form and a short position in an asset or a productive activity through an *unfavorably taxed* organizational form. Although clientele-based arbitrage may also involve taking a long position in a tax-favored asset and a short position in a tax-disfavored asset, the nature of clientele-based arbitrage depends upon whether the taxpayer starts out with a relatively high or a relatively low marginal tax rate. For the high-tax-rate taxpayer, clientele-based arbitrage involves taking a long position in a relatively tax-favored asset (one that bears a relatively high degree of implicit tax), and a short position in a tax-disfavored asset (one that bears relatively more explicit tax). For the low-tax-rate taxpayer, clientele-based arbitrage involves taking a long position in a tax-disfavored asset and a short position in a tax-favored asset.

6.2 Organizational-Form Arbitrage

Immediate Tax Rebates When Taxable Income is Negative

Suppose that the same asset could be held in two differentially taxed organizational forms and that the asset bears no implicit tax.[1] Further suppose that taxpayers' marginal tax rates are always positive; that is, when taxable income is negative, the government shares in the loss by sending a check to the taxpayer. In such circumstances, the taxpayer could create infinite wealth. For example, assume that a taxpayer invests in a single premium deferred annuity (SPDA) that appreciates in value at the rate of R per period before tax for two years. Tax on the appreciation is deferred until the end of year two. Also suppose that the investment is financed by borrowing at before-tax rate R. Interest payments are deductible at the end of each year. The taxpayer undertakes an additional loan at the end of the first period equal to the after-tax interest that accrues in the first period. For marginal tax rate t, each dollar employed in the strategy gives rise to an after-tax dollar return of

$$\text{After-tax SPDA accumulation} \quad - \quad \text{After-tax loan repayment}$$
$$= [(1 + R)^2(1 - t) + t] \quad - \quad (1 + R(1 - t))^2$$
$$= R^2 t(1 - t) > 0,$$

and without restrictions or frictions, the taxpayer would continue to borrow to increase wealth without limit as long as t remains positive. For example, if we assume R = 10% and t = 40%, the taxpayer accumulates $2.40 after tax on a 0 net-investment position per thousand dollars borrowed and invested in a 2-year SPDA contract. That is, a $1000 investment in the SPDA accumulates to $1,126 after tax (or $1,000(1.12 × .6 + .4)) and is financed at an after-tax cost of $1,123.60 (or $1,000 × 1.06^2) for a net benefit of $2.40. The government provides a rebate of tR on the interest expense in the first year and collects tax on the cumulative SPDA interest in year two. This is not consistent with investor equilibrium. To prevent unlimited arbitrage of this form, most tax systems, including that of the U.S., do not provide tax rebates for negative taxable income. Instead, such amounts are carried forward to offset positive amounts of taxable income that may be generated in the future. We consider this tax structure next.

No Tax Rebates on Negative Taxable Income

All taxpayers are endowed with some amount of wealth to invest each period. Wealth consists of human capital and physical capital, such as that inherited or that earned in previous periods and not consumed. Both types of capital can generate investment returns that are taxed implicitly, explicitly, or both.

Suppose that a taxpayer generates taxable income of Y and faces a marginal tax rate of t. If the taxpayer were to pay tY of tax, she would be left with Y(1 - t) after tax. Now suppose that the taxpayer can invest in an organizational form that provides complete tax exemption on investment returns (such as the savings

---

[1]Examples include riskless corporate bonds (our benchmark asset) and depreciable assets that give rise to income taxed at ordinary rates and depreciation deductions for tax purposes that are equal in present value to the path of economic depreciation, as discussed in Chapter Five.

Table 6.1 Example of Organizational-Form Arbitrage

Salary	$ 100,000
Tax before arbitrage strategy (at a 40% tax rate)	40,000
After-tax salary without arbitrage strategy	$ 60,000

Arbitrage strategy
Borrow $1,000,000 @ 10%
Invest proceeds in a tax-exempt savings account @ 10%

Salary	$100,000
Loan one year later	(1,100,000)
Savings account one year later	1,100,000

Tax:		
Salary	100,000	
Interest Expense	(100,000)	
Interest Income (exempt)	0	
Taxable income	0	
Tax @ 40%		0
After-tax salary *with* arbitrage strategy		$ 100,000

portion of a life insurance policy). If the taxpayer could borrow at tax-deductible rate R per period, and invest the proceeds of the loan in the tax-exempt organizational form at the same rate R per period, the taxpayer could wipe out all tax on the Y dollars of taxable income (but could not increase wealth by more than tY because of the absence of tax rebates on negative taxable income). We can illustrate this organizational-form arbitrage with the following example. (Table 6.1 presents a summary.)

> Example: Suppose our taxpayer will earn $100,000 in salary over the forthcoming year. Before any tax-arbitrage activity, she would pay tax at a 40% rate on this income, producing a tax of $40,000. Suppose that the before-tax interest rate on riskless fully taxable bonds is 10%. The taxpayer's $40,000 tax liability can be reduced to zero by borrowing, at the beginning of the year, an amount equal to $100,000/.10, which is $1,000,000, and investing the proceeds of the loan in a tax-exempt insurance product through a life insurance company that holds riskfree taxable bonds yielding 10%. The $100,000 in salary is used to pay the $100,000 of interest (or $1,000,000 × .10) on the loan. As a result, taxable income becomes zero because it is computed as salary minus the interest that is paid on the loan. But this is not troubling to the taxpayer, since the savings portion of the insurance policy has now grown to $1,100,000 (or 1.1 × $1,000,000), $100,000 more than the $1,000,000 loan. On surrendering the tax-exempt insurance policy and paying off the loan, our taxpayer is left with $100,000 after tax, an amount equal to her before-tax salary.[2]

---

[2] Under the U.S. tax rules, if taxpayers surrender life insurance policies, they are taxable at ordinary rates on the excess of what they realize from the policy (that is, policyholder dividends and surrender

Chapter 6   Arbitrage and the Effects of Restrictions and Frictions

Note that this illustration of organizational-form arbitrage involves a long position in bonds invested through a favorably taxed organizational form (life insurance) and a short position in bonds invested through an unfavorably taxed organizational form (a loan that generates ordinary taxable income to the lender and a corresponding deduction for the borrower each period). As a result of this arbitrage activity, salary income becomes tax exempt. Moreover, this process can be repeated with respect to future income as well.

Of course, if the tax-exempt savings vehicle were literally a life insurance policy, some amount of "term" (or pure) insurance must be purchased that may be of no value to someone lacking a bequest motive. But in the absence of tax-rule restrictions, an arbitrarily small amount of term life insurance would be sufficient to take advantage of tax-free savings in the policy. Moreover, in the absence of frictions, taxpayers could offset their purchase of term insurance on their lives by *selling* insurance policies on their lives to other investors or investment intermediaries. In more realistic settings, however, this would prove to be quite difficult and costly.

Restrictions on Organizational-Form Arbitrage

Arbitrage of the type described above could be prevented by placing limits on taxpayers' ability to deduct interest from their taxable income. For example, if taxpayers were permitted to deduct interest only to the extent of other taxable investment income earned (that is, no net interest deduction), the organizational-form arbitrage described above would fail to eliminate tax on salary income. Such restrictions would prevent the taxpayer from making the after-tax cost of borrowing lower than the after-tax return available on the exempt savings vehicle. The U.S. Tax Code provides a similar restriction in Code Section 163(d). This section allows a tax deduction for interest only to the extent that the taxpayer generates taxable investment income, which includes interest, dividends, rents, royalties, and capital gains.

Prior to the Tax Reform Act of 1986, up to $10,000 of interest was deductible per year in excess of investment income. The interest deduction limitation does not apply to corporations, and it only became applicable for individuals in 1969.

An exception to the interest deduction limitation is provided for home mortgage interest in the U.S. But taxpayers cannot really exploit this exception in a way that enables them to effect organizational-form tax arbitrage. After all, one must actually buy a house to qualify for a mortgage. Any arbitrage opportunity available through home ownership should be reflected in the purchase price of the home, creating an implicit tax. Moreover, the 1986 and 1987 Tax Acts place a ceiling on the deductible amounts of home-mortgage interest.[3]

---

proceeds) over the premiums that they paid into the policy. Instead of surrendering their policies, however, investors have had the opportunity to borrow desired funds, using the accumulated amounts in their policies as collateral for the loan. This transaction was not taxable. Since the loan is fully secured by the insurance policy, the borrowing rate on the loan can be the same as the earning rate in the policy, so borrowing on the accumulated earnings in the policy has succeeded in creating tax exemption on the investment income. The 1988 Tax Act added several new restrictions on borrowing the savings portion of insurance policies issued after 1988.

[3] Still, individual taxpayers, who had built up equity value in their homes, wishing to borrow money to finance consumption should have found mortgage financing to be tax-favored relative to

A second set of restrictions to limit organizational-form arbitrage relates to the types of life insurance policies that allow tax-free buildup of savings. Recall that an insurance policy has two components: a pure insurance (or term) component that protects against loss of life, and a savings component. The savings component helps ensure that funds are available to pay future insurance premia, although they can be withdrawn from the policy. Section 800 of the U.S. Tax Code requires a minimum ratio of term insurance to savings in the policy.[4] The reason for allowing tax-free buildup of savings in a life insurance policy in the first place was to encourage the purchase of life insurance. When tax-free buildup of life insurance savings was first permitted, interest rates were quite low relative to the rates observed in the late seventies and throughout the eighties, and transaction costs prevented the organizational-form arbitrage described here. With higher interest rates and refinements in insurance policies (such as Universal Life Insurance), more restrictions became necessary. In fact, minimum term-to-savings ratios were never defined in the U.S. Code until special restrictions were imposed on insurance products in the 1984 Tax Act. The restrictions ensure that if a taxpayer wishes to use the tax-free savings feature of cash value life policies to a substantial extent, a nontrivial portion of additional savings deposits must be allocated to the purchase of additional term insurance.[5]

So, in the absence of restrictions and market frictions, if taxpayers invest through a tax-exempt organizational form, financed by loans that generate tax-deductible interest expense, they could eliminate all income taxes. As we demonstrate next, however, it is not necessary that the investment give rise to complete tax exemption of returns to enable the elimination of taxes on income.

Organizational-Form Arbitrage with a Partially Tax-Exempt Savings Vehicle

Assume that a savings vehicle exists that allows for a partial exemption of investment income. For example, suppose that the taxpayer is taxed on 75% of investment appreciation each year (that is, the inclusion rate, g, is equal to .75).[6] In the absence of limitations on interest deductions (for example, Code Section 163(d)), the taxpayer could eliminate taxes on Y dollars of income by borrowing at the beginning of the year at an interest rate of R and investing this amount in the tax-favored savings vehicle, which also generates earnings at rate R per period. The amount to be borrowed, B, is $Y/[R(1 - g)]$, as shown in Table 6.2.

As Table 6.2 illustrates, the arbitrage strategy allows the creation of Y dollars of tax deductions with a zero net investment. This eliminates taxable income. For example, if $Y = \$100,000$, $R = 10\%$, and $g = .75$, then $B = Y/[R(1 - g)] = \$4,000,000$. This generates $400,000 of interest expense and $300,000 of taxable income from

---

consumer financing in the U.S. after the 1986 Tax Act. Not surprisingly, mortgage financing grew at a much more rapid rate in the U. S. in 1987 than did consumer financing.

[4] As mentioned earlier, in the absence of frictions, this would not be a binding constraint. The taxing authority can exploit the presence of frictions in choosing its restrictions.

[5] As the popularity of using cash-value life insurance policies has grown, so has the frequency with which legislators have proposed changes in the tax laws that would eliminate the tax-favored status of this organizational form.

[6] This would correspond to Savings Vehicle III in Chapter Three.

Chapter 6   Arbitrage and the Effects of Restrictions and Frictions

the arbitrage strategy, a net tax deduction of $100,000 as desired. Moreover, the value at year-end of the investment undertaken with the loan proceeds is exactly equal to the interest plus principal on the loan. Organizational-form arbitrage involving a partially tax-exempt asset has resulted in the complete elimination of taxes on the Y dollars of initial income.[7] Note that this strategy works for any amount of tax exemption ($g < 1$).

Table 6.2 Organizational-Form Arbitrage Strategy: Partially Tax-Exempt Savings Vehicle

Initial Taxable Income	Y
Arbitrage Strategy:	
Borrow B dollars at rate R, yielding a tax deduction of BR.	
Invest B dollars at rate R, yielding taxable income of BgR.	
Net Tax Deduction is BR - BgR = BR(1 - g).	
Choose B so that the net tax deduction equals initial taxable income, Y; that is, BR(1 - g) = Y.	
=> B = Y/[R(1 - g)]	
=> Net tax deduction	$\dfrac{Y}{}$
Net taxable income	0
After-tax cash position:	
Initial income	Y
Loan position	- B(1 + R)
Investment position	+B(1 + R)
Tax	$\dfrac{0}{}$
Terminal position after tax	$\underline{\underline{Y}}$

Full Taxation with Deferral and Organizational-Form Arbitrage

Next, we demonstrate that when the tax-favored organizational form involves deferral of taxation, but investors are eventually taxed fully on all investment income (as with a single premium deferred annuity (SPDA)), taxpayers can reduce but not eliminate their income tax. To illustrate, assume that a taxpayer will earn income of $100,000 in the forthcoming year and the before-tax interest rate is 10%. She now borrows $1,000,000 and invests in an SPDA. The interest deduction in the first year is $100,000, which, in the absence of restrictions on the deductibility of interest, eliminates taxable income. If the SPDA were cashed out at the end of the first year, however, the $100,000 in taxable income would reappear from the interest earned through the SPDA. So the SPDA must be held for at least two years to succeed in postponing any tax payments.

Assume, for simplicity, that the taxpayer has no other taxable income beyond the first year (other than potential interest income from the SPDA). If

---

[7] Note that the asset in the capital gains savings vehicle must earn at the same rate as the borrowing rate to effect this arbitrage. We assume that neither asset bears implicit tax. Thus, as discussed below, a non-dividend-paying stock could not be used to effect this form of arbitrage if such stock bears implicit tax; that is, if the risk-adjusted before-tax return on stock is below that on fully taxable assets such as bonds.

refunds for negative taxable income are not allowed, the interest required to carry the loan creates excess interest deductions, which must be carried into the future until taxable income becomes available (on cashing out the SPDA) to offset the interest deductions. Although the loan creates an interest deduction in the first year, it creates only deferred interest deductions thereafter until the SPDA is cashed out, because there is no other taxable income against which to deduct the interest expense. Cashing out the SPDA creates more than enough taxable investment income to deplete the full amount of the deferred interest deduction. In effect, the loan becomes a short position in an SPDA after the first year, in that interest accumulates on the loan at the fully taxable rate, but it doesn't give rise to a tax deduction until the taxpayer generates other taxable income. The taxpayer has acquired an n-year SPDA financed with a 1-year ordinary loan and an n-1 year SPDA to be issued one year hence. What the taxpayer has achieved by way of tax savings is a function of the length of the deferral period. The tax on the first year's income is postponed until such time as the SPDA and the loan position are cashed out. In the extreme (that is, when the SPDA and the loan position are maintained indefinitely), this strategy results in the elimination of the tax on salary income. This is developed more precisely in Appendix 6.1 at the end of this chapter.[8]

The Effects of Frictions on Organizational-Form Arbitrage

Let us now reconsider opportunities to engage in organizational-form arbitrage in the presence of market frictions (but without tax rule restrictions), using savings vehicles that allow full exemption of investment earnings (such as the savings portion of a life insurance policy). Suppose that, because of special costs incurred to invest in a particular savings vehicle, the taxpayer loses a fraction, f, of the before-tax rate of return, R, from the vehicle; that is, the taxpayer realizes only $R(1 - f)$ of the before-tax return in the savings vehicle. Alternatively, the frictions might relate to special costs incurred to borrow funds to finance other investments, in which case the before-tax borrowing rate becomes $R(1 + f)$, even when the loan is a riskless one. In the case of investing in life insurance policies, the special costs arise, in part, from the presence of sales people who are paid to teach taxpayers how life insurance policies work; from administrative personnel, who are necessary to keep track of policies as well as file reports; and from auditors, who are necessary to assure policyholders that their money really is being invested in riskless bonds (or in whatever types of securities the insurance company advertises).

Suppose that a taxpayer with current taxable income of Y dollars seeks to effect organizational-form arbitrage by borrowing at rate R to invest in a tax-exempt savings vehicle. The tax-exempt savings vehicle, however, yields a return of only $R(1 - f)$ due to the presence of frictions. The taxpayer must borrow Y/R at the start of the year to generate sufficient interest deductions to reduce taxable income to zero. This generates RY/R, or Y dollars of interest expense, an amount equal to the income to be sheltered. The Y dollars of income is just sufficient to pay the interest on the loan and reduce taxable income to zero. The investment made

---

[8] For an 11 year period (that is, 10 years of deferral beyond the receipt of salary), a 40% tax rate, and a 10% before-tax interest rate, the tax is reduced in present value terms by nearly 50%.

with the loan proceeds generates a return of only R(1 - f)Y/R or Y(1 - f) in the tax-favored savings vehicle. Note that fY of the original Y dollars of income has been lost, not due to the payment of taxes, but due to market frictions. It is as if the taxpayer paid an explicit tax at rate f. We can see from this that frictions have the same effect on investment returns as implicit taxes, and from time to time, we will refer to frictions as a type of implicit tax.

As a specific example, suppose that administration costs require the insurance company to reduce the rate of interest offered on the savings account to 9% when the rate on equally risky fully taxable investments yield 10%. As a result, f would be equal to .1 (since 10%(1 - f) = 9%). Note here that f is found by using exactly the same formula as that used to compute implicit tax rates. By borrowing at a tax-deductible rate of 10% and investing at a tax-exempt rate of 9%, the taxpayer can convert $100,000 of taxable income into $100,000 × .9 or $90,000 of after-tax insurance-related interest income.

As a variation on the above example that incorporates frictions on the *borrowing* side of the transaction as well, suppose that cash cannot be borrowed at the 10% riskless rate because the lender incurs administrative costs. If the $100,000 of prospective taxpayer income comes from salary, the lender may worry that the taxpayer will quit his job and never receive the salary, which represents an important part of the lender's collateral. The lender may run a credit check on the taxpayer to alleviate this concern partially, but such information is costly to obtain and to process. For this reason, suppose the lender charges a 12% interest rate on the loan even though the taxpayer knows that the loan is riskless.

At a 12% interest rate to borrow funds, the taxpayer now need only borrow $100,000/.12 or $833,333 to create sufficient interest deductions to eliminate the taxable salary income, rather than $1 million as before. At a before-tax rate of investment return of 9%, the $833,333 in life insurance savings earns $75,000 of interest. So although explicit income taxes are eliminated, these market frictions act as implicit taxes. The $100,000 salary is transformed into only $75,000 of after-tax life insurance savings. It is as if the taxpayer incurs an implicit tax of $25,000. The implicit tax rate is 25%. It is equal to the 12% borrowing rate minus the 9% lending rate divided by the 12% borrowing rate. Alternatively, it is equal to the before-tax salary of $100,000 minus the "after-implicit tax" life insurance investment income of $75,000 divided by the before-tax $100,000 salary. This is exactly the same formula used to compute implicit tax rates in Chapter Five.

Where does the implicit tax go? In this case, it goes two-thirds to the lender and one-third to the insurance company. Unlike the implicit tax examples in Chapter Five, however, the implicit tax collected here is allocated to the lender and the insurance company to cover transaction-related business costs and may inure to no one's benefit. That is, society would have been better off if these costs could have been avoided, although this might not be possible to achieve.

Note that for taxpayers with explicit marginal tax rates below 25%, natural market frictions are sufficient to prevent organizational-form arbitrage from reducing taxes, and tax-rule restrictions become unnecessary. A taxpayer with $100,000 in salary income and an explicit tax rate of 20% retains $80,000 after tax by not using the organizational-form arbitrage strategy and only $75,000 by employing the strategy.

We have assumed full exemption of the returns to investing in an insurance policy. To achieve this in the U.S. requires that the taxpayer never cancel the insurance policy and that the policy be held until death. At that time, all income tax is forgiven on the tax-free accumulation (so-called "inside buildup") in the policy. If the policy were cashed out, however, it would be taxed in a manner similar to an SPDA (except that interest income would be forgiven on amounts paid to cover term insurance premiums). As discussed earlier, the effects of borrowing and investing the proceeds in a savings vehicle that eventually taxes some of the interest income, reduces the scope for organizational-form arbitrage relative to the case in which interest income is forever exempt from tax.

Can a pension account be used successfully to effect organizational-form arbitrage as an alternative to using insurance accounts? Recall that organizational-form arbitrage requires a short position in a relatively tax-disfavored organizational form and a long position in a relatively tax-favored organizational form. In the absence of restrictions on the tax-deductibility of pension plan contributions, taxpayers could eliminate taxes on salary income by depositing their salary into a pension account. While funds are invested in the pension account, no taxable income is recognized. During retirement, however, taxpayers must pay tax on amounts they withdraw from their pension accounts.

If instead of withdrawing funds, taxpayers borrow during retirement to finance their consumption, they would continue to avoid paying tax on any of the accumulated pension earnings in retirement. In fact, if taxpayers were to pledge the assets in the pension fund as collateral for the loan, the borrowing rate should, in the absence of frictions, be equal to the before-tax return on assets held in the pension fund. If taxpayers plan it just right, on the date of their deaths, the amount of their loan (including accumulated interest) would be exactly equal to the accumulation in the pension fund. The secured creditors would then receive the assets in the pension fund to pay off the loan, leaving no assets to pay the tax liability to the taxing authority.

The simplest way to see how this works is to suppose that the taxpayer plans to work until he dies, consuming 100% of earnings each year. If, for example, salary is $100,000 per year, the taxpayer can consume the entire $100,000 of salary each year by simply depositing the entire salary into a pension account and borrowing $100,000, pledging the pension account as collateral for the loan. Neither the interest nor principal on the loan will be repaid until death, at which time the accumulation in the pension account will be equal to the accumulated interest and principal of the secured note. Note that this strategy works despite the absence of a tax deduction for interest on the loan; after all, taxable income is already $0 each period, and we have ruled out a tax rebate on negative taxable income. So, interest-deduction limitations are ineffective at preventing organizational-form arbitrage with this strategy.

Not surprisingly, because of the availability of the pension fund as a savings vehicle, other restrictions have been introduced that do prevent the arbitrage from taking place. These include (1) limitations on the amount of compensation that can be deposited into a pension fund each year (as under Code Section 415 in the U.S.) and (2) limitations on how long pension funds can be left to accumulate tax free without being withdrawn. In particular, rules have been added over the years that require taxpayers to remove pension assets from their pension accounts during retirement. For example, under current rules, taxpayers must begin to draw down pension assets no later than April 1 of the calendar year following the one in which they become 70.5 years old, at a rate no slower than the annuity rate for their life expectancy at the attained age.

Beyond these two restrictions, the IRS would probably contest in bankruptcy court a situation in which the taxpayer's estate had no assets to pay the tax due on the accumulated pension assets because the taxpayer had pledged all of the pension assets as collateral on loans to finance consumption. In fact, to retain the tax deductibility of the pension contribution, restrictions prevent the taxpayer from assigning the pension assets as collateral on a loan. As a result, the lender's property rights become unclear: without collateral guarantees, the lender would have to charge a higher rate than the before-tax riskless rate of interest on the loan. As we saw with insurance savings, such frictions act as an implicit tax on taxpayers that employ this particular strategy.

Similar arguments can be made with regard to an SPDA. Complete tax exemption could be achieved if an account holder could borrow on the SPDA and never cash it in. This would require that the SPDA and the loan on the SPDA be of equal size on the death of the taxpayer, and, once again, that the lender could seize the assets in the SPDA to satisfy the loan ahead of the claims of the taxing authority. Alternatively, complete exemption could be achieved if the IRS were to forgive any income tax that is owed by the taxpayer on death. Such forgiveness is expressly granted for life insurance policies, but not for SPDAs.

Although organizational-form arbitrage strategies are theoretically possible in many cases, market frictions often, for all practical purposes, prevent their implementation. And where market frictions are insufficient, tax rule restrictions are often introduced to prevent most of these arbitrage opportunities.

Buying and Selling Implicitly Taxed Assets to Effect Organizational-Form Arbitrage

In all of the preceding examples, organizational-form arbitrage was effected by taking positions in an asset that bore no implicit tax (except possibly through market frictions). But organizational-form arbitrage can also be accomplished with assets that bear implicit taxes, as long as the asset is held long and short in ways that give rise to differential tax treatment. For example, in the absence of restrictions, taxes on salary income could be eliminated by holding both a long and a short position in the same capital asset, such as a common stock.

In a frictionless market setting, a taxpayer could sell stock short and use the cash proceeds from the short sale to purchase an offsetting long position in the stock. The net investment position is zero, and the pre-tax investment returns are perfectly hedged. The strategy requires taking sufficiently large positions so that the stock will either increase or decrease in value, before the tax year ends, by the amount of taxable income, say $100,000, that the taxpayer wishes to shelter.

If the stock increases in value, the short position can be "closed out" by purchasing additional shares and tendering them to the broker who lent the shares to the taxpayer in the first place. This results in the recognition of a $100,000 loss from the short position, which wipes out the salary income. Of course, the taxpayer has an offsetting gain of $100,000 on the remaining long position in the stock, but this is not taxed until these shares are sold. If the stock decreases in value, the long position can be closed out simply by selling the stock to recognize a $100,000 loss.

If the tax rules provide that only fraction L of the loss is deductible against ordinary income, then the magnitude of the arbitrage transactions need only be scaled up by a factor of $1/L$ to preserve the outcome of zero taxable income. Either way, after the loss is taken, the position that was sold can be repurchased to restore the investor to a perfectly hedged position. This position can then be held until death. This locks in a $100,000 (or $100,000/L) unrealized gain. If capital gains realized at death are tax exempt, as they are in the U.S., the taxpayer escapes the tax.[9] Thus, capital assets can be used to achieve complete tax exemption via organizational-form arbitrage transactions just as with life insurance accounts.[10]

As in previous examples, market frictions and several tax-rule restrictions prevent taking advantage of the fact that gains and losses are typically recognized for tax purposes only when sales take place. First, capital loss limitations prevent taxpayers from offsetting excessive amounts of ordinary income with capital losses. The current restriction in the U.S. is $3,000 per year for individuals, with any unused losses allowed to be carried forward indefinitely to be used against future gains. The restriction on corporations is even tighter: capital losses are only deductible against capital gains, and while such losses can be carried *back* for three years, they can be carried forward for only five years before the carryforwards expire. Second, under the so-called **wash sale rules** (Code Sections 1091(a) and 1256) capital losses are not deductible currently if substantially similar assets are repurchased within 30 days of sale. This means that the investor's position must probably be exposed to a nontrivial degree of risk for a 30-day period to permit the deduction of the capital loss. Third, hedging rules preclude losses from being deducted unless the taxpayer's investment positions differ substantively from perfectly hedged positions; that is, there must be nontrivial risk of overall gain or loss.

Note, however, that one way to avoid the first two restrictions (the capital-loss limitation and the wash-sales rule), is to have an equity interest in a broker-dealer partnership.[11] As we discussed in Chapter Four, broker-dealers realize ordinary income and losses (rather than capital gains and losses) on their securities transactions. Their securities positions are treated as inventory used in

---

[9] If capital gains were taxable at death, but taxpayers consume all income as it is earned, the taxing authority would once again be in a position in which there are no assets in taxpayers' estates with which to satisfy the claim.

[10] In countries where capital gains are taxable at death at the same rate as the losses are deductible, capital assets can be used to achieve organizational-form arbitrage in exactly the same way as we used SPDAs. Losses are recognized "early and often," and gains are deferred.

[11] A securities dealer can be a corporation, a partnership, or a proprietorship. A dealer's profits must be derived from a merchant's markup of the products it sells to its customers in the ordinary course of business and not from market appreciation. A dealer regularly buys and sells securities to customers with a view to profiting from making a market in these securities. Such firms as Goldman Sachs, Salomon Brothers, and Morgan Stanley engage in broker-dealer activities.

Chapter 6   Arbitrage and the Effects of Restrictions and Frictions

the broker-dealer business. As a result, broker-dealer partnerships were commonly used by taxpayers seeking to defer the recognition of their taxable income during the 1970s when tax rates on ordinary income were as high as 70%. The Tax Reform Act of 1986 prevents a partner from deducting a loss from a partnership business against her other income unless she is actively engaged in the business (such as being an active trader in a broker-dealer business).

One particularly common strategy used in the past to effect tax arbitrage of this sort was to take "straddle" positions in commodity futures. This involved buying a futures contract on some commodity for delivery in one month and a sale of a futures contract on the same commodity for delivery in a different month. This is called a spread with two legs. When the price of the underlying commodity changes, one leg of the spread typically increases in value, and the other leg typically decreases in value by a similar amount. Under the tax rules, the spread is not considered a wash sale, and the investment position is not deemed to be riskless (there is, in fact, some amount of risk in the position), because the contracts involve delivery of the commodity in different months.

To assure further that their overall investment position was not too risky, investors commonly used multiple spreads, called butterflies. The typical strategy was to sell the loss legs in one year and the gain legs during the following year to defer recognition of other taxable income. To illustrate, let's consider an example based on real transactions as shown in Table 6.3.

Table 6.3 An Illustration of the Use of a Series of Futures Spreads to Effect Tax Losses Without Significant Risk of Economic Loss

(Dollar amounts represent purchases (+) or sales (-) in millions of dollars)

Delivery Month	GNMA Futures Contracts			T Bond Futures Contracts			Taxable Gain (or Loss)
	3/80	6/80	9/80	3/80	6/80	9/80	
Trade Date							
1	+$38.5[a]		-$38.4[b]	-$39.7[b]		+$39.7[a]	$0
2	-$37.6[c]	+$37.6[a]			+$38.8[a]	-$38.8[c]	
	($0.9)					($0.9)	($1.8)
3		-$36.8[c]	+$36.7[d]	+$38.0[d]	-$38.0[c]		
		($0.8)	$1.7	$1.7	($0.8)		$1.8

Date 1 = October 4, 1978
Date 2 = October 30, 1978
Date 3 = April 27, 1979

[a] Opened a long position for 424 contracts in assets with this market value.
[b] Opened a short position for 424 contracts in assets with this market value.
[c] Closed out a long position for 424 contracts in assets with this market value.
[d] Closed out a short position for 424 contracts in assets with this market value.

Losses result from closing out long positions at lower prices than those at which they were opened, or closing out short positions at higher prices than those at which they were opened. Gains result analogously.

In early October of 1978 (date 1), an investor acquired 424 March-1980 Ginnie Mae (3/80 GNMA) and 424 September-1980 Treasury Bond (9/80 T Bond) futures and sold a like number of September-1980 GNMAs and March-1980 T Bond futures.[12] By the end of the month, interest rates had risen slightly, causing the long positions to decline in value and the short positions to increase in value. On October 30, 1978, the loss legs of the spreads were closed out, and similar (but not identical) positions were opened in the June-1980 contracts. This gave rise to tax losses of $1.8 million, locking in a gain of similar magnitude to be recognized on April 27, 1979 when the remaining open positions were closed out. The overall gain was approximately $0 (actually the investor realized a small gain of $18,563).

Tax rules require that the potential economic gain be substantial relative to the tax benefit from the transactions for losses to be deductible currently and gains to be deferred. Congress has since passed further restrictions to eliminate the opportunity to use these techniques to avoid paying tax. In effect, because it was so costly and time-consuming to enforce the rules, they gave up trying to decide which spreads had economic purpose and which spreads were used only to reduce taxes. Numerous cases similar to this one were in dispute with the taxing authority for over a decade.

6.3   Clientele-Based Arbitrage

Clientele-based arbitrage strategies involve the reduction of explicit tax liabilities at the expense of increasing implicit tax liabilities, or *visa versa*. Such strategies arise when (1) taxpayers can take both long and short positions in differentially taxed assets, at least one of which bears some implicit tax, and (2) taxpayers face different marginal tax rates. In most tax regimes, statutory tax rates are progressive, with marginal tax rates rising with taxable income. Progressivity in the tax rate schedule is an attempt to achieve an equitable distribution of tax burdens (or to redistribute income). At the same time, since the tax system is used to encourage various economic activities, assets are taxed differentially. As we have discussed, the result of taxing assets differentially is the creation of a system of implicit taxes, where the prices of tax-favored assets are bid up such that their before-tax rates of return fall below those of equally risky but less tax-favored assets. Without frictions or restrictions, we demonstrate below that clientele-based arbitrage results in all taxpayers facing the same marginal tax rates in equilibrium. In addition, all assets would bear the same total (implicit plus explicit) tax rate. To preserve the ability to redistribute income through progressive marginal tax rates, many tax rules attempt to prevent clientele-based arbitrage.

In the absence of tax rule restrictions, a particularly simple example of clientele-based tax arbitrage involves purchasing tax-exempt bonds with a loan

---

[12] Ginnie Mae securities are issued by the Government National Mortgage Association. These securities represent an interest in a pool of mortgages. The security holder receives the principal and interest on the mortgages after paying a small service charge. These securities (so-called "Ginnie Mae pass-throughs") are guaranteed by the Government National Mortgage Association and the full faith and credit of the U.S. government.

that gives rise to tax-deductible interest. While this strategy can succeed in eliminating explicit taxes, it also creates an implicit tax liability.

Let's again assume a situation in which $100,000 of salary income is expected over the forthcoming year, and the statutory tax rate is 40%. Taxable bonds yield 10% before tax and taxpayers can borrow at this rate in unlimited quantities. Finally, suppose that municipal bonds yield 7% tax free. Note that municipal bonds bear an implicit tax of 30% (or (.10 - .07)/.10).

To eliminate income tax on $100,000 of salary, we borrow $1,000,000 (or $100,000/.10) and invest the proceeds in municipal bonds to earn $70,000 (or $1,000,000 × .07) after tax. Note that we have converted salary income taxed explicitly at 40% into municipal bond interest income taxed implicitly at 30%. As the example illustrates, clientele-based arbitrage enables high tax-bracket tax-payers to convert income that would be taxed at high explicit marginal rates into income that is taxed at lower implicit tax rates. If low tax-bracket taxpayers can take short positions in tax-favored assets, they could profitably pursue the opposite strategy.

In the example above, when taxpayers face tax rates below 30%, they would find it undesirable to borrow for the purpose of purchasing municipal bonds. For example, if taxpayers face tax rates of 25% on the first $50,000 in salary and 40% on the next $50,000, the optimal strategy would be to borrow enough to reduce taxable income, not from $100,000 to $0, but only to $50,000. This is achieved by borrowing $500,000 at a 10% rate of interest and investing the proceeds in municipal bonds at a 7% rate of interest to yield $35,000 in tax-exempt interest. The net position after tax is

$$\$50,000(1 - 25\%) + \$35,000 = \$72,500.$$

By contrast, a strategy of no borrowing would leave

$$\$50,000(1 - 25\%) + 50,000(1 - 40\%) = \$37,500 + \$30,000 = \$67,500,$$

and borrowing $1 million to eliminate all explicit taxes would leave $70,000 (or $1,000,000 × 7%).

In an attempt to preserve a more progressive tax-rate structure, Congress imposes restrictions on such clientele-based arbitrage. In addition to the interest-deduction limitations we discussed earlier, Code Section 265 prevents the deduction of interest on loans used to purchase certain assets that yield tax-exempt income, like municipal bonds.[13] Note that for taxpayers facing explicit tax rates less than the implicit tax rate on municipal bonds (the cutoff point is 30% in the above illustration), this restriction has no effect. Moreover, the restriction may have no effect on more highly taxed taxpayers if there is a positive spread between the riskless interest rate and the rate at which taxpayers can borrow. For example, if taxpayers must pay interest at a rate of 12% to borrow when equally risky taxable bonds earn only 10%, the implicit tax rate becomes 41.67% (or (.12 - .07)/.12). Since this exceeds the explicit tax rate of 40% on the last $50,000 of salary

---

[13] A generous *de minimus* rule applies, however. Corporations may hold up to 2% of their total U.S. assets in tax-exempt securities or receivables without running afoul of Section 265. Still, this limit can be a problem for businesses that sell goods or services on credit to tax-exempt entities. See the *Wall Street Journal* (November 29, 1990) for a description of how IBM issued tax-exempt securities, backed by installment debts owed to it by municipalities, to avoid Section 265 problems.

income, market frictions are sufficient to prevent this clientele-based arbitrage strategy from being profitable.

For many years banks and insurance companies were allowed to engage in clientele-based arbitrage; they could deduct interest on loans used to buy municipal bonds.[14] As long as the implicit tax rate on municipal bonds was below their explicit tax rate on fully taxed income, these firms could profit by engaging in clientele-based arbitrage. The 1981 Tax Act placed restrictions on these organizations by limiting their ability to deduct interest on loans to finance *new* purchases of municipal bonds. Subsequent tax acts further restricted these activities. We will explore this issue more fully in Chapter Sixteen.

As indicated earlier, it is unprofitable for taxpayers with low marginal tax rates to borrow to purchase tax-favored assets. But the reverse strategy would be profitable if permitted. These taxpayers would prefer to issue municipal bonds, for example, and invest the proceeds in taxable bonds. If they could issue the bonds at a 7% before-tax rate of return and buy fully taxable bonds that return 10% before tax, their taxable income would increase until their marginal tax rate was equal to 30%. The clientele-based arbitrage opportunity disappears at that point.

Clientele-Based Arbitrage Involving Investments in Tax-Favored Assets Other than Tax-Exempt Bonds

While restrictions exist on borrowing to finance the purchase of municipal bonds, no such restrictions exist on borrowing to buy such tax-favored investments as stocks, land, equipment that is eligible for accelerated depreciation, or a host of other tax-favored investments. If the marginal total tax rate (implicit plus explicit) reflected in market prices for tax-favored investments is below a taxpayer's explicit tax rate on other fully taxed income, the taxpayer can borrow to purchase such assets to effect clientele-based arbitrage. Since U.S. corporations are not subject to limitations on interest deductions, such clientele-based arbitrage activities are especially relevant for them. This is particularly so following the passage of the Tax Reform Act of 1986, because this act set corporate marginal tax rates above those for individuals and partnerships.

But assets that are tax-favored due to accelerated tax deductions are not as effective in bringing about clientele-based arbitrage as are **tax-exemption-type shelters** such as municipal bonds. To see this, suppose our taxpayer (who has $100,000 of taxable income, taxed at a rate of 25% on the first $50,000 and 40% on income above $50,000) can invest in equipment that yields an immediate tax deduction equal to the investment cost. This investment yields a risk-adjusted pretax return of 7% or 70% of the return to fully taxable assets. Recall from Chapter Four our demonstration that if an investment project gives rise to an immediate tax deduction equal to its cost and all future income is fully taxable at the same rate, this is equivalent to granting tax exemption to the project returns. So if funds can be borrowed at a rate of 10% and deducted at a tax rate of 40% to yield an after-tax cost of 6%, and if the loan can be used to purchase equipment

---

[14] Corporations other than banks and insurance companies were also allowed to do this in limited quantities, as discussed in the preceding footnote.

Chapter 6 Arbitrage and the Effects of Restrictions and Frictions

yielding a return of 7% after tax, then clientele-based arbitrage will have been achieved.

But note that only $50,000 worth of equipment can profitably be purchased. Beyond this, equipment purchases yield tax deductions at a rate of only 25% although the subsequent income will be taxed at a rate of 40%. Under these circumstances, the after-tax rate of return on investment becomes

$$\frac{1.07 \times (1 - .4)}{1 - .25} - 1 = \frac{.642}{.75} - 1 = -14.4\%$$

So it only pays to invest $50,000. And since the $50,000 investment is assumed to yield an immediate tax refund of $50,000 × 40% or $20,000, the arbitrage strategy calls for a loan of only $30,000.

The $50,000 investment grows to $53,500 (or $50,000 × 1.07) in one year, at which point its entire return is taxed at 40%, leaving $32,100 (or $53,500 × .6) after tax. In addition, the $30,000 loan accrues $3,000 of interest, deductible at 40% for a net interest cost of $1,800 after tax. After repaying both the $30,000 loan and interest on the loan, the taxpayer realizes a tax saving of only $300 (or $32,100 - $31,800) from the strategy. This compares with a tax saving of $5,000 when borrowing $500,000 to buy municipal bonds. The savings is only $R_b(1 - t)$ or 6% as much as with municipal bonds because only 6% as much debt was used to purchase the tax-favored investment (or $30,000/$500,000).

For all practical purposes, then, very little income can be converted from being taxed at personal rates of 40% to being taxed implicitly at 30% over a one-year horizon using these tax-favored investments. Since municipal bond investments do not require deductions against other taxable income to achieve tax exemption, they can shift much larger amounts of taxable income from explicit to implicit taxation. This helps to explain why special restrictions apply to the deductibility of expenses incurred to generate tax-exempt interest income that do not apply to these other types of tax-favored assets.

Equilibrium Relations Among Assets that Bear Both Implicit and Explicit Taxes

In the absence of frictions and restrictions, arbitrage opportunities will be available unless all assets in the economy are taxed at the same total rate. If there exists a partially taxable asset (where fraction g of income is taxed), a fully taxable asset, and a tax-exempt asset (bearing implicit tax at rate t_{Ie}), then the partially taxable asset must bear implicit taxes in an amount, t_{Ig}, that satisfies:

$$(1 - t_{Ig})(1 - gt) = (1 - t_{Ie}),$$

which implies that:

$$t_{Ig} = \frac{t_{Ie} - gt}{1 - gt} . \tag{6.1}$$

To preclude arbitrage possibilities on investing in the fully taxable and the tax-exempt assets, the implicit tax on the tax-exempt asset, t_{Ie}, must be equal to the ordinary tax rate, t. Substituting this equilibrium condition into 6.1 yields

$$t_{Ig} = \frac{t_{Ie}(1 - g)}{1 - gt_{Ie}} \, . \tag{6.2}$$

For example, if fully taxable bonds yield 10%, municipal bonds yield 7% (in which case, t_{Ie} = 30%), and g is equal to .4 for the partially taxable asset of equal risk, then t_{Ig} is equal to 20.5%. This implies that the pretax return on such an asset must be 7.95% (or 10%(1 - t_{Ig}). This yields 7% after tax (or 7.95% × (1 - .3 × 4)).

Market Equilibrium with Constant-Marginal-Tax-Rate Investors

The nature of equilibrium changes dramatically if the returns to different assets are taxed at the same rates for some taxpayers but not for others. For example, tax-exempt entities such as universities and municipalities face marginal tax rates of 0% on both taxable bonds and tax-exempt bonds. Absent restrictions, such taxpayers could profit by buying taxable bonds and selling tax-exempt bonds as long as a positive spread remained between the rates on the two securities. The equilibrium for tax-exempt investors requires that all assets bear zero implicit tax. But then arbitrage opportunities would arise for taxpayers facing positive marginal tax rates. Such taxpayers would buy tax-exempt municipal bonds and sell fully taxable bonds to create sufficient interest deductions to eliminate their taxable income. As a result, no one would pay any taxes. In addition to the tax rule restrictions we have already discussed to prevent high tax-bracket taxpayers from engaging in clientele-based arbitrage, additional restrictions prevent municipalities and other tax-exempt taxpayers from issuing arbitrarily large quantities of tax-exempt securities. Instead, they can issue tax-exempt securities only for certain qualified purposes.

One form of clientele-based arbitrage still seems to remain for municipalities. They can finance profit-making ventures that they own by issuing tax-exempt securities. That is, they can deduct the interest costs on tax-exempt securities from before-tax profits, and pay tax only on the remaining taxable income (so-called "unrelated business income") at corporate rates. Suppose that the profit-making business returns the risk-adjusted before-tax rate of return, R_b, and is financed at rate $R_b(1 - t_{Im})$, where t_{Im} is the implicit tax rate on municipal bonds. Then taxable income is $R_b - R_b(1 - t_{Im})$ or $R_b t_{Im}$ on a zero net investment. If the corporate tax rate is t_c, the municipality earns after-tax profits of $R_b t_{Im}(1 - t_c)$. For example, if R_b is equal to 10% and t_{Im} is equal to 30%, then the municipality earns 10%, financed by issuing municipal bonds at a 7% rate (or 10%(1 - .3)). The 3% profit, taxed at a 40% corporate tax rate, leaves a profit of 1.8% of the gross investment after tax on a zero net investment. Most municipalities do not run profit-making activities to profit from this arbitrage possibility. Perhaps market frictions, such as an inability to manage such activities efficiently or limits on the amount of tax-exempt debt they can issue, inhibit municipalities from undertaking this form of clientele-based arbitrage.

A similar situation is faced by **broker-dealers**. Suppose there exists a common stock that pays a fully taxable dividend of 10%, representing all of its annual return. Another stock pays a 0% dividend and all of its returns come in the form of tax-favored capital gains that are taxed at a 20% rate per year. Assume that the before-tax return on the capital-gains stock is 8.75%, resulting in an after-tax return of 7% (or 8.75%(1 - .2)). If all taxpayers, other than broker-dealers, pay tax at 30% on interest and dividends and 20% on capital gains, everyone other than broker-dealers is indifferent among holding municipal bonds, taxable bonds, the 10% dividend-yielding stock, and the 8.75% capital-gains-yielding stock. But broker-dealers pay tax at ordinary rates on securities gains and take tax deductions at ordinary rates on losses. Given these before-tax rates of return, broker-dealers could profit by selling short the 8.75% capital-gains stock and buying the 10% dividend-yielding stock. This enables the broker-dealer to lock in the 1.25% spread in before-tax rates of return between the two securities. The more highly correlated their price movements, the more precise the hedge. As long as the broker-dealer's tax rate is less than 100%, it earns arbitrage profits on the spread in the before-tax rates of return on these two types of securities. There are no restrictions to prevent this type of activity. Only frictions might prevent the arbitrage from being cost-effective. This also raises the question as to whether stocks can face different expected returns as a function of their dividend yields. We will consider this issue in Chapter Seventeen.

Summary of Key Points

We emphasized the importance of market frictions and tax rule restrictions in preventing either organizational-form or clientele-based arbitrage. The twin objectives of a progressive tax system and a tax system that seeks to encourage certain economic activities over others (taxing unequally the returns to different assets) are rather in conflict. Only through a combination of tax rule restrictions and market frictions is it conceivable that we can attain both goals.

1. Many of the detailed provisions of the Tax Code represent restrictions on taxpayers' ability to effect tax arbitrage.
2. As numerous as these restrictions might appear to be (and they are indeed numerous; we've mentioned only a few of the more important ones here), they are far fewer in number than would be required if implementation of "tax arbitrage" strategies were costless.
3. Most of these costs arise because information is costly and is not symmetrically held by all taxpayers in the economy. This is a point we will consider more thoroughly in the next chapter.
4. Organizational-form arbitrage arises when taxpayers take a long position in an asset through a tax-favored organizational form and a short position in the asset through an unfavorably taxed organizational form.
5. Clientele-based arbitrage arises when taxpayers face different tax rates and when assets are taxed differentially, which gives rise to implicit taxes.
6. Organizational-form arbitrage can be used to reduce the tax on income to zero over investment horizons as short as for one tax year. This requires only that the returns on the long position held through the tax-favored organizational form are taxed at a lower rate than are the losses from the short position held through another tax-disfavored organizational form.

7. If the organizational-form arbitrage strategy involves a long position in an asset that gives rise to deferred taxable income and a short position that yields potential tax deductions, and the tax system does not provide tax rebates for negative taxable income, organizational-form arbitrage will not reduce the tax rate on income to zero.

8. If there are frictions in the market that prevent the taxpayer from earning the full before-tax rate through the favorably taxed organizational form, the taxpayer cannot eliminate taxes. Such frictions are equivalent to an implicit tax, although such taxes may not be paid to any other taxpayer in the economy.

9. Frictions and restrictions are necessary to prevent both organizational-form and clientele-based arbitrage.

10. Clientele-based arbitrage involves a conversion of taxable income from an explicitly taxed to an implicitly taxed form, or visa versa.

11. Asset returns can be exempt from explicit taxes either through the nontaxability of future returns (as with municipal bonds in the U.S.) or through immediate deductibility of investment followed by full taxation of returns. While both types of investments may be equally desirable to hold in small quantities, the presence of progressive tax rates makes tax-exempt bonds more desirable to hold in large quantities if both types of assets bear equal implicit taxes.

12. Related to the point above, were it not for tax-rule restrictions relating to interest deductions, tax-exempt bonds would be more effective in clientele-based arbitrage strategies than would assets that achieve tax exemption due to the deductibility of investment cost.

13. In the absence of market frictions and tax-rule restrictions, a market equilibrium cannot exist in which one taxpayer faces equal marginal tax rates over income from two different assets while another taxpayer faces unequal marginal tax rates over income from the same two assets.

14. Frictions-related implicit taxes represent a dead-weight cost to society that a social planner seeks to reduce. On the other hand, clientele-based implicit taxes are typically collected by some other taxpayer. Dead-weight costs to society result from these latter transfers only to the extent the tax system encourages the "wrong" set of economic activities to be undertaken or gives rise to an "undesirable" distribution of wealth.

Appendix 6.1

Full Taxation with Deferral and Organizational-Form Arbitrage

In this appendix we demonstrate formally that if funds are borrowed; the interest on the borrowed funds is tax deductible each period; the proceeds of the loan are used to invest in an organizational form that yields a pretax rate of return each period equal to the interest rate on the loan; and the income is tax-deferred, then taxpayers can reduce, but not eliminate, the tax liability otherwise due on other sources of taxable income such as salary.

Suppose a taxpayer will earn Y dollars of taxable income in the forthcoming year. One possible strategy is to pay tax on this income at rate t and invest the after-tax proceeds for n - 1 periods at rate R in an SPDA contract. At time n the after-tax accumulation will be

$$Y(1-t)[(1 + R)^{n-1}(1 - t) + t]. \tag{6.3}$$

Alternatively, Y/R dollars could be borrowed for n periods, with the proceeds used to purchase an SPDA. Assume that while the interest expense of Y dollars in the first year wipes out the other taxable income, the interest expense after the first year must be carried forward for n - 1 years until the SPDA is cashed out and generates interest income. The net after-tax accumulation from this organizational-form arbitrage strategy is

$$(Y/R)[(1 + R)^n(1 - t) + t]$$
$$-(Y/R)[(1 + R)^{n-1}(1 - t) + t]$$
$$=(Y/R)[(1 + R)^{n-1}(1 - t)R]$$
$$=Y(1 - t)(1 + R)^{n-1} \tag{6.4}$$

In comparing 6.3 and 6.4, we can see that in the absence of the organizational-form arbitrage strategy, $Y(1 - t)$ is invested in an SPDA for n - 1 periods. The arbitrage strategy allows $Y(1 - t)$ to be invested at the same rate R for n - 1 periods but with no tax at all on the interest income.

If the accumulations under each strategy are discounted for n - 1 periods at the after-tax SPDA rate, the present value of expression 6.3 (no arbitrage activity) is $Y(1 - t)$ and of expression 6.4 (with arbitrage activity) is[15]

$$Y(1 - t)(1 + R)^{n-1}/[(1 + R)^{n-1}(1 - t) + t].$$

For n - 1 = 10, R = 10%, and t = 40%,

$$Y(1 - t) = .6Y$$

and

$$Y(1 - t)(1 + R)^{n-1}/[(1+R)^{n-1}(1 - t) + t] = .7964.$$

So the arbitrage strategy reduces the tax on Y dollars of income by nearly half, from 40% to 20.4%.[16]

---

[15] Note that as n grows large, the present value of expression 6.4 approaches Y, and tax exemption is nearly achieved.

[16] We leave it as an exercise to the reader to verify that if the SPDA yields only 9.75% per year while borrowing rates remain at 10%, for n - 1 = 10, the arbitrage opportunity disappears entirely. If, on the other hand, the SPDA yields 9.9%, the arbitrage strategy results in income being taxed at 29%, which reduces the tax burden by more than 25% relative to paying an explicit tax at 40%.

Discussion Questions

1. What is organizational-form arbitrage? Give an example of organizational-form arbitrage that would create infinite wealth for a taxpayer. What conditions are necessary to prevent this from happening?

2. What is clientele-based arbitrage? Provide an example of such a strategy. Is clientele-based arbitrage restricted to high tax-bracket taxpayers?

3. If half the interest earned on the savings portion of an insurance policy were taxable, would it still be possible for taxpayers to eliminate their taxable income, in the absence of tax-rule restrictions and market frictions? Illustrate your answer to this question by assuming that the taxpayer's taxable income before arbitrage strategies is $100,000 and the before-tax interest rate is 10%.

4. Suppose that insurance policies were fully tax-exempt but (a) policies pay less than the fully taxable bond return to cover the costs of the insurance company and (b) loans can be secured only at a higher rate than the fully taxable bond rate to cover the lenders' costs. Can we use an insurance-policy strategy to eliminate the tax on the $100,000 of taxable income? What is the implicit tax rate on this strategy? How does it arise and where does it go? Would every taxpayer want to use this strategy?

5. List some tax-rule restrictions that prevent organizational-form arbitrage. How do they succeed in preventing arbitrage?

6. In the absence of tax-rule restrictions, how could pensions be used to effect organizational-form arbitrage? What restrictions are necessary to prevent pensions from being used in this manner?

7. Provide an example of organizational-form arbitrage using corporations and partnerships. What is an example of organizational-form arbitrage involving a long-term investment in common stocks? What restrictions are in place to limit taxpayers' abilities to avoid taxes from undertaking these strategies?

8. How could a high tax-bracket taxpayer take advantage of a situation in which the implicit tax rate on a tax-exempt asset is different from the marginal tax rate on income from a fully taxable asset? How would a low tax-bracket taxpayer take advantage of this situation? What impediments (both frictions and restrictions) exist to limit a taxpayers' ability to take advantage of this arbitrage possibility?

9. With a progressive tax-rate system, show that it doesn't pay to reduce your explicit tax rate on fully taxable income to below the implicit tax rate on tax-exempt securities. Under what conditions would you choose not to engage in clientele-based arbitrage when your marginal tax rate exceeds the implicit tax rate on tax-exempt securities, even absent restrictions on the deductibility of interest on loans?

10. Suppose that there were no tax-rule restrictions preventing a municipality from buying taxable bonds financed by tax-exempt bonds yielding a lower before-tax rate of return. What arbitrage strategy should the municipality

adopt? When does the opportunity disappear? Once the municipality no longer has arbitrage opportunities, what arbitrage opportunities must exist for taxable investors? When do these opportunities disappear? When will neither tax-exempt nor taxable investors face arbitrage opportunities simultaneously? What tax-rule restrictions are necessary to prevent this form of clientele-based arbitrage?

11. Under what conditions is it tax-advantageous for municipalities to undertake profit-making ventures? Why don't we see more municipality-operated activities? Can you think of some taxable business ventures that are currently operated by municipalities? Would the same arguments apply to other tax-exempt entities such as universities, hospitals, and charities?

12. Consider the example just below equation 6.2 in the text (near the end of the chapter). What arbitrage strategies would be available if the partially tax-exempt asset yielded 8.5%? 7.5%?

Problems

1. Suppose that taxable bonds maturing in five years yield 10% per year before tax.
   a. What risk-adjusted appreciation rate on a nondividend-paying common stock is required for the following taxpayers to be indifferent between investing in bonds and stock for five years:
      1. taxpayers paying a 30% tax rate on taxable bond interest and a 30% tax rate on capital gains when realized; and
      2. taxpayers paying a 30% tax rate on taxable bond interest and a 50-50 chance (the outcome being independent of the stock return) of a 20% and a 30% tax rate on capital gains when realized.
   b. If the taxpayer in (a.2.) were the marginal investor setting prices in the marketplace, what would be the implicit tax rate on the returns to stock?
   c. If the taxpayer in (a.2.) were the marginal investor setting prices in the marketplace, what arbitrage strategies would be available in a frictionless setting to the following investors:
      1. a broker-dealer facing a 40% marginal tax rate;
      2. a tax-exempt entity;
      3. an individual taxpayer, who can deduct interest expense on borrowing, and who faces a 40% tax rate on ordinary income and a 30% tax rate on capital gains and losses.
      4. an individual taxpayer, who can deduct interest expense on borrowing, and who faces a 40% tax rate on both ordinary income and capital gains, and a 30% tax rate on capital losses.

d. Suppose we have an investor that faces a 30% tax rate on dividends and an expected tax rate of 20% on capital gains when they are realized five years from now. If a stock pays an annual dividend at the end of each year equal to 5% of the stock price at the beginning of the year, what appreciation rate on the stock is required to enable a 7% after-tax return per year over a 5-year period?

e. What would be the implicit tax rate on the returns to the stock in (d)?

2. Following a substantial earthquake, a major west-coast university suffered $100 million in property damage. Suppose that this loss enabled the university to borrow an additional $100 million worth of tax-exempt bonds. The university issues 20-year zero-coupon bonds yielding 7% to maturity; that is, the university will pay bondholders $100 million $\times$ 1.07^{20} or $386.97 million at maturity. Any gift money raised from friends of the university can be invested to earn 10% in riskless taxable bonds.

a. How much must the university raise in gifts to pay off its bond obligation at maturity?

b. How would your answer change if the bonds had a 30-year maturity rather than 20 years?

Chapter 6 Arbitrage and the Effects of Restrictions and Frictions

CHAPTER 7
The Distinction Between Effective
Tax Planning and Tax Minimization

Although the world would be manifestly easier to understand if economic exchanges could be undertaken free of all transaction costs, such costs are pervasive. Moreover, different ways of organizing economic activity give rise to differences in transaction costs. But we also wish to emphasize that different ways of organizing economic activity give rise to differences in tax costs. Hence the efficient organizational choice is not necessarily the one that minimizes transaction costs, once taxes are considered as well.

Similarly, it would be short-sighted to suggest that efficient organizational choice is determined by minimizing taxes, since different tax plans generally give rise to differences in transaction and other nontax costs. If these nontax cost differences are viewed as implicit taxes, on the other hand (after all, this is a tax-planning text), then the (deceptively) simple decision rule of seeking to minimize taxes is an efficient one. But we cannot emphasize too strongly the importance of these nontax costs in forging efficient tax plans.

Casual observation suggests that the effect of taxes on the way that production and exchange is organized in the economy is pervasive. It is equally indisputable that organizational arrangements arise because information is asymmetrically distributed among economic agents. Workers must often be monitored or offered incentives to induce them to perform in owners' best interests. Customers must often be offered warranties to induce them to buy products, and still a variety of consumer protection groups exist. Independent third parties are required to audit the financial statements of publicly owned corporations. And even in the absence of regulatory requirements, many firms voluntarily pay substantial sums to third parties to verify certain information disclosures designed to facilitate economic exchanges among parties who are not equally well informed.

In many contracting problems, a desire to achieve tax minimization encourages precisely the same organizational arrangements as do solutions to incentive problems among differentially informed and opportunistic agents. When this occurs, outside observers (such as researchers, consultants, corporate raiders, investment bankers, and regulators) face a so-called "identification problem" in sorting out which economic force is responsible for the observed contractual relations.

On the other hand, tax considerations and information-related transaction cost considerations often have conflicting implications for efficient organizational design. Sometimes tax considerations dominate in importance, and sometimes information considerations dominate. But frequently, both factors are important and trade-offs must be made. Because of the need to make these trade-offs, efficient tax planning is often quite distinct from tax minimization. We develop this theme in this chapter and illustrate it in several later chapters.

Thus far, uncertainty has not been prominent in our discussion. We begin to remedy that here. In particular, we distinguish between two types of uncertainty:

- **symmetric uncertainty**, where all contracting parties are equally well informed, but still uncertain, about what the future cash flows from an investment might be, and
- **strategic uncertainty**, where the contracting parties are not equally well informed about what the future investment cash flows might be. We further distinguish between two types of information asymmetry regarding future cash flows. The first arises when one contracting party has control over an action choice that affects future cash flows, where the action choice is *unobservable* to other contracting parties (so-called "hidden action" or "moral hazard" situations). The second type of information asymmetry arises when one contracting party has observed a characteristic of the production function she cannot control that affects future cash flows, and that characteristic is only imperfectly observable by the other contracting parties (so-called "hidden information" or "adverse selection" situations).[1]

In this chapter, we illustrate how each form of uncertainty gives rise to efficient tax planning strategies that require sacrificing tax minimization.

7.1 The Effect of Progressive Income Taxes on Risk Taking

We begin with a demonstration of how a progressive income tax system may force some taxpayers to become less inclined to take on risky investments than they might otherwise be. Suppose the tax rate schedule is as follows:

---

[1] For further elaboration, see Kenneth J. Arrow, "The Economics of Agency," in *Principals and Agents: the Structure of Business*, edited by John W. Pratt and Richard J. Zeckhauser (Harvard Business School Press, 1985), pp. 37-51.

Chapter 7   The Distinction Between Effective Tax Planning and Tax Minimization

- If income is positive, you pay a tax of 40%.
- If income is negative, the tax rate is 0%; that is, you get no tax refund.[2]

You have $100,000 to invest in 1 of 2 projects. One of the projects is riskless, yielding a certain profit of $20,000. The alternative project is risky, yielding a profit of $150,000 half the time and a total loss of $100,000 half the time. Since each outcome for the risky project is equally likely, the expected pretax profit is $25,000 (or .5 × $150,000 + .5 × (-$100,000)). For the moment, assume that you are indifferent between a particular payoff with certainty and a risky payoff with equal expected value. In other words, you are risk-neutral.

In which project would you invest in the absence of taxes? Given your indifference toward risk, you would choose the project providing the highest expected pretax profit. That project is the risky project, by $5,000 ($25,000 - $20,000).

How does the presence of a progressive tax affect project choice? Quite dramatically, as reflected in the following after-tax profit numbers:

Riskless Project: $20,000 × (1 - .4) = <u>$12,000 after tax</u>

Risky Project: .5 × [$150,000 × (1 - .4)] + .5 × (-$100,000)
                      = <u>-$5,000 after tax</u>

The riskless project is now *preferred* over the risky one by $17,000 after tax, despite being the inferior choice (by $5,000) in the absence of taxes. Why? Because the tax is progressive, the expected tax is $22,000 higher for the risky project than for the riskless one. This is but an example of a more general feature of a progressive tax system: the average tax rate paid increases with the variability of taxable income levels. So, even when taxpayers are risk neutral, they exhibit risk aversion towards assets with variable pretax returns.[3,4]

The 1986 Tax Act introduced a regressive component into the tax rate schedule for individuals; that is, due to a 5% surtax over certain ranges of income, the tax rate climbed from 15% to 28% to 33% and then dropped back down to 28% for high levels of taxable income. For some taxpayers, the regressive drop in rates from 33% to 28% induced a preference for risky investments, even if the expected pretax return is no higher than that on riskless assets.[5]

---

[2] Assume for the purposes of this example that tax losses can neither be carried back nor forward to offset income earned in other years. We touch on the effect of carrybacks and carryforwards later in the chapter and take a closer look at them in the next chapter.

[3] For further discussion, see John C. Fellingham and Mark A. Wolfson, "Taxes and Risk Sharing," *The Accounting Review* (January 1985).

[4] Prior to the 1986 Tax Act in the U.S., taxpayers could "average" their income over several years to mitigate (but not eliminate) the effects of progressive taxes in the presence of wide swings in income over time.

[5] These rates were in effect from 1988 through 1990. The same regressive structure exists under the 1990 Tax Act but at slightly higher tax rates.

7.1   The Effect of Progressive Income Taxes on Risk Taking

7.2 Tax Planning in the Presence of Risk-Sharing and Hidden-Action Considerations

Contracting in Capital Markets

In Chapter Six, we discussed in very general terms how market frictions drive a wedge between the buying and selling prices of assets, and this helps to prevent tax-arbitrage opportunities from being used to eliminate income taxes. We illustrated the effects of the borrowing rate for funds exceeding the lending rate on the desirability of effecting organizational-form and clientele-based arbitrage. We now examine this issue more closely.

Suppose there were no restrictions on the deductibility of interest on loans that are fully secured by single premium deferred annuities (SPDA). Would we expect the pretax rates of return on the annuity contract to be the same as the rate paid on the loan? The answer is no. The insurance company offering the deferred annuity contract must charge for its operating costs, as must the bank lending the funds.

What kind of operating costs exist for the insurance company? The insurance company has a sales force that earns commissions for educating the public about the nature of deferred annuities. The company must also manufacture an information system to keep track of all of its assets and its policyholders, as well as invest in a system of internal control to ensure that all funds received are invested and to assure all prospective policyholders that it is solvent. Moreover, the company must incur costs to create contracts that specify clearly its property rights and those of its policyholders in various contingencies. Annual operating expenses of companies offering deferred annuities have averaged 1.75% to 2% of funds invested.[6]

What kinds of costs are there for the lender? The lender must also manufacture an information system and a system of internal controls and incur costs to write contracts. The lender must also pay brokers (e.g., loan officers) to identify appropriate borrowers. In addition, the lender must invest resources to investigate the insurance company whose deferred annuity secures the loan. The lender must become convinced that the insurance company assets backing the deferred annuity are adequate to pay market rates of return to annuity holders. Moreover, the lender must incur costs to ensure that the deferred annuity cannot be cashed out by the owner and put to alternative uses without the lender's knowledge. Otherwise, the loan would not really be secured. All of these costs add up. As a result, it is not unusual for the spread between the riskless borrowing rate and the secured lending rate to exceed 300 basis points or 3%.

For example, one simple way to engage in secured borrowing is to borrow from a brokerage house or bank, pledging your stocks as collateral. Such loans are essentially riskless to the lender because investors are initially permitted to borrow up to only 50% of the value of the stock. The broker can sell stocks if they decline in value to the point where they begin to jeopardize full repayment of the

---

[6] *Fund Action* (February 11, 1991), p. 3.

Chapter 7   The Distinction Between Effective Tax Planning and Tax Minimization

loan. Despite the apparent riskless nature of the loans, brokerage houses frequently charge interest rates well above the cost of borrowing (a 2% spread is common). In part, this spread pays for the costs that brokers might incur if forced to sell customers' shares in big market drops (such as that which occurred on October 19, 1987 or October 13, 1989), and customers sue because they allege they did not receive fair treatment.

Of course, one would expect that extremely large investors, including groups of individual investors, can arrange for lower spreads, perhaps as low as .5%. These low transaction costs result from economics of scale, since most of the transaction costs discussed above are fixed in nature. If this is a correct characterization, such large investors would indeed have less difficulty borrowing to invest in some tax-favored savings vehicle like deferred annuities, which is the kind of tax arbitrage that we discussed in Chapter Six. As a result, the tax system must impose restrictions on these activities. Perhaps the threat of these large, low-cost transactors has led to the specific restriction that secured borrowing to finance the purchase of single premium deferred annuities would render the interest expense nondeductible.

With secured borrowing to purchase deferred annuities ruled out by tax rule restrictions, let's now consider whether things look much different with *unsecured* borrowing. The rates on unsecured borrowing can be dramatically higher than the rates on secured borrowing. Moreover, unlike the case of secured borrowing, the borrowing rates for unsecured loans tend to increase with the level of borrowing for a given individual. The reason for this is fairly straightforward and relates to strategic uncertainty. Borrowers cannot always be trusted to act in ways they promise to act. That is, they may take actions that imperil the cash flows that stand behind the contracts (since they do not bear all of the costs of reduced cash flow), and lenders typically cannot observe such actions.

To illustrate, suppose your entire life savings of $100,000 is invested in riskless bonds, and you have no liabilities. You go to the bank and apply for a $50,000 loan. You tell the bank that the loan is to finance a vacation and an investment, and you prefer not to invade your $100,000 savings account for these purposes. With $100,000 in riskless assets, we might suppose that the bank need not charge much of a default premium.

But suppose the vacation and investment you had in mind entailed liquidating your savings account, going to Las Vegas, and betting $150,000 on the color red in a single spin of a fair roulette wheel. Would the bank be very happy? Not likely. If you win, you make a profit of $150,000 less a small fee for the use of the bank's $50,000 for the bet. If you lose, you lose only your $100,000 since you will default on the bank loan. Assuming that winning and losing are equally likely, your expected profit, ignoring the small fee for the "rent" on $50,000 for one day, is $25,000 (or ($.5 \times \$150,000 + .5 \times (-\$100,000)$)). Your expected winnings of $25,000 are precisely equal to the bank's expected loss.

But you can do even better by taking on more risk. Suppose your strategy were to bet everything on the number "7 red" with a 40-slot roulette wheel. Now the payoffs are $6,000,000 (or $40 \times \$150,000$) with probability 1/40, less $50,000 to repay the loan, for a net return of $5,950,000; and $0 with probability 39/40. For this bet, the expected terminal cash position is $148,750 (or $\$5,950,000 \times 1/40$), and

7.2   Tax Planning in the Presence of Risk-Sharing and Hidden-Action Considerations the expected profit increases to \$48,750 (or \$148,750 - \$100,000). The bank is repaid only 1 time in 40. As a result, its expected dollar payoff is \$1,250 on a \$50,000 investment. Of course, your expected profit (and the bank's expected loss) could be made arbitrarily close to \$50,000 by increasing the actuarially fair risk further; for example, if your number comes up after the first spin, reinvest everything on another spin.

The limited personal liability provided by the bankruptcy laws encourages unsecured debtors to engage in riskier investments, since they do not bear fully the cost of such risks. An unfortunate aspect of this incentive problem is that an unsecured borrower, who definitely intends not to buy risky assets, may have no cost-effective way of convincing the lender that this is the case.

One way to lessen the problem is for the borrower to establish a reputation for not taking strategic advantage of the lender (for example, by building up a good credit history with the lender). Tax shelter syndicators and investment advisors are very aware of the benefits of establishing a reputation as we will discuss when we cover the topic of tax shelters. But the moral here is that information costs resulting from strategic uncertainty increase further the wedge between borrowing and lending rates.

No wonder lenders often write extensive loan covenants into loan agreements that restrict borrowers' behavior. But such covenants are costly to write because there are so many possible future contingencies, some of which cannot even be foreseen at the time of contracting. These covenants are also costly to monitor. As a result, they cannot completely prevent opportunistic behavior on the part of borrowers. And further, restrictive covenants can prove costly to borrowers, by hindering their activities in costly ways. As suggested in Chapter Six, these costs can reduce dramatically the number of capital market transactions that can be exploited to reduce taxes in a cost-effective way.

Contracting in Labor Markets

In this section, we consider employee compensation contracting in simple settings. We begin with a single-period setting where there are no hidden action (moral hazard) problems; that is, the employer need not worry about the employee's taking actions on the job that are unobservable to the employer and that may improve the employee's welfare at some expense to the employer. This will enable us to expose easily the nature of the **identification problem** that we discussed earlier.

Suppose that the employee is subject to a constant tax rate independent of compensation received. The employer, on the other hand, is subject to a progressive income tax. If profits are high, so is the tax rate. While it might seem unusual that employees have constant tax rates and employers have progressive tax rates, this is not really so. Suppose, for example, that the employees are highly paid executives, whose marginal tax rates are constant; and the employer is a start-up venture with expenses that currently generate net operating losses, but with profits expected in the future. In such a setting, the tax-minimizing contract is one that loads up on compensation to the employee when profits are high (in the future) and the tax deduction to the employer for compensation paid is worth the

Chapter 7   The Distinction Between Effective Tax Planning and Tax Minimization

most. Similarly, compensation should be minimized when profits and tax rates for the employer are low (which they are at the present time).

In the compensation plan above, the employee foregoes current income for future compensation that is tied to the firm's profits. Note how this contract looks like an incentive-based arrangement despite the absence of any incentive problems. This arrangement could arise due to tax motives or incentive motives, or both. This is what we mean by an identification problem. Such problems make it difficult to untangle the reasons we observe various contractual arrangements. Without a rich understanding of the situation, outside observers could easily misinterpret the economics of the contractual arrangements.

To illustrate, suppose the firm assigns a manager to undertake a risky project. The project yields a pretax profit, before employee compensation expense, of $400,000 half the time and -$100,000 half the time. As in our earlier example, the tax rate is 40% when taxable income is positive and 0% otherwise. This tax schedule applies to both the firm and its employee.

Assume that both the employee and the firm's owners are risk-neutral. The employee has job alternatives that pay the equivalent of $75,000 in salary. This means that the firm must offer a compensation contract that matches the after-tax salary of $45,000 (or $75,000 × (1 - .4)) available elsewhere.

What sort of compensation contract should the employee be offered? Note that a $75,000 salary contract would *not* be efficient from a tax-planning standpoint. Why? Because half the time (when a loss is generated) the employer would obtain no tax benefit from the salary payment. It would be better to pay nothing when profits are negative and a bonus of $150,000 when profits are positive. Since each situation occurs half the time, the *expected* pay is $75,000, and this satisfies the compensation requirements of the employee.

The expected after-tax cost of this arrangement to the firm is $45,000 (or .5 × $0 + .5 × $150,000(1 - .4)). This is $15,000 less than the expected after-tax cost of a $75,000 salary contract. The savings results from avoiding a compensation payment of $75,000 when the tax rate is 0% rather than 40% (a tax difference of $30,000), which occurs half the time.

Conflicts between Risk Sharing and Tax Minimization

Let us now suppose that the employee is risk averse, while the employer is indifferent towards risk. Since the employee is willing to pay to avoid risk, whereas the employer does not mind bearing risk, it is desirable, from a **risk-sharing** standpoint, for the employee to be offered a pure wage contract, independent of the firm's profitability. This would result in the employer bearing all the risk of profit uncertainty.

But if the employee faces a constant tax rate and the employer an increasing tax rate, a pure wage contract results in an increase in joint tax payments relative to the tax-minimizing contract (a bonus contract that shifts all the risk to the *employee*). So, the two parties will find it desirable neither to minimize taxes nor to shield the risk-averse party from all risk. Instead, they will trade off the two forces. Technical Note 7.1 provides an illustration.

7.2 Tax Planning in the Presence of Risk-Sharing and Hidden-Action Considerations

Now let us expand our compensation contracting problem by introducing **hidden action** concerns and contracts that extend over several time periods. Tax rates will be allowed to vary over time, and the employer will be concerned with aligning employee incentives with the employer's interests.

In particular, suppose the employer's tax rate today is greater than it will be in the future. Such a configuration of tax rates favors immediate salary over deferred compensation: it is preferable to take tax deductions when the employer's tax rate is highest, which it is presently.

Further suppose that the employee faces the opposite configuration of tax rates: low today and high in the future. This further reinforces the desirability of accelerating compensation payments: the employee recognizes taxable income when tax rates are low.

Finally, suppose that the employee can earn at least as much on marginal investments after tax as can the employer. This also favors current compensation, since deferred compensation effectively results in the employer investing on the employee's behalf. So the tax-minimizing contract is clearly one that "loads up" on current compensation.

But now suppose that the employee works in a firm in which a durable good is manufactured under conditions of conflict between employer and employee interests. In particular, assume that the employee can take one of two actions. Action 1 involves working hard and causes the product to last W periods. Alternatively, the employee can take action 2, which involves shirking, in which case the product lasts S periods, where S is less than W. The employee prefers action 2 to action 1, but the market value of increased product durability is assumed to exceed this personal cost difference. In other words, if the employer could observe the employee's actions, the employer would be willing to pay a bonus for hard work that more than compensates for the personal cost to the employee of the additional effort.

We also assume that bankruptcy constraints and labor laws prevent the employer from exacting a large penalty from the employee in the event that the product is observed to last only S periods, revealing that the employee has shirked. Finally, assume that the employee's objective is to maximize lifetime consumption, where consumption tomorrow is almost as good as consumption today. Consumption takes place as compensation is received.

Then, ignoring tax considerations, the efficient incentive arrangement entails deferring compensation to the employee until after the manufactured product has been observed to last more than S periods, revealing that the more costly (and more valuable) action has been rendered by the employee. But this is in direct conflict with the tax-minimizing contract, which would accelerate compensation to take advantage of the changing tax rates over time. The production efficiency gains from deferring compensation may be insufficient to compensate for the resulting additional tax payments, and in general the two considerations must be traded off.

In the example above, tax rates for the employer and the employee were such that immediate salary reduced taxes relative to deferred compensation.

Suppose that the tax rates over time were reversed such that for tax reasons alone, deferred compensation is the desired contract. To defer compensation with a deferred compensation contract the employee must be an unsecured creditor of the employer. When the employee is an unsecured creditor, she will want to ensure that the firm remains solvent. This may result in the employee passing up positive net present value projects if they also increase the risk of the firm's defaulting on the deferred compensation contract. As with previous examples, tax minimization may have to be sacrificed to align incentives properly.

7.3 Tax Planning in the Presence of Hidden Information Considerations

The examples considered thus far have illustrated how the organizational arrangements encouraged by focusing narrowly on tax minimization may conflict with those encouraged by risk-sharing or hidden-action considerations. We turn next to an example in which tax minimization may not be achievable because of hidden information problems. The classic setting in which this arises is in the sale of an asset (such as the used car market). The seller is assumed to be better-informed than the buyer about the quality or value of the asset being sold.

Suppose that a firm has generated large tax losses in past years and currently has net operating loss carryforwards (NOLs) that are about to expire unused or will not be used before tax rates drop. Suppose further that it is widely understood that if a profitable firm merges with our NOL firm, some taxes can be saved. It is a common occurrence that sellers of assets are better-informed about the value of the assets for sale than are prospective buyers. If the owners of the NOL firm know that the firm is worth more than the expected value assessed by prospective buyers given their limited information, there may not exist a mutually agreeable price at which to sell the firm. Stated a bit more formally, if high value firms are unable to distinguish themselves in the marketplace from low value firms, high value firms may be forced to withdraw from the market unless the tax gains are large enough to offset the bargain sales price (for high value firms) that clears the market.

Of course, the sale of a business does not represent the only means by which the owners of the NOL firm could cash in the wasting asset that NOL carryforwards represent. But as we will discuss in future chapters, all of the substitutes (including issuing stock, repurchasing debt, effecting a sale and leaseback of depreciable assets, among many other candidates) involve transaction costs that are nontrivial. And such costs may overwhelm the tax benefits of restructuring. So in a friction-filled world, the common occurrence of NOL carryforwards, which is clearly not a tax-minimizing state of affairs, need not imply inefficient tax planning.

A related situation in which the taxpayer may rationally forego tax benefits involves the sale of a depreciable business asset to recognize an immediate tax loss at ordinary rates. In this case, the asset has declined in value by more than the accumulated tax depreciation to date. The alternative to a sale of the asset is to recognize the loss in the future through depreciation deductions, but in a present value sense this is undesirable unless tax rates are expected to increase significantly in the future. Or it might be desirable to sell an asset that has appreciated in value if the gain is taxed at favorable rates and the new buyer is permitted to depreciate the asset at ordinary tax rates based on the stepped-up (to market value) tax basis. In both cases, buyers and sellers may agree that they could gain by trading the asset. Where the seller is better informed about the value of the asset than is the buyer, however, they may fail to reach mutually agreeable contractual terms.

Tax Planning and Organizational Design

When a complex organization is composed of distinct legal entities, its left pocket is often taxed differently from its right pocket. This consideration applies not only to multinational enterprises but also to enterprises that operate exclusively within a single country. Sources of differences in taxation across legal entities include (1) multistate taxation, (2) industry-specific taxation, (3) size-specific taxation, and (4) special rules relating to net operating losses and tax credits. In the NOL and tax credit case, tax rules often prevent these attributes from offsetting the tax liability of any other entity in the consolidated group following a merger. Since shifting income from one pocket to the next may require considerable coordination, tax rules often induce a greater degree of centralization of management than would otherwise be optimal. Conversely, since centralization for tax-planning purposes may undermine the efficiency of decentralized decision-making for nontax reasons, it is often desirable to sacrifice tax benefits to achieve these other goals. Tax rules are not unique in affecting organizational design. Similar issues arise with respect to myriad legal rules and regulatory policies such as trade laws and antitrust laws.

Related considerations arise in the choice between local and foreign suppliers of goods used in production. Suppose that local supply is more cost-effective, ignoring taxes, than is foreign supply (for example, because of lower monitoring costs, lower coordination costs, and lower transportation costs). But **vertical integration** with a foreign supplier may enable the recognition of profits in a tax jurisdiction where the tax rate is lower. One means by which this can be effected is through judicious transfer pricing (subject to the scrutiny of the taxing authority as we discuss in greater depth in the chapters on multinational tax planning). On the other hand, judicious transfer pricing for tax-planning purposes may pollute the planning and control features of a transfer pricing system in a decentralized firm where important information is widely dispersed.

Another example in a multinational organizational setting where tax and nontax considerations often conflict is in the choice between setting up a foreign subsidiary and a foreign branch. The laws and property rights that apply to foreign subsidiaries and foreign branches often differ in important ways, as do the tax treatments of these two organizational forms.

While taxpayers typically wish to report low levels of taxable income to the taxing authority, they often wish to report high levels of income to investors. In the U.S., as in many other countries, businesses often maintain more than one set of books. Profits reported to the taxing authority may differ significantly from those reported to investors. Still, most transactions that reduce taxable income also reduce income reported to shareholders.

For example, whenever a firm owns assets for which the market value is below book value for tax purposes, an immediate write-off is available if the assets are traded, but this would also typically require recognition of a financial reporting loss. The many companies that purchased oil, silver, or gold mining properties in the early 1980s fall squarely into this category. Even if buyers and sellers agree completely on asset values, sellers might be concerned that the sale of such assets at a loss would increase their cost of capital by an amount exceeding the tax savings. Alternatively, managers whose compensation is tied to reported profitability might rationally forego tax savings due to an inherent conflict of interest. In this latter case, the sacrifice of tax savings is due to a hidden action problem. Shareholders might prefer that the manager sell assets to reduce taxes in this circumstance, but as outsiders they may lack the requisite information to discipline the manger who chooses not to do so.

Conflicts of interest between management and shareholders often arise in proposed merger transactions. There are often considerable tax benefits available through a merger. But incumbent managers may find it in their best interest to erect barriers that make such transactions expensive to undertake. We will take up this issue in greater depth in the chapters on mergers and acquisitions.

An example of where tax planning and financial reporting considerations may conflict that has received considerable attention by economists involves the choice among alternative inventory valuation methods. LIFO (last-in, first-out) is an inventory accounting method that minimizes taxes (in those countries where it is an acceptable accounting method) when prices are rising and tax rates are not increasing over time. If LIFO is used for tax purposes in the U.S., however, it must also be used for financial reporting purposes. As such, taxable income can be reduced only by reducing profits reported to shareholders, lenders, and other interested parties, and this may discourage the tax-minimizing strategy.

In certain countries, the tax/financial-reporting conformity rules are far broader than in the U.S. In Japan, for example, most tax deductions are unavailable unless they are reflected in income reported to third parties as well. So whereas the use of a faster depreciation method for tax purposes than for financial reporting purposes is quite common in the U.S., it is nonexistent in Japan. In fact, deferred tax accounting, which reflects timing differences in income and expense recognition for tax and financial reporting purposes under generally accepted accounting principles in the U.S., is simply not practiced in Japan.

Financial reporting concerns may extend to regulators as well as investors. For example, U.S. banks must maintain a minimum level of "regulatory capital" to preserve operating independence from bank regulators. Moreover, the quantity of federally insured demand deposits that banks are permitted to issue is tied to regulatory capital. To the extent transactions that reduce taxable income also reduce regulatory capital (and most do), banks may rationally sacrifice tax savings. This is particularly true of banks that face a relatively high probability of failure and low levels of regulatory capital, because such institutions find it particularly attractive to borrow money at the riskless rate by issuing insured demand deposits.

Political Cost Impediments to Tax Planning

We stated in Chapter Five that politicians, the public at large, and lobbyists (seeking to secure tax favors for certain private parties), often scrutinize the level of taxes paid by public corporations. And perhaps because the concept is not well understood, corporations that pay substantial sums of implicit tax, but little explicit tax, are not always viewed as paying their fair share of the tax burden. When firms that are in the public eye succeed in reducing taxes in socially unacceptable ways, the public often has a way of "getting even." Effective tax planning for certain organizations requires a more subtle calculus in this case.

Other Informational Cost Impediments to Tax Planning

Tax planning is a huge business. Billions of dollars are spent each year in the U.S. alone to secure professional assistance in reducing tax obligations. In addition, billions of dollars are spent each year in maintaining records to support taxpayers' claims concerning their tax obligations. Finally, billions of dollars are spent each year in legal and administrative fees to write and to enforce contractual agreements that are designed, in part, to reduce the joint tax burdens among contracting parties. Effective tax planning must be viewed relative to the costs of implementing these strategies. Although complex contracts may succeed in reducing more conflicts of interest among contracting parties, simple contracts are often observed in practice. Similarly, simple tax-planning strategies may be more efficient from an overall cost standpoint than more complicated strategies that would result in reduced tax payments.

Summary of Key Points

1. A progressive tax-rate system encourages taxpayers to invest as though they were more risk averse than they really are. This is because with progressive taxes, average tax payments increase with the variability of taxable income.
2. Market frictions cause the borrowing rate for funds to exceed the lending rate. These costs are high in part because borrowers cannot always be trusted to act as they promise. In particular, they might have incentives to take actions that are unobservable to lenders and that have unfavorable implications for their cash flows. This in turn impairs borrowers' abilities to repay their debts.

3. In realistic market settings, where information differences among contracting parties are pervasive, efficient tax planning may deviate substantially from tax minimization.

4. Lenders seek to enhance the collectibility of loans by writing extensive loan covenants that restrict borrowers' actions. But such covenants, which are costly to write and to monitor, are imperfect in preventing opportunistic behavior by borrowers. Moreover, restrictive covenants may restrain borrowers from taking actions that would be beneficial to both the borrower and the lender.

5. In organizational contracting problems, it is often difficult for outside observers, such as consultants, corporate raiders, investment bankers, regulators, or researchers, to determine whether contracts tied to profits are motivated by incentive considerations, tax considerations, or both. This identification problem makes it difficult to know what economic problem gave rise to the contractual microstructure.

6. When an employer is risk neutral and an employee is risk averse, a pure wage contract allocates risk-bearing between the parties in an efficient manner, ignoring taxes. If a profits-based compensation contract is preferred for tax purposes, however, tax considerations and risk-sharing considerations will be in conflict, and the two forces must be traded off.

7. Under conditions of moral hazard (hidden action problems), a deferred compensation contract might have attractive incentive features. If, under such circumstances, an immediate salary is preferred for tax reasons, a conflict arises between the two forces, and they must be traded off.

8. Tax-savings strategies might naturally be sacrificed where there are hidden information problems. The seller of an asset is generally better informed than are prospective buyers about the quality or value of the asset being sold. Tax considerations might favor the sale of an asset to realize a loss that reduces taxable income. Prospective buyers, however, will have difficulty in distinguishing whether the motivation for selling the asset is to secure tax benefits or that the asset is no longer as productive as the seller asserts. As a result, the asset might not be sold because the buyer is rationally unwilling to pay full value for the asset, and tax benefits would be sacrificed.

9. Tax-planning considerations often conflict with nontax considerations in such organizational design issues as hierarchical structure (the degree of centralization and vertical integration) and whether to organize certain operations as branches or subsidiaries.

10. Many tax-planning strategies affect financial reporting to shareholders and other less direct "stakeholders" of the firm. Many tax-reducing strategies require transactions that reduce income reported to these other parties. To the extent such strategies convey information to outsiders that cause nontax costs of the business to increase, tax reduction may be discouraged.

11. Effective tax planning must be viewed relative to the costs of implementing the requisite strategies. In addition to certain organizational inefficiencies such strategies may introduce, these costs include securing professional advice, record-keeping, and the administrative costs of writing and enforcing contracts.

Technical Note 7.1

Example of Conflict between Risk Sharing and Tax Minimization

In this example, we assume the employee is risk averse. In particular, we assume her preference for cash compensation increases with the square root of the level of compensation. To illustrate the degree of risk aversion reflected in such preferences, the employee is indifferent between an after-tax payment of $30,000 for certain and a 50-50 chance of a payment of $10,000 and $60,718. The expected value of the risky payment is $35,359, so the employee requires a risk premium of $5,359 (or $35,359 - $30,000) for this level of risk.

Following the example in the text, we assume that the employee must be offered a compensation contract that is at least as attractive as a $75,000 salary. The employer's tax rate is 40% when profitable and 0% otherwise, and each occurs half the time. The employee's tax rate is 40% of any compensation received.

The employer's objective is to minimize expected after-tax compensation expense subject to the constraint that the risk-averse employee be offered a competitive compensation package. If we let c_1 and c_2 denote the compensation payments when the firm is and profitable and unprofitable, respectively, then the optimal contract satisfies:

$$\underset{c_1, c_2}{\text{Minimize}} \quad .5[c_1(1 - .4)] + .5c_2$$

$$\text{Subject to } .5\,[c_1(1 - .4)]^{1/2} + .5\,[c_2(1 - .4)]^{1/2} \geq [\$75{,}000(1 - .4)]^{1/2}$$

The solution is to pay $117,187.50 when profitable and $42,187.50 when unprofitable. The expected compensation payment is $79,687.50 before tax and $56,250 after tax ($.5 \times \$117{,}187.50 \times (1 - .4) + .5 \times \$42{,}187.50$). This contract sacrifices tax savings to a considerable degree because of risk-sharing considerations. In particular, a payment of $42,187.50 is made half the time without any tax benefit. In the tax-minimizing contract, compensation is paid only when the firm is profitable and faces a 40% tax rate.

The contract also sacrifices efficient risk sharing to a considerable degree because of tax considerations. In particular, an expected compensation payment of $79,687.50 is made, rather than the $75,000 that would result from a pure salary contract, which would allocate risk efficiently. Despite a nearly $5,000 increase in expected pretax compensation, however, the expected after-tax compensation cost declines by $3,750 (from $60,000 in the case of a $75,000 salary contract to $56,250 here), because some compensation is shifted to times when the firm's tax rate is high. Figure 7.1 demonstrates this graphically.

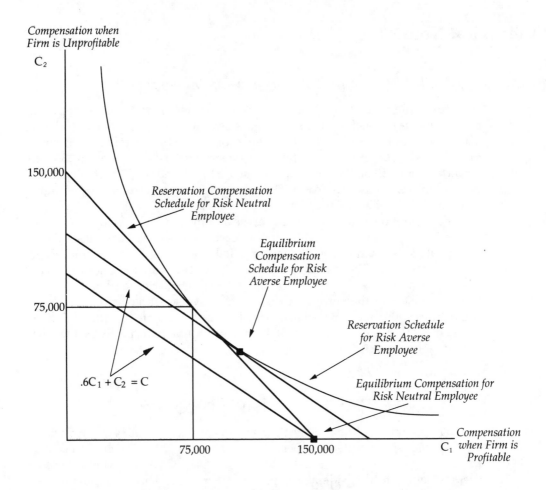

FIGURE 7.1

Chapter 7   The Distinction Between Effective Tax Planning and Tax Minimization

Discussion Questions

1. True or False? Discuss.
   a. Hidden information problems arise when symmetrically informed parties hide information from each other.
   b. Hidden action problems arise because it is costly for principals to monitor the actions of agents.
   c. Symmetric uncertainty about future cash flows causes employees to prefer salary to deferred compensation contracts.
   d. In a progressive tax-rate system, risk-neutral investors prefer volatile assets over riskless assets because they can average their tax rates.
   e. In a progressive tax-rate system, risk-neutral investors will have a demand for portfolio diversification.

2. What role do hidden-action problems play in causing the borrowing rate for funds to be greater than the lending rate? Can we eliminate hidden- action problems? Why or why not? How does the difference in borrowing and lending rates affect the taxpayer's ability to undertake clientele-based arbitrage?

3. What is an "identification problem?" Illustrate conditions under which there might be an identification problem involving: employee-employer compensation contracting; sale of an asset; a merger. Why is it important for outsiders to recognize when an identification problem may be present?

4. If employers are risk neutral and employees are risk averse, why is a salary contract optimal, ignoring tax and asymmetric information considerations? Under what conditions in employee compensation contracting are tax and risk-sharing considerations in conflict? As a result of these conflicts, do employees bear more risk than if the goal were simply to allocate risks efficiently?

5. In the presence of hidden-action problems, under what conditions will a deferred compensation contract both minimize taxes and provide desirable work incentives for employees?

6. How do hidden-information problems affect the costs of corporate restructuring? Might the tax benefits of such restructurings be sacrificed because of these problems?

7. How might tax considerations conflict with financial reporting considerations? How might tax savings be sacrificed to achieve organizational design efficiencies or to mitigate political costs?

Problems

1. Suppose the tax rate is 30% if taxable income is positive and 0% if taxable income is negative. Consider the before-tax payoffs to the following three projects:

   a. Riskless: 10% for sure

   b. Moderately risky: 30% half the time
                               -10% half the time

   c. Quite risky: 300% one time in 10
                               -20% nine times out of 10

   Required:

       i. Calculate the before-tax and after-tax expected rates of return for each project.

       ii. How does variability of returns affect the expected tax rate? Why?

       iii. Does this tax structure encourage or discourage high-technology start-up ventures?

2. An owner-manager of a firm is contemplating the sale of the firm to any one of a number of prospective buyers. The firm has net operating loss carryforwards (NOLs) that are known to be worth $50 million more to the buyers than to the seller.

   While the current owner knows the value of the firm, the prospective buyers are uncertain whether the firm is worth $500 million (including the extra $50 million value in NOLs) or $700 million. Each possibility is deemed to be equally likely by the relatively poorly informed buyers.

   Required:

   a. How much should buyers offer to acquire the firm?

   b. Will the seller always accept the highest rational offer made?

   c. How does the analysis change if the uncertain values of the firm are $500 million and $540 million rather than $500 million and $700 million?

Chapter 7   The Distinction Between Effective Tax Planning and Tax Minimization

CHAPTER 8
The Importance of Marginal Tax Rates and Difficulties in Calculating Them

Where differences in tax rates exist across taxpayers, across time, across organizational forms, and across economic activities, taxpayers have incentives to contract with one another in ways that may alter their marginal tax rates. In Chapter Six, we demonstrated that with differentially taxed assets and the absence of frictions and restrictions, clientele-based arbitrage ensures that all taxpayers face the same marginal tax rates. We also showed that tax rule restrictions and market frictions reduce the set of circumstances in which clientele-based arbitrage can be implemented effectively. In this chapter, we show that the restraint on tax arbitrage is linked to complications in determining the appropriate tax rate for decision-making purposes.

We begin with a consideration of the strategies that an entity might undertake to alter its marginal tax rate via tax-arbitrage techniques. The tax-planner's problem is to minimize a broadly defined measure of tax (current and future) given the history of decisions and outcomes that brought the firm to where it is today. Most investment and financing decisions are undertaken in an uncertain environment. Once plans are implemented, events unfold; given the outcomes of the process, entities must decide how to alter their investment and financing decisions. And given these outcomes, many entities would prefer to undertake clientele-based arbitrage strategies to change their marginal tax rates if it were costless to do so. Restrictions and frictions curtail such strategies. We analyze how much clientele-based arbitrage an entity should undertake. We consider the tax-planning strategies available to a high tax-bracket firm (such as a firm with lots of profits that is not subject to the alternative minimum tax) and then discuss tax-planning strategies for low tax-bracket firms (such as those with net-operating loss, investment tax credit, or alternative minimum tax credit carryforwards).

We follow this with a discussion in Chapter Nine of dynamic tax-planning strategies: that is, how to plan today for future contingencies. There we emphasize that in making investment and financing decisions, entities anticipate that once strategic plans have been put into place, the results of these strategies will throw them out of equilibrium. Due to uncertainty, taxpayers will find themselves in different clienteles than if they had been endowed with perfect foresight. Optimal tax planning requires that the tax advantages and costs of altering clienteles be considered at the outset in making investment and financing decisions. Making an investment/financing decision today but disregarding the tax advantages of altering clienteles as future events unfold would produce an optimal tax plan only if it were costless to alter clienteles. However, a sequence of myopic (that is, one-step ahead) decisions will generally produce an inferior result to a plan that takes advance account of the costs of restructuring activities.

8.1   Tax Planning for a Change in Clienteles

Marginal Tax Rate

In Chapter Five we showed that differentially taxed assets give rise to implicit tax in that the before-tax rates of return on more heavily taxed assets exceed those on more lightly taxed assets. In Chapters Six and Seven we showed that transaction costs act as implicit taxes and can be viewed as a component of them. Although the differential-taxation component of the implicit tax is the same for all investors, the frictions component of the implicit tax is more idiosyncratic. It depends not only on the individual or entity attempting to undertake clientele-based arbitrage, but also on the microstructure of a transaction.

We have argued that high marginal-tax-rate taxpayers have an incentive to hold assets that are granted tax-favored treatment under the law and that low tax-rate investors prefer to hold tax-disfavored assets. And if the costs of buying and selling assets are not too high, taxpayers with relatively extreme (high or low) marginal tax rates have an incentive to engage in tax arbitrage.

We define the **marginal tax rate** as the present value of current **plus deferred** income taxes (both explicit plus implicit) to be paid per dollar of additional (or marginal) taxable income (where taxable income is grossed up to include implicit taxes paid). Notice here that we extend the definition of marginal tax rate to include the effect of a current dollar of taxable income on future-period tax liabilities. And since total taxes are important to investment decisions, the marginal tax rate includes the implicit tax as well as the explicit tax. Sometimes we will focus only on the explicit tax component of the marginal tax rate, and sometimes we will focus only on the implicit tax component. When we do, we will refer to these as the **marginal explicit tax rate** and the **marginal implicit tax rate**, respectively.

To illustrate, suppose a corporate taxpayer has generated an excess of tax deductions over taxable income in the past. The result is $10 million of net operating loss carryforwards (NOLs). Such NOLs can shelter future taxable income. Suppose further that investment and financing plans are fixed and that they will give rise to future taxable income of $4 million per year beginning one year from today. The statutory corporate tax rate is 40% and will remain at this level. What is the marginal explicit tax rate on an immediate dollar of fully taxable income if the firm discounts after-tax cash flow at 7% per year?

Note that in the absence of NOLs, an extra dollar of taxable income would trigger an immediate tax of $.40, so the marginal explicit tax rate is 40%. But with $10 million of NOLs, the firm faces no immediate tax liability on an extra dollar of income. Does this mean its marginal tax rate is 0%? Far from it. The prospect of earning $4 million per year of taxable income means that the firm will begin to pay taxes in three years. So an extra dollar of taxable income today would trigger a tax payment of $.40 in 3 years. The present value of this tax is $.40/$1.07^3$ = 32.65 cents, so the marginal explicit tax rate in this case is only 32.65%.

If the current statutory rate of 40% was scheduled to change in, say, one year to 25%, then the current marginal explicit tax rate of our NOL firm would be 20.41% (or $.25/1.07^3$), although the rate for a firm without NOLs would remain 40%. Analogously, if the statutory rate was scheduled to increase to 50% in 1 year, the current explicit marginal tax rate of our NOL firm would be 40.81% (or $.50/1.07^3$). This illustrates that in the face of tax rate changes over time, the marginal tax rate of NOL firms can exceed that of firms paying taxes at the full statutory rate.

The marginal tax rate is also affected by the presence of rules that tie certain tax deductions to the level of taxable income. For example, under U.S. law, medical deductions, miscellaneous itemized deductions, and the deductibility of certain losses on passive investment activity are tied to the level of taxable income. In the case of medical and miscellaneous deductions, higher income leads to a permanent loss of deductions, and in the case of passive loss deductions (for example, on real estate activity), higher income may lead to a postponement of the deduction.

To illustrate the effect of these factors on the marginal tax rate, suppose that an extra dollar of income reduces tax deductions permanently by $.10 and postpones the deductibility of $.50 of losses for 5 years. The current statutory tax rate is 40% and it will be 45% in 5 years. If the after-tax discount rate of the taxpayer is 7%, the marginal tax rate on a dollar of current taxable income is calculated as follows:

	$1.00	of additional income
+	$0.10	permanent loss of tax deduction
+	$0.50	temporary loss of tax deduction
=	$1.60	of additional taxable income currently.

This gives rise to $1.60 × 40% = $.64 of additional current tax.

An additional deduction of $.50 in 5 years at a tax rate of 45% reduces taxes, in present value, by $.50 × 45%/$1.07^5$ or $.16. The overall increment to tax on the dollar of extra taxable income, then, is $.64 - $.16 = $.48, so the marginal tax rate is 48%.

We also define the **average tax rate** as the present value of current plus deferred income taxes (both explicit plus implicit) divided by the present value of taxable income (where taxable income is again grossed up to include implicit taxes paid). This measure captures a taxpayer's tax burden better than does conventional measures such as **effective tax rates**.

There are at least two popular definitions of **effective tax rates**: (1) For financial reporting purposes it is the sum of currently payable and deferred tax expense divided by net income before tax. Both the numerator and the denominator exclude implicit taxes. Moreover, the tax expense figure is insensitive to the timing of tax payments (that is, a dollar of taxes paid currently is treated no differently from a dollar of taxes to be paid many years into the future). (2) For "tax reformer" (for example, Citizens for Tax Justice) purposes, the effective tax rate is defined as taxes paid currently divided by net income before tax. The numerator excludes not only implicit taxes but also tax deferrals (that is, timing differences in calculating income for tax purposes and for financial reporting purposes).

We argue that effective tax rates have little economic meaning. And while average tax rates may be used to gauge the extent to which taxpayers are paying their fair share of taxes, they are not very useful for tax-planning purposes. In making such economic choices as investment or financing decisions, it is the marginal tax rate that is important.

Problems with Effective Tax Rates

Let us now show why using effective tax rates can be very deceiving. Assume that the before-tax rate of return on fully taxable bonds is 10% and that the municipal bond rate is 7%. This implies that the implicit tax rate is 30%. We know that an investor prefers municipal bonds if her marginal tax rate on holding taxable bonds (all of which is explicit) exceeds that on holding municipal bonds (all of which is implicit).

This is pretty straightforward. To set the stage for our analysis of the marginal tax rate, let's now complicate things a bit by assuming that it is possible to sell taxable bonds and to buy municipal bonds. Note that this transaction could be accomplished by either taking out a loan and using the proceeds to buy municipal bonds (in which case interest deductibility is restricted by the tax rules) or by selling some current holdings of taxable bonds and using the sale proceeds to buy municipal bonds (in which case tax-rule restrictions do not apply).

Let's suppose we undertake this transaction through an up-and-running partnership whose operating decisions (such as selecting what products to produce) have already been determined. These operating decisions will give rise to $600,000 in taxable income. Recall that partnership income is taxed at the individual partner level. Suppose that the ordinary tax rate for each of the partners, t_p, is 40%. For the moment we will ignore the restraints on the deductibility of interest on loans to finance the purchase of municipal bonds. Suppose that the partnership borrows $6,000,000 for one year at the beginning of the year. This financing decision gives rise to $600,000 in deductible interest expense. If the proceeds of the loan are used to buy municipal bonds, the taxable income from the partnership would be zero. As a result, the so-called **effective tax rate** at the partnership level would be zero. The partnership income *is* taxed to the partners, however, at the 30% implicit tax rate on municipal bonds rather than at their 40% ordinary rate on taxable income. The partners are able to accomplish some tax reduction (though not 100% as the effective tax rate implies) by using clientele-based arbitrage to switch from paying explicit taxes on ordinary taxable income to paying implicit taxes on tax-favored assets. The $6,000,000 invested in municipal bonds at 7% yields $420,000 in after-tax income, exactly 70% of the $600,000 in taxable income of the partners before the investment and financing decisions were undertaken.

Although the effective tax rate has been reduced to zero, suppose the partnership continued to borrow at a 10% before-tax rate and purchase municipal bonds with the proceeds at a 7% before-tax rate of return. This creates negative taxable income at the partnership level, which is passed through to the partners.[1] The arbitrage remains profitable until the taxable income of the partners is reduced to such a level that their own personal tax rates on ordinary income become 30%.[2]

This illustration points to a another difficulty with effective tax rate measures. The effective tax rate of the partners on their $600,000 of partnership income would be negative in this case. The negative effective tax rate arises because the calculation ignores the considerable sums of municipal bond interest, earned and taxed implicitly, while including fully the tax savings on the interest deductions. This is hardly a meaningful rate in the face of a 30% implicit tax on municipal bond income. Moreover, the effective tax rate measure provides no guidance in identifying desirable clientele-based arbitrage strategies; for example, it does not indicate when to stop borrowing and investing the loan proceeds in municipal bonds.

8.2 Dynamic Tax-Planning Strategies for Low Marginal-Tax-Rate Firms

To this point, we have developed concepts at a fairly general level of analysis. We now illustrate some of the idiosyncratic tax-planning considerations that arise when taxpayers engage in clientele-based arbitrage in the presence of (1) market frictions and (2) uncertainty regarding future taxable cash flows. We will proceed by way of a case study. Here we illustrate how firms with net operating loss carryforwards and investment-tax-credit carryforwards calculate marginal tax rates to determine tax clienteles for investment and financing purposes under conditions of both market frictions and uncertainty. Similar considerations apply to firms that face foreign-tax-credit and capital-loss carryforwards, as well as

---

[1]We are assuming that the so-called "passive loss limitations" on partnership activities do not prevent partners from taking current tax deductions for their share of partnership loss. And, for pedagogical reasons, we are once again assuming that it is possible to deduct interest on loans used for the purpose of buying or holding municipal bonds. We will have more to say about passive loss limitations in the chapter on tax-sheltered investments.

[2]Note that if each partner does not have identical marginal explicit tax rates, partners may disagree on how much borrowing is desirable. As long as the partners know the amount of borrowing at the partnership level, however, they could adjust the level of borrowing on personal account, if necessary.

alternative-minimum-tax-credit carryforwards due to substantial tax prefer-ences (such as accelerated depreciation).

Net Operating Loss Carryforwards (NOLs)

For our case study, suppose that you have just been hired as the resident tax-planning genius in a U.S. corporation with accumulated NOLs of $20 million. These carryforwards will expire in three years. You are to devise a plan to use these NOLs to the best advantage of the corporation. The following facts are given: (1) the riskless before-tax rate at which the corporation can invest in corporate bonds is 8%, (2) the riskless before-tax rate at which the corporation can invest in preferred stocks issued by other domestic corporation is 6%, and 80% of this return is exempt from taxation,[3] and (3) the corporate tax rate is a flat 40% of taxable income.

Through long-term supply contracts, your corporation has committed itself to a fixed set of operating decisions. As a result, it would be extremely costly for the firm to alter its operating plans. The operating income from these supply contracts before interest and taxes (NIBIT) fluctuates year to year. Let us assume that each year's NIBIT is independent of the previous year's NIBIT. In any one year, there is a .6 probability that NIBIT will be $15 million and a .4 probability that NIBIT will be -$10 million. These payoff prospects will apply each year for the next three years, at which point the firm will liquidate. You should ignore any direct tax consequences that could occur on liquidating the firm. You should also assume that investors are risk-neutral and that after-tax cash flows are discounted at a 6% rate (to simplify the analysis). Bear in mind that if the firm generates sufficient income to use up all of its NOLs and begins paying taxes, but subse-quently generates a net operating loss, the firm can carry the loss back three years and obtain a refund of taxes paid (without interest) by filing an amended tax return.

Your firm's current cash position is $30 million. The firm has a contractual obligation to customers not to pay dividends to shareholders until the long-term supply contract is completed (in three years). You may invest idle funds in either bonds or preferred stocks. Moreover, you face no restrictions on the deductibility of interest on bonds that you issue. Remember that corporations do not receive a tax deduction (at least, not explicitly) for preferred-stock dividend payments.

You have been told by your investment bankers that the corporation faces an increasing cost schedule of risk-adjusted rates for bonds that it might issue. More specifically, the corporation can borrow at 8.4% plus .04% for each $1 mil-lion of incremental borrowing (that is, the first $1 costs 8.40%, the millionth dollar costs 8.44%, the second millionth dollar costs 8.48%, etc.). The corporation can issue preferred stock at a cost of 6.3% plus .03% for each $1 million of incremental preferred stock that is issued.

---

[3]As discussed in earlier chapters, the fraction of dividend income that is exempt from taxation for corporate investors varies from country to country. It also varies for a given country depending upon whether the dividend is paid by a domestic corporation or a foreign corporation and depending upon the fraction of voting stock owned by the corporate investor. Finally, the rules have changed over time within a given jurisdiction. The 80% exemption is used for illustrative purposes only, although it is the relevant exemption rate in certain jurisdictions (such as the U.S.) in certain circumstances.

Chapter 8   The Importance of Marginal Tax Rates and Difficulties in Calculating

Table 8.1 Client Summary Report

Year	Past Years' Incomes ($ millions)	Expected Marginal Explicit Tax Rate	Amount of Bonds Issued	Amount of Preferred Stock Issued	Idle Cash Invested in: Bonds	Preferreds
1	—					
2	15					
2	-10					
3	-10, -10					
3	-10, 15					
3	15, -10					
3	15, 15					

Although the bonds or preferred stocks the firm might issue are of equal risk to those they might purchase, note that the firm's borrowing rate is above its lending rate. The difference (or "spread") represents a deadweight cost (or friction) to the firm. It could be due to the firm's inability to convince lenders of its true default risk or to other borrowing costs such as legal, investment banking, and accounting fees.

Your task is to suggest an optimal investment and financing strategy for your corporation in light of the firm's operating history, prospects, and commitments. To do a complete job, you should provide the plan for each possible realization of operating income over the three years. Your client's investment and financing choices include: (1) issue or repurchase its own preferred stock, (2) issue or repurchase its own corporate debt, and (3) buy or sell corporate bonds or preferred stocks issued by others.

The report to your client will include a summary table like Table 8.1. In other words, you must construct seven tax plans, one for each possible pattern of NIBIT at each date. At the start of the second year, NIBIT in the first year will have been either $15 million or -$10 million. At the start of the third year, NIBIT will have been the sequence -$10, -$10 (2 years of misfortune) or -$10, $15 (1 stroke of bad luck followed by a favorable outcome), etc.

Moreover, you have been asked to consider the conditions under which the corporation would be better off merging with another fully taxable corporation. You should also give some thought here to how the desirability of a merger is affected by the prospect of a change in future tax rates.

Tax-Planning Analysis for the NOL Firm[4]

Let us now attack your assignment. The firm's investment opportunities include fully taxable bonds (yielding 8% before tax) and 80%-tax-exempt preferred stocks (yielding 6% before tax). The firm will be indifferent between these two invest-

---

[4]To test your skills, you may wish to to solve the tax-planning problem before proceeding.

8.2 Dynamic Tax-Planning Strategies for Low Marginal-Tax-Rate Firms

ment opportunities when they yield equal after-tax returns. This occurs when the corporate tax rate, t, satisfies the following relation:

$$\underbrace{8\% \ (1 - t)}_{\substack{\text{After-Tax} \\ \text{Return on} \\ \text{Bonds}}} \qquad = \qquad \underbrace{6\% \ (1 - .2t)}_{\substack{\text{After-Tax} \\ \text{Return on} \\ \text{Preferred Stocks}}},$$

$$\text{or } t = \underline{29.41\%}.$$

When the firm's tax rate is 29.41%, bonds and preferred stocks give rise to returns that are taxed at the same total (implicit plus explicit) tax rate, and both return 5.65% after tax. The tax on bonds is all explicit while the tax on preferred stock is mostly implicit. More precisely, preferred stocks are taxed implicitly at 25% (or $(8\% - 6\%)/8\%$) and explicitly at 4.41% (or $29.41\% \times 20\% \times 6\%/8\%$); that is, 20% of the 6% dividend is taxed explicitly at 29.41%. The explicit tax rate is the explicit tax as a fraction of the fully taxable yield of 8%. When the firm's tax rate is above 29.41%, preferred stocks provide greater after-tax rates of return than bonds, and when the firm's tax rate is below this level, investment in bonds is more attractive.

It is costly for your client to issue bonds or preferred stock to engage in profitable clientele-based arbitrage because there is a wedge between borrowing and lending rates that grows with the amount of borrowing. The firm can issue bonds at the rate of 8.40% plus 4 basis points per $1 million and can issue preferred stocks at the rate of 6.30% plus 3 basis points per $1 million.

In the absence of these borrowing premiums (that is, if bonds could be issued at 8% and preferred stocks at 6%), your firm could use clientele-based arbitrage if its marginal explicit tax rates, t, were above 29.41% and below 25%. At tax rates above 29.41%, it would issue bonds and purchase preferred stocks since the preferred stock return of $6\%(1 - .2t)$ would exceed the after-tax borrowing cost of $8\%(1 - t)$. At tax rates below 25%, it would issue preferred stocks to purchase bonds since the after-tax return on bonds of $8\%(1 - t)$ would exceed the 6% cost of issuing preferred stock. This arises because the corporations that hold preferred stocks are taxed on a portion of the preferred stock dividends they receive, while preferred stock issuers can deduct none of the preferred stock dividends they pay. In this case, when our client's explicit tax rates are between 25% and 29.41%, there are no arbitrage possibilities. Idle funds are best invested in

Table 8.2 Desirable Investment and Financing Strategies in the Absence of Borrowing Premiums on Bonds and Preferred Stocks

Tax Rate	Strategy	Arbitrage Profit	Explanation
0 - 25%	Issue Preferreds, Buy Bonds	$8\%(1 - t) - 6\%$	Profit>0 for t<25%
25% - 29.41%	Issue No Securities, Idle Cash in Bonds	–	$8\%(1 - t)>6\%(1 - .2t)$
29.41% - 40%	Issue Bonds, Buy Preferreds	$6\%(1-.2t) - 8\%(1-t)$	Profit>0 for t>29.41%

Chapter 8   The Importance of Marginal Tax Rates and Difficulties in Calculating

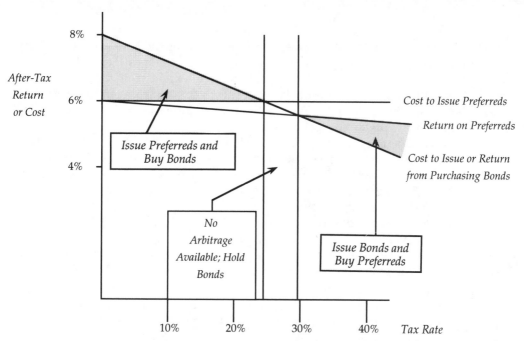

FIGURE 8.1   Desirable Investment and Financing Strategies:
No Borrowing Premiums on Bonds and Preferred Stocks

bonds rather than preferred stocks as indicated earlier. This is summarized in
Table 8.2 and Figure 8.1.

In the presence of borrowing premiums on bonds and preferred stocks,
clientele-based arbitrage becomes desirable over a narrower range of tax rates. If
the cost of issuing preferred stock is 6.3%, buying bonds with the proceeds of a
preferred issue becomes desirable only if the marginal tax rate is below 21.25%
(since 8%(1 - t) - 6.3% > 0 for t < 21.25%). And if the cost of issuing bonds is 8.4%,
buying preferred stocks issued by other corporations with the proceeds of a bond
issue becomes desirable only if the marginal tax rate exceeds 33.33% (since 6%(1
- .2t) - 8.4%(1 - t) > 0 for t > 33.33%). When the borrowing cost schedule is

Table 8.3 Marginal Tax Rate, t*, at which Issuing Preferred Stock (at the Rate of
6.3% + .03% per Million Dollars) to Buy Bonds (at the Rate of 8%) is Neutral

Incremental Preferred Stock Issuance, P (in $ millions)	Marginal Tax Rate, t*
$ 0	21.3%
10	17.5%
20	13.8%
30	10.0%
40	6.3%
50	2.5%
60	-1.3%

t* solves .08(1 - t*) = .063 + .0003P

8.2   Dynamic Tax-Planning Strategies for Low Marginal-Tax-Rate Firms

progressive (that is, the borrowing rate increases as the amount of borrowing increases), the corporation needs ever more extreme marginal tax rates to effect profitable clientele-based arbitrage by issuing either preferred stocks or bonds. In Table 8.3, we show the marginal tax rates at which issuing preferred stock to buy bonds is optimal, and in Table 8.4, we show the marginal tax rates at which issuing bonds to buy preferred stock is optimal.

For example, issuing $30 million of preferred stock to buy bonds would not be profitable unless the corporate tax rate were lower than 10% (as shown in Table 8.3). The last dollar of preferred stock issued costs 7.2% (or 6.3% + 30 × .03%). At this cost, buying fully taxable bonds results in profitable clientele-based arbitrage when t is less than 10% (so that 8%(1 - t) - 7.2% > 0). Similarly, issuing $15 million of bonds to buy preferred stocks would not be profitable unless the corporate tax rate were higher than 38.5% (as shown in Table 8.4). The last dollar of bonds that are issued costs 9% (or 8.4% + 15 × .04%), and at this cost, investing in preferred stock is profitable if the tax rate exceeds 38.46% (so that 6%(1 - .2t) - 9%(1 - t) > 0).

Table 8.4 Marginal Tax Rate, t**, at which Issuing Bonds (at the Rate of 8.4% + .04% per Million Dollars) to Buy Preferred Stock (at the Rate of 6%) is Neutral

Incremental Bond Issuance, B (in $ millions)	Marginal Tax Rate, t**
$ 0	33.3%
5	35.1%
10	36.8%
15	38.5%
20	40.0%

t** solves .06(1 - .2t**) = (.084 + .0004B) (1 - t**)

We can now summarize the optimal investment and financing strategy as a function of the marginal tax rate, t. This is illustrated in Figure 8.2 and described below. The firm's strategy for low tax rates (t < 21.25%) is to issue preferred stock and buy bonds. This is region I in Figure 8.2. Since the cost of issuing preferred stock is increasing in the amount issued, the firm should stop issuing preferred stock when the cost of issuance is equal to the after-tax rate of return earned on fully taxable bonds. How much preferred stock should the firm issue? It should issue P million dollars worth, where P solves

$$.08(1 - t) = .063 + .0003P. \tag{8.1}$$

For example, at t = 15%, $16.67 million of preferred stock should be issued.

When the tax rate is in the range of 21.25% to 33.33%, the firm cannot engage profitably in clientele-based arbitrage. It should issue no securities. The firm should invest its idle cash in bonds when the tax rate is between 21.25% and 29.41% (region II in Figure 8.2) and in preferred stocks when the tax rate is between 29.41% and 33.33% (region III in Figure 8.2).

The firm's strategy for high tax rates (t greater than 33.33%) is to issue bonds and buy preferred stocks (region IV in Figure 8.2). Since the cost of issuing bonds is increasing in the amount issued, the firm should stop issuing bonds when the after-tax cost of issuing them is equal to the after-tax rate of return from investing

Chapter 8 The Importance of Marginal Tax Rates and Difficulties in Calculating

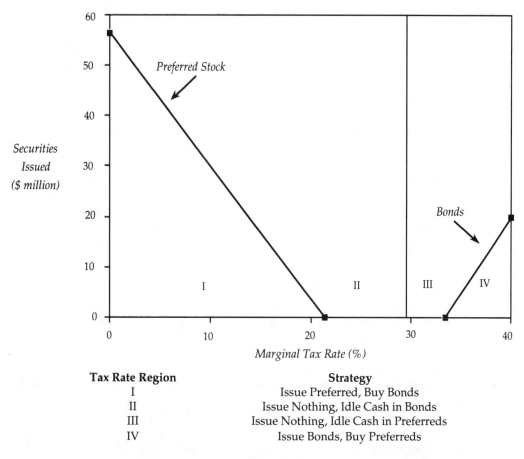

FIGURE 8.2   Desirable Investment and Financing Strategies in the
Presence of Borrowing Premiums on Bonds and Preferred Stocks

the proceeds in preferred stocks issued by other corporations (or 6%(1 - .2t)). How
much should the firm borrow by issuing bonds? It should issue B million dollars
worth, where B solves

$$.06(1 - .2t) = (.084 + .0004B)(1 - t). \qquad (8.2)$$

For example, at t = 37%, $10.48 million of bonds should be issued.

Once we have decided on the optimal amount and type of clientele-based
arbitrage for different marginal tax rates, the firm must now determine its
marginal tax rates to implement the desired tax plan. These marginal tax rates will
differ depending on when income is received and the history of income realizations. Let's take a closer look at these calculations.[5]

---

[5]Although the approach we adopt below is perfectly valid for the problem we face, it is generally safer,
in multiperiod problems under uncertainty, to work backward from the terminal (or final-period)
cash flows to the present. We will employ this dynamic programming approach in later chapters.

8.2   Dynamic Tax-Planning Strategies for Low Marginal-Tax-Rate Firms

Beginning of Year 1 Analysis

Since the firm started the year with $20 million of NOL carryforwards, it will not begin to pay tax until it generates $20 million of taxable income. Since the firm realizes income of either $15 million or -$10 million in any year, the firm must realize $15 million of income in at least two of the next three years or else it will never pay any explicit taxes. And if income of $15 million occurs twice and a loss of $10 million occurs once, the NOLs of $20 million just get used up.

The NOLs would also get used up, and taxes would begin to be paid, if operating income of $15 million is realized only once and interest income of $25 million can also be generated from bond investments ($-20 + 15 - 10 \times 2 + 25 = 0$). But as shown below, this requires a larger issuance of preferred stock, with the proceeds used to buy bonds, than would be desirable. To see this, note first that if the firm invested a dollar in fully taxable bonds at an 8% annual rate of interest, it accumulates to $1.2597 in 3 years, of which $.2597 is taxable income. With $30 million of cash on hand at the beginning of year 1, the firm could earn interest income of $7.79 million in 3 years (or $.2597 \times $30 million). In addition, if the firm generates $15 million of net-operating income the first year, followed by -$10 million of net-operating income in year 2, an additional $1.2 million (or $15 million $\times$ 8%) plus $0.5 million (or ($1.2 million + $15 million - $10 million) $\times$ 8%) of interest income can be generated in years 2 and 3, respectively.

Even if the firm generates investment income by investing in fully taxable bonds, if it realizes $15 million in operating income only once in 3 years, it is left at least $15.51 million short (or $25.00 - $7.79 - $1.20 - $0.50) of using up its NOLs by the end of year 3.[6] To eliminate the $15.51 million shortfall, the firm must invest at least $59.72 million more in bonds (or $15.51 / .2597) at the beginning of year 1, financed by issuing preferred stock. But such a level of preferred stock issuance could not be justified at any positive tax rate. At the $59.72 million level, the last dollar of preferred stock issued would cost the firm 8.09% (or 6.3% + .03% $\times$ 59.72) which exceeds the pretax return of 8% on bonds. This can also be seen from the $60-million-dollar row of Table 8.3, where it is indicated that the marginal tax rate would have to be negative for this strategy to be profitable. Therefore, the interest income on bonds will never change the marginal tax rate for your client. This is so because the level of interest income on bonds is never great enough to affect whether, or in what year, the NOLs are used up. The strategy here is to exploit low or high tax rates until the cost to issue bonds or preferred stocks becomes too high to engage in further clientele-based arbitrage.

Let us now turn to the possible income realizations, the probabilities of realizing these incomes, and the marginal tax rates. These are displayed in Table 8.5. Remember that the probability of realizing $15 million of operating income is 60%. So the firm could realize $15 million of operating income three times in a row with probability .216 (or .6 $\times$ .6 $\times$ .6). There are eight possible sequences (cases). These cases are ($15, $15, $15), ($15, $15, -$10), ($15,-$10, $15), ($15, -$10, -$10), (-$10, $15, $15), (-$10, $15, -$10),(-$10, -$10, $15), and (-$10, -$10, -$10).

---

[6]The shortfall will be larger if the $15 million operating income realization takes place in year 2 or 3 rather than in year 1.

Chapter 8   The Importance of Marginal Tax Rates and Difficulties in Calculating

Table 8.5 Expected Marginal Tax Rate at the Beginning of Year 1

Year 1	Year 2	Year 3	Probability	Year NOLs Used Up	Marginal Tax Rate
15	15	15	0.216[a]	2	0.377[d]
15	15	-10	0.144[b]	2	0.377
15	-10	15	0.144	3	0.356[e]
-10	15	15	0.144	3	0.356
Other four cases			0.352[c]	Never	0.000

[a] $.6^3$
[b] $.6^2 \times .4$
[c] $1.0 - .216 - .144 \times 3$
[d] $.4/1.06$
[e] $.4/1.06^2$

Expected marginal tax rate before clientele-based arbitrage strategies
$= .216 \times .377 + .144 \times (.377 + .356 + .356) + .352 \times 0$
$= 23.84\%$

The marginal tax rate conditional on realizing a particular sequence of outcomes is the present value of the tax to be paid on an extra dollar of fully taxable income for that case. That is, if the NOL will be used up in year 2, which is one year from now, the marginal tax rate is .377 (or .4/1.06). That is, an additional dollar of taxable income today will trigger an extra $.40 of tax one year from today when the NOL is used up. At a discount rate of 6% after tax, this is equivalent to paying a marginal tax of 37.7 cents in year 1. Similarly, if income does not become taxable until year 3, the present value of the marginal tax rate is 35.6%. The expected marginal tax rate at the beginning of year 1 before any clientele-based arbitrage is undertaken is 23.84%. This is calculated by multiplying the probabilities of each income realization by the marginal tax rate corresponding to that income pattern and adding them all up (or, in this case, 37.7% × (.216 + .144) + 35.6% × (.144 + .144) + 0% × .352 = 23.84%).

Given this marginal tax rate, our earlier calculations indicate that the best strategy is to issue no new securities.[7] There are no profitable clientele-based arbitrage strategies available. On the other hand, idle cash should be invested in bonds to yield an expected 6.1% after tax (or 8% × (1 - .2384)) versus 5.6% (or 6% × (1 - .2 × .2384)) if invested in preferred stock of other companies.

Beginning of Year 2 Analysis

The marginal tax rate will be affected by the income realization in the first year (either $15 million or -$10 million), so you must undertake two separate analyses of what to do in year 2. We begin with the case in which year 1 operating income is $15 million. Table 8.6 provides the details behind the marginal tax rate calculations.

---

[7]In this chapter, we assume that the decision-maker is risk-neutral and that the costs of switching from one clientele to another over time are zero. If these assumptions were relaxed, it might be inappropriate to use the expected marginal tax rate to determine optimal investment and financing strategies. Instead, we would calculate the expected utility of the decision-maker across the alternatives, taking account of the costs of changing strategies over time. We will address this issue to some extent in the next chapter.

Table 8.6 Expected Marginal Tax Rate at the Beginning of Year 2 (Given $15 Million of Income in Year 1)

Year 1	Year 2	Year 3	Probability	Year NOLs Used Up	Marginal Tax Rate
15	15	15	0.360	2	0.400
	15	-10	0.240	2	0.400
	-10	15	0.240	3	0.377
	-10	-10	0.160	Never	0.000

Expected marginal tax rate at the beginning of year 2 before clientele-based arbitrage strategies: 33.06% (or 40% × (.36 + .24) + 37.7% × .24 + 0% × .16)

With a $15 million income realization in year 1, the expected marginal tax rate before clientele-based arbitrage strategies is 33.06%. At this rate, it remains optimal not to issue any new securities. However, idle cash should now be invested in preferred stock rather than in bonds.

Let's turn next to the case in which year 1 operating income is -$10 million. Table 8.7 shows that the marginal tax rate in this case is only 13.58%. Here the corporation should issue preferred stock and buy bonds. The amount of securities to issue is found from

$$.063 + .0003 \times P = .08 \times (1 - .1358),$$

where P denotes the amount of preferred stock to issue (in millions of dollars). Solving for P, $20.45 million of preferred shares should be issued. In addition, idle cash should be invested in bonds.

Table 8.7 Expected Marginal Tax Rate at the Beginning of Year 2 (Given -$10 Million of Income in Year 1)

Year 1	Year 2	Year 3	Probability	Year NOLs Used Up	Marginal Tax Rate
-10	15	15	0.360	3	0.377
	Other three cases		0.640	Never	0.000

Expected marginal tax rate at the beginning of year 2 before clientele-based arbitrage strategies: 13.58%.

Beginning of Year 3 Analysis

Four possible pairs of income realizations could have occurred coming into year 3:

	Year 1	Year 2
(i)	-10	-10
(ii)	-10	15
(iii)	15	-10
(iv)	15	15

An optimal strategy must be determined for each of these four cases.

In case (i), the marginal tax rate is 0%, since the firm cannot use up its NOLs even if income in year 3 is $15 million. Therefore, the firm should issue preferred stock until the marginal cost of doing so is equal to the 8% after-tax rate the

Chapter 8   The Importance of Marginal Tax Rates and Difficulties in Calculating

Table 8.8 Summary of Optimal Strategies

	Preceding Year Incomes	Marginal Tax Rate	Bonds* Issued	Preferred Stock* Issued	Idle Cash Invested in:
1	—	23.84%	$0.00	$0.00	Bonds
2	15	33.06%	0.00	0.00	Preferreds
	-10	13.58%	0.00	20.45	Bonds
3	-10, -10	0.00%	0.00	56.67	Bonds
	-10, 15	24.00%	0.00	0.00	Bonds
	15, -10	24.00%	0.00	0.00	Bonds
	15, 15	40.00%	20.00	0.00	Preferreds

*In millions of dollars.

corporation can earn by investing in bonds. As determined by equation 8.1, the firm should issue $56.67 million of preferred stock. In addition, idle cash should be invested in bonds.

In case (iv), the marginal tax rate is 40%, since no unused NOLs remain even if income in year 3 is -$10 million. Therefore, the firm should issue bonds until the after-tax marginal cost is equal to the 5.52% after-tax rate the corporation can earn by investing in preferred stocks. The desired amount of bonds is $20 million as determined by equation 8.2. The proceeds should be invested in preferred stock.

Cases (ii) and (iii) are symmetric. If income in year 3 is $15 million, the marginal tax rate becomes 40%. Otherwise it becomes 0%. Since the probability of the former outcome is .6, the firm's expected marginal tax rate is 24% (or .6 × .4). At this tax rate, issuing either type of security is undesirable, and idle cash is invested in bonds.

In Table 8.8 we summarize the optimal strategies. Although this case analysis already appears complicated, in more realistic settings the firm has many more tax-planning options available to it.[8] Issuing preferred stock to buy bonds is not necessarily the most effective way to exploit the firm's temporarily low tax rate. The firm might consider a number of other strategies:

- Enter into deferred-compensation contracts with employees.
- Sell some equipment to high marginal-tax-rate taxpayers that can better use accelerated depreciation deductions, and lease back the equipment at a bargain rental rate, thereby realizing an implicit tax subsidy.
- Form an R&D partnership with high marginal-tax-rate taxpayers to allow them to obtain the tax benefits from writing off R&D expenditures in exchange for current income.
- Retire any current outstanding debt and issue preferred stock (or issue common stock if it bears high implicit taxes).

[8]The analysis becomes more complex if future income can give rise to losses that create net operating loss carrybacks after the net operating loss carryforwards have been temporarily used up. This has been analyzed formally by Terry Shevlin, "Estimating Corporate Marginal Tax Rates," *Journal of the American Taxation Association* (Spring, 1990), pp. 51-67. Shevlin also uses a simulation procedure (to capture uncertainty in future taxable income) to estimate explicit marginal tax rates for 200 publicly traded corporations.

- Consider a merger with a company that faces a higher marginal tax rate. A highly taxed organization might be able to pay more for the right to use the firm's NOLs than they are worth internally to the firm. However, in a friction-filled world, there is good reason to expect that NOL companies will not be able to sell their losses for anywhere near $.40 on the dollar (the statutory tax rate in the case):

  1. For many profitable corporations, the marginal tax rate may be less than the explicit statutory rate for reasons we have already discussed (i.e., organizational-form or clientele-based arbitrage opportunities).

  2. The cost to evaluate a prospective merger partner can be very large, and buyers must charge for these costs. In addition, buyers must worry about hidden information problems as we discussed in Chapter Seven.

  Note that if the firm's future tax rates are decreasing because of statutory decreases in rates and it cannot use up its NOLs internally before statutory tax rates decline, a merger with a high-tax-rate firm becomes more desirable than when tax rates are constant or increasing through time.

Of course, costs to implement a tax-motivated restructuring apply to all of these alternatives. A sale and leaseback requires contracting costs, monitoring costs, and possibly explicit tax costs like depreciation recapture, as we will discuss more fully in later chapters. R&D limited partnerships may be very expensive to organize and operate and may suffer from severe incentive problems as we discuss in the chapter on tax shelters. Retiring debt is also not costless to the firm. As always, efficient tax planning requires that these frictions be considered very carefully.

8.3 Tax-Planning Analysis for Firms with Investment Tax Credit Carryforwards (ITCs)

Suppose that instead of NOLs, your firm had ITCs of $5 million that expire in one year. Suppose that ITCs can offset 75% of the tax on ordinary income in any tax year (that is, if tax on ordinary income is $100, then $75 of ITCs can be used to reduce the final tax bill to $25). Assume that if taxable income is negative:

1. the corporation will receive a refund of back taxes at the rate of 40% of the loss, but

2. the firm will also have to repay past ITCs used at the rate of 75% of the tax refund.

The net effect of conditions (1) and (2) above is a refund, per dollar of taxable loss, equal to 10% (or $(1 - .75) \times .4$) of the loss. Your new task is to prescribe an optimal strategy for investment and capital structure for the beginning of year 1. In addition, your client would like to know how sensitive this optimal strategy is to changes in the probability of the firm's operating income being equal to $15 million. In particular, what if the probability changed from 60% to 70%? Or what if it changed to 50% and tax losses give rise to no refund rather than a 10% refund?

Note that at a 40% tax rate, each dollar of taxable income gives rise to $.40 in tax and $.30 of ITC utilization. With $5 million of ITCs, $16.67 million (or $5 million/.3) of taxable income is required to use up all the ITCs. Unless the ITCs are fully used up, the marginal tax rate is 10%: each dollar of taxable income gives rise to $.40 in tax and $.30 in tax credits.

From the calculation above, even if $15 million in operating income is generated, this is $1.67 million short of using up all the ITCs. Unless further taxable income is generated, the marginal tax rate would remain 10%. The same marginal tax rate applies if income of -$10 million is realized. At a 10% tax rate, it is clearly preferable to invest idle cash in bonds rather than preferred stocks. Indeed, if the marginal rate remains below 21.3% after investing idle cash in bonds, the earlier analysis indicates that it would pay to issue preferred stock to purchase bonds.

On the other hand, once other taxable income increases by $1.67 million, all available ITCs are used up, and the marginal tax rate increases to 40% following the realization of $15 million of operating income, which occurs with a 60% probability. This happens when $20.833 million (or $1.67/.08) of the available cash is invested in bonds. At this point, the marginal tax rate jumps to 28% (a 40% marginal tax rate with 60% probability plus a 10% marginal tax rate with a 40% probability). At this tax rate, bonds are still the preferred investment vehicle for idle cash, but it is not profitable to issue preferred stock to buy bonds.

Sensitivity Analysis:

1. If the probability increases to 70% that operating income will be $15 million, the only change is that the marginal tax rate jumps to 31% (or $.7 \times .4 + .3 \times .1$) after $20.833 million in cash is invested in bonds. At this rate, preferred stocks provide a higher after-tax return than do bonds, so the remaining $9.167 million in cash is invested in preferred stock rather than bonds.

2. If the probability of realizing $15 million in operating income decreases to 50%, and tax losses give rise to no refund, then once the ITCs are used up following the realization of $15 million of operating income, the firm's marginal tax rate jumps only to 20% (or $.5 \times .4 + .5 \times 0$). At this marginal tax rate, the firm should invest the remainder of the $30 million in bonds. The firm should also issue preferred stock to buy even more bonds. The desired amount of preferred stock to issue, P, in millions of dollars solves

$$.063 + .0003 \times P = .08 \times (1 - .2).$$

So the firm should issue $3.333 million of preferred stock.

Concluding Remarks

These cases were designed to illustrate the calculation of marginal tax rates in the presence of tax loss and tax credit carryforwards and in the presence of uncertainty regarding future taxable income. They were also designed to link marginal tax rates to investment and financing clienteles and to show how a firm may change clienteles through time as its income level changes.

We have assumed that it is costless to change clienteles as circumstances warrant, but in reality this is not so. In the next chapter, we will consider how the costliness of changing clienteles affects the desirability of alternative tax-planning strategies.

Summary of Key Points

1. To calculate the marginal tax cost of a dollar of fully taxable income requires that the effect on the value of future-period tax liabilities be included. One must also include the effects of additional income on the availability of tax deductions and tax credits.

2. Effective tax rates are commonly used to determine the average rate of tax paid by taxpayers. Two popular definitions exist, both of which fail to include implicit taxes and a proper adjustment for the present value of future taxes to be paid.

3. Properly adjusted to include implicit taxes and the present value of deferred taxes, average tax rates allow comparisons across taxpayers of tax burdens per dollar of income. But such tax rates provide little guidance for identifying tax clienteles.

4. For a given configuration of risk-adjusted pretax rates of return on various assets, marginal tax rates sort taxpayers into investment and financing clienteles.

5. Clientele-based arbitrage exploits differences in the total (explicit plus implicit) marginal tax rate that applies to income from different assets. The result of undertaking clientele-based arbitrage is typically to reduce the total marginal tax rate.

6. When statutory tax rates are constant over time, firms that experience net operating loss carryforwards (NOLs) typically face lower marginal tax rates than those that do not.

7. In the presence of NOLs and other carryforwards, the current marginal tax rate is sensitive to future changes in statutory tax rates.

8. In realistic settings, it is rather challenging to calculate the marginal tax rate.

9. As marginal tax rates change over time, so do investment and financing clienteles.

Discussion Questions

1. True or False? Explain.

   a. In undertaking tax-planning strategies, the effective tax rate has no meaning.

   b. In calculating marginal tax rates for the purpose of determining investment and financing clienteles, it is appropriate to ignore deferred taxes.

   c. By borrowing, taxpayers can always reduce their personal tax rate on partnership income to the implicit tax rate on municipal bonds.

   d. The marginal tax rate of firms with net operating loss carryforwards (NOLs) is below that of firms currently paying tax by a discount factor reflecting the delay in when the NOL firm is expected to begin paying taxes.

2. How is the marginal tax rate affected by the presence of rules that reduce current tax deductions by a fraction of incremental income? How is the marginal tax rate affected by the presence of rules that postpone current tax deductions or tax credits by a fraction of incremental income?

3. A case in the chapter describes the tax-planning options available to a firm with net operating losses. Carefully review that analysis. What tax rate makes the firm indifferent between holding preferred stocks and bonds? Why? How can the firm use this information to effect clientele-based arbitrage? If the cost of issuing preferred stock and bonds is increasing in the amount issued or borrowed, how does this affect the clientele-based arbitrage strategies? How does the tax planner compute the probabilities of the firm realizing different operating incomes over the planning horizon? How would you estimate the corporation's marginal tax rate? What decisions can you make using the marginal tax rate? In the case, why would the firm never issue both preferred stock and bonds at the same time? Why do we nevertheless often observe firms with both bonds and preferred stocks in their capital structure?

4. What alternative investment and financing instruments can firms use to alter their marginal tax rate? Why might the firm prefer to repackage its capital structure (the mix of financial instruments it issues to finance operations) instead of changing its operating decisions to effect clientele-based arbitrage?

5. How difficult is it in reality to compute the corporation's marginal tax rate? Why? What are the factors that are really important? If we observe that a firm has net operating losses, does this mean that the firm has not hired a very smart tax-planning strategist?

CHAPTER 9
Dynamic Tax-Planning Considerations

Efficient tax planning requires identifying appropriate taxpayer-specific investment and financing clienteles. This is relatively straightforward in a static environment. But when decisions have uncertain consequences over many tax years, such clienteles depend on the reorganization costs of altering investment and financing policies in response to changes in taxpayers' circumstances. In the presence of uncertainty regarding future pretax cash flows and the tax rules themselves, a premium is placed on contracts that offer flexibility in tax planning to respond to unexpected changes in tax status. But building flexibility into contracts does not come free. For example, it may require a degree of mutual trust among the contracting parties (as in discretionary employee-bonus plans) that cannot be sustained. In addition, flexibility typically requires greater contracting costs.

To illustrate, suppose a firm knows that because its tax rate is high in the current period, it should finance new projects with debt to take advantage of explicit tax deductions for interest payments. The firm is unsure of its future tax rate. It could issue equity, instead, but the implicit tax deduction provided by an equity issue is usually of less value than the explicit tax deduction of bond interest if the firm is fully taxable. A more flexible approach would be to borrow money for one year, and if the firm's tax rate in one year's time remains high, it can issue debt for an additional year. However, certain fixed costs associated with issuing debt make it more economical to issue longer-term debt. Efficient tax planning here requires trading off the transaction cost savings from issuing less flexible debt (that is, long-term debt) against the restructuring cost (or the cost of being in the wrong clientele if this is less than the restructuring cost) in the event the firm's tax rate declines in the future and bonds become more expensive than equity.

Note that the problem cannot be solved simply by issuing callable debt. Lenders also incur fixed costs each time they undertake an investment. They pay brokerage fees and incur costs to investigate the credit risk of the borrower. Still, callable debt does have interesting flexibility features that may make it tax-efficient despite the costs it imposes on the investor.

As another example, let's consider the question of whether to buy or lease depreciable assets, such as office buildings or manufacturing equipment. As we have discussed before, depreciable assets are tax-favored under the present tax system of generous depreciation allowances. As a result, the efficient owners from a tax standpoint are those with the highest marginal tax rates. Those with lower marginal tax rates are better off leasing.

Suppose a firm's tax rate is currently very high, but there is a significant chance that its rate will decline in the future at which point it would no longer be tax-efficient to own depreciable assets. Under what conditions should the firm purchase the depreciable assets? The answer depends on the probability that the firm's tax rate will decline as well as the resulting cost of being in the wrong clientele. If it leases the asset, it bears the cost of being in the wrong clientele now, when its rate is high. The cost of being in the wrong investment or financing clientele at some future date, if the firm's tax rate changes, depends on several factors. We explore three of them here:

- the reversibility of the tax plan,
- the adaptability of the tax plan, and
- the ability to insure against adverse changes in tax status.

9.1   Reversibility of Tax Plans

In some contracts, if tax rates or tax rules change in ways that make existing agreements inefficient, the contracts can be voided. If the contract can be voided upon the occurrence of specified tax-related contingencies, then the contract allows for the **reversibility of tax plans**. Consider the following examples.

1. In closely held U.S. corporations, there is always a risk that the IRS will view a salary payment to an owner-manager as a disguised dividend. This would mean that the corporation loses its tax deduction for the payment. The corporate minutes of many closely held organizations provide that if the IRS claims that owner-employees have received excessive compensation, and treats these payments as disguised dividends, the recipients shall return the payments to the corporation. In other words, the transaction is reversed due to the unfavorable tax treatment accorded the transaction, and the firm avoids the cost of being in the wrong clientele for paying a dividend.

2. Many municipal bonds that are used to fund private activities include standard clauses in the contract that provide for a refund to the investor in the event that the IRS deems the bonds to be taxable because they are not issued for an exempt purpose.

3. Many public utilities have issued preferred stock with mandatory redemption features (i.e., the corporation is required to redeem the shares of investors over a period of say five to ten years). This contractual feature could prompt the IRS to argue that the preferred stock should be classified as bonds, because preferred stock is supposed to have unlimited life.

   Now, why would the IRS wish to have the preferred stock treated as bonds for tax purposes? After all, preferred stock dividends are not tax deductible, whereas bond interest is. The reason relates to the investor side of the contract. In particular, while U.S. corporations are exempted from paying tax on a substantial fraction of the preferred stock dividends paid by other U.S. corporations, they are fully taxable on bond interest. And what are the likely tax characteristics of the issuer of the preferred stock? As we described in Chapter Eight, they are likely to have relatively low marginal tax rates. So they cannot use interest deductions as effectively as can other more highly taxed entities.

   An interesting incentive problem may arise if the IRS, upon auditing the tax returns of issuers of redeemable preferred stock, argues that the securities are really bonds rather than preferred stocks. If the issuer agrees to this interpretation, the dividend payment is treated as interest, and a valuable tax deduction results. This would result in a double deduction. The borrower already received an implicit deduction by issuing the preferred stock at a reduced dividend rate to reflect the tax-favored status of dividends to corporate investors. Classifying the securities as bonds at a later date gives rise to an explicit deduction as well. Of course, the preferred stockholders might sue the issuer or the issuer's lawyers in this case. Moreover, the firm's reputation in the capital market might be severely damaged, and this could raise the cost of finance in the future. Finally, if investors were concerned about this incentive problem, they would demand a higher return to compensate them up front, which could prove costly to the issuer.

   To mitigate this incentive problem, the indentures for securities issued by such firms as Public Service of New Mexico, which has issued several series of mandatory redeemable preferred stock, include an indemnity clause. If the holders of the preferred stock lose the dividend-received deduction, Public Service of New Mexico promises to increase the yield. However, they also reserve the right to redeem the entire series immediately in this case. Note that Public Service doesn't *guarantee* to redeem the entire series, however, perhaps because it may be efficient for them to be issuing bonds at that time anyway.

4. An exception to the rule that dividend payments are nondeductible to the U.S. corporations that declare them relates to dividends paid on shares held by Employee Stock Ownership Plans (ESOPs). An ESOP is a type of pension plan that invests primarily in the stock of the employer on behalf of its employees. The tax-deductibility of such dividends has been controversial ever since it was first introduced into the law. To

guard against adverse changes in the law, some shares issued to ESOPs (typically convertible preferred stock) contain provisions making the shares callable at the issuer's discretion in the event the dividend deduction is eliminated.[1]

9.2   Adaptability of the Tax Plan

Most tax plans cannot be reversed without excessive cost. **Adaptive tax planning** is designed to offset the cost of being in the wrong clientele following unexpected changes in tax status where reversibility is impossible or impractical. We discussed this in Chapter Four in the context of corporations that find the partnership form of organization to be tax-advantageous following changes made by the 1986 Tax Act in the U.S. Many corporations would like to have reorganized as a partnership subsequent to the Act. However, for most of them the tax and nontax costs of the reorganization exceeded the tax benefits. If these firms knew when they first organized that the law would change in the future to favor partnerships, many of them might have organized as a partnership from the start. We also discussed ways in which corporations could undertake transactions that would move them closer to *de facto* partnership tax treatment without undergoing changes in legal organizational form. In particular, the corporate tax burden is mitigated when the corporation distributes pretax profits to owners, employees, and other factor suppliers in forms that are tax-deductible at the corporate level. For example, owner-employees could tie their compensation more closely to their firm's profitability.

If a firm purchases depreciable assets and its tax rate declines, the costs of selling the assets may far outweigh the benefits. In addition to the costs to broker the deal, the transaction might give rise to ordinary taxable income as well as taxable capital gains, as we will discuss in the chapters on real estate investments. Moreover, for tax purposes, the new owner may not be able to use as generous a depreciation schedule as the old owner. For example, office buildings purchased during the period 1981-1984 in the U.S. were depreciable over a 15-year period on an accelerated basis. If the building were sold after 1986, however, its new owners would be entitled only to straight-line depreciation over 31.5 years (or 40 years for alternative minimum tax purposes).

But if the firm's objective in selling the property is to transfer the rights to depreciation deductions to a higher-bracket taxpayer, better alternatives might be available. In particular, it could be less costly to restructure other assets and equities of the firm. For example, tax-favored assets like municipal bonds or common stocks might be sold and replaced with ordinary income-producing assets, like high-yield bonds, at reduced transaction costs. Or firms might issue stock and purchase bonds with the proceeds. If the firm can use these substitutes at sufficiently low cost, it would not be very costly for the firm to be in the wrong investment clientele if tax rates (before adaptive tax planning takes place) decline unexpectedly.

---

[1] See, for example, Morgan Stanley's "Leveraged ESOP Presentation for Unocal Corporation," February 15, 1989, p. III-3.

Transaction Costs and Tax Clienteles

Let's illustrate how the joint presence of transaction costs and uncertainty with respect to future tax status can influence tax clienteles. Suppose you are choosing between two investments, fully taxable bonds yielding 10% per year and tax-exempt bonds yielding 7% per year. Both investments have *three-year* maturities. At the time of investment, you are unsure (because of the uncertain profitability of your other investments already in place) as to whether your tax rate will be 40% over the 3 years or 0%. You assess a 70% chance of the former. This makes your expected marginal tax rate 28% (or $.7 \times 40\% + .3 \times 0\%$).

Note that if you are risk-neutral, and if you must choose one investment or the other and hold it for the entire three-year period, you would be better off choosing taxable bonds. At an expected tax rate of 28%, taxable bonds yield 7.2% after tax while tax-exempt bonds yield only 7%.[2]

Now let us consider what your optimal strategy would be if you could sell your asset and purchase the other at the end of the first year at an annualized cost of 1% after tax. Suppose that at the end of the first year you will discover whether your tax rate for the next 2 years (as well as for the year just ended) will be 40% or 0%.

Note that if you purchase taxable bonds, you will wish you had purchased exempt bonds if your tax rate turns out to be 40%. At a tax rate of 40%, exempt bonds yield 7% and taxable bonds yield 6% after tax. But if the annualized cost of switching from taxable to tax-exempt bonds is 1% after tax, there would be no advantage to switching, and you will be stuck earning 6% after tax in years 2 and 3.

On the other hand, if you purchase exempt bonds and your tax rate turns out to be 0%, you will wish you had purchased taxable bonds, since taxable bonds would yield 10% after tax, or 3% more than tax-exempt bonds. But at least you could secure a 9% return in years 2 and 3 (10% less the 1% annualized transaction cost) by switching to taxable bonds.

So taxable bonds continue to yield an expected after-tax return of 7.2% per year when switching is allowed at the end of the first year at an annualized cost of 1% after tax. But investing in tax-exempt bonds and switching to taxables if tax rates turn out to be 0% yields 7.4% *per year*, calculated as follows:

Tax Rate	Probability	First Year After-Tax Return	Return in Years 2 and 3
40%	70%	7%	7%
0%	30%	7%	9%*

*10% taxable bond less 1% transaction cost

Expected after-tax accumulation per dollar invested:

$$\$1(.7 \times 1.07^3 + .3 \times 1.07 \times 1.09^2) = \$1.24$$

---

[2] If you are sufficiently risk-averse, you might prefer the tax-exempt bonds since they yield 7% for sure whereas taxable bonds yield 10% after tax 30% of the time and 6% after tax 70% of the time. Although taxable bonds generate a higher *expected* return, the return is also riskier due to tax rate uncertainty. Note that tax-exempt bonds are taxed at a known implicit tax rate.

The expected rate of return per year is $1.24^{1/3} - 1$ or 7.4%. In this case, tax-exempt bonds emerge as the investment of choice due to the greater value of the restructuring option.

We leave it as an exercise for the reader to verify that in the absence of transaction costs, *taxable bonds* would be the investment of choice. They would yield 7.7% per year after tax, versus 7.6% for tax-exempt bonds. In the absence of transaction costs, optimal decisions can be made simply by knowing the expected tax rates. This is no longer true in the presence of transaction costs.

Adaptability in Investment and Financing Decisions

In the presence of tax rate uncertainty and transaction costs, it can pay to purchase or issue short-term securities at less favorable yields relative to longer-term securities. Short-term securities introduce an element of flexibility that is valuable in such circumstances. For similar reasons, it might pay to issue callable securities or to purchase puttable securities, even if such options are costly; or it might be desirable to issue (or purchase) securities that can be repurchased (resold) in the marketplace at low cost.

This problem is related to the one of choosing the efficient duration of legal agreements where there is a tradeoff between the fixed costs of writing contracts and the deteriorating efficiency of the agreements over time as circumstances change. In our tax-planning problem, one of the sources of deteriorating efficiency of the agreements is the possibility of being in the wrong tax clientele due to unexpected changes in tax rates.

9.3 Ability to Insure Against Adverse Changes in Tax Status

Tax status can change unexpectedly for at least two reasons besides uncertain future profitability:

- uncertainty about how the taxing authority and the courts will interpret the tax laws, and
- uncertain future legislative changes in the tax law.

In a number of countries, including the U.S. and Canada, a taxpayer can reduce tax-treatment uncertainty by requesting an advance ruling from the tax authority on how a proposed transaction will be treated for tax purposes. In the U.S., such requests must include a comprehensive statement of facts describing the proposed transaction, along with a documentation of the relevant points of judicial, statutory, and secondary authority. The legal costs of such requests are typically in the $15,000 to $30,000 range, but some requests can be quite a bit more costly, especially those involving complicated multinational corporate reorganizations. Of course, there is a risk in seeking such clarification of the rules. The IRS may rule unfavorably and will likely audit the return unless the return is filed in a manner consistent with the ruling. As a result, the taxpayer might have been better off undertaking the transaction without a ruling request, taking an aggressive position on the tax return, and hoping that the IRS would either ignore the issue or that the examining agent would rule favorably.

A second way that a taxpayer can secure insurance against unexpected tax treatment is to purchase professional legal opinions. Tax-sheltered limited partnership investments are notorious for the many facets of the investment for which tax treatment uncertainty exists. In fact, the Securities and Exchange Commission requires that all limited partnership prospectuses contain an extensive section on "Income Tax Aspects" of the investment, which thoroughly discusses uncertainties regarding tax treatment. General comments and warnings such as the following are common:

> As the General Partner has not requested a ruling from the IRS respecting any of the tax consequences of the Partnership, there is an inherent and substantial risk that such benefits claimed might be challenged in whole or in part by the IRS. Such risk is materially increased by reason that direct authority is lacking in several areas involved and that certain of the tax incidents discussed herein are under continuous IRS review.

> (Granada 4, p. 36, 9/23/85)

It is also common to publish the professional opinion of legal counsel in the prospectus. For example:

> With respect to the material tax issues and tax advantages anticipated by an investment in the Partnership, Reynolds, Allen and Cook, Incorporated, counsel to the General Partner and the Partnership, is of the opinion that the significant tax benefits in the aggregate, as anticipated from an investment in the Partnership as discussed herein, probably will be realized by the Partners.

> (*Ibid.*)

Given a legal tax opinion, investors can (and typically do) sue the lawyers in the event that significant expected tax benefits, on which legal counsel has expressed a favorable opinion, are disallowed by the IRS.

The two forms of insurance discussed above both dealt with uncertainty over existing tax rules. But some forms of insurance also exist regarding legislative changes. For example, in November 1984, the U.S. Treasury Department announced its proposal to overhaul the federal income tax system. Among many proposed changes was one to reduce maximum federal tax rates to 35% as of July 1, 1986. Because lower tax rates reduce the value of depreciation deductions, many limited partnerships that invest in real estate and other depreciable assets were having trouble raising funds in the face of this uncertainty. In response to investor concern, a number of partnership contracts provided that the limited partners' share of profits would be increased if the tax proposals were passed. An example is the Stanford Capital Realty Fund, Ltd.:

> The General Partner has agreed, in the event of reduction in the Maximum Tax Rate effective for any year prior to 1990, to reduce its interest in Net Sale or Refinancing Proceeds available for distribution after the

Capital Return Date (that is, after limited partners have already received distributions from the partnership equal to 100% of their initial investment), to attempt to mitigate any adverse impact upon Limited Partners of such a reduction in the Maximum Tax Rate.

The Prospectus then gives the tax-rate-contingent formula for sharing profits and works through an example based on tax-loss projections given in the prospectus. If the maximum Federal tax rate on July 1, 1986 were to decline to 35% in the example, "[t]he percentage of Net Sale or Refinancing Proceeds to which the Limited Partners would be entitled would increase from the current 83.33% to 95.17% (and the General Partner interest would decline from 16.67% to 4.83%)."

Another uncertainty back in early 1986 related to the fate of the Investment Tax Credit (ITC) in the pending tax bill. Although tax reform was discussed throughout 1986, there was considerable doubt as to whether a tax bill would be passed at all. Conditional on passage, it was uncertain whether the ITC would disappear and if so, whether the elimination would be retroactive to January 1, 1986, July 1, 1986, January 1, 1987, or some other date. To insure against loss of ITC benefits for investors, PLM, a major syndicator of equipment leasing deals, wrote contracts in early 1986 guaranteeing that if investment tax credits were lost between January 1, 1986 and July 1, 1986 (and they were), PLM would guarantee a generous level of leasing income to investors.

A third example involves the creation in 1985 of a limited partnership (Enserch Exploration Partners, Ltd.) by Enserch Corporation.[3] The prospectus describing the transaction extolled the virtues of being taxed as a partnership but warned of the risk that legislation could be passed, the result of which would subject the partnership to corporate taxation. To induce investors to purchase units in the partnership in the face of this risk, unit-holders were given an option to resell their units to the issuer at a price linked to the initial offering price if the unfavorable legislation were passed.

The illustrations above involving Stanford Capital Realty, PLM, and Enserch are all examples of **tax indemnities**. The issuer of securities indemnifies the investor against less favorable tax treatment than that promised. Such indemnities may conserve costs in that investors need not research the tax rules as comprehensively, given the insurance. On the other hand, the contracting parties should also be sensitive to the allocation of risk if they are risk averse. Tax indemnities typically allocate all of the tax risk to one party, and this is not always efficient. But concentrating the risk in the hands of one party may provide efficient incentives for lobbying against unfavorable changes in tax rules. It may also induce the insuring party to effect adaptive tax planning (i.e., organizational restructuring) following changes in tax rules.

As another example of tax indemnities, $15 billion worth of so-called (tax-exempt) industrial revenue bonds, issued between 1982 and 1985, contained indentures that would increase interest rates (by as much as 300 basis points, that is, 3%) if statutory corporate tax rates were cut prior to the maturity of the bonds. The objective here was to compensate the bondholders in the event the value of

---

[3] See Donald Christensen, William Moore, and Rodney Roenfeldt, "Equity Valuation Effects of Forming Master Limited Partnerships," Unpublished working paper (January 1989).

the tax exemption feature of their bonds was diminished. As a result of the enactment of the 1986 Tax Act, along with lower tax rates, the interest on such bonds increased by $300 million.[4]

Tax indemnities also arise in connection with employee stock ownership plans (ESOPs). Loans made to the ESOP by certain qualified lenders for the purpose of purchasing stock have been eligible, since 1984, for tax exemption of 50% of the related interest income. Lenders reduce the rate at which they are willing to make such loans because of the 50% interest exemption. It is typical for the firm sponsoring the ESOP to agree to compensate the lender for a variety of adverse changes in the tax law that affect the value of the 50% exemption.[5] In a document entitled "The Decision to Establish a Leveraged Employee Stock Ownership Plan" (1989), Merrill Lynch Capital Markets describes the typical tax indemnities as follows (pp. 20-21):

> Tax indemnities are meant to protect the investor from three risks: (a) a change in statutory tax rates, (b) a change in tax law affecting the investor's 50% interest exclusion, and (c) a disqualification of the employer's ESOP debt or plan. Risks (a) and (b) can be categorized as taxable events and mitigated by a provision which adjusts the ESOP rate up or down to the taxable equivalent rate of return to which the investor originally committed. Risk (c) is an event under the employer's control. Should the employer cause the ESOP debt or plan to become disqualified, the ESOP rate would be grossed-up to the taxable equivalent yield and the employer would reimburse the investor for any penalties and/or other costs or taxes incurred by the investor.

Still another example is the indemnity that Bankers Trust New York Corporation provided to its preferred stock shareholders in August 1989. The Prospectus Supplement for its "Fixed/Adjustable Rate Cumulative Preferred Stock, Series D," on page S-9, contains a section entitled "Changes in the Dividends Received Percentage." Recall that U.S. corporations receiving dividend income from other U.S. corporations are exempted from taxation on a large fraction of the income (Internal Revenue Code Section 243). In the case of the Bankers Trust preferred stock issue, the relevant fraction (often referred to as the "dividends received deduction percentage") is 70%. The Prospectus Supplement contains the following provision:

> If one or more amendments to the Internal Revenue Code of 1986, as amended (the "Code"), are enacted that change the percentage specified in Section 243 (a) (1) of the Code or any successor provision (the "Dividends Received Percentage"), then the (Dividend) Rate ... for Dividend Periods commencing on or after the effective date of such change shall be adjusted by multiplying the Rate ... by a factor, which will be the number determined in accordance with the following formula, and rounding the result to the nearest basis point:

---

[4] *Fortune* (November 9, 1987), p. 120.

[5] See Lawrence N. Bader and Jenny A. Hourihan, *The Investor's Guide to ESOP Loans* (Salomon Brothers, Inc.), March 1989.

$$\frac{1 - .34 (1 - .70)}{1 - .34 (1 - DRP)}$$

For purposes of the above formula, "DRP" means the Dividends Received Percentage applicable to the dividend in question.

A final way to insure against unfavorable changes in tax laws is to purchase investments that will be affected *favorably* by the tax law changes (or take short positions in securities that will decline in value if the tax laws are changed). For example, if you were concerned about unexpected declines in federal tax rates, you might wish to avoid the purchase of municipal bonds, the prices of which are likely to fall if tax rates are reduced as they become less tax-favored.[6] Similarly, a syndicator of real estate deals might sensibly have taken short positions in the common stock of real-estate investment companies prior to passage of the 1981 or 1986 Tax Acts in the U.S. The 1981 Act was extremely favorable to real estate and the 1986 Act was rather unfavorable, so a loss on the short position would have occurred in 1981 and a gain would have resulted in 1986. These gains and losses would have offset the changes in profitability from the syndication business.

9.4 Tax Planning when a Taxpayer's Marginal Tax Rate is Strategy-Dependent

In many tax-planning situations, the firm's marginal tax rate is affected by the very decisions that the firm undertakes to alter its investment and financing activities. For example, if the firm buys bonds with the proceeds of a preferred stock issue, the additional taxable cash flows generated from the bond interest income can affect the computation of the marginal tax rate. If clientele-based arbitrage activities do alter a firm's marginal tax rate, it cannot rely on its initial calculation to make an optimal decision. This is what we mean when we say that the computation of the marginal tax rate is **strategy-dependent**. Strategy-dependence increases the complexity of tax-planning.

We have already illustrated the concept of strategy dependence in Chapter Six where we showed that a taxpayer subject to a progressive tax would wish to engage in certain clientele-based arbitrage transactions only in limited volume. The reason is that as the transactions alter the investor's marginal tax rate, the attractiveness of further transactions decreases.

Unanticipated changes in tax rules and tax status should be viewed as the rule rather than the exception for most taxpayers. It is important to factor in such uncertainty into the tax-planning process, and to be prepared to plan one's way out of being situated in undesired clienteles as nature resolves the uncertainty. Our objective is to provide you with tools necessary to approach this task in a systematic and rational fashion.

---

[6] For empirical evidence of this, see James M. Poterba, "Explaining the Yield Spread between Taxable and Tax-exempt Bonds: The Role of Expected Tax Policy," in *Studies in State and Local Public Finance*, edited by Harvey S. Rosen, pp. 5-49 (University of Chicago Press), 1986.

Summary of Key Points

1. Because it is costly to change investment and financing clienteles as tax status changes, taxpayers place a premium on strategies that allow activities to be reorganized at low cost.

2. Contractual arrangements that can be voided upon the occurrence of specified tax-related contingencies introduce an element of reversibility into tax plans.

3. Adaptive tax planning is designed to offset the cost of being in the wrong clientele following unexpected changes in tax status where reversibility is impossible or impractical.

4. In the presence of transaction costs to change investment and financing clienteles, taxpayers need to know more than simply expected marginal tax rates to choose efficient tax-planning strategies. For example, it is important to know the probability distribution of tax rates as well as the costs of changing investment and financing strategies in the event that changes in tax rates cause investors to be in the wrong clienteles.

5. Uncertainty about how the taxing authority and the courts will interpret the tax laws, uncertainty about future legislative changes in tax law, and uncertainty about future income represent sources of change in tax status that may place taxpayers into undesirable investment and financing clienteles.

6. Tax-treatment uncertainty can be mitigated by requiring an advance ruling from the taxing authority on how a proposed transaction will be treated for tax purposes.

7. Professional legal opinions can also reduce tax-treatment uncertainty. Such opinions are often published for the benefit of third parties who rely on representations made regarding favorable tax treatment of particular contractual arrangements.

8. In many contracts, one party explicitly indemnifies other parties against tax treatment that turns out to be less favorable than that promised. Such provisions are designed to reduce the costs of contracting.

9. A taxpayer's marginal tax rate is often affected by the very investment and financing strategies implemented to take advantage of its initial tax status. This adds an element of "recursion" to tax planning. We refer to marginal tax rates in this case as being strategy-dependent.

Appendix 9.1[7]

To close our discussion of dynamic tax planning and make a link to our first "applications" chapter, which is on compensation planning, we consider a tax-planning problem relating to "medical expense reimbursement plans." In the U.S., medical expenses (including insurance premiums) are tax-deductible only to the extent they exceed 7.5% of so-called "adjusted gross income." So if your salary plus other income were equal to $100,000, you could not normally deduct the first $7,500 in health care costs.

If your employer establishes a qualified plan, however, you can have part of your salary paid into a medical reimbursement plan. The salary you contribute into the plan will not be taxed to you. And the reimbursements you receive for medical expenses will not be taxable. The end result is that you obtain tax deductions for your medical expenses.

But there is a hitch. You must decide at the beginning of the year how much to contribute to the plan. Any excess of contributions over reimbursements for the year is nonrefundable. Instead, the excess goes to cover administrative costs of the plan.

Suppose your tax rate is 30%. Let C denote your contributions into the plan, and let M denote your medical expenses for the year, which are uncertain in amount as of the beginning of the year. If you set C too low (below M), you sacrifice 30 cents worth of tax benefits for each dollar of unfunded medical expenses. Why? You lose a tax deduction of M - C dollars. On the other hand, if you set C too high (above M), you will lose the excess at an after-tax cost of 70 cents for each dollar of excess funding.

Note that as stated, this is a "newsboy problem": if you underfund (you "stock out" of inventory) you lose 30 cents per dollar of underfunding; and if you overfund (you have excess perishable inventory that must be scrapped), you lose 70 cents per dollar of overfunding. The optimal amount of funding is some amount *below* your best guess of medical costs because of the higher cost of overfunding than underfunding.

Now how does this relate to dynamic tax planning? On the adaptability dimension, if your demand for medical services falls below your funding level, you may be able to accelerate routine checkups or medical treatments that would normally be undertaken the following year; or you might try to arrange to prepay for next year's medical insurance. As for reversibility, if you tax plan "cooperatively" with your employer, then your employer could agree to supplement your salary in the event your medical expenses fall well below funding levels. In this case, you might be inclined to fund substantially more than in the case in which all overfunded amounts are forfeited to the plan. Of course, the tax-planning advantages of these arrangements must be balanced against the administrative costs of implementing them.

---

[7] This section was stimulated by a problem developed by Evan Porteus for a decision sciences course taught in the Stanford MBA program.

Discussion Questions

1. What does it mean if a tax plan is reversible? Give some examples to illustrate this concept. What costs are associated with contractual provisions that make tax plans reversible?

2. What is the meaning of the terms "adaptability of tax plans?" Give some examples to illustrate the concept. What are the costs of undertaking such plans?

3. Why might a firm offer insurance against adverse changes in tax status? Do you think we see a great deal of this form of insurance? Why or why not?

4. Why might the taxing authority agree to provide advance rulings on the tax treatment of proposed transactions? Why might it refuse to make rulings in some cases?

5. Why would a taxpayer be willing to pay a lawyer to provide a written opinion to a third party of the tax treatment to be accorded a particular set of transactions?

6. What is meant by the term "strategy-dependence" as it relates to the computation of the marginal tax rate? How does strategy-dependence affect the computation of the marginal tax rate? How does it affect decision-making strategies?

7. How could a company that holds significant quantities of oil in inventory protect itself against the risk of an excise tax being imposed on the sale of oil?

8. Consider the illustration in Section 9.2 where an investment choice was being made between taxable and tax-exempt bonds in the presence of tax rate uncertainty and transaction costs.

    a. Would you prefer to invest in 3-year taxable bonds or 3-year tax-exempt bonds (yielding 10% and 7% pretax, respectively) if the annualized cost to switch from taxable to tax-exempt bonds (or *vice versa*) at the end of year 1 were 3% rather than 1%?

    b. If instead of 3-year bonds that yield 10% per year (taxable) and 7% per year (tax-exempt), you could buy 1-year bonds at yields of 9.75% for taxables and 6.83% for tax-exempts, would you do so?

Problem

Suppose you operate a very profitable sole proprietorship (keep dreaming). Your current-year marginal tax rate is 40% but you expect it to increase to 50% next year due to legislative changes.

Your business includes exclusive rights to distribute microcomputer software packages in specified geographical areas. Your typical gross margin on software sales for the programs distributed is an impressive 50%.

The end of the year is approaching and you wonder whether a special price reduction to promote sales in the current tax year would be desirable. You assess that a 10% across-the-board price reduction for the remainder of the year will generate $400,000 of new sales, but $800,000 of normal sales for the rest of the year will be made at a 10% discount.

Moreover, $1,000,000 of *next* year's sales will be cannibalized. That is, a 10% price cut will result in $1,000,000 of next year's product line being sold this year for $900,000, and $800,000 of normal sales for the rest of this year will yield only $720,000 in revenues, but you will also pick up $400,000 in new sales this year.

a. How much better or worse off would you be *before and after tax* if you employ the year-end sales strategy and it goes according to plan?

Your clientele fall roughly into three categories: corporations (their tax rates typically will not change from this year to next year); retail stores that sell to individuals who are not entitled to tax deductions for the purchase of your software; and stores that sell to small businesses, many of whom face tax rate increases similar to yours. (Suppose such businesses take tax deductions for the purchase of software in the year the software is acquired.)

b. How are these clienteles likely to respond differently to the temporary price cut?

CHAPTER 10
Compensation Planning

In this chapter, we discuss the tax-planning aspects of employee-compensation planning. As in many of the applications chapters, the two themes that we stress are (1) the importance of considering all parties to a contract and (2) the nontax features of the tax-planning alternatives. To begin, Table 10.1 lists a number of categories of compensation, along with their tax treatment to the employee.[1]

Table 10.1 Compensation Alternatives

Category	Employee tax effect
Nontaxable fringe benefits	Never taxed
Pensions	Deferred tax with tax exemption on investment returns
Incentive stock options (ISOs)	Deferred tax at capital gains rates
Deferred compensation	Deferred tax at ordinary rates
Nonqualified stock options (NQOs)	Deferred tax at ordinary rates
Interest-free demand loans	Deferred tax at ordinary rates
Interest-free term loans	Immediately taxed at ordinary rates
Cash salary	Immediately taxed at ordinary rates

Many compensation experts (including those who contribute to the popular press and tax journals) have concluded that the compensation alternatives listed in Table 10.1 are ordered in terms of decreasing desirability. In fact, however, once a global contracting perspective is adopted (one that takes account of both tax and nontax considerations of both the employer and employee) none of the compensation alternatives listed in Table 10.1 can be ranked unambiguously.

---

[1] The idea for proceeding in this fashion was stimulated by the chapter on compensation planning in Ray M. Sommerfeld's book, entitled *Federal Taxes and Management Decisions*, published by Richard D. Irwin (1983-84 edition). Our approach to solving the compensation planning problem differs substantially from his, however.

For example, as we have already demonstrated in Chapter Three, tax reasons alone may favor cash salary over deferred compensation even though it accelerates the date at which the employee must pay tax. In particular, we showed that salary can be the preferred choice by a wide margin when

1. the employee's tax rate is increasing over time,
2. the employer's tax rate is decreasing over time, or
3. the employee can earn at a higher after-tax rate on investment than can the employer.

Moreover, salary can be tax-preferred to deferred compensation even when the employee's tax rate is decreasing over time. For example, the tax rate of many nonmanagement employees dropped from the 25% vicinity to 15% with the passage of the 1986 Tax Act. A deferral of compensation might seem quite desirable under such circumstances. After all, it enables employees to reduce tax payments by 40% per dollar of compensation received (from $.25 to only $.15). Yet in most businesses, salary was tax-preferred in such circumstances. Why? Because the employer's preference for an immediate tax deduction was even stronger than the employee's preference for deferred taxation.

To illustrate this point, consider a corporate employer facing a 46% tax rate in 1986 and a 34% tax rate in 1988. For each $1 of salary deferred from 1986, the employer could afford to pay only $.82 (or $1(1 - .46)/(1 - .34)) in compensation in 1988 (plus after-tax earnings on investment for two years). Each compensation alternative had a present cost to the employer of $.54 after tax. To the employee taxed at a rate of 25%, the $1 salary was worth $.75 after tax. Even at the 15% tax rate in 1988, however, the $.82 in deferred compensation, plus interest for 2 years, had a present value of only .82(1 - .15) or $.70 to the employee. So, despite the employee's drop in tax rate, salary was tax-preferred relative to deferred compensation. If the deferred compensation payment was set at the level that would have made the employer indifferent between salary and deferred compensation, salary would have provided the employee with 75/70, or in excess of 7% more, in after-tax compensation than would deferred compensation.

On the other hand, for more highly-paid employees that faced a 50% marginal tax rate in 1986 and a 28% rate in 1988, deferred compensation was the superior arrangement from a tax standpoint: $1 of salary in 1986 was worth $.50 after tax, and the $.82 in compensation, deferred until 1988, was worth $.59 after tax (or $.82(1 - .28)). This is 18% more than current salary.

Or to go one step further, suppose the employer is a tax-exempt entity, like a university, a municipality, or a charitable foundation. Such entities could have afforded to pay $1 plus after-tax earnings for 2 years for each dollar of compensation deferred from 1986 to 1988. Even if the employee could earn the same after-tax return as the tax-exempt employer, a highly compensated employee in this circumstance would keep $1(1 - .28) or $.72 after tax on the dollar received in 1988, and this is 44% *more* than the $.50 retained on salary received in 1986. Moreover, the employee is unlikely to be able to earn as high an after-tax return as can the tax-exempt employer, thereby providing an additional benefit of compensation deferral. Despite the substantial tax savings, most of these organizations failed to establish compensation deferral programs. Unless the nontax costs of entering into deferred compensation arrangements were extremely high, substantial tax savings were left "lying on the table."

10.1 Salary versus Fringe Benefits

Now that we have illustrated the importance of considering the tax implications of compensation plans to all of the contracting parties, let's consider some of the other compensation alternatives. Let us begin with fringe benefits such as employer-provided term life insurance or business meals. Whether fringe benefits are preferred to salary depends on two factors:

1. whether employees can deduct, on their own tax returns, the cost of fringes they pay for themselves, and

2. the extent to which employees place personal value on employer-provided fringes relative to their cost to the employer.

To illustrate the importance of these two factors, let us consider the following cases.

Example 1: Suppose the employer contemplates paying $1,400 for group term life insurance and group health insurance in lieu of $1,400 in additional salary.

Since the employer receives a $1,400 tax deduction whether the expenditure is for salary or insurance, the employer is indifferent between the two alternatives. Suppose the employee is in a 30% tax bracket. While $1,400 in salary gives rise to $980 in cash after tax, the fringe benefits are nontaxable, so the employee keeps $1,400 worth of benefits after tax. If, on the other hand, the employee were to purchase the fringes directly and could not take a tax deduction for their cost, $2,000 of salary would be required to buy the same benefits:[2]

$$\$2,000(1 - .3) = \$1,400.$$

One problem here is that if these benefits are to qualify for tax-favored treatment, they must be offered on a nondiscriminatory basis to essentially all employees. Unlike cash salary, fringe benefits such as life and health insurance cannot be traded for other commodities very easily. To some employees, the personal value of the benefits could be less than $980 (or $1,400(1 - .3)), the after-tax value of the salary alternative. For example, although costly to the employer, some employees with absolutely no bequest motive find life insurance to be a worthless benefit. For such employees, salary is a more efficient compensation

---

[2] Part or all of the health insurance premiums may be tax-deductible for some employees. An "itemized deduction" for medical expenses (which includes insurance costs) is currently permitted in the U.S. to the extent they exceed 7.5% of "adjusted gross income." In addition, part of the life insurance premium paid by the employer may be taxable to the employee.

Note that **total income** less exempt income (e.g., municipal bond interest income) equals **gross income**. Gross income less **"deductions for adjusted gross income"** (such as business expenses other than those incurred as an employee), equals **adjusted gross income**. Adjusted gross income less the greater of the **standard deduction** and **itemized deductions** (including limited amounts of medical expenses, state and local income and property taxes, interest, charitable contributions, and miscellaneous itemized deductions) and personal exemptions equals **taxable income**. The tax on taxable income is equal to the preliminary tax from the statutory tax rate schedule less tax credits.

component despite the tax-favored treatment accorded these benefits. A related problem arises when a wife and husband receive redundant benefits from their respective employers, such as health insurance that covers the entire family.[3]

Example 2: Employer reimbursement of business meals and entertainment expense.

Suppose an employee incurs expenses of $5,000 for business meals and entertainment for the year. If the employee is reimbursed for these expenses, the reimbursement is nontaxable and no expense deduction is allowed to the employee. If, on the other hand, the employer provides a salary supplement, the payment is taxable but the employee is eligible for a tax deduction.

Prior to the 1986 Tax Act in the U.S., whether the employer reimbursed the employee or provided a salary supplement was largely a matter of indifference to both parties. Although reimbursement would be nontaxable to the employee, the expenses would also become nondeductible, so this "fringe benefit" was really equivalent to the payment of ordinary cash compensation and a deduction. Under the post-Tax Act rules, on the other hand, reimbursement can be better or worse than supplemental cash compensation.

Under the current rules, an employee's business meals and entertainment

1. are only deductible as miscellaneous itemized deductions, and
2. are only deductible to the extent of 80% of the expenditure.
3. Moreover, miscellaneous itemized deductions are deductible from taxable income only to the extent they exceed 2% of "adjusted gross income" (which is taxable income plus itemized deductions plus personal exemptions).
4. If the employer reimburses the employee, the employee reports no income or deductions, but then the employer can only deduct 80% of the reimbursement.

Suppose the employee faces a 30% marginal tax rate, has adjusted gross income (e.g., salary) of $100,000, and has other miscellaneous itemized deductions of $2,500. Assume that the employer's marginal tax rate is 40%. Under the post-1986 rules, should the employee be reimbursed or should the employer simply offer the employee a "bonus" or "salary supplement"?

A $5,000 reimbursement costs the employer:

$$\$5,000 - 40\% \times 80\% \times \$5,000 = \$3,400.$$

The employer is indifferent between this and a salary supplement of $3,400/(1 - 40\%) = \$5,667.[4] Both cost the employer $3,400 after tax. For the employee, the

---

reimbursement leaves $5,000 after tax. On the other hand, the salary supplement leaves the employee better off:

$$\$5,667 - 30\% \times (\$5,667 - 80\% \times \$5,000 + 2\% \times \$5,667) = \$5,133$$

or $133 more after tax.

The salary supplement is fully taxable and the expenses are 80% deductible, but the additional adjusted gross income of $5,667 reduces allowable itemized deductions by 2%. The $133 savings consists of (1) an extra $1,667 deductible by the employer at 40% and taxable to the employee at only 30%, a savings of $167, and (2) additional taxable income to the employee of 2% of $5,667 or $113 taxed at 30%, a cost of $34.

On the other hand, if the employer were a tax-exempt entity, reimbursement would always be the desirable strategy. The employer is indifferent between $5,000 in reimbursement and $5,000 in salary supplement. A $5,000 salary supplement leaves only

$$\$5,000 - 30\% \times (\$5,000 - 80\% \times \$5,000 + 2\% \times \$5,000) = \$4,670$$

or $330 less than reimbursement after tax.

Going one step further, if the other miscellaneous deductions of the employee of the tax-exempt entity had been only $500 rather than $2,500, the difference would have been even more dramatic: a $5,000 salary supplement would leave:

$$\$5,000 - 30\% \times (\$5,000 - 80\% \times \$5,000 + \$1,500 + 2\% \times \$5,000) = \$4,220$$

or $780 less after tax.[5]

Of course, there are nontax factors to consider here as well. These include the incentive effects as well as the administrative costs of reimbursement plans. Reimbursement plans may encourage overspending, although the absence of such an arrangement may lead to underspending.

10.2 Compensatory Loans

To facilitate the purchase of a home upon moving to a new area, key employees are frequently offered interest-free loans as part of their hiring package. Such loans are also used to facilitate the exercise of stock options. The tax treatment depends on the type of interest-free loans, of which there are two broad categories:

1. **demand loans** (repayable upon employer demand; may be made for a specified term if repayment is required upon termination of employment); and

2. **term loans** (repayable at a specified future date, whether employed by the firm at that time or not).

---

[5] The extra $1,500 taxable income term arises because miscellaneous itemized deductions are only allowed to the extent they exceed 2% of adjusted gross income (AGI). Since AGI, before the salary supplement, is $100,000 (2% of which is $2,000), and other miscellaneous deductions amount to only $500, the next $1,500 (or $2,000 - $500) of miscellaneous itemized deductions are nondeductible.

Since they are more common and more interesting for tax-planning purposes, we will concentrate on demand loans.[6] The tax implications of demand loans are that

1. the employer realizes no tax deduction and the employee realizes no taxable income when the loan is made, and
2. as time passes, the employer imputes compensation expense (and the employee imputes compensation income) equal to the riskless interest rate times the loan amount; the employer (employee) also imputes interest income (expense) of equal amount. In other words, we pretend, for tax purposes, that a loan is made at the riskless rate of interest and that the employer pays the employee additional salary equal to the interest on the loan.

At first blush, it might appear that neither the employer nor the employee have any net tax deduction or taxable income: imputed compensation is exactly offset by imputed interest. However, the employee can invest and earn interest on the proceeds of the loan. For example, suppose the riskless before-tax rate of interest is 10%. At the beginning of the year, the employer makes a $50,000 interest-free loan to an employee for one year and reduces year-end salary by $5,000. The employee invests the proceeds of the loan at 10%. This results in the following:

$50,000 × 10%	=	$5,000	imputed compensation income
($50,000 × 10%)	=	($5,000)	imputed interest expense
$50,000 × 10%	=	$5,000	actual interest income (and cash)

Net: $5,000 pretax cash, taxed as salary.

So a one-year interest-free loan at the beginning of the year in exchange for a reduction in year-end salary is the equivalent of cash salary.

But now let's alter the circumstances. Suppose that at the beginning of the year, the employer and employee anticipate that their tax rates will remain constant over the next two years. Consequently, salary and deferred compensation are equally desirable, and, as a result, a salary contract is selected.

Suppose it turns out that towards the end of the year, it becomes apparent that the employer's tax rate in the following year will be higher and/or the employee's rate will be lower. One possible tax-planning response is to reduce salary toward year-end and provide an interest-free demand loan. This will defer the income until the interest on the loan is earned with the passage of time. If a deferral of more than one year is desired, the loan can be made for a longer period of time, but then it must be made contingent upon the continued employment of the employee. This can work fine if there is mutual trust between the employer and the employee, but there could be problems otherwise.[7]

This way of using interest-free loans to defer income recognition is intriguing, because

---

[6] Term loans give rise to immediate income taxation in an amount equal to the "present value" of the forgiven interest under the loan.

[7] One of the requirements to be allowed deferred compensation treatment is that the employer and employee sign an agreement before the beginning of the compensation period.

Chapter 10   Compensation Planning

1. the employee need not be an unsecured creditor of the employer as is required with deferred compensation arrangements, and

2. the arrangement can be used to respond to unexpected changes in tax rates that take place during the period (in other words, interest-free loans score high on the adaptability dimension).

10.3 Cash Bonus Plans

Another compensation arrangement that may satisfy the demand for flexibility when tax rates change unexpectedly over time is a bonus plan, where the bonus is paid at year-end and the amount of bonus is at the discretion of the Compensation Committee of the Board of Directors rather than being set by a pre-specified formula. With mutual trust between the employer and the employee, the bonuses can be timed strategically to coincide with high tax rates for the firm and low tax rates for the employee. Although such plans are extremely common in practice, they are probably used more for incentive reasons than for tax-planning reasons.

As an example, Chrysler Corporation accelerated the timing of its 1990 incentive compensation payouts to managers. Such payments are typically made in January but were moved up a month. The 1990 Tax Act increased tax rates for most Chrysler executives, beginning January 1, 1991. The president of Chrysler indicated that the change in timing was made because "tax rates are higher next year." (*Wall Street Journal*, December 24, 1990)

General Motors Corporation, by contrast, considered but rejected a proposal to make executive incentive payments in December of 1990 rather than January of 1991. While the switch "would have cut taxes for GM's top-ranking executives, (it would) have increased the tax bite for managers further down the ladder." (*Wall Street Journal*, February 8, 1991)

10.4 Stock-Based Compensation Components

Management compensation packages typically include one or more types of equity-based compensation components. The most common are stock options and stock appreciation rights (SARs). A stock option is a right to acquire stock at a specified price (exercise price) for a specified period of time (until the expiration date of the contract). Employee stock options are typically granted with an expiration date of five to ten years, and at an exercise price equal to the price of the underlying stock at the date of grant. Although the options may be quite valuable in that the expected return to the employee from owning the options may be substantial, the granting of options typically is a nontaxable event.[8]

---

[8] If an option is granted at an exercise price below the price of the underlying stock at the date of grant (so called "in-the-money" options), compensation expense (income) equal to the excess of the stock price over the exercise price of the option may have to be recognized by the employer (employee) at the date of grant. Of course, the value of the option may be significantly greater than simply the difference between the current value of the stock and the exercise price of the option. Moreover, some

Instead, taxation of the compensation is deferred until the option is exercised (unless the option is a so-called "incentive stock option" as discussed later).

Stock appreciation rights provide employees with cash payments equal to the change in market value of the firm's stock over some specified period of time. Taxation occurs when the employee has the right to receive the appreciation on the stock that has occurred since the date of grant. As with stock options, the employee does not make a payment to the firm in the event that the stock price declines below its value at the grant date. As a consequence, the expected return to the employee can far exceed the expected appreciation on the stock.

To illustrate, suppose the current stock price is $20 per share, and this is the price at which the stock option or the SAR is granted. The future stock price is uncertain, and for illustrative purposes, assume that its value on the expiration date of the option or the SAR is uniformly distributed between $10 and $40. That is, its future price is certain not to be below $10 or above $40, but every point in between is equally likely.[9] This uncertainty can be represented as in Figure 10.1.

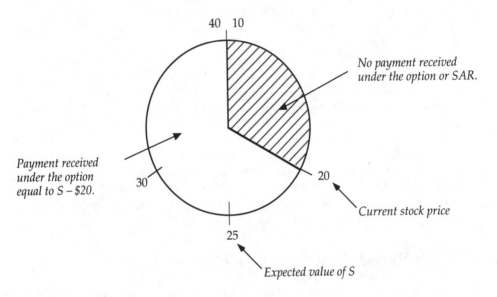

FIGURE 10.1 Distribution of Future Stock Price, S

The expected value of the future stock price is $25 (or ($40 + $10)/2). If the future stock price turned out to be equal to the expected value of $25, the employee would receive $25 - $20 or $5 in cash from the SAR. Similarly, the employee would pay $20 to exercise the option to purchase stock worth $25, thereby realizing a "bargain" of $5. The $5 bargain could be converted into cash by selling the

firms (for example, Digital Equipment Corporation) have imposed restrictions on the exercise of options that are granted at an exercise price below the stock price. Such restrictions postpone the recognition of taxable income until such time as the restrictions lapse.

[9] A uniform distribution for stock prices is not descriptively accurate for securities. The assumption is made here for pedagogical reasons.

Chapter 10   Compensation Planning

underlying stock in the market for $25. But the expected cash value of the option exceeds $5. Why? Because if the terminal stock price is less than $20, the employee receives $0 rather than a negative sum, whereas the employee keeps 100% of the terminal stock price in excess of $20. Since the stock price finishes "in the money" (that is, above $20) two-thirds of the time, and when it finishes in the money, its expected value is $30 (or ($40 + $20)/2), the expected amount to be received under the option is $6.67 (or 2/3 × ($30 - $20)). This means that the expected *option* value relative to holding stock, is $1.67 (or $6.67 - $5.00), to be paid at the expiration date of the option or SAR.

Suppose that the present value of the $1.67 excess of future option value over stock appreciation is $1.25. Then a year-end grant of 20,000 SARs or stock options would be equivalent, ignoring taxes and other considerations (such as risk-sharing and incentives), to a bonus of $25,000. Unlike a bonus, however, the granting of a stock option or SAR does not give rise to immediate taxation. Instead, compensation deferral is achieved. This may or may not be desirable from a tax-planning standpoint depending upon the current and future tax rates of the employee and the employer. If compensation deferral is desirable, however, it may be a useful alternative to a deferred salary or deferred bonus arrangement. Such deferrals require an agreement prior to the services being rendered by the employee while deferrals through options do not.

Differences Among Financial Reporting Rules for Long-Term Cash and Stock-Based Compensation Arrangements

For a variety of reasons, managers are not indifferent to the level of profits they report to shareholders and third parties for any given performance. Different methods of compensation have different financial reporting implications. For example, a deferred cash compensation arrangement for work to be performed over a particular year typically gives rise to compensation expense for financial reporting purposes over the period in which the services are rendered (which is one year in this case). A stock appreciation right, which may have the same cost to the employer at the date of grant, does not give rise to compensation expense until the stock appreciates in value in the future. And a stock option that is granted at an exercise price equal to the extant price of the underlying stock, *never* gives rise to compensation expense in the U.S. under current financial reporting rules. Hence, firms that wish to avoid the recognition of compensation expense for financial reporting purposes, thereby increasing reported profits, have a natural preference for stock options over other forms of compensation.[10]

Tax and Financial Reporting Issues Relating to Incentive Stock Options and Nonqualified Stock Options

As mentioned earlier, not all employee stock options are taxed the same. There are two types of options: nonqualified stock options (NQOs) and incentive stock

---

[10] The Financial Accounting Standards Board has, from time to time, proposed changes in financial reporting rules to neutralize these considerations, but they are unlikely to achieve this goal. The venture capital industry has been very vocal in its opposition to changes in the financial reporting rules.

Date:	Option Granted	Option Exercised	Stock Sold
Stock Price:	S_g	S_e	S_s
Example:	$10	$15	$25
Tax consequences to the employee:			
NQO	None	Ordinary income of $S_e - S_g = \$5$	Capital gain of $S_s - S_e = \$10$
ISO	None	None	Capital gain of $S_s - S_g = \$15$

FIGURE 10.2

options (ISOs). The Tax Reform Act of 1986 reduced the attractiveness of ISOs to a considerable extent. Indeed, the 1986 Tax Act made it desirable in many cases to replace existing ISOs with NQOs. But there are financial reporting implications of this strategy as we see below.

The time line in Figure 10.2 should prove useful in comparing NQOs and ISOs. While NQOs provide ordinary income to employees at the exercise date, ISOs provide capital gains and at a later date. Although it might seem as though ISOs dominate NQOs, especially prior to the 1986 Tax Act when the capital gains rate was so much more favorable than the ordinary tax rate, such a conclusion commits the fallacy of unilateral tax-planning. It is also important to consider the tax consequences to the employer.

The employer receives no tax deduction for the compensation paid to employees via ISOs. In contrast, NQOs give rise to an ordinary tax deduction for the employer at the same time and in the same amount as the ordinary income recognized by the employee.

Suppose the employer and the employee always face the same tax rate. Then NQOs are preferred to ISOs. With NQOs, no net tax is paid on the stock price appreciation between the grant date and the exercise date since the tax paid by the employee is equal to the tax reduction achieved by the employer. By contrast, tax *will* be paid with an ISO, although it will be delayed until the stock is sold and the tax will be at capital gains rates. This is due to the asymmetric tax treatment of the employer and the employee under ISOs.

If the employer's tax rate exceeds the employee's, NQOs are even more preferred compared to ISOs (the net tax paid becomes negative with the NQO). But if the employer's tax rate is below the employee's, the ISOs could be preferred.

So for employees facing high tax rates, ISOs may have a place in the compensation programs of companies with low tax rates (like start-up companies or other companies with net operating loss (NOL) or investment tax credit carryforwards). In addition, due to the increase in the capital gains tax rate in many circumstances under the 1986 Tax Act (not only relative to ordinary tax rates but in absolute terms as well), ISOs are likely to diminish substantially in popularity, if not disappear altogether (at least until capital gains once again become taxed substantially more favorably relative to ordinary income).

One of the interesting tax-planning features of ISOs is the ability to "disqualify" them and convert them into NQOs or even cash compensation if tax rates

Chapter 10 Compensation Planning

change in the "right way." For example, suppose 100,000 ISOs were issued in 1984 at an exercise price of $10 apiece by a company with NOL carryforwards. In 1986, the firm became profitable unexpectedly. As a result, its tax rate jumped to 50% (including state income tax), and its stock price increased to $30. The bargain element in the ISOs was then $20 × 100,000 = $2,000,000. The firm could then afford to substitute 2 NQOs exercisable at $10 apiece for each ISO, since the compensation component of each NQO would have been deductible at a tax rate of 50%.[11]

Suppose that the executives holding the ISOs were also in the 50% tax bracket, although they expected to be in a 30% bracket in 1989, when they anticipated selling the stock. Also assume that executives discounted after-tax cash flows at a rate of 5%. Under these circumstances, exercising the ISOs would have resulted in an expected after-tax present value gain of $2,000,000 × (1 - .30/1.05^3) = $1.5 million. By contrast, exercising twice as many NQOs would have resulted in an expected after-tax present value gain of 2 × $2,000,000 × (1 - .5) = $2.0 million or one third more after tax. If the employee's tax rates had averaged 40% in 1986 rather than 50%, the difference would have been even more dramatic: $1.5 million with ISOs, as before, versus 2 × $2,000,000 × (1 - .4) = $2.4 million with NQOs or 60% more after tax with NQOs.

For those firms who failed to offer cash or NQOs in exchange for ISOs in 1986, there were still substantial advantages to doing so in 1987 (and 1988 and beyond). For example, a corporation facing a 40% marginal tax rate could afford to exchange each ISO for 1/(1 - .4) = 1.67 NQOs. If executives in 1987 faced a marginal rate of, say, 35% on average, they could keep:

1.67 × $2,000,000 × (1 - .35) = $2.17 million after tax with NQOs in 1987

versus

$1.5 million with ISOs or still nearly 45% more with NQOs.

Many firms that could have saved substantial sums in taxes by swapping NQOs for ISOs, or simply paying cash to employees to surrender their ISOs in 1986, failed to do so. Why? One possibility is that they were simply unaware of the advantages. But there is at least one fly in the ointment that we alluded to earlier, and that is that swapping NQOs for ISOs has important financial reporting implications. In particular, under present accounting rules, if ISOs or NQOs are issued at an exercise price equal to the current stock price, the employer need never report any compensation expense despite the obvious fact that considerable value has been transferred to employees through the granting of options. But if NQOs are issued in exchange for ISOs when the exercise price is *below* the current market price, compensation expense must be recognized for the difference.

In our example where two NQOs were substituted for each ISO, $4 million of compensation expense would be recognized for financial reporting purposes. Rightly or wrongly, many firms (especially smaller high-tech firms) are very reticent to reduce income that is reported to shareholders.

---

[11] That is, the exercise of an ISO would have cost the shareholders $30 - $10 or $20. The exercise of two NQOs would have cost the shareholders 2 × ($30 - $10) or $40 before tax, but only $40 × 50% = $20 after tax, the same as with one ISO.

Compensation in Venture-Capital-Backed Start-Ups

The ISO-NQO tradeoff has a counterpart in start-up companies backed by venture capital firms. In many circumstances, management of the start-up ventures are given common stock and the venture capitalists are given convertible preferred stock. To provide incentives and rewards for managers, the price at which the preferred stock can be converted into common is often made contingent on the performance of the company: if the company does well (say, in terms of accounting measures of performance), the conversion price to the venture capitalists increases.

The higher conversion price on the preferred stock is effectively a bonus to members of the management group who hold common shares. The higher the conversion price, the smaller the number of new shares issued to the venture capitalists and the more each remaining share is worth to managment. This bonus is taxed to managers as deferred capital gains on their shares. And the bonus is not tax-deductible to the company. Note that a cash bonus would result in immediate tax to managers at their personal tax rate. While this may appear worse than the stock-based bonus arrangement, the cash bonus would also yield an immediate corporate tax deduction. So a larger tax-deductible cash bonus could be afforded than a non-deductible stock-based bonus. As with NQOs, the cash bonus arrangement is typically more efficient for tax reasons.

Comparison of Stock Appreciation Rights and Stock Options

When stock appreciation rights are compared to nonqualified or incentive stock options, it is important to take account of what happens to stock prices at points in the time between the grant date and exercise date of the option, as well as between the exercise date and the date the stock is sold. The reason for this is that stock appreciation rights yield income to the employee (and tax-deductible compensation expense to the employer) each period.

To illustrate, suppose a stock appreciation right, a nonqualified stock option, and an incentive stock option are issued with an "exercise price" equal to the current stock price of $10. The stock, which pays no dividends, increases in value by one dollar each year for the next four years, which is the length of the life of the stock appreciation right. The options expire in two years when the stock price is $12, and the stock that is acquired upon exercise of the option is sold two years later at a price of $14. Table 10.2 indicates the tax consequences to the employee and the employer for the three alternative stock-based compensation instruments.[12]

Note that for the special case where the ordinary tax rate of the employee is equal to that of the employer, the total tax consequences to the two parties across the alternatives are shown in Table 10.3. This suggests that among the alternatives, stock appreciation rights are the most attractive from a tax standpoint, followed by nonqualified options, with incentive stock options least tax-

---

[12] We ignore the cash flow differences between stock appreciation rights and stock options. The latter requires the employee to experience an extra cash outflow at time 2, and a cash inflow at time 4, equal to $10, the exercise price of the option.

Chapter 10   Compensation Planning

Table 10.2 Tax Consequences to Employees and Employers of Three Stock-Based Compensation Alternatives.

Event	Options Granted				Options Exercised				Stock Sold	
Time Period	0		1		2		3		4	
Stock Price	$10		$11		$12		$13		$14	
Tax Consequences to:*	ee	er	ee	er	ee	er	ee	er	ee	er
SAR	0	0	$-t_p$	$+t_c$	$-t_p$	$+t_c$	$-t_p$	$+t_c$	$-t_p$	$+t_c$
NQO	0	0	0	0	$-2t_p$	$+2t_c$	0	0	$-2t_g$	0
ISO	0	0	0	0	0	0	0	0	$-4t_g$	0

*SAR = stock appreciation right
NQO = nonqualified stock option
ISO = incentive stock option
ee = employee
er = employer
t_p = employee's ordinary tax rate
t_c = employer's ordinary tax rate
t_g = employee's capital gain tax rate

favored. If the employee's tax rate on ordinary income is below that of the employer, the preference ordering among the three compensation alternatives is preserved, with the magnitude of the tax differences increased.[13]

Table 10.3 Total Tax Consequences of Three Stock-Based Compensation Alternatives When the Ordinary Tax Rates of Employees and Employers Coincide.

Time	0	1	2	3	4
Instrument:					
SAR	0	0	0	0	0
NQO	0	0	0	0	$-2t_g$
ISO	0	0	0	0	$-4t_g$

What about financial reporting consequences? While nonqualified stock options and incentive stock options need never give rise to compensation expense for financial reporting purposes, stock appreciation rights yield compensation expense at the same times and in the same amounts as tax expense is recognized. Rightly or wrongly, such financial reporting considerations often appear to swing the choice in favor of the more expensive compensation arrangements from a tax standpoint.

Concluding Remarks

We have now discussed all the compensation components listed in Table 10.1 except for pensions. This is the topic of our next chapter.

---

[13] If the employee's tax rate is well *above* the employer's rate (for example, if the employer faces current or future tax loss carryforwards), the preference ordering could be reversed.

Summary of Key Points

1. In determining the desirability of compensation alternatives, the tax consequences to both the employer *and* the employee must be considered.

2. Although employees prefer to receive taxable compensation at times and in ways that result in the income being taxed at lower rates, *holding the compensation amounts fixed*, employers prefer to pay tax-deductible compensation at times and in ways that result in the payments being deductible at high rates. By adjusting the *level* of compensation to reflect the tax costs and benefits of the compensation alternatives, the interests of employers and employees can be made to coincide.

3. Although certain fringe benefits yield tax deductions for employers and tax-exempt benefits for employees, such benefits are inferior to taxable cash compensation if employees place little personal value on the fringe benefits.

4. Reimbursement of business meal and entertainment expenses is tax-favored over salary supplements in the U.S. where the employer faces low tax rates, but salary supplements can be preferred when employers face high tax rates.

5. In comparing compensation alternatives, such nontax factors as administrative cost differences and differences in employee incentive effects may overwhelm the tax factors in importance.

6. Interest-free demand loans can yield tax treatment similar to deferred compensation arrangements. And while they are more flexible than other deferred compensation arrangements in some respects, they also require a great deal of mutual trust between the employer and the employee to be used effectively for tax-planning purposes.

7. Discretionary cash bonus plans can be a very effective tax-planning tool in that bonuses can be timed strategically to coincide with high tax rates for the employer and low tax rates for the employee. But such plans also require a great deal of mutual trust between the employer and the employee to be used in this fashion.

8. The popularity in the U.S. of incentive stock options (ISOs) in the early and mid-1980s may have resulted from committing the fallacy of unilateral tax planning. Nonqualified stock options (NQOs) impose more tax on employees but yield significantly higher tax benefits for employers.

9. Many ISOs that could have been swapped for NQOs following passage of the 1986 Tax Act at *very significant* tax savings were not swapped. One possible explanation for this is the adverse financial reporting consequences of this tax-saving transaction: it would require the recognition of considerable sums of compensation expense in reports sent to shareholders and creditors.

10. Managers in venture capital-backed start-ups are often compensated in ways that yield deferred capital gains rather than immediate taxation

at ordinary rates. Like ISOs, however, such compensation arrangements yield no tax deduction to the firm and therefore may be inferior to cash compensation alternatives. As in the ISO-NQO-SAR comparisons, the more tax-efficient compensation arrangement often yields reduced income for financial reporting purposes. Some firms are apparently more interested in looking rich to investors than they are in looking poor to the tax collector.

Discussion Questions

1. Why is the list of compensation alternatives in Table 10.1 not necessarily ordered from most desirable to least desirable for an employee?

2. Why might salary be preferred to deferred compensation even if the employee's tax rate is falling over time? Illustrate your answer using the changes in the 1986 tax rules. Was salary preferred for both highly and lowly compensated employees?

3. With the change in marginal tax rates in the 1986 Tax Act, would it have been tax-disadvantageous for tax-exempt institutions such as Stanford University to establish deferred-compensation arrangements in 1986 for their employees? Why might such institutions not have established these programs at that time?

4. What are the tax benefits of a fringe benefit such as employer-supplied life and health insurance? What are the nontax costs associated with such a program? Why would some employees prefer salary to the insurance program?

5. When is it efficient for the employer to reimburse the employee for business meals and entertainment expenditures? How does the 2% limitation on miscellaneous itemized deductions affect the decision? What nontax factors might influence the decision?

6. Illustrate how a demand loan can serve to defer compensation. Why does such a program require mutual trust between employees and their employers?

7. When are discretionary bonus plans attractive tax-planning vehicles? Are there incentives for the employer to renege on the bonus? If there are such incentives, what prevents the employer from reneging?

8. Is each statement true or false?
   a. The expected return on stock appreciation rights always exceeds the expected return on the underlying stock.
   b. The financial reporting differences for compensating employees with stock appreciation rights and stock options leads small start-up companies to prefer granting stock appreciation rights to their employees.
   c. A "non-qualified option" is preferable to an "incentive stock option" for tax purposes.
   d. The 1986 Tax Act made incentive stock options less attractive.

Problems

1. The data table below shows employee and employer current and future tax rates, and after-tax borrowing or lending costs, for different levels of deferred compensation that might be provided to the employee. Note that the employee's current tax rate decreases (and the future tax rates increase) the larger the amount of compensation that is deferred. This reflects the progressive nature of personal tax rates. In addition, the employee's after-tax opportunity cost of funds increases in the amount of compensation deferred. This reflects the employee's increasing desire for funds to finance current consumption as the amount of compensation deferral increases.

Amount of compensation deferral	t_{co}	t_{c5}	t_{po}	t_{p5}	r_{c5}	r_{p5}
$0	35%	40%	40%	35%	8%	6%
$20,000	35%	40%	35%	35%	8%	7%
$40,000	35%	40%	30%	35%	8%	7%
$60,000	35%	40%	30%	40%	8%	7%
$80,000	35%	40%	25%	40%	8%	8%
$100,000	35%	40%	25%	45%	8%	9%

t_{co} = employer's current marginal tax rate;
t_{c5} = employer's marginal tax rate in five years;
t_{po} = employee's current marginal tax rate given the compensation deferral amount shown in the first column;
t_{p5} = employee's marginal tax rate in five years after receiving the deferred compensation payment corresponding to the salary deferral shown in the first column;
r_{c5} = employer's annualized after-tax rate of return on marginal five-year investments; and
r_{p5} = employee's annualized after-tax rate of return on marginal five-year investments;

a. Ignoring nontax considerations, what is the optimal level of compensation to be deferred for five years? Explain briefly.

(Answer: between _____ and _____ thousand dollars.)

b. How much better or worse off would the employee be on the first dollar of salary deferred if the employer paid the deferred compensation amount that makes it indifferent between salary and deferred compensation?

c. How much better or worse off would the employee be on the 100,000th dollar of salary deferred?

d. Suppose that the deferred compensation contract is structured so that it is payable only if the employee remains within the employ of the firm. Further suppose that such a condition: (1) reduces the likelihood of employee turnover; and (2) increases employee performance (since the employee wishes to avoid being fired). How do these considerations affect the desirability of a deferred compensation arrangement?

e. Suppose that the arrangement described in (d) is implemented, and the amount of compensation deferred is $60,000. Two years after the agreement is signed, the employee reports that her tax rate has decreased unexpectedly (and temporarily) to 20%. The employee further reports that her tax rate will increase to 45% in years 3, 4, and 5 (it *was* expected to be 40% as per the table). Considering both tax and nontax factors, what determines whether the deferred compensation arrangement should be restructured to accelerate income into year 2 rather than year 5?

2. The May/June 1990 issue of the *Crystal Report on Executive Compensation* describes a compensation benefit program for executives employed by Sears, Roebuck called the Tax Benefit Right (TBR):

A TBR apparently entitles the executive-recipient to a cash repayment equal to the value of the company's tax deduction with respect to a related compensation payment. Hence, if the executive is receiving $100,000 of compensation—perhaps from an option exercise, or from a bonus—and if Sears' corporate marginal tax rate is 34%, then the executive with a TBR not only receives the $100,000 payment, but also a second payment of $34,000—or the amount the company stands to save in reduced taxes by deducting the original payment of $100,000.

Perhaps to reassure its shareholders that TBRs are not yet another raid on their pocketbooks, Sears goes to the trouble to point out that the TBR "... would itself be deductible by the Company ... for federal income tax purposes, and the Company or its subsidiaries will receive the benefit, if any, from such deduction."

Now if no TBR were being granted, shareholders would, in the example just cited, lay out $100,000 for the compensation payment and receive back $34,000 from the government in reduced taxes. Hence, net shareholder cost for the transaction would be $100,000 - $34,000, or $66,000.

With a TBR attached, shareholders now pay out $134,000 to the executive and receive a deduction of a like $134,000. Given a 34% corporate tax rate, the deduction yields tax savings of $134,000 × 34%, or $45,560. Hence, the new cost to the shareholders rises from $66,000 without a TBR to $88,440 with a TBR—for a cost increase of—guess what—34%.

What motivations might the Sears, Roebuck Compensation Committee of the Board of Directors have in adopting the Tax Benefit Right plan? Under what conditions is it a shareholder ripoff and under what conditions is it beneficial for shareholders?

Chapter 10   Compensation Planning

CHAPTER 11
Pension and Retirement Program Planning

Pension plans have become extremely important components of the compensation package of employers and employees. As we stressed in Chapter Three on alternative savings vehicles, (1) contributions into the plan are tax deductible up to prescribed limits, (2) earnings on pension investments are tax exempt, and (3) employees defer payment of tax until they receive payments from the plan.

In this chapter, we discuss the tax advantages of pension funds and highlight the nontax costs and benefits of using them. We first discuss different types of pension plans and then compare them to salary. We then discuss pension plan investment strategy (for example, stocks versus bonds) and funding strategy (how much to put into the plan). In the last section of this chapter, we discuss the growing importance of post-retirement health care plans as they relate to supplemental benefits to employees.

11.1   Types of Pension Plans

There are two major categories of pension plans: defined contribution plans and defined benefit plans. In a **defined contribution** plan the employer and, in some cases, the employee make contributions into an account that will accumulate pension benefits on behalf of the employee. As its name implies, a defined contribution plan specifies contributions into the plan. For example, employees might be required to contribute 5% of their compensation to receive a matching 10% contribution by their employer. The employee's ultimate pension benefit depends on the amounts contributed into the plan and on investment performance. The employer does not guarantee the amount of its employee's pension benefit. In this regard, corporate defined contribution plans are similar to individual retirement accounts (IRAs).[1] Certain individuals are allowed to contribute up to $2,000 per year into an IRA account.

Pension plan contributions can be invested in a variety of asset classes, including common stocks, bonds, limited partnerships, and real estate. Contribution limits for pension plans are far more generous than for IRAs. Examples of corporate defined contribution plans include profit-sharing plans, money-purchase plans, 401(k) plans, and thrift plans. For example, a profit-sharing plan might require the employer to contribute a fixed fraction of the salary of the employee if profits exceed designated levels and a lesser fraction if profits fall below these levels. Employees are often given a choice among different investment alternatives (for example, a bond fund, a stock fund, and a guaranteed annuity from an insurance company, which promises to pay the employee a specified annual amount in retirement).

In a defined contribution pension plan, the employer deposits the contribution into an employee account. The contributions are tax deductible, and the earnings on the assets in the account are tax exempt. An employee's withdrawals from the account in retirement are taxed as ordinary income. Moreover, the tax rules require that employees begin withdrawing, by April 1 following the year in which the employee reaches age 70.5, an amount that is not less than would be available from a fixed life annuity at that time (although the withdrawal amount can be based on a *joint* annuity payable over the lives of the employee and a beneficiary). On the other hand, except in the case of death or disability, the employee typically must pay a 10% excise tax in addition to the regular tax on withdrawals prior to age 59.5 (prior to age 55 for early retirees).

A **defined benefit** pension plan promises the employee a stated benefit at retirement, often based on salary and/or years of service, usually in the form of an annuity. Defined benefit plans are either flat benefit plans or salary-related plans. A flat benefit plan (usually provided to union employees) stipulates that the employee will receive a fixed dollar amount per year based on years of service (for example, $20 per month per year of service not to exceed 25 years). A salary-related plan typically provides a benefit that is a percentage of an employee's salary. For example, a final pay plan might provide the employee with an annual annuity of 2% of her average salary over her last five years of employment for each year she worked for the firm. For example, if the employee's salary averaged $120,000 in the last five years of her fifteen years of employment before leaving the firm at age 50, she could receive a pension at age 65, the firm's normal retirement age, of $36,000 per year (or $15 \times .02 \times \$120,000$). To fund these promises, employers contribute to a pension trust. Unlike defined contribution plans, employees need not worry about the investment performance of the assets in the pension fund if there are sufficient assets in the fund to support these promised benefits.

It is more difficult to value the promises to employees in a defined benefit plan than in a defined contribution plan. Each year, actuaries determine the

---

[1] Under the 1986 Tax Act, only individuals not covered by other pension plans *or* whose incomes are less than $50,000 can still make tax-deductible contributions to an IRA account. Existing plans need not be terminated. Non-deductible contributions may also be made to an IRA account. Such contributions are taxed in a manner similar to single premium deferred annuities.

required contributions to fund the target retirement annuity for defined benefit plans. They estimate the discount rate to value the retirement liability, the terminal salary to forecast the amount of the annuity, the life expectancy of employees (and their survivors), the earnings rate on assets in the pension fund, the expected employee turnover rates, and the possibility of the employees' disability and death. With all these assumptions, it is difficult to define very precisely the corporation's pension liability and its funding requirements. As a result, by changing the assumptions, actuaries have considerable latitude in determining the tax-deductible funding requirements of pension plan sponsors.

More than $1.5 trillion of assets were invested in U.S. defined benefit pension plans at year-end 1988. This is nearly twice the amount invested in defined contribution plans.

11.2   A Comparison of Salary and Pension Compensation

Because of the tax exemption on the returns to the assets in the pension account, it might appear that a contribution to a pension dominates an equal dollar amount of salary. But even ignoring nontax factors, this is not so in all cases. Suppose an employer contemplates depositing $1 into a defined contribution pension fund for its employee. If t_{co} is the corporate tax rate today, the after-tax cost to the corporation of the contribution would be $\$1(1 - t_{co})$, the same as the after-tax cost of $1 of salary. As a result, the employer is indifferent between paying $1 of salary and making a $1 pension contribution.

For the employee, $1 invested in the pension fund grows in value to $\$1(1 + R_{cn})^n$ in n periods, where R_{cn} is the before-tax rate of return on assets invested in the pension account.[2] Just what this before-tax return might be depends on the assets held in the pension account. As we discussed in Chapter Four, the implicit tax on shares prior to the 1986 Tax Act in the U.S. was likely to have been quite high. Only a fraction of realized capital gains were taxable, the tax on the gains could be deferred, and investors could avoid the capital gains tax on shares by holding them until death (perhaps borrowing to finance their desired level of consumption) or by donating appreciated stock to charity. We have argued that the annualized tax rate on shares could have been as low as 10% per year, far below the tax rate on taxable bonds. This implies that the before-tax risk-adjusted returns on shares would be well below the before-tax returns on bonds.

If employees compare the after-tax accumulation in a pension with that of taking a current salary and investing the after-tax amount on their own for n periods, their after-tax accumulations would be

Pension: $(1 + R_{cn})^n (1 - t_{pn})$ (11.1)

Salary: $(1 - t_{po}) (1 + r_{pn})^n$,   (11.2)

---

[2] R_{cn} might be different for investments in the pension fund than outside the pension fund. For example, pension funds are not permitted to invest in certain kinds of assets. In addition, pension funds cannot invest as general partners in partnerships without attracting corporate taxation on their share of the income. Pension funds also face some corporate taxation on the income they earn as limited partners in partnerships that engage in borrowing.

where r_{pn} is the after-tax rate of return per year available on personal investments, t_{po} is the current marginal tax rate of the employee, and t_{pn} is the marginal tax rate of the employee at time n. Pensions will be preferred to salary when

$$\frac{(1 + R_{cn})^n}{(1 + r_{pn})^n} > \frac{(1 - t_{po})}{(1 - t_{pn})}. \qquad (11.3)$$

When tax rates are constant over time, pension provides higher after-tax accumulations than salary as long as the before-tax return on pension investments exceeds the after-tax return on non-pension investments. But suppose that the employee could earn after tax at the same rate as the pension fund could earn before tax. A possible example here is the savings component of a "cash value" (whole life or universal life) insurance policy. In this case, ignoring nontax considerations, the only motivation for a pension plan would be declining marginal tax rates for the employee.[3] Of course, cash value life insurance policies do bear transaction cost-related implicit taxes, as we discussed in Chapter Six, so pension investments would normally be expected to provide an investment return advantage.

An important disadvantage of pension plans for some employees is that a pension investment is very illiquid. Particularly for younger employees, pension investment may entail greater postponement of consumption than they desire. And while the opportunity to borrow to finance consumption can mitigate this disadvantage, the mitigation may be very slight (if there is any mitigation at all) when there are significant transaction costs associated with borrowing and where interest expense on personal borrowing is not fully tax-deductible. In such circumstances, employees may require a rate of return far greater than R_{cn} per period after tax for them to prefer pension compensation over salary.[4]

Since pension compensation yields future taxable income to the employee, whereas salary yields current taxable income, pensions become more desirable the lower are future tax rates relative to current tax rates. In this regard, the 1981 and 1986 Tax Acts in the U.S., both of which reduced tax rates, provided particularly strong incentives to undertake pension investments prior to the reduction in rates. These Acts provided huge windfalls to older employees, many of whom had been expecting to face nearly twice as high a marginal tax rate in retirement as they may end up facing.

Perhaps in recognition of this windfall, the 1986 Tax Act introduced a number of new rules that limit the advantages of pension plans for high-income taxpayers, including a substantial reduction in the maximum potential tax-deductible pension plan contribution for many high-income employees. As a

---

[3] Of course, a deferred compensation contract might provide a higher after-tax accumulation than either a pension *or* salary in this circumstance, particularly if the employer funds the deferred compensation plan by purchasing cash value life insurance policies on the lives of its employees. RCA invested $200 million in such plans in 1985. Conversations with program designers indicate that RCA incurred an annualized cost of slightly less than 1% of the $200 million invested. At a 9% interest rate, this translates to an implicit tax rate of approximately 10%.

[4] A strong preference for current consumption over future consumption can be reflected in a high value for r_{pn} in expression 11.2. That is, the employee can be viewed as attaching a high after-tax value to being able to invest after-tax salary in current consumption.

result, numerous firms were led to provide supplemental pension benefits for their employees that are essentially deferred compensation plans (that is, the employer loses an immediate deduction for the compensation and is taxable on the income earned on invested funds).

Excise Tax Complications

An interesting investment planning problem confronts U.S. taxpayers with ample accumulations in their qualified retirement programs. The 1986 Tax Act introduced a new 15% excise tax that applies when benefits to a participant from all qualified plans (including IRA accounts, 401(k) plans, defined benefit plans, etc.) exceed the maximum of $150,000 and $120,000, indexed for inflation after 1986. The excise tax clearly reduces the benefit of accumulating funds in a pension plan. With a 15% excise tax in addition to the regular tax on pension plan distributions in excess of $150,000, a pension beneficiary facing a 30% tax rate pays tax at the rate of 45% on the excess pension fund distribution.

When the tax rate on pension fund distributions exceeds the current tax rate on salary income, taxpayers must trade off the advantages of investing at a before-tax rate of return in the pension account against the higher tax rate on pension income. For example, suppose a taxpayer currently faces a 30% tax rate and expects to face a 40% tax rate in retirement. Pension investments earn 10% per year and personal investments yield 7% after tax.

If the investment horizon is 10 years, a dollar of current salary reinvested at 7% after tax yields

$$\$1(1 - .3) \times 1.07^{10} = \$1.38.$$

A dollar of current pension contribution invested at 10% yields

$$\$1 \times 1.1^{10} \times (1 - .4) = \$1.56.$$

This is 13% more than current salary despite the high tax rate in retirement. But if a 15% tax were added to the 40% regular tax rate, the after-tax pension accumulation would fall to $1.17, which falls short of the salary accumulation by $.21.

Note, however, that an increase in the investment horizon may enable the tax-free compounding of the pension to overcome the disadvantage of even the 15% excise tax. Over a 20-year horizon, for example, the salary would accumulate to $2.71 after tax (or $1(1 - .3) \times 1.07^{20}$), while the pension would accumulate to $3.03 (or $1 \times 1.1^{20} \times (1 - .4 - .15))$. So the pension now does better by 12%.[5] A 20-year horizon is not as long as might appear at first blush. After all, most pensions are removed periodically over the retiree's life rather than in a lump sum at the time of retirement.[6]

The 15% excise tax on excess distributions may discourage investment in risky assets. For example, consider the case of a taxpayer who would accumulate an amount that falls just short of the level that triggers the 15% excise tax if the

---

[5] Note, however, that a single premium deferred annuity accumulates to $3.11 (that is, $1(1 - .3) [1.1^{20} \times (1 - .4) + .4])$. This is 3% more than the pension accumulation. On the other hand, a pretax return on the SPDA of only 9.5% per year would yield only $2.86.

[6] Special tax rules apply to lump-sum distributions from certain retirement plans in the U.S. Favorable tax treatment can result which leads some retirees to elect lump-sum distributions.

pension is invested in riskless bonds. If, instead, the taxpayer invests the pension fund in stocks and realizes a high rate of return, the gains above the riskless rate on bonds will be subject to the excise tax. On the other hand, if the stock experiences poor performance, the taxpayer would escape the excise tax. This asymmetric tax treatment can cause taxpayers to invest more conservatively in their pension accounts. As discussed in Chapter Seven, progressive tax rates can induce a degree of risk aversion in deciding on the investment policies of the fund.

Rates of Return on Investments In and Out of Pension Accounts

We have assumed implicitly that investors earn a higher rate of return in the pension account than they could investing on their own. Although it may seem unlikely that the employee can earn at a higher after-tax rate of return outside the pension account than inside the account, it is certainly possible. Let us consider the following examples:

1. Employees may be forced to invest in common stock in the pension plan (for example, this is a common feature of Employee Stock Ownership Plans), and such assets may bear high implicit taxes.

2. Some employees might be forced to borrow to meet consumption needs because the rules of their pension plan preclude them from surrendering their pension accounts (or tax rules prevent them from using the pension fund as direct security for a loan). As a result, they may have to pay a large implicit tax on the pension fund investment return if borrowing rates are high relative to lending rates.

3. Family tax-planning strategies may also permit investment deductions to be taken at high tax rates and income to be taxed at low rates (at the household level). That is, the high income parent might take tax deductions for part of the cost of investments early in the life of a tax-sheltered project, and later in its life gift their interest in the shelter to lower tax-bracket family members if the project starts producing income. As a result, the after-tax rates of return at the household level could exceed the before-tax rates of return in pension accounts.

4. Alternative savings vehicles such as investing in life insurance policies or single premium deferred annuities may provide before-tax rates of return that are close to those available to employees in pension plans.

Anti-Discrimination Rules

A major disadvantage of pension plans (defined benefit as well as defined contribution plans) is that highly compensated employees and a certain percentage of the firm's moderately compensated employees must be included in the firm's pension plan to qualify for tax-favored treatment. While highly compensated employees (generally the older employees) might want pension accounts, moderately compensated employees (particularly the younger ones) typically prefer to consume now, to save later in their life, and to fund their pension plans when their tax rates are higher in the future.

As a result, if lower-income employees prefer salary to pension, they will not be willing to give up $1 of before-tax salary for $1 of pension contribution. For example, they might value the $1 pension contribution at only $.80. But the corporation is indifferent between paying $1 of salary and depositing only $1 into a defined contribution pension plan. In many cases, the more highly compensated employees must end up covering the $.20 shortfall. They do so indirectly by trading off more than a dollar of salary reduction for each dollar they receive in pension contributions. The less generous pension benefit ceilings under the 1986 Tax Act make the cost of subsidizing lower level employees too high, relative to the limited pension benefits available, for an increased number of pension plans.

The 1986 Tax Act tightened up the anti-discrimination requirements. To qualify for tax-favored treatment, the ratio of contributions of highly compensated employees to total contributions became more limited. Forcing more employees who prefer salary to pension into the plan reduces the benefit of maintaining corporate pension plans for those who want such plans. This is another form of implicit tax.

Empirically, pension benefits, particularly in defined benefit plans, have been heavily skewed to older employees in the economy, which is efficient for tax planning purposes for reasons we have already presented. The actuarial rules that determine whether the plan is "top heavy" (too many highly compensated employee dollars going into the plan) make it easier to skew benefits to the older and more highly compensated employees than would be possible with a defined contribution plan.

11.3 The Stocks-versus-Bonds Puzzle

It is somewhat surprising that 40 to 50 percent of pension dollars (in both defined contribution and defined benefit plans) have been invested in common stocks over the years. For example, in 1986, private pension plans (such as corporate, partnership, and self-employed retirement plans) held 51% of their $815 billion in common stock, and public pension plans (such as public employee pension plans) held 34% of their $484 billion in common stock.

Some have argued that corporate pension fund managers are willing to abandon investment in tax-disfavored assets (for which pension funds are the natural clientele) to garner the higher total rates of return available in stock. Until high-yield bonds came into vogue, it was not possible to earn risk premiums without investing in stock. But Fischer Black and Irwin Tepper, in two separate articles, had a good counter to this line of attack.[7] They argued that the corporation could secure the risk premiums without sacrificing the tax benefits of investing in bonds.

Their strategy was to effect organizational-form arbitrage as outlined in Table 11.1. Suppose that a firm initially has $1 in its pension fund invested in stock that earns a risky return of $\tilde{r}_c$. This is Plan A in Table 11.1. Alternatively, if the firm sells the stock and buys bonds in the pension plan, it will earn a return of R_b in the

---

[7] See F. Black, "The Tax Consequences of Long-Run Pension Policy," *Financial Analysts Journal*, (July August, 1980), pp. 1-28, and I. Tepper, "Taxation and Corporate Pension Policy," *Journal of Finance* (March 1981), pp. 1-14.

Table 11.1 Stock Investment in the Pension Fund (Plan A) Compared to Bonds in the Pension Fund Along with Debt-Financed Stock on Corporate Account (Plan B)

	Investment	Return	Example
Plan A			
Pension:			
Purchase Stock	$1	$\tilde{r}_c$	15%
Plan B			
Pension:			
Purchase Bonds	$1	R_b	10%
Corporation:			
Issue Bonds	-$1	$-R_b(1 - t_c)$	-6%*
Purchase Stock	$1	$\tilde{r}_c$	15%
Net Position (Pension Plus Corporation)			
Purchase Stock	$1	$\tilde{r}_c + R_b t_c$	19%
Plan B - Plan A	$0	$R_b t_c$	4%

*For $t_c = 40\%$.

pension plan. If the corporation now borrows $1 on corporate account when its marginal tax rate is t_c, and buys common stock with the proceeds of the loan, its net after-tax rate of return on corporate account is $\tilde{r}_c - R_b(1 - t_c)$ on this strategy. The total return on the pension fund investment in bonds and the corporate investment in stock, financed by issuing bonds, is $\tilde{r}_c + R_b t_c$. This is Plan B in Table 11.1. This exceeds the return from investing in stocks by $R_b t_c$.

Note that the risk of the two strategies is exactly the same. The return from Plan B exceeds that from Plan A by a sure $R_b t_c$, irrespective of what happens to stock prices. The advantage of undertaking this organizational-form arbitrage arises from the corporation's ability to borrow on corporate account to secure the interest deduction and to invest the proceeds in the pension fund through the strategy illustrated in Table 11.1.

There are, however, a few holes in the above argument. First, we have assumed that the corporation pays no tax on the return to investing in shares on corporate account. In fact, taxes must be paid, although the annualized tax rate on shares may be well below t_c as we argued in Chapter Four. On the other hand, if the firm were to hold its *own* shares on corporate account, the return *would be tax-exempt*.

If the effective annualized tax rate on shares held on corporate account is t_{cs}, then a slight change in arbitrage strategy displayed in Table 11.1 is required. In particular, the corporation will now need to issue $1/(1 - t_{cs})$ dollars of bonds and invest the proceeds in stock to maintain the same level of risk in Plan B and Plan A. As Table 11.2 shows, as long as the effective annualized tax rate on shares held on corporate account, t_{cs}, is below the ordinary tax rate, there remains an arbitrage opportunity, although it is not as large as when we assumed t_{cs} to be equal to zero (as we did in Table 11.1).

Chapter 11   Pension and Retirement Program Planning

Table 11.2 Stock Investment in the Pension Fund (Plan A) Compared to Bonds in the Pension Fund Along with Debt-Financed Stock on Corporate Account (Plan B)

Effective Annualized Tax Rate on Shares Held on Corporate Account, t_{cs}, is Positive (Versus Zero in Table 11.1)

	Investment	Return	Example
Plan A			
Pension:			
Purchase Stock	$1	$\tilde{r}_c$	15.0%
Plan B			
Pension:			
Purchase Bonds	$1	R_b	10.0%
Corporation:			
Issue Bonds	$-\$1/(1 - t_{cs})$	$-R_b \dfrac{(1 - t_c)}{(1 - t_{cs})}$	-7.5%*
Purchase Stock	$\$1/(1 - t_{cs})$	$\tilde{r}_c \dfrac{(1 - t_{cs})}{(1 - t_{cs})}$	15.0%
Net Position (Pension Plus Corporation)			
Purchase Stock and	$\$1/(1 - t_{cs})$	$\tilde{r}_c + R_b \dfrac{(t_c - t_{cs})}{(1 - t_{cs})}$	17.5%
Issue Bonds	$-t_{cs}/(1 - t_{cs})$		
Plan B - Plan A	$0	$R_b \dfrac{(t_c - t_{cs})}{(1 - t_{cs})}$	2.5%

*For t_c = 40% and t_{cs} = 20%.

Table 11.2 indicates that the annual tax advantage of funding the pension plan with bonds rather than stock is equal to the pretax interest rate on bonds times $(t_c - t_{cs})/(1 - t_{cs})$. This amount is increasing in the corporate tax rate, t_c, and decreasing in the corporate tax rate on shares, t_{cs}. Since the 1986 Tax Act both decreased t_c and increased t_{cs}, the tax advantage of investing the pension fund assets in bonds has diminished.

The analysis in Tables 11.1 and 11.2 has ignored the nontax costs associated with implementing the arbitrage strategy. Bondholders cannot be sure that the corporation will maintain the position in bonds in the pension fund. After all, the pension fund has its own trustees, who could decide to revert to a strategy of investing in stocks in the pension fund after the loan was in place. This uncertainty increases the risk for bondholders. As a result, they might charge a higher rate of interest on the loan to cover their monitoring costs. Moreover, the firm could go bankrupt, and in bankruptcy it is not possible for the bondholders to claim the accumulated value of the $1 of bonds in the pension plan. Pension beneficiaries have first claim against the pension plan assets. As a result, the bondholders must look to the risky stock portfolio on corporate account as security for their loan, which most likely would cause the borrowing costs to increase further.

For example, if the before-tax borrowing rate were 13.33% instead of 10%, the after-tax cost of the debt would have been 8.0% (or 13.33%(1 - .40)). At this rate, the arbitrage opportunity in Table 11.2 would just disappear.

Related to the point above regarding nontax costs to implement the arbitrage plan, it is worth noting that the arbitrage argument doesn't work as well for defined contribution plans as for defined benefit plans. Whereas the assets in defined benefit plans can be viewed as being owned by the employers that promise beneficiaries a certain level of benefits, the assets in defined contribution plans are owned by the beneficiaries. If beneficiaries in defined contribution plans wish to earn the risk premium on stock, they must effect the organizational-form arbitrage on personal account by borrowing to purchase stock.

With limited interest deductibility for individuals, and with a large spread between the rate at which individuals borrow and the rate at which they can earn on bonds held in the pension plan, such organizational-form arbitrage strategies become too expensive to be profitable. Consequently, nontax factors (in particular, the desire to earn risk premiums on stock relative to bonds) may lead pension fund beneficiaries to prefer nontrivial amounts of stock to be invested in their pension funds, despite the implicit tax such tax-favored investments bear.[8]

11.4 Does it Pay to Maintain an Overfunded Pension Plan?

Many U.S. corporate pension funds are overfunded today by wide margins, because (1) the stock market boomed during the decade of the 1980s and (2) interest rates (in real terms) have been relatively high, reducing the present value of the pension liabilities. There are several advantages and disadvantages of overfunding a pension plan. These are discussed below.

1. Expectations of changing tax rates

In 1986, U.S. corporations facing a marginal tax rate of 46% knew that in 1987 their marginal tax rate would fall to 40% and could anticipate that their marginal tax rates would fall further to 34% in 1988. This encouraged overfunding in 1986. Moreover, each dollar invested in the pension plan in 1986 grows at the before-tax rate R_{cn} until it is withdrawn from the fund. By reducing its future funding, when its marginal tax rate is 34%, the corporation realizes a return bonus of 22% (or (1 - 34%)/(1 - 46%) -1). This opportunity did not go unnoticed by General Motors Corp. GM made a "special, unrequired contribution ... of $1.04 billion (in 1986) ... to its U.S. pension plans to take advantage of tax deductions."[9] As another example of strategic timing of pension plan contributions and "reversions," Exxon terminated several of its overfunded pension plans in 1986, when it was experiencing "tax-free" status due to net operating losses for tax purposes.[10]

The Internal Revenue Service is well aware of the benefits of generous levels of pension funding when tax rates are high. During 1990, the Service announced its intention to conduct 18,000 audits of defined benefit pension plans for the 1986 tax year, expecting to raise hundreds of millions of dollars in additional tax

---

[8] The authors of this text have put their money where their mouths are in this respect. We have invested more than half of our defined contribution pension funds in stocks.

[9] *Wall Street Journal* (September 16, 1987), p.16.

[10] See Mitchell A. Peterson, "Pension Terminations and Worker-Stockholder Wealth Transfers," (Working Paper, M.I.T. Department of Economics), May 2, 1989.

revenues. In particular, it targeted plans that assumed unrealistically low interest rates on investments and unrealistically early retirement dates for plan participants.[11] Such assumptions imply larger current funding requirements to meet promised retirement benefits.

2. Possibility of an excise tax

If the corporation were to surrender its pension plan and capture the excess pension assets, it may face an excise tax in addition to the regular corporate tax on these assets. For example, the 1986 Tax Act imposed a 10% excise tax on excess assets withdrawn from a terminated pension plan in most circumstances, and the excise tax was raised to 15% in 1988 and 20% in 1989.[12] Did the imposition of excise taxes affect the number of terminations? Apparently so. While $6.6 billion of pension plan assets reverted to their corporate sponsors upon termination of their pension plans in 1985, and another $4.3 billion in reversions took place in 1986, only $1.9 billion and $1.1 billion worth of reversions occurred in 1987 and 1988, respectively.[13]

The firm does not have to surrender its pension fund, however, to recapture its excess assets. It can (1) reduce future funding levels by changing plan assumptions and (2) increase promised pension benefits for its employees in lieu of salary increases or bonuses. Reducing salary to employees or contributions to the plan will increase the corporation's current taxable income and reduce the level of overfunding in the plan.

Nontax considerations affect these choices. Employees might not give up a dollar of salary (or bonus) for an extra dollar of pension benefit. For them, the cost of borrowing to meet current consumption needs might exceed the returns that they can earn on this form of deferred compensation as we discussed earlier. To compensate such employees, the employer might have to sweeten pension benefits so substantially that it might not be advantageous to take this path to reduce overfunding in the plan. In addition, even if employees prefer pension to current salary, the 15% excise tax on excess pension benefits to employees imposed under the 1986 Tax Act might make it tax-disadvantageous for these employees to accept an increase in their pension benefits.

3. Investment alternatives with overfunded assets

Being able to earn at the before-tax rate of return in the pension fund, as compared to the after-tax rate of return on corporate account, is one of the advantages of overfunding the plan. Generally, the risk-adjusted rate of return on assets in the pension fund will exceed the rate of return on marginal investments undertaken on corporate account. This is true even if the firm can generate superior profits at the corporate level. After all, the firm can borrow to fund the pension plan while still undertaking the superior corporate investments. This dominates not funding the pension plan. Interest on the debt that is used to fund the pension contributions is tax-deductible at the corporate level, while investment returns on assets in the pension account are tax exempt. Of course, we must

---

[11] *New York Times* (June 2, 1990), p. 22.

[12] The 1990 Tax Act raises the excise tax rate to 50% in certain circumstances.

[13] Peterson, *op. cit.*

not forget that nontax costs associated with convincing lenders that the firm has superior investments could increase borrowing costs to such an extent that the firm should forgo funding the pension plan.

Since the corporation "owns" the excess assets in the pension plan, its best investment strategy is to hold high explicitly taxed assets such as high yielding risky bonds.[14] If the firm commits to a policy of holding bonds in its pension plan, the borrowing rate on the bonds used to finance the contributions would be less than if the corporation undertook more risky investment strategies in the plan. As discussed earlier, however, it is difficult to commit to such an investment policy in advance. Once again, the deadweight costs associated with issuing risky debt would reduce the advantage of overfunding the plan.

Moreover, prior to the 1986 Tax Act, corporations held 50% of their pension fund assets in stock and 50% in bonds. The rate of return advantage of investing the excess assets at the before-tax rate would be reduced by 50% of the implicit tax on shares. For example, if bonds returned 10% before tax and common stocks generated a risk-adjusted return of only 7% before shareholder-level tax, the combined pension fund portfolio would have returned 8.5% (or $.5 \times 10\% + .5 \times 7\%$), for an implicit tax rate of 15% (or (10% - 8.5%)/10%). Moreover, the corporation could invest in other tax-advantaged assets, like cash-value life insurance policies. So the tax advantages of overfunding the pension fund may have been small.

Following the 1986 Tax Act, however, the tax disadvantage of investing pension plan assets in stocks became considerably less. The implicit tax on shares should have become relatively low. As a result, U.S. and foreign pension funds became excellent candidates for increased investment in U.S. stocks.

The 1987 Tax Act restricted the level of overfunding in a defined benefit pension plan. Corporations cannot deduct further contributions if the assets in the plan exceed 150% of the termination liability. To reduce the probability of hitting this funding limit, many corporations are moving their asset mix toward bonds. As we will see in the next section, however, the desirability of stocks relative to bonds as a pension fund investment can be affected greatly by dynamic tax-planning strategies.

4.   Dynamic tax-planning strategies

Why have corporations invested so much of their pension assets in tax-favored assets, especially stock? As we have already noted, this was particularly mysterious prior to the 1986 Tax Act, because one important reason the corporation has for overfunding its pension fund is that it can earn at a higher rate after tax in pension account than on corporate account. Holding stocks reduces this advantage.

As we discussed earlier, another reason for overfunding is to take advantage of expected declines in tax rates. How can a firm overfund its pension plan? Actuaries, in setting pension contribution levels, are likely to assume conservative (low) earnings rates on pension assets to ensure that pension promises to beneficiaries can be fulfilled. The lower the assumed rate of return on investment,

---

[14] To the extent that there is ambiguity regarding who owns the excess assets in a pension fund (the employer or employees), there may be an additional nontax cost to overfunding the pension plan.

the greater is the current funding requirement if the pension fund is to have sufficient assets to meet promised payments. If the assets in the pension fund are invested only in riskless bonds, the actuary is forced to select a rate of return that is very close to the rate earned on the bonds. If actuaries set the earning rate at this level, it would not be possible to overfund the pension plan.

But if the fund invests in stocks, the actuary might choose a lower earning rate on the assets to cushion it against adverse changes in the market value of the fund's common stocks. For example, the actuary might wish to prevent the fund's market value from falling below a prescribed level more than 5% of the time. The greater the possible variation in the returns on the pension assets, the greater is the chance that the initial market value of the fund's assets will fall to this level at some future date. On the other hand, the greater the initial market value of the fund, the less likely that it will fall to this prescribed value given the variation in the returns on the underlying fund. By setting a low earning rate (or equivalently, a low discount rate to be used in calculating the present value of the promised future pension payments), the actuaries can "authorize" an increase in funding to the desired level. The firm then can build up its excess assets by investing, in part, in common stock. At a later time, when it switches into bonds, the actuary will typically increase the assumed earnings rate on pension assets, thereby indicating an overfunded pension plan. Tax rules require that the excess assets in the pension fund be amortized over a number of years by reducing contributions each year. Thus, for this period of time, the firm can achieve the advantage of investing at the before-tax rate in bonds. It can also realize the tax rate advantage from advance funding if tax rates should fall in the future.

5.   Net operating loss firms

Empirical evidence suggests that net operating loss (NOL) firms cut back on pension contributions to the extent they are legally permitted to do so. While, on average, pension funds were overfunded on a termination basis during the 1980s, the pension plans of low marginal-tax-rate firms were not generally overfunded. In fact, many were underfunded. In addition, low-taxed firms, such as start-up ventures, were less likely to sponsor defined benefit pension plans. In fact, they more often favored cash-based or stock-based deferred compensation arrangements to pension plans of *any* sort.[15] The next section helps explain why.

11.5   Deferred Compensation versus Pension

From earlier discussion in this chapter and in Chapter Three, we know an employer is indifferent, from a tax standpoint, between a dollar of current pension contribution (or salary) and

$$\frac{(1 - t_{co})}{(1 - t_{cn})} (1 + r_{cn})^n$$

dollars of deferred compensation in n periods, where t_{co} and t_{cn} represent the employer's current and future tax rates and r_{cn} represents the annual after-tax

---

[15] See Jacob K. Thomas, "Corporate Taxes and Defined Benefit Pension Plans," (Working Paper, Columbia University), September 1987.

rate at which the employer can earn on marginal investments. That is, the employer can afford to pay deferred compensation of $1, plus its after-tax earnings on the dollar in salary or pension contribution postponed for n years, adjusted for changes in its tax rate over time.

For the employee, the deferred compensation payment provides an after-tax accumulation, for each dollar of salary or pension contribution sacrificed, of

$$\frac{(1 - t_{co})(1 + r_{cn})^n}{(1 - t_{cn})} (1 - t_{pn}). \tag{11.4}$$

In comparison, each dollar contributed to a pension plan would yield, in n periods,

$$(1 + R_{cn})^n (1 - t_{pn}). \tag{11.5}$$

Deferred compensation is preferred to pension if

$$\frac{(1 - t_{co})}{(1 - t_{cn})} > \frac{(1 + R_{cn})^n}{(1 + r_{cn})^n}. \tag{11.6}$$

Note that the employee's tax rates are irrelevant to this comparison, because both compensation arrangements give rise to taxation in the future.[16] If the corporate tax rate is expected to be higher in the future (that is, $t_{cn} > t_{co}$) and $R_{cn} = r_{cn}$, then deferred compensation is preferred to pension. For example, if t_{co} is 20% and t_{cn} is 40%, then $(1-.2)/(1-.4)$ is 1.33, which implies that deferred compensation is preferred to pension by 33%. If the employer has a defined benefit pension plan in place under such circumstances, it may pay a corporation to *underfund* (not overfund) the pension plan.

On the other hand, suppose that $r_{cn} = 7.5\%$ and $R_{cn} = 10\%$. Then, deferred compensation is preferred to pension as long as:

$$1.33 > (1.1)^n/(1.075)^n,$$

which will occur if n < 12.5 years.

Other Factors Relevant to the Comparison of Pensions and Deferred Compensation

There are more tax-rule restrictions on funding a defined benefit pension plan than there are with deferred compensation plans. With pension plans there are (1) minimum funding requirements that may force a corporation to take a tax deduction for funding earlier than would be necessary under a deferred compensation plan, (2) higher administration and legal costs than for deferred compensation plans, and (3) many more anti-discrimination rules than for deferred compensation programs.

The objective of the Congress in providing tax-favored treatment to pension plans was to encourage broad-based retirement savings. This led to the introduction of contribution limits and nondiscrimination rules. Deferred compensation arrangements are free from these limits. They can also be used advantageously

---

[16] If the dates of future taxation differ, however, then employee tax rates become relevant to the comparison.

in special tax-planning situations. For example, an executive on assignment for two or three years in a Scandinavian branch office where local tax rates are very high would prefer a deferred compensation program to salary. Income could be received at substantially reduced home-country tax rates upon returning to the home country. The employer cannot target such an individual with a pension plan.

The biggest nontax problem with deferred compensation programs is that to avoid constructive receipt, the employee must be an unsecured creditor of the firm.[17] A pension trust, by contrast, does provide security to the extent it is funded and/or insured. The beneficiary has a claim against the trust and the insurance agency.

Prior to the 1986 Tax Act, U.S. corporations could, and often did, fund their deferred compensation programs by buying single premium deferred annuities with the salary dollars deferred by their employees. The 1986 Act precludes employers from investing in SPDAs on corporate account and avoiding the payment of tax currently on the investment earnings. New types of insurance products, however, have replaced SPDAs as corporate funding vehicles for deferred compensation plans. Moreover, as we will see in Chapter Twenty, there may be ways for corporations to achieve investment outcomes equivalent to SPDAs by entering into certain types of so-called "swap" contracts.

11.6   Funding Post-Employment Health-Care Benefits

The U.S. General Accounting Office has estimated that the accrued liability of U.S. corporations for retiree medical benefit promises made to employees exceeds $400 billion.[18] While this is less than half the accrued liability for pension promises, retiree medical benefits, unlike pension benefits, are largely unfunded. In 1988, the Washington Business Group on Health estimated that only 6% of firms pre-fund retiree welfare benefits. The vast majority operate on a "pay-as-you-go" basis.[19]

What is the best way for a firm to fund retiree medical benefits? In most cases, advance funding of such benefits cannot be done in as tax-advantaged a way as the advance funding of pension benefits. Except in so-called 401(h) plans and collectively bargained Voluntary Employee Benefit Association programs (VEBAs), current tax deductions cannot be taken for advance funding. While deductions *are* available for advance funding through a 401(h) plan, such plans are expensive to administer. Moreover, the annual contribution to such plans cannot exceed 25% of the contributions made to the employer's pension plans. So when a firm's pension plan is overfunded, contributions to a 401(h) plan are not permitted at all.[20]

---

[17] This problem can be mitigated by setting aside funds in a trust on behalf of employees (a so-called "rabbi trust"), but to avoid constructive receipt of income, secured creditors of the firm must have legal priority over the trust beneficiaries to the assets in the trust in the event of bankruptcy.

[18] See the remarks of Theodore E. Rhodes, *Panel on Retiree Medical Benefits*, Fidelity Management Trust Company (Washington, D.C.), January 31, 1989, p.5.

[19] *Ibid*.

[20] In 1990, Proctor and Gamble established a defined contribution Employee Stock Ownership Plan (as described in the next chapter). They had intended to use the plan as a 401(h) program to fund health care benefits, but the taxing authority denied the favorable 401(h) treatment.

There are at least two alternative ways in which retiree medical benefits might be funded:

1. Inform employees that pension benefits will be sweetened and that employees will be made responsible for paying their own medical benefits.
2. Employ a pay-as-you-go plan, whereby the firm pays for employees' expenses as they are incurred in retirement.

The Sweetened-Pension-Benefit Approach

Suppose the firm wishes to cover the cost of a one-dollar future medical benefit (n years from today) for its employee. If pension benefits are supplemented, the employee will receive taxable pension income at time n. After paying tax on this income at personal tax rate t_{pn}, the employee will require a full $1 to pay for the medical benefits, since the expenditure will not be tax-deductible.[21] So the amount of taxable pension benefits required at time n is

$$\$1/(1 - t_{pn}).$$

The cost to the employer of providing this benefit is the amount that must be deposited into the pension plan today, less the value of the tax deduction, at a tax rate of t_{co}, that the employer obtains for the pension contribution. Since the pension fund is tax-exempt, its assets grow at the before-tax rate, R_b. So, to accumulate $1/(1 - t_{pn})$ dollars in n periods, when the funds in the retirement plan earn income at rate R_b per period, the employer must deposit the following amount into the pension fund:

$$\frac{1}{1 - t_{pn}} \times \frac{1}{(1 + R_b)^n}.$$

This would result in an after-tax cost to the employer of

$$\frac{1}{1 - t_{pn}} \frac{1}{(1 + R_b)^n} (1 - t_{co}) \qquad (11.7)$$

The Pay-as-You-Go Approach

In the absence of advance funding of the benefits through a tax-qualified trust, the employer usually receives no current tax deduction. Instead, the employer secures a tax deduction in the future (at time n) when the benefit payment is made. If the benefit is provided to the employee as a fringe benefit through a group health benefit plan, as is typical, the employee is not taxed on the receipt of the benefit. This means that the employer need pay only $1 at time n to satisfy the obligation. If the employer can invest funds on corporate account in the interim at an after-tax rate of rb per year, then the current cost to the employer is

$$(1 - t_{cn})/(1 + r_b)^n. \qquad (11.8)$$

---

[21] As discussed in Chapter Ten, medical costs are deductible in the U.S. as itemized deductions only to the extent they exceed 7.5% of the taxpayer's adjusted gross income, and then only to the extent itemized deductions exceed the standard deduction that is available as an alternative.

Chapter 11   Pension and Retirement Program Planning

Comparing the two alternatives, we see that advance funding through the pension account is the superior choice if

$$\frac{(1 - t_{co})}{(1 - t_{pn})(1 - t_{cn})} \frac{(1 + r_b)^n}{(1 + R_b)^n} < 1. \tag{11.9}$$

Note that in the special case in which the employer's tax rates are constant over time, the pension funding route is cheaper if

$$\frac{(1 + r_b)^n}{(1 + R_b)^n} < (1 - t_{pn}).$$

If r_b were equal to R_b, the unfunded alternative would dominate, because it would allow employees to receive the benefits tax-free, whereas the pension benefits would be taxable.

When might r_b be equal to R_b? When the employer is tax-exempt (e.g., a university or a not-for-profit hospital) or when the taxpaying employer invests idle funds in cash-value life insurance policies without incurring any implicit taxes. Another case in which r_b may be close to R_b is where the corporation funds its health care program by investing in its own common stock. Because a U.S. corporation pays no tax on the dividend or capital gain income it earns from holding its own common stock, the risk-adjusted after-tax return on the stock will be below the pretax bond rate only to the extent the stock bears implicit tax.

But suppose that r_b is less than R_b. Then there is a tradeoff between earning at a higher after-tax rate by advance funding through a pension and providing a tax-exempt benefit to employees by *not* funding the plan. For example, suppose r_b is equal to 7%, R_b is 10%, and the employer's tax rate is constant over time. In Table 11.3, we show the employee's tax rates at time n, t_{pn}, below which pension funding beats the unfunded alternative. At higher values of t_{pn}, it is too costly to forego the advantage of tax exemption for medical benefits, at retirement, available through the unfunded alternative. Note that longer horizons favor advance funding through the pension account since the advantage of tax-free investment becomes more important.

Table 11.3 Employee's Tax Rate, t_{pn}, Below which Pension Funding Dominates Corporate Funding of Reteree Health Benefits

n	$\dfrac{(1 + r_b)^n}{(1 + R_b)^n}$	$t_{pn}{}^*$
5	.8709	.13
10	.7585	.24
20	.5752	.42

n = time horizon (years)
R_b = 10% = Pension fund investment rate of return
r_b = 7% = After-tax rate of return on corporate investments

1. Future medical costs are uncertain. Employees must bear this risk if a supplemental pension plan is used, but not in an unfunded plan or a 401(h) plan.

2. In an unfunded plan, the employee bears the risk of default on the promise. For example, a leveraged buyout of the corporate employer can expose employees to a substantial risk of default on such unfunded obligations.

3. Compensation expense for financial accounting purposes is less for unfunded plans than for the alternatives, although the Financial Accounting Standards Board plans to eliminate most of the differences.

4. Increasing employer tax rates favor unfunded plans: tax deductions are secured at higher tax rates.

5. Unfunded plans are more desirable for employees with high tax rates. So they may be more advantageous where the work-force is predominantly white collar rather than blue collar.

6. There are administrative costs associated with operating 401(h) plans. This can make unfunded plans more desirable than 401(h) plans even when the latter are available. For example, tax exempt entities will typically find unfunded plans preferable to 401(h) plans.

7. Given the magnitude of the unfunded liability, the U.S. Congress probably will be unable to resist tinkering with tax incentives to encourage the advance funding of retiree health benefits. Such changes will surely change the calculus of the cost of the funding alternatives somewhat. But the analysis above should be adaptable to the proposed changes.

Summary of Key Points

1. To encourage saving for retirement, the tax law bestows favorable tax treatment on pension compensation in a great many countries. In the U.S., employers receive an immediate tax deduction for pension contributions, while employees are taxed only when they receive payments in retirement. Moreover, qualified pension trusts are tax exempt, so earnings in the trust accumulate tax-free.

2. There are two broad categories of pension plans: defined benefit plans and defined contribution plans. In defined benefit plans, the employees' retirement benefits are fixed by a contractually specified formula, and there may be considerable uncertainty regarding how much and when the employer will fund the promised benefits. In defined contribution plans, the employer's pension plan *contributions* are fixed by a contractually specified formula, and, depending upon how well the pension fund investments perform, there may be considerable uncer-

tainty regarding how much the employees will receive in retirement benefits.

3. Even when nontax factors are ignored, pensions do not always dominate salaries as a compensation alternative. In particular, if employees' tax rates are expected to increase over time, current compensation may be preferable.

4. When nontax factors are considered, current compensation is preferred to pensions in a broader set of circumstances. Pension plans may force some employees to postpone consumption to a greater extent than they would like.

5. While it is tax-advantageous to invest pension plan contributions in assets that bear little implicit tax (like bonds and other interest-bearing securities), a substantial fraction of such contributions are invested in tax-favored assets, like stocks and real estate. This arises because many risky assets, notably common stocks, are granted tax-favored treatment. Such an investment strategy is sensible only in the presence of substantial transaction costs and a desire to invest in risky assets in the hopes of earning risk premiums. In the absence of transaction costs, such risk premiums could typically be earned in a more tax-favored way by borrowing funds to invest risky assets outside the pension plan and holding interest-bearing securities in the pension plan.

6. An advantage of defined benefit over defined contribution pension plans is the ability to "overfund" the former. This advantage is greatest when employer tax rates are falling over time and when the difference between the after-tax rate of return on pension plan assets and the after-tax rate of return on marginal investments by the employer *outside* the pension plan is highest.

7. Nonqualified deferred compensation arrangements are typically less tax-favored than qualified arrangements, such as pension plans. Not only must the employer defer the timing of the tax deduction in nonqualified arrangements, but the income earned on assets set aside to fund nonqualified deferred compensation is taxed to the employer. Nevertheless, deferred compensation plans face far fewer tax-rule restrictions than do pension plans, making them attractive in a broader set of circumstances. In particular, they are commonly used for highly paid employees who face binding constraints on contributions to qualified retirement plans.

8. Retiree health benefits can be funded in several ways in the U.S. The most tax-advantaged ones involve the use of so-called 401(h) plans or collectively bargained plans, but the availability of these arrangements is restricted. These plans allow a current tax deduction for advance funding, tax-free compounding of investment returns on plan assets, and tax exemption of benefits to employee recipients in retirement.

9. Alternative ways in which to fund retiree medical benefits include sweetening pension benefits (in exchange for making retirees responsible for their own medical expenses) and pay-as-you-go plans, where

the employer pays for employees' expenses as they are incurred in retirement. The benefit of the pension plan alternative is that the employer receives an earlier tax deduction, and funds accumulate free from tax in a pension trust. The benefit of an unfunded plan is that employees can receive retiree benefits free from tax (retiree health benefit payments can be structured as part of a tax-free medical benefit program). The unfunded alternative is more attractive the higher are the employees' tax rates in retirement, the higher is the employer's future tax rate relative to its current tax rate, and the lower is the benefit of tax-free compounding of investment returns in a pension plan.

Discussion Questions

1. What are the major differences between a defined contribution pension plan and a defined benefit pension plan?
2. When is it tax-advantageous for the firm to pay salary instead of an equivalent pension contribution?
3. What are the nontax costs associated with providing pension benefits for employees?
4. Under what conditions will the returns to investing outside the pension fund be greater than the returns to investing inside the pension fund?
5. How does the length of time that the pension contribution will remain in the pension account affect whether pension is preferred to salary? Under what conditions are the duration of the pension investment irrelevant?
6. What is the Black-Tepper stocks-versus-bonds puzzle as it relates to pension planning? Is it still tax advantageous for corporations to hold bonds in their pension accounts subsequent to the 1986 Tax Act?
7. What is the meaning of the term "overfunded" as it relates to a pension plan? What are the advantages and disadvantages to the corporation and its employees of an overfunded pension plan?
8. What role does the actuary play in deciding on whether the fund is over- or underfunded? How does this relate to dynamic planning strategies for the pension fund?
9. What are the tax and nontax factors in choosing between compensating employees by way of a pension plan versus a deferred compensation program?
10. What factors are relevant to determining whether retiree medical benefits should be funded in advance?

Problems

1. Suppose taxpayers were given a new option under the tax law for retirement funding. The new option requires that they forego a current tax deduction for pension plan contributions. Any contribution would accumulate in the pension fund free of tax, and distributions from the plan to beneficiaries would also be tax-free.

   The usual rules provide for current tax deductibility of pension plan contributions and full taxation of pension plan distributions at ordinary tax rates. (The tax rates at which contributions reduce taxes and the tax rates at which distributions increase taxes may differ because they occur at different points in time.)

   a. Who would prefer the new option?
   b. What would likely happen to taxes collected by the government in the short run? In the long run?
   c. What would likely happen to the aggregate amount of savings undertaken through pension accounts?
   d. How would the new option compare to one in which pension plan contributions give rise to current tax deductions, and pension plan distributions are taxed at a rate that coincides with the rate at which deductions were taken (even if ordinary tax rates at the times of distribution are different)?
   e. How would the new option compare to one in which
      - pension plan contributions give rise to current tax deductions,
      - pension plan distributions are taxed at the ordinary tax rates that apply at the time the distributions are made, and
      - if distributions are taxed at a rate above (below) the rate at which contributions were deductible, taxpayers receive a tax credit (pay additional tax) equal to the difference in tax rates multiplied by the pension plan contributions?

2. The accompanying table can be used to make paired comparisons of the desirability of salary, deferred compensation, and pensions as a function of: (1) current and future employee marginal tax rates; (2) current and future employer marginal tax rates; (3) the earnings rates on investment that the employer and employee can achieve; and (4) the number of periods of compensation deferral. Use the table to answer the following questions, and explain how the table enables you to do this. You may wish to refer to the discussion at the end of Chapter Three. To get you started, note that the relative advantage of deferred compensation over salary is given by a/bc^n, where a, b, c, and n are defined in the table and where r_1 is defined to be equal to r_{pn} and r_2 is defined to be equal to r_{cn}.

   a. If $r_1 = r_{pn}$ and $r_2 = r_{cn}$, what do table values greater than 1.00 tell you about the desirability of salary relative to deferred compensation?

b. What portion of the table (i.e., which rows and columns) is relevant to a comparison of salary and pensions? What are the appropriate definitions of r_1 and r_2 in this case? And what do table values greater than 1.00 tell you?

c. What portion of the table is relevant to a comparison of pensions and deferred compensation? What are the appropriate definitions of r_1 and r_2 in this case? And what do table values greater than 1.00 tell you?

You are sitting back in 1986 and have been asked to provide tax-planning assistance in formulating compensation policy for several of your corporate clients. You have three types of clients, each of which has seven types of employees:

Employer clients		t_{co}	t_{cn}
(1)	Tax exempt	0%	0%
(2)	Net operating loss carryforward firm	16%	30%
(3)	Profitable corporation (rates include state income taxes)	50%	37.5%

Employees		t_{po}	t_{pn}
(1)	Maintenance workers	15%	15%
(2)	Young employee anticipating some career advancement and increases in statutory tax rates	28%	40%
(3)	Senior executive	50%	28%
(4)	Moderately high income employee near retirement	40%	25%
(5)	Mid-career nonmanagement employee expecting moderate career advancement and increases in statutory tax rates	34%	40%
(6)	Highly compensated junior-management employee	40%	33%
(7)	MBA student working October to December in the first year of employment and eight months per year in all future years of employment	20%	38%

d. For the case of $r_p = r_c = R_c$, for which employee/employer/length-of-the-employment-contract (EEL) combinations would you recommend that marginal compensation dollars be allocated to:

(1) salary?

(2) deferred compensation?

(3) pension?

e. Consider only employer client #3 and employees #1, 3, and 7. For the case of $r_p = r_c$ and R_c exceeds r_c by approximately 2%, for which of the relevant EEL combinations would you recommend that marginal compensation dollars be allocated to:

(1) salary?

(2) deferred compensation?

(3) pension?

Salary vs. Deferred Compensation vs. Pensions

(a)	0.80	0.80	0.80	1.00	1.00	1.00	1.20	1.20	1.20
n	5	10	20	5	10	20	5	10	20

(b)	(c)				Values for $a/(bc^n)$					
0.70	0.98	1.26	1.40	1.71	1.58	1.75	2.14	1.90	2.10	2.57
0.70	1.00	1.14	1.14	1.14	1.43	1.43	1.43	1.71	1.71	1.71
0.70	1.02	1.04	0.94	0.77	1.29	1.17	0.96	1.55	1.41	1.15
0.80	0.98	1.11	1.22	1.50	1.38	1.53	1.87	1.66	1.84	2.25
0.80	1.00	1.00	1.00	1.00	1.25	1.25	1.25	1.50	1.50	1.50
0.80	1.02	0.91	0.82	0.67	1.13	1.03	0.84	1.36	1.23	1.01
0.90	0.98	0.98	1.09	1.33	1.23	1.36	1.66	1.48	1.63	2.00
0.90	1.00	0.89	0.89	0.89	1.11	1.11	1.11	1.33	1.33	1.33
0.90	1.02	0.81	0.73	0.60	1.01	0.91	0.75	1.21	1.09	0.90
1.00	0.98	0.89	0.98	1.20	1.11	1.22	1.50	1.33	1.47	1.80
1.00	1.00	0.80	0.80	0.80	1.00	1.00	1.00	1.20	1.20	1.20
1.00	1.02	0.72	0.66	0.54	0.91	0.82	0.67	1.09	0.98	0.81
1.10	0.98	0.80	0.89	1.09	1.01	1.11	1.36	1.21	1.34	1.63
1.10	1.00	0.73	0.73	0.73	0.91	0.91	0.91	1.09	1.09	1.09
1.10	1.02	0.66	0.60	0.49	0.82	0.75	0.61	0.99	0.89	0.73
1.20	0.98	0.74	0.82	1.00	0.92	1.02	1.25	1.11	1.22	1.50
1.20	1.00	0.67	0.67	0.67	0.83	0.83	0.83	1.00	1.00	1.00
1.20	1.02	0.60	0.55	0.45	0.75	0.68	0.56	0.91	0.82	0.67
1.30	0.98	0.68	0.75	0.92	0.85	0.94	1.15	1.02	1.13	1.38
1.30	1.00	0.62	0.62	0.62	0.77	0.77	0.77	0.92	0.92	0.92
1.30	1.02	0.56	0.50	0.41	0.70	0.63	0.52	0.84	0.76	0.62

(a) = $(1 - t_{co}) / (1 - t_{cn})$
(b) = $(1 - t_{po}) / (1 - t_{pn})$
(c) = $(1 + r_1) / (1 + r_2)$

where

- t_{co} and t_{cn} are current and future employer marginal tax rates;
- t_{po} and t_{pn} are current and future employee marginal tax rates;
- n denotes the number of time periods (i.e., length of the employment contract);
- r_1 and r_2 denote interest rates; the precise definitions vary depending on the compensation comparison for which the table is used.

CHAPTER 12
Employee Stock Ownership Plans: Myths and Realities

During the first six months of 1989, U.S. corporations acquired more than $19 billion of their own stock to establish employee stock ownership plans (ESOPs). This compares to only $5.6 billion for all of 1988 and less than $1.5 billion per year from the passage of the Employee Retirement Security Act in 1974 through 1987.[1]

Special tax advantages appear to be available to companies using ESOPs. For example, such firms can sometimes deduct dividends paid on ESOP shares, as well as benefit from a tax-subsidized borrowing rate on loans used to buy ESOP shares. There are also important nontax considerations, such as the claimed incentive advantages of employees owning company stock and the use of ESOPs to defend against hostile tender offers by placing shares in the hands of relatively friendly employees. Our analysis brings into question the notion that ESOPs provide unique tax and incentive advantages. Depending on the benchmark against which they are compared, ESOPs can often be inferior along both dimensions.

Our analysis suggests that, particularly for large firms, where the greatest growth in ESOPs has occurred, the case is very weak for tax provisions being the primary motivation in establishing an ESOP. Yet Congress apparently believes that tax benefits explain the growth in popularity of ESOPs over the last few years, since the 1989 Tax Act curtailed tax benefits relating to ESOPs. The case is also weak for employee incentives being the driving force behind the establishment of ESOPs. Although the presence of special tax provisions has enabled management to justify the formation of ESOPs to their boards of directors and to the courts, a major motivation for the growth of ESOPs has been their anti-takeover characteristics.

---

[1]*Pensions and Investment Age*, July 24, 1989, and Joseph R. Blasi, *Employee Ownership: Revolution or Ripoff?* (Ballinger), 1988.

In this chapter we begin with an overview of tax and nontax motivations for adopting ESOPs. This is followed by a closer look at the operational characteristics of ESOPs. Our discussion here includes an evaluation of the risk-sharing and incentive features of these plans. We turn next to a closer look at some of the alleged tax advantages. Finally, we present some evidence on the growing importance of ESOPs in the U.S. and conclude with some brief summary remarks.

12.1   Overview of Tax and Nontax Motivations for Adopting ESOPs

The ESOP is a special type of defined contribution pension plan–like an individual retirement account, a Keogh account, or a Code Section 401(k) plan. The corporation makes tax-deductible annual contributions to the ESOP, which are generally used to buy company stock or to pay down a loan that was used to acquire company stock when the program was initiated. Each year, employees are allocated tax-free company shares, and any investment income accumulates tax free within the ESOP. Employees pay tax when they receive dividend distributions on ESOP shares during their working lives, when they receive other distributions from the ESOP during retirement, or when they otherwise leave the firm and "cash out" of the plan. (However, when employees leave the firm they can "roll" their ESOP shares into an Individual Retirement Account to continue to defer payment of any tax.)

Unlike most other defined contribution plans, the ESOP is required to invest primarily in the stock of the company establishing the plan, and this is commonly taken to mean that the ESOP must hold at least 50% of its assets in the stock of the sponsoring company. Unlike any other defined contribution plan, the ESOP can borrow to buy company stock, to prefund the required number of shares that the firm expects to credit to its employees over the term of the loan. Such plans are called "leveraged ESOPs." As the firm contributes to the ESOP, shares are credited to employees' accounts. Moreover, qualified lenders can exclude 50% of the interest that they receive on the ESOP loan, and the corporation can deduct any dividends that are used to pay down the ESOP loan or are paid directly to employees on their ESOP shares.[2] As we will see, these tax benefits must be balanced against both tax and nontax costs of establishing an ESOP.

The popular press offers these reasons for the popularity of ESOPs: (1) Several important tax benefits are available through an ESOP that are not available through other tax-qualified and nonqualified compensation programs; (2) ESOPs can be used to restructure employee work incentives and retirement benefits; and, (3) ESOPs can be used in corporate finance strategies as substitutes for, or in conjunction with, recapitalizations (changes in corporate capital structures) and leveraged buyouts. For example, ESOPs have been used to sell company divisions to employees. In addition, prior to the 1989 Tax Act, the deductibility of net operating losses (both existing and so-called "built-in losses") against future taxable income were not restricted if a corporate control change

---

[2]Under the 1989 Tax Act, the ESOP must own a majority of the employer's stock for lenders to qualify for the 50% interest exclusion on new ESOP loans.

Chapter 12   Employee Stock Ownership Plans: Myths and Realities

occurred through ownership interests acquired by an ESOP. The 1986 Act restricted the deductibility of such losses upon certain control changes when ownership interests are sold to parties other than ESOPs.

ESOPs have also been used to secure tax deductions on the payment of dividends, to achieve a subsidized borrowing rate on ESOP loans, and to defer the capital gains tax incurred by owners of private companies on the sale of their shares to the ESOP. ESOPs have also been used to allocate interest payments domestically to free up foreign tax credit limitations.[3]

There are other nontax reasons why ESOPs have become popular. Perhaps the most important one is that they have been used effectively to thwart hostile takeover attempts, particularly in the state of Delaware.[4] In early 1989, Polaroid won an important decision in the Delaware Chancery Court, which upheld Polaroid's issuance of 14% of its stock to an ESOP prior to the initiation of a hostile tender offer by Shamrock Holdings. The ESOP helped Polaroid's management defeat Shamrock's bid for its stock because employees voted their Polaroid shares with management. Delaware law requires that a firm wait three years after it acquires a 15% interest in a target before it can merge with the target, unless it can secure an 85% vote of the target's shareholders.[5] The waiting period can impose substantial costs on the acquiring firm if it had plans to use the assets of the target as collateral for interim or longer-term loans to finance a leveraged buyout. Firm management might establish an ESOP because they believe that employee-shareholders are more likely to vote with them than are outside shareholders. As a result, Polaroid's use of an ESOP as a successful takeover defense stimulated considerable interest in ESOPs.[6]

Shareholder approval is typically not required for adoption of an ESOP.[7] In addition, while employees must be granted voting rights in public-company ESOPs, acting on a tender offer is not a voting rights issue, so an ESOP provides a particularly strong tender offer defense. With respect to the Delaware 85% rule, however, stock held by an ESOP is counted as outstanding shares only if the participants have the right to tender their shares confidentially.

ESOPs are also being used to replace existing defined benefit pension programs, to replace other types of defined contribution programs, and to replace

---

[3] The 1986 Act made foreign tax credit limitations a significantly greater concern that it had been previously. The U.S. restricts foreign tax credits to an amount equal to foreign taxable income divided by worldwide taxable income, multiplied by U.S. tax on worldwide taxable income. One way to mitigate this problem is to make foreign-source income, as a fraction of worldwide income, as large as possible. Under Code Section 861, interest generated on domestic debt must typically be allocated partially to foreign activities, thereby reducing foreign-source income. It appears possible to allocate 100% of the interest on certain ESOP debt to domestic income, thereby increasing the allowable foreign tax credits.

[4] According to the *Wall Street Journal* (April 5, 1989), 179,000 companies are incorporated in Delaware, including 56% of the Fortune 500 and 45% of New York Stock Exchange companies.

[5] The three-year waiting period also does not apply if the board of directors and two-thirds of the disinterested stockholders vote in favor of the merger.

[6] For a case study of Polaroid's ESOP, see Robert F. Bruner and E. Richard Brownlee II, "Leveraged ESOPs, Wealth Transfers, and 'Shareholder Neutrality': The Case of Polaroid." *Financial Management* (Spring 1990), pp. 59-74.

[7] Lawrence N. Bader and Jenny A. Hourihan, *Financial Executives Guide to ESOPs: 1990 Update* (Salomon Brothers), January 1990.

post-retirement health care programs. In the case of post-retirement health care programs, some corporations are substituting an ESOP for their previous promise to fund the post-retirement health care costs of their employees.[8] Most post-retirement health-care programs are unfunded and are open-ended as to medical costs. In other words, the corporation makes an unsecured promise to provide health care for employees after they retire, whatever the costs might be. As an alternative, some companies contribute their stock to an ESOP and employees fund their own post-retirement health care costs from their accumulation in the ESOP. By establishing an ESOP, the corporation transfers both the uncertainty of future health costs and the selection of the level of health care to employees.[9] But the advance funding of post-retirement benefits through an ESOP (or any other pension fund) may reduce the risk that the employer will default on the promise to provide the future benefits.

As discussed in Chapter Eleven, however, advance funding of retiree medical benefits through an ESOP is not necessarily tax advantageous. While the employer secures an immediate tax deduction for the contribution into the pension trust, employees eventually pay tax on withdrawals from the fund. By contrast, pay-as-you-go retiree medical benefit plans allow employees to receive tax-free benefits in retirement, but at the expense of a deferred tax deduction for the employer and the loss of tax-free compounding for advance funding. Section 401(h) plans allow the firm to have the benefits both ways: immediate deduction for advance funding and tax-free compounding of investment returns, along with tax-free benefits to retirees. But it is not yet clear whether these benefits are available to defined contribution pension plans, and no more than 25% of a pension plan's contributions (which may be nil for overfunded pension plans) can be invested in a tax-exempt account to be used to provide for tax-free health-care benefits.

That advance funding of retiree medical benefits through an ESOP may be dominated along the tax dimension by other funding alternatives is interesting, because it increases the likelihood that nontax factors (such as an enhanced takeover defense) have a first order effect on the decision to fund such benefits through an ESOP. Since tax considerations are reasonably complicated in the pension area in general, and in the ESOP area in particular, it is important that independent members of corporate boards, and the courts, understand whether there really exist tax benefits for proposed retirement benefit plans. The adoption of such plans may serve the interests of incumbent management, but not shareholders, along nontax dimensions.

There are many substitute vehicles through which the corporation can achieve the many nontax and tax benefits of ESOPs listed above. There are, however, some special tax benefits available to an ESOP that are not available elsewhere. For example, under certain circumstances (far fewer after the 1989 Tax Act than before it), an ESOP can borrow to finance its purchase of company stock

---

[8] Examples include Ralston Purina, Boise Cascade, and Whitman. (*Business Week*, May 15, 1989).

[9] This is not to say that the bargain is one-sided. It may be that the corporation contributes more to the ESOP than the employee gives up in future health-care protection to compensate the employee for bearing the risk of unexpected changes in the cost of health care. On the other hand, employees might manage health-care costs more efficiently when they are responsible for the costs.

Chapter 12   Employee Stock Ownership Plans: Myths and Realities

at a tax-subsidized rate and deduct the interest on the loan. No other pension plan can do this. Moreover, a corporation can take a deduction for dividends it pays on the stock held in the ESOP if the dividends are paid directly to the employees in cash or if the dividends are used to pay down part of an ESOP loan that was used to acquire the company's shares. The ability to deduct from corporate taxable income both dividends on ESOP shares and the interest payments on the ESOP loan enables a part of corporate income to avoid an entity-level tax (as in S corporations, partnerships, and proprietorships). This has become particularly important with the passage of the 1981 and 1986 Tax Acts.

12.2   A Closer Look at the Operational Characteristics of ESOPs

Contribution Limits

It is often claimed that an important tax advantage of an ESOP is that the corporation can make tax-deductible contributions to fund it. This advantage, however, is not unique to an ESOP. Contributions to other pension plans are also tax deductible. In fact, so is straight salary.

Because employees can earn the before-tax rate of return on assets invested in a pension plan, it is generally tax-advantageous to provide at least a portion of compensation in the form of a qualified retirement plan. An ESOP might be more tax-advantageous than other types of pension plans if the corporation can make more generous contributions to an ESOP than to these alternative pension plans. But this is generally not the case. ESOP contributions are limited, as are other defined contribution plans, to 25% of compensation.[10]

As a tax-qualified pension plan, an ESOP cannot discriminate in favor of highly-compensated employees. Indeed, because ESOPs cannot be integrated with social security benefits, while other plans can be, ESOPs face tougher antidiscrimination rules. Therefore, it is difficult for senior management to control a large fraction of the shares of an ESOP. Even if the ESOP owns the entire

---

[10] An ESOP is defined in Code Section 4975 as a stock bonus plan (where contributions may be discretionary or contingent on measures of performance, like company profits), or as a combination stock bonus plan and money purchase pension plan (where contributions are neither discretionary nor conditioned on performance measures). If the ESOP is set up as a stock-bonus plan only, annual contributions are limited to 15% of employee compensation. ESOPs that are a combination of stock bonus and money purchase pension plans face annual contribution limits equal to 25% of employee compensation.

This amount can not exceed $30,000 for any employee, and only up to $200,000 (indexed for inflation after 1989) of compensation is taken into account in determining the percentage allocation to an employee. This $30,000 limit will increase over time with inflation adjustments. That is, the maximum contribution must be less than twenty-five percent of $90,000, indexed to inflation after 1986 once this amount exceeds $30,000. In some cases, employees can contribute more to an ESOP than to other defined contribution programs. For example, since these limits are based on the value of stock acquired at the time a leveraged ESOP was established, advances in stock prices might result in employees being allocated shares whose current market value far exceeds $30,000.

company (as is true of AVIS Corp.), senior management might find it difficult to control a large fraction of the company's stock.[11]

The 1986 Tax Act requires that employee participants in an ESOP be 100% vested at the end of five years (cliff vesting) or, after two years employment with the firm, at least at the rate of 20% for each year of employment. A potential nontax cost of these vesting requirements is that with employee turnover, the remaining employees of the firm might receive an unintended benefit. Indeed, remaining employees might have an incentive to *promote* employee turnover for this reason. An employee can factor expected turnover into his calculations of the amount of current compensation that he is willing to forgo for these expected future benefits. Because of both risk aversion and imperfect information, however, employees might be willing to give up far less in current compensation than the cost of these benefits to the employer despite their tax-favored treatment.

Given these anti-discrimination funding requirements, many ESOPs are funded with contribution percentages far less than the allowable 25% of compensation. For example, Marsh and McAllister indicate that in over 80% of the ESOP plans in firms with over 500 employees, contributions to the ESOP amount to 10% or less of compensation. In a more recent study, Conte and Svejnar find that ESOP contributions average 10% of salary and wages.[12]

The primary reason that these contributions are modest relative to contribution limits, despite the tax advantage of increasing contributions and reducing salary, is that the benefits are not valued highly by lower-level employees. Such employees (particularly young employees) have a relatively strong preference for current over future consumption; they do not wish to save 25% of their compensation to secure future pension benefits. If the firm did contribute a large fraction of their compensation into an ESOP, such employees would be forced to borrow on personal account each year to meet their current consumption needs. Given the dead-weight costs of originating and administering such a loan, a lending institution would require that the borrowing rate substantially exceed its lending rate, even if the lender took into account that an employee will realize a future pension benefit that could be used to pay off the loan.

Note that it is not possible to secure a loan with the future proceeds of a pension benefit without disqualifying the pension plan. Moreover, interest incurred on debt to finance personal consumption may be nondeductible. Given these costs, many employees could not borrow at all, and others might feel that they are still better off with current salary than with deferred ESOP income.

---

[11] The percentage of non-highly compensated employees must be at least 70% of the percentage of highly compensated employees covered in the ESOP. The 1986 Tax Act defines "highly compensated employees" as those who own 5% or more of the company stock, those who earn more than $75,000 in compensation from the company, those who earn over $50,000 and are in the top twenty percent of employee compensation in the corporation, and officers whose compensation exceeds 150 percent of the contribution limit specified in the Code ($45,000 as of January 1, 1987, or 1.5 x $30,000). Union employees can be excluded from the ESOP (and typically are) if the company and the union bargain over contract provisions such as salary, health, and retirement programs.

[12] Thomas R. Marsh and Dale E. McAllister, "ESOPs Tables: A Survey of Companies with Employee Stock Ownership Plans," *Journal of Corporation Law* (Spring 1981), pp. 551-623; and Michael A. Conte and Jan Svejnar, "The Performance Effects of Employee Ownership Plans," Brookings Institution Working Paper (March 1989).

Chapter 12   Employee Stock Ownership Plans: Myths and Realities

Although the corporation could still make pension contributions for these employees, a competitive labor market might force the firm to supplement employee compensation if it is to retain the services of such employees. This extra cost constrains the level of ESOP funding.

Prior to the 1986 Tax Act, the contribution limits were more generous for a defined benefit pension plan than for an ESOP. Generally, a defined benefit pension plan provides the participant with a retirement benefit that depends on the level of final salary and/or the number of years of service. Various funding rules allow the corporation to accelerate the funding of its defined benefit retirement plan. This is not possible with a defined contribution plan.

One motivation for overfunding a pension plan is that it enables the corporate sponsor to earn the before-tax rate of return on investment. The corporation can reduce funding in later years to realize the benefit of overfunding. With the 1986 and 1988 Tax Acts, it became less desirable, as well as more difficult, to overfund defined benefit pension plans. Moreover, it now seems more likely that marginal tax rates will increase than decrease. This further reduces the incentive to overfund. All else equal, it is preferable to fund the pension plan when tax rates are high and expected to fall. As a result, defined contribution pension plans have become more competitive with defined benefit pension plans. This might be another reason why firms have established ESOPs.

Some of the advantage of tax-free accumulation in an ESOP is lost, however, since it is necessary for an ESOP to hold at least 50% of its assets in its company's stock, and common stock is not the most tax-favored security to hold in a retirement plan. This may have been particularly so prior to the 1986 Tax Act. At that time, shares might have borne a high implicit tax as we have discussed elsewhere. That is, the before-tax rate of return on shares on a risk-adjusted basis might have been far below the risk-adjusted returns on fully taxable bonds.

With the 1986 Tax Act, 100% of realized capital gains became taxable. In addition, the corporate dividend-received deduction was reduced from 85% to 80% (and reduced further to 70% in many circumstances following passage of the 1987 Act). As a result, the implicit tax on shares is likely to have fallen and the required risk-adjusted, before-tax rate on shares is likely to have increased. This generally means that the tax penalty for holding company stock in the pension plan has become smaller. This is another reason that ESOPs might have become more popular after the 1986 Tax Act. Moreover, contribution limits and anti-discrimination rules became more uniform across different types of pension plans. Because these rules often represent binding constraints, many corporations have substituted defined contribution plans for their defined benefit plans. Defined contribution plans are simpler, less costly to operate, and less vulnerable to attack by the firm's many constituents.

The 1986 Tax Act imposed an excise tax of 10% on the excess assets of a terminated defined benefit pension plan. This rate was increased to 15% with the 1988 Tax Act and to 20% with the 1990 Tax Act. Prior to 1989, however, corporations were allowed to transfer such excess assets to an ESOP without paying this excise tax. Merrill Lynch, for example, established an ESOP on the termination of its defined benefit pension plan in 1988. In addition, Figgie International, Transco Energy, ENRON, and Ashland Oil terminated defined benefit pension plans and transferred the surplus to a company-sponsored ESOP.

ESOPs provide a form of employee ownership in the corporation. This is an important reason why ESOPs have been championed by certain members of Congress. Employee stock ownership is presumed to align the interests of the employee more closely with the overall goals of the shareholders, relative to a pure salary contract. AVIS, which is 100% owned by an ESOP, emphasizes employee ownership in advertisements. By implication, customers are meant to feel that AVIS's employee-owners are working harder to meet their needs.[13]

While employee ownership of shares may succeed in promoting a commonality of interests between employees and owners relative to straight salary contracts, these incentives might be provided more efficiently in alternative ways. Where employees are risk averse relative to shareholders, efficient risk sharing requires that employees bear little risk of change in the value of the firm. But where their activities affect the value of the firm, and these actions are unobservable to shareholders except at prohibitive cost, it is desirable for incentive reasons to require employees to bear some risk of changes in the value of the firm. Risk averse employees will require additional compensation, however, if they are exposed to risk that is beyond their control. Efficient incentive contracting, therefore, requires a judicious trading off of risk sharing and incentives.[14]

It is useful to think of stock prices as an indirect monitor of employee inputs. The value of the firm can be viewed as being determined jointly by employee actions and actions chosen by others such as competitors, customers, and Nature (that is, random factors). Oftentimes it is possible to devise accounting measures of performance (such as divisional profits or physical output measures) that serve as less "noisy" indirect monitors of employee inputs. The reliance on such measures through incentive compensation arrangements is often a more efficient way (relative to measures based on stock market values) to align the interests of employees with those of shareholders. More generally, both types of measures (stock-based and accounting-based) contain information that is useful in drawing inferences about the effectiveness of employee performance, but stock-based measures are likely to prove far more "informative" with respect to senior management performance than with respect to lower-level employees.[15] As a consequence, the implementation of an ESOP may exact a cost along the incentive contracting dimension.

---

[13] Avis claims that its customer complaints have dropped by 40% since its ESOP was formed. It also claims that its costs are now well below those of Hertz, its competitor, although Hertz's costs used to be lower. There is conflicting evidence, however, as to whether ESOP plan adoptions are associated with increased "productivity." For a discussion of the evidence see Blasi, *op. cit.*, Conte and Svejnar, *op. cit.*, and Joseph E. Cooper, "Employee Stock Ownership Plans and Economic Efficiency," Working Paper (Harvard University), March 1989.

[14] For a particularly clear statement of the problem, as well as its solution, see Bengt Holmstrom, "Moral Hazard and Observability," *Bell Journal of Economics* (Spring 1978), pp. 74-91.

[15] For a comparison of stock-based and accounting-based measures of performance in incentive contracting, see Richard A. Lambert and David F. Larcker, "An Analysis of the Use of Accounting and Market Measures of Performance in Executive Compensation Contracts," *Journal of Accounting Research* (Supplement, 1987), pp. 85-125.

Weirton Steel's 100% employee-owned ESOP decided to take Weirton public again after a successful revitalization of the company. Part of the reason for the sale of company stock was that many of the vested employees in the ESOP did not want to risk undertaking a $500 million expansion of the firm's steel-producing capacity. They preferred a safer position.[16]

It is interesting to note that employee stock ownership was quite common in the 1920s.[17] But due to the market crash begun in 1929, 90% of the stock ownership plans in place before the crash were discontinued by the mid-1930s. Those not terminated restricted participation exclusively to highly paid employees. This is additional evidence that risk-sharing considerations are very important.

The tax rules require that employers allow employees to diversify their holdings at age 55 or 10 years of employment, whichever is later. In the first four years following the passage of this milestone, employees must be permitted to diversify up to 25% of their holdings, and in the fifth year they must be permitted to invest up to 50% of their holdings in nonemployer securities.

If employees receive nontraded company stock when they retire or leave the company, they have the right to put the stock back to the company for cash. Depending on the demographics, it can be very costly for the corporation to redeem these shares. Additional funds might have to be raised at a time when it is very costly to do so. Moreover, the release of shares to the employees of a private company might force the corporation to comply with Securities and Exchange Commission reporting requirements—the threshold is 500 shareholders. These requirements also impose costs.

Prior to the 1987 Tax Act, many ESOP sponsors provided their employees with a defined benefit pension plan offset. Examples include Ashland Oil, Bank of New York, and Hartmarx.[18] In these arrangements, the defined benefit plan might guarantee employees a retirement benefit of, say, 50% of their terminal salary during each year of retirement, but distributions to employees would be made from the defined benefit plan only if the ESOP failed to provide at least that same level of benefits. The defined benefit promise serves as a guaranteed floor. This reduces the employee's risk by essentially providing the employee with a put option. Note that shielding employees from risk also means sacrificing incentives. The 1987 Tax Act restricted the use of these offset provisions.

Firms have discovered other means to reduce the employee's risk of holding company stock in an ESOP. The ESOP can invest up to 50% of its assets in other than company stock, although a comprehensive survey conducted by the U.S. General Accounting Office in 1986 showed that four-fifths of ESOPs invested 75% or more of their assets in sponsoring company stock. The ESOP can also be supplemented with other types of compensation plans to reduce risk. For

---

[16] *Business Week* (January 23, 1989).

[17] Richard J. Patard, "Employee Stock Ownership in the 1970s," *Employee Ownership—A Reader* (National Center for Employee Ownership), 1985, p. 58.

[18] See Daniel Forbes, "The Controversial ESOP Pension," *Dun's Business Month* (November 1986), pp. 40-41.

12.2 A Closer Look at the Operational Characteristics of ESOPs

example, an ESOP might be combined with another defined contribution plan invested entirely in bonds.

Many firms now fund the ESOP with convertible voting preferred stock.[19] Holding preferred shares is generally less risky than holding the company's common stock in the ESOP. Given its superior dividend yield, the preferred will tend to sell at a premium over the common (if convertible into at least one share of common) and retain more of its value than the common stock if the value of the company should fall. If the preferred issue represented a substantial majority of the company's stock, however, it would have little protection in the event that the company does poorly.

Moreover, some ESOPs provide employees with a put option. That is, if the preferred stock happens to be selling below the conversion price when the employee retires or leaves the firm, the employee can put the stock back to the company for the conversion price. This put option is valuable to employees, for it protects them against the risk of a decline in the price of the common stock.

In summary, an ESOP provides a pension savings alternative to more conventional tax-qualified retirement plans, one that provides employees with an ownership interest in the firm. Employee ownership might lead the firm's "productivity" to improve as employees' interests become better aligned with the firm's other shareholders. But such compensation arrangements may be at the expense of other more efficient forms (ignoring taxes), both for risk-sharing and incentive reasons.

Moreover, there can be severe nontax costs if an ESOP must refinance to repurchase shares from departing employees. Shares that are initially contributed to the trust must eventually be cashed out, and high transaction costs might be incurred to accomplish this task, particularly in smaller businesses.

With these nontax costs and benefits of establishing an ESOP in mind, let us turn next to the tax benefits. We discuss primarily the tax advantages of a leveraged ESOP and the tax-deductibility of dividends on ESOP shares.

12.3 A Closer Look at Tax Advantages of an ESOP

Prior to the 1986 Tax Act, there were two basic types of ESOPs: a tax deduction ESOP (in which contributions to the trust give rise to tax deductions) and a tax credit ESOP (in which contributions to the trust give rise to tax credits). The tax credit ESOP was eliminated with the 1986 Tax Act. The 1984 Tax Act added significant tax incentives to encourage ESOPs by providing that (1) shareholders in a closely held company could obtain a tax-free rollover on the sale of their shares to an ESOP, if it attained at least 30% ownership of the company, and if the seller purchased qualified replacement securities such as corporate bonds; (2) the corporation could receive a deduction for dividends paid on ESOP stock, provided that the dividends were paid out currently to employees; and (3) a bank, insurance company, or other commercial lender was permitted to exclude from

---

[19] Our analysis of ESOP announcements in the first four months of 1989 (when there was a surge of new ESOPs formed) from the Dow Jones New Retrieval Service indicates that more than half of all new securities acquired by ESOPs are employer convertible preferred stocks.

income 50% of the interest received on loans to ESOP sponsors, provided that the proceeds of the loan were used to finance the acquisition of employer stock for the ESOP.

The 1986 Tax Act added to these benefits by providing (1) an estate tax exclusion for 50% of the proceeds of certain sales of company stock to an ESOP (subsequently repealed); (2) an expansion of the corporate dividend deduction to include dividends used to repay principal or interest on the loan used to acquire employer securities; (3) a provision allowing mutual funds to be added to the list of lenders eligible to receive the partial interest exclusion on loans to acquire employer securities; and (4) an exemption from the excise tax on reversions from defined benefit pension plans that are transferred to an ESOP (repealed by the 1989 Act). The 1986 Act repealed the payroll-based ESOP tax credit and required that certain employees be allowed to diversify their accounts.

The Fifty Percent Interest Exclusion

Under Code Section 133, banks, insurance companies, or regulated investment companies may exclude from gross income 50% of the interest that they receive on a loan used to buy company stock for an ESOP. Under the 1989 Tax Act, the ESOP must own more than half the employer's stock if *new* loans are to qualify for the 50% exclusion. There are three types of loans: (1) an immediate allocation loan; (2) a leveraged-ESOP loan; and (3) a back-to-back leveraged-ESOP loan. An immediate allocation loan is a loan to the company sponsoring the ESOP. The other two loans are effectively loans to the ESOP itself.

In an immediate allocation loan, the company borrows an amount equal to one year's contribution to an ESOP and transfers qualifying employer securities to the ESOP. The 50% exclusion, including any period of refinancing of the loan, cannot extend beyond a seven-year term. The transferred securities must be allocated to the individual accounts of employees within one year of the date of the loan (hence the term "immediate allocation").

The immediate allocation loan provides an opportunity for tax arbitrage in appropriate circumstances. To illustrate this, note that if lending markets are competitive and if there are no special costs associated with ESOP loans, the risk-adjusted before-tax rate of return on the loan, R_I, will be given by the following relation:

$$R_I(1 - .5t_c) = R_b(1 - t_c)$$

or

$$R_I = R_b(1- t_c)/(1 - .5t_c),$$

where t_c = corporate marginal tax rate;
           R_b = the before-tax risk-adjusted return on fully-taxable bonds; and
           R_I = the required before-tax rate of return on the ESOP loan.

So if corporate marginal tax rates are 34%, this implies that the rate of interest on the immediate allocation loan will be 79.5% of the fully taxable rate.[20] Empirical

---

[20] Property and casualty insurance companies are required to include 15% of any tax-exempt interest that they receive in taxable income. As a result, the insurance company would require a rate of interest

evidence suggests that ESOP loan rates are set between 80% and 90% of the fully-taxable rate, with securitized loans priced at roughly 75% of the prime rate.[21]

Assume for the moment that the corporation already has an ESOP and has determined the magnitude of this year's required contribution of stock. If the firm were to finance the contribution to the ESOP with an immediate allocation loan, the corporation's after-tax interest cost would be $R_I(1 - t_c)$ or approximately 80% of the after-tax cost of an ordinary loan for a 34% corporation that captures most of the tax benefits of the 50% interest exclusion via an interest rate reduction. If the corporation were otherwise planning to repurchase its stock using its internal cash flow, it would be tax-advantageous to use the proceeds of the immediate allocation loan to buy shares in the open market to contribute to the ESOP and use its internal cash flow to pay back some company debt.

Moreover, if the company currently contributes stock to a defined contribution pension plan *other* than an ESOP, it would be tax-advantageous for the company to switch to an ESOP. The seven-year immediate allocation loan is quite valuable. For example, if the before-tax bond rate is equal to 10%, the immediate allocation loan would have a before-tax rate of interest of 8% and an after-tax rate of interest of 5.28% (or 8%(1 - 34%)). If the corporation's ordinary borrowing rate is 10%, its after-tax cost is 6.6%. The immediate allocation loan offers an after-tax savings of 1.32% per year for a maximum of seven years. The present value of this benefit at a discount rate of 6.6% is 7.3% of the principal amount of the loan. This tax advantage was likely an important source of growth of ESOPs.[22]

While the immediate allocation loan is a loan for only one year's contribution to the ESOP, it is also possible for the ESOP to borrow to acquire stock that will fund the contributions to the pension fund for many years. This is called a leveraged ESOP. The ESOP borrows enough such that the loan proceeds can buy sufficient stock to fund, say, the next 15 annual contributions. As with immediate allocation loans, qualified lenders can exclude from taxable income 50% of the interest received on the leveraged ESOP loan.

---

that is 82% of the fully-taxable rate (or $R_I = .66R_b/(1 - 1.15 \times .5 \times .34)$). See Lawrence N. Bader and Jenny A. Hourihan, *The Investor's Guide to ESOP Loans* (Salomon Brothers), March 1989. Partnerships can create dual-class ownership, where one class receives the partially tax-exempt interest and other partners receive fully taxable interest. High marginal-tax-rate taxpayers, like corporations facing a 34% tax rate, would be the natural holders of the tax-exempt piece.

[21] See Steven Kaplan, "ESOP Notes," personal correspondence (March 31, 1989), Merrill Lynch, *Employee Stock Ownership Plans* (October 1988), Shearman and Sterling, *ESOPs; What They Are and How They Work* (January 1989), and Douglas A. Shackelford, "The Incidence of the Interest Income Exclusion in Leveraged Employee Stock Ownership Plans," Working Paper (University of Michigan), August 1988. Care must be exercised in gathering evidence on these rates. Because of the 50% exclusion, it pays for a lender to set a high rate on an ESOP loan and a lower rate on fully taxable loans. The tax laws impose restraints on this, but there is still room to set rates opportunistically. To test this, loans should be separated into two piles: those where the lender has no other business dealings with the buyer and those where the lender also engages in non-ESOP transactions with the borrower. Care must also be exercised to determine the correct risk adjustment to be made in comparing interest rates across loans.

[22] The government also subsidizes any deadweight costs that are uniquely incurred to underwrite the ESOP loan. The lender deducts its costs to process and underwrite the loan while the borrower pays less than 100% of the these costs through the interest break. Further, the 50% interest exclusion encourages the bundling of other services with the loan to secure a 50% income exclusion on revenues generated from these other services.

Chapter 12   Employee Stock Ownership Plans: Myths and Realities

If a leveraged ESOP borrows and buys company stock, the stock is placed in a so-called "suspense account." Each year as the corporation makes tax-deductible cash contributions to its ESOP, stock is released from the suspense account and allocated to the accounts of the participants. The contribution is then used to pay down the loan. The corporation can deduct up to 25% of compensation each year, the same as for an unleveraged ESOP. It also can deduct the interest payments that it contributes to the ESOP to pay the interest on the ESOP loan. Also, any dividends that are paid on the stock allocated to the participants or on the unallocated shares held in the suspense account can be used to pay down the loan. These dividends are tax deductible to the corporation.

It is often claimed that a leveraged ESOP is tax-advantageous because the corporation can make tax-deductible principal repayments on its ESOP loans. As we have already noted, however, all compensation payments are tax-deductible to the corporation. However, the 50% exclusion of interest on the loan and the deductibility of certain dividends *are* tax-advantageous. These options are not available with other plans.

It is difficult to quantify whether the corporation should use an immediate allocation loan or a leveraged-ESOP structure. The term of the leveraged-ESOP loan can extend for as many years as the company wishes to commit to contribute stock to its ESOP.[23] It must, however, pay down the ESOP loan under set guidelines over its life to retain the 50% exclusion. The immediate allocation loan can only extend for a period of seven years. But it can be a term loan in which all principal is repaid at maturity. Each year the corporation can issue another immediate allocation loan to fund that year's contribution to its ESOP. Although a leveraged ESOP loan is initially a much larger loan than an immediate allocation loan, the size of the loan falls each year as the principal on the note is reduced.

Another advantage of immediate allocation loans over leveraged ESOP loans is that where share prices are increasing over time, immediate allocation loans yield larger tax deductions for a given cost of buying shares deposited into the ESOP. The reason for this is that in a leveraged ESOP, tax deductions are based on the value of the stock at the time the shares are first acquired, whereas in the immediate allocation plan, the deductions are based on share prices at the time the shares are allocated to participant accounts.[24] An offsetting consideration for some plan sponsors is that financial reporting income will be lower, due to higher compensation expense, when immediate allocation loans are used and share prices are increasing over time. Depending on the length and size of the ESOP program, the present value of the tax benefits could be greater with an immediate allocation loan than with a leveraged-ESOP loan.

If future legislation were to limit the tax benefits of ESOP programs, the long-term loan might prove more or less attractive than the immediate allocation

---

[23] Although the term of the ESOP debt is limited by the number of years to which the employer will commit to making ESOP contributions, the maturity of the loan is restricted to ten years if the employer uses the "principal method" of allocation to release shares from the suspense account. Generally, the proportional method is used, wherein shares are released from the suspense account in proportion to interest and principal that is paid on the loan.

[24] For a more extensive analysis of this issue, see Howard A. Freiman, *Understanding Leveraged ESOP Economics* (Fidelity Management Trust Company), June 1989.

loan depending upon the particular "grandfather" provisions included in the legislation. It is interesting to note that many ESOP loans are written with provisions that guarantee the lender a benchmark after-tax rate of return that floats with the return on a taxable loan of comparable risk (for example, Treasury bills plus some fixed number of basis points). The rate of interest on the loan changes if statutory tax rates change or if the percentage of interest that is tax-exempt were to change, a form of insurance as discussed in Chapter Nine. The corporation could be at a disadvantage if Congress were to limit tax-deductible contributions to defined contribution plans and, as a result, prevent the corporation from making tax-deductible contributions to its pension plan of sufficient size to pay down the loan.

The back-to-back loan is very similar to the leveraged ESOP loan. In this case, the corporation borrows to purchase company stock and transfers the company stock to the ESOP in exchange for an ESOP note. There are two separate loans, one from the qualifying institution to the corporation, and one from the corporation to the ESOP trust. To qualify for the same tax treatment as the leveraged-ESOP loan, the repayment schedule and the interest rate must be essentially identical. If not, the back-to-back loan is limited to a term of seven years, and it must be paid down at least as rapidly as the corporate back-to-back loans. Moreover, leveraged-ESOP loans cannot be accelerated in the case of a default. As a result, many lenders prefer back-to-back loans. Also, the lender might feel more secure dealing with a corporation than with a trusteed pension plan. A pension plan never borrows except to finance a leveraged ESOP. The body of law concerning the property rights of the parties to leveraged-ESOP transactions is not well established.

The leveraged-ESOP structure has been used in a number of leveraged buyout transactions. It has also been used to accomplish such corporate finance objectives as (1) implementing a share repurchase program, (2) selling a division to employees, (3) placing a large block of the company's stock in employee (friendly) hands, and (4) taking a company private. However, there are several problems with this structure. The company must project future employee contributions. Overestimating the required payments would cause the employer to borrow an amount in excess of the actual annual requirements. Prepaying this excess amount of debt would result in the allocation of shares to the participants' accounts. Employees could benefit at the expense of the other shareholders.

The Deduction of Dividend Payments

Under Code Section 404(k), the corporation can deduct dividends to an ESOP if (1) the dividends are paid in cash directly to ESOP participants, (2) the dividends are paid to the ESOP and it distributes them to participants within 90 days of the close of the plan year, or (3) the dividends on ESOP stock (whether in the suspense account or allocated to participants) are used to make payments on an ESOP loan as described in Code Section 404(a)(9). The ability to take a deduction for dividends used to make payments on an ESOP loan was introduced by the 1986 Tax Act.

The deductibility of dividends eliminates the entity-level tax on part of the corporate income. In the extreme, if all the shares of a corporation were owned by its employees, and the corporation paid out tax-deductible dividends equal to its pre-dividend taxable income, all of the corporation's income would be taxed only once at the individual shareholder level. It is not entirely clear, however, that this should be taken too literally. The 1984 Act contained a provision empowering the Treasury to disallow dividend deductions to the extent they are deemed to "contribute to tax avoidance." Presumably this would be invoked if profitable businesses sought to distribute all profits as tax-deductible dividends. On the other hand, the provision may simply be a "paper tiger."

To see that dividends which are deductible to the corporation and paid on ESOP shares to participants convert the corporate tax to a single level of taxation under most circumstances, assume that the corporation is currently contributing $10 million to an ESOP at the end of each year. Further assume that this is less than the maximum contribution permitted of 25% of compensation.[25] Assume that the employer pays a dividend of $3 million at year-end on the ESOP shares and that this dividend is paid directly to the participants. Now suppose the corporation alters its policy by contributing $13 million to the ESOP instead of the usual $10 million and by reducing employee salary by $3 million. As a result, while salary is reduced by $3 million, employees receive $3 million in dividends from the ESOP. Employee pension accounts grow in value by the return on the pension assets less $3 million distributed as a dividend, but the corporation contributes an additional $3 million to the ESOP. So the accumulation in employee ESOP accounts, as well as their *current* compensation (salary plus dividends), is unaffected by this change in policy. From the corporation's viewpoint, the before-tax cash outflows are also exactly the same whether the corporation contributes to a qualified stock-bonus plan and pays a dividend on these shares or it contributes to an ESOP.

For example, assume that employee salaries, before the ESOP plan was adopted, totaled $50 million. If $10 million was also contributed to a stock bonus plan and $3 million in dividends were paid, the total pretax cash outflows would be $63 million. Under the ESOP plan, with dividends paid currently to employees, cash outflows would be $47 million in salary, $13 million in contribution to the ESOP, and $3 million in dividends on the ESOP shares. The total of $63 million is exactly the same as if the corporation contributed to a stock-bonus plan. After tax, however, the corporation is better off because it secures a tax deduction for $3 million of dividends. So if corporate tax rates are 34%, the corporation can eliminate just over $1 million in tax per year from the dividends paid to employees through securities that they hold in their ESOP accounts. Moreover, the firm and certain employees can avoid paying some social security taxes on their reduced salary. In effect, as employees accumulate securities in their ESOP accounts, they receive tax-deductible dividends from the corporation that convert income that would have been taxed at the corporate level, and then again at the personal level, to income that is taxed only once at the personal level.

Notice, however, that this plan works only if employees are not up against the 25%-of-compensation limit to contributions. If the corporation is already funding contributions to an ESOP to the maximum allowed under the tax rules,

---

[25] As discussed earlier, very few plans actually face binding constraints on the contribution limit. This is particularly so for public companies.

12.3   A Closer Look at Tax Advantages of an ESOP

it could not increase its funding and reduce current compensation as assumed in the analysis above unless a leveraged ESOP structure is used and dividends are used to pay down ESOP loans.

Corporate deductions can also be secured when dividends are used to make payments on an ESOP loan. As was true of paying out dividends to ESOP participants, using dividends on allocated ESOP shares to pay down the ESOP loan creates a marginal tax deduction equal to the amount of the dividends.[26]

To see this, let's return to our previous example, in which the corporate sponsor of the ESOP contributes $10 million in fresh cash to pay down the ESOP loan. This, in turn, releases $10 million of stock from the "suspense account"; that is, $10 million worth of previously unallocated shares are allocated to the accounts of employees. Now suppose that instead of reinvesting $3 million of dividends on allocated ESOP shares, the $3 million of dividends is used to pay down the ESOP loan further. This gives rise to an extra $3 million in tax deductions to the employer and leaves employees exactly where they were before; that is, employees receive an extra $3 million in new ESOP shares but lose $3 million of ESOP dividends, neither of which affects their current tax liability.

Dividends on unallocated shares that are used to pay down ESOP loans do not provide additional tax benefits beyond those provided by the dividends on *allocated* shares that are used to pay down the ESOP loans. Returning to the previous example, assume that in addition to dividends in the amount of $3 million on the allocated shares used to pay down the loan, the firm pays an additional $4 million of dividends on unallocated shares, and these dividends are also used to pay down the loan. The $4 million dividend releases $4 million of additional shares that are then allocated to employees.

To leave employees in exactly the same position as before, the corporation can reduce its nondividend ESOP contribution from $10 million to $6 million. Employees then receive a total of $13 million of new allocated shares: $6 million from fresh cash contributions coupled with the $3 million dividend on allocated shares and the $4 million dividend on unallocated shares. Total tax deductions to the corporation still totals $63 million.

It would be tax-disadvantageous, however, for the corporation to use the dividends on the unallocated shares, not to pay down the loan, but instead to add them to the suspense account. For if it were to select this route, the $4 million dividend on the unallocated shares would be tax-deductible neither when contributed to the ESOP nor when eventually distributed to employees. So these dividend payments support a larger ESOP program.

An additional advantage results when employees wish to add to their pension savings beyond the 25%-of-compensation limits. They can exceed the limits by using dividends to make payments on the ESOP loan. On the other hand, except in small, privately held corporations, it is very uncommon that employees wish to invest so heavily in pension savings, especially in a plan that is so poorly diversified.

---

[26] We have benefitted from discussions with Michael Prouting and Lawrence Bader on this point.

Chapter 12   Employee Stock Ownership Plans: Myths and Realities

ESOPs Financed with Equity Providing Dividend Pass-Through versus Debt-Financed Pension Plans Investing in Debt Securities

In the preceding discussion, we demonstrated that if, for nontax reasons, employer stock were held in the retirement plan or other corporate programs, an ESOP (with the 50% exclusion for interest income on ESOP loans) could be used profitably to effect tax savings. In this section we demonstrate that, ignoring the advantage of the 50% interest exemption on qualified ESOP loans, as well as other less important special tax features, ESOPs are dominated by other pension funds that avoid investing in employer equity securities. We further argue that in many relevant cases, the interest rate subsidy resulting from the 50% exclusion of interest income roughly compensates for the tax *disadvantage* of ESOPs. So in the end, whether ESOPs are desirable, particularly for publicly-traded companies, depends largely on the nontax benefits of employee ownership of employer shares.

To establish that ESOPs with dividend pass-through to employees are weakly dominated by debt-financed defined contribution pension plans, our analysis proceeds in stages. We begin by analyzing the after-tax cash flows to employees and employers when $1 is contributed into a pension plan, financed by debt bearing interest at rate R_b. The pension plan in turn invests in interest-bearing securities yielding rate R_b per year. The tax rates of the employer and the employee are t_c and t_p, respectively.

At time 0, the employer borrows $1 and deposits it into the pension plan, a net cash flow of $0. A tax deduction of $1 for the contribution to the retirement plan, however, yields a tax savings of t_c for the employer, so total cash flow is $+t_c$. Each year thereafter, through retirement, the employer pays out interest of Rb, which is tax deductible at rate t_c. Finally, at retirement in n years, the employer repays the $1 principal amount of the loan and the employee cashes out the pension. By this time, the pension assets have grown in value to $(1 + R_b)^n$, and the employee is taxed on this amount at rate t_p.

Case I: Debt-Financed Pension Fund

	Today (time 0)	Annually Through Retirement	At Retirement (n years)
Cash Flow to:			
Employer	$+t_c$	$-R_b(1-t_c)$	-1
Employee	0	0	$+(1+R_b)^n(1-t_p)$

Next, compare these cash flows to those that result from the employer forming an ESOP, financing the $1 contribution to the trust with a preferred stock paying a dividend of R_b per period.[27] Dividends are reinvested in the trust rather than paid out each year to the employee.

---

[27] Although the dividend rate (on a risk-adjusted basis) on preferred stock issued to other corporations eligible for the dividend-received-deduction might be expected to be *less* than the taxable bond rate, R_b, we consider here the case in which the preferred stock is held in the tax-exempt pension trust. To keep employees whole, relative to Case I, the dividend yield must be the full taxable rate, R_b.

12.3   A Closer Look at Tax Advantages of an ESOP

Case II: Preferred Stock-Financed ESOP with Dividends Reinvested in the Pension Plan

Time Period

Cash Flow to:	Today (time 0)	Annually Through Retirement	At Retirement (n years)
Employer	$+t_c$	$-R_b$	-1
Employee	0	0	$+(1+R_b)^n(1-t_p)$

Except for the annual cash outflow for the employer to service the security issued to fund the pension plan, cash flows are identical to those for the debt-financed retirement plan. Here, however, the dividend payments are nondeductible, so while the employee is indifferent across the alternatives, the employer is worse off by $R_b t_c$ per period. Note that Rbt_c is simply the tax shield from interest deductibility available in Case I but not Case II.

Finally, consider the case of an ESOP financed with employer preferred stock, but where these dividends are paid out to the employee each period (Case III).

Case III: Preferred Stock-Financed ESOP with Dividends Passed Through to Employees

Time Period

Cash Flow to:	Today (time 0)	Annually Through Retirement	At Retirement (n years)
Employer	$+t_c$	$-R_b(1-t_c)$	-1
Employee	0	$+R_b(1-t_p)$	$+1-t_p$

Note that while the cash flows to the employer in this case coincide with those in Case I (debt-financed pension plan), those for the employee are not directly comparable since both interim and terminal cash flows are different. To make them comparable, suppose the employer reduces the employee's salary by R_b per period, contributing this amount to a non-ESOP pension plan that earns interest at rate R_b per period. In this case, the interim cash flows to the employee will be $0, just as in Case I.

To see how the ESOP with dividend pass-through compares with a debt-financed pension, then, we need only compare the terminal after-tax cash flow to the employee in this case with that in Case I (since all other cash flows to both parties now coincide). The supplementary pension plan for the employee accumulates to the future value of an annuity of R_b dollars for n periods with interest at rate R_b per period. This is equal to:

$$R_b[(1 + R_b)^n - 1]/R_b \text{ or } (1+R_b)^n - 1.$$

This is fully taxable at rate tp, so the after-tax amount is:

$$(1+R_b)^n (1-t_p) - (1-t_p).$$

We can now add this supplementary pension amount to the $1 - t_p$ available from the ESOP, and this leaves

$$(1+R_b)^n (1-t_p).$$

This is exactly the same terminal amount the employee receives in Case I, the debt-financed pension plan.

While a comparison of Cases I and III makes it appear as though the ESOP (with dividend pass-through) is equivalent to the debt-financed non-ESOP pension plan, this is only because we have allowed the ESOP to invest in preferred shares that have no equity-like features to them. That is, the dividend yield is the full interest rate, and there is no capital gain component to it. But in fact, the ESOP assets must be invested primarily (that is, at least 50%) in employer common stock or convertible preferred stock, and these securities almost always have an expected capital appreciation component.[28]

Case II can be viewed as a case in which the ESOP is financed with nondividend-paying common stock. The interim cash outflow of R_b can be interpreted as the non-deductible sinking fund contribution required to cover the appreciation in the share of stock that the employer will have to repurchase from the employee at time n.

More typically, the employer securities contributed to the ESOP will have a dividend yield somewhere in between those for Cases II and III. In such circumstances, the employer will be worse off relative to a non-ESOP pension plan, by the value of a tax deduction on the difference between the current yield on the ESOP securities and the interest rate on debt. In this light, one might view the availability of the tax exemption to qualified ESOP lenders of half the interest income on ESOP loans as a way of neutralizing the disadvantage demonstrated above. The analysis also helps to explain why high dividend-yielding convertible preferred stocks have become so popular as an investment in ESOPs.[29]

If the 50% interest income exemption roughly compensates for the reduced deductibility of the employer cost to service the securities issued to fund the ESOP, then the differences between ESOPs and other pension plans becomes restricted largely to the nontax dimension. In particular, with more employer securities in the ESOP, work incentives are clearly affected, and voting control is clearly enhanced, thereby providing a superior takeover defense (or more pejoratively, enhanced management entrenchment).

---

[28] The preferred stock must be convertible into the common stock of the company at a "reasonable" conversion price, which has not yet been clearly defined. The firm must not be permitted to call the preferred, or if it can, the preferred must be convertible prior to the call. It must be convertible into a readily tradeable stock if traded on a securities market. If no such stock exists, the preferred must be convertible into the issue that contains the most voting and dividend rights among all outstanding shares. This last condition might be difficult to satisfy in certain cases. For example, if an ESOP is formed in conjunction with a leveraged buyout, the structure of the leveraged buyout might be such that it is difficult to know which security has the greatest voting and dividend rights.

[29] Other reasons for the popularity of high dividend-yielding convertible preferred stock include (1) reduced investment risk for employees, although this presumably comes at the expense of reduced incentives, and (2) leveraging of voting-rights in presumably friendly hands (a defense weapon).

12.3   A Closer Look at Tax Advantages of an ESOP

In a survey of 83 ESOPs in 1988, Chaplinsky and Niehaus find, surprisingly, that more than two-thirds of the plans reinvest dividends on ESOP shares in the pension plan rather than distribute them to employees to secure tax deductions for the dividends. For another 13% of the plans, the employer stock is *nondividend-bearing*. Both situations correspond to Case II above, and indicate that ESOPs are not managed to secure the maximum tax advantage.[30] Such ESOPs are substantially inferior from a tax standpoint to a debt-financed pension (Case I), except for any interest subsidy on ESOP loans.

12.4 Evidence on the Growth and Importance of ESOPs in the U.S. Economy in the 1980s

It is unfortunate that the most complete survey available of the prominent features of ESOPs goes only through 1984.[31] The Deficit Reduction Act of 1984 and the Tax Reform Act of 1986 had dramatic effects on incentives to utilize these trusts to take advantage of the tax-favored leveraging opportunities and dividend deductibility. Table 12.1 reveals that at year-end 1988, there were 9,500 ESOPs in existence covering 9.5 million workers. The number of new plans established in 1985 and 1986 (591 per year) was 19% higher than the average over the six years ending in 1984. And the number of new plans established in 1987 and 1988 (727 per year) was 27% higher than 1985 and 1986. A total of 830 new plans were established in 1989, and 480 were established in 1990.[32]

The U.S. General Accounting Office estimates that of the 6,904 ESOPs at year-end 1984, only 4,174 were still active. Approximately 90% of these plans were tax-credit ESOPs. Total assets in ESOPs at year-end 1984 were $19 billion, of which $15 billion were in tax-credit ESOPs ($2,300 per covered employee) and $4 billion were in other ESOPs ($5,700 per covered employee).

Although it was the 1984 Tax Act that introduced the interest income exemption for qualified ESOP loans and deductibility of dividends paid out to employees, ESOP activity accelerated more quickly following the 1986 Act. The 1986 Act contained a number of ESOP and non-ESOP provisions that affected the desirability of ESOPs, as discussed earlier.

Since 1986, leveraged ESOPs in particular have exploded in economic significance. According to the National Center for Employer Ownership, new ESOP borrowings grew from $1.2 billion in 1986 to $5.5 billion in 1987 and $6.4 billion in 1988. In addition, $25.7 Billion in ESOPs were financed or announced from January to early December 1989, the vast majority of which were leveraged.[33] It is perhaps not surprising, therefore, that on June 6, 1989, Dan Rostenkowski, as chairman of the House Ways and Means Committee, intro-

---

[30] Susan Chaplinsky and Greg Niehaus, "The Tax and Distributional Effects of Leveraged ESOPs," *Financial Management* (Spring 1990), pp. 29-38.

[31] United States General Accounting Office, *Employee Stock Ownership Plans*, GAO-PEMD-86-4BR (February 1986).

[32] *Wall Street Journal* (March 12, 1991)

[33] *Pensions and Investment Age* (December 11, 1989).

Table 12.1 Growth in the Number of ESOP Plans and Number of Employees Covered

Year	Number of Plans[a]	Number of Employees Covered[a]
1978	4,028	2,800,000
1984	6,904	6,576,000
1986	8,046	7,800,000
1988	9,500	9,500,000[b]
Average *Increase* per Year:		
1978-84	479	679,000
1984-86	571	612,000
1986-88	777	850,000

[a]Source: National Center for Employee Ownership (Oakland, CA)
[b]Note that this exceeds 7% of the nation's labor force.

duced legislation to repeal the 50% interest exemption on ESOP loans. While this proposal was prompted by concerns over revenue losses to the U.S. Treasury, our analysis suggests that takeover defense may have been at least as important a factor in explaining the growth of ESOPs. Instead, we have argued that takeover defense considerations are likely to have dominated, although the availability of special tax provisions, even if not well understood, was probably important to secure the blessing of corporate boards to adopt the plans.

It is interesting to note that another batch of new ESOPs were hurriedly introduced by dozens of companies following the Rostenkowski proposal in an attempt to beat the new effective date for any adverse tax changes that might result from the passage of legislation.[34] And despite the adverse changes introduced by the 1989 Tax Act in November 1989, large new plans continued to be established.[35] Still, the number of new plans established in 1990 was more than 40% below the number established in 1989.

12.5 Concluding Remarks

An ESOP is an interesting organizational vehicle. It can theoretically be used to eliminate the corporate-level tax entirely, although as a practical matter, gutting the corporate tax is impossible even with complete employee ownership. And depending upon the circumstances, another great cost or benefit is its effectiveness as a defensive weapon. This is a cost when entrenchment allows existing management to secure private gain at the expense of shareholders and when a transfer of control over managerial decision rights to a more efficient group is prevented. It is a benefit, however, to the extent such protection from an outside bid promotes investment by employees in firm-specific capital that improves employee performance. Another important disadvantage of an ESOP is possible distortions in incentive compensation arrangements.

---

[34] *Pensions and Investment Age* (July 24, 1989).

[35] For example, Chevron announced the creation of a $1 billion plan, and Dayton Hudson announced a $400 million plan, both in December of 1989. (*Pensions and Investment Age*, December 11, 1989) And Sears announced a plan to borrow $800 million to finance an ESOP on December 21, 1989. (*New York Times*, December 22, 1989)

As is so often the case in public policy debates, the analysis to date of tax and nontax factors in the use of ESOPs has failed to consider the alternative institutional arrangements that are displaced by ESOPs. We have attempted to repair that omission here, and in so doing, we find ESOPs lacking in particular magic for their corporate sponsors along both tax and incentive dimensions, except perhaps in closely-held businesses. With these usual suspects rounded up, the creation of impediments to changes in corporate control would appear to be the prime motivation for ESOPs.

Summary of Key Points

1. An employee stock ownership plan (ESOP) is a defined contribution pension plan that invests primarily in employer securities on behalf of employees.

2. Special tax provisions apply to ESOPs. For example, dividends paid on employer stock held by the ESOP, and distributed to employees, are tax-deductible to the corporation. In addition, half the interest on certain ESOP loans used to purchase employer stock is tax exempt to qualified lenders, although following the 1989 Tax Act, this benefit is only available, for new ESOP financings, on loans made to ESOPs that own a *majority* of the employer stock.

3. ESOPs may impose substantial risk on employees. This can have favorable incentive consequences, but risk-averse employees will require supplemental compensation for bearing risk that is beyond their control. This may prove expensive. Moreover, other incentive compensation arrangements may be more efficient.

4. Ignoring the benefit of the 50% interest exclusion on ESOP loans, debt-financed pension funds that invest in taxable bonds can be far superior to ESOPs along the tax dimension. It is important that ESOPs be compared to other pension plans, rather than salary plans, in assessing their attractiveness along the tax dimension.

5. While it is tax-advantageous to distribute to employees dividends on employer stock owned by ESOPs, such dividends are often reinvested in the ESOP, thereby sacrificing a corporate tax deduction for the dividends. This indicates that most ESOPs are not operated so as to maximize tax benefits.

6. Since 1986, leveraged ESOPs have grown very dramatically in economic significance.

7. ESOPs are often adopted by companies that are rumored to be takeover candidates. By locking up shares in (presumably) friendly hands, ESOPs add to management's arsenal of takeover-defense weapons.

8. In fact, given that ESOPs do *not* appear to offer unique tax or incentive benefits relative to alternative institutional arrangements, their recent popularity may well be driven by their anti-takeover characteristics.

Discussion Questions

1. What is an ESOP? Why has Congress encouraged their use over the years?

2. Do you think that the explosive growth of ESOPs in 1989 was due to the tax advantages of using ESOPs? What other factors might also have been present?

3. Three claimed tax advantages of an ESOP are that the corporation can make tax deductible contributions to fund the ESOP or pay down the principal on an ESOP loan, that qualified lenders can exclude from taxation 50% of the interest that they receive on the ESOP loan, and that the dividend paid on the shares held in the ESOP are tax deductible under certain circumstances. Do you agree with these claims?

4. What are the incentive effects on employees of establishing an ESOP? How does it compare to the alternatives? How do risk-sharing considerations affect the costs of an ESOP program? Would current compensation be more suitable for some employees than deferred compensation in the form of ESOP shares? Why? How does this increase the cost of using an ESOP?

5. What is an immediate allocation loan? How does it differ from a leveraged-ESOP loan? Is it more tax advantageous to use an immediate allocation loan or a leveraged-ESOP loan? Why?

6. Under what circumstances would it be tax advantageous for the firm to switch from a thrift plan in which employees hold employer stock to an ESOP?

7. If the firm can make tax deductible dividend payments, this converts the double corporate tax to a single tax on that part of the firm's income. Can an ESOP be used to eliminate entirely one level of tax on corporate profits?

8. Would it be tax advantageous to adopt an ESOP to replace a debt-financed pension plan invested in fully taxable bonds? Would it be tax advantageous to adopt an ESOP to replace the employer stock held in a non-ESOP pension plan?

9. How do ESOPs impede hostile takeovers? Why are they more effective at doing so in certain states, such as Delaware? If an ESOP holds more than 15% of the voting stock of a company incorporated in the state of Delaware, and the incumbent management group wishes to avoid being taken over by a hostile suitor, are the incumbents sure to have their way?

10. What ways have companies found to reduce employees' risk from holding company stock in an ESOP? How do such risk-reducing strategies affect employee incentives? How do such risk-reducing strategies affect the tax advantages of ESOPs?

11. Why do so many ESOPs reinvest the dividends paid on the employer shares they hold in the ESOP rather than distribute the dividends to employees? Is this desirable from a tax standpoint?

12. In what ways are ESOPs more attractive to closely-held corporations than to widely-held firms?

Chapter 12   Employee Stock Ownership Plans: Myths and Realities

CHAPTER 13
Multinational Tax Planning:
Introduction and Investment Decisions

In evaluating trade policy and its effect on international capital flows, it is inefficient to focus narrowly on tariffs, quotas, and other nontax subsidies. *Tax policy* also plays an important role in affecting the investment and financing decisions of U.S. and foreign multinational firms. Although tax systems around the world have a great deal in common, they also differ from one another along a variety of dimensions: marginal tax rates can vary from essentially 0% in certain tax haven countries to well over 60% in certain high-tax countries; the definition of income can vary dramatically from country to country; the use of non-income taxes can vary considerably; taxpayers may be taxed only on domestic income or on worldwide income.

Multinational corporations generally establish foreign controlled subsidiaries to conduct foreign operations. These corporations are governed by the laws (including the tax rules) of the host country in which they are resident. Generally, there are two different tax regimes that apply to the taxation of income earned by multinational corporations. Some countries, like the U.S., the U.K., and Japan, tax the worldwide income of their resident companies. Other countries, such as France, employ a so-called "territorial" tax system: France does not tax income from active businesses that is earned outside the country.

Although the U.S. taxes the worldwide income of its citizens and its corporations, it doesn't generally tax income from foreign operations as the income is realized abroad, even if the income comes in the form of cash. Instead, if foreign income is reinvested in bona fide foreign businesses, the U.S. defers taxation of this income until such time as the income is repatriated to the U.S., perhaps by way of a dividend.

Actually, this deferral treatment applies only to income earned by foreign subsidiaries. There is no tax-deferral treatment for foreign partnerships or for income earned by foreign *branches* of U.S. companies, but except for banks and insurance companies, foreign branches are rather uncommon. Moreover, the U.S. does not allow deferral of *passive* income (so-called "Subpart-F" income), such as interest income and securities gains, generated abroad.

Countries like the U.S. that tax worldwide income attempt to mitigate multiple taxation of foreign income by allowing credits (subject to important limitations) to be taken for income taxes paid to foreign governments. Countries differ, however, in their generosity regarding these credits.

Most of the interesting issues in multinational tax planning arise because income is often subject to taxation in more than one tax jurisdiction. In this chapter, we will introduce the basics of multinational tax planning and then concentrate on tax planning for investment decisions of U.S. multinational enterprises. We then turn to empirical evidence suggesting that changes in U.S. tax rules have a significant effect on direct foreign investment in the U.S. You should bear in mind that the structure of multinational tax rules is quite similar in a great many countries. This is no accident. Much of the conformity is the result of tax treaties, most notably the *Model Treaty of the Organization for Economic Cooperation and Development.*

Among other objectives, tax treaties are designed to eliminate double taxation of income earned by multinational enterprises by specifying how individual items of income and expense are to be allocated among different tax jurisdictions. Double taxation may be avoided by either (1) having some items of income taxable in only one country,[1] or (2) providing for a tax credit for foreign taxes paid.[2]

Unfortunately, because of tax treaty ambiguities or differences in policy objectives of the governments representing the various tax jurisdictions, the goal of eliminating double taxation is not always achieved. For example, the foreign income of U.S. taxpayers may be subject to taxation by each host country in which business is conducted *as well as* by the U.S. Moreover, income may be taxed more than once by each jurisdiction. For example, it may be taxed as earned, and it may be taxed as it is transferred from one nation to another. And while the U.S. tax system attempts to mitigate the multiple taxation burden through the foreign tax credit (FTC), we will see in more detail in this chapter and the next how the FTC fails to eliminate multiple taxation entirely. In brief, multiple taxation arises because of FTC limitations and because the definition of taxable income varies widely across taxing jurisdictions. Moreover, the FTC applies only to income taxes, whereas many tax jurisdictions outside the U.S. rely heavily on non-income taxes to raise revenue (for example, value added taxes, prominent in Western European countries and many Latin American countries). Although such taxes are not creditable against U.S. taxes, they do give rise to tax deductions as business expenses.

---

[1] For example, Switzerland, Hong Kong, Belgium, France, and the Netherlands have a territorial tax system whereby profits earned by a foreign branch and dividends received from a foreign subsidiary of a domestic corporation are typically exempt from domestic taxation.

[2] Examples here include the U.S., Japan, the U.K., Canada, Germany, Sweden, and Denmark. Some countries, like Germany and Canada, have a territorial system with respect to the income from countries with which they have a tax treaty, and a worldwide tax system (with a provision for credits for foreign taxes paid) with respect to income earned in nontreaty countries.

Chapter 13   Multinational Tax Planning: Introduction and Investment Decisions

There appear to be several U.S. policy objectives regarding foreign taxation. The first, as stated above, is to relieve taxpayers from multiple taxation of the same income. A second is to aid the U.S. balance-of-payments position (although whether this is a desirable objective is debatable).

For example, although the 1981 Tax Act introduced rapid depreciation (the so-called "accelerated cost recovery system") on top of high investment tax credits to encourage investment, the advantages were bestowed only on investments made in the U.S. The objective of the Act was to increase U.S. domestic capital formation and reduce the flow of U.S. investment abroad. Michael Boskin and William Gale present evidence suggesting that the 1981 Tax Act achieved this objective by reducing U.S. direct investment abroad by $0.5 to $1 billion per year (or 2%-4%).[3]

Similarly, as we discuss later, the 1986 Tax Act encouraged many U.S. multinationals to concentrate their worldwide investments domestically or to relocate investments abroad due to binding limits on foreign tax credits. It also encouraged direct investment in the U.S. by foreign multinationals. Of course, in enhancing foreign trade, the government must avoid stepping too heavily on the economic toes of other countries. Taxes are often used as a strategic weapon by governments to attract certain kinds of business to their borders and to achieve certain economic goals. These objectives can be upset through noncooperation from other countries in their setting of tax rules.[4]

A third objective of the U.S. tax rules applying to foreign income is to encourage the development of less-developed countries, and a fourth objective is to achieve so-called "tax neutrality." By neutrality, we mean to allow capital to flow where it can earn the highest return. But this may be impossible to achieve in a world in which there are multiple government units, operating somewhat autonomously, each having different political priorities. We can distinguish between two kinds of neutrality:

Domestic: objective is to tax foreign income and domestic income of U.S. taxpayers similarly.

Foreign: objective is to tax foreign operations of U.S. taxpayers no more than the host-country competitors are taxed. This is designed to preserve the viability of competition.

The objective of foreign neutrality has resulted in rules that allow U.S. corporations to defer payment of U.S. taxes on much of the foreign-source income earned by their foreign subsidiaries until the income is remitted to their U.S. parents. These rules, however, provide a good example of over-inclusiveness. They give rise to transfer pricing games to create either foreign or domestic income when it is advantageous to do so, as well as to considerable efforts to undertake passive investments in low-taxed foreign countries. The foreign tax rules of the three major tax acts in the multinational tax area in the past 30 years (the Revenue Act of 1962, the Deficit Reduction Act of 1984, and the Tax Reform

---

[3] Michael Boskin and William Gale, "New Results on the Effects of Tax Policy on the International Location of Investments," in Martin Feldstein, ed., *The Effects of Taxation on Capital Accumulation* (National Bureau of Economic Research, 1987), pp. 201-19.

[4] In fact, the U.K. reduced corporate and personal rates prior to 1986. Many other European countries have followed suit.

Act of 1986) were motivated by a desire to deal with this over-inclusiveness. In particular, the 1962 Act endeavored to clamp down on the attempt to route income through paper corporations set up in tax haven countries offering income tax exemption or low income tax rates, *without* destroying the deferral privilege for firms undertaking *real* manufacturing and sales activities.

13.1 Overview of Multinational Taxation

As we discuss more fully later, the 1962 Act gave rise to the *controlled foreign corporation* (CFC) rules, along with the passive investment income rules (the *Subpart F income* rules), both of which play an important role in multinational tax planning.[5] We will also see how these plugs in the holes put in place in 1962 gave rise to *new* holes related to how foreign tax credit limitations were to be calculated. Many of the changes relating to international tax rules in the 1984 and 1986 Acts appear to be in response to these defects.

To begin our exploration, we must distinguish between: (1) U.S. taxpayers and foreign taxpayers, and between (2) U.S.-source income and foreign-source income. U.S. citizens (whether they are resident in the U.S. or not), domestic corporations, and domestic trusts are all taxed on *worldwide income*. The same is true of resident aliens, including anyone holding a green card. Nonresident aliens and foreign corporations are taxed by the U.S. only on income derived *within* the U.S. or income that is deemed to be "effectively connected with a U.S. trade or business." We must also recognize that not all income is taxed at the *same time* or at the *same rate*, although we have visited these issues many times in the context of domestic tax issues.

Although there are exceptions, U.S. shareholders are not taxed on the income of foreign corporations (foreign *subsidiaries* of a U.S. corporation) until they receive distributions.[6] Most income, however, relating to multinational business activity that is taxed by the U.S. is taxed *currently*. Examples include income from: (1) direct export by an existing U.S. business, (2) income from licensing arrangements by U.S. businesses with foreign firms, (3) income earned by U.S. citizens and residents employed abroad,[7, 8] (4) a U.S. partner's share of

---

[5] The U.S. lead in this area has been followed by a number of countries, including Japan, Canada, France, the U.K., Germany, and more recently New Zealand and Australia.

[6] All of the income of a personal foreign holding company (so-called PFIC) is taxed currently in the U.S. even if it is not repatriated to the U.S. Briefly, a corporation is deemed to be a PFIC in any year in which more than 50% of its assets are in passive investments, or 75% of its income is deemed to be passive income for that year. Likewise, whether or not repatriated to the U.S., passive (Subpart F) income of controlled foreign corporations (CFCs) is taxed currently in the U.S., as are undistributed earnings and profits that are used by the CFC to buy U.S. property. We will expand on these issues later in this and the next chapter.

[7] A foreign earned income exclusion is permitted of up to $70,000 per year plus "excess housing costs" (housing costs abroad in excess of 16% of U.S. government GS-14 pay scale). The foreign-earned-income exclusion requires physical presence in a foreign tax jurisdiction for 330 days in a consecutive 12-month period. Alternatively, U.S. citizens and residents employed abroad may include all foreign earned income on their U.S. tax return and claim a foreign tax credit for income taxes paid to foreign tax jurisdictions, subject to limits.

[8] An important area of tax planning involves U.S. workers on assignment in a foreign country. Individuals must be compensated for additional tax costs that may depend on personal investment

income earned in foreign partnerships, and (5) the income generated by a foreign branch of a domestic entity.

Operating as a Branch versus a Foreign Subsidiary

There are both advantages and disadvantages of operating as a foreign branch rather than a foreign subsidiary. Advantages arise because:

1. Losses from foreign operations are immediately deductible against U.S. domestic income. This is especially important for start-up operations that can reasonably be expected to generate losses. Moreover, it is possible to incorporate the branch when operations turn profitable to defer future income from U.S. taxation. The cost, however, is that the firm must recapture, as income, previously deducted losses.

2. The U.S. tax law applies to the specific character of a variety of overseas activities. For example, the rules preserve the favorable tax treatment on certain investment activities, like natural resource mining (for example, immediate deduction of intangible drilling costs).

3. Income repatriated from a foreign branch is not considered to be a dividend. As a result, a branch avoids the withholding taxes on dividends that are often paid by a foreign subsidiary, which is often in addition to a tax levied on the earnings of the subsidiary.[9]

4. Property can be transferred to a branch without fear of current taxation on appreciation. Some transfers of property to foreign subsidiaries, however, are taxable.

Disadvantages of operating as a branch arise because:

1. There is no deferral of U.S. tax on the earnings of the branch. In many cases, this is the most important consideration, especially when the host country's tax rate is below that of the U.S. As we will see, this factor became less important for U.S. multinationals after the 1986 Tax Act than it was previously.[10]

---

and other income characteristics. Personal tax rates in many European countries and Japan, especially after the 1986 Tax Act, can far exceed the maximum U.S. rate. Deferred compensation may be an important planning device but will not avoid foreign tax in some countries; that is, what qualifies as deferred compensation in the U.S. may *not* qualify as deferred compensation in certain foreign tax jurisdictions. In addition, some countries are more liberal than the U.S. with respect to taxation of fringe benefits, including education for children, and this can play an important role in determining the optimal way to compensate employees. Because of the highly progressive nature of personal taxes in many countries, it will often pay to spread a 6 to 12 month stay in a foreign country over 2 tax years, rather than concentrate the stay in a single tax year.

[9] Some countries, however, (Canada is an example) impose an additional tax on branch profits in lieu of withholding taxes on dividends. Indeed, in the U.S., the 1986 Tax Act introduced a 30% branch tax on the U.S. branch profits of a foreign corporation unless the branch profits are reinvested in the branch. The rate of branch tax may be lower if the U.S. has a tax treaty with the foreign corporation's country of residence. This branch tax is *in addition to* the regular U.S. tax on income derived within the U.S.

[10] On the other hand, the importance of the deferral provision may have increased for Japanese multinationals.

2. Some countries may require disclosure of data on worldwide operations to tax authorities. This may not only be administratively burdensome, but also may require disclosing sensitive competitive information.

Other considerations arise in the choice between a foreign branch and a foreign subsidiary. Most foreign nations tax branches differently from the way they tax subsidiaries. For example, there is considerable variation in the way loss carryforwards are treated across foreign tax jurisdictions. Although they are typically available to foreign subsidiaries, this is not the case in all countries. Moreover, some countries allow very short carryforward periods, other countries allow some combination of carrybacks and carryforwards, and some countries allow carryforwards of start-up losses only. Although some countries allow branches established in their country to carry losses forward, this is less common than for foreign subsidiaries.

Another consideration is the deductibility of management fees and other expenses paid to the home office. Some countries (such as Switzerland) allow a *subsidiary*, but not a *branch*, to deduct such fees. Domestic subsidiaries are also useful when operations are conducted in Puerto Rico, a U.S. possession. To achieve special tax concessions there, it is often necessary to set up these operations in a separate subsidiary to meet strict percentage requirements along several dimensions. It is also necessary to establish a subsidiary to exploit the export-related tax benefits of a so-called "foreign sales corporation" (FSC). We will return to the issues of U.S. possessions tax benefits and the FSC tax benefits later.

An important nontax consideration is that in contrast to foreign subsidiaries, the liability of branch operations is not limited to assets employed abroad. For this reason, domestic subsidiaries are often used to set up foreign branches to limit legal liability on foreign operations.

Foreign Tax Credits and Subpart F Rules

To understand the advantages of U.S. tax deferral for foreign subsidiaries, it is necessary to understand how foreign tax credits are calculated, as well as how the Subpart F rules work.

To begin with, note that there are two types of foreign tax credits: **direct foreign tax credits** (Section 901) for taxes that are imposed *directly* on the U.S. taxpayer, and **indirect foreign tax credits** (or deemed paid credits, Section 902). Direct foreign tax credits result when a tax is paid on the earnings of a foreign branch of a U.S. company, or when withholding taxes are deducted from foreign remittances to U.S. investors on dividends or other forms of passive income. Indirect foreign tax credits arise when dividends are actually received or deemed to be received from foreign corporations. The potential credit is equal to the taxes paid on the earnings that produced the dividend. These indirect credits are only available to U.S. shareholders owning 10% or more of a foreign corporation. The foreign dividend included in U.S. income is the dividend received *grossed up* to include both the withholding tax and any deemed paid taxes.

We illustrate how the foreign tax credit mechanism works in Table 13.1. Here, we assume that there are two countries, A and B, and a U.S. multinational has established a subsidiary in each country. Both subsidiaries earn $1.00. The local tax rates on income earned in countries A and B are 30% and 20%, respectively. The withholding tax rate on dividends remitted to the U.S. parent is 10% in both countries A and B. That is, each subsidiary must pay to the host government 10% of the dividend it would have paid to its parent. The remaining 90% of the dividend is remitted to its parent.

Table 13.1 Example of How the Foreign Tax Credit System Works

Country	A	B	A + B
Local Taxable Income	$ 1.00	$ 1.00	$ 2.00
Local Tax Rate	30%	20%	
Withholding Tax Rate on Dividends	10%	10%	10%
Local Tax	$ .30	$ .20	$ .50
Withholding Tax on Dividends	$ .07	$ .08	$ .15
Total Foreign Tax Rate	37%	28%	32.5%
Net Dividend	$ .63	$ .72	$ 1.35
U.S. Taxable Income from Foreign Dividends	$ 1.00	$ 1.00	$ 2.00
U.S. Tax @ 34%	$ .34	$ .34	$ .68
Foreign Tax Credit	$ .34	$ .28	$ .65
Net U.S. Tax on Foreign Dividends	$ .00	$ .06	$ .03
Foreign Tax Credit Carryforward	$ .03	$ .00	$ .00

The foreign subsidiary earns $1 of taxable income in Country A. The local tax rate is 30%, so $.30 in local taxes are paid. This leaves $.70 of local income to reinvest abroad or to pay as a dividend. Suppose that the $.70 is paid as a dividend to the U.S. parent. Assume for the moment that the subsidiary in Country B pays no dividend. By treaty with the U.S., Country A assesses a 10% withholding tax on the dividend. As a result, $.07 of the $.70 dividend is withheld, and $.63 is paid to the parent company in the U.S. If t_f is the foreign tax rate on income, and t_w is the withholding tax rate on dividends, the parent receives dividends of

$$(1 - t_f)(1 - t_w)$$

per $1 of dividends paid by the subsidiary to the parent (for example, $1(1 - .3) (1 - .1)$ nets $.63).

The dividend triggers U.S. taxable income to the parent as follows:

	Dividend Received	$.63	
+	Withholding Taxes	.07	(Direct tax paid)
+	Indirect Foreign Taxes	.30	(Deemed paid credit)
=	Total U.S. Taxable Income	$1.00	
	U.S. Tax at 34%	.34	
-	Foreign Tax Credit Allowed	.34	
=	Additional U.S. Tax Due	$0.00	

The deemed paid credit is the tax paid by the foreign subsidiary on the net income that gave rise to the $.70 dividend. That is, the deemed paid credit

$$= \frac{\text{dividend}}{\text{(after-tax) earnings and profits}} \times \text{foreign tax paid.}$$

Since 100% of the after-tax earnings has been paid out as a dividend, the deemed paid credit is 100% of the foreign tax paid or $.30 in this case. As a result of the deemed paid credit of $.30 and $.07 of withholding tax, taxable income on the $.63 of net dividend received is $1.00.

Notice here that only $.34 of the $.37 of total foreign taxes paid can be used currently as a tax credit. The remaining $.03 is carried over to future periods. The foreign tax credit limitation is the minimum of the direct plus indirect taxes paid, and the U.S. tax on foreign source income (or the minimum of ($.07 + $.30, $.34)).

Now suppose that it is the subsidiary in Country B that declares a dividend equal to its income after paying local income taxes, whereas the subsidiary in Country A declares *no* dividend. Given a local income tax rate of 20% (plus an additional 10% withholding tax rate on dividends), we have the following results:

	Dividend Received	$ .72
+	Withholding Taxes	.08
+	Indirect Foreign Taxes	.20
=	Total U.S. Taxable Income (Same as Country A)	$ 1.00
	U.S. Tax at 34%	.34
-	Foreign Tax Credit Allowed	.28
=	Additional U.S. Tax Due	$ .06
	Net Dividend After U.S. Tax ($.72 - $.06)	$ .66

A dividend of $.72 is paid to the parent. It results from the $.80 of after-tax profits earned in Country B, less a withholding tax of $.08. As before, the total U.S. taxable income is $1.00 (or $.72 + $.08 + .$20). The U.S. tax liability on the $1.00 of taxable income is $.34. The foreign tax credit available is the minimum of the U.S. tax on the foreign income ($.34) and the direct plus indirect foreign taxes paid ($.08 of direct tax plus the $.20 of deemed paid credit or $.28). Therefore, the additional tax owed in the U.S. is $.06 (or $.34 - $.28). Since the U.S. parent has $.72 in hand before payment of additional U.S. taxes, it is left with $.66 after payment of the additional U.S. taxes. Note that this is just the same as if the $1.00 had been earned in the U.S. rather than abroad.

In the last column of Table 13.1, we assume that both subsidiaries declare dividends equal to their income after local income tax. Although not all countries do so, the U.S. (and Japan) allows the foreign tax credit limitation to be calculated based on worldwide income, rather than imposing a separate limitation on a country-by-country basis (as Canada and Denmark do). Given the ability to average the foreign tax rates paid on worldwide income, all of the $.65 in foreign taxes paid can be used as a credit against the U.S. tax on foreign income. The $.03 of foreign tax credit carryforward created in Country A (in the absence of a dividend from Country B) is now used up against the foreign source income generated in Country B.

13.2 How World-Wide Foreign Tax Rules Affect Investment Incentives

Should the earnings generated by foreign subsidiaries be distributed to the parent, or should they be reinvested abroad? The answer depends on the length of the reinvestment horizon, the proportion of investment that is represented by retained earnings, and whether marginal investments in the foreign country earn more, after local tax, than marginal investments in the U.S. For sufficiently long investment horizons, a higher after-local-tax rate of return abroad is sufficient to conclude that reinvestment abroad is desirable, as we will show.

One might be tempted to suppose that if tax rates are lower in a foreign country than they are domestically, it follows that after-tax rates of return on marginal investments should be higher in the foreign country. But this ignores the very real possibility that *pretax* rates of return in the foreign country may be lower than that available domestically. In countries where the tax rate on income is relatively low, one would expect competition to force down pretax profitability. In other words, the foreign investments will bear implicit taxes.

For example, let's suppose that you have $100 million to invest in one of two mutually exclusive projects, one at home and the other, of equal risk, located in a lower-tax-rate foreign country. The tax rates, and the rates of return available on the two projects, are given in Table 13.2.

Table 13.2 Tax Rates and Rates of Return to Investing at Home and Abroad

	Tax Rate	Pretax Return	After (Local) Tax Return
Home	55%	22%	9.9% [22%(1 - 55%)]
Abroad	35%	20%*	13.0% [20%(1 - 35%)]

*Note that there is an implicit tax to investing abroad. The implicit tax *rate* is equal to

$$\frac{22\% - 20\%}{22\%} = 9.09\%$$

Marginal dollars invested in the home country earn 22% pretax and 9.9% after a 55% tax. Marginal dollars invested in the foreign subsidiary earn 20% pretax and 13% after a 35% local tax. The foreign investment here bears an implicit tax rate of 9.09% relative to home-country investments and an explicit tax rate of 35% on 20/22nds of the full 22% return (or 31.8%), for a total tax rate of 40.9%, as long as the income is reinvested abroad and not repatriated home. This tax rate is 14.1 percentage points lower than the 55% tax rate that applies in the home country and favors reinvestment of foreign profits abroad rather than repatriation, as shown below.[11]

Why might an implicit tax be associated with investing abroad? Implicit taxes can arise because the foreign country encourages investment by offering generous tax benefits, and competition for the right to garner these benefits

[11] Note that the 14.1% total tax rate advantage of the foreign investment, multiplied by the 22% pretax rate of return available on the home-country investment, explains the foreign country after-local-tax return advantage of 3.1% (or 13.0% - 9.9%).

results in lower before-tax rates of return. Nontax factors can also account for some of the observed implicit tax. Low tax rates are typically offered to lure business that would not otherwise be undertaken in the low-tax jurisdiction. Foreign firms often must bear significant nontax costs to secure special tax benefits, as we will discuss later.

Given the investment opportunities described in Table 13.2, in which country should you invest? The answer depends on the length of the investment horizon. Suppose that you invest abroad for only one year. At the end of the year, the foreign subsidiary divests and repatriates all profits to the home country.

Table 13.3 Investing $100 Million Abroad for One Year at 20% Pretax Versus at Home at 22% Pretax (Amounts in $ Millions)

Invest Abroad		
Before-Tax Liquidating Distribution	120	(Local Taxable Income of 20)
Local Tax (@ 35% Tax Rate)	-7	(35% of 20)
After-Local-Tax Liquidating Distribution	113	(100 represents a nontaxable return of capital originally invested)
Additional Tax at Home	-4	$(20 \times (55\% - \text{FTC of } 35\%))$
Net Liquidating Distribution After All Taxes	109	
After-Tax Rate of Return	9%	$(9/100, \text{ or } 20\%(1 - 55\%))$
Invest at Home	9.9%	$(22\%(1 - 55\%))$

We see from Table 13.3 that over a one-year horizon, investing abroad produces an after-tax return of only 9%. This compares poorly with investing at home, where the after-tax return is 9.9%. More generally, when the tax rate abroad is no greater than the tax rate at home, a one-year investment yields an after-tax return of $R_f(1 - t_d)$ abroad and $R_d(1 - t_d)$ at home, where R_f is the pretax return abroad, R_d is the pretax domestic return, and t_d is the domestic tax rate. The notation we use is summarized in Table 13.4. We see that it is only necessary to compare before-tax rates of return for one-year horizon investments. In our example, investing at home beats investing abroad by 45% (or 1 - 55%) of the 2% pretax return differential (22% - 20%). This amounts to 0.9% (or 9.9% - 9.0%).

Table 13.4 Notation

R_d	=	Pretax (domestic) rate of return in the home country
R_f	=	Pretax (foreign) rate of return abroad
t_d	=	Domestic tax rate
t_f	=	Foreign tax rate
r_f	=	$R_f(1 - t_f)$, the after-local-tax rate of return abroad
r_d	=	$R_d(1 - t_d)$, the after-tax domestic rate of return
n	=	Length of the investment horizon
I	=	Amount invested

What happens if instead of repatriating profits each year as earned, you can reinvest profits abroad at 13% after tax instead of at 9.9% after tax at home? This improves matters. In fact, if you could leave the investment abroad forever, you would earn 13% after tax abroad compared to only 9.9% at home. Let's see what happens if you leave the investment abroad over intermediate-term horizons, say, for 5 years. At the end of 5 years you accumulate

$$\$100 \text{ million} \times 1.13^5 = \$184.24 \text{ million abroad after local tax.}$$

At the end of 5 years, a $184.24 million liquidating distribution can be paid to the parent company at home. This includes after-tax foreign profits of $84.24 million on which home country tax must be paid. We must also compute the foreign taxes paid to determine the amount of pretax profits earned abroad. If the foreign tax rate is constant over time, the taxable home country dividend is equal to the after-local-tax profits earned abroad (*i.e.*, $84.24 million) divided by 1 minus the foreign tax rate, t_f. That is, home country taxable income is equal to

$$\frac{I\,[(1 + r_f)^n - 1]}{(1 - t_f)}, \tag{13.1}$$

where I denotes the amount invested, r_f denotes the after-local-tax rate of return abroad, and n denotes the length of time the investment is made abroad. In our example, this is equal to

$$\frac{\$184.24 \text{ million} - \$100 \text{ million}}{.65} = \$129.6 \text{ million.}$$

To understand why grossing up the after-tax profits repatriated by a factor of $(1 - t_f)$ yields the pretax profit, note simply that

$$\text{Pretax profit} \times (1 - \text{tax rate}) = \text{After-tax profit,}$$

so

$$\text{Pretax profit} = \text{After-tax profit}/(1 - \text{tax rate}).$$

Moreover, the after-tax profit is equal to the after-tax accumulation less the original amount invested, or $(1 + r_f)^n - 1$ for each dollar invested.

The calculations above reveal that upon liquidation in 5 years, the foreign investment yields home-country taxable income of $129.6 million. This attracts an additional home country tax at a rate of 20% (or 55% - 35%) because all taxable income will be taxed at rate t_d less a foreign tax credit at rate t_f. This exacts additional tax of $25.92 million. As a result, the net liquidating distribution retained by the parent company, after both foreign and home-country taxes, is $158.32 million (or $184.24 million - $25.92 million). The 5-year annualized after-tax rate of return from investing abroad is

$$\left[\frac{158.32}{100}\right]^{1/5} - 1 = 9.62\%.$$

Since this is less than 9.9%, the home country after-tax rate of return, you should invest at home. More generally, each dollar of foreign investment, over an n-year investment horizon, yields an accumulation (after paying the home country tax upon repatriation of profits) of

13.2   How World-Wide Foreign Tax Rules Affect Investment Incentives

$$(1 + r_f)^n - \frac{(1 + r_f)^n - 1}{(1 - t_f)} (t_d - t_f),$$

which simplifies to

$$(1 + r_f)^n \frac{(1 - t_d)}{(1 - t_f)} + \frac{(t_d - t_f)}{(1 - t_f)}. \qquad (13.2)$$

This compares with home-country investment for n years, which accumulates to

$$[1 + R_d(1 - t_d)]^n = (1 + r_d)^n. \qquad (13.3)$$

For 1-period investments (n = 1), we see from 13.2 (and recalling that $r_f = R_f(1 - t_f)$) that foreign investment yields

$$1 + R_f(1 - t_d),$$

and domestic investment, from 13.3, yields

$$1 + R_d(1 - t_d).$$

This implies that for short investment horizons, the *pretax* foreign return (R_f) must exceed the *pretax* domestic return (R_d) for foreign investment to dominate domestic investment.

Will foreign investment ever be more attractive than domestic investment if R_f is less than R_d? Yes it will. As the investment horizon increases, the annualized after-tax return from investing abroad will approach 13% in our example, the after-local-tax rate of return, r_f. For example, in 10 years, foreign investment yields 10.27% per year after all taxes, and in 20 years it yields 11.15%. For such investment horizons, investing abroad compares quite favorably with investing at home. With a 20-year horizon, the after-tax accumulation is $168 million more with a foreign investment than with a domestic investment.

Implicit Taxes and Foreign Investment Incentives

Suppose now that tax rates abroad are much more generous and cause implicit tax rates abroad to increase. For example, assume that the foreign country provides generous investment tax credits for investment in that country and that these credits are not available in the home country. To illustrate the effects of increasing the rate of implicit tax on the decision to invest abroad, we now expand our example to allow investment in two other foreign countries. The investment opportunities are summarized in Table 13.5.

Table 13.5 Returns on Investment in Three Countries With Differing Rates of Implicit Tax.

	Effective Tax Rate	Pretax Return	After (local) Tax Return
Home	55%	22%	9.9%
Abroad (Country 1)	35%	20%	13%
Abroad (Country 2)	20%	16.25%	13%
Abroad (Country 3)	0%	13%	13%

Chapter 13 Multinational Tax Planning: Introduction and Investment Decisions

Although the after-local-tax return is the same in each foreign tax regime, the implicit tax rate varies among the countries. While the implicit tax rate in country 1, relative to investment at home, is 9.09% (or (22% - 20%)/22%), the implicit tax rate in country 2 is 26.14% (or (22% - 16.25%)/22%). And, for country 3, because of extremely generous tax benefits, the implicit tax rate is 40.91%. What are the after-tax returns from investing abroad in each of these three tax regimes for different investment horizons? The answer is given in Table 13.6.

Table 13.6 After Repatriation-Tax Returns for Different Investment Horizons

Horizon (years)	1	5	10	20
Abroad$_1$ (implicit tax rate = 9.09%)	9.00%*	9.62%	**10.27%**	**11.15%**
Abroad$_2$ (implicit tax rate = 26.14%)	7.31%	8.07%	8.91%	**10.15%**
Abroad$_3$ (implicit tax rate = 40.91%)	5.85%	6.64%	7.59%	9.13%
Home	**9.90%**	**9.90%**	9.90%	9.90%

*These returns are computed by taking the after-tax accumulation, as given by expressions 13.2 and 13.3, to the (1/n) power and subtracting one.

Notice that for all investment horizons, the lower the implicit tax abroad, the higher are the after-tax returns from investing abroad. While investing abroad in country 1 dominates investing at home by $168 million (for an original $100 million investment) for a 20-year horizon, investing in country 3 falls short of investing at home by $87 million for the same horizon. This occurs even though the after-local-tax rate of return is the same in each foreign country.

What is going on here? Unlike direct foreign taxes and deemed paid foreign taxes, implicit taxes paid in the foreign country are not eligible for the foreign tax credit. Consequently, they are nonrefundable by the U.S. when earnings are repatriated. Like value added taxes, they are effectively *deductible* in calculating home country taxable income, but a deduction reduces home country taxes by only the domestic tax rate ($.55 on the dollar in our example). So whether investment is sensible in the foreign country depends upon the *implicit* tax on investments in the foreign country, as well as on the length of time before the foreign earnings are to be repatriated to the home country, thereby terminating the deferral period.

To see this another way, suppose that tax-exempt securities (like municipal bonds in the U.S.) are available for investment in foreign country 1, where the explicit tax rate is 35%. The before-tax rate of return on fully taxable bonds is 10%, and the tax-exempt bond rate is 6.5%. Assuming that the home country treats the interest on such bonds as taxable income on repatriation, home country investors attract an additional repatriation tax in the home country of 3.575% of the amount invested abroad (or 6.5% × .55), for an after-tax return of only 2.925%. Fully taxable bonds are more attractive to home country investors investing in country 1 than are tax-exempt bonds. As with tax-exempt bonds, fully taxable bonds yield 6.5% after payment of local taxes. On repatriation, however, 4.5% is earned after tax (or 10%(1 - .55)). This is 1.575% more than the return from investing in the foreign tax-exempt bonds. While the tax credit system allows only 55% of the implicit tax to be refunded, it does allow for a full refund of the explicit tax. As a result, foreign investors tend to be attracted to high explicitly taxed assets.

Examples of Tax Jurisdictions in which Tax Rates are Low

Puerto Rico

Under Section 936 of the U.S. Internal Revenue Code, often referred to as the "possessions corporation" provisions, certain types of income earned in Puerto Rico are exempt from U.S. taxation, even when profits are repatriated to the U.S. Although Puerto Rican corporate tax rates reach as high as 45%, 90% of qualified manufacturing income is tax-exempt for the first 5 years of operations and 75% of qualified manufacturing income is exempt for the next 5 years. Moreover, additional years of tax relief (up to 35 years in total[12]) can be secured if operations are located away from San Juan in some of the more remote communities of Puerto Rico.

Besides these tax benefits, Puerto Rico may provide funds to build manufacturing facilities, provide a training allowance to train local labor, and provide exemption from property taxes and customs taxes for a considerable period of time. Given this extraordinary list of benefits, why doesn't everyone locate operations in Puerto Rico? The following partial list of factors might explain why.

To qualify for favorable tax treatment, 80% of the personnel must be Puerto Rican residents and work more than 20 hours per week in the exempt activity. Puerto Rico has a large pool of low-skilled laborers but a small pool of skilled workers. Puerto Rico also has a very high minimum wage rate. Beyond this, there are telecommunications problems, language problems, and infrastructure problems. In addition, there may be difficulties associated with protecting the value of intangible assets, like patents and goodwill. Finally, Puerto Rican tax rates on individuals are very high. This requires that expatriate U.S. workers in Puerto Rico, especially highly compensated managers, be given large salary increases to be "kept whole."

The most active manufacturers in Puerto Rico are drug companies. Why? (This is not meant to be a "loaded" question.) Packing pills in boxes does not require a great deal of skilled labor. Puerto Rico has also attracted a number of high-technology companies that undertake relatively simple assembly operations there.

Puerto Rico is by no means the only tax jurisdiction wherein tax holidays can be secured. But it is unique in not attracting U.S. taxation upon repatriation of profits to the U.S.

Europe

Among European Community (EC) countries, Ireland bids most aggressively to attract new business. It offers a 10% tax rate through at least the year 2000. It also offers favorable financing for plant construction.

---

[12] Special tax treatment is often negotiable with foreign governments. In principle, therefore, tax relief could continue indefinitely.

Chapter 13   Multinational Tax Planning: Introduction and Investment Decisions

The Industrial Development Authority has been authorized by the Irish Government to develop an international financial services center (IFSC) in Dublin. The Irish Government provides incentives for financial service firms to locate in Dublin. These incentives include a 0% tax on income and capital gains accruing to mutual fund-like investments that are managed from the IFSC, and a 10% tax on net income of management companies in the IFSC through the year 2000. The EC has blessed this special tax rate for financial service firms. Moreover, there are no Irish withholding taxes. If a U.S.-based investment company currently located in New York or California relocates and manages money in Ireland, it can defer the payment of U.S. federal taxes for 10 years (and possibly more with extensions). The repatriation of profits from Ireland to the U.S. also does not attract any taxes in a number of states, including New York and California.

An "enticement pamphlet" put out by the Industrial Development Authority (IDA) claims that Ireland has introduced investor protection legislation which complies with EC directives, and, as a result, investment companies set up under the legislation will be marketable throughout the EC. This is a very important consideration in light of the impending integration of the EC. The brochure also claims "an excellent supporting infrastructure, including first class, all-digital telecommunication system, low office accommodation costs, plentiful supply of highly educated and trainable personnel combined with low salary costs, and fully developed banking, accountancy and legal services."[13] The IDA is involved in negotiations with many leading financial service firms including firms from the U.K., Germany, the U.S., and Japan. Some of the firms it lists include American International Group (U.S.), Dresdner Bank (Germany), Eagle Star (U.K.), Sanwa Bank (Japan), and Nat West (U.K.). A total of 111 companies were approved as of May 1990, including 23 firms engaged in corporate treasury management, 11 in captive insurance management, 15 in insurance and reinsurance services, 25 in fund and investment management, 8 in currency and securities trading, and 33 in asset and loan financing.

There are, however, a few catches to locating in Ireland. One is that personal tax rates on income reach a rate above 50% at low levels of income. This is not as onerous for expatriates as it might seem. Expatriates can deduct their ordinary and necessary business expenses, and, perhaps more important, they need only be taxed on the income they spend while living in Ireland. Employers can arrange for a non-Irish corporate affiliate company to pay part of their employee's Irish salary outside of Ireland.

Other European jurisdictions that offer tax incentives to locate operations there include Wales, Switzerland, and the Netherlands. U.S. multinationals do little in the way of manufacturing elsewhere in Europe, in part because tax rates and wage rates are very high.[14] Instead, selling activities predominate in Europe. Of course, the economic unification of the EC in the 1990s could lead to changes here.

---

[13] "The Attractions of Dublin as a Centre for International Fund Management," Industrial Development Authority (Dublin, Ireland), May 1990.

[14] A recent exception on the tax rate dimension is the U.K., where corporate rates were reduced to 35% in 1985. Tax rates were reduced in a number of other EC countries in the second half of the 1980s, but rates are still high compared to those in the U.S.

13.2   How World-Wide Foreign Tax Rules Affect Investment Incentives

Some Eastern European countries have also created incentives for foreign investment. For example, Hungary exempts income from taxation for the first 5 years for certain operations and reduces tax rates by 60% (of the normal rate of 40%) for the next 5 years.

Pacific Asia

The Far East is another source of tax holidays and is much more successful than the EC in attracting manufacturing operations. For example, Malaysia offers five to ten years of full tax exemption, and the actual deal is negotiable. Malaysia also has a large pool of unskilled and semi-skilled laborers.

Hong Kong offers permanently low tax rates (18% maximum corporate rates), a large pool of semi-skilled labor, and excellent banking and telecommunications facilities. Some uncertainty exists, however, regarding Chinese influence when the British lease on Hong Kong expires in 1997.

Singapore is a desirable location if highly skilled labor is demanded. Although it offers five- to ten-year tax holidays, it is becoming selective in what it will subsidize: it has been particularly interested in attracting major manufacturing operations, not simply assembly facilities.

In all of these examples, tax and other subsidies are being offered, not out of the goodness of the local government's heart, but because the tax jurisdiction in question would not otherwise be the location of first choice in the absence of the subsidies. As such, these operations bear implicit taxes in the form of higher costs of operations and/or competition-related reductions in final goods prices.

Investment of Accumulated Earnings and Profits: The Repatriation Decision

Earlier, we compared the attractiveness of undertaking new investments at home versus abroad. We now turn to the *reinvestment* decision. That is, once investment is undertaken abroad, should profits be reinvested there or should they be repatriated as earned?

Let us assume, as we did in Table 13.2, that the home-country and foreign-country tax rates are 55% and 35%, respectively. The pretax and after-tax rates of return available at home are 22% and 9.9%, and those available abroad are 20% and 13%, respectively.

Let us assume that the firm has accumulated $100 million in earnings and profits in the foreign country. Should the $100 million continue to be reinvested locally or repatriated and invested at home? If the $100 million is repatriated, it will attract additional home-country tax of

$$\frac{\$100 \text{ million}}{(1 - .35)} (55\% - 35\%) = \$30.77 \text{ million}$$

after taking advantage of the 35% foreign tax credit allowance. This leaves $69.23 million (or $100 million - $30.77 million) to invest at home at a rate of 9.9% after tax. In general, if RE represents the amount of retained earnings that are repatriated, the amount remaining after paying the home-country tax is[15]

---

[15] This assumes a worldwide tax system, rather than a territorial tax system. This also assumes that the home-country tax rate, t_d, exceeds the foreign-country tax rate, t_f. Otherwise, there would be no repatriation tax due in the home country.

Chapter 13   Multinational Tax Planning: Introduction and Investment Decisions

$$RE - \frac{RE}{(1 - t_f)} (t_d - t_f) = \frac{RE(1 - t_d)}{(1 - t_f)} . \qquad (13.4)$$

If it reinvests this amount at home for n periods at an after-tax rate of return of r_d, the accumulation in n periods is

$$\frac{RE(1 - t_d)}{(1 - t_f)} (1 + r_d)^n . \qquad (13.5)$$

On the other hand, if the firm reinvests the $100 million of retained earnings abroad, it can earn a return of 13% after local tax, and repatriate the accumulated amount at the end of n periods. After repatriation in n periods and payment of the home country repatriation tax, the parent company is left with

$$\$100 \text{ million} \times (1.13)^n - (55\% - 35\%) \text{ tax on } \frac{\$100 \times 1.13^n}{.65} .$$

More generally, reinvesting an amount RE abroad for n periods leaves, after repatriation tax,

$$RE(1 + r_f)^n - \frac{RE(1 + r_f)^n}{(1 - t_f)} (t_d - t_f) = RE(1 + r_f)^n \frac{(1 - t_d)}{(1 - t_f)} , \qquad (13.6)$$

or $69.23 million $\times 1.13^n$ in our example (versus $69.23 million $\times 1.099^n$ if funds are repatriated and invested at home). This means that reinvesting abroad is superior to repatriation for any length investment horizon.

Comparing expressions 13.5 and 13.6, we see that reinvesting abroad dominates repatriation whenever the after-local-tax rate of return on foreign investment, r_f, exceeds the after-tax rate of return on home country investment, r_d. And this is true for *any* length investment horizon. Why is this so? If the firm reinvests retained earnings abroad, it receives, in effect, a current home country tax deduction for the full amount of the pretax earnings that gave rise to reinvested retained earnings. But upon repatriation in the future, all pretax profits earned abroad are taxed at the repatriation tax rate of $t_d - t_f$ (or 20% in our example).

As we demonstrated for pension fund investing in Chapter Three, an immediate tax deduction, followed by full taxation in the future at the same tax rate, is equivalent to allowing tax exemption on the income earned in the interim. Similarly, allowing deferral of the repatriation is equivalent to allowing repatriation tax exemption on the income earned from reinvesting retained earnings abroad. As a result, only the foreign after-tax rate of return versus the home country after-tax rate of return is relevant.

Controlled Foreign Corporations and Subpart F Income

In the situation above, home-country taxation of foreign subsidiary income was postponed merely by reinvesting the foreign subsidiary income locally in active investments. If reinvestment opportunities in active investments are poor, it would be preferable to invest in passive investments abroad, such as Eurobonds, which might provide similar before-tax rates of return as those available by investing in passive assets (like domestic bonds) in the home country. But in many countries, passive income earned abroad is taxed by the home country as it is earned, rather than when it is repatriated. In the U.S., such tax treatment is required under Subpart F of the tax code, and the passive income earned abroad that is taxed in the U.S. is called Subpart F income.

How does this change the firm's decision of whether to invest retained earnings abroad in passive investments? If the pretax rate of return on passive investments is the same abroad as it is at home, then it pays to reinvest abroad whenever there are foreign retained earnings that would attract a home country tax upon repatriation (and this occurs when the home country tax rate exceeds the foreign tax rate). Why is this so? Reinvestment abroad postpones the repatriation tax on the foreign retained earnings: this tax is a fixed nominal amount based on income earned abroad to date. Using our example, if the firm repatriates and invests at home for n periods at rate r_d, it accumulates

$$[\$100 \text{ million} - \frac{\$100 \text{ million}}{.65} (.55 - .35)] (1 + r_d)^n = \frac{9}{13} \$100 \text{ million} (1 + r_d)^n.$$

Suppose instead that the firm leaves the retained earnings abroad and invests in passive assets that yield a pretax return of $R_f = R_d$, and a return of r_d after paying the home country tax. After repatriation in n years, the net accumulation (after paying an additional repatriation tax on only the income that has not yet attracted a repatriation tax) is

$$\$100 \text{ million} \times (1 + r_d)^n - \frac{\$100 \text{ million}}{.65} (.55 - .35).$$

The second term in the expression above represents a fixed amount of tax that is due only on repatriation. It turns out that if the home country imposed an interest charge on the repatriation tax at rate r_d per period, it would be a matter of indifference whether the foreign earnings were reinvested abroad or repatriated. But such a charge is *not* levied. As a result, the longer the retained earnings are reinvested abroad, the lower is the present value of the tax. So reinvesting abroad remains superior to repatriating.

In fact, reinvesting abroad in passive assets can beat repatriation even when the pretax return available on foreign passive assets is *below* that available at home.[16] Most low-tax foreign jurisdictions (such as Ireland or the Netherlands), however, allow firms to reinvest retained earnings in high-yielding passive investments such as Eurobonds, and allow firms to pay dividends to sister subsidiaries in other tax jurisdictions without paying withholding tax.

---

[16] More precisely, each dollar of retained earnings reinvested passively abroad at pretax rate R_f for n years, after which the foreign investment is liquidated, yields

$$[1 + R_f(1 - t_d)]^n - \frac{(t_d - t_f)}{1 - t_f}. \tag{13.7}$$

By contrast, each dollar repatriated immediately and invested at home at pretax rate R_d for n years yields

$$[1 + R_d(1 - t_d)]^n - \frac{(t_d - t_f)}{1 - t_f} [1 + R_d(1 - t_d)]^n. \tag{13.8}$$

Comparing 13.7 and 13.8, R_f can be below R_d and 13.7 can still exceed 13.8, because in the former, no interest is charged on the repatriation tax (the second term).

Chapter 13   Multinational Tax Planning: Introduction and Investment Decisions

Investment and Repatriation Policy
When the Foreign Tax Rate Exceeds the Domestic Tax Rate

In the analysis above, comparisons of foreign and domestic investment accumulations were complicated by the fact that repatriation of foreign earnings gave rise to an additional tax. When the foreign tax rate exceeds the domestic rate, repatriation triggers no additional tax (assuming that there is no foreign withholding tax). With these assumptions, it is straightforward to verify that foreign investment is preferred to domestic investment, for *any* length investment horizon, if and only if $r_f > r_d$; that is, the after-local-tax rate of return abroad exceeds the after-tax rate of return at home. The *same* condition determines whether reinvestment abroad is preferred to repatriation of foreign retained earnings.

Controlled Foreign Corporations

Most U.S. corporations use controlled foreign corporations (CFCs) to invest abroad. A CFC is a foreign corporation owned more than 50% (in terms of voting power *or* market value, the latter condition added by the 1986 Tax Act) by "U.S. shareholders." A "U.S. shareholder" is any U.S. person (including a corporation) owning at least 10% of the voting stock.

Classification as a CFC (Section 951) triggers several possible tax disadvantages:

- Loss of the deferral on Subpart F income, which is passive income and income from certain activities likely to be shifted offshore for the purpose of deferring U.S. taxation. We will describe this in a bit more detail below.
- Loss of tax deferral on earnings and profits reinvested by the CFC in U.S. property (that is, reinvestment in U.S. property is deemed to be equivalent to repatriation of profits to the parent). Such transactions, however, need not give rise to the imposition of withholding tax by the country from which the funds are transferred.
- Gains on the sale or redemption of CFC stock or gain on liquidation of a CFC results in *ordinary* income rather than capital gain up to the CFC's earnings and profits not previously paid out as dividends.

This last feature implies that a CFC cannot accumulate income in the foreign subsidiary for a period of time and then repatriate it to the U.S. parent in the form of a capital gain rather than ordinary income. Of course, if the foreign affiliate were *not* a CFC, this *could* be done. Note that all three of the CFC disadvantages are less important following the 1986 Tax Act than before it, because (1) ordinary U.S. tax rates are reduced, and (2) capital gains tax rates are less advantageous.

Note also that CFC status can be avoided as long as shareholders are willing to share control with other owners. For example, a foreign corporation that is owned 50% by a U.S. corporation and 50% by an unrelated foreign investor would avoid CFC status. Similarly, a foreign corporation can be owned *entirely* by U.S. taxpayers and still avoid CFC status as long as a sufficient number of owners hold less than 10% of the voting stock (11 equal shareholders will do the trick, for example).

A foreign corporation that is *not* a CFC or a foreign personal holding company (the rules for which are quite similar) can invest in assets that yield passive income, like interest-bearing securities, *without* triggering current U.S. taxation. If the investment in interest-bearing securities is made through a foreign corporation in a tax haven country, where the income tax rate is very low, this can offer a very high rate of return after tax to shareholders. Prior to the 1986 Tax Act, as long as CFC status could be avoided, the foreign corporation's earnings eventually could be repatriated to U.S. owners at *capital gains* rates via share repurchases or liquidation. The 1986 Tax Act created a new type of company, however, called a "passive foreign investment company" (PFIC) for which there is no ownership test. A corporation that is not a CFC is classified as a PFIC in any year in which 75% or more of its gross income is passive *or* 50% or more of its assets produce passive income. A year by year test is applied, and as a result, in some years, when a foreign corporation fails the PFIC test, its active income will not be currently taxable in the U.S. Although income from a PFIC is deferred until distributions are made to shareholders or stock is sold, all income is ordinary, and interest is charged on a hypothetical deferred tax liability as if the income had been distributed as earned.

These PFIC rules affect financial service firms that hold passive assets, such as bonds, in the normal course of their foreign operations. For example, a number of financial service firms have formed joint ventures with other European firms. Such joint ventures, which are often located in Dublin, can defer U.S. tax on active income from such activities as making markets in bonds, only in years in which they fail the PFIC test. Many such firms make markets in securities (such as forward contracts on currencies) and hedge their risks by investing in passive assets. The CFC and PFIC tax rules do not allow integration of these transactions in many cases. As a result, the passive income is treated apart from the active income, and the deferral advantage of establishing a corporation in Dublin can be lost in certain years.

As we will discuss in more detail in Chapter Fourteen, it can be advantageous to repatriate income from a foreign corporation in a low-tax jurisdiction if the parent company has a foreign tax credit carryforward from high-tax countries that will soon expire unused.[17] It can also be advantageous for a multinational company to repatriate income from a subsidiary in a high-tax country if income

---

[17] In 1988, Salomon Brothers remitted $1.1 billion of non-U.S. earnings to the U.S., and for financial reporting (but not tax) purposes, it provided for a repatriation tax expense on an additional $200 million of unremitted non-U.S. earnings that were no longer considered to be indefinitely invested outside the U.S. As a result, additional current and deferred U.S. federal income taxes of $130 million and $50 million, respectively, were provided for financial reporting purposes in 1988. If a firm plans never to repatriate foreign earnings, it need not create a deferred tax reserve in the U.S. (thereby increasing its reported earnings). Once Salomon repatriated some of its foreign earnings, it had to establish a reserve for $200 million of deferred income (at a 25% tax rate). Such financial accounting factors can increase the perceived cost for firms to repatriate foreign income. Salomon repatriated this income from Zug, its Swiss subsidiary, because some of its foreign tax credits were about to expire. It took an earnings per share hit because it had booked these earnings at the low tax rates in Zug, and in addition was required to increase its deferred tax reserve for taxes on future repatriations. (*Wall Street Journal*, December 9, 1988)

has already been repatriated from a low-tax subsidiary for non-tax reasons. If worldwide averaging rules apply to the foreign tax credit calculations (as they do in the U.S.), repatriation from a high-tax country typically yields a net tax refund in this circumstance.

Similarly, the PFIC rules can be used to advantage where companies form 50-50 joint ventures with partners in a high-tax country like Japan. For example, Japanese tradition precludes foreign firms from paying out large amounts of dividend income from Japanese companies to significant non-Japanese investors: it is a sign of bad faith if the firm is too aggressive in repatriating income. By holding sufficient quantities of passive investments in the Japanese corporation to trigger the PFIC rules, the firm can "repatriate" its high-taxed income for tax purposes without violating the tradition of retaining earnings in Japan.

We have enumerated some disadvantages of classification as a controlled foreign corporation. There *are* conditions, however, under which CFC status can be quite advantageous. We will consider these conditions later, after we take a closer look at the foreign tax credit limitations. But first, let's take a slightly closer look at Subpart F income.

Subpart F Income

Recall that if a foreign corporation is classified as a CFC, Subpart F income is *not* deferred from U.S. taxation. Instead, the income is deemed to have been distributed to its U.S. owners whether a dividend has been declared or not.

Subpart F has two main components: (1) income from the insurance of risks outside the country in which the CFC is organized, and (2) foreign base company income. Foreign base company income, in turn, has five components: (1) foreign personal holding company income or FPHCI (dividends, interest, rents, royalties, etc.). The 1986 Tax Act expanded the definition of FPHCI to include interest and interest-equivalents received by a bank in its banking business, net gains from the sale or exchange of property that generates passive income (like patents and land), and gains on commodities futures and foreign currency transactions, (2) foreign base company *sales* income, (3) foreign base company *service* income, (4) foreign base company *shipping* income (the 1986 Tax Act repealed the exception for *reinvested* shipping income), and (5) foreign base company *oil-and-gas-related* income.

The Subpart F rules in conjunction with the CFC provisions, are designed to prevent tax avoidance through the formation of paper foreign corporations in a tax haven country to record, but not really actively generate, income from passive investments, sales, services, shipping operations, or oil-related activities. For example, foreign base company *sales income* is income derived from the purchase or sale of personal property such as manufactured goods where the goods are *manufactured outside the country of incorporation as well as sold to a user outside the country of incorporation.*

The insurance component of Subpart F income includes income derived from the insurance of risks outside the country in which the CFC is organized. This is a substantial change from pre-1986 Tax Act rules when Subpart F income included only that derived from the insurance of *U.S.* risks. Moreover, prior to the

1986 Tax Act, even the income from insuring U.S. risks could be postponed. To do this, corporations established insurance companies that avoided CFC status altogether, by banding together with a foreign investor or a large number of U.S. persons.

These considerations clearly influenced the organizational form in which insurance was sold in the insurance market. In 1983, roughly 2000 captive (controlled by U.S. corporations) insurance companies (more than half of them in Bermuda) collected more than $5 billion in premiums or roughly 8% to 10% of the total commercial insurance market.[18] The 1986 Tax Act made insurance income taxable currently as Subpart F income in a variety of circumstances even when the captive insurance company is *not* a CFC (for example, when there is 25% or more total U.S. ownership without regard to the 10% minimum per person).

The 1986 Tax Act also repealed the possessions corporation exception to the Subpart F rules. This means, for example, that corporations no longer generate as much passive income through their Puerto Rican subsidiaries. This affected companies such as Pfizer, Inc., that invested hundreds of millions of dollars in interest-bearing securities in Puerto Rico prior to the 1986 Tax Act to exploit the opportunity to earn largely tax-free income because of the Subpart F exception for possessions corporations. Pfizer, however, was even more clever. It established the Pfizer bank, a foreign CFC, and used its Puerto Rican retained earnings to capitalize the bank. As long as the bank engages in active business activities (commercial lending, etc.), it can avoid paying U.S. tax on income generated on these retained earnings.

For administrative convenience of both taxpayers and the IRS, Subpart F income is modified by the so-called 5-70 Rules. That is, if foreign base company income of the CFC is less than the lesser of $1 million or 5% of the CFC's gross income,[19] then the firm can treat the income as active income and ignore the Subpart F rules. If more than 70% of gross income of the CFC is foreign base company income, then 100% of the gross income of the CFC is treated as Subpart F income. It should also be noted that passive income earned in foreign subsidiaries where the local tax rate is at least 90% of the U.S. tax rate is *not* treated as Subpart F income.[20] These rules provide a potential trap of moderate consequences for taxpayers that aren't careful and a tax planning opportunity for those who *are* very careful. For example, a CFC might find it beneficial to maintain passive investments that generate just less than 5% of its foreign base company income.

Foreign Tax Credit (FTCs)

As indicated earlier, the U.S. attempts to mitigate multiple taxation of foreign income by allowing credits to be taken for income taxes paid to foreign governments. But double taxation is not eliminated in a variety of circumstances.

---

[18] *Price Waterhouse Guide* (Price Waterhouse, 1984)

[19] Ten percent of gross income prior to the 1986 Tax Act.

[20] Prior to the 1986 Act, CFC status was avoided if the corporation was not formed for a "tax avoidance purpose," a less exacting standard than the 90% rule.

- Taxes other than those on *income* (for example, property taxes, value added taxes, and excise taxes) are not eligible for the FTC, although they are deductible as business expenses for U.S. tax purposes.

- The income tax rate in some foreign countries exceeds that in the U.S., and the FTC limitation may prove restrictive here, because the U.S. will not refund more in taxes than would have been paid if the income were earned in the U.S.

- The foreign country may use different *source of income rules* (that is, whether income is deemed to be earned by the foreign corporation or the U.S. corporation), as well as different rules for income recognition and deduction (for example, depreciation rules) than in the U.S.

Foreign taxes can be taken as a *deduction* for U.S. tax purposes rather than as a credit, if desired. This may prove desirable because of the FTC limitation. When the FTC limitation is binding, the U.S. allows a two year carryback and a five year carryforward. Although a foreign tax *deduction* reduces U.S. taxes by only the U.S. tax rate rather than the 100% reduction available when a credit is used, realizing a deduction is better than a potential tax credit that expires unused. The choice of whether to take a deduction or a credit for foreign taxes paid can be changed from year to year under U.S. law.

Tax planning for the utilization of foreign tax credits is among the most important tax considerations in the multinational arena. We will return to this subject in Chapter Fourteen.

13.3 Empirical Evidence on Foreign Acquisitions of U.S. Companies

In the chapters on corporate restructuring, we will present both arguments and evidence suggesting that the 1986 Tax Act discouraged mergers and acquisitions among U.S. companies. When non-U.S. investors face tax rules and investment opportunity sets that differ from those faced by U.S. taxpayers, and where capital is allowed to flow across tax jurisdictions, changes in U.S. tax rules can affect investment incentives of U.S. and non-U.S. taxpayers differently. As we will argue below, such is the case for the 1986 Tax Act and its effect on merger incentives.

To illustrate the advantages of investing abroad, we return to our example summarized in Table 13.5, where we assumed that the home country tax rate was 55% and the tax rates abroad ranged from a high of 35% in country 1 (where the implicit tax rate on investments was rather low) to 0% in country 3 (where the implicit tax rate on investments was rather high). Suppose the home country is Japan (a 55% marginal tax rate) and foreign country 1 is the U.S. subsequent to the 1986 Tax Act. After all, the 1986 Tax Act reduced U.S. corporate tax rates to 34% and eliminated a great many investment incentives. Between the 1981 and 1986 Tax Acts, the U.S. was more like foreign country 3. Generous investment tax credits and depreciation allowances for most operating assets in the U.S. gave rise to substantial amounts of implicit tax (many investments were virtually tax exempt). What does this suggest about foreign investment in the U.S. after 1986 and between 1981 and 1986?

Given differences in statutory tax rates across tax jurisdictions, foreign investors should find investment in the U.S. *more* attractive after 1986 than before. The U.S. has become a tax haven relative to many European countries as well as such countries as Japan, Canada, and Australia, all of which face higher corporate tax rates than the U.S. Investors in such countries may place a higher value on the assets held by U.S. investors than U.S. investors place on them, or at a minimum, the changes in U.S. tax laws should increase the frequency with which non-U.S. investors place a higher value on U.S. assets.

This is an example of how changes in tax rules may alter the natural tax clienteles (that is, the sorting of taxpayers into their most tax-preferred investment and financing habitats) internationally. As a result, agents trade assets (mitigated as always by the tax and nontax costs of trading), because the relative valuations of such assets have changed in response to the new tax rules.

Our characterization of the U.S. as a tax haven for investment after the 1986 Act may appear at odds with the claim that corporate taxes in the U.S. were supposed to have been *increased* by $100 billion under the law, primarily from elimination of investment tax credits and the reduction in the acceleration of depreciation. The resolution of this apparent conflict lies in recognizing that fewer assets bear *implicit* taxes under the 1986 Act. Since more taxes were made explicit, the before-tax rates of return on U.S. investment should have increased, relative to those abroad. Given the increase in explicit taxes, this may not make investment to U.S. investors more attractive, but it does make investment to high-tax non-U.S. investors more attractive. As we have discussed, for a highly taxed foreign investor, most explicit taxes paid in the U.S. will be fully refundable upon repatriation of U.S. earnings (through foreign tax credit mechanisms), whereas implicit taxes are typically only tax-deductible, but not creditable, against taxes paid in the home country.[21]

The 1986 Tax Act favored foreign acquisitions of U.S. businesses for another important reason. As discussed earlier, the Act raised the shareholder-level tax on capital gains. Foreign investors in countries with integrated tax systems, or in countries that otherwise tax capital gains favorably, may be able to avoid much of the shareholder-level tax.[22] As a consequence, such foreign investors should

---

[21] An implication of this argument is that we would expect the increase in demand by foreign investors to be greatest for those U.S. businesses that invest heavily in depreciable personal and real property (like plant and equipment). This argument applies only to countries that impose taxes on worldwide profits and grant tax credits for foreign taxes paid, notably the U.K. and Japan.

[22] By "integration," we refer to a system in which shareholders receive a tax credit for some or all of the corporate tax they have paid indirectly. Shareholders' taxable income is then grossed up to include the amount of the tax credit. Many countries use this system. Complete integration (elimination of double taxation) is provided by Australia, Germany, Italy, and New Zealand. A shareholder credit is provided for half or more of the corporate tax paid in Belgium, France, Ireland, and the U.K. A shareholder credit for less than half of the corporate tax paid is provided in Japan and Spain. In addition, Germany, Greece, Japan, and Norway assess a lower tax rate on distributed profits than on retained profits. Although integrated tax systems generally do not permit full integration with corporate taxes paid in foreign jurisdictions, favorable "stacking rules" for domestic earnings ensure that double taxation largely will be avoided on foreign income as long as domestic profits are sufficient.

acquire more equity interests in U.S. businesses relative to U.S. investors.

While the 1981 Tax Act encouraged U.S. corporations to buy other U.S. corporations (and for foreign firms to acquire fewer U.S. corporations) to achieve rapid depreciation write-offs and to secure investment tax credits, among a host of other factors, the 1986 Tax Act discouraged it. We present striking evidence in support of these predictions in Chapter Twenty-Four. The one exception is debt-financed acquisitions. As we discussed in Chapter Four, debt financing allows corporate profits to be distributed to investors in a tax-deductible way. In the limit, when all corporate-level taxes are avoided, debt financing allows corporations to avoid double taxation (like a partnership structure). The 1986 Tax Act made debt financing highly tax-favored over equity financing because of both the high corporate tax rate, relative to personal tax rates, and the high capital gains tax rates on shares.

It is worth noting that the 1986 Tax Act favored foreign firms over U.S. firms that use leverage (a so-called leveraged-buyout transaction (LBO)) to acquire U.S. companies. As we discuss in more detail in Chapter Fourteen, when a U.S. multinational firm issues debt in the U.S., it must allocate some of the interest that it pays on the debt to foreign operations for purposes of calculating its foreign tax credit limitations. As a result, the U.S. multinational can lose a significant fraction of the interest deduction because of severe limitations on its use of foreign tax credits. The foreign buyer of a U.S. business that forms a U.S. subsidiary and issues LBO debt does not allocate any of the interest it pays on U.S. borrowings back to its parent in the home country because it does not consolidate its parent for U.S. tax purposes. This provides a decided advantage to foreigners that acquire U.S. businesses.

Next, we turn to empirical evidence to test whether foreign incentives to purchase U.S. interests increased following the passage of the 1986 Tax Act. In particular, we compare merger and acquisition activity between U.S. companies to that in which *non-U.S.* companies are represented on the buy side of merger and acquisition transactions around the time of the passage of the 1986 Act in the U.S.

The dollar volume of acquisitions of U.S. firms by U.S. companies increased by 85% during the fourth quarter of 1986 relative to the average during the eight quarters surrounding this period. More precisely, it increased by 66% in the fourth quarter of 1986 relative to the average over the four preceding quarters. Then acquisitions dropped over the four quarters of 1987 to a level roughly 20% below that in the four quarters preceding 1986-4.

In comparison, the dollar value of U.S. acquisitions by non-U.S. companies in 1986-4 increased 430% to $15.52 billion relative to the average over the preceding four quarters of $2.93 billion (see Table 13.7).[23] The level of activity during the fourth quarter of 1986 alone exceeded by 39% the average *annual* dollar volume of such activity for the 1981-1985 period, as reported in *Mergerstat*.

---

[23] The increase is 424% in real terms (as indicated in the column entitled "Constant 1987-4 CPI") and 402% adjusted for changes in the level of the S&P 500 stock index (column entitled "Constant 1987-4 S&P").

Table 13.7 Quarterly Merger and Acquisition Values: Nominal Dollar, Constant Dollar, and Constant Stock Index Amounts: 1985-4 Through 1987-4

U.S. Purchase By Non-U.S. Companies

Quarter	Nominal Amount ($Billions)	Rank Excluding 1986-4	Constant 1987-4 CPI Amount ($Billions)	Rank Excluding 1986-4	Constant 1987-4 S&P Amount ($Billions)	Rank Excluding 1986-4
1985-4	2.13	8	2.25	8	2.66	8
1986-1	3.27	6	3.45	6	3.57	6
1986-2	2.87	7	3.04	7	2.96	7
1986-3	3.43	5	3.60	5	3.80	5
SUM	11.70	26	12.35	26	12.99	26
AVG	2.93		3.09		3.25	
1986-4	15.52		16.19		16.33	
1987-1	10.66	3	11.01	3	9.25	2
1987-2	10.98	2	11.20	2	9.06	3
1987-3	12.82	1	12.93	1	9.92	1
1987-4	9.43	4	9.43	4	9.43	4
SUM	43.89	10	44.57	10	37.66	10
AVG	10.97		11.14		9.42	
PROB*	.0143		.0143		.0143	

* PROB denotes the probability that the sum of the ranks in the four quarters preceding 1986-4 could be as high or higher than the sum of the ranks in the four quarter succeeding 1986-4 by chance alone.

Data Sources: *Mergers & Acquisitions* for nominal values, *Industry Week* for consumer prices, and Ibbotson Associates (*Stocks, Bonds, Bills, and Inflation*) for S&P 500 Index values.

Moreover, while the level of acquisition activity declined over the four quarters of 1987, relative to 1986-4, to $11 billion per quarter, the level of acquisitions in the four quarters of 1987 was 3.74 times as high as during the four quarters preceding 1986-4.[24] Using a simple rank-sum test, the differences in ranks (in nominal dollars, constant dollars, and adjusted for changes in the S&P 500 stock index) could have occurred by chance with probability equal to only .0143.

This evidence is quite consistent with the 1986 Tax Act's having stimulated foreign demand for U.S. businesses. Moreover, the increase in foreign demand for U.S. businesses was approximately offset by the decrease in domestic demand for U.S. businesses. That is, whereas U.S. purchases of U.S. businesses dropped by roughly $8 billion per quarter over the eight quarters surrounding the passage of the 1986 Tax Act, non-U.S purchases of U.S. businesses increased by roughly $8 billion per quarter. Absent a consideration of how changes in tax rules affected domestic and foreign investors differently, one might have concluded, incorrectly, that the 1986 Act was accompanied by only a transitory shift in demand for

---

[24] Activity in 1987 was 3.61 times as high as the four quarters preceding 1986-4 in constant dollar terms and 2.90 times as high adjusted for changes in the level of the S&P 500 stock index.

Chapter 13 Multinational Tax Planning: Introduction and Investment Decisions

mergers and acquisitions during the fourth quarter of 1986. Moreover, foreign purchases of U.S. businesses remained high throughout the ensuing three years, 1988-1990, as shown in Table 13.8.

Table 13.8 U.S. Purchases by Non-U.S. Companies
($Billions, Base Quarter 1987-4)

Quarter	Nominal	Constant CPI	Constant S&P
1988-1	8.91	8.82	8.49
1988-2	12.40	12.16	11.17
1988-3	13.88	13.48	12.62
1988-4	25.97	24.97	23.13
SUM	61.16	59.43	55.47
AVERAGE	15.29	14.86	13.86
1989-1	13.92	13.13	11.70
1989-2	9.60	8.97	7.44
1989-3	17.05	15.50	12.09
1989-4	13.59	12.24	9.50
SUM	54.16	49.84	40.73
AVERAGE	13.54	12.46	10.18
1990-1	12.11	10.72	8.97
1990-2	9.12	8.00	6.42
1990-3	14.69	12.56	12.14
1990-4	5.61	4.75	4.32
SUM	41.53	36.03	31.85
AVERAGE	10.38	9.01	7.96

Data Source for Acquisitions: *Mergers & Acquisitions*

Many large foreign LBOs of U.S. corporations (most notably the Campeau acquisition of Federated Department Stores and the BAT Industries acquisition of Farmers Group) occurred during this period. The number of foreign acquisitions priced at $1 billion or more doubled from 6 in 1987 to 12 in 1988, accounting for more than four-fifths of the increase in total direct investment in the U.S. in that year. In 1988, the U.K. led all other foreign countries in U.S. investments, spending a total of $21.5 billion, followed by Japan with $14.2 billion in U.S. investments.[25] In fact, for the four quarters prior to the 1986 Tax Act, foreign purchases of U.S. firms represented only 7% of all U.S. merger activity. In the 4th quarter of 1986, it jumped to 19%. Foreign purchases represented a large percentage of U.S. acquisitions in years subsequent to 1986: 26% in 1987, 27% in 1988, 22% in 1989, and 26% in 1990.

The argument that the 1986 Tax Act should have increased foreign investment in the U.S. due to the elimination of tax preferences like investment tax credits and accelerated depreciation runs in reverse in 1981. The Economic

---

[25] *San Francisco Chronicle,* "Foreigners Pour Money Into U.S." (May 31, 1989)

Recovery Tax Act (ERTA) of 1981 accelerated depreciation schedules sharply and liberalized investment tax credits somewhat. It is worth noting that foreign acquisitions dropped very sharply in the post-ERTA period, both in absolute dollar terms and as a percentage of total acquisitions. Whereas foreign acquisitions of U.S. companies, as a percentage of total acquisitions, was less than 8% in the post-ERTA/pre-1986 Tax Act period, it was over 20% of the total both immediately before ERTA and immediately after the 1986 Tax Act.

The analysis above ignores other factors that may have contributed to the surge in foreign acquisitions of U.S. businesses in the fourth quarter of 1986. For example, concern by foreign investors over increasing trade restrictions may have prompted acquisitions by foreign manufacturers that sell to U.S. consumers. Another factor is the changes in the magnitude of the trade deficit, although this is not entirely independent of the amount of foreign acquisitions. A related factor is currency exchange rates. Several recent papers document an association between foreign direct investment in the U.S. and the exchange rate between the dollar and other major foreign currencies.[26] In particular, foreign direct investment apparently increases when the dollar is relatively weak, and conversely, although this would not be expected in perfect capital markets.

What is particularly interesting is that the dollar was very strong during the several years immediately following the passage of the 1981 Tax Act and was very weak in the period surrounding the 1986 Tax Act. Consequently, we are faced with an identification problem in sorting out the independent contribution of tax rule changes and exchange rate changes on acquisition behavior of foreign investors. The dollar was also stronger during 1988-89, but foreign acquisitions of U.S. businesses did not fall off in total or as a percentage of all U.S. acquisitions during this period. Moreover, in 1989, Japanese firms acquired $13.7 billion of U.S. corporations (up from $12.7 billion in 1988) even though the yen fell against the dollar.[27]

But it is also interesting to note that Froot and Stein find that the relation between exchange rates and foreign direct investments in the U.S. applies to the manufacturing sector but not to the nonmanufacturing sector. Since it is the manufacturing sector where the investment tax credit and depreciation rule changes are most important, this lends further credence to the role of taxes.

In addition, the weakness of the dollar surrounding passage of the 1986 Tax Act began in 1985. The fact that such a dramatic shift in foreign acquisition activity began during the fourth quarter of 1986 rather than earlier is further evidence suggesting the importance of taxes.

It is also worth noting that Froot and Stein find that the relation between foreign direct investment and exchange rates is not significant for the U.K., Canada, or Japan. And while it *is* significant for West Germany, the coefficient is only one-ninth as large as for the U.S. The one indication in Froot and Stein that

---

[26] For example, see Richard E. Caves, "Exchange-Rate Movements and Foreign Direct Investments in the United States," Discussion Paper No. 1383 (Harvard Institute of Economic Research), May 1988; Kenneth A. Froot and Jeremy C. Stein, "Exchange Rates and Foreign Direct Investment: An Imperfect Capital Markets Approach," (Unpublished working paper), February 19, 1989; and Joel B. Slemrod, "Tax Effects on Foreign Direct Investment in the U.S.: Evidence from a Cross-Country Comparison," (University of Michigan and NBER working paper), January 1989.

[27] *Wall Street Journal* (January 17, 1990)

Chapter 13   Multinational Tax Planning: Introduction and Investment Decisions

exchange rates are important in explaining foreign direct investment in the U.S. is that the relation holds strongly during the 1970s, where tax changes do not seem terribly significant in the U.S.[28]

In fact, further work by Deborah Swenson in her M.I.T. (Department of Economics) Ph.D. dissertation indicates that foreign direct investment in the U.S. occurs most in those industries where capital tax rates were highest and hence implicit taxes were lowest. Moreover, the relation between direct foreign investment in the U.S. is stronger involving buyers from countries with worldwide tax systems than for those with territorial tax systems. She does find, however, that exchange rate changes appear to have marginal explanatory power for foreign direct investment beyond the tax rules.

As for U.S. investment abroad, the evidence indicates that it has increased recently. In 1985, U.S. firms acquired $1.4 billion of foreign firms. This increased to $5.2 billion in 1986, $11.0 billion in 1987, $14.5 billion in 1988, $22.2 billion in 1989, and $18.0 billion in 1990. While there are important nontax factors at work here (like globalization and a desire on the part of many U.S. businesses to get a foothold in Western Europe), there are important tax considerations as well. The U.S. is not the only country to have reduced tax rates and eliminated many tax incentives that gave rise to implicit taxes. In fact, the U.K. did this in 1985, even before the U.S. did. This naturally promoted U.S. acquisition of British companies. Moreover, as we will see in the next chapter, the 1986 Tax Act created a serious foreign tax credit problem for many U.S. multinationals which stimulated acquisitions of businesses that operate in low-tax countries.

Summary of Key Points

1. Generally, two different tax regimes apply to the income earned by multinational businesses. Some countries, like the U.S. and Japan, tax worldwide income of resident companies. Other countries, like France, employ a territorial tax system, where only the income earned domestically (at least for active businesses) is taxed.

2. Worldwide tax systems do not generally tax income from foreign operations as the income is earned abroad as long as the income is reinvested abroad in an active business. Home country taxation is deferred until the income is deemed to have been repatriated to the home country.

3. On the other hand, passive income (so-called Subpart F income in the U.S.) is typically ineligible for home-country tax deferral.

4. Foreign tax credit systems attempt to mitigate multiple taxation of foreign income by allowing credits for income taxes paid to foreign

---

[28] Froot and Stein, *op. cit.* Caves, *op. cit.*, also documents an inverse relation between foreign direct investment and the following variables: equity security prices in the foreign-investor (source) country relative to the U.S.; gross national product of the source country; and lagged profitability of foreign direct investments in the U.S. On the other hand, exchange rate expectations was not found to affect foreign direct investments.

governments. The credits are subject to limitations. The most important for U.S. taxpayers is that the foreign tax credit cannot exceed the U.S. tax on the foreign source income.

5. Some countries, such as the U.S., allow their taxpayers to compute the foreign tax credit limitation on a worldwide income basis. This frees up the foreign tax credit limitation and allows firms that repatriate income earned in low tax jurisdictions to use the otherwise unusable foreign tax credits generated by their high tax subsidiaries.

6. The advantages of investing abroad for a multinational firm facing a worldwide tax system depend on tax and nontax factors. Pretax returns abroad can differ from those available domestically because of differences in implicit taxes. These implicit taxes might arise because of nontax costs that are unique to operating in certain foreign countries. Implicit taxes can also arise because of differences in investment incentives offered across tax jurisdictions. Similarly, explicit tax rates vary across tax jurisdictions, and this encourages investment in the low-tax countries.

7. For multinational firms with high home country tax rates that are subject to taxation on worldwide income by the home country, deciding on which country to invest for one-year horizons requires knowledge solely of *before*-tax rates of return on investments available in the candidate countries. The investment should be made in the country with the highest before-tax rates of return. On repatriation, the profits earned abroad attract additional home-country tax such that the total paid is equal to the home country tax rate on profits earned at home. On the other hand, for very long-lived investments, all that matters is after-tax rates of return. Investment should be undertaken in the country with the highest after-local-tax rate of return. For intermediate investment horizons, the choice depends on the level of the implicit tax. The greater the implicit tax, the longer the deferral period must be before investing in the lower-tax-rate country dominates investing at home. In effect, the firm can defer the higher home country tax on foreign profits reinvested abroad, but this often comes at the expense of earning a lower pretax rate of return on investment abroad than domestically.

8. Whereas explicit taxes are eligible for foreign tax credits and are refunded dollar for dollar, implicit taxes are only deductible. It is very expensive for foreign investors to invest in assets that yield lots of implicit taxes.

9. Once profits have been earned in a low-tax-foreign country, whether they should be reinvested abroad or repatriated to a high tax country that taxes worldwide income depends on whether the after-local-tax rate of return is higher abroad than domestically. If foreign after-tax rates of return exceed domestic after-tax rates of return, it is desirable to reinvest abroad. This is true whether the investment horizon is short or long. Reinvestment abroad effectively allows a home-country tax deduction at the differential tax rate between the home and foreign

countries. Immediate deduction followed by full taxation at the same rate is equivalent to tax exemption of the after-tax income earned from reinvestment abroad.

10. If the pretax returns on passive investment opportunities abroad are about the same as those available domestically, and active investment opportunities abroad are poor, foreign profits earned in low-tax countries should be reinvested passively abroad. This is true even though the passive income is taxed as earned in the home country. Investing passively allows an interest-free postponement of the repatriation tax on previously earned income.

11. There were increased incentives for foreign firms to undertake U.S. investments in 1986 exactly when it became less desirable for U.S. corporations to buy other U.S. corporations. While the 1981 Tax Act encouraged U.S. corporations to buy other U.S. corporations to achieve rapid depreciation writeoffs and secure investment tax credits, foreign investors were discouraged from such acquisitions. The opposite is true of the 1986 Tax Act. The one exception is debt-financed acquisitions. Leveraged buyouts of U.S. businesses were encouraged by the 1986 Tax Act for both U.S. and foreign corporations since corporate rates were set below personal rates and capital gains taxes on shares were increased. Even here foreign firms gained advantages over U.S. firms. While U.S. multinational firms lose a significant proportion of the their interest deductions if they are subject to foreign tax credit limitations, their foreign counterparts do not face such problems.

12. Moreover, the dollar volume of U.S. acquisitions by non-U.S. corporations increased 430% to $15.52 billion in the fourth quarter of 1986 (the quarter following the passage of the 1986 Tax Act) relative to the average over the previous four quarters. On average, foreign acquisitions have been 3.7 times higher from 1987-1990 than in the year prior to the passage of the 1986 Tax Act.

13. Nontax factors could also account for some of the increase in foreign purchases of U.S. businesses. There has been ample concern over possible foreign trade restrictions. The U.S. dollar has also been relatively weak over this period, especially during 1985-1987. Moreover, the U.S. dollar was strong around 1981 when the tax law discouraged foreign acquisitions of U.S. businesses.

14. Unlike the U.S. experience, currency strength and foreign direct investment have *not* been linked strongly in such countries as Canada, Japan, and the U.K. Moreover, the increased investment in U.S. businesses by foreigners has occurred primarily in the manufacturing sector of the economy (where the tax incentives are greatest) and by investors in those countries that have worldwide tax systems (where, again, the tax incentives are greatest).

Discussion Questions

1. Why might countries find that it is mutually beneficial to negotiate bilateral tax treaties? Why might the U.S. adopt a foreign tax credit system?

2. What is the meaning of the term tax neutrality? Is neutrality a worthwhile goal for international tax rules? Would it be a worthwhile goal for the 50 states to pursue within the U.S.?

3. What are the effects on U.S. citizens working abroad of being subjected to a foreign tax in addition to current U.S. taxation of their income?

4. What are the tax and nontax differences between operating as a foreign branch and a foreign subsidiary of a U.S. corporation? What are the advantages and disadvantages of each form?

5. What are foreign tax credits? What is the difference between a direct foreign tax credit and an indirect (deemed paid) foreign tax credit?

6. Under what conditions will foreign tax credits result in the U.S. corporation paying exactly the same tax on foreign income as if this income was earned directly in the U.S.?

7. If tax rates are low in a foreign country, does this imply that expected after-tax rates of return on marginal investments should be higher than on domestic investments? Explain.

8. Is your answer to question seven sensitive to whether the investment funds come from retained earnings or new investment dollars? Explain.

9. We have argued throughout the text that paying implicit taxes is no less costly than paying explicit taxes. Does it matter whether one pays implicit taxes to a foreign government or direct foreign taxes or deemed paid foreign taxes?

10. What are the tax advantages and nontax costs of producing goods and services under the "possessions corporation" provisions in such locations as Puerto Rico?

11. What is "Subpart F" income? How does the taxation of Subpart F income affect the ability of U.S. corporations to defer U.S. taxation on income earned by controlled foreign corporate subsidiaries?

12. How did the 1981 and 1986 Tax Acts affect the incentives of foreign multinational corporations to purchase U.S. businesses? How did the incentives to purchase capital-intensive targets differ from the incentives to purchase non-capital-intensive targets? How did the incentives to purchase U.S. businesses differ for foreign multinationals in countries that impose a worldwide tax system from those in countries that impose a territorial tax system?

Problems

1. A U.S. multinational company owns 100% of two foreign subsidiaries (both are *controlled foreign corporations* or CFCs), one in each of countries A and B.

    Rules

    Each foreign subsidiary pays tax on all local income (that is, income earned in the respective host country) at local tax rates as given in the table at the end of this problem. Local pretax rates of return on passive and active investments are also given. The United States taxes foreign-source income in one of two ways:

    a. (Deemed) income when income is repatriated (for example, when dividends are paid by the CFCs to the parent).

    b. Deemed distributions of Subpart F (passive) income:

       1. If passive income (more precisely, so-called foreign base company income) is less than the lesser of $1 million and 5% of total pretax income for the subsidiary, then no income is deemed to have been distributed to the parent.

       2. If passive income exceeds 70% of total pretax income for the subsidiary, then 100% of the income is deemed to have been distributed to the parent in the year earned.

       3. Otherwise, 100% of only the passive income is deemed to have been distributed to the parent in the year earned, with active income being taxed in the U.S. only as dividends are paid to the parent.

    In this problem we focus primarily on the reinvestment and repatriation problem. We will ignore issues of financing (a topic we take up in the next chapter), and we will consider issues of new investment only indirectly.

    Each of our two foreign subsidiaries has assets in place that give rise to $100 in locally taxed income at the end of each of the next five years, at which point these assets will disappear. The $100 in locally taxed income comes in the form of cash, which is to be repatriated or reinvested. Each company also has $1,000 in cash either to invest (in some combination of active and passive investments in the local economy) or to repatriate to the parent. Any repatriation is treated as a dividend to the extent of previously untaxed earnings and profits (note that Subpart F income is treated as previously taxed income for this purpose). Assume that the $1,000 cash in each of countries A and B represents capital investment, not previously untaxed profits. Therefore, this capital can be repatriated to the U.S. immediately without incurring any U.S. income tax or foreign withholding tax. Once profits are generated, however, distributions come first out of earnings and profits. Further assume that no additional capital can be transferred from the U.S. to the foreign countries, from Country A to Country B, or from Country B to Country A.

Your mission, should you choose to accept it, is to determine an optimal investment and repatriation policy (that is, how much to repatriate and when, as well as how to allocate income that is reinvested in the local economy between active and passive investments) over a five-year horizon. Any cash available in either subsidiary at the end of year five must be repatriated to the parent at that time.

This problem is surprisingly difficult, despite the simple structure we have imposed on it. Make any assumptions you feel are necessary to proceed. If you do not get a satisfying solution in a reasonable amount of time (say, 8 hours), you should describe the tradeoffs you considered in attempting to solve the problem. You may provide qualitative answers where you feel it is appropriate.

Required (You need turn in answers to questions a, b, and c only. You should prepare answers to questions d, e, and f, so that we may discuss them in class. You should ignore the 5-70 Subpart F rules described in (b) (1) and (2) on the first page of the problem in answering parts a through e):

a. Assume that passive income from Country A, passive income from Country B, active income from Country A, and active income from Country B fall into four different "income baskets" for foreign tax credit purposes. (Note that the implication of this assumption is equivalent to what would occur if there were a country-by-country foreign tax credit limitation.)

b. Assume that active income from the two subsidiaries fall into the *same* "overall income basket" for foreign tax credit purposes. Similarly, passive income from the two subsidiaries falls into the same passive income basket. In other words, the foreign tax credit limitation is applied separately to passive and active income, but foreign tax on passive (active) income from Country A can be "averaged" with the tax paid on passive (active) income from Country B.

c. How does the analysis change (qualitatively is sufficient) if the initial endowment of $1,000 in countries A and B will be taxed upon repatriation as an ordinary dividend and treated as neither previously taxed Subpart F income nor repatriation of capital? (You may assume that the nature of this dividend income is such as to place it in the "overall income basket" for foreign tax credit purposes.)

d. How are your answers to parts a and b affected if repatriation is not required to take place at the end of year five but instead income can be reinvested locally for many years before repatriation?

e. Qualitatively, how would your previous answers be affected if withholding taxes on dividends were imposed by Country A? by Country B?

f. Qualitatively, how do the 5-70 Subpart F rules affect your previous answers?

| Country | Tax Rate | Pretax Investment Returns | | Withholding Rate on Dividends |
		Passive	Active	
U.S.	40.0%	10.0%	10.0%	0.0%
A	30.0%	10.0%	9.0%	0.0%
B	60.0%	10.0%	14.5%	0.0%

2. A U.S. multinational firm facing a 40% tax rate at home has a wholly owned foreign subsidiary in a jurisdiction where the tax rate is only 25%. The subsidiary was initially capitalized by a loan that has since been repaid. All that remains in the foreign subsidiary is $150 million of equity. The $150 million represents "earnings and profits" that have already been taxed at a rate of 25% in the host country. Any repatriation of these profits to the U.S. parent would trigger taxable income in the U.S. The host country imposes no withholding tax on dividends repatriated from the foreign subsidiary to the U.S.

a. How much U.S. taxable income would result if a dividend of $150 million were paid by the foreign subsidiary to the U.S. parent?

b. How much additional U.S. tax would be due?

c. How would the net repatriation (that is, dividend less additional taxes) be affected if a 10% withholding tax were levied by the foreign government on the dividend?

d. Suppose the $150 million could be reinvested in active business projects at an annual rate of 13% before tax and 9.75% after local tax in the host country. Alternatively, funds invested in the U.S. earn 15% before tax and 9% after tax.

　　1. Would you prefer to repatriate or to reinvest abroad if your investment horizon is

　　　　a.　1 year?

　　　　b.　5 years?

　　　　c.　10 years?

　　　　d.　20 years?

　　2. How would your answers to (d)(1) change if the host country imposed a 10% withholding tax on dividends?

　　3. Suppose the U.S. tax rate was scheduled to increase to 45% in the next year. That is, any taxable income triggered from current repatriations is taxed at 40%, but any future repatriation will be taxed at 45%. Moreover, the rate earned on funds invested in the U.S. now declines from $15\% \times (1 - 40\%)$ or 9% to $15\% \times (1 - 45\%)$ or 8.25%. How would your answers to (d)(1) change?

　　4. Suppose, once again, that the U.S. tax rate is 40%. But now suppose that active investment opportunities in the foreign country are poor. The 13% pretax investment return applies only to passive investments (such as bonds). And the returns

on these passive investments trigger immediate taxation in the U.S. (as Subpart F income). Funds invested in the U.S. continue to earn 15% before tax. How would this affect the desirability of reinvesting abroad?

e. How would your answers be affected if the $150 million of equity in the foreign subsidiary were "earnings and profits" that had been taxed previously in the host country at a rate of 35% rather than 25%? (Note: this is a rather challenging question.)

CHAPTER 14
Multinational Tax Planning:
Foreign Tax Credit Limitations and
Capital Structure Issues

In this chapter, we take a closer look at foreign tax credits (FTCs) and tax planning issues that arise when foreign tax credit limitations are binding. We also consider some important alternatives to dividends, including interest, rent, royalties, and transfer pricing, to repatriate profits from foreign subsidiaries.

As we noted in Chapter Thirteen, the 1986 Tax Act encouraged foreign investment in the U.S. In addition, it encouraged U.S. firms to reduce their foreign-country local taxes because the FTC limitation will be binding in many more cases subsequent to the 1986 Tax Act than before it. Why is this so? The U.S. corporate tax rate fell below that of such countries as Japan, Germany, and other European countries. And foreign tax rates can be especially high when withholding taxes are incurred on repatriation of foreign profits. As a result, the U.S. will refund less than 100% of foreign taxes paid in more cases than it used to. With binding FTCs, U.S. firms work harder to reduce the foreign taxes they pay in local jurisdictions. This was not as important before the 1986 Tax Act, since firms could average low-taxed foreign source income with high-taxed foreign source income to ensure a full refund of foreign taxes paid. This is now much harder to do. It now pays to reduce the effective tax rate of foreign taxes paid, especially in high-tax-rate jurisdictions.

The international tax-planning story we develop here is similar to the one we told concerning corporations and partnerships in Chapter Four. Corporations are now tax disfavored relative to partnerships. It is costly, however, to convert from a corporation to a partnership, and this creates incentives to increase the magnitude of distributions from corporations to stakeholders that are tax deductible at the corporate level. Similarly, if foreign subsidiaries are tax disadvantageous because their tax rate is above the U.S. tax rate, and it is too costly to relocate the business in low-taxed jurisdictions, there are increased incentives to create tax deductions abroad.

With binding FTC limitations, it becomes desirable for U.S. multinationals to distribute profits from foreign subsidiaries in ways that are tax deductible. Why is this so? Paying taxes on foreign profits at a foreign tax rate above the domestic rate is worse than paying taxes on the same profits at the lower domestic rate. In this chapter, we will discuss how firms use interest deductions on debt, rent on leases, royalties on licenses, and transfer pricing on goods and services to reduce foreign taxes paid in high-taxed jurisdictions. Before doing this, however, we first turn to a more detailed discussion of how the foreign tax credit works.

14.1 Foreign Tax Credits

A worldwide limitation is used to calculate foreign tax credits in the U.S.[1] Japan also uses a worldwide limitation, while Germany, Denmark, and Canada employ a country-by-country limitation. The foreign tax credit limitation is determined as follows:

$$\frac{\text{Foreign-source income}^2}{\text{Worldwide income}} \times \text{U.S. tax on worldwide income.}$$

Note that when the U.S. tax on worldwide income is simply a constant fraction (equal to the U.S. tax rate) of worldwide income, the limitation simplifies to:

$$\text{Foreign-source income} \times \text{U.S. tax rate.}$$

In calculating the FTC limitation, if foreign-source income exceeds worldwide income (due to domestic losses), the U.S. requires that a value of 100% be substituted for the ratio of foreign-source income to worldwide income.[3] In Japan, the ratio is not permitted to exceed 90%.[4]

Example

Suppose a U.S. multinational corporation has two wholly owned subsidiaries, one in each of countries A and B. The local tax rates are 40%, 20%, and 55% in the U.S. and Countries A and B, respectively. Each corporation generates $100 of locally taxed income. After paying local taxes, each subsidiary repatriates after-

---

[1] Prior to the 1976 Tax Act, U.S. firms could elect to use a country-by-country limitation. This was desirable in certain cases when there were losses in some countries and profits in others.

[2] This is total foreign taxable income from all foreign countries using U.S. tax accounting principles for income and expense recognition as well as U.S. source-of-income rules. Foreign-source income only includes income that is deemed to be repatriated in a particular tax year (arising from sources such as dividend income and passive income (Subpart F income)). Worldwide income is the sum of foreign and domestic source income.

[3] This means that U.S. multinationals facing domestic losses may face more significant FTC limitations than do firms that are profitable domestically. In other words, firms with domestic losses may have more difficulty obtaining refunds of foreign taxes paid.

[4] In Japan, the portion of foreign taxes paid by Japanese multinationals at a rate above 50% in any country are ineligible for foreign tax credit relief. In addition, a fraction of tax-exempt income earned abroad by Japanese multinationals is excluded from foreign-source income, making it more difficult to get a full refund of foreign taxes paid.

tax profits. The withholding tax rate assessed by the host country on repatriations to the U.S. parent company is 0% in both countries.[5]

| | Country | | | |
	U.S.	A	B	TOTAL
Taxable income	$100	$100	$100	$300
Foreign taxes (translated to dollars)		$ 20	$ 55	$ 75

Now suppose that A and B repatriate their after-tax income to the U.S.

U.S. taxes before foreign tax credit ($300 × 40%) $120

$$\text{FTC limit:} \qquad \frac{\$200}{\$300} \times \$120 = \$80.$$

Equivalently,

$$\text{FTC limit:} \qquad \$200 \times .40 = \$80.$$

Since actual foreign taxes paid are less than the FTC limitation, all $75 in foreign taxes paid can be taken as a credit against the U.S. income tax liability. This leaves a $45 U.S. income tax liability (or $120 - $75).

If the investment in Country A did not exist, or if the income from Country A were not repatriated, the FTC limit would be (100/200) × $80 = $40, and the remaining $55 - $40 = $15 of foreign tax paid in Country B would be unavailable to credit against U.S. taxes in the current period. Instead, as stated in Chapter Thirteen, the $15 excess foreign taxes paid would be eligible for a 2-year carryback and a 5-year carryforward. Alternatively, the U.S. taxpayer could elect to take a tax *deduction* for all $55 of the foreign taxes paid rather than a credit of $40. Although, all else the same, a credit is preferred to a deduction, a deduction may be desirable in some circumstances if tax credits would otherwise expire unused.

A similar FTC limitation problem would arise if there were a country-by-country FTC limitation and both A and B repatriated their income. In that case, the FTC limitation in Country B would be:

$$\frac{\$100}{\$300} \times \$120 = \$40.$$

Note that if most foreign-source income is from countries where the tax rate exceeds that in the U.S., repatriation will *typically not* trigger extra U.S. tax, but could trigger additional foreign withholding tax on dividends paid to repatriate the income. But repatriation *could* result in a net tax *reduction*, thereby allowing more after-tax funds to be reinvested. Whether there is a reduction in taxes upon repatriation depends upon whether the FTC limitation is binding. That is, repatriating from a low-taxed country could free up the FTC limitation and reduce overall U.S. taxes paid.

To illustrate, suppose in our example that all of the income from the foreign subsidiary in Country A is repatriated, but the income from Country B is not. Given that the tax rate in Country A is below that of the U.S., and that repatriation

---

[5] In most countries, withholding taxes are assessed on repatriations (in addition to the income tax assessed on the earned income) at rates of up to 30% of the gross repatriation. The actual withholding tax rate depends on the form of repatriation (for example, the rate on dividends may differ from the rate on interest) as well as on the tax treaty that exists between the two countries in question.

will attract a higher rate, why would the U.S. parent want to have A's income repatriated? There are many possibilities including:

- fear of nationalization of assets of the subsidiary in Country A;
- poor reinvestment opportunities in Country A relative to the U.S., either because of fierce competition in the relevant markets in Country A or because of high transaction costs in Country A to reinvest passively.[6]

How would taxes be affected if all of the income earned in Country B is repatriated at the same time the income of Country A is repatriated to the U.S.?

Additional U.S. taxable income	$ 100
Additional U.S. tax @ 40%	$ 40
Additional FTC (the overall limit becomes $80 and only $20 has been taken on account of Country A, but the FTC cannot exceed actual foreign taxes paid)	$ 55 (= min(actual, $80-$20))

This results in a net tax *refund* in the U.S. of $55 - $40 = $15.

Alternatively, if there was a 15% withholding tax on the $80 (or $100 - $20) dividend paid by the Country A subsidiary, there would be additional foreign tax paid of 15% x $80 = $12. Now the foreign tax credit limitation of $80 becomes binding since total foreign taxes paid equals $20 + $12 + $55 = $87. The $7 excess of foreign taxes paid over the FTC limitation could be carried back 2 years and forward 5 years. Instead of a $15 refund resulting from the repatriation of income from Country B, only $8 would be available in the current year.

Consider now the case in which Country B income is repatriated, giving rise to $15 of excess foreign tax payments over available credits. If after-tax investment opportunities in Country A are better than those available in the U.S., should the income from the subsidiary in Country A be repatriated to free up the FTC limitation? No, at least not until the foreign tax credits from Country B are about to expire.

Why? If the income from Country A is repatriated (and let us once again assume that there are *no* withholding taxes on repatriation), then the U.S. firm will indeed be able to obtain an additional refund of $15 from Country B taxes paid. *But*, the U.S. company will also end up paying an extra $20 of U.S. taxes on the income from Country A (that is, $100 x 40% less $20 taxes paid in Country A). The net is an additional tax payment of $5.

On the other hand, the additional tax of $5 could be avoided if less income is repatriated from Country A. In particular, if a $60 dividend is paid from Country A rather than the full after-tax income of $100 - $20 = $80, then (1) the excess foreign tax payments would become fully credited and (2) no additional U.S. tax would be due. To see this, note that a $60 dividend from Country A gives

---

[6] This could even include the cost to borrow domestically to finance U.S. activities. Lenders and rating agencies might not agree that the collateral of foreign assets in a foreign subsidiary is as valuable as domestic collateral. Nontax costs could be quite large in this case.

rise to U.S. taxable income of $60 plus deemed paid taxes in Country A. The deemed paid taxes in Country A become[7]

$$\frac{\text{Dividend}}{\text{Earnings and profits of the foreign Subsidiary}} \times \text{Foreign Tax Paid},$$

or

$$\left(\frac{\$60}{\$100 - \$20}\right) \times \$20 = \$15.$$

This means that foreign-source income is $60 + $15 = $75 from Country A and $45 + $55 = $100 from Country B or $175 in total. The foreign tax credit limitation is 40% of this or $70. This is exactly the amount of foreign taxes deemed paid: $15 in Country A and $55 in Country B. Moreover, U.S. tax on $175 of income is precisely $70, so the foreign tax credit exactly offsets the U.S. tax.

So, is it desirable to repatriate? Under the assumption that after-tax investments in Country A earn the same as in the U.S., it would be a matter of indifference whether to repatriate if it is possible *never* to do so (that is, reinvest indefinitely in Country A). This is true even if the excess foreign tax credits from Country B are about to expire unused. On the other hand, if the parent company anticipated that Country A's profits were to be repatriated at *some* point over the next several years, it would pay to *accelerate* the repatriation so that the additional U.S. tax paid on repatriation could be offset by the available excess foreign tax credits from Country B. It might even be desirable to repatriate profits from Country A when the after-local-tax rate of return on investment available in Country A exceeds that available in the U.S.

In this regard, it is interesting to note that Salomon Inc. repatriated $1.1 billion from their Zug, Switzerland subsidiary in the fourth quarter of 1988. According to the *Wall Street Journal*, the move was taken "to make use of certain foreign tax credits which would (otherwise) expire at the end of the year."[8]

Separate Basket Limitations

We have been assuming in our examples thus far that the worldwide foreign tax credit limitation rules freely permit the averaging of tax rates in different foreign countries. But this is not really the case at all in the U.S. The reason is that there exist numerous so-called "separate basket" limitations for various classes of income. The foreign tax credit limitation is calculated separately for each separate basket of income.[9]

---

[7] U.S. tax accounting rules are used to determine earnings and profits, which is an after-tax figure. Under the 1986 Tax Act, the numerator (dividends) is pooled dividends post-1986, and the denominator is pooled earnings and profits post-1986. If dividends paid after 1986 exceed post-1986 earnings and profits, then dividends are assumed to represent a distribution of pre-1986 earnings on a last-in-first-out basis.

[8] *Wall Street Journal* (December 9, 1988).

[9] The U.S. is by no means alone in imposing separate limitations on FTCs for different categories of income, although the specific limitations vary substantially from country to country. For example, the U.K. imposes an item-by-item FTC limitation. But the U.K. also permits wide discretion in how expenses are allocated to income, so FTC limitations may well be less restrictive there than in the U.S.

The motivation for the separate basket approach to FTC limitations is to prevent corporations from undermining the limitations. For example, if a firm faced a severe FTC limitation, it would have incentives to "stuff" income-earning assets into subsidiaries located in tax-haven countries (where tax rates are very low). And to avoid the implicit taxes that often result from investing in active businesses in low-tax countries, there would be a particularly strong incentive to invest in passive assets, such as Eurobonds. This would reduce the average tax rate on foreign-source income and give rise to larger refunds of the foreign tax paid in high-tax countries.

The U.S. tax law permits the averaging of high-tax and low-tax foreign manufacturing income for FTC limitation purposes, but it does *not* permit the averaging of low-taxed passive investment income with high-taxed manufacturing income. This makes it more difficult to receive a U.S. refund for the taxes paid in the high-tax country. More specifically, prior to the 1986 Tax Act, there existed six separate income baskets, the most significant of which included an interest income basket, a foreign oil extraction income basket, and a general overall income basket.

The 1986 Tax Act retained five of the six separate baskets that existed previously and expanded the interest basket to include a broader set of passive income components. Moreover, it introduced four types of additional baskets:

- financial services income;
- shipping income;
- high withholding tax income;[10] and
- dividend income from *non*controlled foreign corporations owned 10% or more by the taxpayer.

The last category above potentially gives rise to an unlimited number of separate income baskets, since a separate foreign tax credit calculation must be made for *each* dividend received from any foreign company in which the taxpayer has a 10% to 50% ownership interest.

To appreciate the significance of the separate basket approach to foreign tax credit limitations, let us reconsider our earlier example. Suppose the subsidiary in Country A generates $75 of passive (Subpart F) income and $25 of manufacturing-related income. It pays a tax of 20% or $20 in Country A. The subsidiary in Country B generates $100 of manufacturing-related income, pays a tax of $55 in Country B, and pays a $45 dividend to the U.S. parent. Because more than 70% of A's income is Subpart F income, 100% of it is deemed to have been distributed to the U.S. parent whether an actual distribution has been made or not. Hence, $200 of foreign income is taxable in the U.S., the U.S. tax on which is $80 (or 40% x $200).

What foreign tax credit amounts are permitted?

Moreover, U.K. corporations often use Dutch "mixer" corporations to conduct foreign activities in different jurisdictions to overcome FTC limitations. The Dutch are less restrictive on averaging foreign source income.

[10] It has been estimated that this provision alone increased U.S. taxes by $1.5 billion per year due to a reduction in available foreign tax credits. See Harry Grubert and John Mutti, "The Impact of the Tax Reform Act of 1986 on Trade and Capital Flows," Working Paper (1987).

On the $75 of passive income, it is the minimum of actual foreign taxes paid and the U.S. tax on the income

$$= \min\left(\frac{75}{100} \times \$20, 40\% \times \$75\right)$$

$$= \min (\$15, \$30)$$

$$= \underline{\$15}.$$

On the $25 + $100 of overall income:

$$= \min\left(\frac{25}{100} \times \$20 + \$55, 40\% \times \$125\right)$$

$$= \min (\$60, \$50)$$

$$= \underline{\$50}.$$

So only $50 of the $60 of foreign tax paid on the $125 of foreign income that falls into the general overall income basket is available as a foreign tax credit. The $10 excess can be carried back 2 years and forward 5. Note that if the $200 of foreign-source income could be lumped into a single basket, as we did in our earlier examples, all $75 of foreign tax paid would be available as a foreign tax credit for U.S. tax purposes.

Prior to the 1986 Tax Act, the separate limitations on interest did not apply if the income was generated from an active trade or business, such as banking. This exception has been eliminated. The one important exception that does exist currently is interest attributable to export financing. Because so many routes for averaging low-taxed foreign income with high-taxed foreign income have been closed by the Act, and because the foreign tax credit limitation should become much more binding due to reduced U.S. tax rates,[11] the incentives for U.S. companies to engage in export financing and to undertake new investments through foreign subsidiaries located in low-tax-rate countries were increased substantially.

14.2 FTC Limitations and the Capital Structure of Foreign Subsidiaries

The 1986 Tax Act caused taxpayers to work harder to reduce their taxes paid in foreign countries. This is a dramatic change in tax-planning strategy in the multinational area. Why? At 34%, the U.S. corporate tax rate is now well below that of Japan, Germany, and a number of other European countries. This is especially so for U.S. multinationals when withholding taxes are incurred upon repatriation of foreign profits. The decline in U.S. tax rates, along with a greater number of separate income baskets used to calculate FTC limitations, means that

---

[11] "Treasury data indicate that the percentage of U.S. manufacturing companies (weighted by worldwide income) that are in an excess foreign tax credit position increases from 20% to 69%" (with the passage of the 1986 Tax Act). See Grubert and Mutti, *Ibid*.

the FTC limitation will be binding in many more cases than it used to be. And this means that the U.S. will refund less than 100% of foreign taxes paid in many more cases than it used to. As a consequence, taxpayers will work harder to reduce their local taxes paid in foreign jurisdictions.

For many U.S. multinational corporations, this was not a particularly important priority before the 1986 Act if low-taxed income could be averaged with high-taxed income to ensure a full refund of foreign taxes paid. But this is now harder to do. It now pays to devote more resources to reduce the effective rate of foreign taxes paid, *especially* in high-tax-rate jurisdictions.

Note that many U.S. corporations *without* foreign operations find themselves in a very similar tax-planning situation following the 1986 Tax Act. As we discussed in Chapter Four, corporations are now tax-disfavored relative to partnerships. Given the costs to convert to partnership form, however, as well as the nontax benefits of operating in corporate form, the vast majority of businesses have remained and will continue to remain in corporate form. But such entities also have incentives to increase the magnitude of distributions from the corporation that are tax-deductible, so as to come as close as possible to achieving *as-if* partnership taxation.

Similarly, in the multinational tax-planning context, where FTC limitations are binding, it becomes desirable to distribute profits from foreign subsidiaries in ways that are tax-deductible abroad. This means that it becomes more attractive to repatriate profits by way of

- interest on debt;[12]
- rent on leases;
- royalties on licenses; and
- transfer pricing for goods and services to shift income from high-tax jurisdictions to lower-tax jurisdictions.

On the other hand, not *all* U.S. multinationals face FTC limitations. There still exist a number of tax jurisdictions that tax income at rates well below those in the U.S., notably Singapore, Malaysia, Ireland, and Hong Kong. If substantial profits are generated in these countries, and the implicit tax on reinvestment is not too high, it may be desirable to reinvest profits in these countries rather than repatriate profits and pay a higher U.S. tax on repatriation.[13] With higher tax rates in some foreign countries, there may be additional incentives to invest in low-taxed countries to free up foreign tax credit limitations. Slemrod finds that investment in low-tax European countries (notably Belgium, Ireland, Luxembourg, and Spain) increased 122% between 1984-1989, but investment increased

---

[12] Partly in recognition of these advantages, certain countries (such as France and Germany) have proposed limits on debt-to-equity ratios for subsidiaries of foreign multinational corporations that are more restrictive than for domestic corporations. For example, a subsidiary of a foreign corporation in France can not borrow more than 1.5 times the subsidiary's share capital to finance its activities (Ernst and Young, *Tax News International*, 1991).

[13] The Income Tax Provisions in Digital Equipment Corporation's (DEC) 1989 financial statements indicates that DEC received large tax benefits from operating in Puerto Rico, Ireland, Singapore, and Taiwan. DEC's effective tax rate was reduced 8% by operating in these countries. Over 63% of DEC's 1989 income was from foreign operations in countries with low tax rates.

only 45% in high-tax European countries (such as Denmark, Germany, and Italy).[14] Recall from Chapter Thirteen that foreign direct investment in the U.S. increased over 300% subsequent to the 1986 Tax Act.

Moreover, an advantage of equity financing of foreign subsidiaries is its flexibility in timing repatriation by way of dividends to coincide with a period of low tax rates in the U.S., as well as its ability to allow foreign profits to be reinvested without imposing a current repatriation tax. By contrast, repatriation by way of interest, rent, and royalties is much less controllable as to timing. Debt contracts and rental contracts, for example, require a certain amount of foreign profits to be repatriated each period.

Counterbalancing this inflexibility of debt contracts regarding periodic distributions is greater flexibility with respect to repatriating the *principal* amount of debt. It is easier to repay principal on a loan and avoid a repatriation tax than it is to do so by retiring stock. Retiring stock is typically treated as a dividend to the extent of "accumulated earnings and profits."[15]

Hines and Hubbard document that in 1984, the average foreign tax rate paid by firms that paid dividends but no interest, rents, or royalties was 34%. By contrast, those that paid interest, rent, or royalties, but no dividends, paid average foreign tax rates of 51%. This is consistent with the arguments made above. Because dividends can be delayed for many years, but interest on debt, rent on lease contracts, and royalties on licensing agreements cannot be, equity financing is desirable in low-tax environments.[16]

Similarly, in high-tax environments, distributions from *pretax* income in a form that is deductible locally is tax-preferred. This makes debt, leases, and licenses desirable financing arrangements. So capital structure should differ across foreign subsidiaries as a function of their tax rates, just as in a purely domestic tax-planning situation.

An additional consideration here that is absent in the purely domestic context is that the different forms of repatriation (dividends, interest, rent, and royalties) may be subject to different levels of withholding tax. And this makes the repatriation alternatives even less perfect substitutes for one another. The repatriation of foreign profits through transfer pricing arrangements, for example, typically avoids withholding taxes entirely.

Because withholding tax rates on different forms of repatriation also vary from country to country (because tax treaties are bilateral rather than multilateral), it is sometimes important to consider alternative *routes* (from one foreign

---

[14]Joel B. Slemrod, "Tax Effects of Foreign Direct Investment in the U.S.: Evidence from a Cross-Country Comparison," University of Michigan and NBER Working Paper (January 1989).

[15]While share repurchases are often taxed as a sale of stock (and therefore taxable to the "seller" only to the extent of gain or loss, and then at capital gains rates), a "proportionate" repurchase (where shares are repurchased from shareholders in direct proportion to the number of shares they hold) is viewed as being the economic equivalent of a dividend and is taxed as a dividend to the extent of earnings and profits generated since 1962. A share repurchase in a wholly owned subsidiary is automatically a proportionate one.

[16]See James R. Hines, Jr. and R. Glenn Hubbard, "Coming Home to America: Dividend Repatriations by U.S. Multinationals," in Assaf Razin and Joel Slemrod, eds., *Taxation in a Global Economy*. University of Chicago Press and National Bureau of Economic Research (1990). See also the comments of Mark A. Wolfson in the same volume.

corporation to another in different tax jurisdictions) through which repatriations can travel to minimize after-tax repatriations. Some of the accounting firms have developed elaborate software to do just this. Price Waterhouse, for example, has a package that considers up to one hundred different routes and allows as many as four intermediate counties to be used in the repatriation strategy.

To see how this works, if an Italian company receives a dividend from a French subsidiary, the withholding tax rate is 15% of the dividend. On the other hand, if the French subsidiary pays the dividend to a Dutch sister subsidiary, the withholding tax is only 5% of the dividend, and if in turn, the Dutch subsidiary passes the remaining dividend along to its Italian parent, there is a 0% withholding tax on that dividend transfer. By routing the dividend through the Dutch subsidiary, the Italian company reduces the withholding tax on its dividends by two-thirds.

Another conduit example involves withholding taxes on interest income. Belgium imposes a 12.5% withholding tax on interest paid to Italian investors, a 10% withholding tax on interest paid to German investors, and a 15% withholding tax on interest paid to U.K. investors. On the other hand, there is no withholding tax on interest paid between taxpayers in Belgium and Luxembourg, and although the withholding tax rate on interest payments between Luxembourg and Germany is 10% (the same as between Belguim and Germany), it is only 10% between Luxembourg and Italy and 0% with the U.K. As a result, Belgium companies borrow through their Luxembourg subsidiaries to effect substantial withholding tax savings.[17]

14.3   Transfer Pricing

When income is taxed at different rates in different countries, it is typically not a matter of indifference how worldwide income is allocated to the various countries. This is especially true in the face of potential limitations on foreign tax credits.

In multinational corporations, many goods and services are routinely transferred among related entities in different tax jurisdictions. The prices at which these goods and services are transferred can have a very important impact on worldwide taxes. Because the entities are related, there would appear to be great tax planning opportunities by setting transfer prices judiciously. For example, in high-tax-rate foreign jurisdictions, transfer pricing represents not only a way to repatriate profits in a tax-deductible fashion, but also a way to avoid the imposition of withholding tax. Congress and the IRS recognize these tax-planning opportunities, and Section 482 of the Code has been made available to the IRS as an important weapon to deal with overzealous tax planning.

Section 482 is only 94 words long, but it "has undoubtedly created more uncertainty and disputes with the IRS (involving) greater amounts of tax dollars than any other part of the law."[18] Section 482 reads as follows:

---

[17] For further discussion, see Alberto Giovannini, "National Tax System versus the European Capital Market," *Economic Policy* (1991).

[18] *Tax Notes* (December 16, 1985), p. 1171.

Chapter 14   Multinational Tax Planning

In the case of two or more organizations, trades or businesses, whether or not incorporated, whether or not organized in the United States, and whether or not affiliated, owned, or controlled directly or indirectly by the same interest, the Secretary or his delegate may distribute, apportion, or allocate gross income, deductions, credits, or allowances between or among such organizations, trades or businesses, if he determines that such distribution, apportionment or allocation is necessary in order to prevent evasion of taxes or clearly to reflect the income of any such organization, trade or business.

The regulations for Section 482 indicate that transactions between related parties must be priced as if they involved unrelated parties; that is, arm's length pricing. The basic problem here, however, is that the circumstances under which the related parties find it desirable to integrate vertically are systematically different from those in which transactions take place at arm's length in the market. Information differences are smaller with related parties than with outsiders. Hence, the notion of an arm's-length price in a related-party transaction is rather ill-defined. A second problem is that the good or service being transferred frequently has no ready market outside the special relationship between the related parties.

The regulations specifically discuss three methods for determining arm's-length prices:[19]

- comparable uncontrolled price (where a similar transaction between unrelated parties can be observed in the marketplace);
- cost plus (20% - 50% markups are commonly used);
- resale price ("This method starts with the selling price to unconnected third parties and works back to an arm's length intragroup purchase price by computing a margin that reflects the intragroup buyer's (1) costs, (2) business efforts, and (3) risk.")[20]

The regulations also mention that if the three approaches above are all inappropriate in the particular circumstances, then any reasonable method to establish arm's length prices may be used. A commonly used alternative is the "profit-split" method, where "each of the related parties is given a fair share of the profits, determined by analyzing the functions performed by each—that is, identifying and assigning a value to each element (e.g., marketing and production) that contributes to the combined profit of the related buyer and seller on the product in question."[21]

To put it mildly, the guidelines in the transfer pricing regulations are unclear. The IRS has a history of considerable unpredictability regarding how it will enforce Section 482. While many multinational corporations might wish that

---

[19] Most countries have transfer pricing guidelines that correspond to those in the U.S. Section 482 regulations. Countries may differ in the preference ordering for using the various pricing methods, however. For further discussion, see Price Waterhouse, *International Tax Review* (September/October 1989).

[20] *Ibid.*, p. 8.

[21] *Ibid.*, p. 9.

the IRS were more consistent in its enforcement in the transfer pricing area, we argued in the introductory chapters that an absence of clear guidelines in this area may be quite a reasonable strategy for the IRS to pursue.

Transfer pricing disputes can yield very significant differences in taxes assessed by the IRS and those proposed by taxpayers. The IRS recommended $662 million in increased taxes due to transfer-pricing adjustments in 1973, and it recommended $4.4 billion in additional taxes due to such adjustments in 1982.[22]

Let's consider three examples of taxpayer-IRS conflict in the transfer pricing area:[23] Eli Lilly, G.D. Searle, and Storage Technology. In all three cases, the conflict relates to transfer pricing between a U.S. parent corporation and a Puerto Rican subsidiary.

In the case of Eli Lilly, the Puerto Rican subsidiary was used to produce tablets and capsules of drugs developed successfully by the parent in the U.S. The parent did not charge the subsidiary for any new research and development costs that it incurred. So the subsidiary received a free option: it shared the gains on research successes, but it bore none of the costs of research failures. Table 14.1 shows return-on-asset data for the parent and subsidiary during 1971-1973, the period covered by the case.[24]

Table 14.1 Eli Lilly's Return on Average Assets Employed (those assets appearing on the books, so certain intangibles developed internally are excluded)

	1971	1972	1973
Parent (consolidated)	20%	24%	30%
Puerto Rican Subsidiary	138%	143%	101%

The G.D. Searle case involves performance data that is even more extreme, as indicated in Table 14.2. Searle is now part of Monsanto. Following its acquisition, Monsanto settled the tax returns for Searle's Puerto Rican subsidiary operations for years *not* before the Tax Court (1976-1982) for $160 million.

Finally, consider the case of Storage Technology for the tax years 1979-1983. In this case, Storage Technology declared bankruptcy, in large measure to forestall the IRS, to which it potentially owed more than to any other of its creditors. Whereas the return on working assets for the parent company ranged from -2% to +7% over the 5-year period 1979-1983, the returns for the Puerto Rican subsidiary ranged from 263% to 303%!

---

[22] Coopers & Lybrand, *Executive Briefing* (December 1989), p. 4.

[23] The data are taken from James Wheeler, "Transfer Pricing: A View from Government and Academia," University of Michigan Working Paper, January 1988.

[24] Believe it or not, this is a case that was decided in the latter half of the 1980s, more than *fifteen* years after the first year covered in the case. And this doesn't even count the years elapsed in dealing with the *appeal* of the court decision.

Chapter 14 Multinational Tax Planning

Table 14.2 Performance Data: G.D. Searle and Its Puerto Rican Subsidiary

	1974		1975	
	Parent	Puerto Rican Subsidiary	Parent	Puerto Rican Subsidiary
Return on average assets employed	(31%)	109%	(42%)	119%
Cost of goods sold/Sales	54%	13%	56%	14%
Operating expenses/Sales	99%	35%	107%	36%

14.4 Transfer Pricing of Intangibles and the 1984 and 1986 Tax Acts

Perhaps the most difficult area of transfer pricing has involved the transfer of intangible assets (such as patents, trademarks, and copyrights) to foreign subsidiaries. Prior to the 1984 Tax Act, it was common for U.S. companies to transfer such assets tax-free (as a contribution of capital to a controlled foreign subsidiary under Section 351). Since the 1984 Act, however, such transfers are considered sales. Still, the uniqueness of such assets makes it difficult to establish an "arm's length" sale price. Similar problems arise when intangibles are transferred by licensing arrangements that provide for the payment of royalties from the licensee to the licensor. Part of the problem here is that "(t)he *form* of pricing arrangements between related parties might be completely different than between unrelated parties" (even in the *absence* of tax considerations).[25]

Transaction cost economic considerations may well justify a cheaper price to a subsidiary than to an unrelated party. Contracting and monitoring costs may be significantly lower for a subsidiary than for an unrelated third party. This may make it easier to exploit economies of both scale and scope. Technology transfer to a wholly owned subsidiary may be far easier to control than would a transfer to outsiders.

The 1986 Tax Act deals with the transfer pricing difficulties in the intangibles area in a drastic way by introducing the so-called "super-royalty" provisions. These rules were a direct response to the perceived abuses in the transfer pricing area involving Puerto Rican subsidiaries. Under these provisions, the taxpayer is required to adjust the transfer price in years *subsequent* to the transfer of technology to reflect the *actual income* the intangible generates. So, for example, if a patent gives rise to the manufacture and sale of a product that turns out to be far more successful than reasonable parties would have predicted at the point of technology transfer, related parties are nevertheless required to adjust the payments to the parent as if the success could have been fully anticipated. A similar adjustment is not allowed, however, if the product proves *less* successful than anticipated.

---

[25] Harry Grubert, "A Proposed Reinterpretation of the Arm's Length Principle in Transfer Pricing," U.S. Department of the Treasury Working Paper (August 3, 1987).

Moreover, the rules provide little guidance as to how profits are to be split between the transferor and transferee of the technology. Among other things, this means that the transfer-of-technology transaction remains "open" indefinitely for audit purposes. This may prove rather costly from a record-keeping standpoint. The provisions clearly serve to discourage the transfer of technology abroad to related parties, an incentive that may exact its own efficiency loss in the domestic economy.

To illustrate the conflicts that arise in the royalty area, the courts, in 1989, decided that Bausch & Lomb's royalty rate on its contact lens technology should be 20% of sales rather than the 5% rate that Bausch & Lomb charged to its Irish subsidiary, which manufactured the contact lens using technology that was developed by Bausch & Lomb in New York. The Irish subsidiary was enjoying a ten-year tax holiday, which provided strong incentives to generate income there. Under the 5% royalty rate, the 1982 return on investment in Ireland was 106%. Under the court-determined royalty rate of 20%, the return on sales in Ireland was reduced to 27%, which is still quite generous.[26]

Super royalty adjustments may result in double taxation. A number of countries have indicated that super royalty adjustments do not yield arm's length prices. Such countries will *not* allow corresponding adjustments in calculating taxable income in their countries.

The IRS does allow firms to negotiate with them for advance approval of intercompany pricing arrangements. Apple Computer is believed to be the first firm to have entered into such an agreement for sales of computers to its Australian unit. The Australian government also agreed to the arrangement.[27] While there are obvious benefits to entering into such advance pricing agreements, there are also important costs to consider. It can be very expensive, for competitive reasons, to disclose the technical product information necessary to secure an advance agreement. Moreover, as circumstances change, the taxing authority need not be bound by an agreement that applied to a very specific set of assumptions.[28]

14.5 Foreign Transfer Pricing Practices in the U.S.

The U.S. has been on the warpath recently against U.S. subsidiaries of foreign multinational corporations. The IRS has been challenging their transfer pricing practices, claiming that foreign multinationals pay too little U.S. tax. For example, in 1986, while U.S.-controlled U.S. corporations reported a 1.7% rate of return on assets, foreign-controlled U.S. corporations reported only a *negative* 0.2% rate of return on assets.[29]

---

[26] For further discussion, see D. Frisch and T. Horst, "Bausch & Lomb and the White Paper," *Tax Notes* (May 8, 1989), pp. 725-34.

[27] *Wall Street Journal* (April 10, 1991), p. 1.

[28] For further discussion, see Joseph L. Andrus, *et al.*, "The New Section 482 Advance Pricing Agreement Procedure: Overview and Analysis," *Tax Notes* (April 22, 1991), pp. 353-361.

[29] See John Turro, "U.S. Congressional Committee Blasts Foreign Firms for Tax Dodging," *Tax Notes International* (August 1990), pp. 797-801.

Chapter 14   Multinational Tax Planning

In Table 14.3, we show, for each year 1983-1987, the U.S. revenues of the subsidiaries of multinational foreign corporations resident in Japan, the U.K., (West) Germany, and Canada. The net income to receipts ratio is also displayed for U.S.-controlled companies and for the foreign-controlled companies for each country. Although the magnitude of the U.S. revenues of these foreign multinationals is impressive, their U.S. net income as a percentage of receipts is extremely low, especially compared to their U.S. counterparts.

Table 14.3 U.S. Revenues of Foreign Multinationals, and a Comparison of Net Income as a Percentage of Receipts Across Countries.

	Revenues ($ Billions)				Net Income/Receipts (%)				
	Japan	U.K.	Ger.	Can.	U.S.	Japan	U.K.	Ger.	Can.
Year									
1983	87.5	65.7	32.1	29.4	2	1	3	-3	-3
1984	112.6	76.9	36.4	31.6	3	1	2	-2	-2
1985	133.5	83.3	42.9	40.5	2	1	2	-1	-1
1986	126.1	83.8	53.4	40.4	3	0	-1	-1	-1
1987	184.9	103.0	62.8	51.5	3	0	3	1	1

Source: Internal Revenue Service

As a result of statistics such as these, the IRS adopted a plan in 1990 to audit 1.3% of the 45,000 foreign-controlled U.S. corporate tax returns filed in 1987. This audit plan represents 55% of the total assets of $959 billion and 52% of the gross receipts of $700 billion of these foreign-controlled corporations in the U.S.[30]

That foreign multinationals have paid so little U.S. tax is not surprising for tax return years prior to the 1986 Tax Act, but it is surprising for tax years subsequent to the Act. To date, most of the audits have concentrated on tax returns for years prior to 1987. But the IRS (and Congress) has expressed great concern with the low levels of U.S. taxable income reported *subsequent* to 1986 as well. The reason this is surprising, at least at first blush, is that the U.S. became a relatively low-tax-rate country subsequent to 1986. It might seem natural for Japanese multinationals, for example, to shift income to the U.S. and away from Japan under such circumstances. But perhaps it is deemed to be important for political reasons to report generous sums of Japan-source income for such companies.[31]

Another motivation for generating low levels of U.S. income is related to so-called "tax-sparing" agreements that exist between significant developing countries and other developed countries. The U.S. has no treaty in which it agrees to spare U.S. tax on income that *could* have been taxed by the host developing country, but was not, so that the developing country could encourage foreign investment. Japan, for example, taxes income repatriated from Singapore at a rate

---

[30] The IRS estimated that transfer pricing on imports alone cost the U.S. $12 billion. The 1990 Tax Act imposed penalties on firms that grossly overprice imports and underprice exports (*New York Times*, February 18, 1990).

[31] Informal conversations we have had with a number of Japanese tax experts suggests that this is deemed to be an important consideration.

of only 17%, rather than 50% in Japan, even though Singapore waives its 33% corporate tax rate for foreign subsidiaries operating in Singapore. As a result, while U.S. firms operating in Singapore face a 34% U.S. tax rate on repatriation of Singapore income, a Japanese firm faces only a 17% tax rate. Japan has similar treaties with Ireland, Korea, Malaysia, and Spain, among others. By using Singapore (or other countries) as a conduit, Japanese multinationals can reduce their worldwide tax bill. For example, if goods and services are supplied from their Singapore subsidiary to their U.S. subsidiary at high prices, the U.S. subsidiary generates low profits, and the Singapore subsidiary generates correspondingly higher profits. But these profits are taxed at a lower rate than in the U.S. and Japan. Germany also has similar sparing treaties with developing countries, including Singapore and Spain.

14.6   Source of Income Rules

Related to the transfer pricing tax rules are the rules governing the "sourcing of income." Sections 861–864 deal with the allocation of worldwide income to U.S. versus foreign source. Whether income is deemed to be U.S. source or foreign source has several important implications. For U.S. taxpayers, it primarily affects the FTC limitations. It is also very important to nonresident aliens and foreign corporations, since they are taxed in the U.S. only on income derived (1) from within the U.S., (2) from business "effectively connected with" the conduct of U.S. trade or business, and (3) from the disposition of investments in U.S. real property.

Among the most significant classes of income and expense in the source-of-income area are (1) inventory, (2) interest, (3) research and development, and (4) headquarters (or stewardship) expenses.

Inventories

Prior to the 1986 Tax Act, income derived from the purchase or resale of tangible and intangible personal property was sourced where *title* to the property passed to the purchaser. Any recapture (such as depreciation or tax credits) was also sourced where title passed to the purchaser.

Income derived from the *manufacture* and sale of personal property, however, is treated as having a divided source. Half of such income is generally sourced where title passes to the purchaser, and the other half is sourced where the property is manufactured. Note, however, that the actual division of the income for computing taxes must be made based on actual prices and costs. The 50% split is used only to determine the source of income (expense) in the computation of the foreign tax credit limitation. Section 865, introduced by the 1986 Tax Act, provides new source rules for the sale of property. If a U.S. resident sells the property, the source of income or loss is U.S. regardless of where the title is passed. If a foreign resident sells the property, the source is foreign.

One important exception is inventory. The sale of inventory continues to be governed by the old rules. Merely passing title abroad will generally not give rise to income taxed in the foreign country. Foreign source income, however, will be generated without any increase in foreign taxes paid, thereby helping to alleviate the FTC limitation. With U.S. corporations finding that FTC limitations have become more binding under the 1986 Tax Act, inventory sales becomes an especially important area of tax planning for many firms that sell to foreign customers.

One must be careful, however, to compare the potential advantages of generating foreign-source income through *direct* sales, as discussed above, with those from forming a "foreign sales corporation" (FSC) through which to route foreign sales. We will not provide details of the FSC rules, but suffice it to say that to encourage export sales, Congress created the opportunity to form such an entity, which typically results in an exemption of 15% of the income earned from export sales. Such sales also give rise to foreign-source income, typically in the amount of 25% of the income. To qualify, the entity must be located abroad (in a tax jurisdiction that enters into a treaty with the U.S. providing for an exchange of information for audit purposes), conduct meetings abroad, and have a Board of Directors that includes local residents.

To understand the nature of the tradeoff in routing sales through a FSC, consider the following example. U.S. Multinational Parent company faces a 34% U.S. marginal tax rate on domestic income. Its foreign subsidiaries are located primarily in tax jurisdictions where the tax rate exceeds that in the U.S. Repatriation of profits from such jurisdictions has given rise to an excess of foreign taxes paid over what the U.S. will allow as a credit.

Suppose we have a product that will generate a taxable profit of $100, whether it is sold directly from the U.S. or routed through the FSC. Assume, as is typical, that the tax rate on income earned by the FSC in the foreign tax jurisdiction, is essentially 0% (e.g., U.S. Virgin Islands).[32] Then a sale through the FSC will trigger U.S. tax of 85% x 34% or 28.91%. If the parent company has foreign tax credit carryforwards that are about to expire unused, then a sale through the FSC could give rise to 25% x $100 or $25 of foreign-source income. This would enable an additional $25 x 34% or $8.50 of FTCs that are otherwise about to expire, to be refunded by the U.S. The result would be a tax rate on the sale of 28.91% - 8.50% or 20.41%.

By comparison, the tax rate paid on a direct export of the inventory would be 34% less any increase in foreign tax credits that may result. If the parent company has foreign tax credit carryforwards that are about to expire unused, then a direct foreign sale would increase foreign-source income, for FTC purposes, by 50% x $100 or $50. This would enable $50 x 34% or $17 of FTCs that are otherwise about to expire, to be refunded by the U.S. The result would be a tax rate of 17% from a direct foreign sale, versus 20.41% from a sale through the FSC.

On the other hand, if there is no binding FTC limitation, sale through the FSC is clearly preferred (28.91% versus 34%). As still another example, if the FTC would otherwise be used up in three years, and the appropriate after-tax discount rate is 6%, then the present value of the tax paid on the direct foreign sale becomes

$$34\% - 50\% \times 34\% + 50\% \times 34\% / (1.06)^3 \text{ or } 31.28\%,$$

---

[32] The motivation of the host country is to promote local employment and development of the local infrastructure, including housing, telecommunications, and banking.

and the present value of tax paid on the sale through a FSC becomes

$$28.91\% - 25\% \times 34\% + 25\% \times 34\% / (1.06)^3 \text{ or } 27.55\%.$$

This would favor sale through the FSC, ignoring any transaction cost differences between the two methods of selling abroad.

Interest

Interest expense incurred in the U.S. is allocated between U.S. and foreign income on the basis of the value of the taxpayer's assets (book or market) that generate U.S. and foreign-source income.[33] Interest allocated to foreign-source income reduces the maximum amount of FTCs that may be refunded by the U.S. The reason is that the FTC limitation becomes more binding as the fraction of foreign-source to worldwide income is diminished.

The requirement to allocate a portion of U.S. interest expense to the foreign operations of a U.S. multinational has become a very significant concern for tax planners since the Tax Act of 1986, because so many firms began facing limits on foreign tax credits for the first time. This concern was exacerbated by the dramatic increase in debt financing in the U.S. since 1984. The interest allocation rules can increase the capital costs of U.S. multinationals relative to their foreign competitors.

Consider the case of a debt-financed acquisition. A subsidiary of a foreign corporation (that in turn has no operations outside the U.S.) can secure a full deduction for any acquisition-related indebtedness it might incur to finance the purchase of a U.S. business. A subsidiary of a U.S. multinational corporation that engages in the very same transactions, however, could lose a significant fraction of the acquisition-related indebtedness due to the required interest allocation to foreign operations.

Recall that the 1986 Tax Act made debt financing highly desirable for U.S. corporations, since they are tax-disfavored relative to partnerships. This encouraged leveraged buyouts of U.S. firms. If U.S. firms have foreign subsidiaries, they must allocate some of the interest on U.S. indebtedness to foreign source income. Reducing foreign source income causes the FTC limitation to become more binding. These Section 861 interest allocation rules cause major problems for banks and other financial service firms. They might be able to use but a small fraction of their available foreign tax credits because their foreign source income is greatly reduced by their U.S. interest expense. The rules do not allow them to net interest income against interest expense before making the allocations. The effects of the interest allocation rules are illustrated in Table 14.4.

As seen in Table 14.4, the U.S. multinational firm earns income of $1,000 in the U.S. (before interest and taxes) and $1,000 (before taxes) in its foreign subsidiary. The foreign tax rate is assumed to be 50% and the U.S. tax rate is assumed to be 30%. In the illustration, we assume that 50% of the interest expense incurred in the U.S. must be allocated to foreign source income. The foreign

---

[33] Before the 1986 Tax Act, it was possible to use the gross income method to allocate the interest expense.

Table 14.4   Illustration of the Effects of Section 861 Interest Allocation Rules on U.S. Multinational Corporations

	U.S. Income	Foreign Subsidiary
Taxable U.S. Income Before Interest	$1,000	$1,000
U.S. Interest Expense	(800)	
(50% Allocated to Foreign Source)		
Foreign Tax @ 50%		500
Dividend		$ 500
Withholding Tax on Dividend (@ 20% rate)		100
Total Foreign Tax		$ 600
Net Dividend		400
U.S. Taxable Income from Foreign Operations	$1,000	
World-Wide Taxable Income ($1,000 + $1,000 - $800)	1,200	
Tentative U.S. Tax @ 30% Tax Rate	360	
FTC Allowed (30% × ($1,000 - $400))	180	
Net U.S. Tax	180	
After-tax Income to U.S. Investor ($1,000 - $800 + $400 - $180)	$420	

subsidiary pays a $400 dividend to its parent, after incurring $500 in foreign taxes and a $100 withholding tax on the dividend repatriation. Total foreign taxes paid are $600 (a 60% tax rate). Without the interest allocation rules, the U.S. would refund $300 of the tax (or $1000 × .30). With interest allocation only $180 of the foreign tax is allowed as a refund, for a loss of $120 (or $300 - $180). To see how this comes about, remember that the FTC limitation is

$$\text{FTC Limit} = \frac{\text{Foreign Source Income}}{\text{World Wide Income}} \times \text{U.S. Tax on World Wide Income}$$

$$\text{FTC Limit} = \frac{\$1000 - \$800 \times .5}{\$1200} \times 30\% \text{ of } \$1200 = \$180.$$

The U.S. multinational nets $420 after all foreign and domestic tax on worldwide income of $1,200. It realizes $1,000 on its U.S. operations before interest and taxes, pays $800 in interest to lenders and $180 in taxes to the U.S., and receives a net foreign dividend of $400.

Let us see how a foreign multinational might fare after tax if it faced exactly the same circumstances. Its results are given in Table 14.5. The income from U.S. and foreign operations is exactly the same as shown for the U.S. multinational in Table 14.4. The foreign multinational's U.S. subsidiary pays $60 of U.S. tax on U.S. net income of $200 (or 30% × $200), and a withholding tax of $28 (or 20% × $140, for a net dividend of $112) on paying dividends of $140 to its foreign parent. The foreign parent faces a 50% tax rate on its $1,200 of worldwide taxable income ($1,000 foreign plus $200 U.S.). Its tentative tax is reduced by the $88 FTC (the total U.S. taxes paid) for a net tax payment to its government of $512. Its after-tax cash flow is $600, 50% of its worldwide income of $1,200. This is $180 (43%) more than its U.S. counterpart.

Table 14.5 Foreign Multinational Buyer of a Leveraged U.S. Corporation

	U.S. Operations	Foreign Operations	Foreign Company's After-tax Cash Flow
Local Taxable Income Before Interest	$1,000	$1,000	$1,000
Interest Expense in U.S.	(800)		
U.S. Taxable Income*	200	200	
U.S. Tax @ 30%	(60)		
Available For Dividends	140		
Withholding Tax @ 20%	(28)		
Local Tax @ 50%		(600)	
Foreign Tax Credit For U.S. Tax Paid (60 + 28)		88	
Net Local Taxes Paid (600 - 88)			(512)
Net U.S. Dividend to Foreign Investor (140 - 28)			112
After-tax Income to Foreign Investor			$ 600

*Taxable in the foreign country upon dividend repatriation

Mitigation of the Interest Allocation Problem

Interest is allocated to all members of the U.S. affiliated group for tax purposes. A U.S. tax return includes income from all subsidiaries owned 80% or more by vote *and* value. This includes all foreign subsidiaries of U.S. parents. In the illustration just discussed, the U.S. subsidiary of the foreign multinational had no subsidiaries of its own, so there was no interest allocation problem.

Where allocation of U.S. interest deductions is costly due to binding FTC limitations, it is possible to substitute preferred stock for debt as a means of financing. Preferred stock dividends are not subject to the interest allocation rules. (Neither are lease payments.) By issuing preferred stock, the firm obtains a tax deduction *implicitly* through a lower before-tax borrowing rate because of the dividend received deduction of 70% to 100% of the dividend received.

Recall in the interest allocation example just discussed that only half the interest was effectively deductible by the U.S. multinational. At a U.S. tax rate of 30%, this meant the interest was deductible at a tax rate of 15%. If preferred stock could be issued at a risk-adjusted dividend yield that is *more* than 15% below that on debt, it would be the preferred financing alternative.[34]

Another way to avoid allocating interest expense to foreign operations is to undertake U.S. borrowing through a U.S. subsidiary that is less than 80% owned by the majority shareholder. In such a case, the subsidiary could not be consolidated for U.S. tax purposes, so the interest would not get allocated to the parent's foreign-source income.

Ford Motor Co. used exactly this strategy to avoid having to allocate interest expense abroad on the debt created in its $3.35 billion acquisition of Associates

---

[34] In 1990 Coke redeemed all of its $300 million dutch auction preferred stock financing. The dividend rate on the stock was 6.05%, which became more expensive than debt financing, after tax, because of a change in its foreign tax credit situation. (*Corporate Financing Week*, December 10, 1990, p. 5).

Chapter 14   Multinational Tax Planning

Corp. from Paramount Communications.[35] This enabled Ford to preserve significant sums of foreign tax credits that would otherwise have become unavailable. To accomplish this, Ford sold off 25% of Associates by issuing money market preferred stock with voting rights. This "deconsolidation" arrangement is not without cost. Preferred stock dividends are not (explicitly) tax-deductible to the issuer, although an implicit deduction is available, as discussed above, because 70% of the dividends received are excluded from the taxable income of U.S. corporate shareholders.

For tax reasons it is also useful to concentrate the ownership of preferred stock in the hands of a small number of holders to secure a larger dividend-received deduction for the investors. But a concentrated investment may be unattractive to investors who seek diversified holdings as well as liquidity.[36] Deconsolidation entails other costs as well. Unwinding the affairs of the subsidiary, for example, can be much more complicated when outside parties are involved in the business. To secure the tax benefits from deconsolidation, Ford was precluded from reconsolidating its subsidiary for five years. If Ford's ownership position in Associates were to exceed 80% of the *value* of Associates in any year during the five-year period, however, it would again be required to allocate the interest expense of Associates to foreign-source income for that year, although it would *not* regain any of the other benefits of consolidation. If Associates were to become unprofitable, its losses could become difficult to use for tax purposes. Moreover, its preferred stock issue is only callable after three years. While a few other companies, such as Exxon, have also deconsolidated some of their U.S. financing operations, not many other corporations have followed suit.

Interest on nonrecourse debt that is secured exclusively by U.S. assets is allocated entirely against U.S. income. So secured borrowing in the U.S. reduces worldwide income while leaving foreign-source income intact. With increasing problems associated with binding FTC limitations under the 1986 Tax Act, there are increased incentives to undertake secured borrowing in the U.S. On the other hand, the requirement that the financing be nonrecourse may exact its own cost.

Since only U.S. interest is allocated to foreign source income, many U.S. multinationals are substituting foreign borrowing for U.S. borrowing as a source of capital for their foreign subsidiaries. They are reducing the equity in their foreign subsidiaries, particularly in high-tax jurisdictions where debt financing is especially desirable. This not only reduces foreign taxes paid in the high-tax foreign jurisdiction, it also reduces Section 861 interest allocation costs. The costs of borrowing abroad, however, might be quite high for many foreign subsidiaries: they might not have sufficient capital abroad to lever themselves to meet their desired financing requirements. Moreover, they can run afoul of the "thin-capitalization" rules of such countries as Germany, France, and Switzerland.

---

[35] *Wall Street Journal* (October 12, 1989).

[36] If the preferred stock is issued to five or fewer investors, the investors can also borrow against their preferred stock without jeopardizing their dividend-received deduction.

Research & Development

Tax rules require multinational firms to allocate part of R&D expense to foreign-source income for purposes of calculating foreign tax credit limitations. There have been many legislative changes over the past 15 years in how these allocations are made. Prior to August 14, 1981, if more than 50% of research expenses were incurred in the U.S., then 40% of these expenditures, wherever incurred, were apportioned to U.S. source income. The remainder was apportioned based on sales. This rule was suspended by the 1981 Tax Act, which allowed U.S. R&D to be allocated entirely to U.S. source income. With the 1986 Tax Act, however, 50% of domestic R&D became allocated entirely to U.S. income and the remaining 50% was allocated on the basis of gross income or gross sales of the U.S. parent and all foreign subsidiaries. As of 1991, 64% of research expenses incurred in the U.S. are apportioned to U.S. source income, and 64% of foreign research expenses are apportioned to foreign source income. The remainder is apportioned based on sales or gross income.[37]

Headquarters (or Stewardship)

The regulations do not prescribe a method for allocating head office expenses to U.S. and foreign income, but they do provide that the method selected not produce a result "substantially disproportionate" to the actual stewardship activities. The rules governing allocation of stewardship expenses between domestic and foreign activities frequently differ among tax jurisdictions, exposing the investor to the hazard of nondeductibility of part of such costs in any tax jurisdiction. Head office expense might be allocated on the basis of (1) executive time spent, (2) gross receipts of subsidiaries, or (3) unit sales.

14.7   U.S. Tax Treatment of Foreign Investors

Prior to 1984, a 30% withholding tax was imposed on interest paid to foreign persons, although this rate was reduced by treaty in many circumstances. The 1984 Tax Act eliminated the withholding tax in most circumstances. It did so primarily for two reasons: (1) U.S. borrowers were raising funds through foreign finance subsidiaries to avoid the tax; and (2) the withholding tax discouraged the use of the growing Eurobond market as an efficient source of capital to finance U.S. activities.[38]

In the absence of a treaty, dividends paid to foreign persons are subject to a 30% withholding tax (just as most interest was prior to 1984). Again, treaties reduce this rate in many circumstances to 5%-15%, depending upon the country

---

[37] For further details, see KPMG Peat Marwick, *High Tech Tax Update* (January 1991).

[38] "In the period immediately preceding passage of the 1984 Tax Act, American corporations accounted for 25% of all of the bonds sold on the Eurodollar market, and more than $100 billion of treasury issues are held by foreigners." (*New York Times*, July 15, 1984). The article goes on to speculate that if the U.S. Treasury were to issue unregistered bearer bonds (which provides anonymity) to foreigners, it would face a large demand. The Treasury subsequently did issue a limited form of bearer bonds for foreigners.

in which the investor is resident and depending upon whether the investor owns a controlling interest in the distributing corporation (in which case the rate is typically 5% or 10%).

Capital gains on the sale or exchange of U.S. capital assets are typically not subject to U.S. taxation. An exception is gains on the sale of ownership interests in U.S. real property.

Summary of Key Points

1. While the 1986 Tax Act promoted foreign investment in the U.S., it also encouraged U.S. firms to increase their efforts to reduce the local tax bill of their foreign subsidiaries. The U.S. became a tax haven relative to many other countries, such as Germany and Japan. The decline in U.S. tax rates meant that the foreign tax credit (FTC) limitations became binding in many more cases than they did previously.

2. A binding FTC limitation means that the U.S. will refund less than 100% of foreign taxes paid. Under such conditions, it pays U.S. multinationals to reduce the effective tax rate on foreign income, especially in high-tax-rate jurisdictions.

3. With binding FTC limitations it becomes desirable for U.S. multinationals to distribute profits from foreign subsidiaries in ways that are tax deductible abroad. Otherwise taxes would be paid on foreign profits at a foreign tax rate that is above the domestic rate. Examples of ways to distribute profits in a tax-deductible manner include (a) interest on debt issued by a foreign subsidiary, (b) rent on leases of a foreign subsidiary, (c) royalties on licenses granted to a foreign subsidiary, and (d) the judicious use of transfer prices for goods and services exchanged among entities in the same affiliated group.

4. With binding FTC limitations, it still pays for a U.S. multinational to invest in low-tax jurisdictions. Such investment could help free up FTC limitations in high-tax countries by generating additional foreign-source income without incurring very large local tax expenses.

5. The FTC limitation is found by taking the ratio of foreign-source income to worldwide income and multiplying this ratio by the U.S. tax on worldwide income. If the U.S. tax rate is a constant fraction of worldwide income, the FTC limitation simplifies to foreign-source income multiplied by the U.S. tax rate.

6. If most foreign-source income comes from countries where the tax rate exceeds that in the U.S., repatriation will typically not trigger additional U.S. tax, but it could trigger additional foreign withholding tax on the dividend paid to repatriate the profits.

7. If income has been repatriated from a low-tax country because of poor reinvestment opportunities, or for other nontax reasons, then the decision to repatriate profits from a high-tax country could actually yield a net *reduction* in U.S. taxes. In effect, the repatriation from the

high-tax country yields a refund of foreign taxes in excess of the repatriation tax in the U.S.

8. FTC limitations in the U.S. are calculated separately for a variety of categories of income (so-called separate basket limitations). This is done to prevent firms from stuffing investments into tax-haven countries to increase foreign-source income and reduce the average foreign tax rate to below the U.S. rate.

9. For example, U.S. law permits the averaging of high-tax and low-tax foreign manufacturing income for FTC limitation purposes, but not the averaging of low-tax passive income with high-tax manufacturing income.

10. Equity financing of foreign subsidiaries offers flexibility in timing repatriation to coincide with a period of low tax rates in the U.S. It also allows reinvestment of foreign profits to be undertaken without imposing a current repatriation tax. Rents, royalties, and interest payments are less controllable. Debt contracts, however, do offer one significant advantage over equity in terms of an opportunity to return investment funds to the parent company without triggering a repatriation tax. In particular, the repayment of the principal on a loan is not deemed to constitute a repatriation of profits, whereas any repurchase of stock is treated as a dividend.

11. The tax rules influence the capital structures of foreign subsidiaries. While equity financing is desirable in low-tax environments to defer the recognition of profits at home, debt financing (and other substitutes) is desirable in high-tax environments to distribute pre-tax income in a form that is tax deductible locally.

12. Withholding taxes also affect the financing decision. Different forms of repatriation, such as dividends, rents, and royalties, are often subject to different levels of withholding tax. Moreover, withholding tax rates vary from country to country. As a result, it is sometimes important to consider alternative routes through which to repatriate foreign income.

13. Transfer pricing procedures may result in the repatriation of foreign profits in a way that escapes withholding tax entirely. Section 482 is used as a weapon against overzealous tax planning and requires that transactions among related parties be priced as if they involved unrelated parties (whatever that means). This is difficult to achieve and administer, and it is the source of a great many disputes between the IRS and taxpayers.

14. The transfer of intangibles between related parties is a particularly vexing transfer pricing problem. What is the value of a particular patent or trademark? What royalty level is sufficient to compensate for the transfer of technology? The "super royalty" provisions in the 1986 Tax Act govern the transfer of intangibles and suggest that royalty levels be adjusted in years subsequent to the transfer to reflect actual income produced. This is not only onerous, it also discourages efficient transfers of technology between related parties.

15. Source of income rules under Sections 861 to 864 regulate the allocation of income and expense to U.S. and foreign source for purposes of determining FTC limitations. The more important items considered here include inventories, interest, research and development, and headquarters expenses. These rules have presented major tax planning problems for U.S. multinationals since passage of the 1986 Tax Act when foreign tax credit limitations became binding for many firms. The requirement to allocate a portion of U.S. interest and research and development expenses to foreign source, thereby reducing foreign-source income, can result in the effective loss of tax deductions on the portions deemed to be foreign source when the FTC limitation is binding.

16. These allocation rules are particularly onerous for U.S. firms that wish to effect leveraged buyouts of companies with significant foreign operations. Such companies will be unable to deduct a portion of the interest payments on debt, the proceeds of which were used to effect acquisitions. A foreign multinational competitor, however, faces no such constraint. Its U.S. subsidiary can deduct from its U.S. taxable income all of the interest it pays on its debt.

17. U.S. firms can mitigate these allocation problems by financing their activities with preferred stock or lease financing rather than with debt. Some firms such as Exxon and Ford have "deconsolidated" financial subsidiaries that issue a lot of debt. By reducing ownership of these subsidiaries to below 80%, deconsolidation allows these entities to deduct all the interest incurred on their debt, because they have no foreign consolidated subsidiaries of their own. Deconsolidation, however, gives rise to other tax and nontax costs.

Discussion Questions

1. In what ways did the 1986 Tax Act encourage U.S. firms to reduce their foreign taxable income?

2. How is the objective of reducing local taxable income in high-tax countries by distributing subsidiary profits in ways that yield local tax deductions similar to that of restructuring domestic corporate activities in ways that more closely achieve partnership taxation (that is, single-level taxation) of corporate profits? Should firms relocate their foreign activities to low-tax countries to reduce the adverse effects of the 1986 Tax Act?

3. Describe some of the ways foreign subsidiaries can reduce local taxable income. Which are most effective? When is it advantageous to employ these strategies?

4. Under what circumstances might U.S. multinationals increase their investment in low-tax foreign jurisdictions?

5. How is the foreign tax credit limitation determined? How does world-wide averaging work? If the firm had no plans to repatriate income from a low-tax country, would it be advisable to do so if foreign tax credit carryforwards from the repatriation of income from high-tax countries were about to expire?

6. Why might a firm wish to repatriate income from a low-tax country? If it does so, is it advisable to repatriate income from a high-tax country at the same time? Why?

7. Why does the U.S. require that repatriated foreign income be separated into baskets by type of income with separate foreign tax credit limitations applied to each basket? Does the presence of separate baskets increase the U.S. tax on foreign income?

8. What are the advantages of using equity to capitalize the operations of foreign subsidiaries? What are the advantages of using debt, or debt-like substitutes such as royalty arrangements, to finance foreign operations?

9. What differences in the capital structures of multinational corporations and their subsidiaries should we observe as a function of the foreign subsidiaries' tax rates? Is there any empirical evidence to support these predictions?

10. How do withholding taxes affect the investment and financing decisions of multinational firms? How do they affect the routes in which, and the forms through which, income is repatriated?

11. What is the import of Section 482 for firms forming subsidiaries in foreign tax jurisdictions? Do taxpayers have much freedom in setting prices of goods and services that they transfer to and from their own subsidiaries?

12. What difficulties arise in valuing intangibles that are transferred to or from related entities? What are the "super royalty" provisions? How might these provisions affect the location and magnitude of research and development expenditures of U.S. multinationals?

13. What factors might explain the relatively low levels of taxable income reported by foreign-controlled U.S. corporations as compared to U.S.-controlled domestic corporations in the 1980s? How might these factors have operated differently during the last half of the 1980s and into the 1990s, relative to the first half of the 1980s?

14. How does the definition of foreign-source income affect the computation of the foreign tax credit limitation? Why does the U.S. allocate different items of U.S. income and expense to foreign sources for purposes of computing the FTC limitation? Are the effects of these allocations more severe for companies that concentrate their investment in high-tax or low-tax foreign jurisdictions? Why?

15. How does the allocation of interest income to foreign source affect the cost-effectiveness of U.S. multinationals effecting leveraged buyouts of other firms? Do foreign competitors have a distinct advantage over their U.S. counterparts in bidding for U.S. firms? What forms of restruc-

turing might U.S. multinationals undertake after a successful LBO to reduce their worldwide taxes?

16. What financing alternatives can the U.S. firm employ to reduce the effect of Section 861's allocation of U.S. interest to foreign source? What are the benefits and costs of these alternatives?

17. What is a Foreign Sales Corporation (FSC)? Under what conditions might a firm wish to establish a FSC? What are the tax and nontax costs of such an organization?

Problems

1. A U.S. company is planning to form a foreign subsidiary to undertake a profitable project in a country where the tax rate is 25%. The company's tax rate in the U.S. is 35%.

   a. If the withholding tax rate on dividends paid from the foreign country to the U.S. is 20%, how much U.S. taxable income will be recognized for each dollar of dividends *received* by the U.S. parent?

   b. Assuming this is the only foreign-source income for the U.S. company, what will be the additional U.S. tax liability (after foreign tax credit) for each dollar of dividend received?

   c. Suppose all foreign profits could be repatriated to the U.S. parent by way of interest payments on debt rather than by way of dividend payments. This would reduce foreign taxable income to zero. How much more or less worldwide profit after tax would result (for a one-year investment horizon) per dollar of foreign income before interest and foreign taxes:

      • if withholding tax rates on interest were 0%?

      • if withholding tax rates on interest were 30%?

   d. Suppose that profits earned in the foreign country can be reinvested at a rate of 10% before interest and taxes, the same as in the U.S. How does the desirability of debt versus equity financing change as the investment horizon increases?

2. Refer to Problem 1 in Chapter Thirteen.

   a. How would the analysis change if the U.S. multinational could issue debt bearing interest at a rate of 10%, rather than equity, to capitalize its investments in Countries A and B?

   b. How would your answer to (a) change if the withholding tax rate on interest were 15% rather than 0%?

3. Suppose dividend payments were made tax-deductible in calculating corporate taxable income in the U.S. Assume that if dividends are received from foreign subsidiaries, and the U.S. parent in turn distributes the dividends to its shareholders, then shareholders are permitted to take foreign tax credits for the foreign taxes they have paid indirectly. Foreign tax credits are limited, however, to an amount equal to shareholders' U.S. tax rate multiplied by the foreign-source income they have received.

For example, suppose a wholly owned subsidiary in a foreign country earns $1.00 of pre-tax income, pays local tax of $.20, and declares a dividend of $.80 to its U.S. parent. The U.S. parent in turn declares an $.80 dividend to its shareholders, thereby avoiding taxable income on the receipt of the dividend. Shareholders must recognize $1.00 of taxable income ($.80 in dividends plus $.20 of indirect foreign taxes paid) and are eligible for a foreign tax credit of up to $.20. The tax credit is equal to exactly $.20 if their U.S. tax rate is 20% or more.

How might this affect the propensity of tax-exempt investors to invest in purely domestic versus multinational businesses?

CHAPTER 15
Capital Structure and Dividend Policy

Legislative changes in tax rules alter relative tax rates across taxpayers domestically and internationally, across time periods, across economic activities, and across legal organizational forms. These changes affect not only *explicit* tax rates but also the *implicit* tax rates that apply to the returns from investing in various economic activities. When implicit and explicit tax rates change, tax clienteles often shift as well. When they do, taxpayers will often prefer to change their investment and financing strategies. The costs of such changes, however, restrain reorganization activity.

Just as changes in tax rules produce a new set of desired investment and financing strategies, so can a change in taxpayers' economic circumstances. Once again, market frictions prevent full adjustment. Since reorganization of economic activities is costly, the amount of and nature of the recontracting that follows a change in tax regimes or economic circumstances depends on the nature of and magnitude of these costs, which are often specific to certain taxpayers and to particular economic activities.

In this chapter, we employ these ideas to shed light on the *capital structure policy* of firms. Our view of capital structure policy is broad: it encompasses the many financing alternatives that are substitutes for debt and equity. We do not assume that the firm's investment policies are fixed. We allow firms to sell off or retain investments already in place and to undertake new investments. We also consider whether the firm should alter other capital structure components to effect clientele-based arbitrage. Investment decisions are important components of this expanded view of capital structure policy. Most textbooks in corporate finance adopt a narrow focus, where the analysis is often limited to determining the relative advantages of debt versus equity as corporate financing alternatives.

The nontax costs to alter clienteles have an important influence on the desirable financing and investment mix. Differences in reorganization cost across assets and equities make changes in investment and financing strategies imperfect substitutes for one another as economic circumstances change. Moreover, because costs are particular to each taxpayer, different taxpayers can be led to respond in radically different ways to changes in the economic environment.

We also stress the role of history in influencing capital structure policy. Firms make planning decisions in an uncertain environment, and as uncertainty is resolved, they respond to changes in their circumstances. They must redesign an organization that already has plans in place and an operating history. They lack the luxury of starting afresh to design a new organization as the economy changes.

In analyzing capital structure policy, many finance textbooks assume that firms undertake investments that cannot be altered. They assume that operating cash flows and investment-related tax deductions (such as depreciation allowances) are also fixed. This limits the firm's response to an unexpected change in its economic circumstances (such as unexpectedly weak sales that give rise to net operating loss carryforwards) to changes in its debt/equity mix. For example, if the firm generates net operating losses, it reduces its level of debt to avoid interest payments and increase taxable income, thereby reducing net operating losses. These simplifying assumptions are designed to focus attention on important debt/equity mix issues. In Chapter Eight we assumed that the firm's operating decisions were fixed to illustrate how to compute the firm's marginal tax rate before adjustments were made to its capital structure. But we also noted that selling depreciable assets (or depreciation benefits) and repurchasing fully taxable debt are substitute tax-planning strategies for changes in the capital structure.[1]

In this chapter, we illustrate some of the many capital structure alternatives that represent imperfect substitutes for effecting clientele-based arbitrage. In Chapter Eight, we demonstrated how changes in a firm's prospects for generating net operating loss carryforwards affected its marginal tax rate, and in turn affected the amount of bonds and preferred stock to be purchased or issued. In this chapter, we expand the set of investment and financing alternatives that the firm might employ. We follow this discussion with an illustration of how firms' operating histories affect capital structure planning. Because of nontax costs to restructure, firms may find it desirable to hold both tax-favored and tax-disfavored assets at the same time. They can also find it desirable to finance operations by issuing tax-favored securities without repurchasing tax-disfavored securities that have been issued in the past.

We also consider whether corporations should issue debt or equity in light of tax reforms in the U.S. in the 1980s, and we examine the important role of nontax factors on the appropriate choice. In Chapters Four and Six, we showed that without frictions, the 1986 Tax Act would result in organizational form arbitrage; that is, the partnership form of organization would displace the corporate form in many circumstances. In this chapter, we introduce the notion

---

[1] For a related discussion see Harry DeAngelo and Ronald W. Masulis, "Optimal Capital Structure Under Corporate and Personal Taxation," *Journal of Financial Economics* (March, 1980), pp. 3-29. They introduce the notion of substitutes in capital structure planning. They assume, however, that the firm's investment decisions are fixed and, as a result, tax shields such as interest deductions must be traded off against depreciation deductions.

that from a tax standpoint, issuing debt to finance new investments is a substitute, albeit an imperfect one, for converting the corporation to partnership form.

15.1 Imperfect Substitutes in the Capital Structure Decision

When the tax status of a firm changes, it generally will consider whether to alter its capital structure and/or its asset allocations. Low-taxed firms would wish to acquire tax-disadvantageous assets (which bear high explicit taxes) and sell tax-advantageous assets (which bear high implicit taxes). For example, a firm that purchases equipment (eligible for rapid depreciation) when its tax rate is high may find it efficient to sell the equipment and perhaps lease it back when its tax rate falls. And evidence indicates that the presence of tax loss carryforwards reduces the likelihood of a firm issuing debt (and increases the likelihood of a firm issuing equity). For example, Mackie-Mason found that for 1,418 new security issues made by U.S. corporations during the period 1977 to 1984, a one standard deviation increase in tax loss carryforwards reduced the probability of issuing debt, and increased the probability of issuing equity, by roughly 8 percent.[2]

Since managers are generally better informed than are outsiders about a firm's prospects, corporate restructurings can serve to inform market participants that a change in the firm's tax-paying status has occurred. Since tax-paying status and real profitability are affected by many of the same events, and therefore are correlated positively, tax-induced changes in asset structure or capital structure could be accompanied by changes in the prices of publicly traded securities. Note that it is expensive for a firm to choose a capital structure that suggests it expects to be a high-tax firm when it really does not expect to be. This fact helps to make capital structure changes credible signals of firms' prospects.

Empirical evidence is consistent with the tax-clientele hypothesis that changes in the firm's future prospects are highly correlated with its current capital structure and asset mix. For example, when firms announce debt-for-equity swaps, their share prices increase. The opposite is true of leverage-decreasing exchange offers. Moreover, equity issues and convertible debt issues are associated with reductions in stock prices, whereas equity repurchases are associated with increases in stock prices.[3] This evidence increases our confidence in using capital structure data to make inferences about a firm's tax-paying status, and we will expand on this theme in Chapters Sixteen and Seventeen.

Direct Changes in Capital Structure

Firms for which marginal tax rates are expected to change from a low level to a high level have incentives to issue nonconvertible (or "straight") debt rather than

---

[2] Jeffrey K. Mackie-Mason, "Do Taxes Affect Corporate Financing Decisions?" *Journal of Finance* (December, 1990), pp. 1471-1493.

[3] See Larry Y. Dann and Wayne H. Mikkelson, "Convertible Debt Issuance, Capital Structure Change and Financing-Related Information: Some New Evidence," *Journal of Financial Economics* (June 1984), pp. 157-86, especially Table 9; Ronald W. Masulis, "The Impact of Capital Structure Change on Firm

common stock, warrants, preferred stock or convertible debt. Although the required before-tax rate of return on straight debt will be higher, on a risk-adjusted basis, than on those alternatives, interest payments are tax deductible.

More specifically, the tax system encourages those firms with the highest expected marginal tax rates to issue "straight" debt bearing interest that is fully deductible from taxable income. Among firms that issue straight debt, the tax law encourages those with the highest expected marginal tax rates to issue the least secured debt. Risky debt, the most risky of which includes so-called "junk" bonds, promises investors a higher fully taxable yield to compensate for the possibility of default. These risk premiums are deductible as paid even though they represent payments that compensate for expected future defaults on the principal of the loan. This tax advantage to the issuer is a tax disadvantage to the holder of these instruments, and encourages low-marginal-tax-rate taxpayers to hold them.

Reorganization costs affect whether the firm issues short-term or long-term debt. For example, it is typically more expensive to issue a sequence of short-term debt instruments than to issue one long-term debt obligation. But not all firms can "afford" the luxury of issuing relatively cheap long-term debt. If a firm's marginal tax rate should fall because of operating losses, it could no longer use the tax shields of the long-term debt cost-effectively. Because of the larger recapitalization costs associated with long-term debt, the lower-cost financing alternative might have been to roll over short-term debt. Hence, issuers of long-term debt signal either that they expect to remain in high marginal tax brackets or that they expect reorganization costs to be low.[4]

The tax rules encourage firms with expected marginal tax rates below those of the marginal holder of straight debt to finance operations in ways that provide smaller explicit tax subsidies; for example, convertible debt, operating leases, warrants, preferred stock, common stock, limited partnerships, and joint ventures. The implicit tax subsidy paid to the firm by the suppliers of these forms of capital motivates the firm to issue each of these classes of debt or equity.

Firms with the lowest marginal *explicit* tax rates are encouraged for tax reasons to issue those instruments that offer the largest *implicit* tax subsidy. As a result, these firms tend to finance their operations with preferred stock and common stock. Firms that finance with convertible bonds are likely to have greater marginal tax rates since convertible bonds provide to the issuer both explicit tax subsidies (through interest deductions) and implicit tax subsidies (through the reduced risk-adjusted yield that results because capital gains are tax-favored to investors). On the other hand, when management is better informed about the prospects of their firm than are outside investors, equity issues might entail "giving away too much of a bargain" to outsiders, because of the discount necessary to sell equity, as we have argued before.

Value: Some Estimates," *Journal of Finance* (March 1983), pp. 107-26; and Clifford W. Smith, Jr., "Investment Banking and the Capital Acquisition Process," *Journal of Financial Economics* (January-February 1986), pp. 3-29.

[4] Note that as with the choice between debt and equity, it is costly for a firm that does not expect to generate enough taxable income to use the interest deductions cost-effectively to imitate the behavior of a firm that *does* expect to generate enough taxable income to use the interest deductions cost-effectively. The cost relates to being in the wrong tax clientele.

Since convertible bonds seem to have some undesirable tax characteristics, their popularity is somewhat surprising. Although low current deductions for interest (relative to straight debt) are consistent with a lower marginal tax rate for issuing firms (relative to firms issuing straight debt), conversion into common stock is likely to take place in profitable times for the firm when its stock price is high and it is generating taxable income. This alters the firm's capital structure in a less desirable way, given its good fortune, than an alternative more efficient tax policy of having the bonds convert into straight debt using the stock price to determine the timing and amount of the conversion value. This makes it seem unlikely that the issuance of convertible bonds is motivated primarily by tax considerations.

In the latter part of the 1980s, a special type of convertible preferred stock began to be used occasionally to finance acquisitions in transactions that involve considerable amounts of borrowing, so-called "leveraged buyouts." In such transactions, the buyers of a company first take out a short-term ("bridge") loan from a bank to purchase a controlling interest in the target. The new owners then arrange for the acquired firm to issue convertible preferred stock. This is particularly appropriate from a tax-planning standpoint when net operating losses arise in conjunction with the control change (for example, because of large severance payments to employees and losses from asset sales). This preferred stock is special in that it is convertible into debt, most likely at a time when the firm is generating taxable income. Such convertible preferred stock was issued in the leveraged buyout of RJR-Nabisco by Kohlberg, Kravis, Roberts in 1989.

Those firms with significant uncertainty about their future tax status are another important class that form a natural clientele for particular financial instruments. These firms must use relatively more costly financing and investment policies to respond quickly to changes in their marginal tax rates. For example, as discussed earlier, they would tend to use short-term debt when their tax rate is high. Alternatively, if their marginal tax rates are highly correlated with reported income, "income bonds" would be a particularly tax-efficient form of financing. Such bonds require payments that depend on the level of corporate income. In this way, large tax-deductible payments are made to bondholders only when income and tax rates are high.

Although some scholars have puzzled over why so few corporations have issued income bonds, many corporations do in fact issue them indirectly. Common examples of indirect income bonds include:

1. risky bonds with high fixed coupon payments that are payable only if the issuer is solvent,
2. operating leases where lease payments are tied to revenue,
3. patent royalty agreements,
4. employee bonus plans where the bonus is tied to profitability,
5. pension plans where funding is timed to coincide with high tax rates, and
6. nonqualified employee stock option plans if there is a positive correlation between the stock price and the profitability of the firm.

As with payments to income bondholders, many of these contracts provide for payments that depend upon the realization of revenues or "profits" that could be manipulated by management. In addition, some of these indirect income bonds may be more or less effective in generating tax deductions when the firm's tax rate is high. These substitutes for income bonds are more prevalent than direct income bonds, perhaps because of greater nontax costs to issue direct income bonds.[5] We turn next to a consideration of other substitutes for debt and equity in the capital structure decision.

Changes in Capital Structure Linked to Employee Compensation Contracts

Payouts from deferred compensation contracts that are based on either the passage of time or are tied to future performance become more attractive when the employer's tax rate is expected to be higher in the future.[6] Increased pension funding is also more desirable when tax rates increase, so defined benefit pension plans can be more attractive than defined contribution plans because of greater flexibility in timing tax-deductible contributions.

Changes in Capital Structure Linked to Customer/Supplier Contracting

Firms that expect increasing tax rates would prefer not to enter into contracts that defer their taxable income. Installment sales agreements, for example (wherein taxable income from the sale of goods is realized in proportion to principal payments received on a note issued by the seller to finance the buyer's purchase), become less attractive from a tax standpoint under such circumstances. Installment sales become more attractive, however, once the tax rate of the firm has increased and is expected to remain high.

Another way to shift income across periods is to sell or buy on credit, using credit terms that differ from market terms. Credit terms that are more favorable or less favorable than market terms translate into a higher or lower "price" charged for the goods or services that are being financed. For example, if the seller of a good offers the buyer cheap financing, this results in a higher sale price. In turn, this leads to higher current taxable income but lower future interest income

---

[5] Another possibility is that the taxing authority would reclassify direct income bonds as equity. See also John J. McConnell and Gary G. Schlarbaum, "Return, Risks and Pricing of Income Bonds, 1956-76 (Does Money Have an Odor?)," *Journal of Business* (January 1981), pp. 33-63; John J. McConnell and Gary G. Schlarbaum, "Evidence on the Impact of Exchange Offers on Security Prices: The Case of Income Bonds," *Journal of Business* (January 1981), pp. 65-85; and Sang Yong Park and Joseph Williams, "Taxes, Capital Structure, and Bondholder Clienteles," *Journal of Business* (April 1985), pp. 203-24.

[6] There may also be a rather severe identification problem in sorting out whether the compensation packages that are observed are driven by tax considerations, incentive considerations, or both. See Merton H. Miller and Myron S. Scholes, "Executive Compensation, Taxes, and Incentives," in William F. Sharpe and Cathryn M. Cootner, eds., *Financial Economics: Essays in Honor of Paul Cootner* (Prentice-Hall, 1982), pp. 179-215; Clifford W. Smith, Jr. and Ross L. Watts, "Incentive and Tax Effects of Executive Compensation Plans," *Australian Journal of Management*, vol. 7 (December 1982), pp. 139-57; Clifford W. Smith, Jr. and Ross L. Watts, "The Structure of Executive Compensation Contracts and the Control of Management," Working Paper 81-7 (University of Rochester, Center for Research in Government Policy and Business, March 1984); and Myron S. Scholes and Mark A. Wolfson, "Taxes and Employee Compensation Planning," *Taxes* (December 1986), pp. 824-34. See also Chapter Seven of this text.

to the seller. It also leads to lower taxable income to the buyer as the asset is expensed for tax purposes and correspondingly higher income to the buyer because of a lower interest expense deduction in the future.[7]

Note how careful one must be here in linking changes in capital structure to changes in tax status. A firm that generates net operating loss carryforwards may actually issue debt (at below-market rates to finance the sale of assets) rather than issue equity, and yet this may still lead to a reduction in its tax burden! To understand how taxes affect financing and investment decisions requires that we know much more about firms than simply how their debt-to-equity ratios change.

Changes in Capital Structure Linked to Investment Policy

Lease obligations represent an important capital structure component. When the tax rate of a firm increases, it may be efficient to buy rather than lease long-lived assets. As we discussed earlier, it is tax efficient for low-tax firms to lease rather than buy durable assets. In an interesting paper, Shaw provides striking evidence that firms are likely to engage in leasing to exploit low marginal tax rates. In particular, 85% of the firms in his sample that sold tax benefits under "safe harbor lease" contracts during 1981 disclosed tax loss or credit carryforwards and at least $50 million in capital expenditures in their 1980 annual reports. Because of the transfer of depreciation shields, the pre-tax financing cost of a lease will be below that of straight debt on a risk-adjusted basis.[8]

Since lease financing is tied to a particular asset, it may introduce lower information costs than other implicitly taxed financing alternatives such as equity, which is a residual claim against all of the firm's assets. On the other hand, a hidden action problem arises in that leased property tends to be maintained less carefully than owned property, and hence is less valuable than owned property.[9] As a result, optimal capital structure will depend not only on the firm's tax status but also on the nature of its information problems (that is, the contracting cost component of implicit taxes associated with various elements of the capital structure).

---

[7] The 1984 Tax Act introduced new original issue discount (OID) rules to limit the use of *below*-market-rate loans to increase the reported sale price of an asset. Under the new rules, the interest rate on a loan is below the market rate when it is below the "applicable federal rate" (a riskless government bond rate matched to the term of the loan). Although firms that issue risky loans at this riskless rate clearly issue a loan with a below-market interest rate, it is not treated as such under the tax code. Even with the new OID rules, many tax-planning opportunities still exist to use below-market-rate demand loans effectively in the compensation programs for employees. This is discussed in Myron S. Scholes and Mark A. Wolfson, "Compensatory Loans to Executives Before and After the Tax Act of 1984," Stanford Working Paper (September 1985).

[8] Wayne H. Shaw, "Measuring the Impact of the Safe Harbor Lease Law on Security Prices," Cornell University Working Paper (August 1987).

[9] See Michael C. Jensen and William H. Meckling, "Theory of the Firm: Managerial Behavior, Agency Costs and Ownership Structure," *Journal of Financial Economics* (October 1976), pp. 305-60; Mark A. Wolfson, "Tax, Incentive, and Risk-Sharing Issues in the Allocation of Property Rights: The Generalized Lease-or-Buy Problem," *The Journal of Business* (April 1985), pp. 158-71; and Clifford W. Smith, Jr. and L. MacDonald Wakeman, "Determinants of Corporate Leasing Policy," *Journal of Finance* (July 1985), pp. 895-908.

15.1   Imperfect Substitutes in the Capital Structure Decision

Moreover, the firm need not stop at buying its own equipment. It could lease equipment to other companies with lower marginal tax rates. General Electric Credit Corporation (GECC) and many commercial banks have extensive leasing divisions. It has been estimated that GECC paid roughly 70 cents on the dollar for over $1.5 billion in tax benefits related to safe harbor leasing contracts in 1981.[10]

This discussion suggests that investment policy changes can substitute for capital structure changes as a potential response to changes in tax status. Other examples include:

Purchase Other Companies: If a firm expects its tax rate to increase, it might purchase other companies that have NOLs. As we discuss more fully in Chapter Twenty-Six, this was a fairly common strategy until its use was severely limited by the 1986 Tax Act. Even prior to the 1986 Act, the strategy did not drive the firm's effective tax rate to zero. The firm paid an implicit tax on acquiring the tax shelter; that is, it shared the tax advantage with the shareholders of the acquired company. For example, if a purchase premium (including all costs of effecting the purchase) of 30 cents is paid for each dollar of tax loss carryforward of a target company, the acquiring company's implicit tax rate would be 30%. An imperfectly competitive market for corporate combinations could leave a buyer with a larger share of the tax benefits and, therefore, a lower implicit rate of tax. There are various other ways in which taxes and information problems interact to determine the efficacy of mergers and other asset restructurings.[11]

Research and Development (R&D): The firm that faces an increase in tax rates could increase the scale of its own internal R&D programs. Some firms contract out R&D programs (either directly or through limited partnerships) for the same tax reasons that they lease rather than buy capital equipment. Internal R&D programs can create tax credits and the immediate deductibility of expenditures incurred in running them. As with ownership of depreciable assets, conducting R&D "in house" also mitigates costly incentive problems that would otherwise naturally arise when the research is conducted by outsiders or conducted by insiders but financed with outsiders' funds through a partnership or joint venture (as described in more detail in Chapter Nineteen).

Other Tax-favored Investments: Firms' tax rates affect their advertising and charitable contribution policies. Those firms facing lower future tax rates because of legislative changes or reduced prospects for profitability might increase their current advertising and charitable contribution budgets. This would reduce current taxable income (at a high marginal tax rate) in exchange for increased future income from sources such as sales generated by advertising

---

[10] See Clyde P. Stickney, Roman L. Weil, and Mark A. Wolfson, "Income Taxes and Tax-Transfer Leases: General Electric's Accounting for a Molotov Cocktail," *Accounting Review* (April 1983), pp. 439-59, especially p. 443.

[11] See Ronald J. Gilson, Myron S. Scholes, and Mark A. Wolfson, "Taxation and the Dynamics of Corporate Control: The Uncertain Case for Tax-Motivated Acquisitions," in John C. Coffee, Jr., Louis Lowenstein, and Susan Rose-Ackerman, eds., *Knights, Raiders and Targets: The Impact of the Hostile Takeover* (Oxford University Press, 1988), pp. 271-299.

Chapter 15   Capital Structure and Dividend Policy

campaigns designed to have a long-term impact on demand. Similar incentives exist to increase market research and personnel costs to lay the foundation for expansion of product offerings. In addition, the firm could replace nontaxable municipal bonds with taxable high-yielding interest-bearing securities. More generally, firms in low tax brackets tend to avoid tax shelters such as real estate, advertising, and R&D (unless they sell the tax benefits to highly taxed entities), and high tax-paying firms naturally hold municipal bonds, high dividend-paying common and preferred stock, and a variety of other tax-sheltered investments.

Multinational Investments: The explicit marginal tax rate of U.S. multinational firms is lower, in present value terms, on foreign-source income generated in certain countries (such as Ireland and Hong Kong) than it is on domestic income, because the U.S. tax on this income (other than so-called Subpart F income, which is passive income) is deferred until it is repatriated to the U.S., as discussed more fully in Chapter Thirteen. Certain countries (such as Japan, Germany, and a number of other European countries), however, impose higher tax rates than does the U.S. (especially subsequent to the 1986 Tax Act). Limitations on the use of foreign tax credits partly depend on the distribution of worldwide income, borrowing policies, and tax rates. As we discussed more fully in Chapters Thirteen and Fourteen, depending on the implicit tax rates on investment in these foreign countries and whether a firm's tax rates are expected to increase in the future, the U.S. multinational may find it tax advantageous to produce abroad or to repatriate foreign profits to the U.S.

When a firm's profitability increases, its demand for tax shelters may increase or decrease, depending on whether the increase comes primarily from low tax-rate jurisdictions or high tax-rate jurisdictions. A change in the firm's tax status can have dramatic implications for its multinational investment and financing decisions, especially with respect to its repatriation policies.

15.2 Implications of Tax Clienteles and Transaction Costs for the Efficient Design of Experiments

In the preceding section, we explored some of the ways in which the economic balance sheet of a firm might be reorganized in response to a change in its tax status. These reorganization opportunities are only suggestive of a broad menu of possible strategies available to firms with changing prospects for profitability. One point should be kept clear: firms have strong incentives to engage in (costly) tax planning that exploits cross-sectional and across-time differences in marginal tax rates. Although there are ample opportunities for them to do so, costs might preclude them from exploiting many of these opportunities. As such, the marginal tax rate could be quite different from the rate that a naive analysis would suggest: namely, either zero or the maximum statutory rate. To determine the "correct rate" requires consideration of many tax planning options, the way tax benefits are shared among the various tax clienteles (that is, the distribution of implicit taxes), the cost of switching from one clientele to another, and the fundamental underlying uncertainty not only of prospects for future profitability but also of the tax rules themselves.

To illustrate some of the possibilities,[12] we have conducted a pilot study on the relation between financing, asset allocation, and compensation policies of 60 firms that went public during 1979 and whose financial statements were available in the library of the Stanford Business School.[13] These firms are interesting because a majority of them start with tax loss carryforwards and tax credits, without any previous history of taxable income. This contrasts with companies that were once profitable, experienced financial distress, and changed components of their asset and capital structures. Because of the costs of restructuring operations or the costs of reorganizing specific elements of their capital structures, these firms could not achieve the "first-best" tax-planning solution.

A seasoned firm with tax loss carryforwards would prefer to have no debt in its capital structure. If there were no reorganization costs, it would prefer to use such strategies as refinancing its outstanding debt with equity. Such reorganization plans, however, cannot be achieved without cost. For example, some debt may be redeemable only at par, although its market value may be far less. Moreover, the costs to exchange public debt (as reflected in the premium paid to effect the exchange) could easily be large enough to wipe out the tax advantage of redeeming the debt. Since the remaining outstanding debt becomes less risky on an exchange of equity for some fraction of the firm's debt, a premium must be paid to induce debtholders to agree to make the exchange. The increase in the value of the risky debt is at the expense of shareholders. Therefore, debt might remain in the capital structure of firms with tax loss carryforwards. Although this appears anomalous, it is perfectly sensible in the presence of sufficiently high reorganization costs, such as those associated with the transfer of value from equity holders to debtholders in "de-leveraging" transactions. For reasons such as these, casual empirical observers might conclude incorrectly that firms are not following optimal tax-planning policies or that taxes appear not to affect the capital structure decision.

Leasing provides another example of a tax-related restructuring problem. Although changing from leasing to owning could reduce agency costs and other costs, it might not be possible for a firm to switch in the short run. Because of depreciation and investment tax credit recapture provisions of the tax laws, it may be desirable to write contracts that preclude a firm from terminating its lease. Similarly, a firm with a large portfolio of appreciated municipal bonds might find it too costly to sell such assets (due to the acceleration of the capital gains tax) despite a drop in its marginal tax rate that would render a *new* purchase of municipal bonds suboptimal.

By focusing exclusively on the behavior of seasoned firms, we may well miss changes in policies that are related to changes in tax status. With costly restructuring, the most efficient response to a change in tax status for some firms will be to change leasing policy first; for others to change debt policy; for still others, to change asset allocations. Tests devised to account for changes among

---

[12] Further evidence is presented in the next chapter on bank investment and financing policies.

[13] We are grateful to Mark Mazur for assistance in collecting and in structuring the data.

a set of policies could be more informative than those focused on a single variable or focused on a cross-section at a single point in time. There is a "downside" here as well. Since we argue that the "dimensionality" of the tax planning problem is so large relative to that reflected in the traditional experiments, improved specification of the problem might require the estimation of too many relations simultaneously.

Because of these reorganization costs, we were particularly interested in considering the tax-planning behavior of young companies that chose to go public. A high fraction of these firms begin public life with tax loss carryforwards. History should pollute their decisions much less than it would for seasoned companies. And our evidence suggests that tax status does affect their decisions. For example, these firms use relatively little debt and rarely have pension plans. On the other hand, deferred compensation tied to future profitability (and hence tax status) is pervasive. Moreover, only 4 of the 60 firms in our pilot study used the last-in, first-out (LIFO) method to value inventories: when prices are rising and tax rates are not, LIFO minimizes taxable income. None of these four LIFO firms had net operating loss, investment tax credit, research and development tax credit, or foreign tax credit carryforwards during the 3 years after going public, although 34 other sample firms had such carryforwards, something that could occur by chance only 3.5% of the time.

The 1983 balance sheet and income statement of Genetic Systems Corporation reveals that since its inception in 1980, it has suffered losses. It has established investment partnerships with profitable firms, committed to noncancelable operating leases, financed research and development through limited partnerships, issued incentive stock options for tax purposes to a far greater degree than non-qualified options, issued warrants and common stock, held interest-bearing marketable securities on corporate account, and issued little long-term debt. It has no pension plan. These are good examples of the expected associations of capital structure, asset structure, and compensation policy with the tax-paying status of the firm.

15.3 Debt Financing and the Cost of Reorganization

In this section, we illustrate the difficulty that a firm might face in attempting to repurchase its outstanding long-term debt. If the firm's economic circumstances change and it finds that its marginal tax rate is low, it would be tax-advantageous to repurchase its fully taxable debt and issue implicitly taxed assets such as preferred stock. In recent years, many corporations have issued large amounts of debt, often using the proceeds to repurchase their stock or to pay out large dividends. Some corporations have been acquired using debt in "leveraged buyouts." Other corporations have been taken private by their own managers, using leverage to finance the purchase of their stock (management buyouts).

Although highly taxed firms might find it tax-advantageous to issue debt, they must also consider the nontax costs associated with refinancing this debt if their economic circumstances should change. Redeeming long-term debt can be costly because long-term debtholders often require a premium to tender their securities. This "hold-up" premium comes at the expense of the stockholders, as illustrated below. As a result, only certain types of firms are suitable for high debt-to-equity ratios.

To illustrate the nature of the hold-up premium, let's make the following assumptions: (1) The before-tax rate of return on fully taxable bonds is fixed at 10%. (2) Several years prior to an unexpected realization of $200 million in net operating loss carryforwards (NOLs) our firm issued $100 million of long-term bonds to finance investments. (3) The corporate tax rate is 40%. (4) Bondholders face a tax rate of 40% on interest income, and they discount after-tax cash flows at a rate of 6%. (5) Bondholders face a lower tax rate on capital losses than on ordinary tax deductions due to capital loss limitations, a lower statutory rate on capital gains and losses, or both. To dramatize the difference, we assume for purposes of this illustration that capital losses yield no tax refunds to bondholders. (6) The risk-adjusted required before-tax rate of return on shares is 7% (or 3% lower than equally risky bonds because of reduced shareholder-level taxes). (7) Finally, the firm's investments will be productive for one additional period and will have no salvage value at that time. The firm is required to repay its debts to the extent it owns assets at the end of the period. Before any restructuring, the NOL firm finds itself in the position shown in Table 15.1.

Table 15.1 Payoffs to Debt and Equity Before Restructuring

| Investment Outcomes | Probability | End-of-Period Assets Before Interest and Tax Payments* | Debt | | Equity* |
			Interest*	Principal*	
Good Results	.5	$130	$10	$100	$20
Bad Results	.5	$ 90	$10	$ 80	$ 0

* Dollar amounts in millions.

We assume that there are only two possible end-of-period asset values before interest and tax payments, $130 million in good times and $90 million in bad times, and each can occur with a probability equal to one-half.[14] The expected value of end-of-period assets (before distributions) is $110 (or $.5 \times \$130 + .5 \times \$90$). Let us assume that even with restructuring, the firm will not be able to use up all of its NOLs. Nor will it be able to sell its NOLs to another firm. This ensures that the firm will pay no corporate taxes.

The value of the equity for the firm described in Table 15.1 is:

Expected Future Value of Equity (.5 × $20 + .5 × $0)	$10.00
Present Value of Equity ($10/1.07)	$ 9.35

---

[14] From here on, we drop the "million" label from all dollar amounts.

The value of the debt for the firm described in Table 15.1 is:

Expected Future Value of Debt:

Principal (.5 × $100 + .5 × $80)	$90.00
+ Interest (.5 × $10 + .5 × $10)	10.00
- Tax on interest (.4 × $10)	(4.00)[15]
	$96.00
Present Value of Debt ($96/1.06)	$90.57

So the total value of the firm is $99.91, consisting of $9.35 of equity and $90.57 of debt. Can the firm restructure and make its shareholders better off? Note that an all-equity firm would be worth $102.80 (or $110.00/1.07). This is $2.89 more than the value of the firm given its current capital structure. The extra value arises because this NOL firm should be financed with equity and not debt.

Although the *total value* of the firm increases, stockholders would be made worse off if the firm were to issue equity and repurchase debt. The recapitalization plan would fail because of a so-called "free rider" problem. That is, it would not pay any bondholder to tender their bonds to the firm at a price that reflected the risk of default just *prior* to the recapitalization. To see why, suppose you hold $10 of the face amount of the debt (or 10% of the outstanding issue). When the firm offers to pay you $9.057 (or 10% of $90.57), which is the pre-recapitalization market value of the bonds, you should decline to tender your bonds. Why? Because you can realize a higher value for your bonds if others tender but you don't. What would your bonds be worth after restructuring if everyone tenders their bonds except you? We show the payoffs in Table 15.2.

Table 15.2 Payoffs to Debt and Equity if 90% of the Debt is Repurchased at the Pre-Recapitalization Market Value from the Proceeds of an Equity Offering

Investment Outcomes	Probability	End-of-Period Assets Before Interest and Tax Payments*	Debt		Equity*
			Interest*	Principal*	
Good Results	.5	$130	$1	$10	$119
Bad Results	.5	$ 90	$1	$10	$ 79

* Dollar amounts in millions.

After the firm restructures its debt, your bonds would increase in value to $10 (or [10 + 1(1 - .4)]/1.06)) from their value of $9.057 (or 10% × 90.57) just prior to the announcement of the reorganization. The reason for this is that your debt would become riskless. You would receive $11 ($10 in principal and $1 in interest) regardless of whether the firm realizes good or bad results.

[15] Note that in this example, we have assumed that if the firm does poorly, the debtholders first receive fully taxable interest of $10 and then they receive principal payments on their debt of $80. As a result, the debtholders retain only $6 (or $10 (1 - .4)) of the $10 interest payment. From the bondholders' vantage point, however, a superior strategy would be for the firm to default on the payment of its interest on the debt in the event of a bad outcome. After a recapitalization of the firm, bondholders would receive $90 in principal, which is nontaxable. With this as a possible outcome, the bonds would increase in value from $90.57 to $92.46 (or by .5 × $4/1.06). Moreover, this increase in value of the

15.3 Debt Financing and the Cost of Reorganization

Indeed, every debtholder would want to hold out for the highest price (in this case a $100 tender offer for the firm's entire bond issue). If the firm did tender for its bonds at a price of $100, it would have to issue $100 of new stock to retire the bonds. But the new stockholders also know that with only stock and no debt in the firm's capital structure, the firm's market value would rise to $102.80. And the new stockholders would demand a fractional ownership of the firm that provides a future return with a present value equal to their $100 current contribution.

So if the recapitalization were to occur, the old shareholders would retain only $2.80 (or $102.80 - $100) of the restructured firm. By contrast, the market value of the equity *before* the restructuring was $9.35. So, as a result of the restructuring, the market value of the shares of the old shareholders would decline by $6.54 (or $9.35 - $2.80).[16] The bondholders would gain $9.43 on the exchange (or $100 - $90.57). How do they achieve this gain? They achieve it in part from the stockholders and in part from the advantages of clientele-based arbitrage.

Total Gain to Debtholders	$9.43
From Old Stockholders	$6.54
Increase in Value due to a Change in Clientele	$2.89

Prior to the recapitalization, the debt was risky. If the firm had experienced bad operating results, bondholders would have lost $20 in principal. Since this would occur 50% of the time, the present value of the loss is $9.43 (or .5 × $20/1.06). After the recapitalization, the debt would be riskless, and the debtholders would realize a gain of $9.43. Even though there is a gain to alter tax clienteles in this case, the old shareholders would prefer not to restructure unless a mechanism can be found for getting bondholders to agree to share enough of the gain with stockholders to make both classes of investors better off. But it is not obvious how this could be done with multiple investors.

An alternative restructuring strategy would be for the firm to issue stock and invest the proceeds of the stock issue in bonds *without* repurchasing the old bonds. But this strategy, like the one discussed earlier, would continue to make the existing outstanding bonds less risky, thereby transferring value to the old bondholders.

---

bonds would result in no reduction in the value of the stock. The source of the gain is the $4 in tax that is avoided on the interest half the time.

On the other hand, if the shareholders can control whether the payment to bondholders is made in the form of interest or principal, the stockholders may be able to negotiate more favorable terms. As we discuss more fully below, however, it will be quite difficult to renegotiate the debt if there are a number of bondholders. Note that this may be one reason that bond covenants are often written so as to give bondholders the right to declare bonds in default even before interest payments are missed. On the other hand, since bondholders do not always possess the same information about the firm's prospects as stockholders do, it may be impossible to write an effective bond indenture that prevents this situation from occurring.

16 The difference is due to a rounding error.

Chapter 15   Capital Structure and Dividend Policy

Still another approach would be for the firm to make a tender offer for all of the bonds at the market price of $90.57 or somewhat higher. The tender offer could be made contingent on receiving a minimum fraction of the outstanding bonds (for example 95%). If less than 95% of the outstanding bonds were tendered, the firm could commit itself to cancel the tender offer. By offering a price above $90.57, the bondholders and shareholders could share some of the $2.89 tax gain from changing clienteles. Theoretically, both groups could be made better off by the exchange, but small bondholders would still find it undesirable to tender at any price below $100.

Another possible strategy would be for the firm to issue equity and use the proceeds to acquire projects generating taxable income of sufficient risk to leave the value of the existing bonds unaffected. Here, information problems concerning the distribution of future cash flows on any proposed new projects might result in the old shareholders being forced to sell new stock at a discount from market value, and this would impede such restructuring activities.

It is worth noting that a large fraction of the outstanding corporate bonds are held by insurance companies and pension funds. Many corporate issuers place their debt privately with these institutional holders. As a result, the debtholders and the issuers know each other and are in close contact with one another. In this market, if it is in the best interest of a firm to restructure, it is more likely that bondholders and stockholders will reach a mutually agreeable restructuring plan. If institutional holders know each other and can monitor each others' actions, it is more likely that the parties will behave cooperatively. This is particularly so if they expect to interact repeatedly in the future. The mechanisms these institutional investors have attempted to devise to allow restructuring to occur at relatively low cost when the situation warrants it probably have much to do with the growth in the U.S. high-yield debt market in the latter half of the 1980s. Whether such restructuring turns out *in fact* to be of relative low cost remains an open question. Evidence from restructurings in the early 1990s casts some doubt on the effectiveness of these cooperative plans.

15.4 Evolution of the Tax Treatment of Debt and Equity in the U.S.

The tax laws in the U.S. have always treated debt differently from corporate equities. Whereas interest paid on debt is tax-deductible to corporate borrowers, dividends paid on common and preferred stock are not. In addition, whereas gains and losses on the repurchase of corporate bonds are taxable events to corporate issuers, the same is not true of share repurchases. On the investor side, interest from bonds is taxable as ordinary income whether paid out currently or not, while dividends and changes in the value of stocks are taxable only when realized. Moreover, dividends receive tax-favored treatment for corporate shareholders, and capital gains, besides being granted favorable tax-deferral treatment, have also been taxed at rates well below that of ordinary income to many shareholders.

323

15.4   Evolution of the Tax Treatment of Debt and Equity in the U.S.

Since the returns to corporate stock are tax-favored relative to bonds, investors are willing to accept lower pre-tax equity returns, on a risk-adjusted basis, to invest in them. This is similar to what we observe in the market for tax-exempt bonds, where the pre-tax yields are substantially below those of fully taxable bonds. The same can readily be observed in the market for adjustable-rate preferred stocks, held almost exclusively by corporations for whom the dividend income is largely tax exempt.

The pre-tax return differential on corporate common stocks is more difficult to document than it is for preferred stocks and tax-exempt bonds. The variability of stock returns is very large relative to the size of the possible tax effects. Moreover, there is a lack of consensus as to the appropriate risk adjustment to make to stock returns (e.g., single-factor pricing models such as the "capital asset pricing model" versus multi-factor pricing models) so that they can be compared to the returns of equally risky corporate bonds. But the tax-favored treatment of corporate stock in the hands of investors should result in lower risk-adjusted pre-tax returns. This reduction in rates exacts an implicit tax from investors. Symmetrically, the rate reduction represents an implicit tax subsidy to issuers of corporate stocks that compensates, at least partially, for the nondeductibility of dividends.[17]

Note that holding everything else constant, increasing the tax rate to investors on income from share ownership reduces the pre-tax wedge between shares and bonds (and therefore reduces the implicit tax subsidy to issuing shares). This makes stock more expensive for corporations to issue relative to bonds. Similarly, increasing corporate tax rates relative to personal tax rates favors corporate debt financing to the extent that such financing moves taxable income from the corporate sector to the noncorporate sector.

Prior to 1981, top marginal tax rates in the corporate sector were well below top marginal personal tax rates. Top personal rates were 70% from 1965 to 1981 whereas top corporate rates were in the 50% range. In the two decades preceding 1965, top personal rates were in the 90% range. During this period of time, top long-term capital gains rates to individuals ranged from 25% to 35%. Such a configuration of tax rates should have caused common stocks to bear substantial implicit taxes, and corporate debt financing might not have been the least bit tax-favored for many corporations during this period.

With the passage of the Economic Recovery Tax Act in 1981, personal tax rates were reduced dramatically while corporate rates were not. But at the same time, capital gains rates were also slashed. Moreover, with interest rates at record levels, the tax advantage of capital gain deferral was particularly high at this time. With top personal tax rates set at a level just above top corporate tax rates, the 1981 Tax Act began to move incentives in the direction of increased corporate borrowing, although this effect was mitigated by the reduction in capital gains tax rates

---

[17] See Joseph E. Stiglitz, "Taxation, Corporate Financial Policy, and the Cost of Capital," *Journal of Public Economics*, Vol. 2 (1973), pp. 1-34. Also, see Merton H. Miller, "Debt and Taxes," *Journal of Finance* (May, 1977), pp. 261-75; Alan J. Auerbach, "Taxation, Corporate Financial Policy and the Cost of Capital," *Journal of Economic Literature* (September, 1983), pp. 905-40; and Myron S. Scholes and Mark A. Wolfson, "The Cost of Capital and Changes in Tax Regimes," in *Uneasy Compromise: Problems of a Hybrid Income-Consumption Tax*, edited by Aaron, Galper and Pechman (Brookings Institution), 1988, pp. 157-194.

Chapter 15   Capital Structure and Dividend Policy

and high interest rates. By 1984, interest rates had subsided dramatically, reducing the tax-sheltered nature of common stocks to some extent, and this further promoted debt financing over equity financing by corporations.

As always, important nontax factors were also bearing on the corporate financing decisions during the early 1980s. In particular, mature corporations were discovering that it was efficient, from a corporate control standpoint, to restructure by buying back equity with the proceeds of debt issues, thereby committing to distribute "free cash flows" to investors through bond interest and principal repayments.[18] Moreover, increased reliance on strip financing (where institutional investors acquire combinations of junior debt along with equity and/or senior debt to reduce conflicts of interest among classes of investors) and the rise of active bondholders enabled more debt to be issued without the prospect of incurring excessive deadweight restructuring and bankruptcy costs in the event of default on corporate commitments to creditors.[19] But it does not seem appropriate to view these developments as being completely independent of the evolution of the tax law. The tax law may well have provided important incentives for the proliferation of these institutional arrangements.

The 1986 Tax Act had an even more dramatic impact on favoring corporate debt financing. Personal rates were reduced to a level well below that on corporations (28% for wealthy individuals versus 34% for corporations by 1988) and capital gains tax rates were increased dramatically. This, in conjunction with relatively low interest rates, substantially reduces the implicit tax on shares, thereby making equity financing a particularly expensive way to finance corporate investment.

That debt financing has become more tax-favored with the 1981 and 1986 Tax Acts is closely related to the fact that noncorporate forms have become more tax-favored relative to the corporate form of organization. In Chapter Four, we considered the tax advantages of the corporate form of organization relative to the partnership form. There we focused on the two levels of tax imposed on corporate profits versus the single level of taxation on partnership income. We showed that corporations can be tax-favored over partnerships if the corporate-level tax was lower than the personal tax rate of partners *and* if the shareholder-level tax was sufficiently low due to tax deferral opportunities and favorable capital gains tax rates.

We then argued that prior to 1981, the two organizational forms might have been equally attractive in the U.S. or perhaps the tax rules even favored the corporate form. We also argued that the 1981 Tax Act changed the calculus in the direction of favoring partnerships and that the 1986 Tax Act gave partnerships a decided edge for tax purposes. Despite these tax considerations, relatively few corporations changed to partnership form, both because of perceived *nontax*

---

[18] See Michael C. Jensen, "The Agency Cost of Free Cash Flow: Corporate Finance and Takeovers," *American Economic Review* (May 1986), pp. 323-29.

[19] Michael C. Jensen, "Capital Markets, Organizational Innovation, and Restructuring," Working Paper, Harvard Business School (January 1989). Others have argued that high-yield bonds are actually more dispersed in ownership than are holdings of traditional debt, which could *raise*, rather than lower, renegotiation costs. See, for example, Mark Gertler and R. Glenn Hubbard, "Taxation, Corporate Capital Structure, and Financial Distress," in Lawrence H. Summers, ed., *Tax Policy and the Economy* (National Bureau of Economic Research, 1990), pp. 43-71.

advantages of corporate form for widely held companies and due to the costs of *converting* from corporate form.

Given this, it becomes desirable to distribute profits from the corporation to shareholders in ways *other* than by paying dividends; that is, in ways that are tax-deductible to the corporation. If all corporate earnings before interest and taxes could be distributed to investors as interest, the corporation would essentially be converted to a partnership for tax purposes. There would be no entity-level tax imposed on the corporation,[20] and all owners would pay tax at the personal level on interest income. It would be as if the shareholders owned income bonds. In Chapter Eighteen, we discuss limits on the firm's ability to distribute corporate profits in tax-deductible ways, but here we wish to emphasize that debt financing is a tax-favored way to capitalize the corporation whenever the partnership is tax-favored as an organizational form.

Recall from Chapters Thirteen and Fourteen, when we discussed multinational tax planning, that debt financing is also a tax-advantageous way to capitalize foreign subsidiaries located in high-tax jurisdictions. The reason is essentially the same as that here. Equity financing of a foreign subsidiary means that the subsidiary's profits are subjected to local taxation. Upon repatriation of profits by way of dividends, the home country will tax the profits again only to the extent the home-country tax rate is higher than the foreign tax rate. If the home-country tax rate is higher, equity financing enables profits earned abroad to be reinvested and compounded without paying the repatriation tax until the money is brought back home. Like a single-premium-deferred-annuity contract, some of the tax is deferred.

But if the home-country tax rate is *lower*, and the firm faces limits on foreign tax credits, it pays to shift taxable income out of the foreign subsidiary and *to* the parent company. Debt financing is one important way to achieve this. So the 1986 Tax Act not only favors debt financing in the U.S., it also favors debt financing of foreign operations in such countries as Japan and Germany and other high-tax jurisdictions.

It is important to bear in mind, however, that the tax advantages of debt financing disappear for firms that are unprofitable. For such firms, the interest on debt yields no (or a reduced level of) tax benefits. It would be better for such firms to issue securities that are tax-favored in the hands of investors, like common stock or preferred stock. Such securities yield *implicit* tax deductions, since investors are willing to accept lower risk-adjusted returns for these tax-favored securities.

As for empirical evidence, corporate restructuring took a decided turn in the mid-1980s. Corporations in the U.S. substituted debt financing for equity financing. Net new borrowing by corporations exploded to nearly $160 billion a year during 1984-1986 from $66 billion per year from 1978-1983, and the popularity of debt financing continued through the end of the 1980s. The total supply of corporate bonds issued by U.S. corporations increased from less than half a trillion dollars at year-end 1980 to nearly $1.4 trillion worth at year-end 1988.[21] At

---

[20] This ignores any corporate "alternative minimum tax" that may be assessed.

[21] The source of these data is the *Flow of Funds* tabulated by the Federal Reserve Board.

Chapter 15   Capital Structure and Dividend Policy

the same time there was a quantum leap in the magnitude of both share repurchases ($37 billion per year 1984-1986 and $54 billion in 1987 versus $5 billion per year 1978-1983) and other equity retirements via corporate acquisitions ($75 billion per year, 1984-1986, versus $15 billion per year 1980-1983).[22, 23] In 1989, General Electric alone announced a $10 billion stock repurchase program and IBM announced a $5 billion repurchase program. Another eleven companies each announced repurchases exceeding $1 billion. (*Wall Street Journal*, January 2, 1990, p. R8). The replacement of equity with debt resulted in an increase in interest payments per dollar of income before interest and taxes from $.33 during the 1970s to $.56 during the 1980s.[24]

As suggested earlier, the shift in emphasis to debt has been much slower than would be predicted if tax minimization were the only consideration. There are nontax costs to having high debt-to-equity ratios. These include the possibility of incurring deadweight reorganization costs in the event of bankruptcy and the costs of various restrictions that lenders impose on borrowers' activities because lenders cannot monitor borrowers' actions costlessly.

On the other hand, there are also nontax reasons for the increased use of debt by corporations over this period. These include (1) discouraging management from making inefficient investments by removing excess cash in the form of interest and principal payments (so-called "free cash flow") from old stable companies that lack profitable investments in their traditional businesses; (2) aligning the interests of management more closely with those of shareholders through more meaningful compensation schemes that involve management holding stock in highly leveraged companies; and (3) the growth in restructuring techniques that reduce the deadweight costs of a reorganization by avoiding the bankruptcy costs that we referred to above.

Tax and nontax considerations have undoubtedly worked together to cause debt to increase for U.S. corporations. Note, however, that in countries where there is no obvious tax advantage of debt over equity (because corporate profits are not taxed twice),[25] debt has *not* increased as it has in the U.S. in the 1980s. Investment bankers from the U.S. interested in exporting to foreign enterprises the debt-financing techniques (like leveraged buyouts) learned at home, should not be surprised if they have a tough time selling their wares.

---

[22] The 1984 Deficit Reduction Act also eliminated withholding taxes on newly-issued bonds and other evidences of indebtedness that generate portfolio interest income to foreign investors. Bonds purchased by foreigners skyrocketed from less than half-a-billion dollars per quarter over the preceding decade to over ten billion dollars per quarter over the next three years. *Flow of Funds Accounts, Fourth Quarter 1988* (Board of Governors of the Federal Reserve System, Washington, D.C.)

[23] *Federal Income Tax Aspects of Corporate Financial Structures* (Joint Committee on Taxation), January 18, 1989, Table I-A, I-B on pp. 8-9.

[24] Gertler and Hubbard, *op. cit.*

[25] Corporate profits can avoid double taxation in one of two ways: (1) through a corporate tax imputation system, where shareholders receive a tax credit for corporate taxes they have paid indirectly (as in most European countries); or (2) by exempting a significant fraction of capital gains from taxation at the shareholder level (as in Japan).

15.5   Retained Earnings and Dividend Policy

If partnerships are deemed to be tax-advantageous relative to corporations, it is important to determine whether existing corporations should liquidate (so individual investors can reinvest the funds in ways that result in single-level taxation) or whether retained earnings should be reinvested at the corporate level. To answer this question, we begin by ignoring information costs.[26] Suppose a corporation issued equity at its inception and used the proceeds to invest in research and development projects. After deducting the cost of the investment as an expense, it has received a cash return from the project equal to the initial cost of the investment. So, the firm has no taxable income or retained earnings, but it has generated cash equal to the original equity issue. It also expects additional cash income in the future from the R & D effort.

Assume that the firm distributes these cash returns to investors. In the absence of any "earnings and profits" in the corporation, any cash distributions made to shareholders represent a return of capital that is untaxed but reduces the tax basis of shares until the basis falls to zero. As a result, the shareholders have a tax basis of zero on their shares. This basis reduction means that when the shares are sold in the future, taxable capital gain will be increased by the same amount. Moreover, any future after-tax distributions made by the corporation (either by paying dividends or making share repurchases) will generate fully taxable income to the stockholders for the full amount (since the shareholder basis can not be reduced below zero).

When the firm earns another $1 of after-tax corporate income, should the firm retain it or pay out the $1 as a dividend? The answer depends on a number of factors. For example, as we will see in Chapter Eighteen, it depends importantly on whether there exist projects that generate returns above the competitive rate. Where only competitive projects are available, undertaking them through the corporation is approximately equivalent to having investors undertake them on private account following a dividend distribution. If it distributes the $1 as a dividend today, shareholders pay taxes at their own personal tax rates, t_{po}, and reinvest the after-tax income on their own account for n periods at an after tax rate of $R_b(1 - t_{pn})$ or r_{pn} per period.[27] If the firm retains the $1 of after-tax corporate income, on the other hand, and invests it on corporate account, it returns $R_b(1 - t_{cn})$ or r_{cn} per period after tax until it finally distributes the accumulated amount of retained earnings. At that time, shareholders pay tax on the distribution at tax rate t_{pn}. So, we can compare the two alternatives as follows:

---

[26] As we discussed earlier, much of corporate activity might not be displaced because, for nontax reasons, operating in corporate form might dominate partnerships, but these benefits may be overstated.

[27] Note that dividend income is investment income against which investment interest can be deducted. Hence, if t_{po} exceeds the implicit tax on tax-favored investments, borrowing to purchase such assets could reduce the taxpayer's tax burden to a lower level that includes implicit taxes, as we have argued before.

Liquidate and invest on personal
account for n periods:

$$\$1(1 - t_{po}) (1 + r_{pn})^n$$

Retain and invest on corporate
account for n periods before
liquidating:

$$\$1(1 + r_{cn})^n (1 - t_{pn}),$$

where r_{pn} and r_{cn} should be interpreted as annualized rates of return available over the n-period horizon.

The best strategy depends upon two factors: (1) the investor's marginal tax rate today, t_{po}, versus the investor's marginal tax rate in the future, t_{pn} (a decreasing tax rate, or an ability to convert dividend income into a capital gain taxed at a reduced rate, favors dividend deferral), and (2) the corporate versus investor tax rate (a higher corporate rate favors current payout).

Note that if tax rates are constant over time and if corporate and personal tax rates coincide, it is a matter of indifference whether the competitive projects are undertaken in corporate or partnership form, when the corporation is an all-retained earnings firm and shareholders have a zero tax basis in their shares. This is the now-traditional trapped equity argument from the public finance literature.[28] At first blush, this may be a counter-intuitive result. After all, corporate income generates both an entity-level and a shareholder-level tax. The explanation lies in the fact that, marginally, investments financed by retained earnings do not generate a shareholder-level tax.

Notice that investors have an important *timing option* in that they may be able to sell their shares when their tax rates are lower than current rates. For example, if investors find themselves in an alternative minimum tax (AMT) position (a 21% marginal tax rate prior to the 1990 Tax Act, when the rate was increased to 24%) when at other times they are in a 28%, 31%, or even 33% marginal tax rate, they could find that the timing option is quite valuable.[29] Moreover, capital gains can be vastly superior to dividend income in each of the following circumstances: (1) holding shares until death (at which time there is no income tax on the appreciation since the basis in the stock is reset to its market value at the time of death); (2) donating the shares to charity and escaping the tax on the appreciation of the stock; (3) transferring shares to a lower tax-rate taxpayer as a gift; (4) planning for the possibility of a reintroduction of a favorable capital gains tax rate; and (5) realizing gains to offset unexpected capital losses from other ventures.[30]

---

[28] See, for example, Mervyn King, *Public Policy and the Corporation* (London: Chapman and Hall), 1977 and Alan J. Auerbach, "Taxation, Corporate Financial Policy and the Cost of Capital," *Journal of Economic Literature* (September, 1983), pp. 905-40.

[29] Taxpayers that make large charitable contributions of property that has appreciated in value or hold investments in municipal bonds might find themselves subject to the AMT and not eligible for AMT credit in the future. The same is true of taxpayers with substantial sums of state income and property taxes and miscellaneous itemized deductions, none of which are tax-deductible in calculating the AMT. These taxpayers wish to accelerate the recognition of taxable income to the point where the next dollar of income is taxed at their ordinary marginal rate currently and the next dollar of expense reduces taxes at the AMT rate .

[30] Net capital losses are limited to $3,000 per year in the U.S., but they can be offset by realized capital gains.

A second consideration is the after-tax rate of return, r_{cn}, that can be earned on reinvesting the retained earnings at the corporate level for the n periods, as compared to the after-tax rate of return on personal account, r_{pn}. If a corporation that faces a 40% tax rate reinvests corporate profits in taxable bonds yielding 10% before tax, its after-tax rate of return on the reinvestment of corporate income would be 6% while an investor facing a 30% tax rate would earn 7% after tax. This, however, stacks the deck against the corporation. If the individual investor is the marginal investor in bonds, the rate of return on municipal bonds would be 7%, the same as the after-tax rate of return on taxable bonds to the individual investor. But then because the corporation would be an inframarginal investor, it, too, could earn 7% by investing in municipal bonds.

The corporation could also invest the after-tax returns on corporate projects in preferred stock, the dividends from which are largely exempt from corporate taxation. Or corporations (and individuals) could invest the after-tax cash flows in life insurance policies (after carefully considering implicit taxes reflected in how the policy is priced). Optimal corporate decisions depend on identifying the marginal investor setting prices of securities in the market. The choice of payout or retention is sensitive to differences in after-tax rates of return on corporate and personal account and to the length of the reinvestment horizon.

Many claim that dividends are used to signal the firm's future prospects to its stockholders without fully informing competitors about the nature of these prospects. It is also claimed that the payment of dividends (or the repurchase of shares) keeps management's "feet to the fire." They work harder if there is less cash on hand.

Without the signalling advantages of dividend payments, the repurchase of shares is more advantageous than is paying dividends for taxpaying shareholders because (1) it is possible for shareholders to determine for themselves whether to "declare their own dividends" by selling shares: those that want current cash flow can sell shares (tax-exempt shareholders, such as pension funds, can do so at no cost), and (2) unlike dividends, where all funds received are taxed (to the extent of earnings and profits), share purchases are not fully taxable to shareholders because part of the payment is a return of shareholders' initial investment in the firm, which is not taxed currently. In our R&D illustration, however, the sale of shares would result in full taxation at the personal level because the basis in the hands of shareholders was zero. In most situations, however, shareholders have a positive basis in their shares.

No wonder share repurchases have become so significant as a means of distributing after-tax corporate profits to shareholders. The only puzzle is why it took corporations so long to catch on. Indeed, the tax advantage of share repurchases over dividends was *reduced* by the 1986 Tax Act, because of the reduction in the capital gains advantage. On the other hand, share repurchases financed by debt issuances can be highly tax-advantageous when double taxation of corporate profits becomes onerous. Similar advantages to repurchasing a corporation's own shares may be secured by acquiring the shares of *another* corporation with cash or bonds.[31]

---

[31] See, for example, Christopher R. Petruzzi, "Mergers and the Double Taxation of Corporation Income," *Journal of Accounting and Public Policy* (Summer 1988), pp. 1-15.

Summary of Key Points

1. New tax rules, by changing relative tax rates across time, across economic activities, and across organizational forms, change the implicit tax rates on economic activities. When implicit tax rates change, the natural clienteles for these activities also change. Transaction costs, however, restrain taxpayers from adjusting completely to these changes in tax rules. Taxpayers undertake less clientele-based arbitrage than they would were it not for these costs.

2. Like a change in tax rules, change in a taxpayer's economic circumstances can induce the taxpayer to alter investment and financing plans. Once again, however, transaction costs impede the adjustment.

3. Identifying a desirable capital structure policy is broader than simply determining the correct debt/equity mix. Capital structure policy includes the many financing alternatives available to the firm, such as compensation (including pension) policies, supplier-contracting policies, transfer pricing policies among affiliates, preferred stock, convertible debt, warrants, operating and capital leases, *as well as* debt and equity.

4. Changes in investment decisions are substitutes for changes in capital structure policy when new tax rules or altered economic circumstances that taxpayers face yield changes in tax clienteles. Because of transaction costs, however, such substitutes are imperfect. The firm can divest or acquire individual assets or subsidiaries, change capital expenditure policy, form joint ventures, change the level of research and development and advertising expenditures, as well as alter the mix of domestic and international investments.

5. The firm's operating and financing history affects its current operating and financing plans. Because of the idiosyncratic tax and nontax costs associated with changing clienteles, firms respond in idiosyncratic ways to changes in tax rules and changes in their economic circumstances.

6. The tax law encourages low-taxed firms to finance their activities by issuing high implicitly taxed assets. These include preferred stock and common stock. Highly taxed firms are encouraged to finance their activities by issuing high explicitly taxed assets such as risky bonds.

7. Low-taxed firms are encouraged to invest in high explicitly taxed assets such as fully taxable bonds, and highly taxed firms should invest in low explicitly taxed assets such as municipal bonds and other tax-sheltered investments.

8. Outside observers of firm behavior might have difficulty documenting that firms adjust their investment and financing strategies in a manner consistent with changes in their tax status. The reason is that while some firms might adjust specific components of their investment mix, others

might adjust specific components of their financing mix, and still others will adjust components of each.

9. History can lock a firm into a particular investment or financing program. Given a change in economic circumstances, the firm might not be able to adjust its capital structure or financing decisions without the cooperation of others. For example, the firm might not be able to reduce its debt because it would transfer too much value to debtholders at the expense of equityholders. Firms must account for the possibility of these "lock-ins" in setting their investment and financing policies.

10. Given a corporate-level tax, the greater is the implicit tax rate on stocks, the less tax advantageous is debt relative to equity.

11. Because top personal tax rates were 70% from 1965 to 1981, and as high as 90% in the two prior decades, when top long-term capital gains rates to individuals ranged from 25% to 35%, common stock investments bore substantial implicit taxes. Debt financing at the corporate level might well have been tax-*disadvantageous* during this time period.

12. Subsequent to 1981, personal tax rates were reduced substantially relative to corporate rates. Capital gains tax rates were also reduced. Were it not for lower capital gains tax rates, and the high interest rates at the time of the 1981 Tax Act, corporations might have borrowed considerably more than they did. By 1984, when interest rates had fallen substantially, corporations had begun a period of dramatically increased borrowing that was to last for at least half a dozen years. The market value of corporate debt-to-equity ratios, however, did not increase as dramatically because the market value of equity also increased during this period.

13. The 1986 Tax Act increased the capital gains tax rate and lowered the corporate-level tax rate. The personal tax rate was set below the corporate tax rate. This configuration of tax rates encouraged corporations to issue additional debt.

14. If all corporate earnings before interest and taxes could be distributed to investors as interest, the corporation would essentially be taxed as a partnership. But there are limits to the amount of interest that may be distributed to debtholders. For example, shareholders must earn a return. Moreover, nontax costs limit the amount of debt that the firm can support.

15. When all corporate distributions are taxed as dividends, it may not matter whether the firm pays a dividend currently or reinvests earnings and pays out larger dividends in the future. This indifference between current versus future dividends will be present, for example, if personal tax rates remain constant over time, the corporate tax rate is approximately equal to the personal rate, and the reinvestment is in projects that earn normal (that is, competitive) rates of return.

16. Under most circumstances, however, there are tax reasons for the firm to *retain* its earnings. Such a policy gives shareholders an option to receive dividends by selling their shares when their tax rates are lower.

Retention of earnings also gives shareholders the option of avoiding taxes by using their shares to make charitable donations or bequests. On the other hand, the payment of dividends may provide information to shareholders about the firm's future prospects that for competitive reasons can't be revealed directly by management.

Discussion Questions

1. True or False?
   a. Capital structure policy involves deciding on the optimal debt-to-equity ratio for a firm.
   b. Corporations cannot engage in clientele-based arbitrage because tax rule restrictions prevent it.
   c. Many finance textbooks, in comparing the tax advantages of debt and equity, assume that the firm's operating decisions are fixed.
   d. Tax-planning substitutes are always imperfect.
2. When might a firm wish to issue straight debt rather than common stock, warrants, preferred stock, or convertible debt? How do these financing alternatives differ along the tax dimension?
3. Why might it be more costly to roll over short-term debt than to issue long-term debt? When might firms wish to issue short-term instead of long-term debt despite these costs?
4. How might the firm and its customers or suppliers plan for changes in the firm's tax rates? What nontax costs are associated with such plans?
5. How might the firm alter its investment strategies if its tax rate changes? And how might such changes affect financing strategies?
6. When would it be tax-advantageous for a firm to issue equity and to redeem its outstanding debt? Why might it prove costly to effect such a recapitalization? What contracting alternatives might the firm employ to mitigate the nontax impediments to effecting the recapitalization?
7. During what time periods over the last 30 years might the tax rules have favored corporations over partnerships in the U.S.? In other countries? Why? Over what time periods might the tax rules have favored equity financing over debt financing? What are the relations among your answers to the financing question and the organizational form questions?
8. Does it matter whether an all-retained-earnings firm distributes earnings currently by way of a dividend or reinvests these earnings and pays dividends to shareholders in the future?
9. Why have share repurchase programs only recently begun to be significant channels for distributing corporate profits to shareholders? How do they differ from dividends along both tax and nontax dimensions?

CHAPTER 16
Empirical Evidence of Clienteles and the Importance of Nontax Factors in Tax Planning: The Case of Commercial Banks[1]

This chapter presents evidence that pertains to the predictions in Chapter Fifteen regarding effects of changes in tax rules and economic circumstances on capital structure. Our focus is on commercial banks. We examine both how the banking industry responds to changes in tax rules that affect the entire industry and how individual banks respond to changes in their own tax-paying status. The latter study of individual banks allows us to assess the substitutability of various investment and financing strategies and to measure the degree of adjustment to changes in tax status.

We find strong evidence that proposed and actual changes in the taxation of municipal bonds held by banks during the 1980s caused the banks to adjust their holding of these securities. We also show that individual banks changed their economic balance sheets as their tax-paying status changed, but find that they did not adjust investment and financing decisions instantaneously or to the extent they would have if there had been no adjustment costs.

By studying individual bank behavior we are able to measure tradeoffs between tax and nontax costs. By measuring the tax benefits that would have resulted from particular strategies that were *not* undertaken, a lower-bound estimate of the perceived nontax *cost* of implementing these strategies is obtained.[2] We find that banks with low levels of regulatory capital voluntarily realize securities gains to increase book income and bolster regulatory capital, paying substantial taxes as a result. The realization of securities gains (or the postponement of securities losses) increases book regulatory capital, which regulators monitor. This enhances the ability of banks to garner deposits at the

---

[1]This chapter is adapted from research that was conducted jointly with G. Peter Wilson (Harvard Business School).

[2]This assumes that the firm's management is aware of the available tax benefits.

low rate of interest made possible by the Federal guarantee offered to depositors, and to avoid regulatory intervention into their other investment and financing strategies.

We select the commercial banking industry not because banks are proto-typical taxpayers, but because in this industry there are data on a large number of firms that are relatively homogeneous in their investment activities and financing methods. This allows us to develop tests of the trade-offs between tax minimization and nontax costs and to estimate the relation between banks' propensities to realize losses on their holdings of marketable securities and their tax-paying status. Moreover, banks (along with other financial institutions) have enjoyed a variety of special tax provisions that are important to the design of our tests. Finally, we can identify changes in tax policy aimed specifically at banks, that permit us to test how the entire industry responds to a change in tax legislation.

In Section 16.1, we motivate and present results relating to banks' holdings of municipal bonds. As predicted, we find strong evidence of a decrease in municipal bond holdings during calendar quarters in which tax legislation discouraged such investments and an increase in holdings during calendar quarters in which legislative developments encouraged such investments.

In Section 16.2, we test whether differences in tax-paying status across banks give rise to investment and financing clienteles. We find that banks with net operating losses take fewer long positions in tax-favored assets (municipal bonds and direct lease assets) and more short positions in tax-favored assets (preferred stock and common stock) than do tax-paying banks.

Our sample includes many banks with net operating loss carryforwards, and this suggests the importance of nontax costs of restructuring for banks even though bank balance sheets would seem less costly to restructure than the balance sheets of industrial corporations (since most bank assets and liabilities consist of financial instruments). Moreover, the nontax costs are not simply direct costs to buy and sell assets, since many tax-paying banks do not sell marketable securities that have declined in value to realize ordinary tax losses despite low transaction costs.

In Section 16.3, we develop and test a simple model in which banks trade off the tax advantages of realizing securities losses against the costs of reporting reduced regulatory capital and financial reporting income. We find that banks make this trade-off in the predicted manner acting as though nominal book values are important both to regulators (in their consideration of whether to impose constraints on bank management) as well as to shareholders. This evidence indicates that efficient tax planning may be very different from simple tax minimization.

16.1 The Relation Between Changes in Tax Rules and Investment Decisions

As discussed in Chapter Six, the U.S. tax code precludes a deduction for interest expense incurred on debt used to purchase or carry tax-exempt bonds. Prior to the

Tax Reform Act of 1986, banks enjoyed an exemption from this restriction.[3,4] As a result, banks have invested very heavily in the municipal bond market. At year-end 1985, 10% of commercial bank assets were invested in municipal bonds, and banks held over 30% of all municipal securities outstanding.[5] Prior to 1983, banks could deduct all interest incurred to finance municipal bonds.[6] Between 1983 and 1987, however, Congress passed three laws that gradually reduced this deduction from 100% to 0% of the interest incurred to finance *new acquisitions* of municipal bonds. The 1982 Tax Act reduced the deduction to 85% of the interest associated with bonds acquired after 1982 but grandfathered a 100% deduction for bonds acquired before 1983. Similarly, the 1984 Tax Act reduced the deduction to 80% of the interest associated with bonds acquired after 1982 but grandfathered the historical deduction rates for bonds acquired before 1983. Finally, with the exception of interest on debt issued by "small municipalities" (entities issuing less than 10 million dollars of debt), the 1986 Tax Act eliminated the deduction of interest incurred to finance municipal bonds acquired after August 7, 1986 but grandfathered historical deduction rates for bonds acquired earlier.[7]

Near year-end 1985, a legislative proposal was introduced that, if passed, would have precluded any interest deductions incurred in connection with holdings of municipal bonds acquired after December 31, 1985. Although this proposal was never enacted, our empirical analysis considers whether banks responded to this proposal and to its congressional defeat in the first quarter of 1986. These legislative events are summarized in Table 16.1.

The motivation for banks to hold municipal bonds is evident from the following arbitrage strategy:

Position	Return
Long in tax-exempt bonds	R_e
Short in taxable bonds (issue debt) (where d is the fraction of R_b that is tax-deductible)	$-(R_b - R_b dt),$
Net	$R_e - R_b(1 - dt)$

---

[3] The bank exception was challenged by the Treasury Department prior to our sample period. For a dicussion of this and the resulting stock market response, see Silvia A. Madeo and Morton Pincus, "Stock Market Behavior and Tax Rule Changes: The Case of the Disallowance of Certain Interest Deductions Claimed by Banks," *The Accounting Review* (July, 1985), pp. 407-429.

[4] In addition to the bank exemption, all U.S. corporations could (and can still) hold up to 2% of their assets in tax-exempt bonds and still deduct the interest on attributed debt. Although banks represent the only explicit exception to the nondeductibility of interest to purchase or carry municipal bonds beyond the 2% *de minimus* rule, property-casualty insurance companies implicitly have had similar opportunities. Moreover, unlike banks, their opportunity to deduct interest to carry municipal bonds continues beyond the passage of the 1986 Tax Act to a substantial extent.

[5] See Salomon Brothers, *Prospects for Financial Markets in 1986* (1986).

[6] Interest expense incurred in connection with holding municipal bonds is determined by allocating total interest expense to specific assets in proportion to their book values.

[7] Under certain circumstances, a portion of municipal bond interest income is a preference item for purposes of calculating the alternative minimum tax. In addition, if municipal bonds are issued (after 1986) for a "nongovernmental purpose," *all* of the interest is a tax preference item that is subject to the alternative minimum tax.

16.1   The Relation Between Changes in Tax Rules and Investment Decisions

Table 16.1   Legislative Events Relating to the Deductibility of Interest Incurred to Carry Municipal-Bond Investments

Time Period	Predicted Effect on Municipal Bond Holdings	Legislative Event
1) First quarter 1983	-	Deductibility of interest expense allocated to municipal bonds acquired after 12/31/82 was reduced from 100% to 85%.
2) First quarter 1985	-	Deductibility of interest expense allocated to municipal bonds acquired after 12/31/82 was reduced further from 85% to 80%.
3) Fourth quarter 1985	+	Proposal to eliminate the deductibility of *all* interest expense allocated to municipal bonds acquired after 12/31/85.
4) First quarter 1986	-	Congressional defeat of the proposal described in (3) above.
5) Fourth quarter 1986	-	Elimination of the deductibility of *all* interest expense allocated to municipal bonds acquired after 8/7/86.

For $R_b = 10\%$, $R_e = 6.5\%$, $t = 50\%$, and $d = 1$ (interest fully deductible), banks earn an arbitrage profit of 1.5% of the amount invested. Note that the lower is the value of d, the less profitable is the arbitrage strategy. For example, if d is reduced to 80%, the arbitrage profit declines by two-thirds to only 0.5%. The legislative developments in the 1980s all relate to changes in d.

These tax changes lead us to expect that banks reduced their concentration in municipal bonds during the first quarters of 1983 and 1985, increased the level of their municipal bond investment at year-end 1985 and reduced it in both the first and fourth quarters of 1986 as well as in all quarters of 1987 and beyond. In Table 16.2 we report the average percentage of bank marketable securities portfolios invested in municipal bonds ("muni mix") at the end of each quarter from the beginning of 1976 through the first quarter of 1987 for the 150 firms on the quarterly Bank Compustat tape.[8]

In addition to the six "treatment" quarters listed in Table 16.1 (including the first quarter of 1987), there are 38 quarterly percentage changes in the average muni mix. Over these non-treatment quarters, the average muni mix is 43%, the average change in muni mix is -.26%, and the standard deviation in the quarterly change in muni mix is 0.89%. In only one of these 38 quarters did the change in muni mix exceed two percent in absolute value.

---

[8] If banks are the marginal holders of municipal bonds, changes in tax laws could affect bond prices to such a degree that bank holdings in these securities would be unaffected. Had we not found the strong effects that we did, we would have looked more carefully at bond prices.

Chapter 16   Empirical Evidence of Clienteles: Commercial Banks

Table 16.2 Association of Changes in Municipal Bond Investment Mix With Legislative Events

Event period	Direction of the expected change in the muni mix	Actual percentage change in the muni mix[a]	Number of standard deviations from the sample mean[b]	Probability of an observation this extreme occurring by chance[c]
First quarter 1983	−	-3.52%	-3.66	<.001
First quarter 1985	−	-2.15%	-2.12	.020
Fourth quarter 1985	+	+6.36%	+7.44	<.001
First quarter 1986	−	-1.65%	-1.56	.060
Fourth quarter 1986	−	-3.59%	-3.74	<.001
First quarter 1987	−	-2.71%	-2.75	<.010

[a]Relative to an average muni mix of 43% from the first quarter of 1976 through the first quarter of 1987.

[b]The sample mean is -0.23% per quarter over the 38 non-event quarters beginning with the first quarter of 1976.

[c]This assumes a t-distribution; the sample distribution does appear to be normally distributed. We also assume independence across periods.

Table 16.2 provides clear evidence that bank asset management policies are influenced by taxes. For all six of the treatment quarters, the muni mix changed in the direction predicted and these differences are highly significant. The weakest of the results is for the first quarter of 1986 (testing for a reversal of an expected buildup in the muni mix during the fourth quarter of 1985), although even here, the change could have occurred by chance only six times in one hundred. Moreover, the muni mix in the second quarter of 1986 declined 2.18%. If this were treated as an event quarter (as a continuation of the reversal of the buildup from the fourth quarter of 1985), the decline would be significant at the 3% level.

The results in Table 16.2 do not control for the changing aggregate supply of municipal bonds in the market. For example, there was an unprecedented increase in the net supply of municipal bonds during the fourth quarter of 1985. To the extent that this is unrelated to a change in bank tax legislation, it could bias our test results. To guard against this possibility, we obtained quarterly data from 1975-1 through 1987-1 on the aggregate change in supply of municipal bonds and the change in the amount of municipal bonds held by banks.[9] More precisely, both the aggregate and bank data are "seasonally adjusted annual rates of net flows for tax-exempt obligations," as published in the *Flow of Funds Accounts* by the Federal

---

[9] In contrast to the results reported in Table 16.2, the results in Table 16.3 are based on changes in aggregate bank holdings of municipal bonds rather than changes in the average mix of municipal bonds in banks' investment portfolios. Also, the Compustat banks used earlier are a subset of the banks included in the Federal Reserve Board's calculations and the sample period here is slightly longer.

Table 16.3 Association of Changes in Bank Municipal Bond Holdings with Legislative Events, Controlling for Changes in Aggregate Supply

| Event period | Direction of expected change | Net change in muni supply ($billion, annualized) | | | Standardized difference[b] |
| | | Actual | | Predicted for banks[a] | |
		Aggregate	Banks only		
First quarter 1983	-	50.5	-10.5	10.4	-3.12[c]
First quarter 1985	-	59.6	-6.2	11.9	-2.69[d]
Fourth quarter 1985	+	378.6	184.3	64.5	8.59[c]
First quarter 1986	-	-15.5	-56.1	-0.5	-7.98[c]
Fourth quarter 1986	-	20.7	-69.7	5.4	-11.20[c]
First quarter 1987	-	55.5	-7.5	11.2	-2.78[d]

[a]The predicted change in holdings from the regression of bank holdings on change in aggregate supply. Prediction is $0.5 billion + 0.165 × the change in aggregate supply. The t-statistic on the slope coefficient of 0.165 is 4.6.

[b]The difference between the actual and predicted change in bank holdings divided by its standard error.

[c]Significant at less than the 0.001 level, one-tailed test.

[d]Significant at less than the 0.005 level, one-tailed test.

Reserve Board of Governors. For the 43 nonevent quarters during this period, we relate the change in bank holdings of municipal bonds to the change in aggregate supply in the market to calibrate banks' normal share of aggregate supply changes.

A simple regression reveals that banks have increased their ownership of municipal bonds by about $0.5 billion per quarter plus 16.5% of the aggregate change in supply of municipal bonds.[10] Using this prediction model, we generate standardized residual changes in bank holdings of municipal bonds for each of our six event quarters. That is, the residual difference between the actual net change in muni holdings and the predicted net change is standardized by dividing by its standard error. The results in Table 16.3 are even more striking than those reported in Table 16.2. The smallest of the absolute values of the standardized residuals for the event quarter is equal to 2.69. Notably, the standardized residual for 1986-1, the 1 event quarter exhibiting only marginally statistically significant behavior in Table 16.2 (where there is no correction for changes in aggregate supply), is -7.98.[11]

Bank holdings of municipal bonds have continued to decline beyond the first quarter of 1987. According to the Federal Reserve Statistics, commercial bank holdings of tax-exempt securities declined by $31 billion in 1987, by an additional

[10] The slope coefficient has a t-value of 4.6, and the regression exhibits an adjusted R^2 of 34%.

[11] The standardized residual for 1986-2 is -2.73. Moreover, the results are qualitatively unaffected if our prediction estimates are based exclusively on data for the period 1975-1981.

$13 billion during the first half of 1988, by $18 billion in 1989, and by $12 billion during the first three quarters of 1990. This is after increasing by $18 billion per year from 1980-85. This is exactly what we would expect as munis held by banks mature, since they are too costly to replace. Collectively, this evidence indicates substantial industry-wide responsiveness of bank holdings of municipal bonds to legislative changes that alter tax clienteles.

16.2. The Relations Between Marginal Tax Rates and Asset Allocations and Capital Structures

We turn now to investigate whether individual banks alter their investment and financing decisions in response to changes in their marginal tax rates. Specifically, we examine the cross-sectional association between tax status and balance sheet composition.

On the assets side of the balance sheet, we investigate how banks change their holdings of municipal bonds and direct leases as their tax status changes (from being a tax-payer to generating net operating loss carryforwards or vice versa). Like municipal bonds, direct leases are highly tax-favored (due to accelerated depreciation and investment tax credits). Competition for the right to receive such benefits will naturally result in such assets bearing implicit tax through reduced rental rates charged to lessees. Consequently, these assets should be less attractive to firms with tax loss carryforwards.

On the equities side of the balance sheet, the choice among capital notes, preferred stock, and common stock as a means of financing should also be a function of the marginal tax rate of the issuer. Preferred stock and common stock pay dividends that were 85% tax exempt to most corporate investors during 1980-1985 and 80% tax exempt during 1986.[12] Since corporations are the dominant holders of preferred stock, the pretax cost of debt is substantially higher (on the order of 25% higher during the mid 1980s) than that of equally risky preferred stock.

Common stocks offered investors a second component of tax-favored returns relative to the return on capital notes during the period covered in this study. The capital gains earned on common stocks were not only tax deferred, they were also taxed at favorable rates. Since capital notes give rise to interest that is tax-deductible, whereas dividend distributions on common and preferred stock are *not* tax-deductible, we would expect banks with relatively high marginal tax rates to issue capital notes and those with low marginal tax rates to issue common and preferred stock.[13]

A few caveats are in order before we present the regression model that tests these predictions. Although our results are consistent with our belief that banks alter their investment and financing decisions in response to changes in their tax status, our analysis is based on statistical associations rather than on a formal causal model. Also, as indicated in model 16.1 below, we regress tax status on the

---

[12] The 1987 Tax Act reduced this percentage to 70% for most corporations, and subsequent tax proposals have sought (so far, unsuccessfully) to reduce the percentage further.

[13] Subordinated capital notes counted as a form of regulatory capital during the sample period.

balance sheet items discussed above even though we believe that this regression's dependent variable (tax status) determines its independent variables (the balance sheet items) rather than the other way around. This multivariate regression allows us to measure the partial correlations between tax status and specific balance sheet items while controlling for the others. A more ambitious approach would be to develop a system of equations in which the dependent variables are the balance sheet items, and the regressors in each equation include tax status plus the dependent variables from the other equations. A problem with such a model, however, is that without stronger restrictions on the coefficients than our theory allows us to make, the model's parameters cannot be estimated. But we do estimate a form of this model that has one balance sheet item per equation as the dependent variable and tax status as a single common regressor in each equation. The coefficients in this reduced form model measure the statistical associations between tax status and specific balance sheet items. The discussion below emphasizes the results from model 16.1, because it allows us to measure the partial correlations between tax status and the various balance sheet items while controlling for the presence of the other balance sheet items.

We estimate relations of the following form to test these predictions:

$$TAX_{it} = b_{0t} + b_{1t} MUNI_{it} + b_{2t} DLF_{it} + b_{3t} PFD_{it} + b_{4t} COM_{it} + e_{it}, \quad (16.1)$$

where i   denotes firm;

t   denotes year (1980-1986);

TAX   is a dummy variable, taking on the value of 1 if firm i in year t experiences a net operating loss carryforward for tax purposes, otherwise 0;[14]

MUNI   is the book value of municipal bonds divided by the book value of total assets;[15]

DLF   is the book value of direct lease finance assets divided by the book value of total assets;

PFD   is the book value of preferred stock divided by the sum of the book values of preferred stock, capital notes, and common stock; and

COM   is the book value of common stock divided by the sum of the book values of preferred stock, capital notes, and common stock.

To estimate this relation, we assume that the error terms, e_{it}, are independent across banks but not across time. Moreover, the regression intercepts are allowed to vary each year to capture shocks that affect the banking industry.[16]

---

[14] We also run regressions in which TAX takes on the value of 1 if the firm experiences a net operating loss *or* an investment tax credit carryforward. See footnote 22 for an explanation of the relation between the presence of investment tax credit carryforwards and marginal tax rates.

[15] Throughout, total assets is the sum of all asset categories before deduction of any loan loss reserve. Thus, it is the bottom line of the asset side of the balance sheet plus the loan loss reserves.

[16] For example, if industry-wide profits are substantial in a given year, then the related intercept will reflect the associated change in the probability of an NOL for all banks.

The tax status variables are crude proxies for the true marginal tax rate, which is the present value of expected current and future taxes paid on a marginal unit of fully taxable income generated in the current period. This in turn depends upon the probability distributions of future taxable income, tax credits, and statutory tax rates, as well as on the levels of past periods' taxable incomes and tax credits, given the carryback rules for tax losses and tax credits. Given the strength of our results, we did not estimate such marginal tax rates, for it would be a demanding task, albeit a potentially efficiency enhancing one.[17]

The independent variables in equation 16.1 include two categories of assets and two "equity mix" variables.[18] The asset variables (deflated municipal bonds and deflated leases) are both tax shelters. Since explicit tax savings from investing in such tax shelters will exceed the related implicit tax costs only for banks that face relatively high marginal tax rates, we expect the coefficient on direct lease financing assets to be *negative*. A similar argument applies to the municipal bond variable.[19]

The two equity mix variables (deflated preferred stock and deflated common stock) in model 16.1 are tax shelters in the hands of investors who hold them. As a technical aside, because these variables sum to one minus capital notes deflated as above, we cannot include capital notes as a third equity mix variable. The coefficients of the equity mix variables included in the model represent the change in tax-paying status associated with an increase in an equity mix variable (common stock or preferred stock) holding constant the other equity mix variable, offset by a proportional decrease in capital notes. From the earlier discussion, the coefficients on each of these variables are expected to be positive.[20]

Our sample size is 121 firms times 7 years or 847. Each coefficient has the predicted sign, and each differs from zero at conventional levels of statistical significance. The estimated relation is

$$TAX = .034 - .9060 \text{ MUNI} - 2.0298 \text{ DLF} + .2266 \text{ PFD} + .1580 \text{ COM.}$$

If we take these coefficient estimates at face value, they have the following interpretations. An increase in municipal bond holdings from the 25th percentile (MUNI=0.038) to the 75th percentile (MUNI=0.085), holding other factors constant, is associated with a 4.3% decline in the likelihood of the bank reporting a

---

[17] For an empirical application, see Terry Shevlin, "Taxes and Off-Balance Sheet Financing: Research and Development Limited Partnerships," *The Accounting Review* (July, 1987), pp. 480-509, and for a further description, see Terry Shevlin, "Estimating Corporate Marginal Tax Rates," *The Journal of American Taxation Association* (Spring, 1990), pp. 51-67. Also see Chapter Eight of this text.

[18] For a discussion of the motivation for including such variables in a model designed to capture a firm's tax-paying status, see Myron S. Scholes and Mark A. Wolfson, "Issues in the Theory of Optimal Capital Structure," *Frontiers of Modern Finance*, edited by Sudipto Bhattacharya and George Constantinides (Rowman and Littlefield), 1989.

[19] Remember that a high value for the TAX variable corresponds to a *low* tax rate (tax loss carryforwards).

[20] If we had included capital notes and either preferred stock or common stock as the equity mix variables in the regression, we would *not* have been able to conduct one-sided significance tests on the coefficients of the latter variable since our theory does not predict whether low-tax firms are more likely to finance operations with preferred stock or common stock. The specification we have chosen, however, does permit one-sided tests.

net operating loss carryforward. Similarly, holding other factors constant, an increase in direct lease holdings from the 25th (DLF=0) to the 75th percentile (DLF=0.015) is associated with a 3% probability decline. An increase in preferred stock issued from the 25th (PFD=0) to the 75th percentile (PFD=0.10) is associated with a 2.3% increase in the probability of reporting an NOL, and an increase in common stock issued from the 25th (COM=0.738) to the 75th percentile (COM=0.999) is associated with a 4.1% probability increase. These are substantial differentials because only 11% of the observations report net operating loss carryforwards.[21]

The significance of the negative average coefficient on the direct lease financing variable is especially impressive since its estimated value is *positive* 1.13 in 1981, the year in which "safe harbor leasing" was introduced. Some banks sold the tax benefits from leases they had originated under such provisions and this tends to pollute our tests since theory calls for a measure of the *net* tax shelter position held; unfortunately, due to data limitations, we use a gross measure. When 1981 is excluded from the sample, the results are sharpened somewhat, despite the loss of 121 observations.

We also ran a test where the dependent variable takes on the value of 1 when there exists a net operating loss *or* an investment tax credit carryforward. There are costs and benefits of using this proxy for marginal tax rates. The benefit is that the presence of investment tax credits reduces marginal tax rates.[22] There is a problem, however, in using this variable to test for a positive association with direct lease financing assets. Direct financing leases represent the primary source of investment tax credits for banks,[23] so banks without these investments largely avoided the possibility of generating investment tax credit carryforwards. This implies a positive relation between investment tax credit carryforwards and direct lease assets by construction, although our earlier discussion implies that tax planning should reduce the positive relation. The coefficient on direct lease assets was indeed *positive* with this specification.

As indicated earlier, model 16.1 "reverses" the dependent and independent variables relative to what the theory motivating the tests would suggest. Generally, a bank reacts to a change in its tax status by altering its assets and liabilities. As an alternative specification, we also estimate a model in which the asset and equity mix variables are regressed on contemporaneous, lagged, and forward tax status dummy variables. We find that the sum of the coefficients in these regressions is highly significant and of the predicted sign with the exception of the direct lease financing variable.

---

[21]Approximately 23% of the observations report net operating loss *or* investment tax credit carryforwards.

[22]The presence of ITC carryforwards reduces marginal tax rates because the amount of the tax credit available is linked to the regular income tax. Hence, when an ITC carryforward is present, each unit of taxable income frees up a portion of the ITC carryforward to be used to reduce the marginal tax. Moreover, any ITC carryforward present at year-end 1986 was reduced by 17.5% in 1987 and reduced further by a like amount in 1988 if not used up in 1987.

[23]Prior to 1986, tax credits were available only on depreciable property *other* than real property (such as that to house bank operations). The Tax Reform Act of 1986 eliminated investment tax credits retroactive to January 1, 1986.

The results reported in this section are important for at least three reasons. First, they demonstrate a clear link between a firm's financing and investing strategies and its tax status. Myers characterizes as "weak" the empirical evidence on this link and claims that the prospects are bleak for documenting such a relation.[24] One reason for the the weak evidence would appear to be that the literature to date presents univariate tests with regression coefficients assumed constant across diverse industries.[25] Our success in documenting these effects may well be due to our focusing on a homogeneous set of firms that face a relatively simple production environment. Another reason for the weakness of published results is that any variable used to represent tax status (such as a net operating loss carryforward dummy) is endogenous, the result of tax planning strategies that have been undertaken. The preferred variable is what the tax status would have been in the absence of tax planning.[26] This "but-for-tax-planning-action" tax status variable is one that we could calculate with some effort, but given the strength of the results, we elect not to. In considering other industries in which researchers have failed to document clientele effects, the theoretically more powerful "but-for" tax status variable could provide stronger results, as could joint tests that consider a host of tax-planning substitutes.

Second, organization theorists have largely ignored taxes in their attempts to prescribe (or describe) efficient organizational arrangements.[27] Their implicit assumption that taxes are of second order in importance is refuted by our evidence.

Third, researchers have been notoriously unsuccessful in linking financial accounting rule changes to changes in the real economic balance sheets of firms. Since changes in tax rules have cash flow implications that are more direct than are the cash flow implications of financial accounting rule changes, failure to find a relation between tax changes and organizational restructuring would not bode well for the more demanding task of linking organizational changes to changes in financial accounting rules.

---

[24] Stewart C. Myers, "The Capital Structure Puzzle." *Journal of Finance* (July 1984), pp. 575-92.

[25] For an exception, see Jeffery K. Mackie-Mason, "Do Taxes Affect Corporate Financing Decisions?," *Journal of Finance* (December, 1990), pp. 1471-1493, and "Do Firms Care Who Provides Their Financing?" in *Asymmetric Information, Corporate Finance and Investment*, R. Glenn Hubbard, ed. (University of Chicago Press), 1990, pp. 63-103.

[26] For example, it has been documented that there is a negative relation between investment in depreciable assets and debt financing, especially for firms that have a high probability of generating tax loss carryforwards. See Dan Dhaliwal, Robert Trezevant, and Shiing-wu Wang, "Taxes, Investment, and Financing," Working Paper, University of Arizona (July, 1990).

[27] For elaboration, see Myron S. Scholes and Mark A. Wolfson, "Issues in the Theory of Optimal Capital Structure," *Frontiers of Modern Finance*, edited by Sudipto Bhattacharya and George Constantinides (Rowman and Littlefield), 1989.

16.3 The Degree to Which Tax-Minimizing Policies are Sacrificed Due to the Presence of Regulators and other Capital Market Participants

While the results reported above are suggestive of the importance of taxes in influencing investment and financing decisions, evidence presented below suggests that banks forego very substantial opportunities to reduce taxes. In this section, we document this behavior and consider nontax factors that may explain it.

A tax rule that has clear implications for asset management policy of banks is that gains and losses on the sale or exchange of corporate bonds, government bonds, and most other evidences of indebtedness (such as commercial and personal loans), give rise to ordinary income or loss, rather than capital gain or loss. While capital losses may offset only capital gains, ordinary losses are deductible against ordinary taxable income. Therefore, income can be sheltered from taxation by selling or exchanging loans and investment securities that have declined in value and by retaining appreciated loans and securities, although the tax saving from postponing taxable income depends upon expected changes in tax rates, as well as on the after-tax discount rate.[28] For example, the scheduled reduction in marginal tax rates from 46% in 1986 to 40% in 1987 and 34% in 1988 created a greater tax incentive for commercial banks to postpone the recognition of ordinary income in 1986 than in other years.[29]

The unexpected increase in interest rates in the late 1970s and early 1980s gave rise to billions of dollars in potential tax write-offs for banks. In the absence of nontax costs, profitable banks should have realized these losses to save taxes. The evidence, however, suggests that many profitable banks did not postpone taxable income nearly to the extent possible. For our sample of banks over the years 1969 to 1985, unrealized securities losses averaged 14% of shareholders' equity with a standard deviation of 19%. The average unrealized loss across the 130+ banks for which data were available in 1980 and 1981 was in excess of 40% of shareholders' equity! Indeed, a number of banks with unrealized losses on

---

[28] Sources of increasing intertemporal tax rates (and hence reduced incentive to postpone taxable income) include: legislative tax changes (such as those applying to thrifts and life insurance companies following passage of the Tax Act of 1986); the temporary imposition of the alternative minimum tax; and investment tax credit carryforwards.

[29] The propensity of financial institutions to postpone capital gains income should differ from their propensity to postpone ordinary income, especially in the period following the Tax Reform Act of 1986. First, the (long-term) capital gains tax rate has been below that on ordinary income. The statutory rate was 28% (alternative rate) until the Tax Reform Act of 1986. Moreover, this rate could be reduced substantially by exchanging capital assets for installment notes rather than cash. See Ronald J. Gilson, Myron S. Scholes, and Mark A. Wolfson, "Taxation and the Dynamics of Corporate Control: The Uncertain Case for Tax Motivated Acquisitions," *Knights, Raiders and Targets: The Impact of the Hostile Takeover*, edited by John C. Coffee, Jr., Louis Lowenstein and Susan Rose-Ackerman (Oxford University Press), 1987 for an elaboration. Second, whereas the tax rate on ordinary income has been reduced, the tax rate applying to long-term capital gains has been increased. The maximum federal capital gains tax rate is 34% for all banks in 1987 and beyond. Moreover, beginning in 1987, installment sales no longer postponed capital gains taxation on the sale of publicly-traded equities. Changes in installment sales rules were passed in 1984, 1986, 1987, and 1988. In each case, the Congress chipped away at the opportunities to postpone the payment of taxes on capital assets.

Chapter 16   Empirical Evidence of Clienteles: Commercial Banks

their marketable securities portfolios selectively sold portions of their portfolios that had *appreciated* in value, thereby accelerating voluntarily the payment of the tax on the increase in value.

This evidence does not *necessarily* imply, however, that banks deviated from tax-minimizing strategies. It is possible, for example, that profitable banks were taking losses and that banks with tax credit or tax loss carryforwards (or high probabilities of generating them in the future) were not. Two facts are worth noting here. First, there are years in the sample in which 100% of the banks reported unrealized losses on their overall marketable securities portfolios. Second, the vast majority of banks in the sample held substantial amounts of municipal bonds in their marketable securities portfolio at the same time they were experiencing unrealized losses. Since municipal bond investments provide after-tax returns exceeding those for equally-risky taxable investments only if the investor faces a high marginal tax rate, factors other than a low marginal tax rate may have been driving the decision not to exploit the opportunity to reduce taxable income.[30]

Nontax factors that affect the management of the marketable securities portfolio include *asset turnover costs*, concern over the level of *income reported to shareholders*, and *regulatory capital* considerations. Since these securities are rarely "marked to market" for financial reporting or regulatory accounting purposes, even when market value is below book value, their sale has essentially the same effect on financial reporting equity, regulatory capital, and income reported for tax purposes.

Asset turnover costs include any discount a well-informed seller may have to offer a relatively uninformed buyer who is unable to distinguish the assets from those of lesser value, as well as appraisal fees and other "due diligence" costs incurred to reduce information differences between buyers and sellers. Asset turnover costs for marketable securities, however, are likely to be less than for commercial loans, real estate acquired in foreclosures, bank branches, and fixed assets where information differences are more chronic.

There are several reasons why firms may be concerned with the income reported to shareholders and associated balance sheet numbers. First, if management is better informed than are outside suppliers of capital about the value of their firm's assets (including the value associated with management's ability to make good investments), the management may find it worthwhile to convey this private information even if it is costly to do so, particularly when new financing is to be arranged. One way to convey information about the value of the firm's net assets is to sell them. Symmetrically, one of the costs associated with selling assets to realize tax losses is that the sale might increase financing costs by revealing that

---

[30] Several caveats are warranted here. First, beginning in 1983 it became costly (due to foregone arbitrage possibilities as described earlier) to sell municipal bonds that had been owned prior to January 1, 1983. For similar reasons, it became especially costly, beginning in 1987, to sell municipal bonds that had been owned prior to August 7, 1986. Second, while municipal bonds may represent the wrong tax clientele with respect to new investments for banks with tax loss carryforwards, it may be undesirable to sell existing municipal bonds if they have appreciated in value since their date of acquisition, because the tax on the sale may exceed the costs of being in the "wrong" clientele. Finally, banks may be motivated to hold certain municipal debt to generate other profitable business with municipal issuers.

16.3   The Degree to Which Tax-Minimizing Policies are Sacrificed

asset values are below the market's expectations.[31] Second, financial contracts with suppliers, creditors, management, and other stakeholders frequently specify an allocation of property rights that depends on financial statement numbers which will affect asset/liability management policy.[32]

Financial reporting costs are not likely to be great for marketable securities held by banks since both book and market values are provided in reports to shareholders. Nevertheless, the evidence to be presented suggests that bank management believes these costs are important.

Banks are also likely to be concerned about the effects of asset/liability management policy on regulatory capital. For example, a bank that sells marketable securities affects taxable income and regulatory capital by similar amounts. To avoid costly direct intervention by regulators, banks must maintain a minimum ratio of primary capital (which is roughly equal to shareholders' equity plus loan loss reserves) to adjusted assets (total assets plus loan loss reserves). Since 1984, banks have also been required to meet a minimum secondary capital ratio set one-half percent above the primary capital requirement (where certain subordinated debt securities are included in regulatory capital). The regulators also impose some restrictions on investment activity at specified levels of regulatory capital above the minimum level that triggers direct intervention in the management oversight of bank activities.[33] For example, completion of a bank merger requires regulatory approval, which is often tied to regulatory capital considerations.[34]

---

[31] See Michael J. Brennan, "Latent Assets," *The Journal of Finance* (1990).

[32] See, for example, Ross L. Watts and Jerold L. Zimmerman, *Positive Accounting Theory* (Prentice Hall), 1986.

[33] Buser, Chen, and Kane suggest that the cost of regulatory intervention is similar to an implicit tax on bank activities. (Stephen A. Buser, Andrew H. Chen, and Edward J. Kane, "Federal Deposit Insurance, Regulatory Policy, and Optimal Bank Capital," *The Journal of Finance* (March, 1981), pp. 51-60.) Moreover, Kane shows that thrifts failed to realize losses on their mortgage portfolios to reduce their tax bills from 1965-1979 and again in 1983. (Edward J. Kane, *The Gathering Crisis in Federal Deposit Insurance* (MIT Press, Cambridge, MA), 1985, esp. pp. 97-110.)

The industry generated net operating losses from 1980-82. Kane argues that by not selling mortgages, thrifts kept their net worths from falling below the level required to maintain insurance from the Federal Savings and Loan Insurance Corporation. On the other hand, we would argue that banks faced with the prospect of losing the value of net operating loss carryforwards in the event of bankruptcy might *reduce* the riskiness of net asset holdings despite the presence of limited liability.

[34] Banks have consistently effected more mergers throughout the 1980s than any other industry group. Completion of a bank merger requires regulatory approval, which is often tied to regulatory capital considerations. For example, in its 1987 first quarter report to shareholders, Banks of Mid-America, Inc. disclosed the following (p. 10):

> During the second quarter of 1984, Liberty Bank and First Tulsa Bank were notified by the Office of the Comptroller of the Currency ("Comptroller") that they were receiving special supervisory attention and entered into separate administrative agreements with the Comptroller relating to various matters. Both banks are still operating under the agreements ... .

> Among other things First Tulsa Bank is required under its agreement to maintain a level of primary capital of at least 7% of total assets ... As part of the approval of Liberty's consolidation with First Tulsa, the Company made certain commitments to the Federal Reserve Board (including the maintenance of a minimum level of consolidated tangible primary capital of 6.40% of total assets) ...

A bank that maintains a 6% regulatory capital ratio can issue roughly $16 in demand deposits and other obligations for each dollar of additional regulatory capital. Because deposit insurance is provided by the Federal Deposit Insurance Corporation at subsidized rates, banks prefer additional regulatory capital. Their demand increases with an increase in the riskiness of their assets, and decreases but at a decreasing rate, as the market value of shareholders' equity increases.[35]

Restrictions on investment and operating behavior are more likely to be binding and costly the closer the bank is to violating its minimum capital requirements. The cost of these restrictions can be reduced by increasing regulatory capital beyond the required minimum. Moreover, even when regulatory capital is above the minimum required amount, monitoring by the bank examiners imposes costs on banks that decrease in the level of regulatory capital.[36] Just as "nominal" contracts with the taxing authority can cause taxpayers to be quite interested in "managing" the level of their taxable income, so contracts with regulators can cause banks (and other regulated financial institutions) to be quite interested in managing the level of their regulatory capital.

To summarize, regulatory costs consist of three components: direct monitoring costs, costs resulting from restrictions on investment activities, and restraints on the issuance of demand deposits. Each component (and hence the aggregate) is decreasing but at a decreasing rate with increases in regulatory capital. Thus, monitoring costs and costs from restrictions on investment activities decrease with increases in regulatory capital (but never approach a level of zero costs) as the regulators scale back the intensity of audits and restraints on investment activities in response to the reduced exposure to bank failure reflected in the expanding equity cushion. But some degree of oversight is exercised at *all* levels of regulatory capital.

At March 31, 1987, the Company was not in full compliance with its commitments to the Federal Reserve Board. At such date, the Company had under review a number of actions which if implemented would result in compliance with the Federal Reserve Board commitments. These actions include plans to increase its equity capital during 1987 through the issuance of new capital stock as well as possible sales of assets.

[35] A sufficient condition for this is that each dollar of debt financing is issued at the riskless rate of interest. Note that new debt financing need not be demand deposits that are fully federally insured (i.e., $100,000 or less per depositor) to be viewed by lenders as riskless—some of the investments made with the proceeds of the insured demand deposits and the uninsured loans to the bank can be pledged to secure the uninsured loans.

[36] Regulatory capital considerations for thrifts are quite similar to those for banks except that the required level of regulatory capital has been lower for thrifts in recent years. The pretax benefit of increasing regulatory capital (e.g., by selling appreciated assets) has, therefore, tended to be higher for thrifts than for banks. On the other hand, for purely tax reasons, debt, which gives rise to tax-deductible interest expense, is not the natural financing clientele for low-tax entities such as thrifts. This serves to reduce the advantage of increasing regulatory capital. Insurance companies are also interested in the level of regulatory capital. Property casualty companies are permitted to write insurance coverage only up to a specified multiple of their "policy holder surplus capacity reserve." The surplus amount is increased (decreased) by gains (losses) on the sale of bonds. Similar considerations apply to life insurance companies. So regulatory capital planning can quite naturally conflict with tax planning, although the conflict may be rather different across different types of financial institutions, across different firms for a given type of financial institution, as well as for a given firm across time.

16.3   The Degree to Which Tax-Minimizing Policies are Sacrificed

The cost of restraints on the issuance of demand deposits is proportional to the risk premium banks would have to offer to attract deposits in the absence of federal insurance. This risk premium is also decreasing, but at a decreasing rate, as shareholders' equity (and hence regulatory capital) increases.

The earlier reference to "nominal" contracts begs the question of why regulators might rely on only a subset of all available information in implementing regulatory policy. For example, why not regulate based on measures of regulatory capital and earnings that incorporate unrealized holding gains and losses that are reported in banks' annual reports? We can think of at least four possible reasons.

First, a commitment by regulators to use book rather than market value may prevent distortions in banks' investment decisions. Absent such a commitment, banks might be motivated to invest in riskier assets, the market values of which are unobservable by the regulator (and hence noncontractible). This in turn could give rise to greater exposure to government-insured losses.

Second, if regulators are given too much discretion in implementing policy, banks might be motivated to overinvest in producing information to promote favorable treatment by the regulators. In hierarchical arrangements, top management may find it desirable to close down communication channels or to commit to ignoring certain information to discourage overinvestment in information production activities.[37]

Third, allowing bank regulators too much discretion might result in regulators being "captured" by bank managements; that is, there is the possibility of collusion in the hierarchical arrangement, and this may prove to be against the public's interest. Such collusion can be mitigated by restricting communication and invoking bureaucratic rules that ignore certain relevant information.[38]

Fourth, monitoring costs are undoubtedly lower when regulators face a limited number of fixed decision rules that are based on observables. A related explanation here is "bounded regulator rationality."

To determine whether tradeoffs between tax and nontax factors contribute to an explanation of cross-sectional differences in banks' propensity to realize securities gains and losses, we regress realized marketable securities gains and losses, deflated by book value of total assets, RSG,[39] on tax factors, nontax factors, and "nuisance" factors as reflected in equation 16.2:

$$RSG_{it} = b_{0t} + b_{1t} PC_{it} + b_{2t} PC_{it}^2 + b_{3t} LLP_{it} + b_{4t} TAX_{it}$$

$$+ \ b_{5t} USG_{it-1} + b_{6t} MCB_{it} + u_{it} \tag{16.2}$$

where i   denotes firm;

        t   denotes year (1981-1986);

---

[37] See, for example, Paul Milgrom and John Roberts, "Bargaining Costs, Influence Costs, and the Organization of Economic Activity," in *Positive Perspectives on Political Economy*, edited by J. Alt and K. Shepsle (Cambridge University Press), 1990.

[38] See Jean Tirole, "Hierarchies and Bureaucracies: On the Role of Collusion in Organizations." *Journal of Law, Economics, and Organization* (Fall 1986), pp. 181-214.

[39] Note that when securities are sold at a loss, RSG takes on negative values.

Chapter 16   Empirical Evidence of Clienteles: Commercial Banks

PC   is "primary capital," measured as book value of shareholders' equity plus loan loss reserve, divided by book value of total assets;

LLP   is the annual "loan loss provision," deflated by the book value of total assets;

TAX   is a dummy variable, taking on the value of one if firm i in year t experiences a net operating loss carryforward for tax purposes;[40]

USG   is "unrealized securities gains and losses" on marketable investment securities measured as the market value less the book value of marketable investment securities, deflated by book value of total assets; and

MCB   is a dummy variable, taking on the value of one for so-called "money center banks."

From our earlier discussion, the expected signs on the coefficients for primary capital, the square of primary capital, and taxes, are negative, positive and positive, respectively. That is, security gains realizations are expected to decrease as primary capital increases (but at a decreasing rate) and as tax rates increase. (Once again, recall that a high value for the tax variable denotes a low tax rate.)

The loan loss provision variable is included to provide a simple test for income management; that is, management's strategic choice of accounting policies designed to affect the levels of reported income. The loan loss provision possesses three properties that make it especially appropriate for this purpose. First, it typically represents a very large fraction of income. Second, conventional wisdom suggests that there is a large discretionary component to the loan loss provision. And third, it is the only income statement item whose effect on income reported to shareholders is either not matched by an effect on regulatory capital at all or is matched by an effect of opposite sign on financial accounting income. To see this, note that an increase in the loan loss provision both reduces shareholders' equity and increases the allowance for loan losses. Ignoring tax effects, regulatory capital is unaffected. If the reduction to shareholders' equity is less than the increase in the loan loss provision due to a reduction in tax expense, then regulatory capital actually increases while financial accounting income decreases as the result of an increase in the loan loss provision. This allows us to distinguish between behavior motivated by regulatory capital considerations and that due to financial reporting considerations.

The expected sign of the coefficient on the loan loss provision variable in equation 16.2 depends upon whether firms seek to offset or reinforce the effect of the loan loss provision on net income reported to shareholders.[41] Both objectives

---

[40] We also run regressions in which TAX takes on the values of one if the firm experiences a net operating loss *or* an investment tax credit carryforward.

[41] An example of earnings management is provided by First Bank System during the third quarter of 1986. According to the *Wall Street Journal* (October 10, 1986; p. 10), "First Bank System's results were bolstered by $197.8 million in gains on massive securities sales … [T]he Minneapolis-based bank

are forms of earnings management. In the former case, the expected sign on LLP is positive, and in the latter case it is negative.[42] Given the competing hypotheses, we conduct two-sided tests of significance of the coefficient on this variable.

The beginning-of-period *unrealized* securities gains and losses is included in the regression to control, in part, for the nondiscretionary component of realized securities gains. The sign of its coefficient is expected to be positive. Finally, because money center banks were subject to regulatory guidelines that differed from those of other banks,[43] we include as an independent variable, a dummy variable taking on the value of one for money center banks only.

We compute unrealized securities gains and losses using market value information from bank annual reports. Since we collect a complete set of data for the years 1980-1986, and since we use beginning-of-period values for unrealized securities gains and losses in the regression, the regressions are based on six years of data (1981-1986).

Over the period 1981-1986, the average primary capital ratio ranges from 6.6% (1981 and 1982) to 7.4% (1986), and marketable securities as a fraction of total assets ranges from 15.7% to 17.4%. Net operating loss carryforwards are reported in just under 11% of all bank-years, ranging from 5% in 1981 to 17% in 1986.[44]

Results

The primary capital and tax variables all have the predicted signs and are significant at conventional levels. The positive coefficient on the loan loss provision variable is consistent with the argument that realized securities gains and losses are chosen strategically to "smooth" the level of income reported to shareholders by offsetting the income effect of the bad debt expense. More specifically, each $1 of increase in the loan loss provision, holding constant primary capital, tax status, and the other "control variables," is associated with nearly a $.05 increase in realized securities gains.

The finding that realized securities gains are higher when regulatory capital is low, holding other factors constant, is consistent with the argument that as regulatory capital falls, banks are more inclined to sacrifice tax benefits by selling appreciated securities (or postponing the sale of losers) to improve their regulatory capital positions. Similarly, as regulatory capital increases, banks can

---

holding company sold nearly $3 billion of its $7.5 billion investment portfolio, which is invested mostly in government securities. The huge gains were needed to help counter write-offs of bad assets totaling $336.2 million, about 10 times more than a year earlier."

[42] While we have chosen to focus on the relation between realized securities gains and loan loss provisions, both of which have discretionary components, other dependent variable candidates, such as gains from the sale of capital assets (e.g., intangible assets and bank buildings) represent another promising avenue that might be pursued. As an example, Shawmut National Corporation recognized a gain of $114 million upon the sale of its interest in its Boston headquarters. Shawmut indicated its intention to allocate $60 to $65 million of this gain to increasing its reserves for Third World loan losses and to add much of the remainder to other reserves. (*Wall Street Journal*; July 1, 1988; p. 21).

[43] Beatty et al., *op. cit.*

[44] Just over 23% of the observations had net operating loss *or* investment tax credit carryforwards, ranging from 21% in 1981 and 1985 to 25% in 1983 and 1984.

Chapter 16   Empirical Evidence of Clienteles: Commercial Banks

better afford to postpone the sale of appreciated securities (or accelerate the sale of losers) to save on taxes.

Realized securities gains and losses are associated nonlinearly with primary capital. When primary capital is equal to 3% of assets, each $1 decrease in primary capital is associated with nearly a $.02 increase in realized securities gains (or with nearly a $.02 *decrease* in realized losses). When primary capital is equal to 5% of total assets, each $1 decrease in primary capital is associated with a $.01 increase in realized securities gains. And when the primary capital ratio is 7.5%, changes in primary capital and realized securities gains are unrelated. If we compare two moderate-sized banks, each of which reports $10 billion of total assets, one of which has primary capital of $400 million and the other which has primary capital of $600 million, the less-well-capitalized bank (for regulatory purposes) is expected to generate roughly an extra $2 million per year in realized securities gains, holding constant other factors.

The positive coefficient on the tax variable is consistent with a greater willingness on the part of high-tax-rate banks to take losses on their marketable securities portfolios to reduce taxes. Similarly it is consistent with a reluctance on the part of high-tax-rate banks to take gains to improve their reported profitability and regulatory capital position, but at a tax cost.

More specifically, holding nontax factors constant, banks reporting net operating loss carryforwards realize, on average, an additional $200,000 in securities gains per billion dollars of assets. For a bank reporting five years of net operating loss carryforwards and 10 billion dollars of assets, the model predicts an extra $10 million of realized securities gains over the five years above and beyond any effects of loan loss provisions and regulatory capital on realized securities gains.

As expected, the coefficient on beginning-of-year unrealized securities gains is consistently positive and significant in most of the six years. The coefficients on the money-center-bank variable are not significant and appear to add little to the regression.

Summary of Key Points

The evidence suggests that banks are more inclined to take actions that reduce taxes when the costs of doing so, in terms of the effects on income reported to shareholders and regulators, are relatively small and the magnitude of the potential tax benefits is large. The evidence is consistent with the following statement made by Douglas McEachern, then a partner at Touche Ross and Chairman of the AICPA's Committee on Savings and Loans:[45]

> "In dealing with clients and others, I often end up in discussions that focus on a transaction basis and ask 'what is the GAAP result of this

---

[45] The statement was made at a roundtable discussion on generally accepted accounting principles and regulatory accounting principles, held at the University of Southern California during October of 1987. (*Proceedings of the October 8, 1987 Roundtable Discussion on Generally Accepted Accounting Principles and Regulatory Accounting Practices*, edited by Jerry L. Arnold (University of Southern California), January 1988)

transaction? What happens for tax purposes? What happens under regulatory accounting practices and lastly, unfortunately, in some cases, what is the economic result of this?' Unfortunately, many of the transactions that are being undertaken by the industry, especially by the savings and loan industry, and by Wall Street, are driven by and designed around the accounting result."

1. We test the predictions of the theory that banks adjust their assets and liabilities to changes in their tax circumstances as the clientele principle suggests.

2. The presence of nontax costs prevents firms from making an immediate and complete adjustment to a change in tax circumstances. This requires that we conduct joint tests using several asset and liability management responses and that we look for restructuring responses over a period of time.

3. In our macro tests, we document a strong response in bank holdings of municipal bonds to legislative changes in tax rules that affect the banking industry. In this situation, asset turnover costs are low and the date of a change in tax circumstances is relatively well documented.

4. Being able to document strong responses in asset allocations among alternative investments (e.g., a change in municipal bond holdings) to changes in tax rules for the industry as a whole is a warm-up to more demanding investigations in situations wherein the nontax costs of balance sheet restructuring are higher and the date of a change in the tax circumstances of a particular bank is more elusive.

5. We also document a significant association between tax status and firms' investment and financing decisions both across firms at a given point in time and over time.

6. We further provide evidence of nontax costs associated with restructuring economic balance sheets that impede tax-related restructuring. In particular, banks do not follow tax minimization strategies with regard to the management of their marketable securities portfolio due to the presence of regulatory capital costs, financial reporting costs, and other transaction costs.

7. Regulatory costs are costs that a bank incurs when its nominal regulatory capital is low. Such a bank is relatively more constrained as to its investment and financing activities than is a bank with more regulatory capital. Banks with low regulatory capital are also subject to more extensive monitoring by bank regulators. Perhaps most important, the level of regulatory capital affects the level of insured deposits that a bank can issue.

8. We show that banks reporting increases in their loan loss provision, which reduces reported earnings to shareholders (with little effect on regulatory capital), tend to realize securities gains (and/or defer losses) to smooth reported earnings. This is striking in that the market value of

the marketable securities portfolio is disclosed to shareholders in published financial statements.

9. Banks with low levels of regulatory capital defer the realization of securities losses and realize securities gains to increase regulatory capital. As regulatory capital increases, banks have historically taken larger securities losses but at a decreasing rate, holding everything else equal.

10. Banks are more willing to take securities gains when they are experiencing net operating loss carryforwards, everything else being equal.

11. Bank managers act as if regulators and shareholders underutilize publicly available information about unrealized securities gains and losses in their oversight of banks. We offered several explanations for why it might be rational for regulators actually to underutilize the information. Managers are apparently willing to sacrifice tax benefits to manage the level of income reported to these parties.

Discussion Questions

1. What events might cause a change in the marginal tax rate of a corporation? What difficulties exist in measuring firms' responses to changes in their tax circumstances?

2. What are the advantages of studying banks if the goal is to measure firms' responsiveness to changes in tax circumstances?

3. Why might banks have invested heavily in municipal bonds prior to 1983? What tax rule changes affected their desire to acquire municipal bonds subsequent to 1983? Should banks acquire municipal bonds following passage of the 1986 Tax Act? Why?

4. Describe the tests used in the chapter to measure whether the banking industry responds to legislative changes in tax rules regarding the deductibility of interest on loans used to buy municipal bonds. Why might it be important to control for the aggregate supply of municipal bonds in conducting these tests?

5. When a bank's tax status changes from that of paying taxes to a net operating loss position, what changes might the bank's management contemplate making to its asset holdings? Why? What changes might management consider making to the bank's liabilities? What factors might restrain management from undertaking these actions?

6. To test for an association between marginal tax rates and changes in asset and liability management, a tax status variable is used that takes on the value of one when a bank experiences a net operating loss carryforward for tax purposes; otherwise, the variable takes on a value of zero. Why is the tax status variable a crude proxy for the marginal tax rate? If you had an unlimited budget, what tax variable would you want to construct?

7. What is the difference between a predictive test and an association test? Consider whether we predict tax status as a function of investment and financing strategies or whether we predict investment and financing strategies as a function of tax status.

8. What does the evidence suggest about the relation between banks' tax-paying status and their asset and liability holdings? Does this support the clientele principle?

9. Why might a tax status indicator that considers only one year of net operating loss carryforwards mask bank management's adjustment of assets and liabilities to a change in marginal tax rates? What other indicators might be tried and why might they be more effective?

10. Do you think that the direct lease holdings of the bank would adjust quickly to a change in tax circumstances? Why? Why would it be preferable to use net rather than gross lease holdings?

11. Why might it be tax advantageous to realize securities losses and postpone securities gains? When might it not be advantageous?

12. Is there evidence that banks do not follow tax minimizing strategies?

13. What nontax variables affect the decision to realize securities losses? Are the transactions costs of selling marketable securities very large?

14. What are the important financial reporting costs of realizing securities losses and postponing gains?

15. How is regulatory capital affected by the realization of securities losses and gains? Why do regulators use book rather than market values in implementing certain regulatory policies when both are readily available?

16. How might the desire to conduct merger activity affect a bank's willingness to realize securities gains and losses?

17. How does the evidence on bank's realization of securities losses demonstrate a tradeoff between tax management and the management of other line items on the income statement? What is the magnitude of the tradeoff? Are you surprised by the magnitude?

CHAPTER 17
Empirical Evidence of Implicit Taxes
And Tax Clienteles II

For many years, finance specialists have investigated whether firms can influence their market values by varying the fraction of after-tax earnings and profits distributed to shareholders as dividends. For some taxpayers, in particular U.S. individual investors who pay tax on dividends at their full marginal rates, the receipt of dividends is tax-disadvantageous. Prior to the 1986 Tax Act in the U.S., individual investors had a particularly strong demand for capital gains over ordinary income (such as interest and dividends), because (1) part of any realized capital gain was excluded from taxation and (2) the tax on the capital gain could be deferred until the asset was sold.

Moreover, investors could escape the capital gains tax by making charitable contributions of appreciated securities (subject to alternative minimum tax considerations)[1] or by holding appreciated securities until death, at which point the capital gain receives a tax-free step-up in basis to market value. While the 1986 Tax Act eliminated, at least temporarily, the ability of taxpayers to exclude part of any realized capital gain from taxable income, the opportunity to *defer* the capital gains tax remained, as did the opportunity to escape the tax by way of charitable contribution or bequest.

If U.S. individual investors are the marginal holders of stock, we would expect (1) stocks to bear implicit taxes relative to bonds and (2) low-dividend-paying stocks to bear more implicit taxes than high-dividend-paying stocks. In other words, we would expect the before-tax risk-adjusted returns on stocks to be below those of bonds and the risk-adjusted returns of low-dividend-paying stocks to be below those for high-dividend-paying stocks, as illustrated in Figure

---

[1] The unrealized capital gain on appreciated securities donated to charities increases "alternative minimum taxable income." Such income is taxed to individuals at a marginal rate of 24% (21% preceding 1991) if the alternative minimum tax exceeds the regular tax.

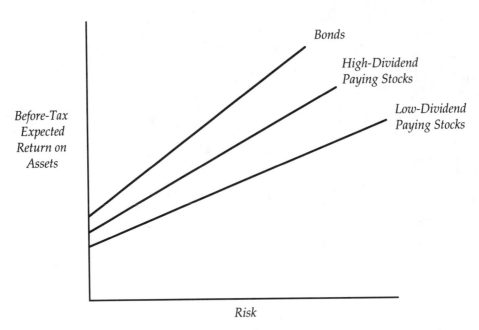

Before-Tax
Expected
Return on
Assets

Bonds

High-Dividend
Paying Stocks

Low-Dividend
Paying Stocks

Risk

FIGURE 17.1   Returns versus Risk for Differentially-Taxed Assets

17.1. The empirical evidence is inconclusive regarding these propositions. In particular, it is unclear from the evidence whether there is a differential in the before-tax rates of return on high and low-dividend-paying securities. It is also unclear whether stocks bear implicit taxes relative to bonds. In part, this is because the expected magnitude of the tax effects on stock returns relative to bond returns is small compared to the variability of returns. That is, available empirical methods are not powerful enough to control for risk differentials between stocks and bonds so that the unique effect of taxation can be isolated.

If dividends *are* tax disadvantageous relative to capital gains, it appears that firms can make shareholders better off by repurchasing their shares in lieu of paying dividends. Some care must be exercised here, however, because a pro rata purchase of outstanding stock from each shareholder would be taxable as a dividend. But as long as shareholders do not retain the same proportionate interest in the firm after the repurchase as before it, shareholders who tender their shares are taxed the same as if they had made a regular sale of stock.

There are two tax advantages of a share repurchase over a dividend. First, the entire amount of a dividend distribution is taxable as ordinary income to the extent of accumulated earnings and profits of the firm. By contrast, if the distribution takes the form of a share repurchase, tax is paid only on the excess of the purchase price over the shareholder's basis in the stock. This reduces the present value of the tax. Second, shareholders who wish to defer realizing capital gains income need not tender their shares to the company; that is, the natural candidates for tendering shares are tax exempt and foreign investors who escape U.S. taxation.

As mentioned in Chapter Fifteen and discussed more fully below, many firms routinely repurchase shares. On the other hand, many firms still pay out a considerable amount of their returns to their shareholders in the form of dividends. This is inconsistent with tax-minimizing behavior. There are, however, some nontax reasons why a firm might pay dividends. These include: (1) recurrent dividend payments remove excess cash from the firm, thereby disciplining management wanting to finance pet projects by forcing them to return to the capital markets for financing—it might be more difficult to raise money to finance bad projects; (2) removing excess cash forces management to work harder and be more efficient so that cash obligations, such as those related to promised interest and principal payments, can be met; and (3) increasing the dividend could signal, to the firm's lenders and shareholders, managements' expectations of future increases in earnings.

17.1 The Implicit Tax on Shares

In 1961, Miller and Modigliani (MM) demonstrated that in a perfect market setting neither the returns to shares nor share values are affected by the proportion of the share return that comes in the form of dividends versus capital gains.[2] Their perfect market assumption rules out the interesting cases of the effects of differential taxation of capital gains and dividend income and of other informational and transaction cost imperfections on the return to shares. Their model, however, serves as a useful benchmark case.

The MM argument is quite simple and persuasive in their idealized setting. In owning shares of stock, investors receive dividends and capital gains income. The total return per dollar invested to owning shares over a holding period from t-1 through t, R_{ct}, is:

$$R_{ct} = \frac{d_t}{P_{t-1}} + \frac{P_t - P_{t-1}}{P_{t-1}}$$

where P_t and P_{t-1} are the prices of the shares at time t and t-1, respectively, and d_t denotes dividends paid at time t to shareholders of record at time t-1.

As an example, if P_{t-1} is \$100, P_t is \$110, and d_t is \$5, then the before-tax rate of return to holding shares is

$$\frac{\$5}{\$100} + \frac{\$110 - \$100}{\$100}$$

$$= .05 + .10 \text{ or } 15\%.$$

The 15% return includes a 5% dividend yield and a 10% capital gains return. The dividend yield and the capital gains return are typically uncertain when the shares are acquired. For most companies, however, the dividend yield is far more certain over short horizons, such as a year, than the capital gains return, since d_t does not change frequently or by large amounts.

MM showed that a shareholder would not pay more for a company's stock if more of the income came in the form of dividends rather than capital gains, or

[2] Merton H. Miller and Franco Modigliani, "Dividend Policy, Growth, and the Valuation Of Shares," *Journal of Business* (October 1961), pp. 411-33.

vice versa. To see why, suppose that shareholders prefer dividends to capital gains and that a non-dividend-paying stock (exactly the same in all other respects to our dividend-paying stock) was selling for only $98, $2 below the dividend-paying stock. While the dividend-paying stock returns 15%, the non-dividend paying stock's total return is 17.3% (or $115/$98 - 1), since the end-of-period price of the shares includes all of the future cash flow, and this is identical across the two companies. But then investors who prefer dividends can buy the non-dividend-paying stock at $98 and sell about 4.3% of their stock at $115 to realize $5 of cash flow. Since we have assumed that there are no transaction costs or taxes, the $5 in cash flow from selling .043 shares is equivalent to the dividend realized on the dividend-paying stock, and the remaining .957 shares are worth $110, the same as the dividend-paying stock.

The smart investors created home-made dividends: for $98 they replicated the dollar payoff on the dividend-paying stock that is selling for $100. Under these circumstances everyone would prefer holding the non-dividend paying stock and selling the dividend-paying stock until prices are the same on both types of shares. Otherwise, arbitrageurs could make a sure profit of up to $2 per share by selling the high-dividend-paying stock short (which can be done costlessly in a perfect market setting) and buying the low-dividend-paying stock to hedge the risk of their position.

When we add taxes and transaction costs to the analysis, various issues come into focus. First, the $5 of dividends from the dividend-paying stock may be taxed differently from the $5 resulting from the sale of 4% of the stock to create home-made dividends. For example, if the tax on ordinary income, t_p, is 40%, the investor retains only $3 of the dividend after tax. On the other hand, suppose the investor qualifies for an exclusion of 20% of any realized capital gain on the sale of shares. If $5 worth of stock is sold at a price of $115 per share, and $100 was originally paid for the shares, the capital gain is $.65 (or $5 - ($5/$115) × $100). With a 20% capital-gain exclusion, the tax is $.21 (without an exclusion the tax would be $.26). So, with home-made dividends, the investor retains $4.79 (or $4.74 without an exclusion). Most of the $5 of sales proceeds is a nontaxable return of capital. By not selling the entire stock position, the investor defers the payment of capital gains tax on the unsold shares.

The nondividend-paying stock provides investors with the option of whether to take a dividend. Moreover, investors can "declare" their home-made dividends when their tax rates are lower, or they can defer the dividend indefinitely to escape all taxes on the gain.[3]

Some have argued that investors prefer to receive dividends because it is very costly for many investors to sell small quantities of shares to create home-made dividends. For these investors cashing a dividend check may be far less costly. If this were true, it would seem tax-advantageous for the firm to establish share-repurchase programs in lieu of paying dividends. In this way, shareholders who wish to create home-made dividends could do so; and those who wish to reinvest in the company would simply not tender their shares.

---

[3] If firms were to issue dividend-protected warrants, they could declare dividends and still enable investors who purchase the warrants, rather than common shares, to avoid taxable dividend income. (Jeremy Bulow made this observation.) We revisit strategies such as this one in Chapter Twenty.

Chapter 17 Empirical Evidence of Implicit Taxes and Tax Clienteles II

In Table 17.1, we show how U.S. corporations have distributed cash to shareholders between 1977 and 1988.[4] Notice that even though share repurchases are tax-advantageous for most shareholders, U.S. corporations pay out large amounts of dividends. In 1983, for example, U.S. corporations paid out $54.9 billion in dividends and repurchased only $7.7 billion of their own shares. The amount of share repurchases have grown dramatically since 1983.

Note that the increase in share repurchases and cash acquisitions since 1983 does not appear to have come at the expense of dividend payments. Dividend payments continued to grow at roughly the same 10% rate per year in the years following 1983 as in the years preceding 1983. Instead, it appears that the share repurchases have been part of programs (1) to return free cash flows to shareholders rather than reinvest them in new capital expenditures and (2) to restructure U.S. corporations by substituting debt for equity in the firm's capital structure.

Cash acquisitions represent cash paid by one company to purchase the shares of stockholders in another company in a corporate acquisition. From a tax standpoint, such transactions are akin to share repurchases, and like repurchases, cash acquisitions have increased substantially since 1983.

Table 17.1 Cash Distributions to Shareholders (Billions of Dollars)

Year	Cash Acquisitions	Dividend Payments	Share Repurchases
1977	$ 4.3	$29.4	$ 3.4
1978	7.2	32.8	3.5
1979	16.9	38.3	4.5
1980	13.1	42.6	4.9
1981	29.3	46.8	3.9
1982	26.2	50.9	8.1
1983	21.2	54.9	7.7
1984	64.2	60.3	27.4
1985	70.0	67.6	41.3
1986	74.5	77.1	41.5
1987	62.2	83.1	54.3
1988*	32.6	43.0	26.0

*Through the first two quarters of 1988.

If all investors were like our tax-paying investor, the prices of non-dividend paying shares would have to be bid up relative to the prices of dividend-paying shares for investors to be indifferent to holding them. Generally, a firm's board of directors declares the amount of the cash dividend and sets the record date and the payment date for the dividend. The dividend is payable to shareholders who are on the company's book of records on the record date. To prevent the wrong stockholders from receiving the dividend, most exchanges in the U.S. set the ex-dividend date for a stock to coincide with the exact lead time necessary to change the company's records. The ex-dividend date is the date on which investors who

[4] Laurie Simon Bagwell and John Shoven, "Cash Distributions to Shareholder: Alternatives to Dividends," *Journal of Economic Perspectives* (Summer 1989), pp. 129-140.

buy shares do not receive the dividend because their names will not be added to the record book until after the record date.

Elton and Gruber first proposed a model to test for the presence of tax effects in the pricing of shares on ex-dividend dates.[5] They assumed that investors were not risk-averse in deciding whether to sell their shares the night before the stock goes ex-dividend at price P_b or wait overnight to sell their shares at price P_a. If they sell their shares at P_b, they pay capital gains tax on their gain; if they wait to sell at P_a, they receive the taxable dividend and pay a lower capital gains tax because they receive a lower price for their shares on the ex-dividend day. If there were no tax effects of the differential taxation of dividends and capital gains, the share would sell for price P_b on the night before the ex-dividend date and at price P_b-d on the ex-dividend date. That is, P_a would be equal to P_b-d. But with differential taxation of dividends and capital gains, indifference between selling the night before the ex-dividend date and waiting until the next day requires that

$$P_b - gt_p(P_b - P_o) = P_a - gt_p(P_a - P_o) + d(1 - t_p),$$

where g is the capital gains inclusion rate, t_p is the investor's marginal tax rate on ordinary income, d is the amount of the dividend, and P_o is the investor's basis in the stock. Simplifying this expression we find that

$$\frac{P_b - P_a}{d} = \frac{(1 - t_p)}{(1 - gt_p)}. \tag{17.1}$$

If g is less than 1, we expect that the price fall-off on the ex-dividend day will be less than the amount of the dividend. Investors prefer to sell the stock before the ex-dividend date, or they require a higher rate of return to carry the stock across the ex-dividend date. For example, if t_p is 40%, and g is equal to 80%, then $(1 - t_p)/(1 - gt_p)$ = .83, and the stock price should fall by only 83% of the dividend amount. If the dividend were $5, the stock price would fall by only $4.17. Thus, if the ex-dividend day price is $110, the price the night before the ex-dividend date would be $114.17. The before-tax return for the investor holding through the ex-dividend date would then be .73% even though the after-tax rate of return is assumed to be 0 over this short holding period.[6]

In fact, if investors have different marginal tax rates, and we assume that it is expensive to sell stock short, we would expect higher dividend-yielding securities to attract lower marginal-tax-rate shareholders than would lower dividend-yielding securities. Indeed, some tax-exempt pension funds tilt their common stock holdings toward higher dividend-yielding securities. Because of these clientele effects, the relative price fall-off on the ex-dividend day could be less for high-dividend-yielding stock than for low-dividend-yielding stock.

---

[5] Edwin J. Elton and Martin J. Gruber, "Marginal Stockholders Tax Rates and the Clientele Effect," *Review of Economics and Statistics* (February 1970), pp. 68-74. See also Edwin J. Elton, Martin J. Gruber, and Joel Rentzler, "The Ex-Dividend Day Behavior of Stock Prices: A Re-Examination of the Clientele Effect: A Comment," *Journal of Finance* (June 1984), pp. 551-556.

[6] With an expected positive appreciation in share prices, we would expect the share price to fall by slightly less than the amount of the dividend in any case. For example, if the expected return on stocks were 15% per year, the expected one-day return would be .04%.

Chapter 17 Empirical Evidence of Implicit Taxes and Tax Clienteles II

The early tests of these propositions appear to support an effect of differences in tax treatment of dividends and capital gains. They also support the notion that lower tax-bracket investors are attracted to higher dividend-yielding shares. During the mid-1960s, stocks appeared to fall, on average, by 80-90% of the dividend on the ex-dividend date.[7] With investors facing a 50% inclusion rate on capital gains at that time, equation 17.1 implies that the marginal tax rate of investors setting prices in the stock market during this period was 33%. In 1986, stock prices fell by about 90% of the dividend. With capital gains taxed at only 40% of the tax rate on dividends, this implies that the marginal tax rate of investors setting prices in the stock market was 16% in this period. In 1987, when the highest capital gains tax rate was 28% and the highest personal tax rate was 38.5%, stocks also fell by about 90% of the dividend amount.[8]

Barclay studied the behavior of U.S. stocks in the period preceding adoption of an income tax in 1913.[9] His evidence indicates that stocks fell, on average, by the full amount of the dividend during the period. He also found that the price decline on ex-dividend days was the same for low dividend-paying stocks and high dividend-paying stocks.

Poterba and Summers provide evidence, using British stock market data, that ex-dividend day price behavior is related to differences in tax treatment of dividend income and capital gains income.[10] But Hayashi and Jagannathan, using Japanese data, document that stock prices fall by the full amount of dividends on ex-dividend days.[11]

Finally, Shaw investigates the ex-dividend day behavior of publicly-traded master limited partnerships that generate distributions to unit holders. Because the distributions are nontaxable (they represent a return of capital), one would expect the value of the securities to decline by a dollar for each dollar distributed to investors. Curiously, the securities decline by *more* than the distribution amount.[12]

Although many of these tests appear to document differential tax effects of dividends and capital gains, they suffer from several problems. Perhaps most important, they implicitly assume that arbitrage possibilities are too expensive to

---

[7] Elton and Gruber, *op. cit.*, and Avner Kalay, "The Ex-Dividend Day Behavior of Stock Prices: A Re-examination of the Clientele Effect," *The Journal of Finance* (September 1982), pp. 1059-70.

[8] Roni Michaely, "Ex-Dividend Day Stock Price Behavior: The Case of the 1986 Tax Reform Act," Unpublished Working Paper, Stern School of Business (New York University), June 1988.

[9] Michael J. Barclay, "Dividends, Taxes, and Common Stock Prices: The Ex-Dividend Day Behavior of Common Stock Prices Before the Income Tax," *Journal of Financial Economics* (September 1987), pp. 31-43.

[10] James M. Poterba and Lawrence Summers, "New Evidence that Taxes Affect the Valuation of Dividends," *Journal of Finance* (1984), pp. 1397-1415.

[11] Fumio Hayashi and Ravi Jagannathan, "Ex-Day Behavior of Japanese Stock Prices: New Insights from New Methodology," Discussion Paper 30, Institute for Empirical Economics, Federal Reserve Bank of Minneapolis (July 1990). Note that most Japanese stocks pay dividends only once a year, so a 1% annual dividend on a typical Japanese stock is as large as a quarterly dividend for a stock that yields 4% annually.

[12] Wayne H. Shaw, "An Examination of Ex-Dividend Day Stock Price Movements: The Case of Nontaxable Master Limited Partnership Distributions," Working Paper, Cornell University (May 1990).

exploit. To illustrate, suppose you manage a pension fund that is tax exempt on dividend and capital gains income or you are a broker-dealer who pays tax on dividends and capital gains at full corporate rates (no capital gains exclusion allowance). If investors like you were the marginal investors over the ex-dividend date, the fall-off in price on this date would be approximately equal to the amount of the dividend. Suppose you believe that a stock will fall by less than the amount of the dividend. If you buy the stock the night before the dividend and hold until the opening of trading the next morning, you will earn a positive rate of return before tax. Ignoring risk for the moment, you will continue to buy the stock until the expected return is zero over night. This is true even if you face a high tax rate as a broker-dealer.

For example, if you could sell short the stock of a company (not going ex-dividend) whose returns were very highly correlated with the returns of the stock that was about to go ex-dividend, you would make an almost sure return without bearing capital costs or risk. And you would continue to undertake these activities until the before-tax expected returns on this strategy were zero.[13] As a pension fund manager, you could undertake the same strategy. You could buy stocks the night before an ex-dividend date, using the proceeds from the sale of stocks *not* going ex-dividend on that date to finance the transaction. As long as the basis risk (the lack of perfect correlation between the returns on the ex-dividend day stocks and the stocks that are liquidated from the portfolio) is low, the returns on this strategy will be more or less riskless.

Given these arbitrage opportunities, it is of questionable propriety to use ex-dividend day price behavior to measure the tax effect of dividends on share returns. Dividend-paying and non-dividend-paying stock might display the same amount of implicit tax around ex-dividend days.

One reason we *might* observe a differential in returns over ex-dividend dates is because short-term traders must incur some costs to effect a transaction, and these costs could overwhelm the arbitrage profit opportunities for stocks with small dividend yields. For investors who plan to sell their stock anyway, however, the transaction costs are irrelevant. Their only cost is the uncertainty of the price moves that occur by holding the stock for one extra day. Part of the extra return on the ex-dividend date might be necessary to induce risk averse investors to hold the stock for this extra day.[14] As transaction costs have fallen to trade securities, and as new hedging vehicles such as futures and options have become more popular, it has become even harder to detect an ex-dividend day effect on share price.

There are other problems with using short-term price movements around ex-dividend dates to estimate marginal tax rates of individual investors. One is that corporations might buy shares around ex-dividend dates to capture dividends. If a corporation holds stock around an ex-dividend date (for a period of

---

[13] But even for broker-dealers, the short-selling costs might be nontrivial, and regulatory constraints may prevent them from effecting too much arbitrage of this sort. They could lose their tax and regulatory status as broker-dealers.

[14] See, for example, Avner Kalay, *op. cit.*, and Merton Miller and Myron S. Scholes, "Dividends and Taxes: Empirical Evidence," *Journal of Political Economy* (March 1982), pp. 1118-1141.

Chapter 17   Empirical Evidence of Implicit Taxes and Tax Clienteles II

at least 46 trading days including the ex-dividend date) it can exclude a generous fraction of the dividend received from taxation. This dividend-received deduction reduces the marginal tax rate of corporations holding common stock. For example, assume that the corporation can exclude from taxation 80% of the dividend received. Let us assume that the corporation buys, for $115, a stock that is about to go ex-dividend for a $5 dividend. If the corporation sells the shares for $110 on the ex-dividend date, it realizes a $5 capital loss and a partially taxable dividend of $5. Assume that the corporate tax rate is 45% on ordinary income and 30% on capital gains income. Also assume that it can use capital losses to offset its other capital gains. Although the corporation earns a pretax profit equal to zero, it earns an after-tax profit of $1.05 (or $5(1 - .45 × .2) - $5(1 - .3)).

During the late 1970s and early 1980s, many corporations with huge realized capital gains from real estate transactions bought the common stocks of companies that were going to pay large dividends to effect this arbitrage strategy. The tax rules in the U.S. were tightened up with the 1984 Tax Act to prevent corporations, who received large dividends, from realizing the capital loss. But corporate arbitrage opportunities are still available in many circumstances.

Many corporations have also engaged in "dividend-capture" programs to manage their short-term cash positions. That is, they buy dividend-paying common stock prior to ex-dates and sell similar securities (or options and futures) to hedge out the risk of their holdings. If they are not the marginal holders of stock, they expect to make a positive after-tax return with little risk. The 1984 Tax Act prevented firms from selling in-the-money call options (that is, options whose underlying stock price is above the exercise price) or using other risk-reducing activities and still claiming the dividend-received deduction. Moreover, corporations (subsequent to the 1984 Tax Act) lose the dividend-received deduction on the amount they borrow to finance the stock position over the ex-dividend date.[15]

Despite tax-rule restrictions and market frictions, many corporations continue to engage in some forms of dividend capture. Since their marginal tax rate on dividend income is less than that on capital gains income, the active participation by such investors in the market could, in principle, cause share prices to fall by *more* than the amount of the dividend on the ex-dividend date. Unlike fully taxable investors, some corporate investors prefer dividends to capital gains for tax purposes.

Moreover, dividend-capture strategies have not been restricted to U.S. investors. Japanese institutional investors have been *very* active traders of U.S. stocks immediately preceding ex-dividend dates, often accounting for millions of shares in trading volume on a single day for a single company.[16]

Given these short-term traders, and the effects of different traders on the prices of securities around ex-dividend dates, it might not be possible to deduce whether broker-dealers, corporations, or individual investors are the marginal

---

[15] There are, however, important *de minimus* exceptions to this rule. Dividend-received deductions are not lost if the amount of dividend-paying stock held is below a corporation's book value of stockholders' equity.

[16] For example, see "Tax Maneuver By Japanese," *New York Times* (August 26, 1987), p. 32 and "Japanese Firms Dart In and Out of Market, Chasing Dividend Stock—and Lifting Volume," *Wall Street Journal* (January 27, 1988).

investors setting prices in the stock market using the ex-dividend date experience. But what about over longer holding periods? Do we observe differences in the rates of return on portfolios of equal risk that differ in terms of dividend yields? In particular, do high-tax-bracket investors require return premiums to hold high-dividend-yielding stock portfolios over the long term? We will attempt to provide some insights into the answers to these questions.

A number of factors might prevent stocks from bearing substantial implicit taxes and high-dividend-yielding stocks from bearing less implicit taxes than low-dividend-yielding stocks. For example, individual investors may be able to convert dividend income into untaxed income by way of organizational-form arbitrage. Ignoring nontax costs for the moment, investors can borrow on personal account using their dividend-paying stocks as collateral for the loan. The interest expense could then offset their dividend income. By investing the proceeds of the loan in tax-exempt savings vehicles such as life insurance contracts or pension accounts, investors could effect organizational-form arbitrage.

To illustrate, if the dividend yield on a $100 stock is 4% and interest rates are 10%, the taxpayer could borrow $40 (or 4%/10% × $100) on personal account to generate sufficient interest deductions to eliminate the tax on the dividend. The taxpayer would receive $4 in dividends from the stock and realize a deduction for interest of $4 (or .10 × $40).

The cost of this strategy to the taxpayer is the increased riskiness of a leveraged stock position. To mitigate the increased riskiness, the investor could use the proceeds of the loan to invest in a cash-value life-insurance policy. The earnings on the savings within the policy accumulate tax free. The result of this strategy is that investors have a stock position that is equally risky as an unlevered stock position, and they have converted their dividends into equal amounts of untaxed interest income. That is, the return on the $40 loan proceeds invested in the insurance policy is $4. This is exactly equal to the dividend, but because of organizational-form arbitrage, it escapes taxation.[17]

The problem with this strategy, however, is that taxpayers might not be able to borrow at the riskless before-tax rate of interest. They might be required to pay a premium rate on their loan because of hidden-action problems. Lenders may not be sure that the loan proceeds will be invested in the insurance account, nor that they can access the savings portion of the policy in case of a default. Beyond this, the insurance policy might offer a lower rate of return on its savings account than the before-tax riskless rate because of operating and other costs. As a result, investors would pay an implicit tax on shares.

For example, suppose the borrowing rate is 12% when the before-tax riskless rate is 10%, and the life insurance policy offers only 9% on the savings portion of the account. The investor would now need to borrow $33.33 (or $4/.12) to generate $4 of interest expense. Investing $33.33 in the insurance policy at a 9% rate generates $3 of income. So, the implicit tax rate on dividend income would be 25% (or ($4 - $3)/$4). Investors with marginal tax rates below 25% would not

---

[17] See Merton H. Miller and Myron S. Scholes, "Dividends and Taxes," *Journal of Financial Economics* (December 1978), pp. 333-364.

undertake this strategy. Because of market frictions and the reduction of personal tax rates in the 1986 Tax Act, many investors find these types of conversion strategies too expensive to implement.

The empirical evidence has been mixed as to whether long-term holders of high-dividend-yielding stock earn higher before-tax rates of return than long-term holders of low-dividend-yielding stock. Most studies, however, *do* find a premium to high dividend yields. Using the differentials in before-tax returns, the studies have tended to conclude that the tax rates of the marginal holder of stock are in the range of 25% to 56% over the various periods studied.[18]

Black and Scholes estimated a marginal tax rate of about 20%, but they also concluded that there was so much noise around this estimate, they could not determine convincingly whether the marginal tax rate was really even positive.[19] They used a long-run measure of dividend yield to avoid the effects of short-term traders on share prices around ex-dividend dates. More specifically, they allocated stocks to portfolios according to their historical dividend yields, and held these portfolios intact over long holding periods. Stocks that exhibited high dividend yields in the previous year were placed in high-dividend-yielding portfolios; stocks with low dividend yields were placed in low-dividend-yielding portfolios. They then measured the differences in realized returns and the differences in realized dividend yields on their constructed portfolios to estimate the tax effect. The assumption, which was borne out by the data, was that stocks with high dividend yields (low dividend yields) would tend to continue to be high-dividend-yielding stocks (low-dividend-yielding stocks) in the future. Many of the other studies really used short-term measures of dividend yield, and their results are very sensitive to the measures selected.

Black and Scholes argued that the characteristics of stocks with high dividend yields were substantially different from the characteristics of stocks with low dividend yields. As a result, investors who concentrated in either high or low dividend-yielding stock because of differences in their marginal tax rates would be taking on enough extra risk by deviating from a diversified strategy of holding both types of stock so as to erase the tax benefits of concentration. Blume extended the work of Black and Scholes and found that stocks with high dividend yields had higher before-tax rates of return than lower dividend yielding stocks, but he also found that stocks that paid *no* dividends also had higher before-tax rates of return.[20]

Keim discovered that the firms with the highest dividend yields and the lowest dividend yields were small firms. Moreover, in another study, he found that most of these return differences occurred in January.[21] There must be more going on here than just tax differentials. It would be hard to believe that investors

---

[18] See, for example, Robert H. Litzenberger and Krishna Ramaswamy, "The Effects of Dividends on Common Stock Prices: Tax Effects or Information Effects?," *Journal of Finance* (May 1982), pp. 429-443.

[19] Fischer Black and Myron S. Scholes, "The Effects of Dividend Yield and Dividend Policy on Common Stock Prices and Returns," *Journal of Financial Economics* (May 1974), pp. 1-22.

[20] Marshall Blume, "Stock Returns and Dividend Yields: Some More Evidence," *Review of Economics and Statistics* (November 1980), pp. 567-577.

[21] Donald B. Keim, "Size-Related Anomalies and Stock Return Seasonality: Further Empirical Evidence," *Journal of Financial Economics* (June 1983), pp. 13-32; and "Further Evidence On Size Effects

require a greater rate of return on high-dividend-yielding securities (and non-dividend-paying stocks) only in January.

Chen, Grundy, and Stambaugh update the tests using data into the 1980s, and use relatively powerful statistical techniques to estimate the effects of dividend yields on before-tax rates of return.[22] They could not distinguish the returns on high-dividend-yielding portfolios from low-dividend-yielding portfolios because their results were too sensitive to the measures used to control for differences in risk among the portfolios.

The effect on stock prices of differences in taxation of dividends and capital gains remains an open question. If there is a long-run tax effect on security returns because of differentials in dividend yields, it is very difficult to measure using available techniques.

17.2 Implicit Taxes on Securities other than Common Stocks

Tax-Exempt Bonds

While the evidence on the magnitude of implicit taxes on common stocks is unclear, there *is* evidence of implicit taxes on other securities in the market. For example, in Table 17.2 we show estimated implicit tax rates on one-year and twenty-year municipal bonds.[23] The implicit tax rates implied by the one-year maturities indicate that high-marginal-tax-rate investors are the marginal investors in the municipal bond market. The implied marginal tax rates fell from the 50% range in the late 1970s, to the 45% range in the early 1980s, and to the 32% range with the enactment of the 1986 Tax Act. The long-term municipal bonds exhibit much lower implicit tax rates. This might be due, in part, to differences in risk and differences in the call features associated with long-term municipal bonds compared to taxable bonds. Still, as with short-term municipal bonds, the implicit tax rate on long-term munis has declined markedly since the late 1970s, when personal tax rates were as high as 70%.

Adjustable-Rate Preferred Stocks

As discussed earlier, it is possible that individual investors are not the marginal investors in stock, particularly high-dividend-yielding stock. As noted, corporate investors actually prefer dividends to capital gains. Indeed, corporate investors

---

and Yield Effects: The Implication of Stock Return Seasonality," Ph.D. dissertation (University of Chicago), 1982.

[22] Nai-Fu Chen, Bruce Grundy, and Robert F. Stambaugh, "Changing Risk, Changing Risk Premiums and The Dividend Yield Effect," *Journal of Business*, Part 2 (January 1990), pp. 178-206.

[23] As described fully in Chapter Five, the implicit tax rate is computed by subtracting the yield on municipal bonds from the before-tax yield on fully taxable bonds and dividing the difference by the yield on fully taxable bonds.

Table 17.2 Marginal Tax Rates Implied by Taxable and Tax-Exempt Interest Rates, 1955 - 1988

Year	1-Year Maturity	20-Year Maturity
1955-59	41.1%	20.6%
1960-64	45.4	24.0
1965-69	37.6	21.8
1970-74	42.1	19.0
1975	40.8	21.7
1976	47.5	27.6
1977	50.7	32.2
1978	49.3	34.6
1979	49.8	35.5
1980	48.5	30.8
1981	46.3	22.9
1982	42.4	15.4
1983	44.5	20.6
1984	44.1	22.2
1985	39.7	19.7
1986	32.5	14.8
1987	33.4	19.0
1988	31.5	15.5

Source: Salomon Brothers, *Analytical Record of Yield Spreads*, from James M. Poterba, "Tax Reform and the Market for Tax-Exempt Debt," *Regional Science and Urban Economics* (August 1989), pp. 537-562.

appear to be the marginal holders in the short-term variable-rate preferred stock market. Such securities, which provide no capital gains, typically bear substantial implicit taxes (of between 25% and 30% in 1986, and somewhat less following the 1986 Tax Act).

17.3 Clienteles: Who Holds U.S. Debt and Equity Instruments?

In Table 17.3 we show the proportion of corporate debt and stock held by various investors as of the end of 1987. At that time, the largest holder of U.S. equities was the U.S. individual investor. But the proportion of the outstanding common stock held by these investors has been falling over time. In 1952, they held about 92% of the outstanding common stock, falling to 87% by 1962, 77% by 1972, and 69% by 1982. Currently, they hold less than 60%. Notice that life insurance companies and pension funds hold 27.4% of the outstanding stock. In 1952 they held less than 5%, rising to about 8% by 1962, 16% by 1972, and 23% by 1982.

Foreign investors hold 6.1% of the stock. This is also up from earlier periods. For example, foreigners held only 3% of U.S. equities in 1980, although they held 5% in 1968. With the elimination of the capital gains exclusion in the 1986 Tax Act, foreigners and U.S. pension funds were encouraged to buy more U.S. equities because shares should bear less implicit tax. Since many foreign investors escape capital gains taxes, they prefer to hold U.S. equities that provide them with greater before-tax rates of return. On the other hand, some foreign investors,

369

17.3   Clienteles: Who Holds U.S. Debt and Equity Instruments?

Table 17.3 Holdings of U.S. Corporate Equity and Bonds, 1987 (Billions of Dollars)

Sector	Year-end balance, 1987	Percent of total
Corporate equities (excluding mutual funds)	$2,853.2	100.0
Household sector[1]	1,697.4	59.5
Foreign investors	173.4	6.1
Mutual savings banks	7.0	0.2
Insurance and pension funds	782.7	27.4
Life insurance companies	83.2	2.9
Private pension funds	460.6	16.1
State and local government retirement funds	172.6	6.0
Other insurance companies	66.3	2.3
Mutual funds[2]	181.7	6.4
Brokers and dealers	10.7	0.4
Corporate bonds[3]	1,180.9	100.0
Household sector[1]	92.9	7.9
Foreign investors	157.6	13.3
Commercial banks	71.3	6.0
Savings and loans	37.6	3.2
Mutual savings banks	14.5	1.2
Insurance and pension funds	734.7	62.2
Life insurance companies	388.3	32.9
Private pension funds	157.4	13.3
State and local government retirement funds	135.2	11.4
Other insurance companies	53.9	4.6
Mutual funds[2]	54.2	4.6
Brokers and dealers	18.8	1.6

[1] The household sector consists of individuals (which include self-administered pension plans such as IRAs, Keoghs, etc.), charitable organizations, foundations, and private trusts. The Federal Reserve has estimated, for 1982 year end, that 83 percent of equity held by the household sector was owned by individuals, and that 63 percent of corporate bonds held by the household sector was owned by individuals; the remainder was held by charitable organizations, foundations, and private trusts.

[2] The great majority of mutual fund shares are owned by the household sector.

[3] Corporate bonds include bonds issued by foreigners held by U.S. persons. Other types of debt (for example, trade debt, mortgages, and bank loans) are excluded. Source: Board of Governors of the Federal Reserve System, "Flow of Funds Accounts: Financial Assets and Liabilities, Year End, 1964-87," September 1988.

notably foreign pension funds, worry about the withholding taxes they must pay on U.S. dividend income. We will return to this issue in Chapter Twenty.

As for corporate bonds, over 13% are held by foreign investors and 62.2% of these bonds are held by insurance and pension funds. Individual investors hold a relatively small proportion (less than 8%) of the outstanding supply of corporate bonds. Their holdings as a percentage of the total have fallen off during the 1980s. In the 1970s, they held as much as 20% of the outstanding supply of corporate bonds.

As Table 17.3 indicates, foreign investors are major holders of U.S. equities and bonds. Like individual investors, foreign pension fund investors have a preference for U.S. capital gain income over U.S. dividend income. Unlike interest income, U.S. dividend income is subject to withholding taxes, typically at a rate of 10% or 15% on the gross dividend payment, depending on the treaty the U.S. has with the country in which the investor is resident. As with interest, there is no withholding of tax on capital gains income.

Given different investors with different demand for dividends and capital gains, a natural question that arises is whether there is a way to separate out the components of the returns to common stocks, so that the parties that prefer dividends can claim *them* and the parties that prefer capital gains can claim *them*. The answer is that there are a variety of ways to do this. Some involve investing in derivative securities such as options or futures contracts. Some involve setting up mutual funds or partnerships to split returns to stock into dividend and capital gains components and issuing separate claims to each (a so-called "dual fund"). Still others involve creating securities such as futures contracts, "unbundled stock units," and dividend-protected warrants. In Chapter Twenty, we return to this theme and illustrate some of the opportunities available. We wish to emphasize that the availability of these opportunities to separate out components of asset returns to different investors makes it difficult to predict how large the implicit tax rate on various assets like stocks might be.

Summary of Key Points

1. If capital gains are tax-favored to the marginal investor in stocks, relative to dividends and interest income, we would expect stocks to bear implicit tax relative to bonds. We would also expect the implicit tax to be larger, the smaller is the dividend yield on stocks.

2. Empirical evidence is consistent with these propositions, but not conclusive. The difficulty in pinning down tax effects is that nontax factors, such as risk and firm size, are difficult to hold constant across assets that are taxed differently.

3. If individual investors are the marginal holders of common stock, shareholders could reduce their tax liability if firms were to distribute corporate profits by way of share repurchases rather than dividends.

4. While there are probably nontax advantages to declaring dividends rather than repurchasing shares, such benefits are not well understood.

5. Share repurchases in the U.S. have increased dramatically in amount since the early 1980s, as have cash purchases of shares in corporate acquisition transactions. At the same time, corporate debt outstanding has increased markedly.

6. Evidence suggests that U.S. stocks have tended to fall by only 80-90% of promised dividend payments on ex-dividend dates. The 80% figure applies to a period during which capital gains were highly tax-favored to individual investors. The 90% figure applies to more recent experience.

7. Because of myriad tax-arbitrage opportunities of investors who do not prefer capital gains over dividends for tax purposes (for example, tax-exempt investors, broker-dealers, many U.S. corporations, and foreign institutional investors), it is difficult to interpret ex-dividend day price behavior of stocks as indicative of the identity of the marginal investor.

8. Through borrowing, individual investors may be able to mitigate the tax disadvantages of dividends, but such strategies are limited by transaction costs. Individuals may also mitigate the dividend tax by avoiding high-dividend-yielding stocks, but this may result in poorly-diversified portfolios.

9. While high-dividend-paying stocks tend to earn a pretax premium over low-dividend-yielding stocks, so do nondividend-paying stocks. Moreover, both nondividend-paying stocks and high-dividend-paying stocks tend to be associated with smaller firms. This creates an identification problem in sorting out the explanation for return differences across firms with different dividend policies.

10. Where risk differences across differentially-taxed assets are relatively easy to control, it is less difficult to document significant effects of taxation on asset prices. For example, tax-exempt bonds and adjustable-rate preferred stocks bear substantial implicit taxes relative to fully-taxable bonds. The former are held primarily by high-tax individuals and corporations, and the latter are held almost exclusively by corporate investors eligible for the dividend-received deduction.

Discussion Questions

1. Would we expect the returns on high-dividend-yielding stocks to exceed the returns on low-dividend-yielding stocks on a risk-adjusted basis? Why or why not?

2. How might an investor convert dividends into unrealized capital gains? Does this strategy increase the investor's risk? If so, how might the investor reduce the risk of this strategy? What are the costs of undertaking this strategy? How do these costs affect the returns to the strategy?

3. Why might the implicit tax rate on municipal bonds be greater for short-term than for long-term municipal bonds?

4. Does the fact that tax-exempt investors hold such a large fraction of the outstanding bonds imply that the implicit tax rate on shares is low? What about the effect of these investors on the before-tax return on bonds?

5. What effect does a withholding tax on dividend payments to foreign investors have on the investment decisions of such investors?

6. What should happen to the market value of warrants, convertibles, and executive stock options when a dividend distribution is made? How does this compare with the valuation effects of a share repurchase of

Chapter 17 Empirical Evidence of Implicit Taxes and Tax Clienteles II

equal dollar magnitude? How might this affect management's desire to declare dividends?

7. If some investors prefer dividends to capital gains, while others prefer capital gains to dividends, how might a firm allow shareholders a choice of the form the return takes?

8. Why might a firm declare dividends despite a tax disadvantage to doing so?

CHAPTER 18
Converting Corporations to Partnerships through Leverage: Theoretical and Practical Impediments

As discussed in earlier chapters, U.S. tax reforms in the 1980s have introduced significant tax disincentives to operate in the corporate form relative to organizational forms that impose no entity-level tax. We have witnessed two types of responses to this shifting of the costs across organizational forms:

1. direct conversion of **regular corporations** to organizational forms that avoid entity-level tax; and
2. changes in capital structures of corporations that allow them to avoid some of the entity-level tax by distributing corporate profits to capital suppliers in forms that are tax deductible.

In this chapter, we examine the degree to which corporate restructuring can result in tax treatment, for income earned by corporations, that is similar to that achieved in partnerships. We find that the presence of tax rule restrictions alone is sufficient to prevent corporations from avoiding double taxation on at least the competitive portion of their pretax return streams. Corporate returns above the competitive rate face double taxation. This is true of returns to both human capital and physical capital, even where the latter is 100% debt-financed. Moreover, market frictions lead firms to moderate their propensity to issue debt, causing part of even the competitive return to corporate activity to be taxed twice.

18.1 The Tax Advantages of Debt: A Simple Model

Assume that the corporation has an investment project that will return Y dollars of taxable income and cash before interest and taxes. The required investment in the project is $1. For an all-equity-financed firm, the after-tax return on the investment would be

$$Y(1 - t_c)(1 - t_s),$$

where t_c is the corporate marginal tax rate and t_s is the annualized shareholder-level tax rate. If shareholders sell shares, they pay tax at rate gt_p, where g is the fraction of realized income from shares that is taxable and t_p is their marginal tax rate at the time of sale. Shareholders, however, can defer the realization of capital gains and in some cases avoid paying capital gains taxes entirely by donating stock to charity or by realizing a stepped-up basis on death. Moreover, capital gains tax rates are not necessarily constant over time (both g and t_p can change), and shareholders have an option to time their realizations strategically to coincide with periods of relatively low tax rates. As a result, the marginal tax rate on the returns to shares on an annualized basis, t_s, is lower than the current values of gt_p.

To ease notation, we define t_d by the following identity:

$$(1 - t_d) = (1 - t_c)(1 - t_s).$$

From the identity above, t_d can be interpreted as the total tax rate that shareholders pay on income earned by their all-equity-financed corporations. The subscript "d" is chosen to denote a "double" tax, once at the corporate level (t_c) and then again at the shareholder level ($t_s(1 - t_c)$). With this notation, the after-tax return to shareholders from investing in an all-equity-financed corporate project that yields Y dollars of corporate taxable income is

$$Y(1 - t_d).$$

If the firm were to finance the project with debt instead of equity, which reduces taxable income by the interest payments at rate R_b, the after-tax return to stockholders would be

$$(Y - R_b)(1 - t_d),$$

and the after-tax return to the firm's bondholders, given personal tax rate t_p, would be

$$R_b(1 - t_p).$$

If the interest on the debt, R_b, was equal to Y, then corporate taxable income would be zero. The corporate-level tax would disappear, and the firm's debtholders would realize a return of

$$R_b(1 - t_p) = Y(1 - t_p).$$

This could happen if the firm's only shareholders were its bondholders and all of the firm's income were paid out as interest. In effect, the firm's owners (the bondholders) would be taxed as if they were partners in a partnership, and the income earned by the corporation would escape an entity-level tax.[1]

In general, this strategy will not work. A corporation must have shareholders if it is to avoid the so-called "thin capitalization" rules (which denies interest deductions on the portion of "debt" that is recharacterized as equity). In principle, the firm's capital structure could consist of some form of strip financing where each investor acquires both debt and equity in constant proportions and the firm

---

[1] The corporation could still face corporate-level capital gains taxes on its liquidation. A partnership does not pay partnership-level taxes on any gains realized on the sale of its assets.

Chapter 18 Converting Corporations to Partnerships through Leverage

"overpays" on the debt component of the package. In the extreme, if interest rates are set high enough, the stock portion of the strip would receive no return and have a market value of zero. Were it not for tax rule restrictions, this ruse would avoid the double taxation of corporate income. All the payments on the debt would be tax deductible even though they included equity returns (in the form of interest) to shareholders. The IRS, however, would consider this arrangement to be a sham. For debt to be distinguished from equity under Code Section 385, there must be a disproportionate interest in the profits of the firm: the debt and equity holders cannot be one and the same investor, directly or indirectly through related party ownership of securities. A significant proportion of the shares must be held by shareholders who are not also bondholders. This necessity defeats the ability of strip financing with above-market-rate debt to eliminate the corporate tax completely. Moreover, when bondholders and stockholders are different investors, severe conflicts of interest between the investor groups can arise in highly leveraged organizations.[2] As a result, partnerships remain tax-advantageous relative to corporations.

18.2 Corporate Taxation of Economic Rents versus Competitive Returns

Surprisingly, if the corporation earns a non-competitive rate of return on its investments (that is, a return above its cost of capital), its shareholders must pay a full corporate and personal tax on these excess profits even if the firm finances the investments with debt. To illustrate, assume that the corporation finds an investment project that will return Y percent before interest and taxes (for example, 20% a year on a risk-adjusted basis, when the risk-adjusted borrowing rate is 8% before tax). If the project is financed with equity, shareholders pay a full double tax on the corporate income and are left with $Y(1 - t_d)$ after corporate-level and shareholder-level taxes.

Suppose that shareholders finance their equity investment in the corporation by borrowing on personal account at rate R_b. In that case, their after-tax annualized net return, assuming the interest on their personal debt is tax-deductible at rate t_p, would be $Y(1 - t_d) - R_b(1 - t_p)$. This appears as Case I in Table 18.1. But to use these interest deductions fully, shareholders must have investment income from other sources. That is, because of the restrictions imposed by Section 163(d), interest deductions in any tax year cannot exceed realized investment income.[3]

If the same investment undertaken by the corporation was instead undertaken through a partnership, the after-tax return to investors would be $Y(1 - t_p)$.

---

[2] For further discussion, see Jeremy I. Bulow, Lawrence H. Summers, and Victoria P. Summers, "Distinguishing Debt from Equity in the Junk Bond Era," *Debt, Taxes, and Corporate Restructuring* (Brookings, 1990), pp. 135-172.

[3] One way to generate investment income is to realize capital gains on shares. But if shares are sold early to enable the deduction of interest expense, shareholders lose some of the advantage of deferral of the shareholder-level tax. In other words, t_s increases, and this increases t_d as well.

If the partners borrowed on personal account to finance this project, their net return would be $Y(1 - t_p) - R_b(1 - t_p)$ or $(Y - R_b)(1 - t_p)$. This is Case II in Table 18.1.

Case II serves as a useful benchmark against which to evaluate the taxation of corporate investment returns, since there is no double taxation of partnership investment income. Note also that the net return to partnership investors would be the same whether the borrowing is undertaken on personal account or through the partnership. As we will see, this is not true for corporate investors.

A comparison of Cases I and II in Table 18.1 reveals that personal leverage does nothing to eliminate the double tax on the all-equity corporate investment. If, instead, the corporation borrows to finance this project at the corporate level, it returns to shareholders $(Y - R_b)(1 - t_d)$. This is Case III in Table 18.1. Here, the advantage of the partnership form over the corporate form, even for 100% debt-financed investments, is

$$(Y - R_b)(t_d - t_p).$$

Corporate-level financing succeeds in eliminating double taxation on R_b of income (the competitive return), but not on the excess.

To illustrate, if $Y = 20\%$, $R_b = 8\%$, $t_c = 34\%$, $t_p = 28\%$, and $t_s = 20\%$, then a corporate debt-financed investment (Case III) yields an annual profit to shareholders after interest and taxes of $(20\% - 8\%)(1 - 34\%)(1 - 20\%)$ or 6.34% of the amount invested in the project, versus 8.64% (or $(20\% - 8\%)(1 - 28\%)$) to partnership owners. The excess return to the partners is 36% higher than to corporate shareholders.

Table 18.1 The Degree to which Debt Financing Avoids Double Taxation

	Form of Debt-Financed Investment	Net After-Tax Return to Investor	Double Tax Avoided?
Case I.	Equity-Financed Corporation	$Y(1 - t_d) - R_b(1 - t_p)$	Not at all
Case II.	Debt-Financed Partnership	$(Y - R_b)(1 - t_p)$	Completely
Case III.	Debt-Financed Corporation	$(Y - R_b)(1 - t_d)$	On R_b only
Advantage of a debt-financed partnership over an equity-financed corporation:		$Y(t_d - t_p)$	
Advantage of a debt-financed partnership over a debt-financed corporation:		$(Y - R_b)(t_d - t_p)$	
Advantage of a debt-financed corporation over an equity-financed corporation:		$R_b(t_d - t_p)$	

$Y \equiv$ Taxable project return before taxes;

$R_b \equiv$ Pretax interest rate on debt;

$t_d \equiv$ Total tax rate to shareholders on income earned at the corporate level. The rate equals t_c, the corporate tax rate, plus $t_s(1 - t_c)$, where t_s is the annualized shareholder-level tax rate paid on gains from holding corporate stock:

$$(1 - t_d) = (1 - t_c)(1 - t_s);$$

$t_p \equiv$ Tax rate paid on ordinary income earned at the personal level, including income earned by partnerships (passed through to its partners) and interest income or expense.

Because of nontax factors, however, the pretax return on projects might differ between corporations and partnerships. To generate the same after-tax return as partners, the pretax return on the corporate project would have to increase from 20% to 24.36%.

Moreover, because of such nontax factors as restructuring costs, it might be undesirable to finance projects with 100% debt even if the taxing authority would allow it.[4] This would further favor partnerships. For example, if projects were only 50% debt-financed at the corporate level (and 50% debt-financed at the personal level), the project would have to earn 25.82% in corporate form to provide the same after-tax return as the 20% partnership project.[5] In other words, corporate profitability before interest and taxes would have to be 5% higher for the 50% debt-financed corporation than for the 100% debt-financed corporation to provide identical net returns to shareholders. The reason is that personal borrowing shields income from tax at rate t_p whereas corporate borrowing shields income from tax at the higher rate t_d.

The Effect of Borrowing for Multiple Periods

Some firms borrow a sufficient amount to wipe out their current taxable income. Does this strategy convert the tax rate on the total return (the required plus the excess return) to the personal tax rate as in a partnership? The answer is no. To illustrate this point, let us assume that the firm earns Y percent per year in perpetuity on a project and borrows at rate R_b to finance it. Its before-tax excess return is $Y - R_b$ each year.

To eliminate its entire before-tax income, the firm could borrow an additional $(Y - R_b)/R_b$ dollars. The interest payments on this loan would be supported by the annual project cash flows of $Y - R_b$.

But what would the firm do with the loan proceeds? If it cannot pay out the loan proceeds to its stockholders (perhaps due to loan covenant restrictions), and it invests in competitive projects, it would earn at rate R_b per dollar invested in the additional projects. This generates taxable income of $(Y - R_b)$ (or $((Y - R_b)/R_b) \times R_b$). This strategy leaves the firm exactly where it started before undertaking additional borrowing.

Alternatively the firm might attempt to engage in some form of clientele-based arbitrage. That is, it might take a long position in tax-favored assets financed with debt that gives rise to fully deductible interest payments. For example, suppose the firm were to purchase tax-exempt assets, such as municipal bonds, with the loan proceeds. Even if the tax rules allowed the firm to deduct interest following the purchase of such assets, the firm could only convert the corporate-level tax rate to the marginal tax rate that sets prices in the tax-favored

---

[4] On the other hand, in the event of bankruptcy, there may also be benefits from transferring control of the firm to a management team that can do a better job than would the incumbents. See, for example, Philippe Aghion and Patrick Bolten, "An 'Incomplete Contract' Approach to Bankruptcy and the Financial Structure of the Firm," Technical Report No. 536, Institute for Mathematical Studies in the Social Sciences (Stanford University Economics Department), 1988.

[5] Remember that risk is held constant across these financing alternatives, because any equity investment in the corporation is financed by borrowing on personal account. This avoids a comparability problem.

asset market. That is, while explicit taxes would be reduced, so would pretax returns on the investment, an implicit tax.

If the corporation borrows $(Y - R_b)/R_b$ to eliminate corporate taxable income and is permitted to pay out the entire loan amount to its stockholders, either as a dividend or as a repurchase of shares, this would not eliminate the double taxation either. Shareholders would realize current taxable income on the distribution.[6] The amount of taxable income normally depends on whether the distribution is a dividend or a share repurchase, as well as on the magnitude of "earnings and profits" in the corporation and the shareholders' basis in shares. If the shareholders have a zero cost basis in their shares (after all, the projects are all debt-financed), then any distribution will be fully taxable as a dividend or a capital gain. In this case, after paying the shareholder-level tax, the firm's shareholders retain

$$\frac{(Y - R_b)}{R_b} (1 - gt_p)$$

where, as before, g denotes the fraction of the income that is fully taxed at rate t_p.

Note that if shareholders can reinvest this after-tax amount at rate R_b, before tax, they generate an annual after-tax cash flow stream of

$$(Y - R_b) (1 - gt_p) (1 - t_p).$$

Compare this to the annual cash flow to partners in a partnership if they finance a project at rate R_b that returns Y percent per period in perpetuity:

$$(Y - R_b) (1 - t_p)$$

So the corporation cannot avoid a second level of tax on the excess return on corporate projects through additional corporate borrowing, even if the proceeds are distributed to shareholders. This is true even if the distribution takes the form of a share repurchase and shareholders have some cost basis in their shares. In that case, g would be less than one, but it would still be positive, resulting in one more round of taxes than in a partnership.

To illustrate this point, let us assume that the firm can generate a perpetual annual return of 20% on its $1 debt-financed investment. The required annual return on projects of this risk is 8%. On the strength of these cash flows, it borrows an additional $1.50 (or (.2 - .08)/.08) for a total loan of $2.50 per $1 of investment and pays no taxes each year. The firm requires $1 for investment in the project, which generates $.20 of taxable cash income per year, forever. After it pays $.08 in interest to bondholders for the $1 borrowed, the corporation is left with $.12 of before-tax income. By borrowing $1.50 more, at an interest rate of 8%, it pays an additional $.12 in interest each year. As a result, its net income is $0 (or .2 - .08 - .12), assuming that no additional corporate taxable income is generated with the excess $1.50 loan.

But the firm must do something with the additional $1.50 debt proceeds. If it could pay out the $1.50 to its shareholders, the payment would be at least partially taxable as a dividend or as a capital gain. If the entire distribution is

---

[6] If the firm had no accumulated earnings and profits, many state laws would prevent the firm from distributing the loan proceeds to shareholders.

Chapter 18   Converting Corporations to Partnerships through Leverage

taxable at a rate, t_p, of 28%, shareholders would net only $1.08 (or $1.50 \times (1 - .28)$). The present value of the same opportunity in partnership form is $1.50, a perpetuity of $(Y - R_b)(1 - t_p)$, discounted at $R_b(1 - t_p)$ or $(.2 - .08)(1 - .28)/.08(1 - .28)$.

The Effect of Recapitalizing and Distributing the Loan Proceeds

If the firm has undertaken a project that returns Y percent per year, forever, and has issued debt at an interest rate of R_b to finance the entire project, then it would realize $(Y - R_b)(1 - t_c)$ per year after corporate-level tax. Since shareholders can defer paying the tax on this excess return until they realize a gain, their annualized effective shareholder-level tax rate, t_s, is usually less than t_p. For example, because of deferral opportunities, t_s might be only 20% when t_p is 28%. For the firm's shareholders, the present value of this investment opportunity is

$$\frac{(Y - R_b)(1 - t_d)}{R_b(1 - t_p)}.$$

Substituting the parameter values from our illustration yields

$$\frac{(.2 - .08)(1 - .34)(1 - .2)}{.08(1 - .28)} = \$1.10.$$

With full borrowing and immediate taxation of the gain at the shareholder level, the present value of the investment opportunity is $1.08 (or $1.50(1 - .28)$). Without borrowing, and with deferral of the shareholder-level tax, the present value of the opportunity is $1.10. More generally, the firm must trade off realizing shareholder-level taxes earlier than necessary against the advantage of converting the corporate-level tax rate to the shareholder-level tax rate (for example, 34% to 28%) on corporate taxable income. Recapitalization may not be a tax-advantageous strategy for fully taxable shareholders. Note, however, that with heterogeneous shareholders, a partial recapitalization allows shareholders for whom deferral is unimportant (for example, pension funds) to step forward to liquidate their interests in a share repurchase.

Let us define gt_p as the shareholder-level tax today, and t_{sn} as the annualized shareholder-level tax rate if the capital gain is realized in n years. Then in the presence of a perpetual investment opportunity yielding Y dollars per year per dollar of investment, the advantage of a 100% leveraged recapitalization of the firm with a complete payout to shareholders today, compared to borrowing an amount only up to the required investment level, is

$$\frac{(Y - R_b)}{R_b}\left[(1 - gt_p) - \frac{(1 - t_c)(1 - t_{sn})}{(1 - t_p)}\right]. \tag{18.1}$$

As seen in the expression above, if gt_p, t_{sn}, and t_p are equal to each other (which requires, among other things, that $g = 1$; that is, no capital gains exclusion), then the advantage of leverage is to allow corporate income to be taxed at the personal rate rather than the corporate rate. If deferral of the capital gain is quite tax advantageous (that is, gt_p exceeds t_{sn}), then some or all of the advantage is offset because shareholders are forced to pay taxes early. In fact, in our example, it was a net tax disadvantage to increase leverage for this reason.

18.2   Corporate Taxation of Economic Rents versus Competitive Returns

Gains to Tax-Exempt Holders of Common Shares

As seen from expression 18.1, tax-exempt holders gain if corporations lever up to eliminate corporate taxes and distribute the proceeds of the loan to shareholders. They gain $t_c(Y - R_b)/R_b$ by escaping the corporate-level tax on their investment. Using our illustration, tax-exempt holders realize \$1.50 after tax. If the corporation were to pay corporate tax, the present value of the firm would be only \$.99 (or $.66 \times \$1.50$) to these tax-exempt entities. So, if tax-exempt institutions succeed in pressuring corporations to restructure (that is, add leverage and use the loan proceeds to pay out dividends to shareholders), they gain, although this may be at the expense of individual shareholders. So, on net, it might not be tax-advantageous to restructure.[7] On the other hand, if the distribution is made by way of a share repurchase rather than a dividend, the conflict may be mitigated, since tax-exempt holders can step forward to sell their shares at no tax cost.

Foreign investors may also benefit from a strategy of corporate leverage and share repurchase. Such investors are exempt from U.S. capital gains taxation, but they face withholding taxes on dividends that range from a rate of 5% to 30%, depending upon the treaty the foreign investors' home countries have with the U.S. The degree to which the foreign investor benefits also depends upon how the home country taxes U.S. dividends and capital gains, as well as whether the home country allows a foreign tax credit for U.S. taxes paid on dividends.

Finite Duration Debt

If the firm's cash flows were to generate abnormal profits forever, there is some advantage, at least for tax-exempt entities and certain foreign investors, for the firm to increase its leverage and make payments of the loan proceeds to stockholders. When the firm faces the prospect of earning abnormal profits for only a limited time, however, the advantage of corporate leverage is lessened, and the partnership form becomes even more tax-advantageous relative to the corporate form.

To eliminate corporate taxable income, the firm must borrow $(Y - R_b)/R_b$ to generate $(Y - R_b)$ of interest payments each year. If the firm's projects were to generate abnormal returns for only n years, the firm could not afford to pay out the entire loan proceeds to its stockholders. To ensure repayment of the loan, it must retain an amount sufficient to repay the principal on the loan at its maturity in n years. Because interest on the loan will be exactly offset by cash flows from the project, no residual cash flows will be available to repay loan principal unless some loan proceeds are retained within the firm. Assuming that the corporation can invest at the annual rate of R_b, before tax, on marginal investments, netting $R_b(1 - t_c)$ after tax per dollar invested, it must retain an amount ρ such that

$$\rho (1 + R_b(1 - t_c))^n = \frac{(Y - R_b)}{R_b}.$$

---

[7] Increasing the firm's leverage increases the likelihood of bankruptcy. In the event of bankruptcy, shareholders can deduct the capital loss only against other realized capital gains (plus \$3,000) each year. All realized capital gains, however, are fully taxable in the year incurred. This asymmetric treatment might increase the tax on shares. On the other hand, shareholders can time their sales to realize losses earlier than they realize gains.

Chapter 18   Converting Corporations to Partnerships through Leverage

This ensures that the loan can be repaid. So the amount that must be retained is equal to

$$\frac{(Y - R_b)}{R_b} \Big/ (1 + R_b(1 - t_c))^n. \tag{18.2}$$

Note that this retention precludes the corporate-level tax from being eliminated entirely, let alone the shareholder-level tax.

If the firm borrows $(Y - R_b)/R_b$ dollars and retains the amount specified in expression 18.2, it can distribute

$$\frac{(Y - R_b)}{R_b}\left[1 - \frac{1}{(1 + R_b(1 - t_c))^n}\right]$$

to its stockholders. After paying the shareholder-level tax, shareholders retain

$$\frac{(Y - R_b)}{R_b}\left[1 - \frac{1}{(1 + R_b(1 - t_c))^n}\right](1 - gt_p)$$

Compare this to a strategy of *no* additional corporate borrowing beyond that required to finance the project. If the corporation retains the excess profits of $(Y - R_b)$ each period for n periods and reinvests them at rate $R_b(1 - t_c)$, the present value of this annuity, after corporate tax but before shareholder-level tax, would be

$$(Y - R_b)(1 - t_c)\left[\frac{1 - [(1 + R_b(1 - t_c)]^{-n}}{R_b(1 - t_c)}\right],$$

which simplifies to

$$\frac{(Y - R_b)}{R_b}\left[1 - \frac{1}{(1 + R_b(1 - t_c))^n}\right]$$

If this amount is then distributed to shareholders, the net amount available is exactly the same as when the corporation undertook additional borrowing. As a result, there is *no advantage whatsoever* for the corporation to undertake additional borrowing beyond its project financing requirements to eliminate its current taxable income. By contrast, if the project were undertaken through a partnership: (1) the shareholder-level tax would be avoided and (2) the excess returns would compound net of the partnership tax rate, t_p, rather than the higher corporate tax rate, t_c.

Why Do So Many Restructured Firms Seem to Pay No Corporate Tax?

It is commonly believed that corporate restructurings involving significant amounts of newly created debt enable the corporate tax to be eliminated.[8] But we have demonstrated that this is not really so. Why, then, do so many restructured firms seem to pay no corporate tax? Several factors may be at work here.

---

[8] For example, see Laura Saunders, "How The Government Subsidizes Leveraged Takeovers," *Forbes* (November 28, 1988), pp. 192–196.

First, to the extent that debt is issued in sufficient quantity to eliminate corporate taxable income, significant amounts must be distributed to shareholders, thereby triggering immediate realization of taxable gain at the individual level. A study by Jensen, Kaplan, and Stiglin illustrates this phenomenon in the context of the leveraged buyout of RJR-Nabisco by Kohlberg, Kravis, Roberts.[9] Second, to the extent taxable income in the post-restructuring period is temporarily low due to nonrecurring expenses associated with the restructuring, future taxable income at the corporate level can be significant. Examples of such nonrecurring expenses are costs associated with plant closings, the sale of other assets that have declined in value, severance pay for employees, and consulting, legal and certain investment banking fees associated with the restructuring that are currently tax deductible. Third, restructuring may occur during periods of transitory operating losses. And fourth, the restructured firm may invest in tax-sheltered assets that avoid explicit taxes but at the expense of paying implicit taxes through reduced pretax returns on investment.

Whatever the reason, if corporate restructuring does not eliminate all positive net present value projects to the corporation, the corporation will incur a second level of tax on the excess return it generates. Moreover, a second level of tax on projects undertaken in the past, whether positive net present value or not, cannot be avoided due to the shareholder-level tax that results from replacing equity with debt. This misunderstanding may contribute to the desire expressed by many in Congress to remove interest deductibility for some or all of the debt issued by corporations. We now turn briefly to this subject.

Deductibility of Interest on High-Yield Debt

Proposals to eliminate the deductibility of interest on high-yield debt would strain considerably the corporate form of organization. Indeed, the 1989 Tax Act actually included several provisions that restrict interest deductibility on high-yield original issue discount obligations[10] and that limit net operating loss carrybacks that are created by interest deductions when accompanied by so-called "corporate equity reduction transactions," such as leveraged buyouts or large debt-financed stock repurchases.

Partnerships would look much more attractive if interest deductions on debt could not be used to mitigate double taxation of corporate income. While one might argue that few would abandon the corporate form because it achieves risk-

---

[9] Michael C. Jensen, Steven N. Kaplan, and Laura Stiglin, "Effects of LBOs on Tax Revenues of the U.S. Treasury," *Tax Notes* (February 6, 1989).

[10] "For (certain) debt instruments with yields more than five percentage points above applicable federal rates, the Act does not allow the issuer to deduct the discount as interest over the life of the obligation, but puts payers on the cash basis for this deduction. However, the holder must continue to accrue interest income as it accrues according to current law.

"Further, to the extent that yields exceed six points over the federal rate, the excess will be treated as a dividend. As a result, an issuing corporation will not receive a deduction, but holders that are C corporations are entitled to a dividend received deduction." (Deloitte & Touche, *Washington Briefing* (November-December, 1989), p.2)

sharing and liquidity efficiencies among investors, these arguments have not been fully tested.

Moreover, the 1980s witnessed a trend toward active investors and concentrated ownership.[11] This trend reflected, in part, a recognition that in most relevant settings, effective monitoring and managerial performance incentives in organizations requires key decision-makers to have a large stake in organizational performance. Apparently, the favorable incentive effects of concentrated ownership had become increasingly important relative to the risk-sharing benefits that dispersed ownership confers.[12] So partnerships may well become viable as alternatives to even large-scale corporate activity, particularly if there is a substantial difference in the tax cost of the two organizational forms. And unless tax planners could conceive of alternatives to high-yield debt as a means of distributing corporate profits in a tax-deductible manner, corporations would surely begin to lose their dominant position.

Of course, alternatives to high-yield debt will surely be devised in response to legislation precluding the tax deductibility of interest on such debt. For example, trade credit at low interest rates, with corresponding increases in the price of goods and services exchanged, would be one obvious response. Closely related would be the use of bank credit at below-market rates, tied to a requirement to maintain interest-free compensating balances.[13] Operating leases would increase as well, with rental expense substituting for interest. Alternatively, key lenders might demand more managerial input in exchange for tax-deductible compensation and reduced interest rates. Still another response would be to reverse the trend toward deconglomeration of corporate America so as to increase the low-risk debt capacity of the firm. Unfortunately, all of these responses would exact efficiency costs on the economy.

Finally, eliminating interest deductibility on high-yield debt would accelerate the recent trend of foreign acquisitions of U.S. corporations, particularly by investors who reside in tax jurisdictions that do not tax foreign-source income (so-called territorial tax systems). For such investors, the U.S. tax exemption on capital gains means that the shareholder-level tax on U.S. corporate income can be avoided.

Alternatives To Debt To Reduce the Corporate-Level Tax

ESOPs

Employee stock ownership plans (ESOPs) offer three ways to distribute corporate profits to investors in a tax-deductible way: (1) interest on ESOP loans (at specially subsidized rates), (2) employee compensation, and (3) dividends on

---

[11] Michael C. Jensen, "Capital Markets, Organizational Innovation, and Restructuring," Working Paper (Harvard Business School), January 1989.

[12] This trend seems to have diminished in the 1990s.

[13] Such a strategy was widely employed in Japan in the face of interest-rate ceilings prior to deregulation in the 1980s and in the U.S. under interest-rate ceilings specified in Regulation Q prior to deregulation. See Takeo Hoshi, Anil Kashyap, and David Scharfstein, "Bank Monitoring and Investment: Evidence from the Changing Structure of Japanese Corporate Banking Relationships," Working Paper (National Bureau of Economic Research), April 1989.

employee-owned shares. Theoretically, a 100% ESOP-owned firm provides an opportunity to eliminate the corporate tax even if substantial physical capital is invested in the firm. The firm can distribute all of the firm's before-tax income to its employee-owners in the form of either compensation or dividends that are paid on ESOP-held shares. Compensation is tax deductible, and the dividends paid on the shares held in the ESOP are tax deductible if the dividends are paid to employees (or used to pay down an ESOP loan that was used to acquire the shares held in the ESOP). Such strategies are not possible in 100% employee-owned corporations that are not organized as ESOPs, because attempts to distribute, as compensation, 100% of pre-compensation taxable income from a business that requires nontrivial amounts of physical capital, will be met with IRS claims of excessive compensation and disguised dividends.

As discussed more fully in Chapter Twelve, ESOPs have exploded in popularity since 1986, and they provide an opportunity to test the importance of tax and nontax factors that explain their proliferation. For example, to secure ESOP tax benefits, employee ownership must be allocated in ways that may provide poor performance incentives relative to alternative incentive compensation arrangements. As regards special tax treatment, ESOPs can be viewed as being highly tax-subsidized or not subsidized at all depending upon the benchmark against which they are compared. To the extent ESOP plans replace existing stock bonus plans or the investment in employer stock held through a firm's other pension plans, ESOPs offer distinct tax advantages. But to the extent ESOP plans replace debt-financed pension contributions into plans that hold no employer securities, ESOPs may actually be tax-disfavored. If the latter case is the relevant one, then the recent popularity of ESOPs would likely be attributable largely to the voting control they help incumbent managements secure.

Elimination of interest deductibility on high-yield debt would greatly increase the attractiveness of ESOPs. First, employee ownership becomes desirable, since both compensation and ESOP dividends are ways to distribute profits out of the corporation in a tax-deductible manner. And second, with 50% of interest income on qualified ESOP loans tax exempt to qualified lenders, competition results in interest rates on ESOP loans being reduced. This means that high-risk ESOP loans may bear interest rates comparable to those of low-risk fully taxable loans. Unless a different standard for interest deductibility applied to ESOP loans, the formation of ESOPs would clearly expand tax-deductible debt capacity.[14]

Partnerships and Other Organizational Arrangements

The firm could also form a partnership with its shareholders. That is, if the firm undertakes new investments in a partnership with its shareholders, the new investment escapes corporate-level and shareholder-level taxes if all of the income can be passed through directly to the shareholders, who pay tax on this income at their own personal tax rates. But even here, restrictions under Code Section 704(b) prevent certain disproportionate allocations of income to specific

---

[14] The supposed tax advantages of ESOPs did not escape the notice of legislators. As a result, Congress curtailed some of the tax advantages of the interest exclusion as well as the deductibility of dividends in the 1989 Tax Act.

partners unless such allocations have "substantial economic effect." Also, supplier-to-customer transfer pricing opportunities can move income from corporate to partnership form. Franchise arrangements could be used. The supplier or customer entity might be set up with current shareholders as owners. The corporation could then set prices strategically to shift corporate-level income to the shareholder partnership. As we have discussed in earlier chapters, however, Code Section 482 restricts these types of transfer pricing opportunities.

Shareholder-Level Taxes and Pension Funds

At the end of 1987, more than 30% of all U.S. corporate equities were held by pension funds, self-administered pension plans, and insurance companies.[15] A common misconception is that the shareholder-level tax for ownership interests held by these entities is zero. But in fact, pension funds merely enable their beneficiaries to postpone the tax on investment income until it is distributed.[16] While we have discussed before that a tax deduction for pension contributions followed by full taxation of pension benefits is equivalent to tax exemption of pension investment income when the pension fund invests exclusively in zero net present value projects, this result does *not* apply to investment in *positive* net present value projects.

Studies that estimate the revenue consequences to the U.S. Treasury of leveraged buyouts and other forms of corporate acquisitions routinely err in assuming that merger premiums received by pension funds that hold shares in target companies generate no tax revenues.[17] In fact, the return premium generates both (deferred) income tax as well as (deferred) estate tax to be paid by beneficiaries.

18.3 Retained Earnings, Dividend Policy, and Positive Net Present Value Projects

We showed in Chapter Fifteen that if tax rates are constant over time and if corporate and personal after-tax rates of return coincide, it is a matter of indifference whether *competitive* projects are undertaken in corporate or partnership form, when the corporation is an all-retained earnings firm and shareholders have a zero tax basis in their shares. At first blush, this may be a counter-intuitive result. After all, corporate income generates both an entity-level and a shareholder-level tax. The explanation lies in the fact that, marginally, investments financed by retained earnings do not generate a shareholder-level tax.

The analysis changes when positive net present value projects are available to the corporation. In particular, a marginal round of shareholder-level tax cannot be avoided on the return above the competitive rate. To see this, suppose that a project is available that yields income of Y dollars per dollar invested, where Y

---

[15] Board of Governors of the Federal Reserve System, "Flow of Funds Accounts: Financial Assets and Liabilities, Year End, 1964-87," September 1988.

[16] Conversations with Richard Leftwich have clarified our thinking on this point.

[17] See, for example, Jensen, Kaplan, and Stiglin, *op cit.*

exceeds the competitive rate R_b. If the project is financed through retained earnings, and the after-tax profit is distributed to shareholders a year later, the net return to the shareholder per dollar invested is

$$[1 + Y(1 - t_c)] (1 - t_p). \tag{18.3}$$

If, on the other hand, a dividend is declared now, and the project is undertaken outside the corporation (say, through a shareholder-owned partnership or proprietorship), an immediate tax of t_p is levied per dollar of dividend. So t_p will have to be borrowed by the shareholder at rate R_b to finance the entire project. The net to the shareholders becomes

$$(1 - t_p)(1 + Y(1 - t_p)) + t_p [Y(1 - t_p) - R_b(1 - t_p)]. \tag{18.4}$$

The expression above simplifies to $(1 + Y - t_p R_b))(1 - t_p)$. Comparing the after-tax accumulations in the two strategies (reinvest retained earnings in the corporation and pay a dividend later in 18.3 versus pay a dividend now, followed by investment of after-tax dividend plus borrowing in 18.4) reveals that an immediate dividend beats a reinvestment in the corporation by

$$(t_c Y - t_p R_b) (1 - t_p).$$

Even if t_c were no larger than t_p, reinvestment of retained earnings in the corporation would subject the excess return on the project to one additional round of tax. With $t_c > t_p$, the advantage of a current dividend is increased.

The intuition behind this result is as follows. Where shareholders in an all-retained-earnings firm have a zero tax basis in their shares, they face a tax liability equal to t_p on every dollar of net asset value in the firm. Shareholders have an option of paying off the liability now by distributing corporate property to the owners or they can pay the tax later, *with interest*, by reinvesting the corporate income. In the latter case, the interest rate shareholders pay on this liability if corporate distributions are postponed is equal to the rate of return the corporation earns on its investments after paying corporate tax. If the corporation invests exclusively in zero net present value projects, it earns a competitive rate of return and shareholders are indifferent between paying their liability now or later. If the investments generate *excess* returns, however, shareholders would prefer to pay the tax liability now rather than paying interest at the high rate earned on the positive net present value projects.

The foregoing analysis assumes that the positive net present value project can be managed no more effectively in the corporation than in a partnership that might be formed by shareholders to invest corporate distributions in attractive projects. If the positive net present value projects are available only if undertaken within the corporation, then reinvestment of retained earnings in the corporation could prove to be the most efficient strategy.

18.4 Concluding Remarks

We explored the degree to which debt financing can reduce the corporate-level tax on income in the U.S. Although we showed that debt is capable of shielding the competitive rate of return on projects from the corporate-level tax, debt financing cannot shield the positive net present value portion of project returns. Because nontax factors preclude corporate activities from being 100% debt-financed, part of the competitive return to corporate activity is also subject to double taxation.

We also considered alternative mechanisms that would convert the corporate tax to a personal tax (or a partnership tax). These include other claims that give rise to tax-deductible payments to the corporation such as obligations to employees, lessors, and suppliers. As we showed, all these alternatives are limited in their ability to eliminate the corporate-level tax.

Summary of Key Points

1. If all corporate earnings before interest and taxes could be distributed to investors as interest, the corporation would essentially be taxed as a partnership. The firm, however, can not pay out all of its earnings as interest: its shareholders must expect to earn a return. In addition, nontax costs limit the amount of debt that the firm can support.

2. The annualized tax rate on the returns to shares held for more than one year is lower than the capital gains tax rate on shares held for a single year. This results because shareholders can defer payment of the tax. They can also plan for the possibility that future capital gains tax rates will be lower than current rates. Moreover, shareholders can donate appreciated shares to charity or achieve a stepped-up basis at death. Therefore, the shareholder-level tax rate will generally be greater if shareholders are forced to sell shares in a recapitalization such as a debt-for-equity swap than if shareholders can control the timing of the disposition of their shares.

3. If a corporation earns a rate of return in excess of that required on investments of similar risk, its shareholders must pay full corporate and shareholder-level tax on the excess returns even if the required investment in the projects is 100% debt-financed.

4. Shareholders who borrow to buy the shares of an all equity-financed firm cannot avoid the double corporate-level and shareholder-level tax on any of the corporation's taxable income. A corporation that finances its investments with debt, however, avoids the corporate-level tax on the competitive part of the return on the project. But an investment in a partnership avoids double taxation on both the competitive *and* the excess returns on a project.

5. A corporation can borrow more than needed to finance its investments if it has positive net present value projects. As a result, it can generate sufficiently large interest deductions to wipe out the taxable income from the returns on its noncompetitive projects. But the proceeds of the debt issue that are not required to fund corporate projects must be reinvested or distributed. If the corporation invests in competitive-rate-of-return projects, it will generate corporate-level taxable income in an

amount equal to that which it was trying to avoid; if it invests in tax shelters, it substitutes implicit taxes for explicit taxes; if the excess is distributed to shareholders, a tax on dividend or capital gains income must be paid by shareholders at their personal tax rates.

6. If the net present value of the firm's projects is distributed to its shareholders, tax must be paid sooner and at a higher rate than if the net present value was not paid out currently. The corporate-level tax is reduced but the shareholder-level tax is increased. Shareholders such as pension funds and foreign investors prefer that the firm pay out these excess returns. They escape the corporate-level tax and, except for withholding taxes imposed on foreign investors, are exempt from shareholder-level taxes.

7. Since most projects do not generate abnormal returns forever, the corporation cannot borrow sufficient funds to generate interest deductions to wipe out the corporate-level tax and pay out all of the proceeds of the debt issue to its shareholders. The firm's future cash flows would not be adequate to support the payment of interest and the repayment of the debt's principal. The firm must retain sufficient funds to repay the debt, and the corporation generates taxable income on these funds. As a result, it is not tax-advantageous for the firm to borrow to eliminate part of its taxable income in the finite duration case.

8. Employee Stock Ownership Plans can eliminate the corporate-level tax in a 100% employee-owned firm. Since compensation is tax deductible, as are dividends on shares held by an ESOP and paid out to employees, the firm can distribute all of its taxable income to its employees in the form of compensation and dividends to avoid the corporate-level tax. The corporation becomes taxed like a partnership.

9. Substitutes for debt and ESOPs can be used to reduce the corporate-level tax. For example, partnership joint ventures with shareholders, employee compensation arrangements, and supplier/customer relations can be used to reduce the corporate-level tax. All of these vehicles, including debt, however, can only go so far in converting the corporate tax to that of a partnership. On the other hand, the corporate form might provide sufficient nontax subsidies to overcome its tax disadvantage relative to partnerships.

10. In some circumstances, it does not matter whether an all-retained-earnings corporation pays a dividend currently or retains and accumulates the earnings to be paid out in the future. This will be true if the personal tax rate remains constant, the corporate tax rate is approximately equal to the personal rate, and the reinvestment vehicles are projects that earn normal rates of return such as fully taxable or municipal bonds.

11. If an all-retained-earnings firm has positive net present value projects that could be carried out equally efficiently in partnership as in corporate form (a big "if"), it would be tax advantageous for the firm to have the projects conducted by shareholders in partnership form. If, instead,

retained earnings are used to fund the project in corporate form, a deferred tax plus interest, at a rate set equal to the high earning rate on the projects, must be paid when the earnings are finally distributed to shareholders. As a result, shareholders would prefer to undertake the projects outside of the corporation. They would prefer that the corporation restrict its reinvestment of retained earnings to projects that earn competitive rates of return.

Discussion Questions

1. Give examples of the ways in which firms can reduce the corporate-level tax in addition to debt financing? Are these ways effective in reducing the total tax to investors?

2. If a firm has projects that earn abnormal rates of return, can the firm borrow a sufficient amount to generate interest deductions to wipe out all corporate taxable income? Why?

3. If a firm can earn abnormal returns forever, is it tax advantageous to distribute the net present value projects to its tax-exempt shareholders (such as pension funds, foreigners, tax exempt institutions, and insurance companies)?

4. When a firm expects that its projects will generate abnormal returns for only a limited number of years, is it tax advantageous for the firm to borrow sufficient funds to generate interest deductions to wipe out its taxable income and distribute some of the proceeds of the debt issue to its stockholders? Why?

5. Why do we observe many firms generating net operating losses after a leveraged buyout if it is not tax advantageous to borrow to reduce corporate-level taxable income to zero?

6. Does it matter whether an all-retained-earnings firm pays its retained earnings out currently or reinvests these earnings to be paid out in the future? Does it make a difference whether the firm can earn abnormal rates of return on its investment projects?

7. What are the tax and nontax costs associated with an increase in the firm's debt-to-equity ratio?

Problem

A manufacturing corporation owns tangible fixed assets that cost $100 million. The $100 million was financed by an equity offering of equal amount. The assets are specialized and have no value in use other than to produce the sole product that the firm sells to its wholesale distributors. There is no debt in the firm's capital structure. Its reinvestment opportunities are poor, so the firm distributes all profits as earned. As a consequence, the corporation has no accumulated earnings and profits.

The firm's manufacturing activities generate a pretax profit of $10 million per year, year in and year out. This return of 10% of the cost of the fixed assets is equal to the rate of return earned on riskless bonds in the marketplace. The corporate tax rate is 40%, and the personal tax rate on income (including dividend income) is 30%.

a. What is the current market value of the corporate stock?

b. How much better or worse off would the shareholders be if the corporation were to issue $100 million in debt at a rate of 10% and use the proceeds to repurchase stock?

c. What impediments exist to issuing a $100 million loan to repurchase stock?

d. How does the analysis change if the firm's tangible fixed assets yield $40 million of profits before interest and taxes each year rather than $10 million?

e. How does the analysis change for a "tax-exempt" shareholder (for example, a pension fund) if the firm generates $40 million of profits each year before interest and taxes?

f. If debt can only be issued at a rate *above* 10%, and the firm generates income before interest and taxes of $40 million per year, under what conditions will taxable and tax-exempt investors disagree on how to restructure the firm?

CHAPTER 19
Repackaging Ownership Rights through Joint Ventures and Partnerships: Tax-Sheltered Investments

In this chapter, we explore the motivations for and economic consequences of investing in **tax shelters**. The distinguishing characteristic of a tax shelter is that its investment cost can be deducted from taxable income at a rate that exceeds its economic depreciation. As discussed in Chapter Five, highly tax-favored investments typically give rise to implicit taxes in that they are often priced to yield reduced pretax returns relative to less favorably taxed investments.

A great many tax-sheltered investments are undertaken in partnership or joint venture form. Of course, these arrangements are stimulated by a variety of nontax factors: outside investors may bring special research, marketing, or administrative expertise to the venture, not to mention risk sharing benefits. But on the tax dimension, such investments are motivated by a desire to split up and allocate the investment expenditure and investment return in a way that enables investors with different tax characteristics to inhabit their natural tax clienteles.

But these attempts to capture tax benefits through joint ownership arrangements frequently introduce both administrative and other costs resulting from the creation of conflicts of interest among the co-venturers. As in other contexts, taxpayers must trade off the tax benefits against the nontax costs. Naturally, if the nontax costs are too high, it will not be worthwhile to capture the tax benefits. This provides an incentive for investors and managers to establish institutional arrangements that mitigate the costs. We illustrate how this has occurred in certain types of investments.

Another theme of this chapter is that the 1986 Tax Act changed dramatically the natural tax clienteles associated with tax-sheltered investments in the U.S. Among the reasons for this are (1) the introduction of so-called "passive activity loss" rules that apply to individuals and closely held corporations but not to widely held corporations, (2) the fact that many corporations now face higher marginal tax rates than do wealthy individuals, (3) the introduction of the alternative minimum tax for corporate taxpayers, and (4) an increase in the tax rate on capital gains relative to the rate on ordinary income. These, and other tax rule changes introduced by the 1986 Tax Act, have caused a substantial shift in demand for tax shelters from individuals to those corporations not subject to the alternative minimum tax, as discussed more fully below. Such changes in tax clienteles can be a nuisance for investors, but they also provide an opportunity for investment advisors and other intermediaries to contribute to economic efficiency by helping to reorganize investment portfolios in as costless a manner as possible.

In this chapter, we focus on a subset of the tax-favored investments available to investors. In particular, we consider those that give rise to tax losses in the year of investment (possibly the first *several* years of investment), followed by substantial sums of expected taxable income in subsequent tax years. A large number of tax-favored assets satisfy this definition of tax shelters, including: (1) assets, such as tangible business property, that are depreciable at rates faster than the decline in their economic values (particularly if the assets are debt-financed), (2) research and development (R&D) investments, (3) investments in qualified pension plans, and (4) oil and gas investments.

We will take a closer look at investments in depreciable property in subsequent chapters, and we have already discussed pension investments. In this chapter, we focus on joint ventures and limited partnerships as alternative ways for investors to finance such tax-favored investments as R&D and oil and gas exploration.

19.1   Research and Development Ventures

R&D investments are classic tax shelters. Qualifying research expenditures in the U.S. are immediately deductible as incurred under Section 174 of the Internal Revenue Code. Moreover, the sale of successfully developed technology generally gives rise to capital gains. Beyond this, the 1981 Tax Act introduced a generous tax credit to encourage R&D activity.[1] The U.S. is not alone in granting favorable tax treatment to R&D activities. In fact, the tax rules in some countries are far *more* generous than in the U.S.

To illustrate, suppose a corporation makes an R&D investment of $1. Its marginal tax rate is 40%. Any income generated from the investment will be taxed in the future when the corporation's tax rate is expected to be 30%. Suppose that an R&D tax credit equivalent to 10% of the investment expenditure is immediately available. The technology is very risky, as indicated below:

Probability	Payoff	Tax Rate
90%	$ 0 (worthless)	—
10%	$ 11 (successful)	30%

---

[1] Prior to 1986, the credit was 25% of incremental R&D expenditures over the average for the preceding three years, subject to limits. The 1986 Tax Act reduced the credit to 20% of incremental R&D expenditures. It also narrowed the definition of qualified research. The credit was scheduled to expire in 1988, but it was extended.

The expected pretax rate of return is 10% (or $.9 \times \$0 + .1 \times \$11 = \$1.10$ of expected cash return on a $1 investment). But the expected after-tax rate of return is considerably higher, even if we assume that the $11 return in the event of a successful investment outcome is fully taxed at 30%:

$$\frac{\$1.10 \times (1 - .30)}{\$1.00 - \$.40 - \$.10} - 1 = \frac{\$.77}{\$.50} - 1 \text{ or } 54\%.$$

If the research were undertaken by a firm with net operating loss carryforwards or a start-up company with no profits against which to offset the R&D deductions or the R&D tax credits, the after-tax returns would decline dramatically. The after-tax returns would also decline for firms subject to the 20% corporate alternative minimum tax.[2] Still another situation in which the return to R&D would be reduced is where the investor generates substantial sums of foreign-source income, the home country requires the R&D costs to be allocated to worldwide operations, and the foreign country does not allow a deduction for any of the R&D spent in the home country.

For example, suppose the R&D expenditure were deductible at a rate of only 20%, the present value of the R&D tax credit were only 5%, and subsequent income were taxed at a rate of 30%. Then the after-tax expected rate of return would decline from 54% in our first example to only 2.7% (or [$.77/($1.00 - $.20 - $.05)]-1).

One possible response to the unfavorable tax treatment that results in these situations is to undertake the investment anyway and suffer the tax cost. Another reaction to unfavorable tax economics is simply to abandon the investment. The tax rules discourage research expenditures by low-tax firms. On the other hand, low-tax firms can finance the activity in a way that sells off the rights to favorable tax treatment to a party that is in a better position to take advantage of the tax writeoffs.

Such considerations give rise naturally to the creation of limited partnerships (LPs) or joint ventures. Outside investors are allocated the lion's share of the write-offs and a share of the investment returns. The company doing the research receives a management fee and an interest in any revenue generated from licensing or selling the technology.

Shevlin provides empirical evidence that supports the tax motivation for forming R&D LPs.[3] He finds that firms sponsoring R&D LPs are younger and have more net operating loss carryforwards than do firms that conduct R&D in-house. Shevlin also considers off-balance-sheet financing as a nontax motivation for forming R&D LPs, but he finds only weak empirical support for this.

---

[2] The alternative minimum tax applies to U.S. taxpayers that shelter "too much income" from current taxation by exploiting such "tax preferences" as accelerated depreciation and the expensing of intangible drilling costs incurred in connection with oil and gas exploration. If "alternative minimum taxable income" (which is regular taxable income plus adjustments for tax preferences), multiplied by 20% (24% for noncorporate taxpayers subsequent to the 1990 Tax Act, 21% prior to the Act) less allowable tax credits, exceeds the regular tax, then this higher tax is the one that applies.

[3] Terry Shevlin, "Taxes and Off-Balance-Sheet Financing: Research and Development Limited Partnerships," *The Accounting Review* (July 1987), pp. 480-509.

19.1   Research and Development Ventures

As effective as these partnership or joint venture arrangements may be from a tax standpoint, it does not take much imagination to recognize that they can create severe incentive problems. Moreover, such entities require considerable administrative costs to organize, including sales commissions and investment banking fees that can easily run to 10% or more of the total amount invested. In addition, joint venturing of R&D may require disclosures to investors regarding the nature of the research that compromise the firm's competitive advantage.

To illustrate the importance of these costs, even prior to 1982, when wealthy individuals were taxed at rates of up to 70% on investment income (while corporations faced rates below 50%), corporations owned most of their depreciable property outright. Tax incentives notwithstanding, they failed to lease such assets from individuals, and most oil and gas as well as R&D investments were undertaken entirely through corporations.

Firms often have a number of research projects at various stages of development at any given time. Typically, the projects are in related fields. A firm that funds one among several related projects through an LP will have an incentive to spend the LP funds in a way that benefits the projects not being funded by the limited partnership.

This problem can be mitigated to the extent the project is one-of-a-kind; that is, the researcher has no other related projects being undertaken and the skills developed in working on the project are difficult to apply elsewhere. The Delorean Motor Car may be a good example here. In 1978, $20 million was raised to finance this venture through an R&D LP.

On the other hand, Genentech has used R&D LPs fairly extensively. One might expect incentive problems to be rather severe in their case. To the extent that Genentech wishes to establish a reputation as a high quality and trustworthy contract researcher, however, they may find it in their best interest to act in the LPs' best interests. Otherwise, they might have difficulty raising capital in the marketplace in the future.

Genentech did just this in a joint venture with a Houston-based beef manufacturer. The goal of the project was to develop bovine interferon to reduce disease in shipping cattle to market. The beef manufacturer put up several million dollars and Genentech failed to produce a commercially successful product despite high expectations. Although not specified in their contract, Genentech returned all the money to its co-venturer to protect its reputation (and perhaps to avoid litigation costs).

19.2   Oil and Gas Investments

For many years, limited partnerships have been popular as a means of financing oil and gas investments. The motivation for financing oil and gas investments through a joint venture or limited partnership is similar to that discussed earlier in the context of R&D investments; that is, the active investor places a lower value on the tax benefits than do outside investors.

Let's consider some special issues that arise in the course of selling oil-and-gas-related tax benefits. With some simplification, oil and gas investments consist of two phases:

1. drilling a hole, and

2. completing a well if oil and/or gas are present in sufficient quantities–otherwise the hole is plugged and abandoned.

Drilling costs typically run on the order of two-thirds the total cost of bringing a well to the point of production. In limited partnerships, there are two classes of partners: limited partners (LPs), who are the passive investors, and general partners (GPs), the managing investors.

Limited partners are characterized by a relatively strong demand for tax benefits as compared with GPs. To maximize the tax efficiency of the partnership contracts, many of the deals are structured such that the LP pays for 100% of the costs that are immediately tax deductible (mostly drilling costs). The GP pays for all the costs that must be capitalized (mostly completion costs). This type of sharing arrangement is called a "functional allocation" cost-sharing arrangement in the industry. It is by far the most popular type of contract.

With such a cost-sharing arrangement, the after-tax rate of return to LPs routinely exceeds the before-tax rate of return. To see this, recall that immediate deductibility of an investment, followed by full taxation of the returns at the same tax rate, is equivalent to tax exemption. Like R&D investments, as well as other tax-sheltered investments, the after-tax returns on oil and gas investments can actually exceed before-tax returns (and therefore be taxed more favorably than municipal bonds). There are at least three reasons for this.

1. Percentage depletion allowance: 15% of revenues (up to 50% of net income) is explicitly tax exempt (typically about 25% of the income is exempt).

2. Income may be taxed at rates well below the tax rates at which deductions are taken. This may occur because of
   a. statutory changes in tax rates (such as occurred with the passage of the 1981 and 1986 Tax Acts);
   b. a gift of a partnership interest to a low-tax relative after a tax deduction has been taken on the investment at high tax rates; or
   c. deduction at current high tax rates, followed by income at lower rates during retirement or when the alternative minimum tax applies.

3. Part of the income may be subject to more favorable capital gains tax rules, especially if an installment sale is used to sell the partnership interest.

For the 40% taxpayer, if percentage depletion alone exempts 25% of the return from taxation, it would make the after-tax return equal to 117% of the pretax return (or $(1 - .75 \times .4)/(1 - .4)$ or 7/6). Tax rates being lower in the future (condition 2 above), can mean that a 30% tax-bracket investor may be a more efficient investor in a tax shelter than a 40% tax-bracket taxpayer if the future tax rate is expected to decline for the lower tax-bracket investor. For example, the 30% investor, whose tax rate is expected to decline to 20%, and for whom 25% of the income is sheltered by percentage depletion, earns an after-tax return that is 121% of the pretax return (versus 117% for the 40% taxpayer).

As we have indicated on numerous occasions, efficient tax planning is not always the same thing as tax minimization; nontax costs must be considered as well. In functional allocation drilling programs, for example, a desire to maximize the tax benefits naturally leads general partners to complete fewer wells than is optimal insofar as the partnership is concerned.

This arises because costs are incurred sequentially: after drilling takes place, the well is either completed or abandoned. Moreover, the GP alone knows the status of the drilled hole. Since the GP bears 100% of completion costs, but gets less than 100% of any resulting revenues (the typical revenue share is 40%) this creates a so-called "externality problem."

The presence of the externality problem means that the GP will not complete as many wells as would be completed if the venture were organized as a sole proprietorship. In a 100%-owned project, all wells would be completed if the value of the oil in the ground exceeds the cost to remove the oil. But the GP has an incentive to abandon any well in which the cost to remove oil exceeds the GP's *share* of the value of the oil. So the GP has an incentive to abandon a valuable prospect whenever R>C>sR, where R represents oil revenues in the ground, C represents well-completion cost, and s is the GP's share of partnership revenues; that is, whenever the revenues in the ground exceed the cost to remove them but not by enough to compensate the GP.

For example, suppose the GP takes some LP dollars to drill a well. The GP looks down the hole and sees $2 worth of oil. Suppose it costs $1 to complete the well. Obviously, if the GP were a sole proprietor, the well would be completed. (It is profitable to spend $1 to recover $2.) But the GP in the partnership is entitled to receive only 40% of $2 or $.80 if the well is completed, although tax incentives drive the GP to take responsibility for 100% of the completion costs of $1. So it is not in the GP's best interest to complete the well, and there is a $1 opportunity loss from abandonment.

Prospectuses are remarkably candid in recognizing this incentive problem. A typical disclosure is the following one (taken from the "Conflicts of Interest" section of Dyco Petroleum Corporation's 1983 Oil and Gas Program prospectus):

> All drilling program structures involve conflicts of interest. Functional Allocation of costs creates conflicts at the time of well completion, where completion of a commercial but non-profitable well might prove to be in the best interest of the Participants, though not of Dyco. The feasibility of any such completion, as well as the selection of any Leases to be acquired by the Drilling Programs, will be determined solely by Dyco ... (D)ecisions with respect to completion or continued operation, although consistent with industry practice and based on Dyco's best judgment of the well's potential for profit, may not necessarily be in the best interests of Participants. (pp. 45 and 46)

This incentive problem is quite similar to the underinvestment problem in corporations that have risky bonds in their capital structure. In such corporations, shareholders may rationally prefer to pass up positive net present value projects if they must finance the projects themselves, since part of the return may go to creditors by way of reduced riskiness of the debt.

Functional allocation drilling programs are not the only ones that suffer from an undercompletion problem. The same problem exists in so-called **prospect-by-prospect reversionary interest drilling programs,** although here the problem is not entirely tax-induced. In these programs, LPs pay essentially all the drilling and completion costs. GPs obtain no revenue share until LPs have been paid an amount equal to their investment in the prospect. Again, the GP gets a private look down the hole after drilling. Even though LPs pay all the completion costs, there is an opportunity cost to the GP of spending a completion dollar on any well. With limits imposed on the amount that can be invested in the partnership, spending a dollar on completion precludes using that dollar to drill a new hole.

Suppose the GP spends 2 LP dollars to drill a hole. The GP looks down the hole, and sees $2 of oil. It will cost $1 of the LPs' money to complete the well. Once again, it is desirable to complete the well. But the GP doesn't get a revenue share until the LP has been paid an amount that recovers drilling costs (D) plus completion costs (C) in the prospect of $3 (or $2 + $1). Since there is only $2 of oil down the hole, the GP won't get a penny if the well is completed. By contrast, if the GP can take the completion dollar and invest it in a new hole that has any positive probability of returning more than $1, the GP is better off even if the expected amount of oil down the new hole is well below $2. The GP here is rationally led to act as though the drilling costs, that literally represent "sunk" costs, are relevant to the completion decision, although this would be irrational if the project were wholly owned by the GP.

At this point, let's consider some empirical evidence confirming the presence of these incentive problems. Let's also consider how these incentive problems can be, and are, mitigated. Recall that both functional allocation and reversionary interest programs have an undercompletion-of-wells incentive problem when the GP has drilled a marginal well:

$$D + C > R > C \text{ for reversionary interest programs, and}$$

$$R > C > sR \text{ for functional allocation programs.}$$

That is, the GP has an incentive to abandon a well that should be completed because it is expected to return more than the completion cost but not enough to cover the already sunk drilling cost, in the case of a reversionary interest program, or not enough revenue to provide a positive return to the GP given that the GP must bear 100% of the completion cost, in the case of a functional allocation program.

This incentive problem can be minimized by drilling wells that have a low probability of being marginal. This is exactly what characterizes an *exploratory* well. In an exploratory well, there is a high probability that no oil will be found at all and a low probability that a lot of oil will be found (in other words, the probability of a marginal well is relatively low). By contrast, developmental drilling results in a relatively high fraction of marginal wells.

Hence, we would expect functional allocation and reversionary interest programs to be predominantly exploratory. Two other common sharing arrangements, "promoted interest" and "carried interest,"[4] do not suffer from the undercompletion incentive problem described above. We would expect such partnerships to invest a smaller fraction of partnership funds in exploratory drilling. For nearly three billion LP dollars invested in over 600 partnerships tabulated by the Robert A. Stranger Company during the 1970s:[5]

- Less than 1 in 20 functional allocation dollars were devoted to developmental programs, where the chance of drilling a marginal well is rather high.
- Less than 1 in 6 reversionary interest dollars were devoted to developmental programs.
- By contrast, more than 1 in 2 carried interest and promoted interest dollars were devoted to developmental programs.

Recall that functional allocation contracts provide superior allocation of tax benefits relative to the other contract forms, but this favorable tax outcome can only be achieved at the cost of an incentive problem along the completion-of-wells dimension. This incentive problem is relatively unimportant in exploratory programs, so functional allocation arrangements dominate here, but the incentive problem becomes overwhelming in development programs, where the carried interest and promoted interest arrangements dominate.

Mitigation of Incentive Problems

As we discussed earlier in the context of R&D LPs, another way that incentive problems are reduced is when part of the return to the GP comes from establishing a reputation of being a skillful or honest general partner. Empirical evidence indicates that reputation effects are priced in the marketplace: a good track record enables sponsors to charge a higher price for the right to buy into subsequent partnerships.[6]

That functional allocation programs and reversionary interest programs are concentrated in exploratory drilling, and that a good reputation is priced in the marketplace, indicates that economic forces are at work that reduce the severity of the incentive problems between general partners and limited partners. But are these economic forces so powerful that they eliminate incentive problems entirely? Apparently not. Incentive problems are priced as well. In functional allocation arrangements, GPs charge a higher price to buy into exploratory programs than "balanced" programs (those in which roughly 50% of the drilling is exploratory and 50% is developmental) and a higher price to buy into balanced programs than developmental programs, *after standardizing* for risk differences.

Moreover, the results could not have been driven by differences in first-year tax write-offs since the write-offs are actually most generous in the developmen-

---

[4] Promoted interest and carried interest arrangements provide the general partners with a revenue share exceeding their percentage ownership of partnership capital.

[5] See Mark A. Wolfson, "Empirical Evidence of Incentive Problems and Their Mitigation in Oil and Gas Tax Shelter Programs," in *Principals and Agents: The Structure of Business* (Harvard Business School Press), 1985, pp. 101-125, 221-224.

[6] See Wolfson, *op. cit.*

tal programs. More precisely, the first-year tax write-off, as a fraction of the investment cost, was 80% in exploratory programs, 84% in balanced programs, and 87% in developmental programs. Yet the price was highest in the exploratory programs. Also, this relation between price and riskiness of drilling does not exist in promoted interest or carried interest program structures where there is little or no incentive problem related to riskiness of the wells to be drilled.

Other ways to mitigate incentive problems have been devised. Two that are discussed here are: (1) the GP could purchase LP interests, and (2) marginal wells could be "farmed out."

Aligning Incentives by Having the GP Purchase Some LP Ownership Interests

Suppose that the GP buys percentage p of the LP interests. In functional allocation programs, recall that absent reputation considerations, the GP completes wells whenever $sR > C$; that is, the GP's share of revenue exceeds completion cost. The socially desirable policy is to complete whenever total revenues exceed the completion cost; that is, $R > C$.

If the GP buys fraction p of LP interests, the GP policy becomes to complete wells whenever $sR + (1 - s)Rp > C$. The larger is the percentage of the LP interests purchased by the GP, the lower is the probability that a socially costly noncompletion of wells will result. To illustrate, let's reconsider our earlier example in which the GP observes $2 of oil down the hole, it costs $1 to complete the well, and s, the GP's share of partnership revenues, is equal to 40%. Without any LP interest owned by the GP, the GP will not complete the well since

$$sR < C \text{ (or } \$.80 < \$1).$$

But if the GP acquires a 25% LP interest, then completion yields

$$sR + (1 - s)Rp$$

$$= \$.4(2) + \$.6(2)(.25) = \$1.10 > \$1.00,$$

and the GP will now be $.10 better off completing the well than not completing it. This is not to say that GPs *should* purchase LP interests. After all, there are costs to doing so that relate to the motivations for forming the limited partnership in the first place:

1. the greater demand by the LPs for tax benefits;
2. a desire on the part of the GP to share economic risks with nonmanaging investors; and
3. financing constraints.

Empirically, GPs commonly do purchase nontrivial amounts of LP ownership interests. The price charged to buy into a partnership should be higher, all else the same, the larger the LP interest purchased by the GP. Similarly, the performance of the partnership should be better.

Farmouts

Another potential means of mitigating incentive problems is to farm out marginal wells. If there is $2 of oil in the ground and it takes $1 to complete the well, then the GP should be able to "farm out" (that is, to sell the right to complete the well) for up to $1. But farmouts introduce their own problems:

1. Farmouts are costly. The GP must negotiate a sale. Moreover, a sale might result in the GP's providing valuable information to the buyer regarding the surrounding land, which the GP prefers to keep private.
2. Farmouts create their own incentive problems, which can be severe. The GP has an incentive to claim that all wells are marginal, farm them out, and save the completion costs. Moreover, to avoid being "caught" farming out productive wells, GPs may have an incentive to farm out wells too cheaply, so as to make it appear that the wells are more marginal than they really are.

For example, suppose the GP observes $3 of oil down a hole. Completion cost is $1, and the GP's share of revenues, s, is 40%. If farmouts are not permitted, the GP will choose to complete the well since the GP nets $.4 \times \$3 - \$1 = \$.20$; and as a result the LP realizes $.6 \times \$3 - \$0 = \$1.80$.

But suppose the GP can farm out the well for $1. Now the GP gets $.4 \times \$1 - \$0 = \$.40$; and the LP gets $.6 \times \$1 - \$0 = \$.60$. This is twice as good for the GP as completion, but it is only one-third as good for the LP. The prospect is worth $2 (or $3 - $1) to complete in-house or twice as much as the farmout price. So it may be desirable for the partnership agreement to discourage farmouts despite the fact that they are desirable for the economy as a whole in that at least someone completes a well where oil revenues exceed completion costs.

Alternative arrangements exist that are similar to farmouts. One is to have a functional allocation sharing arrangement only on the first hole drilled on a prospect (Hilliard Fund has done this); thereafter, a promoted-interest sharing arrangement can be used. What does this accomplish? After an exploratory well is drilled successfully, it becomes desirable to develop the area. Development gives rise to a much higher probability of producing a marginal well and, therefore, the potential to create an incentive problem. By switching to promoted interest on development wells, the undercompletion problem is eliminated, although this benefit comes at some tax cost. An alternative arrangement would be a "balanced" program with different sharing arrangements for exploratory and development prospects.

Another approach would be to form two partnerships. After exploratory drilling is conducted under a functional allocation arrangement, all future drilling is conducted by a second (nonfunctional allocation) partnership to do the development work (Woods Petroleum has done this). This is similar to the previous case, except that with two distinct partnerships, their respective partners can sort themselves out better in terms of tax characteristics.

19.3 The Tax Reform Act of 1986 and Shifting Tax-Shelter Clienteles

As suggested earlier, the 1986 Tax Act caused corporations to be more natural co-venturers in such tax-sheltered investments as R&D than was true previously. For example, limited partners faced severe limitations on the deductibility of passive activity losses. The 1986 tax rules require all non-corporate taxpayers to separate their income into three baskets (actually many more baskets than three once multinational tax issues are considered, as we saw in Chapters Thirteen and Fourteen):

1. portfolio income (such as, dividends, interest, royalties, and capital gains),
2. other passive income (including income from partnerships and joint ventures where the taxpayer does not "materially participate" in the activity giving rise to the income),[7] and
3. active income.

Under the 1986 Tax Act, passive losses cannot be deducted against other types of income until the underlying investments are sold. For individual investors, losses from most tax shelter activities represent passive activity losses. As a result, their demand for tax shelters to shield portfolio income and active income from taxation was reduced dramatically beginning in 1987.

Individual investors may still have a demand for tax shelter for two purposes:

1. Many investors generate passive income from old tax shelters. Such investors can postpone the taxation of such income by making new investments that give rise to passive losses.
2. Many new investment vehicles have been structured to generate passive income to investors.[8] Investors can combine such investments with tax shelters to postpone recognition of such investment income.

Oil and gas investments represent one of the only ways in which wealthy individual investors may still generate passive losses that can offset taxable portfolio income and active income. The only requirement is that the investment not be held in limited-liability form. The typical arrangement involves individuals purchasing working interests in oil and gas properties. To compensate for the exposure reflected in the unlimited liability, investors simply purchase commercial insurance. The new law continues to allow immediate deductibility of drilling costs (except for large integrated oil companies who must capitalize 30% of these costs and amortize them over a five-year period). Percentage depletion is also retained. Still, in many circumstances, corporations are more efficient investors in oil and gas properties than are individuals under the new bill. This is explained more fully below.

---

[7] Material participation requires the taxpayer to be "involved in operations on a basis that is regular, continuous, and substantial."(IRC Section 469(h)).

[8] Such investments are sometimes referred to as PIGs (passive income generators).

In addition, many limited partnerships have been reorganized to generate partnership taxable income of approximately $0 rather than substantial losses in the early years of operation. One way to accomplish this is to cut back on borrowing within the partnership.[9] For example, in the first 6 months of 1987, income-oriented equipment leasing partnerships that were publicly registered with the Securities Exchange Commission raised 141.5% more funds than during the first six months of 1986. In contrast, shelter-oriented equipment leasing partnerships raised 52.5% *less* in 1987 than in 1986. Similar results are found in oil and gas partnerships: income-oriented public deals raised 62.6% more funds during the first 6 months of 1987 than in 1986, whereas shelter-oriented funds raised 67.8% less in 1987 than in 1986.[10]

The passive loss limitations do not apply to widely held corporations. Moreover, after the 1986 Tax Act, U.S. corporate investors generally face higher marginal tax rates than do wealthy individuals. Consequently, it is fully taxed corporate investors that represent the natural clients for most tax-sheltered investments under the 1986 Tax Act.

Changing Reputational Considerations with the Passage of the 1986 Tax Act

According to the *Wall Street Journal* (June 8, 1989), 12 million investors invested about $100 billion into limited partnerships in the 1980s. As individual demand for tax shelters has fallen, so has the incentive of program sponsors to maintain their reputations for performing well on behalf of limited partners. It is interesting to note that 1989 saw an unprecedented deterioration in the financial condition of limited partnerships. The *Wall Street Journal* estimates that limited partnerships representing $5 to $10 billion worth of investment became "financially troubled."[11]

In the face of decreasing tax rates during the 1980s, however, investors were encouraged to invest in tax shelters even if the pretax return was expected to be lower than the historical average. For example, suppose your current tax rate is 50%, and you expect it to be 30% in two years, at which time you will collect whatever income results from your investment. Your tax shelter investment is fully deductible at your current tax rate of 50% and the liquidation value of the tax shelter will be fully taxable at your future rate of 30%. In the past, such investments have earned an average of 10% per year before tax (that is, $1.21 in 2 years for each dollar invested). How would you fare if the investment yielded a pretax return of 15% per year *below* the historical average; that is, negative 5% per year (or $.90 in 2 years per dollar invested)?

Note that the historical average return of $1.21 in 2 years is more than one third higher than $.90. The after-tax return from this investment that produces a 10% pretax loss over 2 years (or -5% per year) is

---

[9] Individual taxpayers with passive income who continue to have demand for tax shelter can undo the "deleveraging" of their partnerships by borrowing on personal account and treating the interest payments on their home-made leverage as itemized deductions, if they have generated other investment income against which to deduct the interest.

[10] The source of these data is Robert A. Stanger & Co. (Shrewsbury, N.J.), as reported in the *Wall Street Journal* on July 23, 1987.

[11] Class-action lawyers have been much less distraught about this somewhat predictable turn of events than have investors.

Chapter 19   Repackaging Ownership Rights through Joint Ventures and Partnerships

$$\frac{\$.90\ (1 - 30\%)}{\$1.00\ (1 - 50\%)} = \frac{.63}{.50} = 26\%.$$

This after-tax return of 26% over 2 years actually exceeds the historical average pretax return of 10% per year.[12]

Summary of Key Points

1. Tax shelters are tax-favored investments that enable investors to postpone or eliminate permanently substantial sums of explicit taxes.

2. Because such investments typically bear substantial *implicit* taxes, however, they are not desirable for everyone.

3. While limited partnerships and joint ventures offer a tax-advantageous way of financing tax-sheltered investments in the presence of differences in tax status across different investors, such arrangements are not without cost. And while such tax-planning devices have flourished, they are *far* less prevalent than would be expected in the absence of such costs.

4. Investments in research and development as well as oil and gas exploration are highly tax-favored in most countries. Such investments are very commonly undertaken with an investment partner, both for tax and nontax reasons.

5. All joint investments create conflicts of interest. The party responsible for making decisions for the venture has an incentive to act in ways that are in its own best interest, and this may not coincide with the actions that the co-investor would prefer.

6. The presence of conflicts of interest creates demand for ways to reduce the costs of these conflicts. Monitoring, incentive contracts, performance bonds, warranties, and lawsuits are all responses to this demand.

7. Building a reputation is an important way to reduce incentive problems, but it is not a panacea. Just as there may be incentives to build a reputation to improve the terms on which transactions can be made in the future, there may also be incentives to "harvest" one's reputation. There appears to have been a tangible "return" to possessing a favorable reputation in the tax shelter industry during the 1960s through the mid-1980s, but these reputations may have been "cashed in" at the expense of investors following the 1986 Tax Act, as the importance of maintaining a good reputation was reduced.

---

[12] This was approximately the situation the authors of this text believed they faced with respect to a particular tax-sheltered investment in 1986, so we decided to undertake the investment. Alas, not all good decisions lead to good outcomes. We would have been thrilled to have earned a pretax return as high as -5% per year on the investment. Unfortunately, so would a few of our friends.

8. In the oil and gas industry, the most tax-advantageous way to allocate investment costs to investors facing disparate tax situations is typically along functional lines: drilling costs are allocated to investors who have the greatest demand for immediate tax shelter, and capitalized costs are allocated to the other investors. Such an arrangement introduces an incentive problem with respect to the completion of wells: the party responsible for incurring the well-completion costs prefers to complete fewer wells than do the other investors.

9. While institutional arrangements to reduce this incentive problem have been employed, such arrangements do not eliminate all incentive problems.

10. Changes in tax laws often have a dramatic effect on the natural tax clienteles for various investments. The Tax Reform Act of 1986, for example, reduced very substantially the demand in the U.S., by individual taxpayers, for investments in tax-sheltered partnerships. At the same time, corporate demand for such investments was increased, except for corporations that already shelter substantial sums of income from taxation.

Discussion Questions

1. What are tax-sheltered investments?

2. Are the following statements true or false?
   a. Limited partnerships can be used to split up and allocate the components of investment cost and income from tax-sheltered investments.
   b. Corporations are the marginal investors in tax-sheltered investments.
   c. The 1986 Tax Act caused investors to prefer tax-sheltered investments that minimize the use of debt to finance its activities.
   d. The alternative minimum tax has reduced the demand for tax shelters.

3. What is an R&D tax shelter? How does the taxation of returns in an R&D investment affect its required before-tax rate of return? What role does the R&D tax credit play in the analysis?

4. Why might individual investors have a demand for tax shelters? Why might they shy away from investing in tax shelters? How has the 1986 Tax Act affected individual investors' demands for tax-sheltered investment?

5. What are the tax and nontax motivations for forming research and development joint ventures or limited partnerships?

6. What incentive problems are created by forming research and development joint ventures? How are these problems mitigated?

7. In oil and gas limited partnerships, what is a functional allocation program? Why might the LPs enter into a contract to pay 100% of the costs that are tax deductible immediately while the GPs pay for all the costs that must be capitalized?

8. What incentive problems are introduced by allocating oil and gas exploration costs along functional lines? When is it in the interest of the GP to complete wells in such a situation? Under what conditions would limited partners prefer that wells be completed by the general partner? How can the GP mitigate the incentive problem? How would we expect the types of drilling (exploratory versus developmental) to differ between these programs and carried interest or promoted interest programs?

9. What are the advantages and costs of allowing general partners to "farm out" marginal wells to third parties?

10. What effect does the GP's ownership of some LP interests have on partnership incentive problems? Why? How does this relate to incentive problems in widely owned corporations?

CHAPTER 20
Repackaging Ownership Rights: Tax and Nontax Considerations

As we have discussed in previous chapters, different assets give rise to future cash flows that vary not only in magnitude but also timing, riskiness, form (for example, passive versus active, ordinary versus capital), and source (for example, domestic versus foreign). For both tax and nontax reasons, it is often undesirable for any one individual or entity to retain ownership of the entire package of cash flows that an asset represents. This motivates a repackaging of ownership rights to assets that allows some of the risk and return components to be sold off to parties that value the components most highly. Repackaging ownership rights is a growing area of interest for firms and investors around the world.

Vehicles that are used domestically and internationally to effect the repackaging include (1) financial contracts such as futures, forwards, options, and warrants; (2) securities, such as contingent-interest bonds, that promise their holders payoffs that depend upon the value of another asset such as the Standard & Poor's (S&P) 500 Index or the price of a commodity (say, oil or silver); and (3) organizational forms such as partnerships (often used to parse out the returns to real estate and other investments), investment companies (sometimes used to sell components of investments to different investors, as in so-called "dual funds"), tax-exempt entities (insurance policies, governmental entities, and pension funds), or special purpose organizations such as real estate investment trusts. In this chapter we explore how investors exploit differences in their tax status by using these tools to create new contracts, securities, or legal organizational forms that unbundle the components of investment returns and parse them out to the parties that value them most highly. We demonstrate that the tax-planning uses to which such tools can be put are very broad.

A number of these vehicles fall into the category of so-called "synthetics" in that they mimic the performance of underlying assets. An example here is an equity contract that pays the total return on an underlying index such as the

S&P 500 Index. The holders of these synthetics do not receive certain rights of shareholders that they would if they held the underlying securities directly (such as the right to vote shares, or the right to receive income in the form of dividends).

The taxation of the returns to many of these vehicles, particularly in an international setting, is far from cut and dried. This is an area where the architects of the tax rules find it difficult to predict how the rules will affect taxpayer behavior. Moreover, care must be exercised to avoid designing such specific rules that slight variations in the features of financial products would result in various forms of tax arbitrage. This forces the creation of regulations that are not defined very precisely. In this regard, the final designers of the regulations are often the tax planners themselves.

We highlighted this problem in Chapter Two. Because tax systems are designed to achieve a variety of social goals, tax rates vary across investors, time periods, and activities. But the very tax rules that encourage some taxpayers to undertake socially desirable activities, encourage *other* taxpayers to exploit ambiguity in the rules and, as a result, lead to some socially undesirable economic activity. When taxpayers have gone "too far" in their efforts to avoid taxes, the architects of the tax rules fight back by changing the rules. Sometimes they are successful, but sometimes new opportunities for taxpayers are created that have unintended consequences. Often, the unintended consequences come about from the usage of the vehicles we discuss in this chapter.

With financial engineering, many different combinations of assets, securities, and "synthetics" can lead to economically similar cash flows. Yet taxing authorities often impose different tax treatment across the economically similar bundles. For example, although a convertible bond is equivalent to a warrant and a straight bond, its periodic return is taxed as interest, just like a bond. The market typically does a better job than the taxing authority in sorting out the economic characteristics of securities.

At first blush, it might appear sensible to decompose a transaction into its constituent parts and tax each part accordingly (for example, tax a convertible bond as a warrant and a straight bond, which is issued with original issue discount). The taxing authority typically does not do this, but at times this approach is taken.[1]

The decomposition approach, however, faces practical obstacles. It is not always obvious how to decompose a contract into its constituent parts. Assets can be decomposed in multiple ways that are equivalent, except for taxes. Moreover, this approach could reduce tax revenues once the tax consequences to all parties to the contract are taken into account. For example, decomposing a contract into its constituent parts might provide tax deductions for U.S. taxpayers without a corresponding tax cost to the counterparty to the trade. This is particularly true

---

[1]For example, on February 26, 1991, the IRS issued proposed regulations (revising previously proposed regulations issued in 1986) concerning contingent-interest debt obligations that pay off, in part, based on the value of an asset index. Previous regulations did not separate the bond into a straight bond part and a contingent piece, and require that taxpayers value the separate pieces and be taxed on each piece separately. The new regulations require that certain new issues of contingent interest bonds be bifurcated in this manner.

Chapter 20   Repackaging Ownership Rights: Tax and Nontax Considerations

when one party to the contract is a tax-exempt entity, such as a governmental agency in Europe or the Far East.[2]

Should the taxing authority adopt a more conceptual approach, wherein it attempts to determine whether a particular set of transactions is motivated solely for tax purposes and recharacterize such transactions to afford a less tax-advantageous outcome for the taxpayer? Perhaps so, but as a practical matter, the taxing authority can only guess what is behind a complicated string of transactions.

What is the authority to do? For the most part it has given up in the financial innovation market. It takes a long time to issue rules and regulations when new financial contracts emerge, sometimes many years. It is difficult to issue regulations in an area that is so fluid and relatively easy for taxpayers to restructure. Perhaps this is the only reasonable approach that the taxing authority can take. If the technology of producing new vehicles to repackage ownership rights is such that innovations can be produced cheaply, one way to increase the cost of such innovation is to increase tax treatment uncertainty. But while this may reduce the volume of undesirable arbitrage activities, it also inhibits the growth of important and legitimate contractual innovations that increase economic efficiency.

In the international environment, synthetics provide an excellent opportunity to explore how changes in investment technology (a reduction in information costs) lead to new products that reduce tax collections of governments around the world. In this chapter, we illustrate this by analyzing the effect of these technologies on the elimination or mitigation of withholding taxes on dividend and interest transfers that stem from securities holdings, and we explore the difficulty of writing regulations that prevent tax planners from avoiding withholding taxes around the world. We also demonstrate how tax rule uncertainty has impeded various approaches to solve the withholding tax problem. We close with a discussion of corporate finance and the use of forward-like contracts to (1) increase the debt capacity of corporations without incurring some of the usual nontax costs of doing so, and (2) convert the passive income of multinational corporations into income that is not taxed currently.

20.1 Repackaging Ownership Rights: Mitigation of Withholding Taxes on Dividends and Interest

In this section, we illustrate the use of organizational forms, financial contracts, and securities to mitigate the withholding tax on dividend and interest payments. Most taxing authorities require that part of the dividend or interest payment be

---

[2] This is essentially what is likely to happen as a result of the new proposed regulations concerning contingent interest bonds referred to in footnote 1. These regulations apply only to certain types of contingent interest bonds. The ones that are to be bifurcated yield larger current tax deductions to U.S. issuers because the accrued contingent interest becomes currently deductible to the issuer (whereas previously, it was only deductible upon payment), and currently taxable to the holder. If the holder is tax-exempt, there is a net revenue loss to the taxing authority.

withheld on payments to foreign portfolio investors.[3] Many corporate, individual, and tax-exempt investors pay these taxes. For the reasons explained below, unless the tax rules change substantially, we believe that investors will avoid payment of more and more of these taxes over time. First we show how organizational forms such as partnerships and regulated investment companies can be used to mitigate the dividend withholding tax problem. We then discuss how financial contracts such as options, futures, and swap contracts can achieve the same result. Last, we show how securities that provide payoffs that are contingent on the performance of other securities can be used to reduce the dividend withholding tax problem.

Organizational Form

Consider a situation in which we have two taxpayers that are located in different tax jurisdictions and are taxed differently on various types of income. In particular, one taxpayer is a large pension fund resident outside of the U.S. Its total assets are $5 billion of which $1 billion is invested in a diversified portfolio of U.S. stocks that pay dividends at the rate of 4% per year. The stocks also generate capital gains and losses.

Note that the annual dividend income on the portfolio of U.S. stocks is $40 million per year (or $1 billion × 4%). The pension fund is located in a country that has a treaty with the U.S. The treaty specifies a withholding tax on dividends at the (reduced) rate of 15%. Interest and capital gains, however, are exempt from withholding tax. The 15% withholding tax on dividends exacts $6 million per year in U.S. tax liability ($40 million dividend income × 15%). Moreover, since the pension fund is exempt from domestic tax in its home country, there is no scope for receiving a refund of U.S. tax through a foreign tax credit mechanism.

Our second taxpayer is a large U.S. corporation that holds $500 million in short-term U.S. Treasury securities or bank certificates of deposit that pay interest at a rate of 8% per year. These assets yield taxable interest income of $40 million per year (or $500 million × 8%). The interest is taxed at the corporation's ordinary tax rate of 40%, so the tax on $40 million of interest income is $16 million.

How can we marry these two very different, completely unrelated taxpayers to exploit their differential tax situations? There are many possibilities. For example, the two taxpayers could form a regulated investment company or a partnership, neither of which attracts an entity-level tax.

How does this work? The nonU.S. pension fund contributes $1 billion of U.S. stock to the venture. In exchange, it receives a claim to 100% of the interest income of the investment company plus any capital gains and losses on the stock. The U.S. corporation contributes $500 million in interest-bearing securities to the venture and receives a claim to 100% of the dividend income of the investment company. The flows are shown in Figure 20.1.

---

[3] For example, the U.K., France, Germany, Japan, Italy, Canada, and Switzerland require withholding taxes of 15% on dividends and interest to taxable U.S. portfolio investors. All of these countries, except Canada, also withhold a 15% tax for tax-exempt investors. Canada forgives the withholding tax for tax-exempt investors. Since 1984, the U.S. does not withhold tax on interest payments made on most U.S. bond obligations.

Chapter 20 Repackaging Ownership Rights: Tax and Nontax Considerations

Note that the pretax returns to the parties from participating in this new investment vehicle are identical to what they were before. The nonU.S. pension fund earns $40 million plus capital gains and losses on the $1 billion stock portfolio, and the U.S. corporation earns $40 million each year.

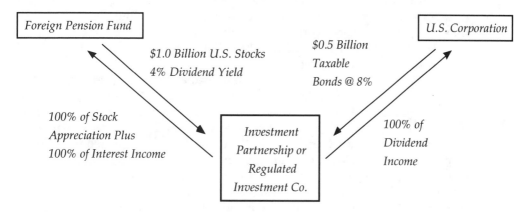

FIGURE 20.1 Marrying the Foreign Pension Fund and the U.S. Corporation

But now the foreign pension fund pays no tax, since the U.S. imposes no withholding tax on interest earned from Treasury securities or bank certificates of deposit. Moreover, the tax on the U.S. corporation has also been reduced. Instead of $40 million in interest income, it now generates $40 million in dividend income, much of which is exempt from taxation due to the corporate dividend-received deduction. For example, if 75% of the dividends are exempt, the tax rate on dividends becomes 10% (or 40% × (1 - 75%)). So the tax on $40 million of dividend income becomes $4 million, whereas it was $16 million (or $12 million *more*) before.

The total tax on the pension fund and the corporation from the income earned on their ownership positions in the new investment vehicle is $4 million ($0 for the pension fund and $4 million for the corporation). Compare this to the initial tax liability of $22 million ($6 million for the pension fund and $16 million for the corporation). The tax savings from the repackaging is $18 million per year.

This increases the after-tax return on the $1.5 billion investment by 1.2% per year. The pension fund receives a $6 million extra return on its $1 billion investment or 0.6% per year, and the U.S. corporation earns an extra $12 million on its $500 million investment or 2.4% per year. Whereas before, the U.S. corporation earned an after-tax return on its investment of 8% × (1 - 40%) or 4.8%, it now earns 8% × (1 - 40%(1 - .75)) or 7.2% after tax. This is a 50% increase in after-tax return!

Of course, nothing prevents the two parties from splitting up the savings in a different way. For example, suppose the U.S. corporation was promised only a 6 2/3% pretax return. This could be operationalized by having the corporation contribute $600 million of interest-bearing securities to the venture, rather than

$500 million, in exchange for a claim to all of the dividends on the billion dollar stock portfolio.

With this arrangement, the corporation would net 6 2/3% × (1 - .4(1 - .75)) or 6.0%, a bonus return of 1.2% per year. This is still 25% better than the 4.8% after-tax return available from direct holdings of interest-bearing securities. The pension fund now nets interest income of $48 million (or $600 million × 8%) rather than after-tax dividend income of $34 million (or $40 million × (1 - .15)). This provides a bonus return of 1.4% (or $14 million on an investment of $1 billion) relative to holding stock directly.

The organizational arrangements described above are similar to those that have been used in the marketplace. Examples include "dual funds" (like the Gemini Fund and Americus Trusts). Such arrangements typically create two classes of shares, allowing the dividend stream to be purchased separately from the capital gain stream. More specifically, dual funds are regulated investment companies (such as closed-end mutual funds) that create two classes of shares. One class of shares, called the capital shares, receives all of the capital gains returns, and the other class of shares, called the income shares, receives all of the dividend returns on an underlying portfolio of common stock.

Many tax-exempt entities (such as corporate pension funds) hold the stocks comprising the S&P 500 Index to mimic its performance. Suppose a pension fund holding the index were to sell off the right to receive next year's dividends on the stocks in the index to a corporation that values the dividends more highly. The corporation could replace its holdings of fully taxable bonds or adjustable-rate preferred stocks (that yield substantially less than equally risky fully taxable bonds but are taxed more favorably), with claims to dividends on the S&P 500 stocks.

As we have argued before, pension funds are not the most tax-efficient investors in a capital gain-yielding security such as the capital share, because such tax-favored assets are likely to bear substantial implicit taxes. As demonstrated in the following sub-section, however, the pension fund can convert the income from the capital share into ordinary interest income by selling a stock index futures contract.

As pension funds and corporations engage in these strategies in increasing volume, they influence the required rates of return on dividend-paying securities. If domestic corporations became the marginal investors in stocks, the before-tax rates of return on dividend-paying securities to shareholders would be less than those on non-dividend-paying securities. Implementing these strategies, however, is costly for corporations and pension funds. Nontax restrictions (such as regulated investment company rules and labor department rules regarding investments of pension funds) restrain corporations and pension funds from being too aggressive in applying these strategies. Even the taxing authority has restricted their use, at least in the U.S.: a regulated investment company filing a registration statement subsequent to June 12, 1989 can no longer allocate dividends disproportionately to the income shareholders for purposes of exploiting the dividend-received deduction.[4] But this restriction does not (yet) apply to

---

[4]See Revenue Ruling 89-81 relating to Code Section 852—Regulated Investment Companies (June 14, 1989).

Chapter 20   Repackaging Ownership Rights: Tax and Nontax Considerations

partnerships, and it does not preclude allocating the dividend income to different investors for purposes other than exploiting the dividend-received deduction.[5]

Nontax Considerations

There are several possible disadvantages of repackaging ownership rights to stocks. An obvious one is that the repackaging costs (including investment banking and legal fees) may be nontrivial. Another is that the individual ownership claims may be less liquid than the underlying assets. Still another is that conflicts of interest may arise between the owners of different classes of shares.

For example, in the case of splitting up a stock portfolio into a claim to dividends and a claim to capital gains and losses, the parties owning the dividend claim prefer that the investment portfolio be weighted toward higher dividend-yielding stocks, whereas the capital shareholders prefer just the opposite. This will make it more difficult for the portfolio manager to engage in any sort of active trading of securities to enhance overall portfolio returns due to the conflicts between the claimants. There will also be conflicts regarding how much pressure the investors will wish to place on corporations to increase dividends. Issues such as these made it difficult for the various dual funds to attract a large following of investors despite the promise of great tax savings.

Using Financial Contracts to Avoid Withholding Taxes

Futures and option contracts are used by both domestic and international investors as an alternative to stock and bond investments and as a way to take long positions as well as to hedge investment risks. It turns out that being long a call option (a right, but not an obligation, to buy a security at a fixed price) and being short a put option (a right, but not an obligation, to sell a security) is essentially equivalent economically to being long a futures contract if the exercise prices and expiration dates on the options are chosen appropriately.[6] Options with standardized terms are traded on organized exchanges; other options are created and traded privately. Most of our discussion in this section focuses on futures contracts because they are easier to describe, but options can be used equally well to illustrate how ownership rights can be repackaged to secure tax benefits.

A futures contract is a standardized contract traded on an organized exchange such as the Chicago Mercantile Exchange. A futures contract is a contract to buy a commodity, such as the S&P 500 Stock Index, at some future date at a fixed price determined at the time the futures contract is entered into. For example, suppose the current spot price, S, is $400 (for example, the current price

---

[5] The U.S. tax law restricts the use of partnerships that parse out the components of partnership income to different investors in ways that do not reflect underlying risks in the cash flows.

[6] If the exercise price of the option is set equal to the forward stock price, the relation is exact for so-called European options and forward contracts. The forward stock price is described below in equation 20.1. A European option can only be exercised at maturity. A forward contract is settled at the end of a set term, such as six months: at the end of the term, the party that acquires the underlying asset forward takes delivery of the underlying asset. A futures contract is similar to a forward contract, but a futures contract is "settled" each day. That is, any gain or loss on the futures position is settled in cash at the end of the day. We ignore this distinction between futures and forwards in our analysis.

at which the S&P 500 portfolio of stocks could be acquired is $400), and the price for future delivery of the commodity in one year is $416. The buyer of the futures contract agrees to buy the index in one year for $416. No money changes hands when the contract is struck. It is a commitment to buy in the future. Buyers and sellers generally post security or margin to assure that they can fulfill on their commitments.

A forward contract is the private market counterpart to a futures contract. It has broader rights and is less standardized than a futures contract. In many more cases than a futures contract, a forward contract ends up resulting in actual delivery of the underlying commodity. While a futures contract is written with a clearing corporation and is settled each day, a forward contract is generally settled only at maturity. Each party to a forward contract is at risk with respect to the performance of the counterparty.

Let's compare investments in stock and futures in a no-tax world. Assume that in one year, the value of the S&P 500 stocks, S^*, can take on only two values, either $340 or $540, and the current value of the index is $400. A futures-contract investor agrees to buy the index at the futures price, F, in one year. Suppose that the stocks in the index will pay dividends, D, of $16 over the coming year (a dividend yield of 4%), and the before-tax bond rate is 8%.[7] To find the futures contract price that must prevail to prevent arbitrage opportunities from being present, we compare the two alternative investments:

	Cash Flows Today	Cash Flows in One Year	
Future Value of S&P 500, S^*		$340	$540
Strategy A			
Buy S&P 500 Index ($-S + S^*$)	-$400	$340	$540
Collect Dividends ($+D$)		16	16
Total		$356	$556
Strategy B			
Buy Futures ($+S^* - F$)		$340 - F	$540 - F
Buy $S of Bonds ($-S + S(1+R_b)^n$)	-$400	432	432
Total		$772 - F	$972 - F

Current spot price, S, = $400; Dividend, D, = $16; Taxable bond rate, R_b, = 8%; Futures contract expires in $n = 1$ period.

Notice that the risks of the two investment strategies are the same. The only source of uncertainty is S^*, the terminal value of the index, and both strategies include a long position of equal magnitude in S^*.[8] Moreover, the current cash outlays for the two strategies are the same. To prevent arbitrage, the futures price F must be set such that the returns to the two strategies are the same. That is, F must satisfy

---

[7] For simplicity, assume that the dividends are all paid on the expiration date of the futures contract. Alternatively, $16 is the future value of the dividends as of the expiration date of the futures contract.

[8] For this reason, equation 20.1 below holds for *any* stock price distribution. We chose the two-outcome case for simplicity only.

Chapter 20   Repackaging Ownership Rights: Tax and Nontax Considerations

$$-S + S^* + D = -S + S^* - F + S(1 + R_b)^n$$

or

$$F = S(1 + R_b)^n - D. \qquad (20.1)$$

The futures price will be above the spot price by a factor of one plus the before-tax rate of interest, R_b, compounded for the number of periods until the futures contract expires (one period in this example), minus the future value of the expected dividends to be paid on the index. In this example, the futures price is \$432 - \$16 = \$416.

Buying bonds and entering into a futures contract on a stock index such as the S&P 500 Index, is exactly the same as buying the underlying index (other than voting and other shareholder rights). That is, if we define S^* to be the value of the stock index on the date the futures contract expires, then an investment of S dollars in bonds and a long position in a stock futures contract at the price specified in equation 20.1 provides the following future payoff:

$$S(1 + R_b)^n + \{ S^* - [S(1 + R_b)^n - D]\} = S^* + D$$

Taxation of Futures

Under the 1981 Tax Act, year-end holdings of regulated futures contracts in the U.S. are treated as though they are sold at market value at year-end. That is, they are "marked to market." All gains and losses on futures contracts (including the year-end adjustments) are aggregated, and 40% of the net gain (loss) is treated as a short-term capital gain (loss), and 60% of the net gain (loss) is treated as long-term. Note that prior to the 1986 Tax Act (with the 60% tax exemption for long-term capital gains), a taxpayer with a 50% marginal tax rate faced the following tax rate on futures:

$$.4 \times 50\% + .6 \times .4 \times 50\% = 32\%.$$

This is 36% less than the ordinary tax rate of 50%.[9]

Who Sets the Price in the Futures Market?

Let us now suppose that because of tax considerations, futures prices are *not* set according to 20.1. More generally, suppose that

$$F = S(1 + R_b)^n - D + A, \qquad (20.2)$$

where A is an adjustment factor for taxes that makes the marginal investor in futures indifferent between an investment in the stock index and an investment in a portfolio of bonds and a stock-index future. Suppose that the marginal investor setting prices in the futures market faces a tax on dividend income at rate t_D, a tax on capital gains from direct holdings of stocks at rate t_s, a tax on returns from the futures contract at rate t_F, and a tax on bond interest at rate t_p. Further suppose that R_b and D are normalized so that $n = 1$. Then equation 20.1, adjusted for taxes, requires that the futures price satisfy

---

[9] Options contracts are not taxed like futures. They are taxed like securities. The price an investor pays for a call option or warrant is the basis in the investment. Gain or loss results on a sale or lapse of the contract. If exercised, the purchase price of the option is added to the exercise price of the option to determine the investor's basis in the security. The buyer of a put option who exercises the option, is considered to have undertaken a short sale of the underlying security.

$$\underbrace{S^* - (S^* - S)t_s + D(1 - t_D)}_{\text{After-tax stock return}} = \underbrace{(S^* - F)(1 - t_F)}_{\substack{\text{After-tax} \\ \text{return on} \\ \text{futures}}} + \underbrace{S[1 + R_b(1 - t_p)]}_{\substack{\text{After-tax} \\ \text{return on} \\ \text{bonds}}}.$$

Solving for the futures price, we find that

$$F = \{S[1 + R_b(1 - t_p) - t_s] - S^*(t_F - t_s) - D(1 - t_D)\}/(1 - t_F). \tag{20.3}$$

For the special case of $t_p = t_s = t_F = t_D$, we obtain the same solution as in the absence of taxes (that is, equation 20.1). Note that this is the equilibrium we would expect if the marginal investors are pension funds (and other tax-exempt entities) or broker-dealers. If, in equation 20.2, the value of the adjustment factor, A, were different from zero, tax-exempt investors and broker-dealers (even if they face high marginal tax rates) would encounter arbitrage opportunities. If A were positive, these investors would find futures to be priced too dearly, and in the absence of market frictions, they would achieve arbitrage profits by buying stock, financed with bonds, and selling futures. For an investment level of S, the arbitrage profit would be equal to:

Stock return	-	Bond repayment	-	Futures return	
$(S^* + D)$	-	$[S(1 + R_b)]$	-	$\{S^* - [S(1 + R_b) - D + A]\} = A.$	

If A were negative, tax-exempt entities and broker-dealers would face a different arbitrage strategy: purchase futures, sell stock short, and invest the proceeds of the short sale in bonds.[10] This, too, would yield an arbitrage profit equal to A. On the other hand, these strategies are not costless to implement. It is more difficult for a broker-dealer to short the stocks in the index because of the up-tick rule (a stock can only be sold short following a transaction in which its price moves up by at least 1/8 of a $1); and in volatile markets, it is difficult to transact in multiple markets at the same time. Pension funds must also incur transaction costs of moving in and out of the stocks in the index and the futures contract.

Strategies for Other Investors When Broker-Dealers Set Prices

If prices are set according to equation 20.1, profit opportunities may exist for investors who face different tax rates on interest, dividends, capital gains, and futures. For example, if equation 20.1 holds true, and if the tax rate on gains from holding stock is lower than the tax rate on income from futures, then individual investors would prefer to hold stocks rather than invest in bonds plus futures. Other investors, however, would prefer positions in futures contracts. For example, let's return to the investment problem of our foreign pension fund and U.S. corporation.

---

[10] A study done by Cornell and French (*Journal of Futures Markets*, 1983) indicates that futures prices are set at a level below that implied by equation 20.1, but this study is based on 1982 data, when the contracts were first introduced. A later study by Cornell (*Journal of Futures Markets*, 1985), using 1983 data, indicates that prices *are* consistent with equation 20.1.

For the foreign pension fund, buying futures and bonds yields the same pretax return as that from buying stock. But withholding taxes on dividends are avoided. As for our U.S. corporation, if the price of the futures contract is set according to equation 20.1, a profit opportunity exists, because the corporation can buy an index fund (such as Vanguard's Index-500 or Merrill Lynch's Index Trust) and sell a futures contract to hedge the market risk. Let's examine this strategy:

	Current Payoffs	Future Payoffs
Buy Index Fund for S Dollars	-S	$S^* + D$
Sell Index Future for a Price of F	0	$-(S^* - F) = -(S^* - S(1 + R_b) + D)$
Total Payoff	-S	$S(1 + R_b)$

Note that the before-tax return on this strategy is exactly equal to the return from investing in bonds, but a large fraction of the income is exempt, because it comes in the form of dividends eligible for the dividend-received deduction. Not *all* of the return is received in the form of dividends, however, unless the dividend yield on the stock portfolio happens to be as high as the taxable bond rate. There is, therefore, a component of the return that is taxed as a capital gain. This component is equal to

$$(S^* - S) - (S^* - F) \text{ or } F - S.$$

Substituting for F from equation 20.1, $F - S$ is equal to $R_b S - D$. Even if the capital gains tax rate is equal to the ordinary tax rate, this is an improvement over holding bonds due to the dividend-received deduction secured on the portion of the return that comes in the form of dividends.

Note that if the corporation were to borrow at rate R_b and purchase stock with the proceeds, along with taking a short position in stock index futures, it could achieve tax arbitrage. Except for transaction costs, its pretax return and net investment outlay would be zero, but it would generate a positive after-tax return.

Three restrictions were introduced by the 1984 Tax Act to prevent corporations from being too aggressive in using these strategies. These include: (1) portfolio interest on loans used to purchase dividend-paying common stock is not deductible under Section 246(a) of the Code; (2) corporations must hold stock for more than 46 days (including the ex-dividend date) to be eligible for the dividend-received deduction (up from 15 days prior to the 1984 Tax Act); and most important for our purposes here, (3) the 46-day holding period is not satisfied if "substantially similar property" is held in a short position (such as by selling futures to hedge the stock positions). What constitutes substantially similar property, however, is subject to debate, and this provides ample scope for aggressive taxpayers to attempt to secure tax gains from futures-related trading strategies.

Reducing Withholding Taxes through Swap Contracts

Interest rate swap and currency swap agreements are rapidly growing financial products that facilitate the management of global asset and liability risk. Parties that commonly enter into swap agreements include commercial banks, investment banks, insurance companies, domestic and multinational corporations, foreign governments, and U.S. and foreign government-sponsored entities. Swap contracts reduce the transaction costs of dealing in international markets and, as a result, their use tends to unify disparate local markets around the world.

A swap contract is a rather simple financial agreement. Two counterparties agree to swap payments tied to different indices at specified intervals of time. These payments are usually netted. Perhaps the simplest of the swap agreements is the fixed-for-floating interest-rate swap. Here, one counterparty, A, agrees to pay a fixed rate of interest, say 10% per year, to another counterparty, B. A, in turn, receives a floating rate of interest (often tied to "LIBOR")[11] on, say, $100 million "notional amount" (so-called, because neither party puts up the $100 million) for each of the next 10 years. Let us assume that the floating interest rate is initially 10% per year and that the agreement requires no investment by either party since the value of receiving $10 million a year (10% of $100 million) and paying $10 million a year, is zero (since the payments are netted).

If interest rates later fall, say to 8%, A's agreement to pay $10 million a year for 10 years and now to receive only $8 million a year is valuable to B. A must pay B $2 million each year if interest rates remain at a level of 8%. If just after the contract was signed, interest rates fell from 10% to 8%, B would have a receivable and A would have a payable with a present value of approximately $13.4 million. Unlike futures contracts, swaps are not settled for cash each day, and this enhances the ability of various entities to use swap contracts in tax-planning strategies. We expand on this property in the analysis below.

The swap market has exploded from a level of $4 billion in notional amounts outstanding in 1984 to over $2.5 trillion in notional amounts outstanding at the end of 1989.[12] The market has evolved from one concentrated in standard interest-rate swaps, such as the one described above, to one that now includes substantial amounts of cross-currency swaps, options on interest-rate swaps, interest-rate caps and floors, floating-for-floating swaps, and swaps involving commodities and indices. Yet comprehensive tax rules have not been formulated for this burgeoning market.[13]

Let's return once again to the withholding tax problem for our foreign pension fund. Recall that the foreign pension fund invests $1 billion in U.S. stocks with an annual dividend yield of 4%. It loses $6 million per year in U.S. withholding tax ($40 million dividend income × 15%). Suppose that a U.S. pension fund also invests $1 billion in common stocks yielding 5% in the home country of the foreign pension fund, and this country also imposes a 15% withholding tax on dividend payments to foreign investors. The U.S. pension fund incurs $7.5 million per year in withholding taxes. Because both pension funds want to diversify their portfolios across international borders, they are willing to pay the foreign withholding tax on their dividend income if necessary.

---

[11] LIBOR is the London interbank offering rate for international lending and borrowing transactions.

[12] Saul Hensel, "Is the World Ready For Synthetic Equity?" *Institutional Investor* (August, 1990), pp. 54-61.

[13] Edward D. Kleinbard, "Equity Derivative Products: Financial Innovation's Newest Challenge to the Tax System," *Texas Law Review* (Vol. 69, 1991), pp. 1-57.

Chapter 20   Repackaging Ownership Rights: Tax and Nontax Considerations

But they can do better. To see this, assume that the foreign pension fund invests its $1 billion in the stocks that the U.S pension fund wants to hold, and the U.S. pension fund invests its $1 billion in the stocks that the foreign pension fund wants to hold. Then they swap the returns each year on the portfolio investment that each counterparty made in their home country on a notional $1 billion. The gains to this arrangement are shown in Figure 20.2.

Figure 20.2. Swap of Stock Returns between U.S. and Foreign Pension Funds to Mitigate Their Respective Withholding Tax Problems

---

Assume the U.S. market appreciates by 30%, including a 4% dividend yield.
Assume the foreign market appreciates by 25%, including a 5% dividend yield.

Returns *without* Entering into a Swap Agreement

	Foreign Pension Fund	U.S. Pension Fund
Holdings	$1 billion U. S. stocks	$1 billion foreign stock
Capital gain	$260 million	$200 million
Dividend income	40 million	50 million
Withholding tax @ 15%	(6) million	(7.5) million
Net return	$294 million	$242.5 million

Returns After Entering into a Swap Agreement

Foreign Pension Fund buys $1 billion of *foreign* stocks rather than U. S. stocks and swaps the return on $1 billion of foreign stocks for the return on $1 billion of U.S. stocks.

Pretax return from holding $1 billion of foreign stocks	$250	million
Withholding tax	- 0 -	
Cash flows from swap contract:		
Receive return on $1 billion of U.S. stocks	300	million
Pay return on $1 billion of foreign stocks	(250	million)
Net after-tax return to Foreign Pension Fund	$300	million

U.S. Pension Fund buys $1 billion of *U.S.* stocks rather than foreign stocks and swaps the return on $1 billion of U.S. stocks for the return on $1 billion of foreign stocks.

Return from holding $1 billion of U.S. stocks	$300	million
Withholding tax	- 0 -	
Cash flows from swap contract:		
Receive return on $1 billion of foreign stocks	250	million
Pay return on $1 billion of U.S. stocks	(300	million)
Net after-tax return to U.S. Pension Fund	$250	million

The gain under the swap agreement, relative to direct holding of U.S. stocks by the foreign pension fund and foreign stocks by the U.S. pension fund, is equal to the withholding tax savings of $6 million plus $7.5 million or $13.5 million.

If the return on the foreign investment portfolio in the first year is 25%, and the return on the U.S. investment portfolio is 30%, the foreign counterparty would receive a swap payment of $50 million (30% - 25% or 5% of the $1 billion notional amount) from the U.S. pension fund. As a result, the U.S. pension fund nets a return of $250 million or 25% of $1 billion (30% on the $1 billion invested in the

---

20.1   Repackaging Ownership Rights: Mitigation of Withholding Taxes on Dividends

U.S. stocks or $300 million, less a $50 million swap payment). Note that this is exactly the same as the before-tax return it could have achieved by investing in the foreign portfolio directly. Similarly, the foreign pension fund nets a return of 30%, the same before-tax rate of return as if it had invested in the U.S. directly. Because net swap payments are not subject to a dividend withholding tax, the swap contract allows the foreign and the U.S. pension funds to save $13.5 million annually in foreign withholding taxes on the dividend payments.[14]

This swap arrangement, however, is not free from costs. Both pension funds seek relatively passive investments, a diversified portfolio of securities in a foreign country. It is more costly to design a swap agreement on a portfolio that has a composition which changes significantly over time.

For example, if the foreign pension fund manager wishes to trade securities in his U.S. stock portfolio, he would have to call the U.S. pension fund manager to add or delete securities from the swap portfolio. It is unlikely that the U.S. pension fund manager would have the same incentives to secure the best prices in buying or selling the designated stocks as would the foreign pension fund manager. Also, the U.S. fund manager would require compensation for the time and expense required to trade someone else's portfolio. Moreover, it is costly for pension fund managers to find the proper counterparties abroad. There is also a credit risk to worry about. Excessive risk taking or simply bad luck on the part of a counterparty can give rise to default on a promised swap payment. Unanticipated regulatory changes can also imperil promised payments.

There is some uncertainty as to whether net payments on notional amounts based on *any* index or commodity escape withholding tax, which is particularly important to pension funds and tax-exempt institutions. In 1990, such payments on interest rate swaps were ruled not to be subject to withholding tax.[15] In the

---

[14] An alternative approach that might be employed is for each pension fund to buy and hold the desired stocks, being careful to sell the stocks just before they go ex-dividend and repurchase them just after they go ex-dividend. In this way, all returns come in the form of capital gains, and withholding taxes on dividend income are avoided. Indeed, this strategy is commonly employed by pension funds holding high-dividend-yielding foreign stocks. But the transaction costs of using this strategy can be very high.

Note that if the withholding tax rate on dividends is 15%, a stock paying a 2% quarterly dividend (or 8% per year) attracts a withholding tax equal to 0.3% of the value of the stock each quarter. If it costs one-quarter of one percent to sell and repurchase shares around the ex-dividend date, the transaction costs would exact an implicit tax nearly as great as the explicit withholding tax. More precisely, replacing the withholding tax with transaction costs would reduce the effective tax rate on the dividends from 15% to 12.5% (or $(.25\%/.30\%) \times 15\%$).

Note further that for lower dividend-paying stocks, it would not pay to sell the stock to avoid the withholding tax. For example, a stock paying a 1.5% quarterly dividend (or 6% per year) attracts a withholding tax equal to 0.225% of the value of the stock each quarter. This is less than the assumed transaction cost to sell and repurchase the stock.

On the other hand, the withholding tax problem disappears for nondividend-paying stocks. While this provides incentives for foreign investors to tilt their holdings in favor of nondividend-paying stocks, nontax factors can operate in the opposite direction. In particular, the payment of dividends can provide valuable monitoring information to investors. This may be especially true for foreign investors who find other forms of monitoring relatively expensive to undertake. Moreover, a portfolio of nondividend-paying (or low-yielding) common stocks may simply not provide the desired level of risk and expected pretax return to investors.

[15] Private Letter Ruling 90-42-038 (July 23, 1990). The IRS later announced that the ruling was being reconsidered. See *Investment Dealers Digest* (November 12, 1990).

Chapter 20   Repackaging Ownership Rights: Tax and Nontax Considerations

swap contract involving stock indices, no cross-border dividends change hands—there are only net payments based on an index that could even exclude the dividend portion of the return. If dividends are excluded, the swap agreement might have positive value to one of the counterparties, but this can be handled by making a non-taxable payment to the other counterparty when the agreement is initiated.

It could be less costly and less risky from a tax perspective to interpose an intermediary to effect the swap transactions. To see this, assume that the U.S. pension fund agrees to pay LIBOR to an investment bank and to receive from it the positive returns (or pay to it the negative returns) on some broad-based index such as the Tokyo Stock Price Index (TOPIX) on the notional $1 billion. In turn, the U.S. pension fund invests its $1 billion at LIBOR, and after paying LIBOR to the investment bank, it receives the return on TOPIX each year, on the notional $1 billion. The investment bank, however, by promising to pay the return on TOPIX each year, is actually short the underlying stocks in TOPIX. It can buy the underlying stocks that comprise TOPIX (or a representative subset, other securities, or futures contracts) to hedge out its commitments. The investment bank finds the withholding tax on any dividends that it receives far less of a problem than the pension fund does. For example, it may use the withholding taxes as a credit against its U.S. liability from foreign-source income.

The investment bank could undertake a similar swap program for the foreign pension fund as it did for the U.S. pension fund. Here the investment bank pays the return on the S&P 500 Index to the foreign pension fund, which in turn pays LIBOR to the investment bank on a notional $1 billion. The investment bank invests the $1 billion in U.S. stocks funded by borrowing $1 billion at a rate that is tied to LIBOR. Whether all of these trades are efficient depends on transaction costs. First, the investment bank must either acquire a portfolio of domestic equities or enter into financial futures contracts to hedge its swap commitments. Second, it is likely that the investment bank will incur a borrowing premium on the loan it undertakes to hedge its swap commitments. With the swap program, the foreign pension fund has credit risk along two dimensions: (1) for the receivable that would be created if the stock index appreciates more than LIBOR, and (2) on the loan to the investment bank, assuming the pension fund is the lender.

The foreign pension fund manager must balance these transaction costs against the tax savings available from entering into the swap agreement. It must also compare these net benefits with those available through such alternatives as buying futures contracts on the S&P 500 Index. Of course, if the foreign pension fund wishes to earn the returns on an index that is not traded on an exchange, the swap agreement might well be its only alternative. Swap agreements are private contracts and can be fashioned quite flexibly.

For the swap contracts we have described to succeed in avoiding withholding tax, it is necessary that the host country treat the income from the swap transaction as foreign-source income. For example, the foreign-source income earned by foreign investors is not subject to U.S. withholding tax. Under Sections 871 and 872, the U.S. only imposes tax on income effectively connected with a trade or business in the U.S. Regulations put into place in early 1991 specify that

20.1 Repackaging Ownership Rights: Mitigation of Withholding Taxes on Dividends

income derived from swap contracts based on indices (such as the S&P 500) will be foreign source for foreign investors.[16] This will probably lead to a growth in the number of indices provided by well-known companies such as Standard and Poors Corporation. These regulations probably arose from the recognition that foreign investors would shy away from entering into swap contracts with U.S. counterparties if swap income was not considered to be foreign source.

U.S. pension funds (and other tax-exempt entities) have worried that entering into swap contracts would subject them to unrelated business taxable income (UBTI). If it did, the pension fund would have to pay tax at the corporate rate on the net income derived from the activity (Sections 511-15). The rules exclude interest, dividends, rents, and royalties from the scope of UBTI. Section 512 also excludes from UBTI gain from the "sale, exchange or other disposition" of property other than inventory (or other property held primarily for sale to customers in the ordinary course of business). This latter exception is particularly relevant to pension funds and tax-exempt entities, for they may be able to consider the swap contract as a "sale or exchange" of property.[17]

While the U.S. does not impose withholding taxes on interest payments made to foreigners on U.S. bond investments, many foreign countries do impose such a tax on interest payments made on bonds issued in their country. This was particularly important in Europe in the 1980s. As a result, cross-currency interest-rate swaps were used to circumvent the withholding tax on interest payments.

To illustrate, assume that for business purposes a German entity wishes to invest, short-term, in Italian bonds paying interest denominated in lira. If it buys short-term bonds from Italian entities, these entities must withhold 15% of the interest that they pay to the German entity. Suppose the German entity cannot get a refund from the German government of these withholding taxes (e.g., the entity is tax exempt).[18] An alternative for the German entity is to enter into a swap agreement. For example, a swap dealer might agree to pay floating interest denominated in lira and receive floating interest denominated in deutchemarks from the German counterparty. The counterparty buys short-term German interest-bearing securities. On net, the German entity receives floating rates in lira, exactly the currency and bond investment returns that it desired in the first place. This is called a floating-for-floating foreign currency swap. In the last few years many European countries have eliminated withholding taxes on interest payments due to the wide use of swap instruments. In early 1990, when Italy eliminated its withholding tax on interest payments to foreign holders of domestic Italian bonds, the number of swap transactions that involved Italian interest rates on one leg of the swap fell dramatically. It is likely that the growth in the use of derivative instruments has caused changes in the withholding tax regimes in

---

[16] In January 1991, new Regulation Section 1.863-7 states that income will be foreign source on any "financial instrument that provides for the payment of amounts by one party to the other at specified intervals calculated by reference to a specified index upon a notional principal amount in exchange for specified consideration or a promise to pay similar amounts."

[17] See Kleinbard, *op. cit.*, pp. 28-35.

[18] If the entity was a French, rather than a German business, taxed on a territorial basis, where the interest receipts on the Italian bond are connected with other active income that is not taxed again in France, the tax credits would routinely be unusable.

Chapter 20   Repackaging Ownership Rights: Tax and Nontax Considerations

Europe. Pressure for a reduction in withholding tax on interest is now apparent in Japan as well.[19]

Nontax Considerations: The Allocation of Voting Rights

Beyond the issues surrounding the creditworthiness of contracting parties to which we have already alluded, and beyond the transaction costs (including investment banking fees) that may be incurred to hold claims in a tax-favored manner, the substitution of derivative securities for the underlying commodities can have consequences for real corporate performance. For example, let's revisit the swap contract summarized in Figure 20.2. To save withholding taxes, the foreign pension fund owns foreign stocks and swaps for the return on U.S. stocks. The U.S. pension fund does the opposite. While this arrangement eliminates withholding taxes, note that the parties in possession of voting rights have no economic interest in the underlying assets. As a consequence, they have no incentive to monitor the management of the companies in which they have voting rights.

Securities

Unbundled Stock Units

The withholding tax problem can also be tackled by creating new securities. For example, Shearson proposed to issue so-called Unbundled Stock Units (USU) in December 1988. Companies such as Pfizer, Dow Chemical, and Sara Lee had agreed to exchange some of their outstanding stock for three new securities: (1) a deep discount bond that pays interest at a rate equal to the current dividend yield on the stock plus a large deferred payment in 30 years; (2) a preferred stock with dividends over the next 30 years equal to the *incremental* dividends that the company paid on their common stock above their current dividend, if any, plus a small liquidation payment at the end, and; (3) a nonvoting warrant or "equity appreciation certificate," convertible into stock at the maturity value of the deep discount bond in 30 years. The return to holding the three pieces is approximately the same as that from holding the underlying stock. Foreign investors, who would hold the appreciation warrants, would participate in the returns on the underlying securities without receiving dividends. U.S. corporations could hold the preferred stock, the dividends on which would be eligible for the dividend-received deduction. And the issuing corporation would secure an interest deduction for the interest on the bonds rather than paying nondeductible dividends.

For example, in early December, 1988 the common stock of Pfizer was selling for approximately $56. The bond component of the proposed Pfizer USU would pay interest of $2 per year (equal to Pfizer's dividend yield at the time) and $150 in 30 years. Investors would be required to accrue original issue discount (OID) as interest income on the difference between the issuance price and the maturity value, and Pfizer would be able to deduct the "dividend" and the OID

---

[19] Similar arguments apply to transaction and turnover taxes on securities. Investors who wish to acquire the returns on baskets of securities can do so by using derivative contracts outside the host country and avoid the transaction taxes. For a related discussion, see Joseph Grundfest, "The Damning Effects of a New Stock Tax," *Wall Street Journal* (July 23, 1990), p. A8.

as interest expense. The preferred stock component had a redemption value in 30 years of $2.50. Because it was worth far more than $2.50, holders of the preferred stock would have a substantial built-in loss for tax purposes. Last, Pfizer's equity appreciation certificate required that the holder deliver the other two instruments plus $2.50 to Pfizer to receive a share of stock.

USUs were never issued for a variety of reasons. One important factor was that pension funds wanted to vote their shares, but their equity appreciation certificates carried no voting rights. Another is that the exchange of stock for USUs would have been a taxable event, so taxable investors with accrued capital gains would have found an exchange expensive. Concern was also expressed that U.S. corporations would not find the preferred stock piece of the USUs attractive to hold because of the highly uncertain dividend stream and possible illiquidity.[20] Still another problem relates to unfavorable financial reporting consequences.

Synthetic Bonds

As an alternative structure to USUs, corporations can issue synthetic bonds to finance their activities. A synthetic bond is a debt obligation that provides for contingent payments determined by reference to the change in value of traded securities, commodities, or other publicly traded property. Investors in synthetic bonds issued prior to February of 1991 (and possibly beyond),[21] are treated as receiving interest income, even though the contingent payments might be linked to both the appreciation of, and the dividends paid on, a portfolio of common stocks. The bonds have typically been issued at a low interest rate, and at maturity the holder receives the greater of the bonds' maturity value and the value of some traded property.

Under the proposed regulations in 1991, the synthetic bond must be bifurcated into a straight bond portion and a warrant piece, with each taxed accordingly. To qualify for this bifurcation treatment, the debt must provide for non-contingent payments that are at least equal to its initial issue price. Because of the low interest rate, the bonds would naturally be issued at a substantial original issue discount (OID). The issuers of such bonds are permitted to deduct not only the current coupon on the bonds, but also the OID on the accretion of the bond to par over its life, which is very attractive if the holder is a tax-exempt pension fund or a foreign investor. Moreover, payments above par value on bonds are also deductible as interest.

---

[20] See, for example, *Business Week* (December 19, 1988), pp. 84-85.

[21] In February 1991, the IRS issued proposed regulations affecting the treatment of debt obligations issued after February 20, 1991 that provide for contingent payments determined by reference to the change in value of traded stock, securities, commodities, or other publicly traded property. They responded, in part, to the Republic of Austria's offering of Stock Index Growth Notes (SIGNS), which provide a return linked to the S&P 500 Index. These notes provide investors with deferred income and capital gains on the appreciation in the S&P 500 Index, all taxed as interest. Foreign investors holding this bond would escape U.S. taxation entirely, since no dividends are paid on the investment.

The proposed regulations (Section 1.1275-4(g)), described, in part, below, amend prior *proposed* regulations issued in 1986 (Section 1.1275-4). These proposed regulations might be replaced by new proposed regulations. The tax consequences of many of these synthetic debt issues are rather uncertain.

Chapter 20   Repackaging Ownership Rights: Tax and Nontax Considerations

There are many options available to taxpayers under these regulations. If the bond is convertible into the stock of the issuer, the bond is not bifurcated; if it is settled for cash, however, it *is* bifurcated. If the synthetic bond promises non-contingent payments in excess of initial issue price, the bond is bifurcated; if not, the bond is not bifurcated.[22]

Section 249 of the U.S. tax code prevents the corporation from deducting contingent interest based on the performance of its own stock or that of its affiliates. It can, however, deduct as contingent interest the performance of the stock of a competitor, or of an index such as the S&P 500. Pfizer might agree to pay a 2% coupon and contingent interest based on the performance of Merck or a portfolio of other drug companies. These contracts are similar to the swap contracts described earlier. For a debt obligation to be classified as a contingent interest obligation and not an original issue debt obligation, however, requires that the interest payments not be determinable with near certainty. Therefore, a firm could not agree to pay the returns on LIBOR deferred for ten years. The Service would argue that this was simply a ten-year bond, and the accrued interest would be taxed annually.

Under the 1991 proposed regulations, a tax-exempt entity is an excellent candidate to issue these contingent interest notes. For example, a university might issue a 1% current coupon bond with contingent interest tied to the performance of the S&P 500. The contingent interest would be paid some time in the future. Bondholders would avoid current taxes on dividends, as well as the taxes on the realization of capital gains when stocks are sold to rebalance the S&P 500 portfolio as its composition changes. If the capital gains tax rate were reduced in the future, the bondholder could sell the bonds for a capital gain to a pension fund or some other tax-exempt entity rather than realizing the contingent interest. If the security is to be classified as a bond for tax purposes, the university would have to guarantee a minimum payoff at maturity (a payoff of say $50 on a $100 initial bond price).[23]

If the guaranteed minimum payoff at maturity were set greater than or equal to the initial bond price, the security would have to be bifurcated under the 1991 proposed regulations. The contingent payment would then be treated as a capital gain to the investor, so foreign investors would avoid dividend withholding taxes, and individual investors might secure a lower tax rate than that which applies to interest income.

Salomon Brothers issued contingent interest bonds in August 1986. Their bonds were called 2% Standard and Poor's 500 Index Subordinated Notes (SPINS) due in 1990. The notes bore interest at 2% per annum, and at maturity, the holder received the maximum of (1) the principal amount of $1,000 and (2) the S&P 500 Index multiplied by 3.6985 at a time when the index value was approxi-

---

[22] If the issuer does not promise payments at least equal to the price of the bond, the taxpayer participates in the decline in the value of the security to which payments are linked. In this case, non-contingent payments are treated as principal and contingent payments are taxed as interest when the amounts become fixed (typically at maturity). In effect, these bonds have similar tax treatment to the single premium deferred annuities described in Chapter Three.

[23] Notice here that the holder can swap the returns on the index for LIBOR deferred. This creates a synthetic single premium deferred annuity invested in bonds.

mately 250.[24] Although Salomon might not have been the correct clientele to issue these bonds, since it was a tax-paying corporation and preferred to deduct interest payments currently, it sold the entire issue to Chase Manhattan Bank, which offered similar contracts to its depositors, before banks were precluded from doing so by federal regulators.[25]

Convertible Bonds

It is interesting to note that the 1991 proposed regulations for contingent interest debt allows corporations to increase interest deductions for convertible bonds that are settled in cash rather than convertible into stock. Such securities are bifurcated into a bond and an equity piece. Normally, when convertible bonds are *not* bifurcated, the interest deduction is only equal to coupon payments made.

A convertible bond is a combination of a straight debt issue and a warrant to buy the underlying stock (or other property) of the issuer. It must be issued at approximately par (that is, the face amount of the bond) to avoid original issue discount. As a result, the coupon on the bond is set below market yields to cause the debt portion to trade at below par, such that the sum of the debt value and the warrant value will equal par on issuance. If the convertible bond were bifurcated into the debt portion and the warrant portion, the debt portion would sell for a discount from par (because of the low coupon), and the difference would be treated as original issue discount (OID). This discount is deductible as interest over the life of the bond.

Warrants

Entities such as corporations, international government agencies, and investment banks issue warrants to purchase a broad-based index of securities such as the S&P 500 or the FTSE (the London Financial Times Stock Exchange). Such warrants have been traded on exchanges around the world. No dividends are paid to warrant holders.[26] The warrant price is lower to reflect this fact.[27] Warrant holders can achieve returns that track the returns on the underlying portfolio, and incur no withholding tax on dividends.[28]

---

[24] Morgan Stanley issued a similar warrant on the so-called Major Market Index.

[25] Bankers Trust has issued $500 million of protected equity notes for 8 U.S. pension funds, and over $2 billion worldwide. (*Pensions and Investments*, May 14, 1990)

[26] An example here is the Americus Trust Units that broke the returns on stocks such as IBM, AT&T, and Merck into a Prime and a Score. Primes and Scores are traded on the American Stock Exchange. The Primes are like preferred stocks. They have a fixed redemption price and earn all the dividends on the underlying stock. The Scores are like warrants. They earn only the price appreciation in the underlying stock above the redemption price of the Primes. Another example is the warrants issued by Banker's Trust, Salomon Brothers, and other issuers to buy the Nikkei index (a Japanese stock market price index like the Dow Jones Index in the U.S.).

[27] If warrants are issued on individual securities, and the issuer controls the dividend policy on the underlying security, hidden action problems might result: the issuer can increase the dividend, unexpectedly, thereby reducing the value of the warrant. Jeremy Bulow has suggested to us that firms should issue dividend-protected warrants to reduce this hidden action problem. The only uncertainty is whether the warrant terms can be adjusted to protect the warrant holder completely.

[28] These warrants weren't necessarily issued primarily because of withholding tax concerns. On the contrary, they provide low-cost alternatives for investors to buy broad market participation. Moreover, because warrants are options, their risk changes as a function of changes in the value, composition, and riskiness of the underlying portfolio. If investors wish to maintain a specified level

Concluding Remarks on Withholding Taxes

Over the last 15 years, we have seen dramatic growth in the use of synthetics. Beyond their magnificent contributions in facilitating efficient risk management, these contracts have allowed financial engineers to develop new technologies that have been used to reduce the import of withholding taxes on interest and dividends. We have stressed the case of the foreign withholding taxes on interest and dividends because of the myriad ways to reduce them. And yet we have only touched on a rather limited subset of possible tax-planning strategies. We have also explored how the taxing authorities have responded to the development of these technologies. In the 1990s, we are likely to see continued evolution of these strategies, and the taxing authorities are likely to find it even more difficult to stem the tide. This would appear to imperil the worldwide system of imposing different rates of withholding tax on different forms of international capital flows, a system that has been in place for decades.

20.2 Repackaging Ownership Rights: Other Tax-Planning Motivations

The withholding tax problem is only one of many tax-planning problems that can be addressed by using synthetics. For example, consider the interest allocation problem faced by U.S. multinationals that we discussed in Chapter Fourteen. A few firms have deconsolidated financial subsidiaries (that is, sold off more than a 20% interest in a subsidiary) by issuing preferred stock to unrelated investors. In this way they avoid having to allocate the interest deductions on the debt of the subsidiary to their other foreign source income. One difficulty with this approach is that the firm could regain control of more than 80% of the value of its subsidiary, if the subsidiary were to increase in value, and once again be forced to allocate interest of the subsidiary to the worldwide operations of the parent. One way to avoid this problem is for the firm to enter into a swap contract with the subsidiary. The parent would receive the return on the subsidiary's assets in return for paying LIBOR to the subsidiary. This ensures that any unanticipated increase in the value of the subsidiary accrues directly to the parent rather than the subsidiary, and the parent's percentage ownership in the value of the subsidiary can be managed more easily.

Over the last several years more and more corporations have become comfortable with the use of synthetic instruments as a low cost way to hedge risks and to reduce the costs of regulatory constraints. For example, Canada restricts its pension funds from investing more than 20% of their assets internationally. Countries such as Israel and Chile restrict capital flows out of their countries. Synthetic contracts can be used to comply with the intent of these regulations (that is, to keep the capital in the home country), yet allow investors access to international returns and risks.[29]

---

of risk over time, they may have to buy bonds (and sell warrants), or conversely, as circumstances in the market change. This could create capital gains realizations on the sale of warrants sooner than desired. It could also generate periodic interest income. Warrant terms (such as a changing exercise price) can be devised to mitigate these tax costs.

In the introductory chapter of this book, we noted that our goal was to develop a framework for understanding how tax rules affect business decision making. We also indicated that the framework was applicable to a broad set of regulations *besides* taxes. The above examples of using synthetics to reduce the costs of restrictions on capital flows are an indication of this. Synthetics may also be used to affect the timing of income reported to shareholders and other third parties. One final illustration of this sort we will discuss relates to Japanese banking regulations, which provide for different types of banks. Two that are of interest are the city banks and the long-term credit banks. City banks cannot borrow to fund their activities by issuing long-term notes; while long-term credit banks can borrow long-term to fund activities. While city banks may wish to hedge their own risks by issuing longer-term instruments, they are precluded from doing so because of the regulations. Our framework suggests that they will use new vehicles to satisfy their hedging demands if the costs of doing so are not too high. Indeed they have done just that. City banks issue short-term paper, and through swap agreements with long-term credit banks (LTCB), pay the return on long-term bonds and receive the return on short-term instruments. The LTCBs issue long-term bonds, and invest the proceeds in short-term instruments to hedge their swap commitments.

As technologies change and the costs to create synthetics fall, the creation of myriad new types of organizational forms, contracts, and securities will become common. Tax rules will change to make many of the old vehicles undesirable, but the changes will create an incentive to develop new vehicles. Such tax rule uncertainty, however, dampens participants' enthusiasm for tackling these tax-planning issues. To illustrate a few opportunities along these lines, we turn now to a discussion of the use of synthetics to reduce business risks for corporations and how swap contracts can be used to achieve deferral of income that would otherwise be taxed as Subpart F income. In later chapters, we revisit the use of synthetics as ways to solve some corporate reorganization and estate and gift tax planning problems.

Synthetics and Corporate Finance

In previous chapters we have argued that both the 1981 and the 1986 Tax Acts encouraged U.S. corporations to diminish equity financing and increase financing that distributes corporate profits in tax-deductible ways. Highly leveraged strategies, however, might be very costly if the firm must reorganize its activities prior to or in bankruptcy. Equity serves as a way to cushion the firm against these reorganization costs, especially when outsiders know less about the operations of the firm than do insiders.

Synthetics can be designed to hedge certain of the firm's business risks, thereby reducing the probability of incurring these reorganization costs for a given level of debt. Alternatively, for a given level of risk, hedging allows firms to increase tax-advantageous debt and reduce costly equity. Firms must trade off

---

[29] Bankers Trust-Canada completed the first protected equity note deal in 1988. "The investor was the Shell-Canada pension plan, which was trying to expand its foreign equities exposure but faced legal constraints, said Mr. D'Onofrio." (*Pensions and Investments*, May 14, 1990).

Chapter 20   Repackaging Ownership Rights: Tax and Nontax Considerations

the costs of using synthetics to hedge business risks against the costs (including tax costs) of using equity as a cushion. Firms will tend to hedge the risks of those aspects of their business for which they have little expertise (for example, foreign exchange fluctuations) and concentrate on those aspects in which they know more than outsiders (for example, conducting research and development activities).

Use of Swaps to Achieve Deferral of Subpart F Income

The passive income of controlled foreign subsidiaries of U.S. corporations (CFCs) is taxable each year in the U.S. as Subpart F income, as if the subsidiary paid a taxable dividend to its parent each year. These CFCs, however, can use swap transactions to defer the payment of U.S. tax on Subpart F income, and, as a result, achieve the same risk-adjusted after-tax returns as if they had invested actively abroad. Consider a CFC in a low-tax country that faces an unattractive opportunity set for active investments. Its past investments, however, have been quite profitable. It has accumulated $1 billion of profits from active investments that would be taxed at U.S. rates, less any foreign tax credit, if deemed to be paid as a dividend to its U.S. parent. The CFC can either invest the $1 billion in passive investments that yield Subpart F income, taxable each year in the U.S., or undertake a combination of an active investment and a swap of the return from the active investment for a future payment that will defer the U.S. tax on the investment return until some future date.

To accomplish the deferral, the CFC might invest the $1 billion in a precious metal such as gold bullion that is actively traded in world markets. The entire return on bullion results from its price appreciation.[30] The CFC also enters into a swap agreement to pay the price appreciation on gold at the end of some period of time, say 10 years, and to receive LIBOR deferred for 10 years on a notional $1 billion. In 10 years, the investor receives the accumulated amount invested at LIBOR and pays the appreciated value of the gold on the swap. The gold investment is made so as to employ the CFC's funds.

The likely U.S. tax treatment of this combination gold-swap investment is that the CFC will generate passive, Subpart F income only at the end of 10 years when the swap agreement is settled. The U.S. parent will pay tax on its net swap receipt or payment and the realized profit or loss on its gold investment. The net before-tax accumulation on the combination gold-swap transaction will be the same as if the CFC had invested directly in passive assets at the before-tax LIBOR rate.

Let us assume that LIBOR is 8% and gold is expected to appreciate at 6% per year. This is a reasonable assumption in that the returns on gold appear to be negatively correlated with the returns of other assets in the economy, and, as a result, the price of gold is bid up to reflect its hedging value. At the end of 10 years, if gold does appreciate at the expected rate of 6%, the CFC would receive $.37

---

[30] An investment in land in the CFC's host country or some other country *other than* the U.S., and swapping the return on this land investment for LIBOR, will also work. An investment in *U.S.* land, however, will *not* work, because such an investment would be treated as a deemed repatriation of the CFC's profits.

billion (or \$1 billion $\times$ [$(1.08)^{10}$ - 1] less \$1 billion $\times$ [$(1.06)^{10}$ -1]) from its swap agreement. The gold held appreciates in value to \$1.79 billion (or \$1 billion $\times$ $(1.06)^{10}$). In total, the CFC accumulates \$2.16 billion before tax, the same as investing at LIBOR. Its net swap receivable of \$.37 billion is taxable as ordinary income, and the gain on the gold of \$.79 billion is taxable as ordinary income if the transaction is "integrated." Otherwise it is treated as a capital gain. That is, the CFC can "integrate" the transaction by designating, at the time the transaction is entered into, that the swap transaction is part of a so-called "qualified hedging transaction."

If capital gains rates are the same as ordinary rates, and if gold appreciates at a rate below LIBOR, as expected, the net after-tax result would be the same for the CFC whether or not the transaction was integrated. It would pay U.S. tax at ordinary rates on income of \$1.16 billion. At a 40% tax rate, this would yield an after-tax accumulation of \$1.7 billion (or \$1 billion + \$1.16 billion (1 - .4)). If instead the CFC had invested its \$1 billion at LIBOR for 10 years and realized Subpart F income each year, it would accumulate only \$1.6 billion after tax (or \$1 billion $\times$ $(1 + .08(1 - .4))^{10}$). The present value of the increased accumulation from the gold-swap transaction is \$62 million after tax (or 6.2% per dollar invested) for a 10-year deferral. The longer the deferral, the greater the present value of the tax savings.

If, by chance, gold appreciates by more than LIBOR, the CFC would make a net payment to its counterparty, which is tax deductible from ordinary income. It would realize ordinary income from the returns on its gold holdings, if the transaction were integrated, and capital gains treatment if not integrated. If not integrated, the value of the transaction would be enhanced if capital gains were taxed at more favorable rates than ordinary income. If, on the other hand, gold depreciated in value, the non-integrated transaction would generate a capital loss on the gold holding and an equal amount of ordinary income on the swap. The CFC or its parent might have to defer taking the deduction for the capital loss until it could offset it against a capital gain. In deciding on the form of the transaction, integrated versus non-integrated, the CFC would have to weigh the trade-offs between receiving a favorable capital-gains rate at some time in the future against the possibility that it would generate a deferred capital loss on its gold holdings.

An important issue here is who would be willing to pay interest to our CFC deferred for 10 years if this means deferral of an interest deduction. A natural counterparty for the gold-swap transaction is a tax-exempt entity. It could enter into a swap contract, with the CFC agreeing to receive the returns on gold deferred for 10 years and pay LIBOR deferred for 10 years. It could then invest \$1 billion in LIBOR and hedge its gold investment by selling a series of gold-futures contracts on the Comex in New York each year. There are, however, dead-weight transaction costs to effect these trades. Moreover, the tax-exempt entity would expect to share some of the tax gains with the CFC. If, however, the entity happened to be the pension plan of the parent of the CFC, the tax gains could be completely internalized.[31]

It is worth noting that the credit risk of a swap is greater for deferred payments than for current payments, because the accumulation, which could

---

[31] If the tax-exempt entity were the counterparty to our CFC, it need not remain invested in LIBOR deferred. For example, if a pension fund were the tax-exempt entity and it wanted to achieve the

Chapter 20   Repackaging Ownership Rights: Tax and Nontax Considerations

become quite large, is paid out at the end of the life of the contract and not each year as it accrues. To mitigate the effect of credit constraints, each counterparty could agree to escrow the in-the-money value of the swap or to obtain a letter of credit securing their net payable to their counterparty.

If our CFC prefers an investment alternative to LIBOR, say the S&P 500 Index, the gold-swap transaction works equally well in postponing U.S. taxable income if the counterparty to the swap contract agrees to pay the return on the S&P 500 Index, rather than LIBOR, in 10 years. Alternatively, the CFC could undo the claim to deferred LIBOR in its initial swap contract by entering into a second swap contract to receive the returns on the S&P 500 Index deferred for 10 years and pay LIBOR deferred for 10 years. The new swap offsets the deferred LIBOR returns from the first swap and generates deferred S&P 500 returns from the second swap.

Furthermore, even if the CFC was initially satisfied with the risk and return pattern of the first swap, it could change its mind later. For example, at the end of the first year, it could enter into an additional swap agreement in which it promises to pay LIBOR deferred for nine years and receive the returns on, say, the S&P 500 Index deferred for nine years on a notional amount that is equal to the appreciated value of its initial investment. As a result, the CFC receives, on its $1 billion investment, a net return of LIBOR for the first year and the return on the S&P 500 Index (including dividends) for the remaining nine years, on the accumulated value of its position at the end of the first year. Since a direct investment in the S&P 500 already offers partial deferral of tax on the capital gains part of its return, the relative advantage of investing in S&P 500 swaps to secure deferral of all returns is not as great as investing in LIBOR swaps.

Instead of entering into a series of swaps, it is also possible to enter into an asset allocation swap agreement. In this arrangement, the CFC can change the designated index return (LIBOR, S&P 500 Index, Bond Index) when it so desires. Changing the designated index does not trigger a realization of taxable income. It is possible for the swap contract to include terms that allow the CFC to extend it beyond 10 years. It is also possible to build in options to cancel the swap to provide the CFC with added flexibility. It could time the cancellation of its swaps to effect a realization of income in a year in which it needed more foreign source income (perhaps because some of its foreign tax credits were about to expire unused). Extendable and cancellable swaps provide both the CFC and its counterparty with some comfort when dealing with a risky contracting partner and with deferred payments that create large and unsecured receivables. An alternative possibility is for the counterparties to post collateral to reduce the import of the credit risk. These nontax costs reduce the desirability of employing these techniques.

It is worth emphasizing that the tax rules are always subject to change and reinterpretation. If the rules on deferred swap payments were changed such that

---

returns on French stocks, it could enter into a second swap agreement to receive the returns on some French stock index and to pay LIBOR. Since it is tax exempt, it is indifferent to current or deferred cash flow realizations for tax purposes. Its counterparty, however, might prefer one or the other payment streams.

income were recognized on an accrual or a market value basis, the advantage of tax deferral would be lost.[32]

Summary of Key Points

1. There are important tax and nontax motivations for repackaging ownership rights in ways that transfer parts of the risk and return of holding assets to parties that value them most highly.

2. Vehicles that are used to repackage returns include (a) financial contracts, (b) organizational forms, and (c) securities. All of these vehicles are contractual forms of repackaging of one kind or another. They are in the broad class of synthetic securities that are designed to mimic the financial performance of some underlying assets.

3. The taxation of these synthetic instruments is uncertain in many instances. Many regulations are only in proposed form, and even the proposed regulations change periodically. This makes it difficult for taxpayers to plan their activities.

4. The taxing authority creates this uncertainty, in part, to inhibit the growth of synthetic instruments that have no purpose other than to avoid taxes. As the cost of creating new instruments declines, these vehicles are employed to undertake organizational-form and clientele-based arbitrage strategies. This is particularly so in an international setting, where tax rules differ across taxpayers, time periods, tax jurisdictions, and economic activities.

5. Changes in technology (a reduction in transaction costs) lead to changes in tax rules.

6. Withholding taxes on portfolio dividend or interest income can impede international diversification. Investors can use synthetic securities, however, to mitigate the impact of these taxes.

7. U.S. taxpayers can use partnerships or regulated investment companies to parse out the returns on dividend-paying securities to appropriate parties. For example, a foreign pension fund and a U.S. corporation may form a partnership, wherein the foreign pension fund contributes its U.S. dividend-paying securities into the partnership and the U.S. corporation contributes an appropriate amount of its bond holdings into the vehicle. The foreign pension fund agrees to take the interest on the U.S. corporation's bonds, and the U.S. corporation agrees to take the dividends on the stocks in the portfolio. The pension fund retains the risks of the stock portfolio, and the U.S. corporation retains the risks of the bond portfolio. For the appropriate bond and stock mix, both parties

---

[32] There are other substitutes for this structure. For example, Salomon Brothers established an oil trust that allows holders to buy oil for forward delivery. Since holders receive no interim cash flows, they expect that the price of the trust units will appreciate at approximately the rate of interest, unless the price of the trust shares are bid up (a form of implicit tax) because holders pay no tax on the appreciation until they sell their interest in the trust.

can earn the same before-tax rate of return as they did prior to using the organizational form. Since withholding taxes are withheld on dividend income but not on interest earned on U.S. portfolio investments by foreign investors, the pension fund achieves a higher after-tax rate of return. The U.S. corporation is better off as well, because it exchanges its interest income for dividend income, which is subject to the dividend received deduction.

8. Nontax costs and regulations might preclude this arrangement from being efficient for many taxpayers.

9. Contracts such as futures, forwards, options, and swaps can mitigate the impact of withholding taxes. For example, if a foreign pension fund holds a futures contract to buy the Standard & Poor's 500 Index, and holds the funds that would have been invested in the index in bonds, the foreign pension fund achieves the same before-tax result. It converts dividends into interest that is not subject to withholding taxes. The before-tax return on a futures contract plus the interest on an appropriate amount of bonds provide a pretax return equal to the sum of the capital gains and dividends on the index.

10. Using contracts can be costly. For example, there are transaction costs to buy and sell futures contracts each period. Moreover, taxpayers may be interested in investing in a portfolio for which no ready futures contract exists.

11. Swap contracts provide alternative ways to achieve similar results. A swap contract is a private forward contract (or long-dated futures contract). It can be more tailored to meet investor desires. Being a private contract, however, it is subject to more credit risk of the counterparties to the trade and is less liquid than market-traded futures contracts. With private contracts, the taxing authorities have greater difficulties in specifying tax rules in ways that discourage tax avoidance, while at the same time preserving the nontax benefits of swaps, because the form of the contract can adapt quickly to changing circumstances.

12. Securities can also be devised to achieve similar results. For example, foreign firms can issue index-linked bonds that provide investors with a return linked to the performance of an index such as the S&P 500. If properly structured, the security is treated as a bond for tax purposes, and the return is considered to be contingent interest and is taxable as such. This avoids dividend withholding tax problems, since no dividends are paid on the security.

13. Synthetic instruments are of growing importance to corporations in the U.S. because they can be used to hedge business risks. For example, if the firm has no expertise in forecasting foreign exchange risks, it can hedge these risks with synthetic instruments. By hedging, it reduces the probability of bankruptcy for a given level of equity. Bankruptcy and reorganization costs are expensive for firms. Since corporations prefer to finance with debt (because it is tax efficient to do so), reducing risks

with synthetic instruments allows the firm to have a higher debt-to-equity ratio, but the tax benefits of this must be balanced against the costs of using synthetics.

14. Synthetic instruments can also be used to defer the taxation of Subpart F income. In essence, these instruments can be used to create synthetic single premium deferred annuity contracts for investors.

Discussion Questions

1. What does the expression "repackaging ownership rights" mean? What are the motivations for doing it? Describe some vehicles that can be used to repackage ownership rights.

2. What factors might dissuade investors from using these vehicles to conduct organizational-form or clientele-based arbitrage?

3. If you are an advisor to a foreign investor facing a dividend withholding tax problem on investments in U.S. securities, what strategies might be employed to mitigate the problem? What are the nontax costs of the strategies?

4. What is a swap contract? How does it differ from a futures contract? From a forward contract? Which entities would you expect to set the prices of futures contracts in the market? Why?

5. Do taxable investors form a natural clientele to issue contingent interest securities? If not, who *are* the natural clienteles? What tax and nontax issues arise for investors holding these securities?

6. Why might corporations use synthetic instruments to hedge business risks? What types of business risks might they hedge? What are the costs of using these hedging devices?

7. Synthetic instruments can be used to create synthetic single premium deferred annuity contracts. Explain how this can be done. How might synthetic instruments be used to fund compensation benefits for executives or to fund post-retirement health care benefits?

8. How does uncertainty in tax rules affect investor behavior? What costs does this uncertainty impose on investors?

CHAPTER 21
Real Estate Investments

In this chapter, we continue to explore the theme of parsing out investment returns to exploit differences in tax characteristics across investors. In particular, we consider how the property rights to real estate investment returns should be allocated in the marketplace among property users (residents), property managers, and various classes of more passive investors. We begin with a focus on tax considerations. Then we discuss incentive problems that may render tax-minimizing contracts undesirable.

21.1 Taxes, Rental Rates, and Property Valuation

As discussed more fully in the next chapter, real estate investments receive tax-favored treatment along a number of dimensions: (1) rapid depreciation relative to economic depreciation; (2) potential for multiple write-offs through property resales; (3) deferral of income, especially when installment sales are used; and (4) taxation of some income at favorable rates. Real estate investments have historically borne considerable implicit taxes, attracting high tax-bracket taxpayers as owners and low tax-bracket taxpayers as renters.

To better understand how the tax rules affect the pricing of real estate transactions, we next develop a simple model. Let

V = market value of a piece of property,

M = maintenance cost of the property per period that preserves the value of the property in real terms. In other words, M represents the real depreciation on the property each period plus routine maintenance costs,

R = rental charge on the property per period,

P = property tax per period imposed by the locality,

R_b = interest rate on fully taxable riskless bonds,

t = tax rate on ordinary income,

i = inflation rate, the rate at which R, P, and V increase in value each period, given a policy of spending M per period to maintain the value of the property in real terms. For simplicity, we will assume that the property depreciates at a constant rate of value each period, so M will also increase at rate i per period,

d = fraction of V that is immediately deductible in present value terms in *excess* of economic depreciation.

An investor should be willing to pay the following amount, V, for the property:

$$V = dVt + \frac{(R - M - P)(1 - t)}{R_b(1 - t) - i}. \qquad (21.1)$$

The right-hand-side of 21.1 represents the present value of future cash flows from investing in the property. The first term represents the present value of the tax reduction from accelerated depreciation allowances. It is like an investment tax credit. The second term represents the present value of after-tax rental income in excess of rental expenses. In 21.1, we implicitly assume that amounts spent to maintain the real value of the property (M) are tax-deductible as incurred. While this may be somewhat of an overstatement of the tax benefits derived from property maintenance (since property improvements must actually be capitalized and depreciated over their useful lives), we have also assumed that all income is taxed at ordinary rates in the period earned, which overstates the tax cost.

Note also that our assumption of R, M, and P increasing at a constant rate each period, in perpetuity, enables a particularly simple valuation equation. Given a discount rate of $R_b(1 - t)$ per period, the present value of a perpetual stream of cash flow of \$1 in the first period and $\$1(1 + i)^{n-1}$ in the nth period (that is, the cash flow is growing at rate i per period) is simply $\$1/(R_b(1 - t) - i)$.

Equation 21.1, the investor indifference condition, can be rewritten in another (perhaps more intuitive) form:

$$\underbrace{V(1 - dt)}_{(a)} \underbrace{[R_b(1 - t)]}_{(b)} = \underbrace{(R - M - P)(1 - t)}_{(c)} + \underbrace{V(1 - dt)i}_{(d)} \qquad (21.2)$$

In words, the investor must earn the after-tax risk-adjusted interest rate on investment each period:

- Term (a) represents the net cost of the investment after subtracting the present value of the accelerated depreciation tax shield.
- Term (b) is the after-tax interest rate. This represents the investor's required rate of return per period. Note that the product of (a) times (b) represents the required *total* return on investment each period.

The investor's return comes in two pieces:

- Term (c) is the annual "dividend" portion of the return, the excess of rental income over maintenance costs and property taxes; and

- Term (d) represents the anticipated capital gain portion of the return on the net investment.

Let's now denote by r the after-tax required real rate of return or $R_b(1 - t) - i$. Then a little rearranging of 21.2 reveals that the rental rate on property each period satisfies:

$$R = \rho V \frac{(1 - dt)}{(1 - t)} + M + P. \qquad (21.3)$$

By definition, when the depreciation deductions allowed for tax purposes are equal to economic depreciation, d is equal to zero. In this case,

$$R = \frac{\rho V}{1 - t} + M + P. \qquad (21.4)$$

According to equation 21.4, the rental rate must cover real economic depreciation (including routine maintenance costs), property taxes, and the real after-tax rate of interest on the investment grossed up by a factor of $1 - t$. The gross-up factor is required so that when tax is paid on $\rho V/(1 - t)$ (which is the net taxable rental income), the investor is left with ρV in after-tax income. Since this after-tax income grows at rate i each period, it has a present value of V.[1]

Depreciation allowances are typically more generous, however, than economic depreciation. Moreover, as we discuss more fully in the next chapter, property may be depreciated multiple times over its life as ownership is transferred from one taxpayer to the next. The *additional* depreciation benefit is equivalent to the opportunity to take an *extra* tax deduction for part of the purchase price of the property over the depreciable life of the asset as specified by the tax code. The portion of the purchase price that is eligible for the extra depreciation deductions, however, is only that part *not* represented by the land component of the investment, which commonly runs on the order of 20% of the investment value.

In Table 21.1, we show the present value of the depreciation deduction over various time periods. We assume that 80% of the purchase price of property is permitted an *extra* depreciation deduction in *addition* to economic depreciation, and this amount is deductible at a rate permitted by the statutory depreciation schedule.

Note from Table 21.1 that the depreciation schedule in 1986 is actually more generous than that in 1981 ("bonus" depreciation deduction of $.48 versus $.40), despite the slower nominal rate of depreciation. The reason for this is that the interest rate is substantially lower in 1986, and this *more* than offsets the slower rate of depreciation.[2] On the other hand, the 1986 Tax Act substantially reduced the tax-favored treatment accorded to real property.

---

[1] Cash flow of amount ρV in the first period, growing at rate i per period in perpetuity thereafter, has a present value, given a discount rate of $R(1 - t)$, of $\rho V/[R(1 - t) - i] = \rho V/\rho = V$.

[2] These calculations ignore differences across the different time periods in the ability to earn multiple depreciation writeoffs through property resales. As we will discuss in the next chapter, the desirability of trades was greater in 1981 than in 1986 due to differences in depreciation recapture rules under installment sales.

Table 21.1 Present Value of Depreciation Tax Shelter per Dollar of Investment Over Various Time Periods.

Time Period	Depreciation Schedule	After-Tax Discount Rate*	Present Value of "Bonus" Depreciation Per Dollar of Investment	Present Value of Tax Savings at Tax Rates of 40% Pre-1987 and 25% Post-1986
Late 1970s	200% Declining Balance, Switching to Straight Line, Over 40 Years	5.5%	40¢	16¢
1981-1983	ACRS** (15 Years)	10%	45¢	18¢
1986	ACRS** (19 Years)	7%	48¢	19¢
1987 on	Straight Line Over 27.5 Years	8%	32¢	8¢
1987 on	Straight Line Over 40 Years (foreign-use property and property financed with tax-exempt bonds)	8%	24¢	6¢

*From Salomon Brothers, *Analytical Record of Yields and Yield Spreads*. Our proxy for $R_b(1 - t)$, the after-tax riskless bond rate, is the long-term tax-exempt bond rate. This proxy could overstate the after-tax riskless rate due to the risk of default and the illiquidity of municipal bonds.

**Accelerated Cost Recovery System

Suppose that the marginal investor in property faced a 40% tax rate in 1986 and a 25% tax rate in 1987. Further suppose that the after-tax real rate of interest, ρ, is 2%; M = 3%, consisting of 1% for routine maintenance plus 2% for real depreciation (for example, this corresponds to a 40-year useful life for a structure that represents 80% of the value of the property, with land representing the remaining 20%); and property taxes, P, are 1%. Then rental rates, as a percentage of the value of the property, would be equal to:

$$6.70\% \text{ (or } 2\% \times \frac{1 - .48(.4)}{1 - .4} + 3\% + 1\%) \text{ in 1986, and}$$

$$6.45\% \text{ (or } 2\% \times \frac{1 - .32(.25)}{1 - .25} + 3\% + 1\%) \text{ in 1987.}$$

For 1986, this would translate to rent of $20,100 per year or $1,675 per month for a $300,000 property.

The calculations above suggest that rental rates should have *declined* following the 1986 Tax Act despite the fact that real estate is less tax-favored under the new rules. The reason for this is that tax rates have declined as well.

With lower tax rates, investments giving rise to taxable income require lower before-tax returns to provide a given level of after-tax return.[3]

For example, if property were not granted tax-favored treatment (that is, d = 0), then from equation 21.4, the required before-tax rate of return (that is, pretax rental income), given that income is growing at the inflation rate, i, per period, is R - M - P = $\rho V/(1 - t)$. Suppose that the tax rate of the marginal holder of property is 40% prior to the 1986 Tax Act and 25% after the 1986 Tax Act. If ρ = 2%, then $\rho/(1 - t)$ = 3.33% for t = 40% and $\rho/(1 - t)$ = 2.67% for t = 25%. But given the tax-favored treatment accorded these investments, pretax rental income (of R - M - P), as a percentage of the value of the property, according to the simple model above would be $(1 - dt) \rho V/(1 - t)$ or 2.70% prior to the 1986 Tax Act and 2.45% after the 1986 Tax Act. From these data, we can calculate the implicit tax rate on property investment before and after the 1986 Tax Act:

Pre-1987: $$\frac{3.33\% - 2.70\%}{3.33\%} = 19\%$$

Post-1986: $$\frac{2.67\% - 2.45\%}{2.67\%} = 8\%$$

So implicit taxes would comprise roughly half the total tax burden of 40% before the 1986 Tax Act but only one-third of the total tax burden of 25% following the Act.

21.2 Tax Clienteles

Tax Exempt Entities

As mentioned earlier, high tax-bracket taxpayers represent the natural clientele for investor/lessors in real property, and low tax-bracket investors represent the natural clientele for lessees. Tax-exempt entities like municipalities, hospitals, universities, and certain charitable organizations, however, are an interesting special case.

Since such entities cannot exploit the rapid depreciation benefits (as can high tax-bracket taxpayers), one might suppose that they would be natural candidates for renting. But this is not necessarily so! Unlike low tax-bracket individual taxpayers, such entities may be able to issue tax-exempt securities to finance the purchase of real estate. They *do* face restrictions, however. In particular, they can only issue tax-exempt securities to finance qualifying expenditures, such as the purchase of their own facilities (although there are even limitations here).

Recall that the annual rental cost is given in equation 21.3, and this cost grows at rate i per period. If property were purchased, the tax-exempt entity would also incur real depreciation and maintenance costs (M) and property taxes

---

[3] Of course, this conclusion depends heavily on the assumption that real after-tax rates of return are the same before and after the 1986 Tax Act, an assumption that warrants some scrutiny.

(P). Consequently, the only difference between renting and buying is $\rho V(1-dt)/(1-t)$. Since this savings from buying grows at rate i per period, its present value to the exempt entity is:

$$\frac{\rho V(1-dt)/(1-t)}{R_b(1-t)-i} = V\frac{(1-dt)}{1-t}, \qquad (21.5)$$

since $\rho = R_b(1-t)-i$.

Note from equation 21.5 that when d is equal to 1.0, the tax-exempt investor is indifferent between renting and issuing tax-exempt bonds to buy the property, because the savings from buying the property are just equal to the *cost* of buying, V. In this pivotal case, the investment cost is immediately deductible from taxable income. As a result, if tax rates are constant over time, the asset yields tax-exempt returns. This implies that the property would bear a full implicit tax, and municipalities would be indifferent between renting and issuing tax-exempt bonds to purchase such tax-favored assets.

For less tax-sheltered situations in which d is less than 1.0 (which is certainly the case following the 1986 Tax Act), the savings exceed the purchase price, and buying is desirable. In fact, the 1986 Tax Act requires that property leased to tax-exempt entities be depreciated on a straight-line basis over 40 years. As Table 21.1 indicates, this would imply a value of d equal to .24.

On the other hand, if the tax-exempt entity is not permitted to issue tax-exempt bonds to finance the acquisition of property, the entity's discount rate becomes R_b rather than $R_b(1-t)$, because the entity must then cut back its investments in assets on which it earns the before-tax rate R_b. Even when d is equal to zero (corresponding to the case in which the present value of tax depreciation is equal to the present value of economic depreciation), the tax-exempt entity should find renting desirable when its discount rate is R_b, because the capital gain on the property is tax-favored, and the investment still bears some implicit tax.

Corporations Facing Low Tax Rates

Another interesting special case to consider is corporations with low tax rates (for example, due to tax loss, the alternative minimum tax, or tax credit carryforwards). As discussed in previous chapters, such entities could issue common stocks which, prior to the 1986 Tax Act, may have borne substantial implicit taxes. The cost of issuing such securities may have been closer to the *after-tax* bond rate, on a risk-adjusted basis, than the *before-tax* bond rate. Even after the 1986 Tax Act, such entities can issue preferred stock at a risk-adjusted yield well below the rate on taxable bonds. Would such taxpayers prefer to buy depreciable property for the case of d < 1?

The answer is no. Unlike restrictions on the issuance of municipal bonds by exempt organizations, corporate taxpayers face few restrictions if they issue common or preferred stock. Consequently, low corporate tax rates provide an opportunity for corporations to engage in clientele-based arbitrage.

Indeed, the corporate leasing market is an enormous one. Total leasing volume was $95 billion in 1986 and roughly $100 billion in 1987.[4] In 1985 alone,

---

[4] *Institutional Investor* (November 1987), special section on leasing.

Chapter 21   Real Estate Investments

General Electric deferred nearly $600 million in federal taxes through the leasing activity of its finance subsidiary, General Electric Credit Corporation. Although the 1986 Tax Act made depreciable property less of a tax shelter than previously, thereby reducing the desirability of leasing, the Act also introduced the alternative minimum tax (AMT) at the corporate level. When binding, the AMT rate is only 20% (subject to adjustment for the AMT credit). Moreover, less generous depreciation allowances are permitted for AMT purposes (40-year straight-line for real property).[5]

Home Ownership

As a final special case, we consider the individual taxpayer's decision of whether to purchase a personal residence. Owner-occupied housing is a *very* large portion of national wealth in the U.S. In 1984, there were 61.5 million single-family homes with an estimated market value of $5.3 trillion (or $86,500 per house). This compares with $6.6 trillion in total financial assets in the household sector.[6] Residential property has always been more tax-favored than commercial property. For example, depreciation rules have always been more generous, both with respect to the timing of deductions and the magnitude of depreciation recapture due upon sale of the property. As we have seen, more liberal depreciation allowances result in lower equilibrium rental rates. And this helps to achieve the long-standing legislative objective of promoting affordable housing.

On the other hand, taxpayers are not permitted to take depreciation deductions on their personal residences. Does this mean that everyone should rent, effectively selling the right to take rapid depreciation to a high tax-bracket investor? The answer is no, because there are several important tax advantages to home ownership. The two most important are:

1. Homeowners pay no tax on the rental value of the house, whereas a lessor does. In other words, lease payments are paid from after-tax income, whereas a homeowner can earn the rental value without paying taxes on it.

2. Property taxes are tax-deductible to homeowners but not to renters. Renters pay property taxes indirectly through increased rent, which is nondeductible. While property owners can secure tax deductions for the property taxes *they* pay (as business expenses), they also are taxed on the increased rent they charge to lessees. It is as if the landlord acts as a tax collector for the local government.

Other advantages include:

3. Gains on the sale of a personal residence can be postponed if another home is purchased at a greater price within two years (before or after) the sale.

---

[5] The AMT effectively forces many leasing experts to syndicate leasing deals (that is, to originate leases and sell off the tax benefits to other passive investors) rather than keep them all in-house.

[6] Karl Case and Robert Shiller, "Prices of Single-Family Homes Since 1970: New Indexes for Four Cities," *National Bureau of Economic Research Working Paper #2293* (1987).

4. Gains on personal residences of up to $125,000 for sellers 55 years of age or older are tax-exempt (once-in-a-lifetime option per individual or married couple).
5. Interest on a home mortgage is tax-deductible (within limits) even if the taxpayer has no investment income against which to offset the interest expense. This may enable clientele-based arbitrage.

The tax advantage to homeowners of the tax deductibility of property taxes can be significant. For example, suppose property taxes, P, and property values increase at rate i, which is equal to 5% per year; taxable bonds yield R_b of 10%; and the homeowner's income tax rate is 30%. The homeowner's discount rate is then 7% (or 10% × (1 - .3)). Finally suppose that annual property taxes amount to 1% of the value of the property.

The tax shelter from the tax deductibility of property taxes is the income tax rate multiplied by the property tax payments. The present value of this is

$$\frac{tP}{R_b(1 - t) - i} = \frac{.30 \times .01V}{.10 \times (1 - .30) - .05} \text{ or 15\% of V.}$$

That is, the deductibility of property tax is worth 15% of the value of the property!

Note that with deductible property taxes, it is tax-efficient for homeowners to encourage local governments to provide services that are paid for through the property tax. For example, in addition to lavish parks and public schools and police protection, local governments could also provide gardening and utilities and maintenance services and have homeowners pay for the services through property taxes. This is tax-efficient because property taxes are tax deductible, whereas gardening expenses, utilities, and maintenance services, if paid directly by homeowners, are *not* tax deductible.

Despite these tax incentives, local governments typically do *not* provide these services. There are at least three reasons for this:

1. Heterogeneity of tastes. Not everyone desires the same level of services.
2. Incentive problems:
   a. If utility services provided through property taxes are a function of property value rather than a function of service usage, residents have an incentive to overconsume utilities; and
   b. If local governments provide maintenance services, each individual resident has little incentive to take precautionary measures to reduce the required level of maintenance services. Moreover, not everyone wishes the same level of maintenance quality (back to our heterogeneity-of-tastes problem).
3. Not all homeowners itemize their deductions. Instead, some opt for a flat-rate substitute level of deductions (the so-called "standard deduction"). For these taxpayers, property taxes aren't really deductible. Residents of lower-income neighborhoods are most likely to fall into this category.

The fact that maintenance costs are non-tax-deductible to homeowners and that profits on the sale of their homes are largely tax exempt also provides strong

Chapter 21   Real Estate Investments

incentives for homeowners to perform their own home repairs, as well as to undertake their own capital improvements (unless they are as inept as the authors of this text). Home repairs give rise to tax-exempt income, so even if you are less efficient than an expert, it may pay to do your own repairs. Home improvement activities also convert labor income into deferred capital gain income as the value of the house increases, and deferred capital gain income remains highly tax-favored for personal residence investments even under the 1986 Tax Act.

Since the two biggest advantages of owning a personal residence are tax exemption on the returns to home ownership and deductibility of property taxes, owning is more valuable the higher is the tax rate, so the highest-taxed entities will prefer to own rather than rent. By contrast, the lowest-taxed entities will be better off selling the tax benefits associated with rapid depreciation through reduced rental rates.

There are, of course, very important nontax considerations that affect the desirability of renting rather than buying. For example:

1. *Risk aversion*: Many rightfully fear the possibility of a decline in the value of real estate investments, especially if the property value is a large fraction of their wealth. Home ownership then creates a very poorly-diversified portfolio. Individuals may respond to such risk aversion by leasing property or by entering into shared equity contracts, where they own part and lease part of their property.

2. *Pride of ownership*: There is an intangible value to owning property in the minds of many.

3. *Transaction costs*: Some property users expect to use property for a relatively short period of time before moving to a new location. For them, the cost of buying and selling a home may be excessive.

4. *Hidden-action problems*: Because leased property is not maintained as well as owner-occupied housing, leased property is generally worth less over time than otherwise equivalent owner-occupied housing. Why? Lessees have less incentive to maintain the property because they get less than 100% of the benefits from doing so.[7]

In Chapters Seven and Ten, we discussed these risk aversion and hidden-action problems in the context of employee compensation contracting. Employees who have neither an ownership interest in the businesses that hire them, nor any incentive compensation arrangements, have reduced incentives to work in the best interests of owners. But direct ownership, and indirect ownership through incentive compensation arrangements, imposes risk on employees. In most businesses, it is desirable to trade these two forces off against one another: employees are given incentives without being *overexposed* to risk.

In housing, we see less of a tradeoff. Although rental contracts often contain penalty provisions that encourage lessees to maintain the property, property residents typically own the property outright or they lease the property.

---

[7] For further discussion, see Mark A. Wolfson, "Tax, Incentive, and Risk-Sharing Issues in the Allocation of Property Rights: The Generalized Lease-or-Buy Problem," *Journal of Business* (April 1985), pp. 159-71.

Shared equity mortgage contracts (where the lender takes a partial owner-ship interest in property appreciation in exchange for a lower periodic interest rate on the mortgage) began to become popular in the early 1980s when interest rates were high. Although they continue to exist today, the idea hasn't really caught on. Reasons for this appear to relate to the practical difficulties of administering such contracts. For example, it is costly to determine how to share the cost of capital improvements like putting in a pool or a tennis court or remodeling when the value of the property is unlikely to increase by the same amount as the cost of the improvements. What if the property is sold to a friend or a relative at a non-arm's-length price? What if the co-investors wish to terminate their relationship without selling the property, but there is no reliable information on the market value of the property to serve as the basis for "cashing out" the outside investor? The more effectively such difficulties can be resolved, the more likely it is that these contractual arrangements will flourish in the marketplace.[8]

21.3 Real Estate Partnerships

A different set of incentive problems arises when investors in property are passive with respect to management activities. This is a feature of real estate limited partnerships, which raised substantial sums from investors in the early and mid-1980s (over $8 billion in public syndications in 1986 alone), largely due to the introduction of the accelerated cost recovery system of depreciation in 1981. The 1986 Tax Act altered the nature of this market in many important respects:

1. Depreciation schedules were made dramatically less accelerated, much more so for real estate than for other types of assets. For example, prior to the 1986 Tax Act, real property was depreciable over 19 years using an accelerated depreciation schedule. Under the 1986 Tax Act, residential rental property is depreciable over 27.5 years and commercial property is depreciable over 31.5 years. Moreover, the new rules require straight-line depreciation for all real estate. This means that real estate investments should bear much less implicit tax after the 1986 Tax Act than before it.

   Recall from the chapters on multinational tax planning that a reduction in implicit taxes on investments in the U.S. encourages investment by foreign investors. In this regard, tax factors may have contributed to the dramatic rise in Japanese investment in U.S. real estate since the passage of the 1986 Tax Act.

2. Installment sales are less effective in deferring gains than they were prior to the 1986 Tax Act.

3. Subsequent to the 1986 Tax Act, income or loss from real estate activities is deemed to be passive, whether the investor participates materially in the management of the investment or not. This means that individual

---

[8] Alternatively, taxpayers can hedge their risks by using options, futures contracts, or swap contracts linked to real estate values. Of course, such contracts introduce their own tax and nontax costs.

investors can no longer deduct real estate investment losses against other income. An exception, however, applies for taxpayers earning less than $100,000 in taxable income. They can treat up to $25,000 in real estate losses as active income if they participate materially in management.

These new passive loss rules caused a restructuring of the terms of many deals to attract individual investors. For example, deals became less leveraged subsequent to 1986. Prior to the 1986 Tax Act, real estate partnerships were typically highly leveraged, creating large tax-deductible interest payments early on in the life of the investment. By the first half of 1988, unleveraged public real estate partnerships outsold leveraged ones (50% or more debt-financed property investments) by a factor of 3 to 1.[9] In addition, more loans now include an equity participation feature. That is, the lender reduces the borrowing rate on the loan in exchange for a share of the appreciation in the value of the property. This reduces the front-end tax deductions to the partnership and hence the magnitude of the passive losses. This allows the lender to postpone the recognition of income and therefore encourages the lender to provide financing on more favorable terms.

The lenders in these arrangements are often low-tax-rate entities like pension funds, which may seem anomalous, since they are surely inefficient holders of capital-gains-type investments. Actually, the arrangement turns out to be quite sensible. The contracts are structured so that the equity share is paid off in the form of "contingent interest." Investors deduct these equity payments to lenders as ordinary interest expense. In addition, the more successful the property (the greater the operating income and appreciation in the property), the greater will be the taxable income to the investors and the more valuable will be the interest deduction in the year of property sale. Similarly, the greater the appreciation of the property, the greater the investment income (of which realized capital gains are a component), and the less binding will be the limitation on the deductibility of investment interest under Section 163(d).

For example, suppose a $50 million project financed by a $40 million loan will either increase in value to $90 million or decline in value to $30 million over the next 3 years, and each possibility is equally likely. The expected sales price is $60 million and the expected appreciation rate is 20% over the 3-year period.

The mortgage interest rate is 10%. Suppose that the partners' tax rates will be 40% if the property is sold for $90 million. Further suppose that half the interest would be nondeductible due to investment interest limitations unless and until the property is sold at a profit and that the marginal tax rate on interest deductions above a 5% mortgage rate is only 20%. Then an equity loan that pays a 5% interest rate plus a 10% equity kicker in the form of contingent interest, only if the property is sold at a profit, would reduce the partners' after-tax borrowing cost by 1% or by $400,000 per year after tax: that is, half the interest (5%) or $2 million per year would be made deductible at a rate of 40% rather than 20%.

Fewer investors currently look to real estate deals to provide tax write-offs as in the past. For example, Mackie-Mason and Gordon report that from 1981 to

[9] *Wall Street Journal* (August 4, 1988), p. 23.

1986, net income reported by S Corporations and partnerships averaged -$2.2 billion per year. In 1987, by contrast, income from such entities exploded to $32 billion![10]

Corporations have picked up some of the slack in the demand for real estate (and other) tax shelters, given their relatively high tax rates and given that they are not subject to the passive loss limitations. In particular, where generous depreciation allowances are available, it makes sense for partnerships to be structured with a corporate general partner being allocated a substantial fraction of the tax deductions.[11] This is a dramatic turnabout from the standard practice prior to the 1986 Tax Act, when it was individual limited partners who both sought and were allocated the lion's share of the tax benefits in these ventures.

Sales of public limited partnership interests fell dramatically from the $8 billion level in 1986 to only $3 billion in 1989.[12] Part of the fall-off probably can be explained by the poor performance of the partnerships formed in the 1980s, but as discussed in Chapter Nineteen, the poor performance is itself likely related to adverse changes in real-estate-related tax laws.[13]

The 1986 Tax Act devastated the values of publicly traded sponsors of real estate limited partnerships. On May 7, 1986, *The Wall Street Journal* reported the following:

> "The Senate Finance Committee gave final approval early today to the biggest tax overhaul bill in more than 30 years. ... Senator Bill Armstrong, R-Colorado, warned that the provisions aimed at wiping out tax shelters could collapse large segments of the real-estate market."

Numerous additional articles appeared in the *Wall Street Journal* during the period May 7 through May 12, 1986 on the tax bill, its provisions, the probability of its passing, and its effect on various industries.

As Table 21.2 indicates, publicly-traded sponsors of real estate partnerships fared very poorly over the four trading days that spanned May 7, 1986 through May 12, 1986. The equity value of such firms declined 23% over this period, relative to the overall market.[14] Over the following three-and-a-half years, the equity values of these firms continued to decline. By the end of 1989, they had underperformed the overall market by a factor of over 90%! Investors may have anticipated that Congress would provide some relief to the onerous changes in the 1986 tax law that apply to real estate investment, but these expectations were apparently not fulfilled.

---

[10] Jeffrey K. Mackie-Mason and Roger H. Gordon, "Taxes and the Choice of Organizational Form," Working Paper, April 3, 1991.

[11] The alternative minimum tax restrains the demand of some corporations for such tax shelter. If they secure "too much" accelerated depreciation deductions, the alternative minimum tax is calculated under a *slower* depreciation schedule, and tax will be sheltered at a rate of only 20%, the marginal tax rate when the alternative minimum tax applies.

[12] Data are from Robert A. Stanger & Co. as reported in the *Wall Street Journal* on January 2, 1990.

[13] Indeed, the savings and loan crisis in Texas and Arizona may be related to the overbuilding of commercial properties, encouraged by the tax incentives introduced in the early 1980s and removed by the 1986 Tax Act.

[14] For further details, see Deposition of Mark A. Wolfson, *In re: Brichard Securities Litigation*, U.S. District Court (Northern District of California), No. C-87-2987-CAL, November 9, 1990.

Chapter 21   Real Estate Investments

Table 21.2 Percentage Changes in Stock Prices of a Portfolio of Large Sponsors of Real Estate Limited Partnerships,[a] Relative to the Overall Market, Over the Period May 7 – 12, 1986.

Date	Percentage Change in Stock Price Relative to the Performance of the Overall Stock Market[b]	T-Statistic
May 7, 1986	-7.502%	-5.476
May 8, 1986	-3.891%	-2.840
May 9, 1986	-5.359%	-3.911
May 12, 1986	-8.942%	-6.527
Cumulative Return	-23.389%	-9.378

[a]The companies in the portfolio are the four public companies with more than $300 million in public limited partnership capital, as listed in Table 1 on page 23 of the January 1989 issue of the *Stanger Register*. The four companies are: Angeles Corporation, Equitec Financial Group, Integrated Resources, and Southmark Corporation.

[b]An equal-weighted index of stock prices was created from the four companies in the index. The historical relation (during 1985) between each stock and the overall market (a value-weighted index of all stocks listed on the New York and American Stock Exchanges, excluding ADRs) was calculated, and the portfolio performance was calculated relative to its normal relation to the overall market.

4. Tax credits for the rehabilitation of historic properties were also reduced by the 1986 Tax Act, as was the opportunity to deduct losses from such investments. As with many other changes made in the 1986 Tax Act, these changes represented a reversal of the tax benefits provided to encourage such investments by the 1981 Tax Act.

Did these changes in the tax law affect investment in historic properties? You bet they did. The Preservation Assistance Division of the National Park Service reports that 614 historical renovation projects were approved in 1980, in which $346 million was invested. In 1985, several years after the 1981 Tax Act spurred such investments, 3,117 projects were approved involving an investment of $2,416 million, a 12-fold increase over 1980. But in 1988, such investments were once again on the wane: only 1,092 projects were approved entailing $866 million of investment, a drop of nearly two-thirds from the 1985 level.[15]

It is noteworthy that individual and corporate pension funds represent the biggest growth component in real estate tax shelters. There are really three classes of investors in real estate partnerships: (1) limited partners, the passive investors; (2) general partners, who possess expertise in selection and management of real estate investments; and (3) lenders, who are low-tax-rate entities, and who can soak up lots of ordinary income. Key players that serve in the capacity as lenders or as intermediaries include pension funds, mortgage bankers, insurance companies (inasmuch as earnings on policyholder reserves are tax-exempt), and savings and loan associations. On the intermediation side, although mortgage bankers

---

[15] "Historic Properties Go Begging at National Auction," *New York Times* (October 15, 1989), p.31.

may originate loans, they face high marginal tax rates, so it is efficient for them to sell the right to receive income to pension funds, which they do regularly. The bank earns a syndication fee and a loan servicing fee. There is a potential incentive problem here, however. If the loan goes bad, the bank may not have the same incentive to go after the borrower for payment as it would if it owned the right to the principal and interest. As usual, the bank's concern in preserving its reputation may serve to discipline it.

Let us turn lastly to the contractual arrangement between the limited partners (LP) and the general partner (GP) in real estate partnerships. In such entities, the LP was typically allocated all of the depreciation deductions prior to the 1986 Tax Act. Due to the introduction of passive loss limitations that apply to individuals, this arrangement remains popular only in partnerships where the limited partners are corporations. The GP typically receives a management fee equal to roughly 5% of rents plus 1% to 10% of operating profits. Payments to the GP are tax deductible by the LP.

When the property is sold, the GP typically obtains 15% - 25% of the net proceeds after LPs first achieve some minimum return (commonly 0% to 6% return in addition to a return of their initial investment). This is a form of carried or reversionary interest arrangement.[16] This latter payment is designed to compensate the GP in a way that puts the incentives in the right place with respect to: (1) selection of investment property, and (2) negotiating a good price at which to buy and sell property. It does, however, introduce other incentive problems, of which two will be mentioned.

1. Reversionary interest arrangements encourage excessive mainte- nance.[17] For example, if the GP has a 5% operating profit share and a 20% share of profits on the sale of property, the GP should be willing to spend $1 in maintenance cost to increase the value of property by only $.25

2. Because the GP typically doesn't share in any sale proceeds unless LPs first achieve some minimum return, the GP may not wish to sell the property if it has declined in value. This is so even though it may be desirable to do so for tax reasons (such as to allow limited partners to recognize a capital loss) or for nontax reasons (for example, the GP may lack expertise in managing property in distress situations or may simply face poor incentives to manage the property efficiently).

---

[16] In some cases, the GP may be taxable on the value of this carried interest at the time the partnership is formed rather than when the properties are sold. Unless limited partners can secure corresponding tax write-offs, this contractual arrangement has undesirable tax consequences. Moreover, even when tax write-offs are available to the limited partners, they are of no value to those limited partners that are tax-exempt entities.

[17] This is in contrast to the incentive on the part of renters to maintain leased property poorly.

Chapter 21   Real Estate Investments

Summary of Key Points

1. The return to real estate investment has three components: pretax rental income, capital appreciation, and tax-related cash flows. Rental rates are established in the marketplace so as to provide competitive after-tax returns to investors.

2. Real estate investments have long been granted tax-favored treatment under the law, and this in turn results in tax-subsidized reductions in rental rates.

3. While the 1986 Tax Act reduced substantially the tax-sheltered nature of real estate investments, it also reduced tax rates. The former factor tends to raise rental rates, but the latter may reduce them, and the ultimate effect on rental rates is unclear.

4. Although tax-exempt entities cannot take advantage of accelerated depreciation deductions from owning property, they are better off owning rather than leasing property if owning property permits them to raise more tax-exempt debt than they would otherwise be permitted to raise. On the other hand, if the funds to purchase property come from an endowment fund invested in taxable bonds (on which the entity is tax-exempt), then leasing is the tax-preferred strategy.

5. In contrast to tax-exempt investors, low-tax-rate corporate investors should generally lease rather than buy for tax purposes. This is true even if they can issue tax-favored securities, like common or preferred stock, at a pretax cost of capital approaching the tax-exempt bond rate.

6. Tax laws in many countries, including the U.S., provide special inducements to encourage home ownership. In the U.S., these include tax exemption of the rental value of owned property, deductibility of property taxes, special rules providing capital gains tax relief on the sale of personal residences, and deductibility of interest on home mortgages *without regard* to investment income.

7. The deductibility of property taxes on personal residences encourages homeowners to lobby their local governments to supply many community services that would otherwise be nondeductible if they paid for them directly. Despite this, a host of nontax considerations restrain the supply of such services.

8. There are important nontax factors that enter into the calculus of whether property should be leased or purchased. These include risk aversion (real estate prices can swing widely), pride of ownership, transaction costs (it can be expensive to sell long-lived assets), and incentive problems (leased property is generally less well-maintained than is owned property).

9. The 1986 Tax Act had a dramatic effect on investment activity in the real estate industry. Limited partnerships fell from favor as individuals no longer looked to real estate as a way of sheltering ordinary income from taxation, and the equity values of publicly-traded sponsors of real estate limited partnerships declined dramatically. Pension funds in-

creased substantially their investment in real estate as such assets became less tax-favored under the law, thereby bearing less implicit tax.

10. As in all ventures in which ownership and management are separate, real estate ventures are beset by incentive problems. Incentive contracts serve to mitigate these problems, but not eliminate them. These problems tend to be more severe when the duration of the relationship between owners and managers is short. The 1986 Tax Act had the effect of shortening the duration of relationships between passive investors and syndicator-managers in the real estate industry and may have caused some syndicators to "cash in" whatever reputation they had built up until this time.

Discussion Questions

1. True or False? Explain.
   a. Because the user value of home ownership is not taxed under U.S. law, ownership may dominate renting, purely from a tax standpoint, even for low-tax-rate taxpayers.
   b. The tax-deductibility of property taxes on personal residences and business property favors ownership over renting of these assets.
   c. Tax-exempt organizations should rent depreciable assets rather than own them since they cannot benefit from generous depreciation write-offs.
   d. The more important property maintenance is to preserving the value of a durable asset, the less likely it is that taxpayers will enter into leasing contracts to save taxes.
   e. The corporate alternative minimum tax in the U.S. encourages leasing under certain circumstances.

2. If depreciation rules are made more generous when interest rates increase, does this augment or reduce the effect of changes in depreciation rules on investment incentives?

3. Does the deductibility of home mortgage interest make home ownership tax-favored? How has this changed with the passage of the 1986 Tax Act? And how is the answer affected by the presence of market frictions?

4. How has the 1986 Tax Act affected the economic incentives to form real estate limited partnerships? How have the rights of various ownership claims of limited and general partners changed with the passage of this act?

5. Passive real estate ownership in the U.S. has been largely concentrated in partnership form and in real estate investment trusts (another organizational form that avoids an entity-level tax). Why does this make sense both before and after the 1986 Tax Act even though the 1986 Act made partnerships tax-favored over corporations for profitable businesses?

Problem

In January, 1983, Hotel Partners raised $25 million from investors (limited partners). The partnership purchased a hotel for $20 million in cash plus an installment note (interest only, principal amount due in 10 years) in the amount of $80 million at below-market interest rates issued to the seller of the hotel. The installment note bore interest at a rate of 9%. The market rate of interest on such loans was 13%.

In December of 1988, the partnership defaulted on the mortgage after unsuccessfully trying to sell the hotel at an acceptable price (the best offer was $65 million), and the hotel was repossessed. The partnership was liquidated and limited partners received none of their money back. In fact, they received no cash distributions from the partnership at all during the entire 1983-1988 period.

From 1983-1987, limited partners received the following tax write-offs:

Year	Tax Write-off
1983	$18 million
1984	$15 million
1985	$12 million
1986	$10 million
1987	$ 0

Although limited partners received no cash distributions in 1988, they were required to recognize taxable income in the amount of $30 million. This is equal to the excess of the $25 million they initially invested over the $55 million in tax write-offs they were allowed from 1983-1986. The deductions in 1983-1986 reduced limited partners' tax liabilities at the rate of $.50 on the dollar, while the income in 1988 was taxed at a rate of 28%. Investors discount these after-tax cash flows at 6.5%.

In 1989, a class-action suit was filed by limited partners against the general partners of Hotel Partners alleging that the general partners violated their fiduciary responsibilities to the limited partners by overpaying for the hotel in 1983 and mismanaging the property to secure management fees. The suit calls for a full refund of the $25 million invested.

To support the claim that the partnership overpaid for the hotel, the plaintiffs hired an "expert" who estimated that the property was worth only $70 million at the time it was purchased for $100 million. The $70 million appraisal was determined by discounting projected gross rents less maintenance costs and other operating expenses (and ignoring depreciation expense) of $7 million per year in perpetuity at a rate of 10%.

You have been hired by legal counsel of the general partners to assist in rebutting the claims of the limited partners. In particular, counsel would like to argue that:

1. limited partners lost far less than $25 million due to the tax shelter nature of the investment;

2. the general partners did not overpay for the hotel; and

3. the decline in the value of the hotel between 1983 and 1988 was caused by bad luck (factors beyond the general partners' control) rather than mismanagement.

How can you help?

Chapter 21   Real Estate Investments

CHAPTER 22
Property Transactions[1]

In this chapter we consider how tax rules influence the frequency of property sales. Three crucial tax factors should be considered in every property transaction: (1) changes in depreciation deductions and investment tax credits available to prospective buyers compared to those available to the current owner;[2] (2) the amount of past depreciation (and tax credits) that the seller must recapture as ordinary income in the event of a sale; and (3) the magnitude of the seller's capital gains tax on the sale of property. As we will see in the chapters that follow, these same factors come into play in tax planning for mergers and acquisitions.

U.S. tax reforms in the 1980s included major provisions affecting the tax treatment of depreciable real estate, and these reforms provide a good opportunity to evaluate the impact of tax rules on real estate values. In this chapter, we undertake such an evaluation. We consider both the theoretical impacts and the actual responses of investors to changes in tax rules.

An important feature of the tax rules is that property can be depreciated more than once if it is transferred to another investor. As a result, the market value of real estate depends upon when it is optimal to trade such assets. And optimal

---

[1]This chapter draws heavily on the work of Myron S. Scholes, Eric Terry, and Mark A. Wolfson, "Taxes, Trading and the Value of Real Estate," *The Journal of Accounting, Auditing and Finance* (Summer 1989), pp. 317-340.

[2]For tax purposes, "real property" is real estate, and "personal property" is all other property. Depreciation is the write-off of the cost basis of tangible property, and amortization is the write-off of the cost basis of intangible property. Tangible property includes such items as buildings, machinery, and equipment, while intangible property includes goodwill, trademarks, and patents. Property is depreciated for tax purposes based on the schedule that applies under the tax law at the time the current owner placed it into service.

The 1986 Tax Act eliminated investment tax credits on depreciable business property in the U.S., although for the most part, such credits were only available for investments in "personal property."

trading strategies depend, in turn, upon current and expected future real estate market values. Accordingly, market values and turnover rates for real estate will be determined simultaneously in equilibrium.

A number of models to determine optimal trading strategies for depreciable real estate appear in the literature. They compare the benefits to the new owner of stepping up the depreciable basis of property against the cost to the seller of taxes on its disposition, including both capital gains taxes and a tax on the recapture of past depreciation at ordinary tax rates. Early models of real estate turnover required market prices for properties to be pre-specified and known in advance.[3] Recent papers, however, correct this deficiency by developing models in which the optimal trading strategies of investors and equilibrium market values of depreciable real estate are determined simultaneously.[4]

There are significant differences, however, between the predictions of these models and actual investor behavior. First, the predicted *holding periods* for real estate tend to be much longer than those actually observed. Second, these models predict that a larger proportion of properties would be depreciated on an accelerated (as opposed to a straight-line) basis for tax purposes prior to the 1986 Tax Act than was actually observed. This leaves us with the following question: Do real estate investors in fact behave in a manner that is clearly suboptimal, or are there some important features of the tax code or nontax costs that are not properly captured by these models?

While the prediction failures of these models can undoubtedly be explained partially by their failure to incorporate a variety of nontax factors into the analysis, they also leave out an important *tax* feature; namely, the special tax treatment accorded to installment sales in the U.S. More specifically, Section 453 of the Internal Revenue Code allows investors to defer the payment of capital gains taxes (and, prior to the 1984 Tax Act, also the payment of recapture taxes on past depreciation) arising from the sale of real estate. When these models are extended to allow for the possibility of installment sales, predicted property values and turnover rates increase significantly prior to the 1986 Tax Act. Following the 1986 Tax Act, however, installment sales have only a minor impact upon the market value and turnover rates of real estate.

The changes in the installment sales provisions of the tax law in the U.S. decreased property values and tended to increase rental rates as a fraction of property values. This result suggests that analyses of the 1986 Tax Act that ignore

---

[3] See William B. Brueggeman, Jeffrey D. Fisher, and Jerrold J. Stern, "Federal Income Taxes, Inflation and Holding Periods for Income Producing Property," *AREUEA Journal* (Summer 1981), pp. 148-164, or Patric H. Hendershott and David C. Ling, "Trading and the Tax Shelter Value of Depreciable Real Estate," *National Tax Journal* (June 1984), pp. 213-223.

[4] See David C. Ling and Michael J. Whinihan, "Valuing Depreciable Real Estate: A New Methodology," *AREUEA Journal* (Summer 1985), pp. 181-194; Anthony J. Pellechio, "Taxation, Rental Income, and Optimal Holding Periods for Real Property," *National Tax Journal* (March 1988), pp. 97-107; and Patric H. Hendershott and David C. Ling, "Prospective Changes in the Tax Law and the Value of Depreciable Real Estate," *AREUEA Journal* (Fall 1984), pp. 297-317. Such models have also been developed at the Office of Tax Analysis at the U.S. Treasury Department. For a general discussion of these models, see Leonard E. Burman, Thomas S. Neubig, and D. Gordon Wilson, "The Use and Abuse of Rental Project Models," *Compendium of Tax Research* (Washington, D.C.: Office of Tax Analysis, Department of the Treasury, 1987), pp. 307-349.

the impact of installment sales on property turnover rates will also tend to underestimate the effect of this Tax Act on real estate market values.[5] Moreover, the introduction of installment sales into these models increases dramatically the predicted use of straight-line depreciation for tax purposes prior to the 1986 Tax Act. Thus, the use of installment sales by investors can potentially explain much of the gap that currently exists between the predictions of these real estate turnover models and the actual behavior of investors prior to 1987. Of course, property is sold for nontax reasons as well, but the changes in installment sales rules should have diminished substantially the incentive to trade properties.

We also study how the optimal choice of depreciation method for tax purposes changes over the life of a property.[6] Prior to the 1986 Tax Act, which requires straight-line depreciation to be used for tax purposes, accelerated depreciation is optimal throughout the life of residential rental property. For commercial property, however, we find that straight-line depreciation tends to be optimal in the early years of the property's life, particularly when inflation is low, while accelerated depreciation becomes optimal later in its life.

Property market values and turnover rates tend to be sensitive to changes in the size of the nontax transaction costs that are incurred when investors trade real estate. The assumed size of these costs has varied widely. For example, while Ling and Whinihan assume that these costs equal 5% of the selling price of a property, Pellechio assumes that these costs are zero. Our results indicate that when installment sales are ignored, nontax transaction costs have only a small effect upon the market values and turnover rates for real estate. The capital gains and excess depreciation recapture taxes that are incurred when property is sold are the primary factors that deter investors from turning over real estate rapidly. When installment sales are used, however, real estate market values and turnover rates become very sensitive to the size of the nontax transaction costs associated with property sales. When these transaction costs are very low, property turnover rates and market values will be very high. Conversely, property turnover rates and market values will be low when these transaction costs are high. As a result, closer attention should be given to both the size and nature of these nontax costs.[7]

In this chapter, we also consider the sensitivity of property market values and turnover rates to macroeconomic conditions and to the specific terms of installment notes. In particular, we consider the effects of varying (1) the inflation rate, (2) the duration of the installment note, and (3) the relation between market interest rates and the interest rate specified in the installment note. With respect

---

[5] See James R. Follain, Patric H. Hendershott, and David C. Ling, "Understanding the Real Estate Provisions of Tax Reform: Motivation and Impact," *National Tax Journal* (September 1987), pp. 363-372, and Patric H. Hendershott, James R. Follain, and David C. Ling, "Effects of Real Estate," *Tax Reform and the U.S. Economy* (Washington, D.C.: The Brookings Institution, 1987), pp. 71-97.

[6] Hendershott and Ling (1984, *op. cit*), implicitly assume that the optimal choice of tax depreciation method does not change over the property's life. And Pellechio (1988, *op. cit.*) makes sufficient assumptions to guarantee that each successive owner of the property will rationally choose the same tax depreciation method.

[7] Indeed, a reduction in transaction costs may have induced Congress to tighten up on installment sales rules in 1984, 1986, 1987, and 1988.

Introduction to Property Transactions

to item (3), we consider the additional tax benefits available when below-market interest rates can be built into the installment contract.

22.1 Changing Tax Benefits of Acquiring Assets

Property is depreciated under the tax rules that exist at the time that the latest sale took place. It is important to know the rules both at the time the asset was last acquired and at the time a sale is contemplated. These rules have an important influence over whether it is efficient to sell an asset.

As indicated earlier, depreciation tax rules changed several times in the U.S. during the 1980s. Prior to the Economic Recovery Tax Act in 1981, taxpayers could choose from a range of depreciation methods. The most common methods were the straight line (SL) and the declining balance (DB) methods. A 200% declining balance method, the most rapidly accelerated method, was available for new residential property. Guidelines for property lives were provided in "asset depreciation range" (ADR) tables.

Striking changes in depreciation rules were made by the 1981 Act. This act introduced the accelerated cost recovery system (ACRS), which replaced the ADR system. With ACRS, asset depreciation lives were reduced substantially. ACRS allowed the cost of eligible personal property to be recovered under a 3 or 5-year period for most assets, and real property could be depreciated over 15 years using a 175% DB method switching to SL to maximize depreciation benefits. Owners of low-income housing could use a 200% DB method changing to SL when appropriate. The Deficit Reduction Act of 1984 extended the recovery period to 18 years for real property placed into service after March 15, 1984. A subsequent tax bill changed the recovery period to 19 years for real property placed into service after May 8, 1985.

The 1986 Tax Act lengthened substantially the useful lives of most classes of property. Investment tax credits for personal property were also eliminated. On the other hand, the depreciation schedule was also made more accelerated for personal property (from 150% declining balance to 200% declining balance). The useful lives for real property were extended relatively dramatically, from 19 years to 27.5 years for residential property and to 31.5 years for commercial property. Moreover, unlike the *acceleration* in the rate of depreciation permitted for personal property, taxpayers were required to use the straight-line method of depreciation for real property (other than for low-income housing).

The potential for a tax gain from selling an asset arises because of the possibility of

1. stepping up the basis of the asset to market value to increase depreciation allowances (for example, real estate prices increased significantly during the 1970s and much of the 1980s),

2. changing to a depreciation schedule that allows for faster write-off (e.g., from an ADR (pre-1981) schedule to an ACRS schedule), and

3. changing the number of years over which an asset can be depreciated.

Of these three factors,[8] the most important for real property in a period of rising prices is the increase in the basis of the property on a sale. Note, however, that buyers do not receive the increased depreciation deductions immediately; such deductions are spread out over the "recovery period" of the asset. As a result, the value of the increased deductions depends on the after-tax discount rate as well as on expected future tax rates. The lower the discount rate and the higher the expected tax rate, the more valuable are these future increased deductions.

As explained in greater detail below, the value of these deductions is incorporated into the price of the asset. The buyer must also anticipate that it will be optimal under certain circumstances to resell the property to another investor. As a result, the asset's price includes the anticipated tax advantage of any subsequent resales.

Real estate prices are lower because the seller incurs tax costs on the sale of property. These tax costs include capital gains taxes and ordinary income taxes from the recapture of depreciation. There are also nontax costs to sell the property. These include all of the usual costs associated with finding a buyer, including legal and administrative costs and the costs that arise because the seller is generally better informed about the value of the asset than are prospective buyers (that is, hidden information costs). The property should be sold if the net price received after paying these costs is greater than the present value of the property's cash flows from retaining the property for another period.

On the sale of depreciable property or land that is classified as a business asset (so-called "Section 1231 property"), the seller must pay a capital gains tax on the excess, if any, of the sale price over the adjusted basis in the property plus any past depreciation recaptured as ordinary income.[9] Long-term gains were taxed at favorable rates (subject to the 60% exclusion for individuals) throughout the 1980-1986 period. In addition, losses on Section 1231 property are ordinary losses (not subject to the $3,000 current deduction limitation for individuals and the $0 current deduction limitation for corporations). If a Section 1231 asset is

---

[8] These three factors do not always work in the same direction. For example, an asset acquired prior to the 1981 Tax Act (depreciated under a relatively slow ADR schedule) might have a higher depreciation rate than a used asset depreciated under the otherwise faster ACRS schedule because the ADR asset could have a shorter remaining depreciable life than the ACRS asset.

[9] There are two sections of the tax code that define the amount of depreciation to be recaptured on the sale of property: Section 1245 and Section 1250. Section 1245 property includes all personal property. Section 1250 property includes all residential real property. Commercial real property can be classified as either Section 1245 or Section 1250 property: it is Section 1245 property if any method other than straight-line was used to depreciate the property; it is Section 1250 property if the straight-line method was used to depreciate the property.

For Section 1245 property, all depreciation is subject to recapture. For Section 1250 property, only depreciation in excess of straight-line is subject to recapture. Consequently, all ACRS depreciation is subject to recapture for commercial real estate and for personal property. Only the excess of ACRS depreciation over straight-line is subject to recapture for Section 1250 residential rental property.

Prior to 1981, only a fraction of the excess of accelerated over straight-line depreciation was subject to recapture if residential real property was put into service prior to 1975. For all post-1975 residential real property, however, all of the excess of accelerated depreciation over straight-line is recaptured on the sale of the property.

sold, some or all of the depreciation taken on that asset may have to be recaptured and included as ordinary income.

We illustrate the effects of these tax rules in Table 22.1 for three different cases. The background facts common to all three cases are as follows. A piece of property was purchased some time ago for $100,000, and a total of $40,000 in depreciation expense has been recognized for tax purposes since the date of acquisition. The asset is Section 1245 property, so all past depreciation must be recaptured as ordinary income upon sale to the extent of gain. The asset is sold for cash for an amount that varies across the three cases considered in Table 22.1. The capital gains tax rate is 30%, and the ordinary tax rate is 40%.

In Case 1, the selling price is $75,000, which is less than the initial purchase price of the property but $15,000 more than its tax basis of $60,000 (or $100,000 purchase price less $40,000 of accumulated depreciation). As a result, only $15,000 of past depreciation is recaptured, and no additional capital gains tax results. The seller pays a tax of $6,000 (or 40% of $15,000) on the recaptured depreciation. In Case 2, the selling price of $130,000 is above the initial purchase price of the asset. As a result, all $40,000 of past depreciation is recaptured, with a recapture tax of $16,000, and an additional capital gains tax of $9,000 (or 30% of $30,000) must be paid. In Case 3, the selling price is only $50,000, and this is below the tax basis of the asset. A sale gives rise to an ordinary loss of $10,000, which is fully deductible against other income provided there are no other Section 1231 gains against which the loss would have to be offset first.

Table 22.1 Illustration of the Tax Treatment of the Sale of Depreciable Assets

Assumptions		Amount or Type	
Initial Cost of Asset		$100,000	
Accumulated Depreciation		$ 40,000	
Property Tax Basis (cost less accumulated depreciation)		$ 60,000	
Property Type		Section 1245	
Installment Sale?		No	
Capital Gains Tax Rate		30%	
Ordinary Tax Rate		40%	
	Case 1	**Case 2**	**Case 3**
Sales Price	$75,000	$130,000	$50,000
Gain (Loss) from Sale	$15,000	$ 70,000	($10,000)
Recapture of Depreciation	$15,000	$ 40,000	$ 0
Capital Gain (Ordinary Loss)	$ 0	$ 30,000	($10,000)
Tax on Sale	$ 6,000	$ 25,000	($ 4,000)

If the property sold had been Section 1250 (for example, residential rental) property, and the $40,000 of accumulated depreciation was $10,000 in excess of straight-line depreciation, then only $10,000 of depreciation would have been recaptured as ordinary income in Cases 1 and 2. The capital gain in Case 1 would

Chapter 22   Property Transactions

increase from $0 to $5,000, thereby decreasing the tax on sale by $500 to $5,500; and the capital gain in Case 2 would increase from $30,000 to $60,000, thereby decreasing the tax on sale by $3,000 to $22,000. The tax implications of a sale in Case 3 are the same for Section 1250 property as for Section 1245 property.

In the absence of transaction costs, investors should typically recognize ordinary losses to secure an immediate tax deduction. Such a transaction *will* result in reduced depreciation deductions to the next buyer, but the tax loss from this will be spread over time. Unless tax rates are increasing (substantially) over time, the cost of losing future tax deductions cannot be greater in present value than the gain from the immediate write-off of the loss. An expected fall in tax rates would reinforce the advantage of taking an immediate loss. If tax rates were expected to rise, however, it might pay to wait to receive the deduction at a higher rate.

Similarly, there is a built-in bias against recognizing ordinary taxable income currently in exchange for an equal amount of increased future tax deductions, unless tax rates are expected to increase (substantially) in the future. On the other hand, if the gain can be taken currently at favorable capital gains tax rates and the future deductions can be taken at ordinary tax rates, recognizing a gain currently could be desirable as this is akin to a situation in which tax rates are rising over time.

Installment Sales

By using the installment sale provisions of the tax code, taxpayers could defer the payment of capital gains taxes, and over certain years, the payment of recapture taxes. The definition of an installment sale under Section 453 is fairly broad. Generally, the asset's seller takes back a note from the asset's buyer for some fraction of its purchase price. The essential requirement that must be met to qualify for installment sale treatment is that at least one of the promised payments be made by the purchaser in a tax year that is subsequent to the year of the sale. Under installment sales tax treatment, the gross profit from the sale is recognized over time as the seller receives payments of principal from the purchaser of the property.[10] As a result, the taxpayer could defer payment of the capital gains tax, and prior to the 1984 Tax Act, the taxpayer could also defer the payment of the recapture tax on that part of the asset's sale price covered by the note. Subsequent to the 1984 Act, however, depreciation is subject to immediate recapture regardless of the means of financing the investment.

What is the value of deferring the tax? Suppose that as in Case 2 in Table 22.1, the immediate recapture and capital gains taxes on the sale of the property amounted to $25,000 but that the firm defers the tax payment for 15 years by effecting an installment sale prior to the 1984 Tax Act. This could be accomplished, for example, by having the buyer give the seller a 15-year interest-only

---

[10] See Ronald J. Gilson, Myron S. Scholes, and Mark A. Wolfson, "Taxation and the Dynamics of Corporate Control: The Uncertain Case for Tax Motivated Acquisitions," *Knights, Raiders, and Targets: The Impact of Hostile Takeovers*, edited by J.C. Coffee, Jr., L. Lowenstein and S. Rose-Ackermen (Oxford University Press, 1988), pp. 314-354 for a detailed discussion of the particulars of the tax treatment of installment sales.

installment note equal to the purchase price of the asset. Alternatively, the note could be of longer maturity with some principal payments made prior to maturity.[11] Assuming an after-tax discount rate of 7%, the present value of the deferred taxes (given that the seller's tax rates remain unchanged) would be $9,061 or only 36% of the tax if paid immediately. If the seller expects its tax rates to fall or if the tax deferral period is extended beyond 15 years, the installment sale becomes even more valuable. In fact, a perpetual installment sale causes the present value of the tax on the sale to disappear.

By using installment sales, property should have turned over very frequently between the 1981 and 1984 Tax Acts if there were no offsetting nontax costs to the installment sales. Subsequent to the 1984 Act, however, the recapture tax must be paid on the sale. Only the capital gains tax could still be deferred. If the sale in Case 2 in Table 22.1 took place in 1985, the seller could only defer the payment of the $9,000 of capital gains taxes.

While taxpayers should trade property more frequently if they can use installment sales to defer the payment of taxes due on their sale, this incentive is restrained by the presence of nontax costs associated with the use of installment sales. Installment notes cannot be pledged as collateral for a loan without causing the tax to become due immediately. A seller that requires cash therefore may be forced to borrow unsecured, and the costs of unsecured borrowing typically exceed the costs of secured borrowing. Note also that the interest on installment notes is fully taxable. High-tax-rate sellers of property might prefer to invest the proceeds of the sale in tax-exempt bonds rather than fully taxable notes of equal risk. These factors reduce the value of the installment note.

The analysis below indicates that history can provide an extremely misleading indication of the duration of holding periods for depreciable assets in the future when important tax factors such as depreciation, capital gains, depreciation recapture, and installment sales tax rules change over time. We now turn to our model to examine how these tax rules have affected property turnover rates in the U.S. during the 1980s.

22.2 The Dynamic Programming Model

The model we use to determine the impact of installment sales upon property values and turnover is an extension of the one developed by Ling and Whinihan.[12] Consider a property with a remaining economic life of N years. This property consists of a depreciable structure and nondepreciable land. The property produces before-tax income of I(i) in year i. The value of this property in year n to an investor who will sell it in year n+h is calculated as derived in Technical

---

[11] If the seller pays off part of the principal prior to maturity of the note, each installment payment is allocated first to interest and then to principal. Any repayment of principal is allocated first to deferred recapture of depreciation, taxed at ordinary rates, until all recapture tax is paid; further principal repayments are split in proportion to any gain on the sale. For example, if capital gains represented 20% of the selling price, 20% of the installment note payment would be considered to be capital gain and the remainder a return of capital.

[12] See Ling and Whinihan (1985, *op. cit.*), Hendershott and Ling (1984, *op. cit.*) and Pellechio (1988, *op. cit.*).

Note 22.1. The model also determines the optimal trading strategy that produces this value.

Market-Rate Installment Sales

As mentioned above, installment sales may be used to defer the payment of capital gains taxes (and, prior to the 1984 Tax Act, the payment of recapture taxes) that arise from the transfer of real estate. The deferral of these taxes effectively lowers the cost of selling real estate (relative to the additional depreciation tax savings that results from the step-up in the depreciable basis of the property at the time of sale). This causes property turnover rates to be higher than they would be in the absence of installment sales.

In the analysis that follows, we will assume for simplicity that the installment note issued by the buyer of the property pays interest only until the note matures. That is, entire principal amount of the installment note is repaid with the final interest payment. Under this assumption, the effective number of years of deferral by the seller of the payment of taxes is just equal to the initial maturity of the installment note.

To illustrate the effect of installment sales on property turnover, we begin with the following assumptions:

1. The property has an economic life of 70 years.
2. The before-tax income produced by the property declines in real terms according to a straight-line pattern. For example, if before-tax income is $7 million in the first year, it is $6.9 million, inflation-adjusted, in the second year, and $6.8 million, inflation-adjusted, in the third year.
3. The proportional cost of selling real estate is 5%.
4. The real after-tax discount rate for the property is 3%.
5. The marginal investor is an individual who, prior to 1987, faces ordinary tax rates of 50% and capital gains tax rates of 20% and both ordinary and capital gains tax rates of 31% after 1986.
6. The value of the land, which grows at the inflation rate, initially comprises 25% of the value of the property, but this value ignores the value of the depreciation deductions and any other taxes incurred on the disposition of the depreciable structure.[13]
7. Installment notes bear interest at market rates.

These assumptions are similar to those that others have used, and as we will see, they are consistent with past experience.[14] We repeat our analysis for both a low inflation environment (annual inflation of 4%) and a high inflation environment like that in the early 1980s in the U.S. (annual inflation of 10%).

---

[13] We contrast this assumption with Pellechio (1988, *op. cit.*), who assumes, unrealistically, that the value of land depreciates at the same rate as does the depreciable structure. Note that his assumption implies that the land is worthless when the economic life of the depreciable structure is exhausted. This enables him to obtain a simple valuation solution, but at the expense of introducing implausible assumptions.

[14] Hendershott and Ling (1984, *op. cit.*) and Ling and Whinihan (1985, *op. cit.*) appear to assume a somewhat slower rate of depreciation of real before-tax income. This, in turn, gives rise to somewhat more rapid property turnover.

Results for residential and commercial property are given in Tables 22.2 and 22.3, respectively. Each of the tables contains three separate panels displaying the results for three different tax regimes. Under the 1981 Tax Act regime, installment sales postponed both recapture taxes and capital gains taxes, and very rapid depreciation was available (175% declining balance over 15 years); following passage of the 1984 Tax Act, installment sales no longer postponed recapture taxes and the depreciation schedule became slightly less accelerated (175% declining balance over 18 years); and with the 1986 Tax Act, the depreciation schedule became dramatically less accelerated (straight-line over 27.5 and 31.5 years for residential rental property and commercial property, respectively).

Within a panel, the effects of a 4% and a 10% inflation rate on asset turnovers and initial property values are given for 3 different maturity structures of installment sales: (1) immediate payment of principal (that is, no installment sale), (2) principal repayment in 10 years, and (3) principal repayment in 20 years. In this section, we assume that the installment note bears interest at the market rate. We relax this assumption in the next section, where we assume that interest rates are set opportunistically.

As seen in the top panel of Tables 22.2 and 22.3, in the absence of an installment sale, property is turned over infrequently under the 1981 Tax Act. In Table 22.2, with a 4% inflation rate, the first owner holds the property for 15 years before selling to the next owner who holds the property for its remaining life of 55 years. The column labelled "Initial Property Value" displays the property's initial value to the first holder as a multiple of its value ignoring depreciation benefits. The ratio of 1.39 means that the initial value of the property, taking account of both the depreciation benefits and the right to sell to the next holder, is 39% greater than the initial value of the property without these tax benefits. In Table 22.3, without an installment sale, commercial property is held for 70 years. Its initial property value is 1.36 times its value ignoring the depreciation benefits. The difference between 1.39 and 1.36 indicates a 2.2% incremental value of the property due to its sale to the second holder.

All property is depreciated using the method (straight-line or accelerated) that maximizes tax benefits. If the straight-line depreciation method is optimal for the holder of the property, the number of years that the property is held is enclosed in a box in the tables. Note that straight-line depreciation is never optimal for residential real estate (Table 22.2), but it can be optimal for commercial real estate (Table 22.3), as discussed more fully below.

Without installment sales, little turnover of real estate occurs under these tax rules. While commercial property is never sold, investors optimally trade residential real estate only under conditions of low inflation. For both types of property, investors rationally choose to use accelerated depreciation. These results are at odds with observed investor behavior. Gordon, Hines, and Summers note that during 1981 and 1982, approximately 60% of all real estate held by partnerships was depreciated using the straight-line method for tax purposes.[15] This indicates that investors anticipated selling the property well before the time

---

[15] Roger H. Gordon, James R. Hines, Jr., and Lawrence H. Summers, "Notes on the Tax Treatment of Structures," *Taxation and Capital Formation*, edited by M. Feldstein (University of Chicago Press, 1987), pp. 223-257.

Chapter 22   Property Transactions

at which the depreciable structure became worthless. Beyond this, casual observation suggests that real estate is turned over much more frequently than the above results predict. For example, the May, 1985 issue of *Money Magazine* reports an average holding period of eight years for properties held through limited partnerships.

Table 22.2 The Initial Property Value (as a Fraction of Value Ignoring Depreciation Benefits) and Optimal Trading Pattern for Property Under the 1981, 1984, and 1986 Tax Act Rules

		Residential Real Estate Market-Rate Installment Sales					
Length of Installment Sales (Years)	Initial Property Value*	Optimal Holding Period by Investor (in Years)					
		1	2	3	4	5	6
1981 Tax Act							
A. 4% inflation							
0	1.39	15	55				
10	1.49	15	15	40			
20	1.56	9	10	15	36		
B. 10% inflation							
0	1.24	70					
10	1.33	8	9	13	40		
20	1.42	5	5	6	7	9	38
1984 Tax Act							
A. 4% inflation							
0	1.33	17	53				
10	1.41	17	17	36			
20	1.45	17	17	36			
B. 10% inflation							
0	1.21	70					
10	1.25	14	17	39			
20	1.29	13	15	42			
1986 Tax Act							
A. 4% inflation							
0	1.11	70					
10	1.12	70					
20	1.12	70					
B. 10% inflation							
0	1.07	70					
10	1.07	70					
20	1.08	70					

*Per dollar of property value *ignoring* depreciation benefits and taxes on disposition.

Table 22.3 The Initial Property Value (as a Fraction of Value Ignoring Depreciation Benefits) and Optimal Trading Pattern for Property Under the 1981, 1984, and 1986 Tax Act Rules

Commercial Real Estate
Market-Rate Installment Sales

Length of Installment Sales (Years)	Initial Property Value[b]	Optimal Holding Period by Investor (in Years)					
		1	2	3	4	5	6
1981 Tax Act							
A. 4% inflation							
0	1.36	70					
10	1.42	15 [a]	15	40			
20	1.48	15	15	40			
B. 10% inflation							
0	1.24	70					
10	1.29	11	15	44			
20	1.40	5	5	6	8	9	37
1984 Tax Act							
A. 4% inflation							
0	1.32	70					
10	1.36	17	53				
20	1.40	17	17	36			
B. 10% inflation							
0	1.21	70					
10	1.22	70					
20	1.24	16	54				
1986 Tax Act							
A. 4% inflation							
0	1.10	70					
10	1.11	70					
20	1.11	70					
B. 10% inflation							
0	1.06	70					
10	1.07	70					
20	1.07	70					

[a] Boxed terms indicate use of straight-line depreciation for tax purposes.

[b] Per dollar of property value *ignoring* depreciation benefits and taxes on disposition.

Once market-rate installment sales are considered, significant turnover of real estate occurs, and the model predictions begin to appear more consistent with investor behavior. Under 20-year installment sales and 10% inflation, residential property is traded optimally 5 times over its 70-year life, and the initial value of the property increases by roughly 15% relative to its value in the absence of an opportunity to use installment sales. This happens *despite* the 5% transaction cost incurred each time the property is sold. The initial owner holds the property for 5 years before selling the property to a second investor, who also holds the property for 5 years. The property is then sold to a third investor, who holds the property for 6 years before selling it to a fourth investor, who holds the property for 7 years. The fifth owner holds the property for 9 years, while the final owner holds the property for the 38 years remaining in its life.

As the property ages, the optimal holding period increases, because the value of the depreciable structure declines over time relative to the value of the land. In addition, more turnover results if land comprises a smaller fraction of the initial value of the property. And if property improvements are made periodically, turnover decreases in the early years of the life of property and increases in the later years.

Note that investors always choose to use accelerated depreciation for residential property and, at high levels of inflation, for commercial property. At low levels of inflation, however, investors choose straight-line depreciation during the initial years for commercial property and then switch to accelerated depreciation in the later years. This result can be understood as follows. If commercial real estate is depreciated using an accelerated method, all depreciation is recaptured as ordinary income when the property is sold. (Recall that this is not true for residential real estate.) If this property is depreciated using the straight-line method, however, the entire gain on its sale is taxed as a capital gain. So, an investor who chooses accelerated depreciation over straight-line depreciation realizes larger depreciation tax savings over the period the property is held, but incurs larger tax liabilities when the property is sold. At low levels of inflation and in the early years of the life of the property, the present value of these increased depreciation deductions is less than the present value of the increased tax liabilities incurred upon sale of the property. As a result, investors rationally choose straight-line depreciation for commercial property.[16] The converse holds at high levels of inflation and/or the later years of the life of the property.

Recall that the 1984 Tax Act lengthened the depreciable life of structures to 18 years and, more important, eliminated the opportunity to use installment notes to defer depreciation recapture taxes upon the sale of real estate. As one would expect, the "1984 Tax Act" panels of Tables 22.2 and 22.3 show that property values and property turnover fall significantly from what they were under the 1981 rules. The incremental value of market-rate installment sales also falls significantly. Some churning of real estate, however, still occurs.

With the dramatic slowdown in depreciation rates introduced in the 1986 Tax Reform Act, Tables 22.2 and 22.3 show that there is no longer *any* turnover of real estate for tax reasons, even when market-rate installment sales are considered. The 1986 Tax Act effectively eliminates the tax advantages of market-rate

---

[16] Note that even the last holder of the property uses straight-line depreciation under the 1984 Tax Act when 20-year installment notes are used and the inflation rate is low (4%). This is because the increase in land value triggers an onerous recapture tax when accelerated depreciation is elected and the land is eventually sold.

installment sales.[17] The presence of nontax as well as other tax motives for selling property suggests that the 1986 Tax Act should have prompted an increased interest in tax-free exchanges of real estate (where, under Section 1031 of the Code, there may be no depreciation recapture or capital gains tax to the seller and no step-up in depreciable basis to the buyer).

We also examined whether it was advantageous for a holder who knew that the 1986 Tax Act would reduce depreciation benefits to new owners for sales in 1987 and beyond to sell the property in 1986 to retain the shorter depreciation lives and faster depreciation rates. As it turned out, however, unless the property owner was planning to sell in 1987 anyway, it would not have been optimal to accelerate sales into 1986. Although depreciation rates were reduced and capital gains taxes increased with the 1986 Act, recapture taxes were also reduced because income tax rates were lowered. This latter effect, coupled with the advantage of deferring the tax on the gain in the value of the land, was more important in deciding whether to accelerate property sales into 1986 than the disadvantage of losing some depreciation benefits and paying tax on gains at a higher rate.

To examine the sensitivity of our results to changes in the assumed level of nontax transaction costs, we recalculated the optimal turnover rates and market values for real estate under the 3 tax regimes for levels of these costs ranging from 2% to 8% of market value. Table 22.4 summarizes our results under the 1981 Tax Act for residential property. Without installment sales, the optimal trading strategies of investors and the resulting market values of real estate are rather insensitive to changes in these nontax transaction costs. Even in the absence of nontax transaction costs, the capital gains and recapture taxes incurred when real estate is sold are sufficient to deter investors from turning over real estate very rapidly. The picture becomes very different, however, when we consider installment sales. Now, real estate turnover rates and market values are very sensitive to changes in these nontax transaction costs.

For example, when the inflation rate is 10% and a 20-year installment note is used in the sale of real estate, residential property is optimally traded 12 times during its life when transaction costs are equal to 2% of the selling price of the property, whereas they are traded only 7 times when these costs equal 4% of the selling price of the property. Similar results are found under the 1984 and 1986 Tax Acts. These results can be understood as follows. By deferring the payment of capital gains and recapture taxes through the use of installment sales, investors are able to decrease significantly the present value of the tax costs associated with the sale of the property. As a result, significant nontax transaction costs become necessary to deter investors from turning over real estate very rapidly.

There are both explicit and implicit transaction costs to sell real estate. Examples of explicit transaction costs include legal and brokerage expenses, which are related to several other informational costs associated with the sale of real estate. For example, there is the cost associated with verifying the credit-worthiness of the prospective buyer (which may be explicit if this is done through an intermediary). There are also the costs associated with monitoring the buyer

---

[17] We can imagine a benefit resulting from using installment sales under the 1986 Act if sellers anticipate a reduction in future capital gains tax rates, but we did not model this scenario.

Table 22.4 The Effect of Transactions Costs Upon the Initial Value and Optimal Trading Pattern for Residential Property

1981 Tax Rules
Market-Rate Installment Sales

Percentage Transactions Cost	Initial Property Value	1	2	3	4	5	6	7	8	9	10	11	12	13
4% Inflation														
A. No installment sales														
2%	1.42	15	15	40										
4	1.40	15	15	40										
6	1.38	15	55											
8	1.37	15	55											
B. 10-year installment sales														
2%	1.55	5	5	9	15	36								
4	1.51	15	15	40										
6	1.48	15	15	40										
8	1.46	15	15	40										
C. 20-year installment sales														
2%	1.70	4	4	4	4	4	5	5	36					
4	1.59	5	9	9	15	32								
6	1.54	9	15	15	31									
8	1.51	15	15	40										
10% Inflation														
A. No installment sales														
2%	1.24	70												
4	1.24	70												
6	1.24	70												
8	1.24	70												
B. 10-year installment sales														
2%	1.45	3	4	4	4	4	4	5	5	37				
4	1.35	5	6	9	10	40								
6	1.31	10	15	45										
8	1.29	14	15	41										
C. 20-year installment sales														
2%	1.64	3	3	3	3	3	3	3	3	3	4	4	5	30
4	1.47	4	4	4	5	5	5	9	34					
6	1.38	6	7	9	10	38								
8	1.34	9	9	14	38									

after the sale to protect against possible defaults. Finally, it is costly to determine the fair market value of the property. The buyer may invest in appraisals, inspections, and other information to avoid unpleasant surprises that might not surprise the seller at all.

In our model, we have assumed that all investors are in the same tax bracket. If investors are in different tax brackets, implicit tax costs will arise when high-tax-bracket sellers use installment sales, because they will be receiving fully taxable interest income from installment sales when they would prefer to generate tax-sheltered income such as that arising from tax-exempt bonds.

Below-Market-Rate Installment Sales

In the previous section, we observed that market-rate installment sales can explain much of the gap that exists between the observed behavior of investors and the predictions that are made in published models of real estate turnover. Below-market-rate installment sales represent a second means by which investors can increase the net tax benefits associated with real estate transfers. Even where market-rate installment sales do not create an incentive to churn real estate, the availability of below-market-rate installment sales may generate *significant* turnover of real estate. Moreover, below-market-rate installment sales were very common in the U.S. in 1981-1982 when interest rates were high.

This possibility is illustrated by the following example. Consider a parcel of land that produces fixed annual rent of $7,000, net of property taxes and other recurring expenses (that are paid annually). The land can be sold without incurring any selling costs. The required before-tax rate of return on the investment is 7% per year. The ordinary and capital gains tax rates are 30% for all individuals. Under these assumptions, the intrinsic value of the land remains constant at $100,000 through time. Suppose the current owner, A, purchased this land for $100,000. In the absence of below-market-rate installment sales, it will not be beneficial to trade the land. In contrast, consider the following set of transactions, the first of which involves a below-market-rate installment sale:

  i. A sells the land to B for $150,000 on a 20-year installment basis, with required annual interest payments of 4%;

 ii. B in turn sells the land to C for a $98,000 installment note with principal due in 20 years and with required annual interest payments at the rate of 7% of principal.

Since A is able to defer the payment of capital gains taxes for 20 years, A's after-tax economic gain from the sale of the land is calculated as follows:

Present value of the after-tax payments to be received from the note[18]	$ 104,647
Less: Value of land if *not* sold	(100,000)
After-tax economic gain from sale of land	$ 4,647

---

[18] A receives a pretax annuity of $150,000 × 4% or $6,000 for 20 years. The after-tax annuity is $4,200 per year. In addition, A receives $150,000 in 20 years, of which $50,000 is a capital gain, taxable at a rate of 30%. This leaves $135,000 after tax from the principal repayment. The present value of a 20-year annuity of $4,200 and a lump-sum receipt of $135,000 in 20 years, all discounted at an after-tax rate of 7% × (1 - 30%), or 4.9%, is $104,647.

Chapter 22   Property Transactions

Similarly, the gain to B from the purchase and subsequent sale of the land is given by:

Present value of the after-tax installment payments to be received from C	$ 98,000
Plus: Tax reduction from capital loss[19]	15,600
Less: Present value of the after-tax installment payments to be made to A[20]	(110,409)
After-tax economic gain	$ 3,191

Finally, the gain to C from the purchase of the land is $2,000 (assuming that C never sells the land). Thus, this set of transactions is beneficial to all three individuals. The aggregate economic gain to the three parties is nearly $10,000 on this $100,000 property.

The use of a below-market rate of interest causes the quoted selling price of a property to be artificially inflated above its fair market value. This causes the seller to incur an artificial capital gain; however, as with market-rate installment sales, the seller is able to defer the payment of taxes on this capital gain. Meanwhile, the buyer will be able to claim an artificial capital loss on a subsequent sale of the property. If the property is quickly turned over (as in our example), the capital loss will be taken before the original seller must pay taxes on the capital gain, creating a net gain from the difference in timing of the capital loss and capital gain. The terms of the installment sale can be arranged such that both parties share these timing gains.

In addition to these tax timing gains, below-market-rate installment sales for depreciable property create other benefits. Because the quoted selling price of property is artificially above its fair market value, the buyer will be able to take larger depreciation tax deductions than otherwise. Of course, this does not arise in the above example involving nondepreciable land.

The potential for large-scale tax avoidance via below-market-rate installment sales has been recognized by the tax authorities. As a result, Section 1274 of the Code sets a minimum rate of interest that must be imputed on below-market-rate installment sales. This minimum rate of interest is a riskless rate and is usually several percent below the interest rate appropriate for the level of risk borne by the investor who sells the property on an installment basis. As a result, below-market-rate installment sales may still offer significant benefits.

For the results presented in this chapter, the minimum rate of interest on installment sales given by Section 1274 was assumed to be 2% below the rate of interest that appropriately compensates investors for the risks associated with the installment sales. Tables 22.5 and 22.6 present results for residential and commercial property, respectively. Apart from being more exaggerated, the results are

---

[19] [($150,000 - $98,000) × 30%]. This assumes that the taxing authority would accept these valuations and, hence, the capital loss. This also assumes that B is able to offset the entire capital loss of $24,000 against capital gains or ordinary income in the year of the sale. Even if B were to hold property for awhile before reselling, however, a tax gain would remain.

[20] This differs from the net present value of the after-tax amounts to be received by A only in that the after-tax lump-sum payment to be paid by B in 20 years is $150,000, whereas A keeps only $135,000 due to the capital gains tax. So the present value of B's payments is $5,762 higher.

very similar to those found under market-rate installment sales. For example, under the 1981 Tax Act rules, a 10% inflation rate and a 20-year installment note, property turnover increases from 5 turns to 7 turns. Initial property values increase nearly 30% relative to their values in the absence of installment sales versus a 15% premium when market-rate installment sales are used.

The use of installment sales significantly increased the market values and turnover rates of both residential and commercial real estate prior to the 1986 Tax Act. Subsequent to this Tax Act, however, installment sales have little impact on property values and turnover rates. Prior to this Tax Act, accelerated depreciation was always the optimal depreciation method for tax purposes for residential property. Meanwhile, straight-line depreciation tends to be optimal for commercial property in the early years of the life of a property, particularly at low inflation rates. Interestingly, we find little churning of real estate similar to that given in our above example. Only at low inflation rates and under 20-year installment sales do we find investors buying properties via market-rate installment sales and then quickly turning around and reselling these properties to another investor via a below-market-rate installment sale. The minimum imputed interest rate on installment sales is sufficient to preclude frequent occurrence of this type of churning.

As with our analysis for market-rate installment sales, property values and turnover rates found under below-market-rate installment sales are very sensitive to changes in the assumed level of the nontax costs associated with real estate sales. When these transaction costs are small, very high property turnover rates are found even under the 1986 Tax Act. As these transaction costs are increased, real estate market values and turnover rates fall significantly under all three tax regimes.

Chapter 22   Property Transactions

Table 22.5 The Initial Value and Optimal Trading Pattern for Property

Residential Real Estate
Below-Market-Rate Installment Sales

Length of Installment Sales (Years)	Initial Property Value	Optimal Holding Period by Investor (in Years)							
		1	2	3	4	5	6	7	8
1981 Tax Act									
A. 4% inflation									
0	1.39	15	55						
10	1.70	15	15	15	25*				
20	2.02	9	9	15	15	1*	21		
B. 10% inflation									
0	1.24	70							
10	1.42	9	9	13	39*				
20	1.60	5	5	5	5	7	9	4*	30
1984 Tax Act									
A. 4% inflation									
0	1.33	17	53						
10	1.56	17	17	36*					
20	1.77	17	17	17	1*	18			
B. 10% inflation									
0	1.21	70							
10	1.31	14	17	39*					
20	1.39	11	13	15	31*				
1986 Tax Act									
A. 4% inflation									
0	1.11	70							
10	1.15	70							
20	1.18	1	69*						
B. 10% inflation									
0	1.07	70							
10	1.08	70							
20	1.09	70							

*Market-rate installment sale of property to this investor.

Table 22.6 The Initial Value and Optimal Trading Pattern for Property

Commercial Real Estate
Below-Market-Rate Installment Sales

Length of Installment Sales (Years)	Initial Property Value	Optimal Holding Period by Investor (in Years)							
		1	**2**	**3**	**4**	**5**	**6**	**7**	**8**
1981 Tax Act									
A. 4% inflation									
0	1.36	70							
10	1.59	15 [a]	15	40 *					
20	1.82	9	15	15	1*	30			
B. 10% inflation									
0	1.24	70							
10	1.36	12	15	43*					
20	1.57	5	5	5	5	8	9	4*	29
1984 Tax Act									
A. 4% inflation									
0	1.32	70							
10	1.49	17	17	36 *					
20	1.66	17	17	17	1*	18			
B. 10% inflation									
0	1.21	70							
10	1.27	17	53*						
20	1.32	13	15	42*					
1986 Tax Act									
A. 4% inflation									
0	1.10	70							
10	1.13	70							
20	1.17	1	69*						
B. 10% inflation									
0	1.06	70							
10	1.08	70							
20	1.08	70							

[a]Boxed terms indicate use of straight-line depreciation for tax purposes

*Market-rate installment sale of property to this investor.

22.3 Empirical Evidence

While the preceding analysis provides a logically consistent explanation for why property turnover has been so much faster than that predicted by other models in the literature, it relies on the common use of installment sales. It is reasonable to ask, therefore, whether such transactions are empirically relevant. To address this question, we interviewed personnel at two of the leading managers of real estate: Balcor Properties and JMB Realty. The Balcor and JMB people have assured us that their experience in installment sales is typical of many firms in the partnership industry, the dominant form through which real properties have been held.

Balcor Properties

Balcor controlled over $7 billion in properties at year-end 1988, virtually all of which was held through partnerships. Since the Tax Reform Act of 1986, they have used installment sales infrequently. Prior to the 1984 Tax Act, however, installment sales were the rule rather than the exception. Roughly 90% of the sales involved installment notes with maturities of typically 5 to 7 years, although occasionally the maturities were much longer. The average holding period of property was about 5.5 years. Following the 1984 Tax Act and prior to the 1986 Act, installment sales remained quite common (over 50% of all transactions), but they were not as common as before the 1984 Act.

Since the 1986 Tax Act, Balcor has lengthened the average holding period of properties by nearly 40% to 7.5 years. Still, 7.5 years is quite short relative to our prediction, so a couple of comments are in order.

As mentioned earlier, nontax factors obviously influence property turnover. Important among these factors is a desire on the part of investors to monitor property managers. The price realized on the sale of property provides reasonably objective performance evaluation information.

Another important nontax factor is that most property is owned by partnerships, and claims to partnership units typically do not trade in active secondary markets. Borrowing against these claims for consumption purposes can be costly. For liquidity reasons, property sales can be desirable because they facilitate distributions to partners. The desire for liquidity also explains why installment sales are not used even more than they have been.

The Tax Act of 1986 has made property investments relatively tax-disfavored, especially given that for nontax reasons properties are sold earlier than if pure tax minimization strategies were pursued. Consistent with effective tax planning, these changes in tax rules have resulted in a dramatic shifting of tax clienteles. While taxable investors used to dominate the holding of equity positions in real estate, there has been a dramatic ownership shift after the 1986 Tax Act to pension funds and other tax-exempt investors.

JMB Realty

JMB managed over $20 billion of property at year-end 1988. Prior to the Tax Act of 1986, 80-90% of sales involved installment notes, with the high end of this range represented by the period preceding the 1984 Act. Typical deal terms were 20-

25% cash and 75-80% installment notes. The typical maturity of installment notes was 10 years, although they ranged from 3 to 30 years.

The installment notes typically bore interest at well below market rates. In fact, JMB commonly used the lowest rate explicitly allowed by the safe harbor provisions under the law. As we noted, increasing the nominal sales price resulted in a larger capital gain to the seller (postponed through the installment sale), and a larger step-up in depreciable property (deductible by the buyer against ordinary income).

Since 1986, JMB no longer uses installment sales. Moreover, as with Balcor, there has been a substantial shift in clienteles. Whereas individuals previously owned nearly 100% of JMB properties through partnerships in the early 1980s, institutions now own roughly half of the properties.

Other Evidence

According to a report prepared by the Individual Statistics Branch of the IRS, roughly $10 billion of capital gains were reported by individuals on their 1981 tax returns from 2.1 million installment sale transactions.[21] This is up from $4 billion of such capital gains reported on 1977 returns. The IRS has accumulated similar data for 1985, but we have not seen them. We expect the amounts to be significantly higher than in 1981, since the 1985 data will include partial gains from sales that occurred in the 1981-1985 period, the heyday of installment sales.

We were unable to locate data on the use of installment sales in the corporate sector, but installment sales have played an important role in mergers, acquisitions, and asset sales. We list below a few examples reported in the business press:

- Following the purchase of Federated Department Stores, Campeau sold retail outlets to May Department Stores, Macys, and Marks & Spencers on terms that included $1.25 billion of installment notes due in approximately 10 years. The arrangements successfully postponed about $1 billion of taxable gain or $300-400 million in taxes.[22]

- The First Boston Group's bid for RJR's food business included about $13 billion in installment notes. Had the offer been accepted, $2.5 billion of taxes would have been deferred.[23]

- PepsiCo struck a tentative deal in 1988 with General Cinema to purchase the latter's bottling business for a $1.5 billion interest-only installment note due in 20 years.[24] Because General Cinema's basis in these assets was only $300 million, as much as $1.2 billion of taxable gain (less any depreciation recapture) might have been postponed. Because of an unexpected delay due to Federal Trade Commission evaluation of the proposed transaction, the deal was not completed until 1989. Installment sales rules passed in 1988, and effective January 1, 1989, largely elimi-

---

[21] "Sales of Capital Assets, 1981 and 1982," by Bobby Clark and David Paris, prepared under the direction of Michael Coleman. We are grateful to James Poterba for directing us to this report.

[22] *Forbes* (October 31, 1988), pp. 98-99.

[23] *Wall Street Journal* (November 30, 1988), p. A3.

[24] *Washington Post* (December 2, 1988), p. G2.

Chapter 22   Property Transactions

nated General Cinema's ability to postpone the capital gains tax by using an installment sale. As a consequence, PepsiCo changed the terms to 100% cash and increased the price by $250 million. As a result, General Cinema's after-tax cash proceeds of more than $1.1 billion was approximately the same as with the installment note.[25]

- Beyond this, land development companies have made extensive usage of installment sales, as reported in their financial statements.

Legislative Response

Considering the evidence, it is not surprising that the installment sales rules were tightened up in the 1984 Tax Act, requiring that past depreciation be recaptured at the time of an installment sale.[26] The Senate Report that accompanied the passage of the 1984 Act explained the legislative objective of the change in the installment sales rules as follows:[27]

> The depreciation recapture provisions of (Code Sections) 1245 and 1250 provide a disincentive for taxpayers to rapidly depreciate a property and then sell or exchange it to acquire another piece of property which they could depreciate. It appears that some persons have used the installment sale provisions to avoid the disincentives for 'churning' property contained in the recapture provisions. The deferral of the recapture provisions and capital gains tax accomplished through an installment sale can reduce the disincentive for selling depreciable property. The revision of the installment sales provision contained in the 1984 Act will reduce the incentive for persons to replace property as soon as the tax benefits are exhausted. This change will also make it more difficult for investors to achieve negative tax rates throughout the use of ACRS deductions and rapid sales of property.

22.4 Other Tax Factors Affecting Real Estate Trading

Our analysis has ignored a number of tax considerations that affect property values and optimal trading strategies. These include the minimum tax provisions, the requirement to capitalize "construction-period interest and taxes," "passive loss" limitations and "at-risk" rules for real estate introduced by the 1986 Tax Act, special rules that apply to low-income housing and qualified rehabilitation property, rules applying to wrap-around mortgages when a sequence of

---

[25] *Wall Street Journal* (January 16, 1989), p. A3.

[26] Other tightenings of the law occurred in 1986, 1987, and 1988. For example, it used to be permissible to postpone the capital gains tax on the sale of publicly traded stock by using an installment sale. The 1986 Tax Act changed that. The 1987 Act required interest to be paid (albeit at below-market rates) on the deferred tax from installment sales involving most sales of real property used in a trade or business or held for rental, to the extent that more than $5 million of installment notes are held by the seller. The 1988 Act extended this treatment to most personal property as well (except personal-*use* property like personal residences).

[27] Senate Report Number 169 (Vol I) 98th Congress 2d Session 465 (1984).

installment sales occurs, and the tax-free step-up in basis that occurs when property is inherited from a decedent.

Another tax consideration that deserves special mention is "like-kind exchanges" under Section 1031 of the Code. When two owners of real estate exchange properties, capital gains taxes are postponed (except to the extent of cash and other non-like-kind property received) until a taxable disposition takes place at a later date. Moreover, if residential rental property is exchanged for other residential rental property, there is no recapture of past depreciation. The same is true if depreciable commercial real estate is exchanged for other depreciable commercial real estate.[28]

Because like-kind exchanges do not result in a step-up of the tax basis of the exchanged properties (except to the extent of depreciation recapture), there might appear to be no tax advantage to effecting such an exchange. But in fact, there *can* be an advantage because the exchange may increase the tax basis allocated to the depreciable component of the investment and decrease the tax basis allocated to the nondepreciable land component of the investment.[29] An extreme way to do this is to exchange unimproved land for improved real estate, an exchange explicitly blessed under Section 1.1031(a)-1(c)(2) of the Treasury Regulations, although such an exchange may give rise to recapture of depreciation.[30] In fact, such a transaction gives rise to tax treatment very similar to that achievable with an installment sale following the 1984 Tax Act. On the other hand, these exchanges can be expected to involve more transaction costs than the more straightforward installment sales.

22.5 Conclusions

In this chapter, we have shown that installment sales can have a significant effect on the turnover rates and market values of real estate, especially prior to the 1986 Tax Act. Factoring the installment sales tax rules into previous models of real estate valuation and trading substantially improves the ability of these models to predict investor behavior that accords with that observed. In addition, we have found that optimal property turnover rates and market values become very sensitive to changes in the magnitude of nontax transaction costs associated with real estate sales when these sales are done on an installment basis. This suggests the importance of further research that is designed to determine accurately the magnitude of these costs. Moreover, we do not factor in the effects of uncertainty in real estate prices. Such uncertainty will *increase* the tax benefits of turning over

---

[28] The 1989 Tax Act scaled back opportunities to defer gains from exchanging domestic and foreign real estate as well as opportunities to defer gains on exchange of property among related parties.

[29] For further discussion and examples, see *Tax Free Exchanges Under Section 1031*, Tax Management Portfolios (Bureau of National Affairs), 61-5th (1987).

[30] It might appear that such an exchange would be difficult to effect. In practice, however, it is not. Once the seller of the depreciable property identifies the desired replacement property in the marketplace, an intermediary arranges to purchase the asset through a trust. The like-kind exchange then takes place with the trust. Once the exchange is completed, the depreciable property is sold by the trust to the new owner. The trust records no gain or loss on these transactions.

Chapter 22   Property Transactions

property due to a tax-timing option.[31] If the value of the property appreciates unexpectedly, the property can be sold to generate additional depreciation deductions; if the property depreciates in value it can be retained.

Summary of Key Points

1. Three crucial tax factors in asset transactions are the present value of depreciation deductions (and tax credits), the present value of depreciation (and tax credit) recapture on dispositions, and the present value of capital gains taxes on dispositions.

2. In this chapter, we employ a model to value real property and to predict property turnover rates. The model takes account of the fact that it might be desirable to sell the property prior to the end of its economic life to permit a new owner to depreciate it for tax purposes based on an appreciated purchase price. The model also takes account of the effects of transaction costs, inflation, capital gains taxes, and recapture taxes on asset prices and turnover rates.

3. That it might be desirable to sell used depreciable property to enhance depreciation deductions to a new buyer contrasts with the usual "lock-in" effect on capital assets such as stocks that have appreciated in value.

4. Installment sales have played an important role in real property transactions in the U.S. An installment sale allows the taxpayer to defer payment of realized capital gains and, between 1981 and 1984, to defer the payment of depreciation recapture taxes. An installment sale is a sale wherein the seller takes back a note from the buyer. Taxes become due in proportion to the receipt of principal payments on the note.

5. There are nontax costs associated with using an installment sale to postpone taxes. An important one relates to liquidity. If the installment note is pledged as collateral for a loan, the deferred taxes become due immediately. As a result, if cash flow requirements of a seller are financed by unsecured borrowing, the borrowing costs may be quite high.

6. Without installment sale possibilities, there has been little *tax* motivation to sell residential and commercial property. With installment sales, tax-motivated turnover is greatest prior to the 1984 Tax Act, because both recapture and capital gains taxes could be deferred under that regime. Were it not for a reasonable level of transaction costs, property should have turned over every year.

7. The tax advantage of installment sales was reduced by the 1984 Tax Act. Subsequent to this Act, depreciation recapture could not be postponed under an installment sale.

---

[31] For further discussion, see Joseph T. Williams, "Trading and Valuing Depreciable Assets," *Journal of Financial Economics* (June 1985), pp. 283-308, and Jeremy I. Bulow and Lawrence H. Summers, "The Taxation of Risky Assets," *Journal of Political Economy* (February 1984), pp. 20-39.

8. The 1986 Tax Act further eroded the importance of installment sales as a tool for turning over property to secure tax gains by reducing the gross tax advantage of stepping up the asset basis of property for depreciation purposes.

9. Managers of real estate properties have indeed acted in ways broadly consistent with our analysis. Property turnover rates fell following the 1984 and 1986 Tax Acts, and installment sales were also employed significantly less often.

10. When property is sold for any number of nontax reasons, installment sales remain a valuable tax-planning strategy to defer capital gains taxes following the 1986 Tax Act.

Discussion Questions

1. Are the following comments true or false?

   a. When a tax bill changes depreciation schedules, property owned prior to the change in rules is typically depreciated based on the new schedule.

   b. The only tax reason to sell an asset is to step up its basis for depreciation purposes.

   c. The higher the rate at which future cash flows are discounted, the more valuable are depreciation deductions.

   d. It is desirable to use a high rate of interest on installment notes so that the buyer may secure generous tax deductions for the interest.

2. Taxpayers incur both tax and nontax costs when they sell assets. What are these costs? How can the seller reduce them?

3. Describe the model used to value real estate in this chapter. Ignoring installment sales, why does the model predict such infrequent sales of property (as reflected in Tables 22.2 and 22.3)?

4. How did the 1984 Tax Act discourage property sales?

5. Why does the model suggest that installment sales have little effect on the rate of property turnover under the 1986 Tax Act?

6. What are the tax motivations for using below-market interest rates on installment notes when property is sold? Taxpayers are now required to provide interest on installment notes at a rate no less than that on government securities. To what extent does this eliminate opportunities to secure tax advantages from using below-market interest rates?

7. What is a like-kind exchange under Section 1031? Illustrate the tax advantages of such a transaction. What might have been the motivation behind restricting tax-deferral treatment in a like-kind exchange between related parties?

8. Why might tax-exempt institutions, including pension funds, be the natural holders of real estate in the U.S. subsequent to the 1986 Tax Act? Consider the effects of actual property turnover rates in your answer.

Problem

Some years back, you purchased a piece of commercial real estate for $700,000. You have since accumulated $200,000 of straight-line depreciation on the property for tax purposes. The property is now worth $5 million to a new owner.

    a. If you sold the property for $5 million in cash and your tax rate were 30%, how much would you net after tax?

    b. How much better or worse off would you be if you sold the property for a $5 million interest-only installment note, with the $5 million of principal due in a lump sum in 20 years? Assume that the buyer is *very* reliable and pledges ample collateral besides the building to secure the note. The note pays interest at the rate of 10% per annum. Your alternative to receiving interest income on the note is to invest in tax-exempt bonds yielding 7%. You expect your tax rate to remain 30% over the next 20 years.

    c. Suppose that 10 years after selling the property with a 20-year installment note, it is announced that your tax rate in the future will be 40% rather than 30%. Assume that the tax-exempt bond rate declines to 6% for the remaining life of the installment note.

        1. Should you sell your installment note to a third party for $5 million cash while tax rates are still 30% and recognize the capital gain now, or should you continue to hold the note to postpone the gain?

        2. At what price would you be indifferent to selling the note?

    d. Suppose your alternatives to the installment note were tax-exempt bonds yielding 8% rather than 7%. How would your answers to (b) and (c1) be affected? Assume for (c1) that your after-tax investment opportunity declines to 7%, which is still 1% above the after-tax rate on taxable financial instruments.

Technical Note 22.1

The model used to determine the impact of installment sales upon property values and turnover is an extension of the one developed by Ling and Whinihan. Consider a property with a remaining economic life of N years. This property consists of a depreciable structure and nondepreciable land. The property produces before-tax income of I(i) in year i. The model value of this property in year n to an investor who will sell it in year n+h is

$$V(n,h) = \sum_{i=1}^{h} \frac{(1 - t_o)\, I\,(n + i)}{(1 + K)^i} + \sum_{i=1}^{h} \frac{t_o D(i)\, [V(n,h)] - L(n)]}{(1 + K)^i} + \frac{(1 - b)V^*(n + h)}{(1 + K)^h}$$

$$- \frac{t_g\, [(1 - b)V^*(n + h) - B_s\,(h)\, [V(n,h) - L(n)] - L(n)]}{(1 + K)^h} \left[1 - p_g + \frac{p_g}{(1 + K)^T} \right]$$

$$- \frac{t_o\, [B_s(h) - B_a(h)][V(n,h) - L(n)]}{(1 + K)^h} \left[1 - p_r + \frac{p_r}{(1 + K)^T} \right] \tag{22.1}$$

where

t_o, t_g ≡ the marginal ordinary and capital gains tax rates;

K ≡ the nominal after-tax rate of return required by investors;

$D(i)$ ≡ the tax depreciation rate for the i'th year that the property is held;

β ≡ the proportional selling cost;

$L(n)$ ≡ the market value at time n of the nondepreciable land component of the property;

$V^*(n+h)$ ≡ the market value of the property in year n+h;

$B_a(h)$ ≡ the adjusted basis per dollar of purchase price of the depreciable structure when held for h years;

$B_s(h)$ ≡ the basis per dollar of purchase price of the depreciable structure used to determine capital gains;

p_g, p_r ≡ the proportion of the capital gain and recaptured depreciation, respectively, that can be deferred; and

T ≡ the effective number of years taxes are deferred.

The first term on the right-hand side of equation 22.1 represents the present value of the net income generated from the property, while the second term represents the present value of the depreciation tax savings. The third term gives the present value of the proceeds from the sale of the property in year n+h. The remaining two terms represent the present values of the tax liabilities (capital gains and recaptured depreciation, respectively) that result from the sale of the property.

Solving this equation for V(n, h), we find

$$V(n,h) = \frac{F_1}{F_2},$$ (22.2)

where

$$F_1 = \sum_{i=1}^{h} \frac{(1 - t_o) I (n + i) t_o D(i) L(n)}{(1 + K)^i} + \frac{(1 - b) V^*(n + h)}{(1 + K)^h}$$

$$- \frac{t_g [(1 - b) V^*(n + h) - (1 - B_s(h)) L(n)]}{(1 + K)^h} \left[1 - p_g + \frac{p_g}{(1 + K)^T} \right]$$

$$+ \frac{t_o [B_s(h) - B_a(h)] L(n)}{(1 + K)^h} \left[1 - p_r + \frac{p_r}{(1 + K)^T} \right]$$

and

$$F_2 = 1 - \sum_{i+1}^{h} \frac{t_o D(i)}{(1 + K)^i} - \frac{t_g B_s(h)}{(1 + K)^h} \left[1 - p_g + \frac{p_g}{(1 + K)^T} \right]$$

$$+ \frac{t_o [B_s(h) - B_a(h)]}{(1 + K)^h} \left[1 - p_g + \frac{p_g}{(1 + K)^T} \right].$$

Similar formulas can be derived for the cases in which the sale of the property in year n+h will result in a capital loss or a partial recapture of excess depreciation. The competitive market value of the property in year n will be the value of the property to an investor who holds it for the optimal length of time, i.e.,

$$V^*(n) = \max_{h < N-n} V(n,h),$$ (22.3)

where N denotes the time at which the depreciable structure becomes worthless. Note that the competitive market value of the property at time N will just be the residual value of the land. Thus,

$$V^*(N) = L(N).$$ (22.4)

With this fact, we use equation 22.3 to solve recursively backwards in time from year N to find the current market value of the property and the optimal trading strategy that produces this market value.

CHAPTER 23
Introduction to Mergers and Acquisitions

This chapter is the first in a series on corporate reorganizations, restructurings, and combinations. As discussed in Chapter Twenty-Two, these chapters are a natural extension to the material on tax planning for a single asset like depreciable real estate. We begin here with an overview of the economics of corporate reorganizations from the tax planner's vantage point. The next chapter concentrates on taxable acquisitions, where a target's stock or assets are purchased in a manner that results in a change in the tax basis of the target's assets. The third chapter in the series concentrates on tax-free reorganizations of corporations and spin-offs of subsidiaries. Such mergers and acquisitions may be effected without either a change in the basis of assets inside the corporation *or* a tax on shareholders. Chapter Twenty-Six describes how a reorganization affects the value of both the purchaser's and target's tax attributes, especially net-operating-loss and tax-credit carryforwards. We show how the tax rules provide opportunities to entrench incumbent managers. That is, the tax laws may contribute to management's arsenal of weapons used to defend against hostile takeover attempts.

23.1 Overview of Issues

It is often claimed that the tax laws are largely responsible for the wave of mergers experienced in the U.S. throughout the 1980s. Others have claimed, however, that new financing techniques and other innovations in both capital markets and organizational design facilitated the removal of inefficient managers and that these techniques caused the wave of mergers. In truth, both factors were probably important, as were a number of others.

Many in Congress apparently felt that the tax laws contributed significantly to encouraging the merger wave of the early 1980s in a number of respects. As a result, the 1986 Tax Act increased the costs of effecting mergers and acquisitions through tougher rules. Despite the changes in rules, however, the "merger wave" continued, albeit with notable differences in the types of deals consummated. And anti-merger tax rules have continued to be adopted in legislation subsequent to 1986.

We have argued that tax considerations and information-related transaction-cost considerations often have conflicting implications for efficient organizational design. For example, although mergers might represent an *inefficient* way to achieve tax benefits in a transaction-cost-free world, relative to alternative strategies, it could be the most efficient alternative once we factor information costs into the analysis. In fact, merger-related tax benefits could be *negative* relative to the status quo, but the nontax benefits of a combination could outweigh the tax costs, and mergers may represent the most efficient way to secure the nontax benefits.

Alternatively, although tax benefits might encourage a reorganization, transaction and information costs might outweigh the tax benefits. The formation of partnerships is an example of this conflict. As discussed in earlier chapters, many corporations would realize tax savings if reorganized as partnerships, but the corporate form apparently provides nontax benefits that dominate the tax benefits. Moreover, many reorganizations are not undertaken because the present value of the tax costs outweigh the nontax gains. For example, a firm might wish to sell a division to increase its operating efficiency, but the obligation to pay recapture taxes and capital gains taxes immediately could eliminate the advantage of a sale.

The Many Reasons for Mergers and Acquisitions

There are at least four broad camps that attempt to explain the reasons for acquisitions. Acquisitions occur (1) to improve economic efficiency, (2) to extend the power base of management, (3) to effect transfers of wealth from one class of stakeholders to another, and (4) to secure tax benefits.

In the camp that stresses the improvement of economic efficiency, the arguments typically refer to (1) the advantages of integration to achieve economies of scale and/or scope and (2) gains that result from the removal of inefficient management.

The second camp stresses that the wave of acquisitions can be explained by managerial demand for power, larger salaries, and job security (more broadly, management self interest versus the interest of society). This argument is heard particularly often in relation to conglomerate mergers, which proliferated in the second half of the 1960s. Because of this alleged self interest, management wastes corporate resources acquiring other firms.

Of course, one can adopt a more charitable interpretation of the conglomerate merger movement of the 1960s. Top managers in large corporations may have viewed themselves as running mini internal capital markets, allocating corporate capital in an efficient manner among diverse investment projects. By bringing a number of diverse businesses under one roof and securing good

Chapter 23 Introduction to Mergers and Acquisitions

information about their investment prospects, top management believed it was in a superior position to ration capital wisely as compared to the more decentralized capital market. The poor performance of these companies in the 1970s, however, suggested that they failed to realize these anticipated economies. Indeed, some of the deconglomeration resulting from corporate spinoffs and bust-up acquisitions in the 1980s might have resulted from the realization that in many circumstances, external capital markets are more efficient than internal capital markets at allocating capital to competing projects. In this regard, it is interesting to note that Japanese multinational companies, in the latter half of the 1980s, embarked on a conglomerate merger binge that resembles in interesting ways the U.S. experience in the 1960s.[1]

A third camp emphasizes how a change in corporate control can cause a transfer of some of the wealth of bondholders, employees, and other stakeholders to shareholders. One way to accomplish this is to increase leverage, thereby increasing the risk of default to creditors (such as bondholders, bank lenders, and employees who have been promised certain unfunded benefits such as post-retirement health care) without increasing the level of promised payments. Or it may be accomplished by abrogating unwritten promises to employees, suppliers, customers, or the community to provide certain future benefits for which the firm has already received economic consideration.

In a variation on this theme, some have argued that mergers and acquisitions are motivated by a desire to transfer wealth from stockholders, creditors, and employees to the investment banking community. Investment banking fees in a large deal can easily run into the tens of millions of dollars. These fees, however, remain a small fraction of the value of the assets restructured, and are small relative to the typical merger premium target shareholders enjoy when a purchaser buys them out.

In the fourth camp, we find arguments that the *tax system* drives mergers and acquisitions. These are the arguments on which we will be focusing. Prior to the 1986 Tax Act, there were four major reasons offered to support the tax claim. These include: (1) avoidance of dividend taxation and other taxes via a liquidation of the firm; (2) a step-up in the tax basis of depreciable assets; (3) the transfer of certain tax attributes to an entity that values them more highly; and (4) the tax advantages of debt financing. We turn next to a discussion of each of these claims.

Alleged Tax Motivations for Mergers and Acquisitions

Liquidation

It was often asserted that prior to the rule changes introduced by the 1986 Tax Act, the tax laws encouraged firms to liquidate so that their shareholders could avoid paying tax on both realized corporate profits as well as unrealized profits from the corporation's appreciated assets. This was allegedly accomplished by effecting a sale of assets followed by a liquidation. Let's take a closer look at these claims.

---

[1] For further discussion of this point, see Michael C. Jensen, "The Eclipse of the Public Corporation," *Harvard Business Review* (September - October 1989), pp. 61-74.

A firm that accumulates earnings and does not pay dividends (or pays a low level of dividends) builds up retained earnings (or "accumulated earnings and profits" as the tax code calls it) in the firm. If stockholders retain their shares, they postpone the payment of personal tax on the accumulation of these earnings until the corporation distributes the retained earnings as a dividend (or until shareholders sell their appreciated shares). Moreover, shareholders escape the income tax on their appreciated shares if they donate them to charity or bequeath them to a beneficiary.

Assume that the firm's stockholders are in a 40% tax bracket. Suppose that accumulated earnings and profits of the corporation are $100 and that shareholders have contributed $10 of capital to the firm. Finally, suppose that the current shareholders have a tax basis in their shares of $10, the amount of contributed capital.

Now suppose that the firm distributes $110 (the market *and book* value of all of its assets) to its shareholders. As a result, $100 would be taxable as a dividend to shareholders, and $10 would represent a nontaxable return of capital. After personal tax, shareholders would retain

$$\$100(1 - .4) + \$10 = \$70.$$

Suppose now that instead of paying out $100 as a dividend, and $10 as a nontaxable return of capital, that the corporation liquidated in the U.S. under old Section 337. If the firm distributed $110 in liquidation, the excess of assets received by shareholders over their basis in the stock (that is, $110 - $10) was taxed, not as a dividend, but as a capital gain. Moreover, prior to the 1986 Tax Act, 60% of long-term gains were excluded from taxation. In that case, after tax, the investors would have retained

$$\$100 (1 - .4 \times .4)) + \$10 = \$94.$$

This is 34% more than the $70 retained in a dividend distribution.

With the 1986 Tax Act's elimination of the 60% exclusion on realized capital gains from taxation, shareholders receive the same after-tax results whether the retained earnings are paid out as dividends or as a capital gain from liquidation. In either case, the taxpayer with a 40% marginal tax rate retains only $70 of the $110 distribution, and liquidation of the firm is no longer tax-advantageous under most circumstances.[2]

Prior to the 1986 Tax Act, the firm could achieve exactly the same tax result for its shareholders as that provided by a liquidation simply by repurchasing shares from its stockholders. In fact, a partial repurchase of shares at market price provides some investors an option to defer the realization of their capital gains. This advantage still persists today.

Indeed, as we discussed in Chapter Seventeen, publicly traded firms have repurchased a significant fraction of their shares in recent years. For example, in 1985 and 1986, share repurchases exceeded 50% of dividend payments and 20% of total cash distributions to shareholders.[3]

---

[2] Where shareholders have capital loss carryforwards that they cannot deduct against ordinary income, however, the liquidation route can still prove advantageous.

[3] Total cash distributions to shareholders include cash paid to purchase shares of a target company in a corporate acquisition.

Another claimed advantage of a liquidation prior to the 1986 Tax Act was the ability of a firm to avoid a corporate-level capital gains tax on a sale of its appreciated assets if it liquidated within one year. (This option remained available from 1987 until 1989 to certain firms with market value of less than $10 million.)

To illustrate, assume in the example above that the $110 worth of assets in the corporation had a tax basis to the corporation of only $60 and that the "accumulated earnings and profits" of the company was only $50 rather than $100 as we assumed previously. In other words, the market value of the firm's assets exceed their tax basis by $50. Suppose further that the assets include depreciable property. If the corporation sells the assets for cash, it incurs a tax on the recapture of depreciation to the extent of gain, and it pays a capital gains tax on the excess of the total gain over the depreciation recaptured as ordinary income. If, for example, the original cost of the assets sold was $90, and $30 of past depreciation has reduced the tax basis to $60, then the sale of assets for $110 would yield $30 of ordinary income recapture and $20 of capital gain.

As a result, prior to the 1986 Tax Act, the tax on the $20 of capital gains, at a corporate tax rate of 28%, would have been $5.60 (or $20 × .28). If the capital gains tax rate following the 1986 Act is 34%, the same sale would generate a capital gains tax of $6.80 (or $20 × .34). In addition, the corporation would be required to pay tax at ordinary rates on any recapture of depreciation. And if the corporation distributes the proceeds from the sale of assets to its stockholders, they are subject to another round of tax at their own personal tax rates.

Prior to the 1986 Tax Act, however, the sale of all of the assets of the firm in a Section 337 plan of liquidation, resulted in the firm avoiding the tax assessed at the corporate level on the $20 of capital gain. As a consequence, the shareholders received an extra liquidating distribution of $5.60 on which they had to pay taxes at their own capital gains rates. Liquidation thereby avoided taxation of the capital gain at the corporate level.

Use of the Section 337 liquidation to avoid the double tax on capital gains came to be called the General Utilities doctrine after a case involving General Utilities (a corporate taxpayer) and the IRS Commissioner. The 1986 Tax Act attempted to repeal this doctrine, and the 1987 and 1988 Tax Acts further restricted the firm and its shareholders from avoiding a corporate-level capital gains tax on the sale of appreciated assets. Any liquidation of the firm after a sale of assets now results in a corporate-level capital gains tax (to the extent there *is* a capital gain). Current rules yield tax results equivalent to what occurs upon the sale of all the firm's assets and a subsequent distribution to stockholders of the after-corporate-tax proceeds from the sale.

In addition to avoiding the corporate-level capital gains tax prior to the 1986 Tax Act on the sale of appreciated assets pursuant to a plan of liquidation, the new owners of the assets were able to achieve a step up in the depreciable basis of the assets, as discussed more fully below. This was often referred to as a "tax-free step up."

The liquidation route, however, was not the only way to avoid the corporate-level capital gains tax. For example, the firm could effect an installment sale of appreciated assets to other firms without liquidating and substantially reduce the present value of the corporate-level capital gains tax. As discussed more fully in the preceding chapter, in an installment sale, the corporation sells the asset and takes back a note for all or part of the sale price of the asset. As a result, the capital gains tax is deferred on that part of the sales price that is covered by the note. The capital gains tax becomes due only as the principal amount of the note is repaid. Moreover, as we discuss in more detail in the ensuing chapters, there are other transactional substitutes for liquidation that mitigate the tax effect of the repeal of the General Utilities doctrine.

At the present time, it is still possible to avoid the tax on a liquidation (or the payment of dividends) by effecting a tax-free merger with another firm. In that case, the target shareholders might exchange their firm's stock for stock in the purchaser without realizing a capital gain at either the corporate or personal level. The cost, however, is that the purchaser cannot change the basis of the target company's assets to garner extra depreciation benefits.

Change in Basis of Assets

It is claimed that the tax code provided incentives for mergers designed to minimize corporate taxes by changing the depreciable basis of assets to achieve a higher level and/or a faster rate of depreciation. These are the so-called "step-up-in-basis" mergers. That is, Purchaser P buys Target T's assets and T liquidates, or P buys all of T's stock and elects that the purchase of stock be treated as if it had acquired T's assets and liquidated the firm (a Section 338 taxable stock acquisition). As a result, P steps up the basis of acquired property to market value (acquisition cost). As was mentioned, T may be subject to tax from the recapture of depreciation or the step-up in basis of certain inventories. But prior to the 1986 Tax Act, if T liquidated, it was not subject to the tax on capital gains (if any) on the sale of its assets. A deceleration of depreciation rates and a lengthening of depreciable lives under the 1986 Tax Act reduced the desirability of changing the basis of acquired assets. The change to a less attractive depreciation schedule, along with the repeal of the General Utilities doctrine, reduced the advantage of a step-up merger.

Transfer of Tax Benefits

Firms with net operating loss carryforwards (NOLs) have an incentive to eliminate their NOLs quickly. The same is true of firms with investment tax credit (and other) carryforwards. Although the Code prohibits the direct sale of tax benefits from one company to another, mergers can be used to sell benefits indirectly as we will discuss in Chapter Twenty-Six. The law *does* attempt to restrict the sale of NOLs (including losses not yet recognized, so-called "built-in losses") and the sale of excess tax credits. The 1986 Tax Act made it tougher for a profitable firm to offset the losses of an NOL firm with other taxable ordinary income.

But there are alternative internal reorganization strategies that result in an acceleration of the firm's use of its NOLs. We talked about these in Chapter Fifteen. For example, the NOL firm can issue high implicitly taxed securities such as preferred stock and use the proceeds to buy high explicitly taxed assets such as fully taxable bonds.

Chapter 23 Introduction to Mergers and Acquisitions

Debt-Financed Mergers or Leveraged Buyouts (LBOs)

When a buyer forms a legal entity for the purpose of acquiring a target with a small amount of equity and a large amount of debt, the transaction is usually called a leveraged buyout (or "LBO"). When the officers of the target are involved in forming the acquisition entity to purchase the target company, this is generally called a management buyout. Most LBOs are financed by financial entities such as investment banking organizations, venture capital groups, and banks. These entities, however, do not provide identical services in LBO(21.2) transactions. For example, banks tend to supply more senior debt (that is, debt that has a higher priority in the event of default) and play a less active role in directing the activities of the restructured enterprise.

Many LBO transactions also involve a series of asset sales subsequent to the acquisition to pay down the LBO debt. These are called "bust-up" transactions. For example, after Kohlberg Kravis Roberts & Co. (KKR) acquired Beatrice, it sold many of its subsidiaries to unrelated parties.

It is claimed that the tax deductibility of interest payments encourages acquisitions that result in the substitution of debt for equity. If the target managers maintain low debt-to-equity ratios, and thereby fail to exploit the tax advantages of debt financing, the interest deduction on new debt financing allows purchasers to acquire such targets at bargain prices.

We have argued that tax reforms in the 1980s encouraged further the use of debt in a merger, because the cost of equity financing appears to have increased relative to the cost of debt financing. As we have discussed, a case could be made that the cost of debt and equity financing were roughly equal to one another for many firms, prior to the Economic Recovery Tax Act of 1981. If debt financing has become increasingly tax-advantageous since that time, however, this begs the question of why the corporation cannot borrow (recapitalize) *without* the need to resort to an LBO. Such a question leads one to consider other nontax costs that make one method of recapitalization more efficient than another (tax-equivalent) method. This is a potentially fruitful line of inquiry in that empirical evidence here may shed light on management entrenchment propensities as well as the efficiency of alternative organizational arrangements.

Leveraged buyouts exploded in economic significance beginning in 1984. In 1983, $4.5 billion of LBOs were recorded by W.T. Grimm as reported in *Mergerstat*. In 1984, by comparison, $18.8 billion of LBOs were registered, followed by $19.6 billion in 1985 and a stunning $46.4 billion in 1986. And the $25 billion LBO of RJR-Nabisco by KKR wasn't even conceived by this time. Nor were the Chapter 11 bankruptcy filings of Campeau and other major LBO transactors. This and other problems relating to the junk bond market resulted in a dramatic decline in LBOs beginning in 1989.

Recap of Tax Factors

These four themes, (1) the sale of assets to effect a change in depreciation basis, (2) a tax-free reorganization to preserve the depreciation basis and other tax attributes, (3) the use of acquisitions to increase leverage, and (4) the ability to avoid a corporate-level capital gains tax on the disposition of some or all corporate assets, are featured throughout the next chapters. Moreover, we consider the tax consequences of restructuring to a target's employees, creditors, and shareholders.

23.2 The Four Basic Acquisition Methods and their Tax Implications

The four main methods for P to acquire T are (1) P's taxable purchase of T's stock, (2) P's taxable purchase of T's assets, (3) P's acquisition of T's stock in a tax-free exchange, and (4) P's acquisition of T's assets in a tax-free exchange. To understand the tax implications of a transaction, it is crucial to keep in mind which of the four methods is being used to effect the transaction. We refer to them repeatedly over the next several chapters.

In a taxable purchase of T's stock, shareholders receive cash or notes for their shares. P's basis in T's stock is generally its purchase price. At P's election (under Section 338) P can be treated as if it purchased T's assets directly. As a result, there is a change in basis, and T's tax attributes (other than an ability to use T's NOL carryforwards to reduce T's recapture and capital gains taxes on the asset sale) will be lost. If P does not elect to treat its purchase of T's stock as an asset purchase, however, the depreciation basis in T's assets is not affected and T's tax attributes are preserved. As discussed in Chapter Twenty-Six, there can be significant restrictions on P's ability to use these surviving tax attributes.

In a taxable purchase of T's assets, T receives taxable consideration for the assets, and it must pay recapture taxes and capital gains taxes on the sale. If T's shareholders retain their shares, they do not realize capital gains or losses until T liquidates or otherwise dispose of their shares.

If P acquires T's *stock* in a tax-free exchange under Section 368, T's shareholders will not generally recognize gains on the exchange of their stock for stock of P. In this case, P is not permitted to step up the basis of T's assets. Moreover, P generally retains T's tax attributes, but as in a taxable purchase of T's stock wherein P does *not* elect under Section 338 to treat the transaction as an asset purchase, P might be limited in its ability to use T's net operating losses, capital losses, and tax credit carryforwards.

If P acquires T's *assets* in a tax-free exchange under Section 368 in exchange for P's stock, and T's stockholders exchange their T stock for P stock, the T shareholders do not pay tax on the exchange. P takes a "carryover" basis in T's assets (that is, the tax basis to P is the same as it was in the hands of T), and P will generally acquire T's tax attributes. But, once again, the use of these attributes may be limited.

23.3 Tax and Nontax Costs of Alternative Restructurings

Tax considerations are clearly important in a merger. A step-up in the basis of assets could increase after-tax cash flows. Leverage reduces taxes. A merger may allow NOLs to be used faster than in the absence of a reorganization. And as we will see, mergers can enhance the tax-planning position of firms with potential alternative minimum tax problems.

On the other hand, all of these tax advantages are counterbalanced to a degree by (1) tax costs that are triggered in the event of an acquisition (such as acceleration of capital gains taxes and tax from the recapture of depreciation) and (2) information-related costs incurred in connection with the merger.

If these tax costs and information costs are netted against the tax gain, there may be no net advantage to a merger transaction. For example, although P can attain a tax benefit for a step-up in the basis of T's assets in a taxable merger, the cost to T can exceed P's benefit. In particular, T must recapture depreciation and potentially pay capital gains taxes, as well as incur other tax and nontax costs. As a result, leaving tax benefits on the table can become the value-maximizing strategy.

As another example, some firms experience very significant NOLs that remain on their books for years (examples include Penn Central, Chrysler, Lockheed and U.S. Steel). We infer from this that the costs to eliminate the NOLs must be very significant.

In a non-taxable merger, P does not change the basis of T's assets, and the tax attributes (such as the NOLs, foreign tax credits, and investment tax credits) of the two firms are preserved under certain circumstances. The tax rules attempt to prevent P from both retaining T's tax attributes and changing the depreciation basis in T's assets.

There are many imperfect substitutes for mergers to garner the tax benefits discussed above. Any analysis that singles out mergers and ignores these competitors is focused too narrowly and fails to address the more important strategic question: under what circumstances are mergers the best reorganization alternative?

It is interesting to note that in a perfect market setting in which transaction costs, asset divisibility costs (the costs of dismantling going concerns), and information costs are ruled out, a narrow focus on tax considerations reveals that many alternative internal reorganization strategies have dominated mergers as a way to garner tax benefits prior to the 1986 Tax Act. During this period, firms could achieve the same gross tax benefits in ways that avoided the tax costs associated with mergers.

Following the 1986 Tax Act, the alternative methods have become even more important, because from a tax point of view, it has become more expensive to use mergers and acquisitions. In fact, many of the current tax rules inhibit the restructuring of corporations or the sale of assets even when they are advisable for other economic reasons. Investment bankers, attempting to restructure organizations to enhance operating efficiency, will find that the tax rules impose sufficient costs in many situations to block otherwise desirable reorganizations.

Summary of Key Points

1. Many have argued that tax rules have been largely responsible for feeding the U.S. merger frenzy in the 1980s.

2. Others have argued that the merger wave of the 1980s was the natural result of both a desire to achieve globalization of markets as well as to achieve an unwinding of the excesses of the conglomerate merger boom of the late 1960s. The unwinding was facilitated by innovations in the capital market (notably the high-yield debt market) and innovations in organization design (notably a heavier loading of incentives on top management and more active monitoring of management by large investors).

3. More generally, the motivations for mergers include a desire to improve operating efficiency by exploiting economies of scale or scope or by removing inefficient management, to build empires, to transfer valuable assets from one class of stakeholders to another, and to secure tax benefits.

4. The alleged tax motivations for mergers have included a desire to enhance depreciation deductions, avoid the payment of corporate-level capital gains taxes, transfer valuable tax attributes like net operating loss carryforwards to a company that values them more highly, and create debt to secure interest deductions and thereby reduce corporate taxes.

5. None of the motivations listed in point (4) is unique to mergers and acquisitions. Indeed, some transactional alternatives can achieve the same gross tax benefits at lower cost.

6. All corporate restructurings involve transaction costs. Mergers and acquisitions may dominate transactional substitutes for achieving certain tax benefits if they can be effected at lower cost than the alternatives.

7. Congress has singled out mergers and acquisitions for special tax treatment. This can either be viewed as a naive way to engineer the tax law (to the extent transactional substitutes are ignored) or a rather sophisticated way to engineer the law (if the special treatment is the end result of evaluating transaction cost differences across the alternatives). Remember, we have argued that market frictions can substitute for restrictions in their effect on tax-planning strategies.

8. There are four basic methods for a purchaser to acquire a target (T): a taxable purchase of T's stock, a taxable purchase of T's assets, a tax-free purchase of T's stock, and a tax-free purchase of T's assets. The term "tax-free" refers to the tax consequences of the transaction to the seller. The methods also differ in their consequences for whether the tax basis of the target's assets is stepped up (or down) to market value in the transaction as well as whether tax attributes like NOLs and tax credit carryforwards survive following the transaction.

9. The 1986 Tax Act made it much more costly to effect certain kinds of mergers with U.S. companies, notably taxable mergers and transactions motivated by a desire to transfer tax attributes like NOLs.

Discussion Questions

1. Why is it sometimes difficult to identify whether a merger (or acquisition) has been effected for tax or for nontax reasons?
2. What is a leveraged buyout? What is a management buyout? Why might a firm sell assets after an acquisition?
3. What factors motivate acquisition transactions? Which do you think are most important?
4. What key tax factors might motivate mergers and acquisitions? Which do you think are most important? Are mergers and acquisitions unique in their tax consequences?
5. How does liquidation of a corporation differ from repurchase of shares from the standpoint of avoiding a shareholder-level tax on accumulated earnings and profits? Why might it be tax-disadvantageous for the firm to liquidate?
6. What is the General Utilities doctrine? Did its repeal with the 1986 Tax Act encourage or discourage mergers and acquisitions? Why?
7. What are the tax benefits and costs of a transaction that changes the depreciable basis of an asset? What are the nontax costs to effecting a change in depreciable basis?
8. What are the tax advantages of transferring T's tax attributes to P? Are there transactional substitutes that T might use to secure these advantages?
9. What are the advantages of an LBO to increase the debt-to-equity ratio in a firm over other alternatives?
10. What are the four basic acquisition methods?

CHAPTER 24
Taxable Mergers and Acquisitions

In the last chapter we introduced the economic and tax motivation for corporate combinations and dissolutions. In this chapter we focus on taxable transactions, of which there are two types. A purchaser may buy either the assets or the stock of a target company. In the latter case, the buyer may elect to treat its stock purchase as if it had acquired all of the target's assets and then liquidated the target company. In either case, a stepped-up (or stepped-down) tax basis in the target's assets is achieved. As a result, the acquired inventory will be charged off and the acquired fixed assets will be depreciated from a base equal to their fair market value at the time of acquisition.

On the other hand, tax must be paid on the ordinary income resulting from the sale of inventory, on any depreciation and other ordinary income recapture, as well as on any taxable capital gains. During the 1980s, the tax rules changed concerning the extent to which gain or loss is recognized on the disposition of assets. The 1987 and 1988 Tax Acts, for example, reduced the extent to which assets sold in exchange for installment notes resulted in the deferral of the payment of the tax on capital gain realized on the sale. Prior to the 1984 Tax Act, the payment of depreciation recapture taxes could also be deferred by using an installment sale. The deferral of recapture and capital gains taxes reduced the cost of selling assets. We introduced these issues in Chapters Twenty-Two and Twenty-Three, and we take a closer look at them in this chapter.

In many ways, the analysis of the effects of a sale of an entire company is very similar to the sale of individual assets as covered in Chapter Twenty-Two. In other ways, it differs. The main difference is that an asset sale allows selectivity in choosing the assets to be written up or down to market value. Moreover, there are likely to be information cost differences in the sale of individual assets and the sale of an entire company. We consider these issues in this chapter.

We also consider the sale of a division or a subsidiary of a large firm. When the assets of a subsidiary are sold, stockholders of the selling parent may face *three* rounds of capital gains taxes, once at the corporate level when the subsidiary's assets are sold, once when the subsidiary's appreciated stock is sold (again, at the corporate level), and finally when the selling parent's stockholders sell their shares.

In an acquisition, the overriding considerations are (1) what happens to the target company's tax attributes (including its NOLs), and (2) what happens if the buyer changes the basis in the target's assets. In this chapter, we concentrate on the second question.

To set the stage, in Table 24.1, we describe five cases that cover the broad spectrum of corporate reorganizations, along with their tax consequences. We defer discussion of Case 5, tax-free reorganizations, until the next chapter.

24.1 Tax Consequences of Alternative Forms of Corporate Acquisitions

Table 24.1 lays out the major tax consequences of corporate acquisitions to the target company, the purchasing company, and to the shareholders of the target company. Note that the target company recognizes a gain or loss on the sale if it sells assets (whether or not the asset sale is followed by a liquidation) *or* if it sells its stock and an election is made (under Section 338) to treat the transaction as a sale of assets followed by a liquidation (under Section 336). By contrast, a sale of stock (*not* accompanied by an election to treat the transaction as a sale of assets) or a tax-free reorganization yields no taxable gain to the target company.

As Table 24.1 indicates, taxable gain recognition by the target company is linked to a change in the tax basis of assets acquired (to market value) for the purchaser. Moreover, with the exception of a sale of assets by a target company that is *not* liquidated (Case 1), a change in tax basis of acquired assets by the purchaser leads to a loss of tax attributes, such as net operating loss and tax credit carryforwards.

As for tax consequences to the shareholders of the target company, the general rule is that where shareholders exchange their stock for valuable consideration, they are taxed on the excess of the value received over their tax basis in the shares. Exceptions to this rule include installment sales of stocks (only for shares in private companies subsequent to the 1986 Tax Act) and tax-free reorganizations (Case 5).

Having outlined the basic tax consequences, we turn next to an analysis of factors that are relevant to choosing among the transactional alternatives. We begin with the sale of individual assets by a company that survives the sale (that is, no liquidation of the target company follows the sale). This is a case we have already begun to analyze in Chapter Twenty-Two.

Case 1: Target Sells Individual Assets without Liquidating

This is our benchmark case. In this transaction, there is no change in the identity of the target's shareholders, and they retain control of the firm. Note from Table 24.1

Table 24.1 Income Tax Treatment of Corporate Acquisitions

Tax Consequences	Case 1: Sale of Assets Without Liquidation	Case 2: Sale of Assets Followed by Liquidation (Section 336)	Case 3: Taxable Stock Acquisition (With Section 338 Election)	Case 4: Taxable Stock Acquisition (No Section 338 Election)	Case 5: Tax-Free Reorganization (Section 368)
To the Target Company					
Immediate Recognition of Gain/Loss on Sales of Assets (including recapture of depreciation)?	Yes[a]	Yes[b]	Yes[b]	No	No
To the Purchasing Company					
Change in Tax Basis?	Yes	Yes	Yes	No	No
Transfer of the Target's NOLs, Credit Carryovers, and Other Tax Attributes?	Retained by Seller[c]	No	No	Yes, but Possibly Limited	Yes, but Possibly Limited
To Shareholders of the Target Company					
Immediate Recognition of Gain/Loss on Exchange of Shares for:					
1. Cash?	N.A.	Yes	Yes	Yes	Yes
2. Bonds/Notes?	N.A.	Yes[e]	Yes[d,e]	Yes[d,e]	Yes[d,e]
3. Stock?	N.A.	Yes	Yes[e]	Yes[e]	No

[a] An installment sale may enable some or all of the taxable gain to be postponed. The opportunities here were diminished with each of the 1984, 1986, 1987, and 1988 Tax Acts.

[b] Prior to the 1986 Tax Act, the General Utilities doctrine allowed firms to liquidate without paying a corporate-level capital gains tax. A Section 338 election is the same as an asset sale followed by a liquidation.

[c] Carryforwards may be reduced by gain recognized on the sale. Certain tax credits may also be recaptured.

[d] Prior to the 1989 Tax Act, it was also possible to defer realization of capital gain with long-term notes or bonds in Section 351 transactions as described more fully in the next chapter.

[e] Prior to the 1986 Tax Act, investors could use the installment sale method to defer the realization of capital gain on the sale of marketable stock. Subsequent to the 1986 Tax Act, installment sales succeed in postponing gain only for stockholders of private companies. Other methods also exist for postponing the gain as discussed in the text.

that the target's shareholders do not pay a direct tax on the asset sale (unless they receive a dividend or sell their shares).

If a firm sells assets for a price that exceeds its tax basis (usually its original acquisition price less accumulated depreciation or amortization since acquisition), it realizes a gain. How the gain is taxed depends on the nature of the assets sold. For example, gains from the sale of inventories and accounts and notes receivable acquired in the normal course of business (for services rendered or inventory sold) give rise to *ordinary income or loss*. Gains from the sale of depreciable property and land used in a trade or business (so-called Section 1231 property) yield *capital gains* (except to the extent that past depreciation must be recaptured as ordinary income as described in Chapter Twenty-Two) or *ordinary losses*. Other assets that might be sold, such as stock held for investment, are capital assets, and their sale triggers *capital gains or losses*. Remember that if a corporation suffers a capital loss, the loss can only be used to offset other current or future realized corporate capital gains.

Reducing the Cost of Selling Assets through Installment Sales

As discussed more fully in Chapter Twenty-Two, if the firm sells an asset in exchange for an installment note, the tax on the capital gain can be deferred at the corporate level, at the taxpayer's election (Section 453), until the gain is realized through repayment of the principal of the note. If capital gains tax rates do not increase, this deferral reduces the present value of the capital gains tax. Even if tax rates increase in the future, the taxpayer might still be able to realize the capital gain in the year prior to the increase. Moreover, taxpayers must trade off the increase in expected tax rates against the present value of the deferral. In many ways this situation is similar to a decision to continue to fund a pension fund when the taxpayer fears that tax rates will increase.

Since passage of the 1987 and 1988 Tax Acts, the seller of the asset that elects installment sale treatment is assessed an interest charge (at the federal applicable rate) on the deferred capital gains tax on aggregate installment sales of more than $5 million in any one year. By using an installment sale, the large asset seller still has an option to realize a capital gain if and when capital gains tax rates should fall in the future. Also, the government bond rate may represent an attractive rate at which to borrow funds, although interest is not deductible until paid on this liability. Moreover, it remains desirable for smaller companies to use installment sales to defer the payment of a capital gains tax on the sale of their assets.

To qualify as an installment sale, the tax rules require, since the 1986 Tax Act, that the installment note be non-marketable. Prior to the 1988 Tax Act, however, it was possible to use the note as security against a loan. Many taxpayers (individual stockholders as well as corporations) would pledge their notes and borrow a like amount (perhaps as much as 90% of the face amount of the note). For example, when Campeau acquired Federated Department Stores, it sold off several of Federated's old divisions to pay down acquisition indebtedness, but instead of receiving cash on the sale, the divisions were sold in exchange for an installment note issued by the division buyers. The installment note deferred the payment of the capital gains tax that resulted from the sale of the assets. Campeau could have left the interest-bearing notes on Federated's books as assets that offset other outstanding debt. It did something essentially equivalent: it issued new debt to pay off the old debt. The new debtholders looked to the installment note as the collateral backing their loan.

The installment sales rules also require that the note be issued by the buyer. But in many situations, the asset's seller does not have the expertise to assess the buyer's credit risks, to monitor the buyer, or to follow up on loan collections. The use of the installment note imposes costs on the seller. These costs are likely to be higher for the seller than for an efficient intermediary such as a commercial bank or an investment bank that regularly follows the market.

One method that may reduce these costs for the seller is for an investment bank to act as the initial purchaser of assets from the seller (perhaps through their merchant-banking operations), issuing its own installment note to acquire the asset. The seller's costs of monitoring the investment bank might be far less than the costs of monitoring the ultimate buyer of the assets. The merchant banker can then resell the assets for cash to the same firm that initially wanted to buy the target's assets. This is an approach that has been used in the public utility industry, involving the sale and leaseback of power plants. There is, however, uncertainty as to the length of time that the merchant banker must hold the assets before resale and the degree to which the merchant banker must be at risk to avoid having the taxing authority view the sale as having been made directly to the ultimate buyer. In any case, the buyer and seller of the assets must be aware of the costs of this alternative route to "securing" the loan.

Another cost of the installment note, discussed in Chapter Twenty-Two, is that the asset seller receives an interest-bearing security, the interest on which is fully taxable as ordinary income. But interest-bearing securities may represent the wrong investment clientele for high-tax-rate sellers.

Case 2: Sale of the Firm's Assets Followed by a Liquidation

Prior to the 1986 Tax Act, a corporation could sell all of its assets and liquidate, and avoid the payment of capital gains tax on the sale of its assets. This is the so-called General Utilities doctrine. This doctrine appeared to favor the complete liquidation of the firm over the alternative of selling assets selectively without a liquidation. While a complete liquidation eliminated the capital gains tax, the sale of an asset resulted in an immediate or deferred capital gains tax. The General Utilities doctrine was eliminated with the 1986 Tax Act (but the installment sales method can still be used to defer the tax on the realization of capital gains for asset sales of under $5 million in aggregate per year at the corporate level).

Many tax planners have invented alternative ways to avoid or defer the payment of the capital gains tax on the sale of a firm or its divisions, and some have been successful. As they have been discovered, however, Congress has issued additional rules to curtail their use.[1]

The advantage of a complete liquidation, however, did not dominate selective asset sales in all cases prior to the 1986 Tax Act. When a firm sells its assets and liquidates, it changes the basis of *all* of its assets. The buyer, on the other

---

[1] Prominent examples include so-called "mirror" transactions and "son-of-mirror" transactions.

hand, might have preferred *not* to change the basis of certain of the firm's assets, as demonstrated below.

Assume that

MV   is the current market value of an asset,
Cost   is the cost of the asset,
D   is the accumulated depreciation or amortization taken on the asset for tax purposes, and that
Basis is the tax basis of the asset. It is equal to Cost - D.

Note that when MV < Basis, sale of the asset triggers a loss. If the assets sold are inventory, receivables, depreciable business property or land used in the business, the loss is an ordinary one. To the extent it is preferable to recognize the losses in a future period (perhaps because of higher expected marginal tax rates in the future), selective asset sales would be preferred to a complete liquidation.

When MV > Basis, sale of the asset triggers a gain, and on most of the firm's property, the gain is recaptured as ordinary income to the extent of D. This means that when Cost > MV > Basis (that is, the current value exceeds the tax basis but does not exceed original cost), the gain is all taxed as ordinary income. Only when MV > Cost was a liquidation *potentially* superior to an asset sale prior to the 1986 Tax Act. In such a case, an asset sale would have resulted in a capital gains tax; however, with a complete liquidation under Section 337, the firm avoided the tax on the capital gain. Subsequent to the 1986 Tax Act, the seller faces a corporate-level capital gains tax on the sale of its assets whether or not such sale is followed by a liquidation.

There are several advantages of individual asset sales over a sale of all of a target's assets. For example:

1. If the target sells all of its assets, the buyer typically would prefer not to change the basis in the assets in cases where Basis < MV < Cost. The change in basis gives rise to immediate taxable income, at ordinary rates due to depreciation recapture, and the step up in basis yields additional depreciation benefits only over time. Unless tax rates are increasing over time, this is undesirable.[2] Taking account of both the tax costs of the recapture and the change in depreciation tax benefits, the present value of this asset sale is typically negative. The asset will not generate after-tax cash flows that are high enough to increase the sale price and justify a higher level of depreciation.

2. In most sales of businesses, the sale price exceeds the market value of the individually identifiable assets, often by very substantial amounts. Much of this excess must often be allocated to goodwill, an asset that is not amortizable for tax purposes in the U.S., although its creation does trigger a capital gains tax to the seller following the 1986 Tax Act. This can be a very significant cost of liquidation. A similar consideration applies to the sale of appreciated land.

---

[2] Note, however, that if corporate tax rates are increased substantially in a future tax act, many corporations may find it desirable to sell assets prior to the increase in tax rates to achieve a step up in basis even if the step up attracts ordinary income tax immediately.

3. Investment Tax Credits (ITCs) are subject to recapture on all assets in a complete liquidation.

4. In fact, when the installment method could be used, prior to the 1984 Tax Act, to defer both the tax on the recapture of depreciation and capital gains, an asset sale with an installment sale might have been more tax-advantageous than a complete liquidation. A liquidation only eliminated the capital gains tax and not the recapture tax. Moreover, if the target company distributed to its shareholders the installment notes that it received on the sale of its assets, and if the shareholders continued to hold these notes, they continued to defer paying the target's capital gains tax (and recapture tax).

5. On a liquidation, the target's tax attributes disappear. As we discuss more fully in Chapter Twenty-Six, the loss of these attributes can increase considerably the costs of a sale of all of the firm's assets followed by a complete liquidation.

6. Moreover, the nontax costs to sell an entire firm might exceed the costs to sell single assets or groups of assets.[3]

Case 3: The Purchase of the Target's Stock Followed by a Section 338 Election

Targets are often acquired in hostile transactions. If a target company does not agree to a friendly merger with a prospective buyer, the buyer often makes a hostile tender offer for the target's stock.

A common procedure to effect a so-called Section 338 transaction is for the acquiring corporation to tender for all of the shares of the target, and after purchasing a significant portion of the shares for cash (or installment debt prior to the 1986 Tax Act), to cause a newly formed subsidiary to merge into the acquired corporation under applicable state law (a so-called "freeze-out merger").

If the purchasing company can acquire at least 80% of the target company's stock (all classes except nonvoting preferred), it can decide whether to change the basis in all of the target's assets. If it decides to do so, the law treats the purchaser as if it acquired all of the target's assets on the day it took control and liquidated the old target company. A new target company is assumed to have been born on that date. The buyer has approximately nine-and-a-half months to make its decision. This time delay makes sense, because in a hostile tender offer, the target might be reluctant to show the purchaser the tax basis of its assets. The buyer needs the time to study whether to change the basis of its newly acquired assets.

The target company's private information about the tax basis of its assets, as well as aspects of the firm's operations, sets the stage for it to call on so-called "white knights" to offer a higher value for its stock. A threatened target might show a prospective "friendly" buyer its tax books in advance of the final tender offer.

---

[3] The reverse, however, could also be true. Suppose that firm profitability is commonly known by a buyer and a seller, but a buyer is uncertain of the individual profitability of business components. Then an information problem may exist for selected asset sales, but the problem can disappear if the entire firm is sold.

24.1   Tax Consequences of Alternative Forms of Corporate Acquisitions

The main tax advantages of either a single asset sale or a sale of all of a target's assets is that the acquiring firm can depreciate these assets using a new and presumably higher tax basis than the old firm was using. There are costs, however, to a stepped-up basis in the assets, as we suggested earlier. These include

1. Depreciation "benefits" occur over time and, as a result,
   a. The value of depreciation benefits depends on changes in interest rates. Lower interest rates or expectations for falling interest rates increase the value of depreciation deductions.
   b. Similarly, expectations of falling tax rates reduce the value of depreciation deductions and increase the cost of early recapture. On the other hand, early step-*down* in depreciation basis, accompanied by an ordinary loss of the sale of assets, is more valuable with an expected future decrease in tax rates.
   c. Different depreciation schedules (new versus old assets) alter the value of the asset's depreciation benefits. Under the 1986 Tax Act, the depreciation lives of real property were extended to 28.5 years for residential real estate and 31.5 years for commercial real estate, and the straight-line method of depreciation became mandatory.[4] Although the depreciation lives for certain types of personal property were extended, the depreciation rates were accelerated with the 1986 Act. The net effect of these tax rule changes is difficult to determine without taking account of changes in interest rates.
2. The payment of tax from the deemed sale of assets is immediate. Incremental depreciation benefits, however, only occur over time. The purchaser must "borrow" to pay a tax now for greater future expected tax benefits, and the nontax costs of such borrowing must be considered. Fewer Section 338 elections occur than would be the case in the absence of these nontax costs.
3. If the purchaser makes a Section 338 election, the target company is assumed to liquidate and all of its NOLs and ITCs (and other tax attributes) expire worthless other than that its NOLs and ITCs can be used to pay the recapture and capital gains taxes that result from the election. The purchaser cannot use its NOLs to offset the target's recapture, other ordinary income, and capital gains taxes. The use of the target's NOLs to pay the recapture and capital gains taxes has its costs. If the target's marginal tax rate were zero, either because its NOLs were about to expire worthless, or because it would not be able to generate future profits to use up its NOLs for many years, then the use of the NOLs to pay the tax costs would reduce the buyer's acquisition costs.

---

[4] As discussed in Chapter Twenty-Two, just prior to the 1986 Tax Act, taxpayers could use accelerated depreciation (150%) for residential real property over a 19-year life. Depreciation was only recaptured on the excess of accelerated over straight-line depreciation. For commercial property, there was no depreciation recapture if the property was depreciated using the straight-line method but there was full recapture of depreciation if the taxpayer used an accelerated method.

(Presumably, the target's shareholders would share this gain, as reflected in the price of the target company shares sold.) On the other hand, the target's marginal tax rate, even in the presence of NOLs, might not be zero or even close to it. As we covered in our concept chapter on marginal tax rates, the target's marginal tax rate might be far closer to the statutory tax rate once its other tax-planning opportunities are considered.

4. In the sale of an entire entity, as opposed to a selective sale of assets, a substantial portion of the purchase price may have to be allocated to land, goodwill, and other nonamortizable assets, rather than to inventory and depreciable assets.

Some acquisition costs are deductible, others are amortizable, and still others are added to the basis of specific assets. For example, the costs of obtaining debt financing are generally amortizable over the life of the debt; the costs of obtaining equity financing are neither deductible nor amortizable; and the transaction costs of buying assets are added to the basis of the assets acquired. Although the purchaser's investment banking fees incurred in connection with the acquisition are allocated to the assets acquired, the purchaser's normal investment banking expenses (such as continuing financial advice) are deductible in the year incurred. Section 162 allows the firm to deduct such ordinary and necessary expenses. It is interesting to note that the investment banking firm recognizes its fees as income in the year earned, while the buyer's deduction may be largely deferred. This is an impediment to restructuring.[5]

Prior to the 1986 Tax Act, the sale price was allocated first to cash and cash equivalents, and then the remainder was allocated to the target's other assets in proportion to their fair market values. After the 1986 Tax Act, firms are required to use the "residual method" to allocate the fair market value of the target's assets. With the residual method, the sale price is first allocated to cash and to cash equivalents. Then the fair market value of marketable securities, certificates of deposit, government securities, foreign currency, etc., is allocated. This is followed by an allocation of the fair market value of receivables, inventory, fixed assets, and then intangibles such as customer lists, plans, formulas, etc. Since goodwill is not amortizable, it is not necessary to calculate a fair market value for goodwill with the residual method. The residual method was instituted to reduce the possibility of allocating too much of the sale price of the firm to depreciable assets.

---

[5] This net tax cost to restructuring is ignored in estimates of the tax advantages of mergers and acquisitions. For an example in the context of the RJR-Nabisco LBO, see Michael C. Jensen, Steven N. Kaplan, and Laura Stiglin, "Effects of LBOs on Tax Revenues of the U.S. Treasury," *Tax Notes* (February 6, 1989).

24.2 Tax Consequences to Selling Stockholders

If the target company sells assets without a complete liquidation, there is no immediate tax consequence to its stockholders (unless shareholders sell their shares in the open market, or unless the target company pays out dividends with some of the sales proceeds). On a complete liquidation, shareholders realize a capital gain equal to the difference between the value of the property distributed and their basis in the stock (Section 331).[6] Note that this capital gain can be much larger than the capital gain on the sale of individual assets, because the firm might also have accumulated earnings, and shareholders must pay a tax on these distributions as well.

Prior to the 1986 Tax Act, if selling shareholders received the buyer's non-marketable debt or installment notes, their capital gains tax was deferred. Following the 1986 Tax Act, however, deferral results only if the target's stock is not publicly traded. Even in this case, each shareholder can avoid paying interest on the deferred capital gains tax on only the first $5 million of installment notes.

Alternatives to Installment Sales to Defer the Payment of Tax on the Sale of Assets

Shareholders have other methods by which they can sell their shares and defer the payment of capital gains taxes, although none of these alternatives are without transaction costs of their own. For example, shareholders can use the technique of "shorting against the box."[7] If you own 100 shares of IBM and sell short 100 shares of IBM, this is called shorting against the box. To sell short, you must borrow 100 shares from another shareholder, say a pension fund (or the "box" at your brokerage house), and sell the stock in the open market. Note that since you have both a long and a short position in the same security, your gain on the date of the short sale is locked in. Any subsequent gain or loss on the long position will be exactly offset by the loss or gain on the short sale and vice versa.

If your broker agrees, you can arrange to receive the cash proceeds of your short sale to use for consumption or other investments. If proceeds from the short sale *cannot* be secured from the broker without the payment of interest, however, this strategy becomes costly. In either case, the tax on your gain is deferred until the short sale is closed out by delivering your IBM shares. Moreover, unlike an installment sale, the basis in your stock will be stepped up to market value on death or upon donation to a qualified charity.

As discussed in more detail in Chapter Twelve, an Employee Stock Owner-ship Plan (ESOP) can also be used to defer the realization of the capital gains tax in certain circumstances. Major shareholders can postpone their gains by selling their shares to the ESOP and reinvesting the proceeds in other marketable securities. This important planning tool has been used rather extensively in closely held businesses.

---

[6] As Case 5 in Table 24.1 indicates, gain is not recognized to shareholders on the exchange of stock in tax-free reorganizations. We take a closer look at such transactions in the next chapter.

[7] For a more extensive discussion involving other strategies, including put and call options, see Jack Crestol and Herman Schneider, *Tax Planning for Investors* (Coopers & Lybrand), 1988, pp. 2-9.

Another strategy for avoiding capital gains to shareholders is to contribute shares to a qualified charity in exchange for a cash annuity from the charity. The formal arrangement is called a "charitable remainder trust," because the charity keeps the remaining value of the property contributed to the charitable trust once the donor has received all the front-end annuity payments as specified in the trust agreement. We will discuss this tax planning strategy further in Chapter Twenty-Seven.

Special Considerations when the Target is a Subsidiary of Another Corporation

As mentioned earlier, when a target's stock is sold to a buyer, and the buyer chooses to step up the basis of the acquired assets to market value, there is the possibility of *three* rounds of tax: capital gain to the target's parent corporation, capital gain to the shareholders of the target's parent, and income tax on the deferred sale of assets on the step up in the target's assets.

There are ways to mitigate the tax in this case. We have already discussed the possibility of the target company using up some of its NOL (or capital loss) carryforwards to offset the realized capital gains and ordinary income on the sale of its assets.

Another possibility involves the use of Section 338(h)(10). To illustrate, suppose the target company files a consolidated return with its parent (which requires that the parent own more than 80% of the target). Further suppose that the parent owns another subsidiary that has NOL carryforwards. If the target company is sold, and the buyer and the parent of the target agree to make a Section 338(h)(10) election, the target's parent can use the NOL and capital loss carryforwards of its other subsidiary to offset the realized capital gains and ordinary income from the sale or liquidation of the target's assets. Of course, this might not be the most efficient use of the subsidiary's NOLs.

In addition, there may be nontax reasons to transfer ownership of assets by selling stock rather than selling individual assets, especially where intangible assets are involved. If the target's parent does sells its stock in the target company to a buyer, the parent will incur a capital gains tax on the sale unless it and the buyer agree to make a Section 338(h)(10) election. *With* such an election, however, the buyer can change the basis in the target's assets without causing the target's parent to realize a capital gains tax on the sale of its stock. This avoids one round of capital gains taxes.

Another important use for Section 338(h)(10) elections is where the target subsidiary has substantial NOLs. As discussed more fully in Chapter Twenty-Six, such valuable tax attributes may disappear or at least diminish substantially in value following a sale of the target's stock. A Section 338(h)(10) election allows the target's parent to retain its subsidiary's tax attributes upon the sale of its subsidiary's stock.

24.3 Transaction Cost Issues

As the discussion thus far indicates, the sale of individual assets can be rather tax-advantageous relative to complete liquidation. These tax advantages include:

1. A selective step-up or step-down in the basis of particular assets.
2. Avoidance of the payment of taxes on inventory gains.
3. Avoidance of triggering a shareholder-level capital-gains tax on all of the target shareholder's stock appreciation.
4. Retention of the target company's tax attributes such as its NOLs, ITC, foreign tax credit, and other tax credit carryforwards, and capital loss and other carryovers.
5. Deferral of a capital gains tax via installment sales.

And with the repeal of the General Utilities doctrine, many corporations face a capital gains tax on liquidation in addition to a tax on depreciation recapture and other ordinary income. The benefits of a stepped-up depreciation basis will not overcome these costs unless tax rates are expected to increase significantly in the future. Therefore, most stock transactions will now occur without an election to change the "inside basis" of assets acquired (a Section 338 election). Indeed, from a tax standpoint, it appears that the tax advantages of selective asset sales *dominate* the sale of all of the assets of the firm followed by its liquidation.

Why, then, have we observed so many transactions involving the sale of *all* of a target's assets or the sale of the target's stock followed by a Section 338 election to change the basis in the target's assets (at least, prior to the 1986 Tax Act)? The answer must lie with transaction costs or information costs. The transaction costs of a single asset sale include:

1. The costs of removing individual assets on their sale. This includes not only physical removal costs but also legal costs associated with title transfers. And it is sometimes difficult to transfer assets such as patents and licensing agreements piecemeal. It is often far easier to transfer such assets by transfering stock ownership in the entire entity.
2. Divisibility costs that result from the sale of pieces of a business. The business might not operate as efficiently following a piecemeal sale of assets. In addition, the sale might trigger other costs such as severance pay and the vesting of pension benefits.
3. The usual information costs associated with current owners being better informed about asset values than are prospective owners. Note that such costs are not *necessarily* higher when assets are sold piecemeal than when the entire business is sold.

With individual asset sales, the seller might be able to mitigate transaction and information costs by a sale of the asset followed by a leaseback to change the basis of an asset if this is desirable for tax purposes. A sale and leaseback transaction might conserve transaction and information costs because:

1. the asset is not removed,

2. divisibility problems are reduced,

3. the old management continues to operate the asset and as a result hidden action and hidden information problems are reduced because much of the risk of owning the asset is retained by the initial owner through the terms of the lease contract,

4. it is possible to use an installment sale coupled with a sale and leaseback to defer the realization of capital gains tax, and

5. no investment tax credits are recaptured on a sale and leaseback transaction.

Note, however, that for assets acquired prior to the 1981 Tax Act, it is not possible to change from a class life depreciation schedule to a current depreciation schedule by using a sale and leaseback transaction. This restriction in the 1981 law was introduced to prevent excessive churning of assets. Congress was able to exploit the fact that natural market frictions would impede asset turnover adequately in transactions *other* than those involving sales and leasebacks.

24.4 Conversion of C Corporations to S Status

Prior to the 1986 Tax Act, it was possible for a regular taxpaying-corporation (a so-called C corporation) to convert to an S Corporation without paying any tax or losing any of its attributes on the change in its status. An S Corporation is a pass-through entity, like a partnership, in which no entity-level tax is assessed. Shareholders report their share of the corporation's income and deductions on their own tax returns. If a corporation can meet the strict requirements of an S Corporation, the 1986 Tax Act made it very tax-advantageous for a C Corporation to convert to an S corporation. Among the many restrictions is the requirement that an S Corporation have 35 or fewer stockholders and only one class of shares.

Subsequent to the 1986 Tax Act, a conversion from a C to an S corporation requires that the S corporation retain the historical tax basis of its assets at the time of conversion for a period of 10 years. On the sale of an asset within the 10-year period, the corporation must pay a capital gains tax on any gain accrued prior to the conversion from C to S status ("built-in" gain) at the maximum tax rate on corporate ordinary income in the year of the sale. This requires that assets be appraised at the point of conversion, and there are obvious incentives to appraise the assets at below market value.

With the 1987 Tax Act, C corporations using the LIFO inventory accounting method must, on converting to S corporation status, include the excess value of any FIFO inventory valuations over LIFO valuations as income over a four-year time period beginning with the year of conversion.

Despite the tax advantages of the noncorporate form of organization under the 1986 Tax Act, very few public firms converted from corporate to noncorporate form. The tax and transaction costs associated with converting to a partnership apparently outweighed the perceived benefits for most publicly traded corporations.[8] But while there are both tax and nontax costs to converting from corporate to partnership form, it seems reasonable to suppose that the nontax costs are relatively small for closely held private corporations.

In this regard, recall from earlier chapters that in 1985, there were approximately 75,000 S Corporation elections. In the 5 *weeks* spanning the end of 1986 and the beginning of 1987 there were approximately 225,000 S Corporation elections, or 3 times as many (over this 5-week period) as occurred throughout all of calendar 1985.[9] The number of corporations electing S status continued at a high rate throughout the remainder of 1987 and through 1988 as well.[10]

24.5 Empirical Results: Domestic Merger and Acquisition Activity in the U.S.

In this section, we present evidence suggesting that the 1981 and 1986 Tax Acts had first-order effects on the level of aggregate merger and acquisition activity in the U.S., despite the presence of transaction cost impediments to trade. We begin by considering the dollar value of mergers and acquisitions in the period surrounding the 1981 Act. Recall that this tax bill, by virtue of its introduction of very rapid depreciation under the accelerated cost recovery system, should have stimulated mergers and acquisitions.

Table 24.2 displays the annual values of mergers and acquisitions from 1968 through 1987 in nominal dollars, constant 1986 consumer price index (CPI) dollars, and constant 1986 S&P 500 stock index dollars. The data source for nominal values is W.T. Grimm and Company (*Mergerstat*) for 1968-1985 and *Mergers & Acquisitions* for 1986 and 1987. There is a slight downward bias in the apparent annual trend for 1986 and 1987, since Grimm uses a minimum $500,000 cutoff value for a transaction to be included in its database, whereas *Mergers & Acquisitions* uses a $1 million cutoff value. The dollar volume of merger and acquisition activity increased 86% in nominal terms between 1980 and 1981, from $44.35 billion to $82.62 billion.[11]

The constant CPI dollar increase was 70%, and the constant S&P 500 dollar increase was 96%. In all cases, the percentage increase was approximately *twice* as large as the next largest percentage increase in annual merger and acquisition activity over the 1970-1986 period.

---

[8] For example, one concern on the tax dimension may have been a perceived possibility of adverse changes in rules governing publicly traded firms that converted to partnership form. Indeed, the 1987 Act requires that most newly created public partnerships be taxed as corporations. Moreover, corporations can mitigate double taxation without converting their legal organizational form by entering into arrangements that result in a tax-deductible distribution of corporate profits (for example, income-participation bonds and their equivalents, incentive compensation arrangements, and income-shifting joint venture partnerships). We discussed this at length in Chapter Eighteen.

[9] *Tax Notes* (2/1/88), p. 434, quoting Ronald Perlman.

[10] Jeffrey K. Mackie-Mason and Roger H. Gordon, "Taxes and the Choice of Organizational Form," Working Paper (April 1991).

[11] Throughout this section, where aggregate dollar values are reported, they are based on the subset of transactions for which dollar values are available. Dollar values are not always available, for example, in transactions involving private sellers.

Chapter 24   Taxable Mergers and Acquisitions

Table 24.2 Merger and Acquisition Values: Nominal Dollar, Constant Dollar, and Constant Stock Index Amounts: Annual Figures, 1968-1987

Year	Nominal Dollar Value of M&A Activity ($Billions)	Constant 1986 Dollar Value of M&A Activity ($Billions)	Constant 1986 S&P 500 Index Value of M&A Activity ($Billions)
1968	43.61		
1969	23.71		
1970	16.42	42.48	86.90
1971	12.62	31.15	58.44
1972	16.68	39.62	64.93
1973	16.67	37.42	76.01
1974	12.47	25.75	77.32
1975	11.80	22.23	53.33
1976	20.03	35.77	73.12
1977	21.94	37.09	86.28
1978	34.18	53.93	126.15
1979	43.54	63.06	135.66
1980	44.35	58.88	104.36
1981	82.62	100.04	204.46
1982	53.76	61.52	109.57
1983	73.08	80.45	121.59
1984	122.22	129.02	191.36
1985	179.77	183.23	212.97
1986	201.37	201.37	201.37
1987	174.99	168.77	166.30
AVG 1970-1980	22.79	40.67	85.68
AVG 1975-1980	29.30	45.16	96.48
AVG 1981-1986	118.80	125.94	173.55
1981-86/1975-80	4.05	2.79	1.80
1981-86/1970-80	5.21	3.10	2.03

Data Sources: *Mergerstat* for 1968-1985 nominal values
Mergers & Acquisitions for 1986-1987 nominal values
1985 *Economic Report of the President* for consumer prices through 1984
Industry Week for consumer prices 1985-1987
Ibbotson Associates (*Stocks, Bonds, Bills and Inflation*) for S&P 500 index values

Although not reflected in Table 24.2, the increase in activity in 1981 did not occur uniformly throughout the year, as might be expected. The 1981 Act was not signed into law until August of 1981, although its passage was widely anticipated much earlier in the year. Moreover, while the accelerated cost recovery system for depreciable property was made effective retroactively to January 1, 1981, this could not have been fully anticipated at the beginning of 1981. It is worth noting that merger and acquisition activity in the first quarter of 1981 was no higher in nominal dollar value than during the fourth quarter of 1980, whereas there was a doubling in the dollar value of activity during the second quarter of 1981 and

511

24.5   Empirical Results: Domestic Merger and Acquisition Activity in the U.S.

an additional increase of 40% in activity during the third quarter of 1981. This increases our confidence that the increase in activity in 1981 was at least in part tax-driven.

Looking over a somewhat longer horizon, the average annual dollar value of mergers and acquisitions in the 6 years between the effective dates of the 1981 Act (January 1, 1981) and the 1986 Act (January 1, 1987 for most of the relevant provisions) was $118.4 billion. This is more than 4 times as large as during the 6 years immediately preceding the effective date of the 1981 Act (and more than 5 times as large as during the average over the 11 years dating back to 1970).

In constant dollar terms, the dollar value of mergers and acquisitions during 1981-86 is 2.8 times as large as during 1975-80 (and 3.1 times as large as the annual average during the 1970-80 period). Adjusted for changes in the consumer price index, mergers and acquisitions during 1981-86 rank first, second, third, fourth, fifth, and seventh over the 17-year period 1970-86. The sum of these ranks (22) for 1981-86 could have been this low or lower purely by chance less than once in 3,000.[12,13]

The dramatic increase in merger activity that began contemporaneously with the passage of the Economic Recovery Tax Act of 1981 is not the only "merger wave" of the twentieth century. Three other periods of unusual merger activity have occurred: the late 1890s to early 1900s, the 1920s, and the 1960s. It may be of interest to note that the termination of the merger wave of the 1960s was accompanied by several regulatory events that discouraged such transactions: the Williams Amendments that increased the difficulty and the costs of effecting tender offers; the issuance of Accounting Principles Board Opinions 16 and 17, reducing the flexibility of acquiring firms in regards to their accounting for mergers (forcing many acquiring firms to increase depreciation expense, cost of goods sold, and goodwill amortization for financial reporting, but not tax, purposes); and the passage of the 1969 Tax Act that, among other things, introduced restraints on the transferability of certain tax attributes such as net operating loss carryforwards.

Researchers have documented a negative response in the value of equity to these regulatory events for firms engaged in active acquisitions programs.[14] Moreover, the data in Table 24.2 display an abrupt and dramatic decline in merger activity from the peak in 1968: *Mergerstat* reports $43.6 billion of mergers and acquisitions in 1968, $23.7 billion in 1969 and an average of $14.4 billion per year for the 1970-1975 period, a decline of 67% in nominal terms (and, of course, larger in real terms) from 1968.

---

[12] Adjusted for the level of the Standard and Poor's 500 stock index, the rankings during 1981-86 are first, second, third, fourth, seventh, and eighth out of 17. Such an extreme ranking could occur by chance less than once in 1,000. In nominal dollars, the rankings during 1981-86 are first, second, third, fourth, fifth, and sixth out of 17. Such an extreme ranking could occur by chance less than once in 6,000.

[13] While the significance levels reported for the rank sum tests are in some respects conservative (in that they rely only on ordinal information), they also assume independence across observations, a condition that may well be violated. Consequently, significance levels should be viewed with caution.

[14] See Katherine Schipper and Rex Thompson, "Evidence on the Capitalized Value of Merger Activity for Acquiring Firms," *Journal of Financial Economics* (April 1983), pp. 85-119.

Chapter 24   Taxable Mergers and Acquisitions

As a note of caution, however, it is also worth emphasizing that we have not controlled for contemporaneous nontax factors that may have influenced merger activity over the survey period. For example, the Reagan administration has been viewed as being relatively passive in the antitrust arena, which removes one impediment to mergers and acquisitions. On the other hand, it is not clear that tax policy in general, and the provisions of the 1981 Act in particular, should be viewed as being independent of antitrust policy (or, indeed, other regulatory policies such as those relating to foreign trade).

Among the explanations that have appeared in the institutional literature for the merger activity in the 1980s is the development of the "junk" (that is, high risk/high yield) bond market. The public issues of junk bonds as a fraction of total public bond issues increased from 6.3% in the 1977-80 period to 14.8% in the 1981-86 period.[15] It is also interesting to note that Drexel Burnham began selling junk bonds to effect leveraged buyouts in 1981.

Two comments are in order here. First, Taggart cites evidence suggesting that junk bonds were hardly used in 1984 and 1985 in mergers and acquisitions. Drexel Burnham estimated that such securities were associated with 1.4% and 2.7% of total merger financing in 1984 and 1985, respectively, while Morgan Stanley estimated that junk bonds accounted for 2.6% and 4.5% of the merger financing in those years. Second, even this level of development of this market may be due, at least in part, to a tax-induced demand.

Evidence Relating to the Tax Reform Act of 1986

As indicated earlier, the restructuring of the Tax Code in 1986 should have reduced substantially the incentive of U.S. firms to buy *other* U.S. firms for tax purposes.[16] Taxpayers, however, were given an advance warning of a calendar quarter's duration of the massive changes to take place. The law was passed early in the fourth quarter of 1986, and there was substantial uncertainty as to whether it would pass prior to this time; but the changes in rules did not go into effect, with respect to depreciation, installment sales, net operating losses, ordinary income recapture items, the General Utilities doctrine, and both ordinary and capital gains tax rates, until January 1, 1987.

Table 24.3 displays quarterly merger and acquisition activity (transactions between U.S. companies only) in nominal dollar, constant 1987-4 CPI dollar, and constant 1987-4 S&P 500 Index dollar amounts for the 9 quarters centered on 1986-4, the quarter in which the 1986 Act was passed. The dollar volume of mergers and acquisitions during the fourth quarter of 1986 of $64.65 billion represents a record, in both nominal and real terms, over at least the past 50 years. It exceeds the average volume for the 8 quarters surrounding it by 85% in nominal dollars, 86% in constant dollars, and 93% adjusted for the level of the S&P 500 stock index.

---

[15] See Robert A. Taggart, Jr., "The Growth of the 'Junk Bond' Market and its Role in Financing Takeovers," in *Mergers and Acquisitions*, edited by Alan J. Auerbach (University of Chicago Press, 1988), pp. 5-24.

[16] Recall from Chapters Thirteen and Fourteen on multinational tax planning that the incentives (and experience) for foreign buyers of U.S. businesses was quite different from those of U.S. buyers.

513

24.5   Empirical Results: Domestic Merger and Acquisition Activity in the U.S.

Table 24.3 Merger and Acquisition Values: Nominal Dollar, Constant Dollar, and Constant Stock Index Amounts

Quarterly Figures: 1985-4 through 1987-4

Transactions between U.S. Companies Only

Quarter	Nominal Amount ($ billions)	Rank Excluding 1986-4	Constant 87-4 CPI Amount ($ billions)	Rank Excluding 1986-4	Constant 87-4 S&P Amount ($ billions)	Rank Excluding 1986-4
1985-4	45.93	1	48.60	1	57.26	1
1986-1	29.97	7	31.65	7	32.75	5
1986-2	44.55	2	47.15	2	45.97	2
1986-3	34.86	4	36.65	3	38.67	3
SUM	155.31	14	164.05	13	174.65	11
AVG	38.83		41.01		43.66	
1986-4	64.65		67.44		68.03	
1987-1	21.66	8	22.38	8	18.78	8
1987-2	32.97	6	33.63	6	27.20	6
1987-3	33.66	5	33.96	5	26.04	7
1987-4	35.82	3	35.82	4	35.82	4
SUM	124.11	22	125.79	23	107.84	25
AVG	31.03		31.45		26.96	
PROB*		.1714		.1000		.0286

*PROB denotes the probability that the sum of the ranks in the four quarters preceding 1986-4 could be as low as or lower than the sum of the ranks in the four quarters succeeding 1986-4 by chance alone.

Data Sources: *Mergers & Acquisitions* for nominal values
Industry Week for consumer prices
Ibbotson Associates (*Stocks, Bonds, Bills and Inflation*) for S&P 500 Index values

While these data provide clear evidence of a bulge in activity during the fourth quarter of 1986, we are also interested in documenting a decline in activity post tax reform relative to pre tax reform. Table 24.3 documents a decline in mergers and acquisitions from the 4 quarters preceding tax reform to the 4 quarters succeeding tax reform by 20% in nominal dollars, 23% in constant dollars and 38% adjusted for the level of stock prices as reflected in the S&P 500 index. Using a simple rank sum test, we can reject the hypothesis that the level of post-reform activity was drawn from a distribution with at least as large a mean as was the pre-reform activity, adjusted for changes in consumer prices and the S&P 500 stock index, at levels of 10% and 3%, respectively.

In nominal dollars, the decline in activity is *not* significant at conventional levels using only rank information. But the decline in merger and acquisition activity of $31 billion ($124 billion - $155 billion) is larger than any annual decline between 1970-1986. This could have occurred by chance with probability equal to .0625. The 22% decline in activity (in nominal dollar terms) in 1987 stands in

Chapter 24 Taxable Mergers and Acquisitions

contrast to the average *increase* of over 35% during the 6 years following passage of the 1981 Act.

The data in Table 24.3 include leveraged buyouts. We have argued that the 1986 Tax Act encouraged debt financing, so leveraged buyout activity might be expected to *increase*, although more conventional acquisitions were expected to decrease subsequent to the Act. In fact, *Mergers and Acquisitions* reports $35.7 billion of leveraged buyouts in 1987, versus $30.5 billion in the 4 quarters prior to the fourth quarter of 1986.

In terms of the *number* of merger and acquisition announcements, the decline in 1987 is even more dramatic than indicated in Table 24.3. According to *Mergerstat Review*, U.S. buyers announced 2804 deals in 1985 and 3072 deals in 1986, compared to only 1812 deals in 1987, a 41% drop. Moreover, the number of deals involving U.S. buyers remained well below the pre-1986 Tax Act level through 1990: 1951 in 1988, 2081 in 1989, and 1808 in 1990.

On the other hand, the dollar value of merger and acquisition activity in 1988 and 1989 was very high. U.S. buyers of U.S. businesses accounted for $176.9 billion and $159.9 billion of deals in 1988 and 1989, respectively. As the collapse of the high-yield debt market took effect in 1990, however, the volume crashed to a level of $57.1 billion.

Several factors help to explain the high dollar volume of activity in 1988 and 1989. First, leveraged buyouts (LBOs) continued at a frenzied pace, and this is consistent with the tax incentives provided by the 1986 Tax Act. *Mergers and Acquisitions* reports $43.4 billion of LBOs in 1988 and $61.8 billion in 1989, including the huge RJR-Nabisco transaction recorded in the second quarter of 1989. Second, the 1986 Tax Act provided special tax favors for the bank and thrift industry, favors that promoted acquisitions of weak institutions. *Mergerstat* reports $12.2 billion and $18.6 billion of acquisition in the "banking and finance" industry in 1988 and 1989, respectively. And finally, 1988 and 1989 saw the sale of many divisions of companies that had been merged or acquired in previous years. To the extent such "bust-ups" were part of the plans that motivated the initial take-overs, such divestitures are really attributable to these earlier transactions. In this regard, it may be worth noting that, based upon data reported in *Mergerstat*, the number of divestitures, as a fraction of total merger and acquisition transactions, increased from 37% during 1981-86 to 42% during 1988-89.

Nontax Costs of Reorganization and Transactional Responses

The evidence presented thus far suggests very strongly that changes in the tax laws passed in 1981 and 1986 affected merger and acquisition activity. We have also alluded to nontax costs that diminish the level of activity relative to what would be observed if tax minimization were the goal of corporate managers. In this section, we inquire as to whether there is any evidence of organizational arrangements designed to reduce the magnitude of nontax costs in tax-motivated transactions. In particular, we consider evidence on management buyouts of divisions.

At the broadest level of analysis, we can think of merger and acquisition transactions as being motivated by two categories of economic forces: tax factors and nontax factors. We argued earlier that tax-motivated transactions should have increased in importance during the 1981-1986 period. Suppose that the transaction costs associated with the sellers of assets being better informed than prospective buyers about asset values are lower when shareholders sell the assets to incumbent managers than when the assets are sold to outsiders. To take an extreme example, suppose that the value of the assets available for sale is commonly known by the current management group and the independent members of the Board of Directors, who must approve the terms of sale. Prospective non-manager buyers from the outside, however, are less well-informed regarding asset values. Then ignoring risk-sharing considerations, the nontax costs of a sale will be lower in a transaction with management relative to one involving outsiders.

Suppose further that the source of nontax gains to a merger or acquisition may be either managers or outsiders (although the range of nontax benefits is much wider for outsiders), but that the tax-related gains are common to both prospective buyer groups.[17] When the nontax gains are large, it is outsiders that are most often the source of this value. They can, therefore, often afford to bid more for the right to purchase the firm (or a division) than can incumbent management despite their disadvantage along the hidden information dimension. But when the nontax benefits of the transaction are small relative to the tax benefits, incumbent management will typically be the most efficient purchasers due to their advantage along the hidden information dimension. The 1981 Act should have increased the frequency of cases in which the common tax benefits are large relative to the nontax benefits of mergers and acquisitions. As a consequence, we should observe an increase in the proportion of transactions involving management buyouts.[18]

Turning to the evidence, *Mergerstat* reports annual data on management buyouts of divisions and total divestitures beginning in 1978. As Table 24.4 indicates, there was a significant increase in the fraction of divestitures effected by way of management buyouts in the 1981-86 period relative to the 1978-1980 period. More specifically, the fraction of divestitures in which a public announce-ment was made that an executive of the parent company or members of the selling division's management were included among the purchasing group increased from 6.93% during the 1978-1980 period to 12.22% during the 1981-1986 period. While the total number of divestitures increased by 34% from 746 per year during 1978-1980 to 1002 per year during 1981-1986, the number of unit management buyouts increased by 137% from 51.7 per year to 122.5 per year. Whereas the maximum fraction of unit management buyouts to total divestitures in any given year in the 1978-1980 period was 7.85%, the *minimum* fraction was 10% in 1981-1986, and this occurred in 1981, the transition year. Using only rank information for these fractions, the increased management buyout activity after 1980 is statistically significant at the 1% level.

---

[17] In truth, a component of the tax-related gain may increase with the level of nontax gains to merger, as discussed in Ronald J. Gilson, Myron S. Scholes, and Mark A. Wolfson, "Taxation and the Dynamics of Corporate Control: The Uneasy Case for Tax-Motivated Acquisitions," in *Knights, Raiders and Targets: The Impact of the Hostile Takeover*, edited by John C. Coffee, Jr., Louis Lowenstein, and Susan Rose-Ackerman (Oxford University Press), 1987.

[18] We develop these ideas further within a formal model in "The Effects of Changes in Tax Laws on Corporate Reorganization Activity," *Journal of Business* (January 1990), pp. S141-65.

Chapter 24   Taxable Mergers and Acquisitions

Table 24.4 Unit Management Buyouts
Annual Figures: 1978-1990

Year	Total Divestitures	Management Buyouts	Percentage Management Buyouts	Rank (1978 - 1986)	Rank (1981 - 1990)
1978	820	49	6.0%	9	-
1979	752	59	7.9%	7	-
1980	666	47	7.1%	8	-
SUM	2238	155	6.9%	24	-
1981	830	83	10.0%	6	7
1982	875	115	13.1%	3	3
1983	932	139	14.9%	1	1
1984	900	122	13.6%	2	2
1985	1218	132	10.8%	5	6
1986	1259	144	11.4%	4	4
SUM	6014	735	12.2%	21	23
PROB*				.0119	-
1987	807	90	11.2%	-	5
1988	894	89	10.0%	-	8
1989	1055	91	8.6%	-	9
1990	940	63	6.7%	-	10
SUM	3696	333	9.0%	-	32
PROB*				-	.0190

*PROB denotes the probability that the sum of the ranks in the 3 years preceding 1981 or the 4 years succeeding 1986 could be as high or higher than the actual values (of 24 for 1978-80 and 32 for 1987-90) by chance alone.

Data Source: *Mergerstat Review* (Merrill Lynch)

Note: Data Unavailable Prior To 1978

The results are even more striking in dollar value terms. Whereas the annual dollar value of merger and acquisitions increased by a factor of 3 between 1978-1980 and 1981-1986, the annual dollar value of unit management buyouts increased by a factor in excess of 20.[19]

Moreover, subsequent to the 1986 Act, where the tax advantage to selling divisions was reduced (except for debt-financed transactions), unit management buyouts as a fraction of total divestitures once again decreased. Specifically, only 9.01% of all divestitures during the period 1987-90 were unit management

[19] It is worth noting that going-private transactions, where a public company is taken private, also increased substantially as a fraction of all public takeovers during 1981-86. *Mergerstat* reports going-private data dating back to 1979. Whereas the average number of going-private transactions was 7% of public takeovers during 1979-1980, it was 19% during 1981-1986. Once again, 1981 was a transition year with 10.1% of the public takeovers being going-private transactions. Using only the information reflected in the ranks of these fractions, the relatively low level of going-private activity in the 1979-1980 period could have occurred by chance alone with probability equal to 4%. In addition, the annual

24.5 Empirical Results: Domestic Merger and Acquisition Activity in the U.S.

buyouts, down from 12.22% during the period 1981-86. As Table 24.4 indicates, the decrease in management buyout activity in the post-1986 period could have occurred by chance alone fewer than 2 times in 100.[20]

24.6 Leveraged Buyouts and Tax Revenues

It is sometimes argued that leveraged buyouts (LBOs) generate revenue losses to the Treasury through tax subsidies.[21] Jensen, Kaplan, and Stiglin, however, argue that the typical LBO generates *positive* incremental revenues for the Treasury.[22] They point out five ways in which LBOs do so:

1. Realized capital gains to shareholders;
2. Increased taxable operating income of LBO firms, due to increased operating efficiency;
3. Interest income on LBO debt is taxed;
4. Increased taxable income of LBO firms due to increased capital efficiency; and
5. Subsequent sale of assets by LBO firms generate additional capital gains that are taxed.

The gains in tax revenues are estimated by Jensen, *et al.*, to exceed the revenue losses due to increased interest deductions for LBO firms and reduced dividend income to LBO firm shareholders. In fact, for the typical LBO of $500 million, they estimate increased tax revenues of $110 million, as summarized in Table 24.5. Since they assume incremental taxable income from operating efficiencies and avoidance of wasteful capital expenditures of $250 million and $88 million, respectively, in present value, this represents a tax rate on incremental income of 32.5% (or 110/(250+88)), a respectable rate.

---

average dollar volume of going-private transactions increased by a factor of 14 between the two periods, whereas the dollar volume of all mergers and acquisitions increased by a factor of only 2.7. To the extent going-private transactions are effected by incumbent managers, these data provide further evidence consistent with our management buyout story.

[20] As for going-private transactions, they became the darlings of the leveraged buyout industry in the mid-to-late 1980s, so such transactions, although they virtually ceased in 1990, remained a healthy fraction of all public takeovers during 1987-89.

[21] For example, see Laura Saunders, "How the Government Subsidizes Leveraged Takeovers," *Forbes* (November 1988), pp. 192-196.

[22] Michael C. Jensen, Steven Kaplan, and Laura Stiglin, "Effects of LBOs on Tax Revenues of the U.S. Treasury," *Tax Notes* (February 6, 1989), pp. 727-33.

Table 24.5 Tax Revenue Implications of a Typical LBO
(Taken from Jensen, *et al.*, 1989)
(Amounts in $ millions)

I Typical LBO Features

Prebuyout market value of equity	$360
Buyout purchase price	500
Incremental debt	400
Tax basis of selling shareholder's stock	290
Postbuyout value of equity (in 5 years)	750
Taxable capital gain to prebuyout shareholders (500 - 290)	210
Capital gain to buyout investors (750 - 500)	250

II Incremental Tax Revenues and Tax Losses to U.S. Treasury

Incremental Revenues

Capital gains taxes

At buyout: $210 \times 70\%^a \times 28\%^b$	$41.2
At subsequent restructuring: $250 \times 30\%^c \times 28\%^b \times .62^d$	13.0
Taxes on increased operating income: $100^e \times .25^f \times .34^g \times 10^h$	85.0
Taxes on LBO creditors' income: $400 \times .6^i \times .5^j \times .34^g$	40.8
Taxes from increased capital efficiently:	
$44^k \times .2^l \times .1^m \times .34^g \times 10^n \times 10^h$	29.9
Taxes to selling corporation on subsequent sale of assets:	
$500 \times .2^o \times .5^p \times .34^g$	17.0
	$226.9

Incremental Tax Losses

Tax deductibility of interest payments on debt: $-400 \times .6^i \times .34^g$	-81.6
Taxes on foregone dividend payments: $-.05^q \times 360 \times .7^a \times .28^b \times 10^h$	-35.3
Net Incremental Tax Revenues to U.S. Treasury	$110.0

[a] Percent of stock owned by taxable shareholders at buyout.

[b] Capital gains tax rate.

[c] Percent of stock owned by taxable shareholders at postbuyout sale.

[d] Present value factor for cash flows in 5 years discounted at 10% per year.

[e] Typical operating income prebuyout.

[f] Incremental operating income of 25% postbuyout due to increased efficiency.

[g] Corporate tax rate.

[h] The present value of a perpetuity of one dollar discounted at a rate of 10% per year is $10.

[i] Percent of incremental debt deemed to be permanent.

[j] Percent of debt held by taxable investors.

[k] Typical capital expenditure amount of prebuyout firm.

[l] Typical reduction in capital expenditures *per year* postbuyout.

[m] Reduced capital expenditures is assumed to be returned to shareholders where it earns this rate (10%) per year before tax, whereas the capital expenditure would have been a waste (earning 0% before tax).

[n] The 10% pretax income savings for each dollar of capital spending reduction is expected to recur in perpetuity, so this is the present value factor at a discount rate of 10%.

[o] Sale of 20% of the $500 million of LBO assets is assumed to take place within a year of the LBO.

[p] The basis of the assets sold within a year of the LBO is assumed to be equal to half the sales price, so the other half is a taxable gain.

[q] Reduction of dividend of 5% on $360 million worth of equity.

Although Jensen, *et al.*, deserve much credit for taking a stab at generating these tax revenue estimates, each calculation is controversial. To mention but a few:

1. Some of the accrued capital gains preceding the LBO would have yielded taxable income even in the absence of the LBO as shareholders sold their stock for liquidity and other reasons.

2. Jensen, *et al.*, assume that a $250 million capital gain would be recognized by investors post-LBO (in 5 years) through a restructuring transaction. But some capital gain (possibly a significant amount) would also have been realized even in the *absence* of an LBO, and this is ignored. Moreover, not all restructurings trigger a current tax. Examples include going public and issuing stock to repurchase debt.

3. It is assumed that LBOs are *responsible* for the increase in value of target companies. But some LBOs may result because the market fails to recognize that firms are simply undervalued. To the extent the latter is the case, then some of the stock appreciation (and related capital gains) would have occurred *anyway*. Similar arguments apply to the increased operating income often observed following LBOs.

4. The interest rate on debt and the discount rate used to calculate the present value of the after-tax cash flows are the same, 10%. But one is a before-tax rate, while the other is an after-tax rate. This can substantially understate the lost revenue due to the excess of interest deductions over interest income.

5. The assumed incremental taxes from increased capital efficiency is a reflection of the Jensen "free cash flow" argument: many buyout candidates are those with lots of cash flows that should be returned to investors rather than squandered through unproductive reinvestment. This, too, is controversial. Indeed, some have argued that reduced investment in LBOs is a *problem* in that profitable projects go unexploited.

   The calculations here also assume implicitly that capital equipment does not depreciate in value. This overstates the efficiency gains and incremental tax revenues that result.

6. The calculations ignore the possibility of generating NOLs that are carried back to years when tax rates were 40% or 46%.

Adjustments to reflect the factors above, plus others, would cast the analysis in a rather different light. Whether LBOs generate incrementable tax revenues, and if so, whether the tax rate on incremental income generated is equitable, will continue to be controversial. The answers may well differ from transaction to transaction.

Summary of Key Points

1. As discussed in Chapter Twenty-Two, there are both tax costs and tax benefits to selling individual corporate assets. Similarly, there are tax costs and tax benefits to selling *all* of a corporation's assets in an asset or stock acquisition transaction.

2. Mergers and acquisitions can be effected through a number of transactional forms. These alternative forms yield varying tax consequences to the target company, to the purchasing company, and to the shareholders of the target company.

3. Mergers and acquisitions that allow the buyer to step up the basis of assets acquired typically result in a loss of the target's tax loss and tax credit carryforwards, as well as other tax attributes of the target company. Such transactions also subject the target company to ordinary and capital gains tax. An example of such a transaction is a sale of the target's assets followed by a liquidation of the target company.

4. When the stock of a target company is acquired, the buyer may elect (under Section 338) to treat the transaction *as if* the target's assets had been acquired, followed by a liquidation of the target company.

5. Prior to the 1986 Tax Act, there was a tax advantage to effecting a corporate liquidation following the sale of *all* of a target company's assets: under the so-called General Utilities doctrine, the corporate-level capital gains tax on the appreciation in the value of the assets was forgiven.

6. Corporate liquidations (or stock acquisitions followed by so-called Section 338 elections to step up the basis of assets to market value) introduce tax costs, however. And assets cannot be stepped up in basis *selectively*, although it may be desirable to do so. Moreover, such transactions may cause valuable tax attributes, such as operating loss and tax credit carryforwards, to expire worthless.

7. Although it may be desirable for tax purposes to sell a subset of a target's assets to a buyer, there can be significant transaction cost differences in selling individual assets relative to selling all of the assets.

8. The 1986 Tax Act repealed the General Utilities doctrine and reduced the tax benefit of stepping up the depreciable basis of assets by reducing tax rates and decelerating depreciation schedules. This made taxable acquisitions desirable in substantially fewer cases.

9. Evidence suggests that the 1981 Tax Act contributed to significant increases in mergers and acquisitions in the U.S. The volume of such transactions nearly doubled in 1981 from 1980, and the volume of activity during 1981-1986 was nearly three times the level in the 1975-1980 period, adjusted for inflation.

10. The 1981 Tax Act also encouraged management buyouts of divisions. For example, the fraction of divestitures in which the existing management was among the buyers increased from an average of only 6.9

percent between 1978 and 1980 to 12.2 percent between 1981 and 1986. Moreover, unit management buyouts decreased to 9.0 percent of divestitures during 1987-90 as the 1986 Tax Act made such divestitures less tax-favored.

11. Evidence suggests that the 1986 Tax Act significantly discouraged mergers and acquisitions between U.S. companies. There was an explosion of activity in the fourth quarter of 1986 as firms rushed to transact prior to the effective date of most of the new, less liberal rules. And the volume of activity dropped over 20% in 1987 relative to the 4 quarters preceding the fourth quarter of 1986.

Discussion Questions

1. What are the main tax considerations in the sale of a target's stock to a purchaser?

2. Why is it tax advantageous for the firm to use an installment note in connection with the sale of assets? What are the potential tax and nontax costs of using an installment sale?

3. Why might the use of installment notes in conjunction with assets sales be more important for small than for large corporations after 1988?

4. What are the disadvantages of effecting a change in the basis of all of the firm's assets either by their sale, followed by a complete liquidation, or by a stock purchase, along with an election to treat the stock purchase as a purchase of all of the firm's assets followed by a liquidation?

5. Are many firms likely to make a Section 338 election subsequent to the 1986 Tax Act? What are the benefits and costs of changing the basis in a target company's assets?

6. Since a purchaser can use a target's NOL carryforwards to offset the ordinary and capital gain and recapture tax on the sale of the target's assets, it has been argued that this reduces the cost of achieving a stepped-up basis in assets and makes it advantageous for the purchaser to acquire the target. Do you agree with this line of argument?

7. Under what conditions is it advantageous to make a Section 338(h)(10) election? Is this method preferred to a sale of selected assets using an installment sale?

8. Why might the IRS have convinced Congress to adopt the so-called residual method of allocating the fair market value of a target company's assets to specific assets?

9. What are the advantages of a sale and leaseback transaction to effect a change in an asset's basis?

10. How has merger and other reorganization activity in the U.S. been affected by changes in U.S. tax laws in the 1980s?

11. Refer to Section 24.6 on leveraged buyouts. What adjustments would you make to the Jensen, Kaplan, and Stiglin revenue estimates to gauge the effect of LBOs on tax revenues collected by the U.S. Treasury?

Problem

The House Ways and Means Committee issued a press release on April 12, 1989 announcing that it would hold hearings the next month on tax policy issues relating to mergers and acquisitions, ESOPs, LBOs, and corporate leverage. The Committee had proposed specific legislative options, but had not decided whether to propose changes in the tax treatment of debt and equity or mergers and acquisitions.

The Committee requested testimony and invited public comment on each option, including the impact on specific industries, on the market for corporate control, and on domestic and international markets. The Committee sought comments on fairness and on the tax and economic policy implications of the options, including the strengths and weaknesses of each.

The 1989 Tax Act included legislation that sought to curb LBOs, ESOPs, leveraged recapitalizations, and mergers and acquisitions more generally. Some of the proposed changes were implemented; and a number of others will continue to be debated in Congress over the coming years.

A copy of the press release follows. You have just been hired by a leading investment banking firm, and you made the mistake of mentioning that you had acquired skills in applying tax-planning concepts to corporate reorganization strategies. The partner in charge of your group has asked you to comment on several sections in the press release in a written report of three to five pages. You need not address all sections of the press release in your report. Instead, you can concentrate on those few sections about which you are most passionate and can muster the best arguments. Note, however, that you may be asked to express oral opinions on the other sections not addressed in your write-up.

The Honorable Dan Rostenkowski, D-Ill., Chairman, Committee on Ways and Means, U.S. House of Representatives, announced today that the committee will continue its hearings on tax policy issues with respect to mergers, acquisitions, leveraged buyouts, and recent increases in corporate debt. The hearing will be held on May 16 through 18, 1989, beginning at 10:00 a.m., in the committee's main hearing room, 1100 Longworth House Office Building.

In announcing the continuation of these hearings, Chairman Rostenkowski stated: "The committee plans to continue its comprehensive review of the complex issues surrounding the tax treatment of corporate debt and equity. Earlier this year, the committee conducted five days of public hearings on these issues. Based upon the testimony received by the committee and the interest of the members in these issues, I asked that members submit legislative options for consideration by the committee in a public hearing. In this way, the committee will be provided the opportunity to receive testimony on specific options for change before any decision is made to legislate on these issues.

"The options submitted for review by the members, along with options submitted by staff, are contained in this press release. I want to emphasize that no decision has been made by the committee at this time regarding whether or not to draft legislation proposing to change the tax treatment of corporate debt and equity. The options contained in this press release are listed for purposes of public comment only."

SCOPE OF THE HEARINGS

A. Comments Applicable to All Legislative Options

The committee invites the public to comment on a series of legislative options submitted by members of the committee and staff. Testimony is requested concerning the fairness of each proposal, and the tax and economic policy implications of each option. In addition, the committee requests testimony regarding the practical feasibility and administrability of each proposal. Also, the committee is interested in comments comparing the relative strengths and weaknesses of the various options.

The committee anticipates that if any option is ultimately considered for legislative action, such option would contain fair and adequate transition relief for transactions in which taxpayers have reasonably relied upon existing rules. It is anticipated such relief would be designed so as not to disrupt the orderly conduct of financial markets. The committee invites testimony on the proper scope of transition relief for each legislative option.

The revenue impact, if any, of the following options is unknown. It is anticipated that if any option is ultimately considered for legislation and such option would increase revenues, such revenues would be utilized to finance related options providing some form of tax relief, such as proposals allowing a deduction or credit for payments made by a corporation with respect to equity. It should also be noted that because of budget constraints, the committee anticipates that options which, if enacted, would result in a loss of revenue could only be considered along with companion options which would raise a similar amount of revenue.

The committee requests testimony on the potential impact, if any, of each option on domestic and international markets. In addition, testimony is requested regarding the possible impact of any option on the competitiveness of U.S. corporations with foreign acquirers.

Moreover, with respect to each option affecting foreign persons, the committee is interested in receiving comments on the discriminatory or nondiscriminatory nature of the option, and on proposals for eliminating any perceived or actual discrimination. In addition, comments are requested regarding any potential impact on current and future tax treaties with foreign countries.

The committee also requests testimony on the potential impact, if any, of each option on specific industry segments, such as small business or financial institutions, including possible modifications of options which should be considered by the committee. In addition, testimony is invited regarding whether threshold dollar amount exceptions are advisable with respect to any of the options.

Testimony is specifically requested regarding limiting the applicability of any option to transactions involving a high-dollar threshold, such as $100 million. Another possible restriction would be to apply the proposals only to transactions where the interest incurred exceeds a certain threshold, such as $10 million, or higher, per year or per acquisition. In addition, testimony is requested with respect to the purchase of assets or stock of wholly owned subsidiaries of other corporations, and negotiated purchases of stock of closely held corporations in friendly transactions with owners of such stock or assets. Testimony is also requested regarding limiting the scope of any option to takeovers of a "publicly owned" company (for example, a company with 100, 250 or more shareholders, a company registered under section 12 of the Securities and Exchange Act of 1934, or a company whose shares are listed for trading on an exchange or through NASDAQ).

Chapter 24   Taxable Mergers and Acquisitions

B. Options Modifying the Current Tax Treatment of Corporate Interest

1.   Interest deductions could be denied on debt incurred or continued to purchase 20 percent, or more, of the stock of a corporation in a hostile tender offer, or to purchase assets of a corporation following such a stock purchase (H.R. 158). A hostile tender offer would be defined as one disapproved by a majority of the independent members of the board of directors of the target corporation. In addition, all gain would be recognized at the corporate level in the case of an acquisition of 80 percent, or more, of the stock of a corporation where a significant portion of the stock was purchased pursuant to a hostile tender offer.

2.   The deduction for interest could be denied for debt incurred to finance mergers determined not to be in the public interest, specifically those transactions that result in a significant loss of jobs (H.R. 679). If the merger is expected to reduce employment by more than 100 employees in the location of the establishment, the Federal Trade Commission would determine (i) the economic reasons for the proposed reduction in employment, (ii) the extent of economic losses to those employed by the establishment in which the reduction will occur, (iii) the extent of any economic loss, including a decline in the tax base, of any local government unit and any person in the geographic area in which such establishment is located, and (iv) other findings. If the Federal Trade Commission finds that the proposed merger would have a substantial adverse effect on employment in a county, city or other jurisdiction, the interest deduction limitations would apply.

3.   The deduction for interest payments on certain high-yield or so-called "junk bond" debt could be denied above a specified threshold amount. The threshold exemption would be provided for a certain dollar limit of debt, such as $50 million, on an issue-by-issue or aggregate basis. A junk bond could be defined as an instrument that possesses one, or more, of several characteristics, such as an excessively high interest rate (as measured by some number of percentage points over the prime rate or the applicable Federal rate (AFR)), significant subordination to other debt of the issuer, convertibility into equity, or a noninvestment grade bond rating. Such restrictions could be applied to junk bonds used in a broad class of stock or asset acquisitions, including stock buybacks, or such restrictions could be limited to a narrower class of circumstances, such as hostile takeovers.

4.   The deduction for corporate interest could be reduced by a specified percentage. Under the proposal, the revenues raised by such modification would be utilized to provide a percentage deduction for dividend payments made to corporations. The percentage deduction allowed for corporate interest would be the same as the percentage deduction allowed for dividend payments. This percentage would be determined on a revenue-neutral basis.

5.   The deduction for corporate interest expense could be fully repealed and replaced with a credit to shareholders representing the corporate taxes paid on the earnings distributed to shareholders as a dividend. Depending upon the revenue consequences of such a proposal, the scope of these rules could be modified for companies whose shares are not publicly owned.

6.   A corporate taxpayer's deduction for interest in excess of a specified rate of interest could be disallowed in whole, or in part. The rate above which the interest deduction would be disallowed would be selected by reference to some number of percentage points over the AFR. For example, disallowance could apply to interest in excess of three, six, or nine percentage points over the AFR at the time the instrument was issued. This option would not affect the characterization of an obligation as debt or equity under present law. Special antiavoidance rules could address issues such as the possible ability of taxpayers to issue debt qualifying under the option for full deductibility, which debt subsequently is securitized into a combination of lower-rate instruments, plus higher rate instruments that would not have qualified for full deductibility if issued directly by the corporation.

7.   A normative level of debt to equity of a corporation could be established, such as 80 percent. Any transaction which results in debt to equity levels above this percentage would be penalized, for example, through the imposition of a 50-percent reduction in the deductibility of interest on the debt incurred. The option might also be designed with a different ratio, such as debt to net worth, not counting junk bonds.

8.   The deduction for corporate interest expense could be replaced with an annual percentage deduction based upon the overall capitalization of a company. The percentage deduction for capital would be established on a revenue-neutral basis, according to revenues raised by the denial of the current law deduction for corporate interest. For nonfinancial corporations, overall capitalization would include the sum of recorded shareholders' equity, plus the average of any loans for which the interest rate paid is greater than the percentage rate set for capital deductions. For financial corporations, only equity would be counted toward overall capitalization, but such corporations would be allowed to offset interest expense against interest income, so long as net interest income would be positive.

9.   Corporate interest deductions for interest expense that is not actually paid currently could be deferred with respect to original issue discount (OID) obligations in transactions in which debt replaces corporate equity, until such time as interest amounts were actually paid. The amount of the ultimate deduction could be increased to reflect the time value of the deferral of the deduction. The proposal could be tailored to only apply to OID obligations held by tax-exempt entities and foreign persons.

As an alternative to postponing interest deductions of the issuer, OID from obligations which result in the replacement of corporate equity with debt could be treated as unrelated business income for tax-exempt entities. In addition, foreign holders of such obligations could be subject to full current taxation. Antiavoidance rules would govern situations in which such OID obligations are held through intermediaries.

C. Options Modifying the Current Tax Treatment of Equity Distributions Made by Corporations

1.   A shareholder-level credit could be provided in an amount equal to the corporate tax paid with respect to a percentage of dividends paid by corporations. Shareholders would include in income the total amount of the dividend and the credit, and then would offset income tax liability by the amount of the credit. In this manner, a portion of the corporate-level tax on earnings distributed as dividends would be relieved.

2.   Shareholders could be provided an exclusion from income for a percentage of dividend income.

3.   Corporations could be provided a deduction for a percentage of dividends paid to shareholders. This option could be modified to reduce the deduction to the extent of holdings by foreign and tax-exempt shareholders, or, alternatively, to impose a compensating tax on such shareholders.

Each of the above options could apply to equity raised by a corporation after the enactment of the proposal, or could be applied to both existing and newly raised equity.

D. Options Relating to Investment Banking Fees

1.   A nondeductible excise tax could be imposed on compensation derived by any party earning income in a leverage buyout. The proposal would include a five-percent excise tax on all parties earning a profit in such transactions. In the case of fees earned by managing investment banking firms and other leveraged buyout managers, an additional excise tax on management fees of 20 percent would be assessed, resulting in a total excise tax of 25 percent with respect to fees earned by these parties.

2.   A nondeductible excise tax could be assessed on excessive compensation derived by individuals from services rendered in connection with merger and acquisition activity.

The excise tax rate could be as high as 50 percent, as a means of achieving a substantial deterrent effect. The compensation subject to the excise tax would be an amount that exceeds a specified threshold (such as $50 million a year).

3.   A nondeductible excise tax could be assessed on so-called "two-tiered" rate structures for advisory fees which are based upon the success of an offer. In addition, a nondeductible excise tax could be assessed upon financial advisors both providing an independent appraisal of the target company's assets and playing a role in a tender offer for the same company.

E. Options Relating to the Tax Treatment of Foreign Persons and to Issues of Foreign Investment

1.   With respect to any domestic corporation controlled by foreign persons, an additional amount could be included in the domestic corporation's gross income, to account for interest that would have been disallowed under any of the above options, except for the fact that it was incurred by a related foreign corporation outside the United States. For example, under option B.6 above, the corporation could be required to determine the amount of worldwide interest, if any, paid by related foreign corporations that would be disallowed if paid by a corporation subject to U.S. tax, as set forth in that option. An amount of such worldwide excess interest would be allocated to the investment in the U.S. corporation. To the extent that such excess interest is allocated to the investment in the U.S. corporation, and is greater than interest paid by the U.S. corporation and otherwise disallowed under rules applicable to all corporations subject to U.S. tax, such interest would be treated as additional gross income to the U.S. corporation. For these purposes, rates on non-U.S. dollar denominated debt would be adjusted to comparable dollar interest rates, taking into account anticipated foreign exchange gains and losses. Corporations that fail to properly account for all worldwide interest payments would be subject to mandatory income inclusions. An exemption would be provided for foreign persons operating only in countries certified by the Treasury Department as imposing effective interest deduction rules that eliminate any substantial competitive advantage for investors residing in such countries.

2.   A 30-percent withholding tax could be imposed on interest earned by foreign persons on portfolio debt in the United States. Such a tax was previously required by the Internal Revenue Code until it was repealed in the Deficit Reduction Act of 1984. The 30-percent withholding tax could be applied notwithstanding exceptions such as tax treaties that provide for lower or zero withholding rates on interest payments, or the withholding percentage could be reduced in accordance with existing tax treaties. Under another version of this proposal, the withholding rate could be set at a minimum of five percent on all interest, overriding tax treaties where necessary. As an alternative to requiring withholding on all portfolio interest, an exemption could be provided for interest paid on debt backed by the full faith and credit of the United States.

3.   A corporate taxpayer's deduction for interest paid to certain related parties, in so-called "earnings stripping" transactions, could be limited. For these purposes, an "earnings stripping" transaction could be defined as one in which a corporation's net interest payments (or net payments serving as a proxy for interest, such as certain types of lease payments) exceed a threshold percentage of the corporation's taxable income. Such taxable income would be determined without regard to net interest expense and net operating loss carryovers. The option could be targeted to reach only those cases where the recipient of the interest payments would not be subject to U.S. income taxation on those payments.

4.   An amortization deduction for goodwill could be provided for U.S. corporations. For example, goodwill could be amortized over a 40-year period. A modification of this proposal would allow the amortization deduction for goodwill only in cases where a

taxable acquisition of a U.S. corporation is made. In addition, the proposal could provide an amortization deduction for goodwill only to the extent that goodwill exceeds 10 percent of the value of a corporation's assets. As an alternative, U.S. treaty policy could be reviewed to address situations where foreign countries provide benefits not provided by the U.S. that may give foreign acquirers an advantage over U.S. acquirers, such as the amortization of goodwill.

5.   Gain realized by foreign persons on the liquidation of a U.S. corporation (which is generally exempt from U.S. tax unless the gain is effectively connected with the conduct of a trade or business in the U.S., or the foreign person is an individual present in the U.S. for at least 183 days during the taxable year) could be taxed as a dividend, to the extent of earnings and profits. Gains so treated could be subject to U.S. withholding tax at the 30 percent rate imposed on dividends, or at reduced treaty rates where applicable. This liquidation tax could be imposed notwithstanding contrary provisions of existing tax treaties, or the option could be imposed only where permitted by applicable tax treaties. In a similar manner, gain realized by foreign persons on the sale of stock in a U.S. corporation could be taxed as a dividend, to the extent of earnings and profits, where the gain is not effectively connected with the conduct of a trade or business.

F. Options Modifying the Tax Consequences Relating to Certain Corporate Financing Transactions

1.   A nondeductible excise tax could be imposed upon the value of assets acquired pursuant to certain stock or asset acquisitions. The proposal could be made applicable to the acquisition of a defined amount of stock (such as 50 percent or more), or assets (such as substantially all assets or those assets constituting a discrete line of business) of a corporation. The transactions in which the excise tax would be imposed could be all acquisitions, or could be limited in scope, for example, to hostile takeovers.

The rate of the excise tax could be in the range of three to five percent, depending upon revenue considerations. Revenues raised by such a tax could be used as a revolving fund to help small business and venture capital situations. In addition, exemptions could be provided for transactions under a certain threshold amount (such as $50 million), and for transactions where a full corporate level tax has been paid as a result of the acquisition.

2.   A 50-percent exclusion could be provided for gain from the sale of an asset which is both (i) financed through corporate or individual equity (or savings), and (ii) held for a minimum of three years.

3.   A corporation could be required to recognize gain on its appreciated assets when it borrows against those assets and distributes the proceeds to its shareholders. Such treatment would be similar to current law recognition of gain by a corporation when it distributes appreciated assets. The proposal would only apply to the extent that the distributions exceed the amount of the shareholders' contributions to the capital of the corporation, plus the accumulated earnings of the corporation.

Under the proposal, gain would be recognized to the extent that the liabilities of a corporation exceed the sum of the aggregate basis of all the assets of the corporation, plus any accumulated deficit in earnings and profits. The aggregate basis of all assets would be the basis used in computing earnings and profits. Accordingly, borrowing would not produce gain recognition solely because of accelerated depreciation, or other tax benefits that do not reduce basis for earnings and profits purposes. Any accumulated deficit in earnings and profits would be added to the basis in determining the amount of liabilities that may be incurred before gain is recognized, in order to prevent gain recognition from occurring solely by reason of a corporation incurring losses. Where gain is recognized under the proposal, such gain would be allocated to all of the corporation's assets, including goodwill, and would increase the basis of such assets.

G. Options Relating to Employee Stock Ownership Plans (ESOPs)

1.   The present law rule allowing financial institutions to exclude from income 50 percent of the interest income received with respect to loans to ESOPs or to employers making loans to ESOPs, could be repealed or reduced, in order to reduce the differences in tax treatment between the use of debt and equity in corporate financings.

2.   The deduction for dividends paid on employer securities held by an ESOP could be repealed, or could be repealed to the extent that the dividends are used to repay an acquisition loan. (To the extent dividends would become deductible pursuant to other options which may be considered by the Committee, however, a deduction could be allowed for these dividends.)

3.   Present law rules could be modified so that an ESOP would not be treated as a qualified plan unless the ESOP was a supplemental retirement plan. Accordingly, the employer would be required to maintain another meaningful qualified plan as a means of protection for participants participating in ESOPs that are 100-percent leveraged, or are the only qualified plan maintained by the employer. As an alternative, the exposure of plan participants, in the event a company does not repay an ESOP loan, could be limited by providing that the acquisition of shares by an ESOP could not be 100 percent leveraged.

H. Miscellaneous

Tax benefits could be reduced in the case of noncompliance with one, or more, of certain possible statutory and regulatory requirements dealing with mergers and acquisitions. For example, interest on debt incurred in a transaction not adhering to a specific requirement could be subject to a 50-percent reduction in deductibility. This restriction could be applied with respect to several possible rules governing acquisition transactions. The defense period for outside takeovers could be increased to 60 days. The period in which competing offers can be made during a management buyout could be increased to 90 days. Steps could be taken to minimize insider trading by ensuring that the board charged with deciding among competing proposals is truly independent. At a minimum, a majority of the board would be outside members, and a clear majority (two-thirds) would be needed to approve any management takeover. In addition, while it may not be feasible to have the Securities and Exchange Commission (SEC) approve all leveraged buyouts and other corporate acquisitions on a case-by-case basis, requiring SEC approval of management buyouts could be a safeguard against inside deals.

Furthermore, the committee could recommend that creditors and suppliers be notified when a company's debt to net worth ratio (or other standard) reaches a certain level, so actions can be made with full knowledge of a company's financial condition. In addition, with respect to the differing treatment of goodwill by different countries, the committee could recommend that the SEC selectively waive the so-called "push down rule," which requires that goodwill associated with a purchase or merger remain on the books of a company when it returns to the U.S., even if such amount was written off abroad.

CHAPTER 25
Tax-Free Reorganizations and Divestitures[1]

In the last chapter we concentrated on taxable transactions wherein a corporation either sells its assets to another corporation and liquidates, or more than 80% of its stock is acquired by another corporation and the acquiring corporation elects Section 338 treatment. In either case, the purchaser changes the basis in the assets it acquires but loses the ability to carry over the target's tax attributes, including the target's net operating loss (NOLs), investment tax credit (ITCs), foreign tax credit (FTCs), alternative minimum tax credit, and capital-loss carryforwards.

If the parties can agree to combine in a friendly transaction, they might avoid some tax costs by carefully planning the combination. For example, the buyer might take a carryover basis in the seller's assets by effecting a tax-free reorganization under Section 368. By receiving the buyer's voting stock in exchange for their shares, the target's shareholders avoid realizing a current capital gain. The buyer may also have access to the target's tax attributes (although with limitations) in a tax-free reorganization. In this chapter, we discuss tax-free reorganizations under Section 368.

As an alternative to a tax-free reorganization under Section 368, the rules and regulations under Section 351 can be used if a corporation wishes to divest itself of some assets owned by one of its subsidiaries, and the purchaser does not want to change the basis of the subsidiary's assets. If the deal is friendly, the target's assets can be transferred to a controlled corporation (the buyer could own 100% of the stock), and the parent of the target subsidiary can defer the payment of capital gains taxes on the transfer of the shares of its subsidiary to the controlled corporation. We also discuss such transactions in this chapter.

---

[1] Some of the material in this chapter and the next has been influenced by conversations with Martin Ginsburg, as well as by some of his writings, notably his excellent volumes in the Commerce Clearing House Tax Transactions Library Series entitled *Mergers, Acquisitions and Leveraged Buyouts*, co-authored with Jack S. Levin (1989).

In still other cases a firm might wish to spin off a subsidiary, tax-free, to its stockholders. It can do this under Section 355, so long as certain restrictions are met. We discuss spin-off distributions (pro rata distributions of subsidiary stock to all shareholders), split-off distributions (tax-free distributions of subsidiary shares in exchange for the parent's stock), and split-up distributions (distributions of multiple subsidiaries in a tax-free exchange for the parent's stock).

In all acquisitions, taxpayers must be aware of the possibility that the transaction will be recharacterized under "the substance-over-form" doctrine that we described in detail in Chapter Two. One manifestation of this is called the "step transaction" doctrine. Although a series of formally independent steps appear to satisfy the code and regulations for a particular tax treatment, there is always a risk that these steps will be treated as part of an integrated transaction and be recharacterized in an undesirable way. But "form" appears to be more important in corporate acquisitions than in other transactions.

25.1 Tax-Free Reorganizations Under Section 368

When a noncontrolling interest in a company, say 10% of its shares, is acquired, the selling shareholders are subject to a capital gains tax on their sale. The target company's basis in its assets, however, remains unchanged. Its other tax attributes, such as its NOLs, retained earnings, and tax credits, also remain unchanged.

If a purchaser acquires 80% of a target company's stock, but the buyer does not make a Section 338 election, *or* if the purchaser and the target company adopt a plan of reorganization under Section 368, the tax basis in the target's assets is once again preserved, and the recapture of depreciation and any capital gains tax on the sale of these assets is deferred until their future sale. The other tax attributes of the firm may be carried over, in whole or in part, depending on the proportion of the combined firm that is retained by the target's shareholders. In a tax-free reorganization under Section 368, the selling shareholders who exchange their shares for those of the buyer can continue to defer the payment of any capital gains tax on their shares.

Section 368 defines reorganizations that are tax-free to target stockholders. These include:

1. "B" reorganizations (so called, because it is described in Section 368 (a) (1) (B) of the Code), which are acquisitions of at least 80% of the target company's stock "solely" in exchange for the purchaser's voting stock. There is no need for control to be acquired at any particular time for a B reorganization to apply. There can be a "creeping acquisition" of the target's stock for the purchaser's stock under a plan of reorganization. The purchasing company's basis in the target's stock is the same as the basis of the target's old shareholders, who exchange their stock tax-free for that of the purchaser.

   The purchaser cannot have acquired the target's stock in the past for other than its own stock unless the previous transaction is deemed to be a completely separate transaction. This is an example of where the step-transaction doctrine can wreak havoc on the plan of reorganization.

Prior to acquisition by the purchaser, the target can redeem up to 50% of its own stock to squeeze out the minority shareholders without destroying the "solely for stock rules" of a B reorganization if the target company uses its own money (or its own independent credit) to buy its shares. The target must be careful, however, not to use the purchaser's credit, directly or indirectly, to back its loan.

2. A "C" reorganization is an acquisition of substantially all of the target's *assets* solely in exchange for the purchaser's voting stock. A subsidiary of the purchaser can also acquire the target's assets solely for the purchaser's voting stock, or the purchaser can merge the target into a subsidiary of the purchaser. In a C reorganization, the purchaser can select which of the acquired firm's liabilities it will assume in the reorganization. This is a nontax advantage to this form of reorganization.

   The purchaser's stock must represent at least 90% of the market value of the target's net assets (assets less liabilities) and 70% of the fair market value of the target's gross assets. Otherwise, the C reorganization will fail, and the exchange of the purchaser's stock for the target's assets is considered to be a taxable transaction (unless the transaction qualifies as tax-free under another subsection of 368).

3. An "A" reorganization is a statutory merger under state law. The requirements under an A reorganization are less onerous than under a B or C reorganization. In an A reorganization, the purchaser can buy the target's stock for stock, cash, debentures, or a combination of securities. Consideration other than the purchaser's stock that is paid to target shareholders is called "boot." Target shareholders are taxed on their gains to the extent of boot received, even if the reorganization otherwise qualifies as tax free.

   The buyer can use voting *or* nonvoting stock in an A reorganization. Target shareholders can be offered a menu of buyout terms that involve different forms of payment. For shareholders who receive only stock, the exchange is tax-free. For shareholders who receive the buyer's "boot," the gain is taxed as a capital gain to the extent of the value of the boot.

   In some "A" reorganizations, shareholders are offered an option to receive cash *or* shares, subject to an aggregate limitation on the amount of cash paid to all shareholders (such as 40% or 50% of the total). Following a purchase of shares for cash, there is an exchange of stock for the interest of the remaining shareholders. In such deals, pension funds and other tax-exempt entities, that are indifferent for tax purposes between receiving cash or stock for their holdings of target-company stock, often tender their shares for cash, whereas taxable shareholders often exchange their holdings for stock.

4. A "D" reorganization involves a transfer of assets to another company controlled by the transferor or its shareholders. D reorganizations may be divisive (that is, a spin-off, a split-off, or a split-up), where only *some* of the corporate assets are transferred, followed by a distribution of the transferee's stock and securities to the transferor's shareholders; or nondivisive, where essentially *all* of the corporate assets are transferred, followed by a distribution of the transferee's stock to the transferor's shareholders in a liquidation of the transferor corporation.

5. An "E" reorganization involves a change in the corporate capital structure (such as an exchange of preferred stock for common stock). It is especially important in closely held businesses and in estate planning.

6. An "F" reorganization is one in which there is a mere change in the place of incorporation, name, or organizational form (such as conversion of a mutual savings and loan company to a stock company).

7. A "G" reorganization involves a transfer of corporate assets in a bankruptcy or insolvency situation.

Regulations and case law suggest that other conditions must be met to qualify as a tax-free reorganization. These include a *business purpose, continuity of shareholder interest,* and *continuity of the business.* The stockholders of a target company must maintain a significant equity interest in the combined firm, although the rules here are quite liberal.

The two most common forms of merger include a "forward triangular" merger, wherein the target company merges into a subsidiary of the purchaser, and a "reverse triangular" merger, wherein the subsidiary of the purchaser merges into the target company. The "reverse" merger preserves all of the outstanding contracts of the acquired firm. Acquiring a company's stock can have nontax advantages when property rights are difficult to transfer to a new firm. This is often particularly true of patents and licensing agreements.[2] As a result, a stock acquisition, where the target is the surviving corporation, can have nontax advantages over either a reorganization where the target is *not* the surviving corporation or a sale of the target's assets.

Although tax-free reorganizations yield tax benefits to the target's stockholders, relative to a taxable reorganization, they can exact significant nontax costs. This is particularly so where the primary motivation for the reorganization is to discontinue the target company's business. The continuity-of-business-enterprise doctrine prevents a buyer from discontinuing the target's operations too soon after the reorganization if tax-free treatment is to be preserved.

---

[2] This was an important consideration in Schlumberger's attempt to sell Fairchild to Fujitsu in 1986. Fujitsu was particularly interested in Fairchild's licenses. The deal eventually fell through due largely to political pressures.

Chapter 25   Tax-Free Reorganizations and Divestitures

Tax-Free versus Taxable Reorganizations and Merger Premia

In principle, mergers structured in a way that allows selling shareholders to postpone capital gains taxes should be accompanied by smaller merger premia than those triggering immediate capital gains to shareholders. This means that all-cash deals should be accompanied by higher prices. And indeed they are.[3] But all-cash deals are also more likely to be associated with tender offers and competing bidders, so it is difficult to isolate the unique effect of taxes on merger premia.

Moreover, there are even conceptual difficulties predicting the magnitude of the effect of all-cash deals on merger premia. First of all, as we have discussed, shareholders may be able to avoid tax on appreciated shares even when a taxable merger is effected (for example, by using installment sales, especially prior to the 1986 Tax Act, or by making gifts to low-tax-rate relatives, or to qualified charities, or by being a tax-exempt institutional shareholder). And second, many mergers are motivated by a desire to purchase the tax attributes (such as NOLs and tax credit carryforwards) of a target company. Such attributes only survive in tax-free mergers, and their transfer to buyers may be expected to fetch a premium if the merger comes as a surprise to the market.

Empirical Evidence

Are corporate acquisitions in the U.S. usually taxable or tax-free? Of 640 acquisitions completed between 1970 and 1985 for which data are available:[4]

- 28% were tax-free;
- 54% were taxable; and
- 18% were *partially* taxable (that is, tax-free but some amount of taxable "boot" was paid to selling shareholders).

Note that to qualify as a tax-free transaction, a substantial amount of stock must be issued by the buyer to acquire stock of the seller. Most hostile transactions are cash tender offers. It is interesting to note that *Mergerstat Review* indicates that 62.5% of all public company acquisitions over the 5 years 1984-1988 were all-cash deals. By comparison, only 27.7% of all privately held company acquisitions over this same time period were all-cash deals. So many more of the private deals were likely tax-free (and friendly). *Mergerstat* interprets the evidence as follows (1989, p. 51):

> Acquisitions of publicly traded companies continued to be paid primarily in cash, and continued the trend of the past few years of stock deals over combination payments (that is, combination of cash and stock). Cash is typically the favored method of payment for acquisitions of

---

[3] See, for example, James W. Wansley, William R. Lane, and Ho C. Yang, "Abnormal Returns to Acquired Firms By Type of Acquisition and Method of Payment," *Financial Management* (Autumn 1983), pp. 16-22; Carla Hayn, "Tax Attributes as Determinants of Shareholder Gains in Corporate Acquisitions," *Journal of Financial Economics* (1989), pp. 121-153; and Cathy M. Niden, "Acquisition Premia: Further Evidence on the Effects of Payment Method and Acquisition Method," (Working Paper, University of Pittsburgh), December 1989.

[4] Hayn (*op cit.*)

public companies because it requires less disclosure on the part of the buyer.[5] When issuing securities to the shareholders, the acquiring company is obligated to disclose ample information on its business operations and financial condition so the selling shareholders can determine both the present and potential value of the buyer's securities.

Purchases of privately held companies typically are transacted through an exchange of stock to enable owners of private entities to avoid paying capital gains taxes. Unlike a publicly traded company, which has many shareholders, a privately held business has one owner or a handful of shareholders, usually members of the owner's family. Hence, their concern for tax liability is much greater. Furthermore, in many instances, management owners remain with the company, expecting to contribute to the future growth of the newly merged entity, and thereby profiting from the stock's appreciation.

Table 25.1 summarizes some evidence collected by Hayn on acquisition premia (excess of buyout price paid over the market price preceding the buyout) as a function of whether the acquisition is a tender offer or a merger, on the one hand, and the tax status of the transaction on the other.[6] The table also reports the stock price reaction of acquiring firms in these deals. Estimated premia are larger for tender offers (35.9%) than for mergers (24.0%). And premia are larger for taxable transactions than for tax-free transactions (even controlling for whether there was a tender offer or a merger).

Hayn's evidence also suggests that net operating loss and tax credit carryforwards are twice as likely to be present for targets in tax-free deals than in taxable ones. This makes sense, since tax attributes like net operating loss and tax credit carryforwards often expire in taxable deals. We take a closer look at this issue in Chapter Twenty-Six.

One final piece of evidence is worth noting from Hayn's study. To secure tax-free status for an acquisition, the parties must jump through a number of hoops and *still* there may be substantial uncertainty as to whether the taxing authority will bless the proposed tax-free treatment. As we discussed in Chapter Nine, tax treatment uncertainty is often reduced by requesting a ruling of the tax treatment for a proposed transaction. Hayn identified 199 transactions where it could be determined whether a ruling request was made.

Table 25.2 summarizes the target and acquiring firms' abnormal stock price performance in the period surrounding various outcomes of ruling requests. As the table indicates, the stock price performance of targets *and* acquirers was superior when *no* ruling request was made.[7] Moreover, the stock price perfor-

---

[5] As an additional remark, timing is important in tender offers, and this favors cash deals. A stock deal requires registration with the Securities and Exchange Commission (SEC). A tender offer involving stock cannot be made until the SEC declares the registration statement effective, which can take a considerable amount of time. Although a cash tender offer *also* requires a filing, the purchaser can proceed immediately with a tender offer to the shareholders of a target company, which can place competing bidders at a disadvantage relative to a stock deal.

[6] *Ibid.*, p. 138.

[7] One factor that may contribute to this, besides tax treatment uncertainty, is that the absence of ruling requests may be associated with hostile tender offers.

Chapter 25   Tax-Free Reorganizations and Divestitures

Table 25.1 Acquisition Premium ("Abnormal" Stock Return from -40 to +10 Trading Days Relative to Acquisition Announcement) as a Function of Type of Acquisition

Targets (640 acquisitions)					+29.2%
279 Tender Offers				+35.9%	
	178	Taxable	+39.4%		
	62	Partially Taxable	+31.7%		
	39	Tax-Free	+26.9%		
361 Mergers				+24.0%	
	165	Taxable	+27.6%		
	54	Partially Taxable	+22.7%		
	142	Tax-Free	+20.2%		
Acquiring Firms (518 Acquisitions)					+3.6%
214 Tender Offers				+ 4.7%	
	152	Taxable	+4.9%		
	51	Partially Taxable	+4.2%		
	11	Tax-Free	+4.0%		
304 Mergers				+3.8%	
	156	Taxable	+3.4%		
	25	Partially Taxable	+2.1%		
	123	Tax-Free	+2.2%		

mance was superior when a favorable ruling was made than when an unfavorable ruling was made. More than half of the cases in which a ruling request was known to have been made resulted in an unfavorable ruling (50 out of 93 cases).

Table 25.2 Abnormal Stock Price Performance of Target and Acquiring Firms as a Function of Ruling Request Status

	Target's Abnormal Stock Price Performance from -9 to +5 Trading Days Relative to the Acquisition Announcement (Results for Acquiring Firms in Parentheses)	Target's Abnormal Return Day Before and Day of the Ruling (Results for Acquiring Firms in Parentheses)
No Ruling (106 cases)	+17.2% (+2.9%)	
Ruling Requested (93 cases)	+10.0% (+1.3%)	
43 Favorable Rulings		+7.4% (+0.4%)
50 Unfavorable Rulings		
Deal Completed Anyway (24 cases)		-4.3% (-1.3%)
Deal Abandoned (26 cases)		-5.0% (-1.6%)

It is worth noting that in 100% of the cases in which a favorable ruling was received, the deal was completed. By contrast, more than half of the cases in which an unfavorable ruling was received resulted in the deal being abandoned.

Financial Reporting Considerations

The two methods of financial accounting that apply to business combinations are the "purchase" method and the "pooling-of-interests" method. In the purchase method, assets and liabilities of the acquired company are recorded at market value on the consolidated books. For consolidated reporting purposes, income of the target company is added to that of the purchaser's only subsequent to date of acquisition. In addition, any excess of the purchase price over the market value of the separately identifiable net assets acquired is recorded as goodwill. Goodwill can be a very substantial amount. In the U.S., goodwill must be amortized for financial accounting purposes (although it is not deductible for tax purposes) over a period of 40 years or less.

Tax and financial accounting rules for goodwill amortization vary considerably across countries. In some countries, like Japan, goodwill is deductible for tax purposes (and for financial reporting purposes) over very short periods of time. In other countries, like the U.K., while goodwill is not tax-deductible, it needn't be amortized for financial accounting purposes either, so reported income is higher each period than it would be in the U.S. Many have argued that the tax and financial reporting rules governing goodwill place U.S. companies at a competitive disadvantage relative to non-U.S. companies, in both the capital market and in the corporate acquisition market.

The pooling method of accounting records assets and liabilities of the acquired company at their *historical cost book value*, so no goodwill is created in a pooling consolidation. Consolidated financial accounting income of the enterprise includes the income of the acquired company for the entire accounting period (as if the two enterprises had always been merged together).

Purchase consolidations and pooling consolidations (which are governed by Accounting Principles Board Opinion No. 16) are *related* to taxable combinations and tax-free reorganizations, but they are not the same. In particular, taxable transactions always result in purchase accounting treatment. Tax-free reorganizations often result in pooling treatment, but not always. For example, pooling treatment in the U.S. requires, among a number of other things, that at least 90% of the voting stock of the target company be acquired with the purchaser's voting stock. A, B, and C reorganizations can be consummated without meeting this financial accounting requirement, and a number of tax-free reorganizations end up receiving purchase consolidation treatment.

25.2 Transfers of Property Under Section 351

While most tax-free acquisitions fall under the reorganization provisions of Section 368, a somewhat different tax-free treatment for a target company's shareholders can be achieved under the incorporation provisions of Section 351.

The transaction will qualify for tax-free treatment if the transaction satisfies all of the following conditions:

1. the property (including common stock) is transferred to a corporation (say, Newco) by one or more persons (the "transferors");
2. the transferors receive, in exchange, "stock or securities" of Newco; and
3. immediately after the exchange, the transferors "control" the corporation; that is, they own stock of the corporation possessing at least 80 percent of the total combined voting power and shares of all classes of the corporation's stock.

What is particularly significant about Section 351 is that revenue rulings and court cases have defined "stock or securities" to mean stock or long-term interest-bearing securities. For example, a shareholder of the target company can transfer her shares as well as other property to Newco in exchange for Newco common stock or preferred stock and long-term bonds, and the transfer will be a tax-free exchange as long as at least 10% of the Newco securities issued are stock.[8] Prior to the 1989 Tax Act, Newco could issue long-term bonds (for example, 10-year bonds) for the target shareholders' stock, and the target shareholders would not be taxed currently on the exchange. The target shareholders' combined basis in the stock and long-term securities acquired in the exchange would be equal to their combined basis in the contributed property.

For example, suppose a shareholder's basis in the target company's stock were $2 and the stock had a current value of $10. If the target stock were exchanged for Newco's preferred stock with a fair market value of $1 and 10-year bonds with a fair market value of $9, the exchange would have been tax free. The shareholder's basis in Newco's bonds would be $1.80 (or 90% of $2). If the shareholder later sold or redeemed the Newco bonds for more than $1.80, a capital gains tax would be paid on the difference between the sale price of the bonds and this $1.80 basis.

Note further that if the target shareholder were to die or donate the bonds to qualified tax-exempt entities, the basis in the bonds would be stepped-up, tax-free, to market value. Other than the requirement that some Newco stock be received by the target shareholder in the exchange, the Section 351 transaction was equivalent to an installment sale of the target shareholder's stock, but with the important added advantage that the capital gain on the stock could be *avoided completely* at the time of surrender of Newco securities at death or by way of a charitable contribution.

If the securities issued to the target shareholder by Newco were short-term securities, gain would be recognized up to the market value of the short-term

---

[8] The requirement for at least ten percent stock arose out of a letter ruling in 1978 regarding the National Starch Co. In that letter ruling, the service agreed that 10% of the payment being in the form of preferred stock was sufficient to provide continuity of interest in an incorporation under Section 351 such that an exchange of stock for preferred stock and long-term bonds would be tax-free. In 1980, the service reversed its decision, claiming that a 10% stock interest failed the continuity-of-interest test. But in 1984, it once again concluded in another letter ruling that 10% stock was sufficient to preserve continuity of interest.

securities.[9] In other words, only short-term securities were considered to be "boot" in a Section 351 transfer. If the short-term securities were nontraded and the target company shares contributed to Newco were not publicly traded, the target shareholder may have been able to use the installment method to defer the payment of capital gains tax.

The 1989 Tax Act tightened up the rules by treating *longer-term* debt securities (like ten-year notes) as boot as well. As such, unless the installment sales route were available, gain on the exchange of target stock or assets for Newco bonds and stock would be taxable immediately to the extent of the value of bonds received.

Another advantage of a Section 351 transaction was that the target's old shareholders could use the long-term bonds or preferred stock received in the exchange as collateral against a loan. Following the 1989 Tax Act, this works only for preferred stock. On the other hand, as we discussed in the previous chapter in the context of installment sales, the tax advantage of capital gain deferral (or even elimination) may come at the expense of nontax costs, such as the monitoring costs that must be incurred because of the purchaser's credit risk, or being forced to hold fully taxable bonds or preferred stock if the selling shareholder is more suited to hold other tax-favored assets, such as tax-exempt bonds.

If the target shareholder owns 50% or more of Newco's stock by vote or value, Section 304 might apply to the transaction. If it does, securities paid in exchange for target company shares might be considered to be a dividend. If this were the case, target shareholders would lose the advantage of being able to defer the realization of the capital gain. For this reason, purchasers generally contribute enough cash and other property to control more than 50% of Newco by vote and value.

Let's illustrate a Section 351 transaction with an example that worked prior to the 1989 Tax Act. Then we will discuss how the deal can be modified following the 1989 Tax Act to preserve some of the tax benefits available under the old structure.

Assume that management and some venture capitalists acquired the stock of a company *without* an election under Section 338 to step up the basis of the target's assets. To purchase the stock, the buyers used debt to finance a large portion of the acquisition (an LBO). To pay down the debt, the LBO group wishes to sell a subsidiary of the acquired company. The subsidiary's assets have a fair market value of $20 million and a tax basis of $8 million. If the subsidiary is sold for cash, it would attract an ordinary income and capital gain tax on the $12 million excess of sale price over tax basis. Prior to the 1988 Tax Act, the subsidiary could have been sold by the LBO group to a buyer for a negotiable installment note. The LBO group, in turn, could borrow, say, $18 million from its bank using the buyer's installment note as collateral for the loan. This is called "monetizing" the installment note. With the 1988 Tax Act's new Section 453A, it is no longer possible to monetize the installment note and still defer the payment of the capital gains tax on the sale of the subsidiary.[10]

---

[9] The case law suggests that if the security will be outstanding for less than five years, it will be considered a short-term security.

[10] Industry experts refer to this change in law as the anti-Campeau rule following Federated Department Store's disposition of Foleys and Filenes. See Robert Willens, *Tax and Accounting Issues* (Shearson Lehman Hutton), October 6, 1989.

Chapter 25 Tax-Free Reorganizations and Divestitures

It was possible, however, to produce the same result as installment sale treatment would provide by using the tax-free incorporation rules under Section 351. Let us assume that the buyer of the subsidiary and the LBO group agree to form Newco. The following amounts are contributed to Newco by the buyer of the subsidiary and the LBO group:

	Value (Millions)
LBO group contributes to Newco:	
Subsidiary to be divested	$ 20
LBO group receives from Newco:	
Preferred Stock	$ 2
20-Year Debt	$ 18
P contributes to Newco:	
Property or Cash	$ 50[11]
P receives from Newco:	
100% of Newco Common Stock	$ 50

The debt of Newco is guaranteed by the buyer to reduce the LBO group's monitoring costs on the installment debt. Since the LBO group's objective is to pay down some of its own debt created in the earlier leveraged buyout, it borrows $18 million from its own bank and pledges its preferred stock and 20-year bonds in Newco as collateral for the loan. The payment to the LBO group of at least 10% of the value of the subsidiary in the form of preferred stock satisfies the continuity of interest rules.

Notice that the LBO group holds Newco's debt and avoids paying capital gains tax on the transfer until principal on the note is repaid. This is similar to, but in some ways better than, installment sales treatment for reasons already discussed.

Since the transaction is tax-free, the $8 million tax basis that the LBO group had in its subsidiary assets carries over to the bonds and preferred stock of Newco it receives in exchange. Ten percent or $0.8 million is allocated to the preferred stock, and 90% or $7.2 million is allocated to the bonds. By holding the preferred stock or the bonds, the LBO group can defer the payment of the capital gains tax for at least 20 years. Assume that the after-tax discount rate is 8% and the capital gains tax rate is 40% for the LBO corporation. Further assume that the bank charges the LBO group a fee of $100,000 a year on the $18 million loan above and beyond the interest they will receive.

The capital gains tax on the sale of the subsidiary, if paid today, would be $4.8 million (or ($20 million - $8 million) × .40). If the same capital gains tax were paid in 20 years, its present-value cost would be $1.03 million at an 8% discount rate. The present value of a fee of $100,000 a year ($60,000 after tax) for 20 years is $0.59 million. So, the total after-tax cost using Section 351 is $1.62 million, or roughly one-third of the immediate capital gains tax on the sale. The tax saving amounts to 16% of the value of the subsidiary, far greater than most investment banking fees.

---

[11] This can be a smaller amount. The buyer needs to contribute only enough to "control" Newco by vote and value.

With the 1989 Tax Act, the LBO group could no longer postpone the tax by exchanging stock in the unwanted subsidiary for Newco bonds. But if they accepted $20 million of Newco *preferred stock*, deferral *is* accomplished. Moreover, the preferred stock could be monetized by pledging it as collateral for a loan.[12] As long as the preferred stock of Newco issued to the LBO group is held by 5 or fewer corporate shareholders and the LBO group's stock in Newco constitutes at least 20% of the voting power and value of Newco, the debt-financed portfolio stock rules under Section 246 do not apply; that is, the corporate dividend-received deduction (which is *80%* when the shareholder owns at least 20% of Newco) remains available to the LBO group despite its having monetized the preferred stock.

So while Newco loses the interest deduction by not issuing debt to the LBO group, it should be able to secure an implicit deduction by issuing lower-yielding preferred stock. For example, suppose that an appropriate debt rate for Newco were 12% and that it issues an 8% preferred stock instead. Then Newco receives a 33% implicit tax reduction by issuing the preferred stock. Moreover, the LBO group retains 7.36% {or 8% × [1 - .4 × (1 - .8)]} after tax which compares favorably to the 7.2% (or 12% × (1 - .4)) they would have earned after tax on the 12% installment debt.

On the other hand, the LBO group's bank might be expected to charge a higher fee on a loan secured by preferred stock than on installment debt, and this could reduce some of the benefits of the transaction. One additional factor is that Newco, as its name implies, is a new company with no accumulated earnings and profits. So unless Newco generates earnings, the preferred stock dividend will be treated, not as dividend income, but rather as a nontaxable return of capital. Such distributions reduce the tax basis of the LBO group in the Newco preferred stock, and once the basis is reduced to zero, it begins to generate capital gains income. This is typically tax-disadvantageous to the LBO group relative to 80% exempt dividend income.

Another alternative is for Newco to issue $20 million of (non-dividend-paying) stock to the LBO group. The LBO group could then swap, with tax-exempt institutions, the returns on Newco stock in return for the return on a bond index, where all payments on the swap contract are deferred for, say, 20 years. The LBO group thereby creates a synthetic bond and can monetize it as it wishes. Newco can borrow on its equity to achieve the same debt structure as it had previously. This transaction is functionally equivalent to the old Section 351 transaction. It actually is more tax advantageous, because the LBO group can defer tax on the appreciation in the bond index. Nontax issues such as counterparty credit risk, however, are important factors for firms to consider in contemplating such a transaction.

---

[12] We have benefitted from conversations with Robert Willens of Shearson Lehman Brothers on this subject.

Chapter 25   Tax-Free Reorganizations and Divestitures

Transferring assets to a partnership creates a variation on Section 351 transactions. A reorganization undertaken by SPX Corp. in 1989 illustrates the possibilities.[13]

SPX contributed assets (with a market value of $275 million and a tax basis of $130 million) to a partnership in exchange for a 48% limited partnership interest and a 1% general partnership interest. Goldman Sachs contributed $15 million of cash to the partnership. Like SPX, they too received a 48% limited partnership interest and a 1% general partnership interest. Management contributed a small amount of cash to the partnership in exchange for which they received a 2% limited partnership interest.

The partnership arranged $295 million in loans from banks and the public. The partnership then distributed $246 million in cash and $14 million in partnership receivables to SPX. The consequences? SPX recognized a gain for financial reporting purposes but not for tax purposes. The contribution of property by SPX to the partnership was a tax-free transaction under Section 721. Moreover, the cash distribution to SPX from the partnership was treated as a tax-free return of partnership capital.[14] Had SPX owned more than 50% of the partnership, it could have been taxed on the distribution (under Section 707) as a deemed sale of the assets it contributed to the partnership, but SPX avoided this problem by owning only 49% of the partnership. Tax on approximately $145 million of accumulated gain was thereby postponed even though SPX effectively disposed of a substantial fraction of its interest in the appreciated assets and received cash for the disposition.

25.3 Tax-Free Spinoffs of Subsidiaries

Another way in which unwanted divisions can be shed tax-free is through Section 355. Assume for the moment that a firm has two divisions that we will call D1 and D2. The firm wishes to divest itself of D1. To do so, the firm establishes a new subsidiary, S1, to hold division D1. More formally, the firm forms subsidiary S1 and contributes all the assets of division D1 to it in exchange for 100% of the stock of S1. Assuming that there is a valid business purpose for this restructuring, it will qualify as a tax-free "D" reorganization. Under Section 355, the firm can then distribute the shares of S1 tax free to its stockholders pro rata. The basis of the shares of S1 in the hands of the firm's shareholders is just the apportioned basis in their original holdings of shares, using the (estimated) market values of D1 and D2 as weights. This is called a spin-off.

If the firm distributes the stock of S1 to its shareholders in redemption of a portion of their stock, this is called a split-off, regardless of whether the distribu-

---

[13] We are grateful to several of our students (K. Bettauer, A. Button, G. Gruber, W. Harris, B. Kerzner, M. Novelli, and M. Prouting) for bringing this reorganization to our attention and helping us to analyze it.

[14] Distributions from a partnership do not generate taxable income to a partner unless they exceed the partner's tax basis in the partnership. A partner's tax basis includes the basis of assets contributed to the partnership ($130 million in SPX's case), *plus* the partnership debt attributable to the partner.

tion is pro rata or not. If the firm establishes a second subsidiary, S2, to hold the D2 assets, and distributes stock in both subsidiaries to its stockholders in redemption of a portion of their stock, this is called a split-up. As with the spin-off transaction described above, these, too, are tax-free transactions.

If shareholders receive "boot" in a spin-off, the boot will be taxable as dividend income to the extent of the firm's accumulated earnings and profits. The regulations require that there be a continuity of the spun-off business if the tax-free treatment is to be preserved. It appears that the continuity-of-business requirement is more restrictive under Section 355 than under Section 368 (a tax-free reorganization). To qualify for tax-free treatment under Section 355, the firm's and the subsidiaries' businesses must have been actively conducted for *five years*, and they must not have been acquired in the five years prior to the distribution unless a business was acquired wholly tax free; that is, no boot was distributed in the reorganization.

A corporate spin-off of a subsidiary can be used to advantage prior to a purchaser's tax-free acquisition of a portion of a target company. If the buyer desires to purchase only a portion of the target's assets, the target might be able to spin off the undesired assets in a Section 355 transaction. For example, unwanted subsidiary S can be spun off to shareholders and the remaining assets can be merged into the purchaser. The entire transaction is tax free.

Of course, there are motivations for effecting corporate spin-offs and split-offs *other than* to sell part of the business to outsiders. On the tax side, a number of firms have spun off income-producing real estate and natural resource assets into a trust that enables shareholders to avoid entity-level taxation. Nontax motivations include (1) segmenting diverse assets of a business in separate legal entities to satisfy a creditor's or a customer's wishes; (2) splitting up a closely held business due to shareholder disagreement as to how the business should be run; (3) allowing shareholders that wish to invest more heavily in one of the corporation's lines of business than another to do so; (4) separating regulated from unregulated businesses to facilitate favorable rate regulation; and (5) creating separate equity claims on various parts of the business for employee incentive, takeover defense, or other purposes. It is typically desirable to accomplish the nontax goals listed above without triggering recognition of taxable gain from the restructuring.[15]

More than 25 public company spin-offs were completed in 1988 alone. Examples include Sun Co., which spun off its U.S. exploration and marketing businesses; DEKALB, which spun off its energy, oil-well service, and agricultural genetics businesses into three separate entities; and Holiday Corporation, which spun off more than $2 billion worth of Holiday Inns before they were acquired in a tax-free transaction by Bass PLC.

---

[15] Several studies have documented that stock price reaction to corporate spin-off announcements is favorable (prices increase by three percent, on average, over the two-day period that ends on the day the *Wall Street Journal* reports the event). See, for example, G. Hite and J. Owers, "Security Price Reactions Around Corporate Spinoff Announcements," *Journal of Financial Economics* 12 (1983), pp. 409-436; J. Miles and J. Rosenfeld, "An Empirical Analysis of the Effects of Spin-Off Announcements on Shareholder Wealth," *Journal of Finance* 38 (1983), pp. 1597-1606; and K. Schipper and A. Smith, "Effects of Recontracting on Shareholder Wealth: The Case of Voluntary Spin-offs," *Journal of Financial Economics* 12 (1983), pp. 437-467.

25.4 Other Tax-Free Divestiture Vehicles

Like-Kind Exchanges

Under Section 1031, a swap of one business for another is taxable only to the extent of boot received. To qualify for tax-free treatment, the business must either be actively managed (for example, swapping portfolios of investment securities would not qualify) or in very similar lines of business. Examples of such transactions include General Electric's exchange of its consumer electronics business in 1987 for Thompson SA's medical equipment business; Borden's swap of its Wyler powdered soft drink business in 1987 for Thomas J. Lipton's Pennsylvania Dutch pasta and noodle business; and the two major swaps of cable television properties completed by Times Mirror in 1987 and 1988.

Involuntary Conversions

When property is divested involuntarily due to its destruction, theft, or condemnation, any gain that would normally be taxable from the receipt of insurance proceeds or a legal settlement can be postponed (under Section 1033) if the proceeds are used to invest in "qualifying replacement property," that is, property that is "similar or related in service or use" to the lost property. Not surprisingly, what constitutes qualifying replacement property is not always clearcut.

A celebrated case in which involuntary conversions occupy center stage involves four major oil companies: Getty, Texaco, Pennzoil, and Chevron. It is a fascinating case that illustrates some of the tradeoffs invariably made between tax and nontax factors in tax planning.

In December 1983, Pennzoil made a tender offer for up to 20% of Getty stock. On January 3, 1984 Getty and Pennzoil agreed on terms that would result in Pennzoil receiving a three-sevenths interest in Getty assets. On January 5, Texaco expressed interest in purchasing *all* of Getty and on January 6, the Getty board agreed to allow Texaco to purchase 100% of Getty stock for $10.0 billion.

Pennzoil then sued Texaco for inducing Getty to breach its contract to transfer an interest in Getty assets to Pennzoil. In November 1985, a jury awarded Pennzoil in excess of $11 billion ($7.5 billion in actual damages, $3.0 billion in punitive damages, and $0.6 billion in pre-judgment interest). In April 1987, after Pennzoil refused to settle the matter with Texaco for $2 billion, Texaco declared bankruptcy. In December 1987, Pennzoil agreed to a $3 billion settlement with Texaco, and it received that amount in April 1988.

After considering alternative ways to invest the money received from Texaco, Pennzoil disclosed in a 13-D filing (which must be filed with the Securities Exchange Commission shortly after a 5% or greater interest in a company has been accumulated) that it had invested $2.1 billion in 31.5 million shares of Chevron, an 8.8% interest. Under "Purpose of Transaction" in the 13-D filing, Pennzoil states: "In addition to the expected benefits from ownership of the shares, including potential appreciation in the shares, Pennzoil believes that its investment in the shares may provide Pennzoil the opportunity to defer for an indefinite period a portion of the federal income taxes that would otherwise be payable currently on the litigation settlement proceeds which Pennzoil received from Texaco in 1988. Pennzoil may decide to continue to expend up to an amount equal to the original Texaco settlement net proceeds ... to purchase additional shares for investment from time to time."

Chevron was not overjoyed with the news of Pennzoil's stake. It immediately sued Pennzoil for filing a false and misleading 13-D filing. Among other things, Chevron complained that "Pennzoil has failed to reveal its true interest, which is to influence Chevron management decisions and/or force an extraordinary restructuring of Chevron which would provide Chevron assets to Pennzoil, and thereby to use proceeds of the $3 billion Texaco settlement and receive favorable tax treatment of the the settlement and defer tax liability attaching to the settlement." Chevron further claims that Pennzoil's ability to postpone taxation (of $800 million to $1 billion) depends on Pennzoil's being able to become actively involved in the management of Chevron, a prospect that Chevron does not relish. Among other things, Chevron wanted the court to force Pennzoil to divest itself of Chevron shares.

Pennzoil disagreed with Chevron's tax theory. The former chief executive officer of Pennzoil, J. Hugh Liedtke, in a May 11, 1990 declaration (in Support of Motion of Summary Judgment), indicated: "It is my belief that although an 8-11% investment in Chevron stock may not provide us with an optimum position with the IRS regarding tax deferral under Section 1033 of the Internal Revenue Code, we nonetheless have a sound position on that issue." (Paragraph 34).

On the subject of trading off tax and nontax factors, Liedtke also stated the following: "During most of 1988, I was interested principally in acquiring a majority or complete interest in a company in the oil and gas business since such an investment was most likely to maximize our tax position. However, ... tax considerations were secondary to making a sound investment. During that time, I was unable to locate any feasible alternative which satisfied Pennzoil's long term investment objectives since the companies considered either were fully priced (i.e., did not possess a potential for significant appreciation in value) or were unavailable, or both. During that time, I also considered the possible acquisition of oil and gas properties. I rejected that option, both because the possibilities I looked at were fully priced and because they were not suitable from a tax standpoint." (Paragraph 7)

Summary of Key Points

1. The 1986 Tax Act increased the desirability of selling operations in tax-free ways in the U.S. There are myriad ways to do this, including tax-free reorganizations (Section 368), tax-free incorporations (Section 351), tax-free creation of partnerships (Section 721), spin-offs (Section 355), tax-free exchanges (Section 1031), and, under special circumstances, involuntary conversions (Section 1033).

2. The most common of the tax-free routes are A, B, and C reorganizations under Section 368 of the tax code. "A" reorganizations are statutory mergers, B reorganizations involve an acquisition of at least 80% of target company's stock "solely" in exchange for the purchaser's stock, and C reorganizations involve an acquisition of all of the target company's assets solely in exchange for the purchaser's stock.

3. Conditions that must be met to qualify as a tax-free reorganization include a business purpose, continuity of shareholder interest, and continuity of the business.

4. Merger premiums are smaller, on the average, in tax-free transactions than in transactions that impose immediate taxation on the selling shareholders.

5. Financial accounting consequences of reorganizations can differ significantly from their tax consequences and are often alleged to influence the form (for example, cash versus stock) such transactions take.

6. Tax planners have displayed considerable ingenuity in crafting transactions designed to provide sellers with access to cash without triggering a tax on the sale of the assets.

7. Corporate reorganizations is an area where nontax factors often dominate tax factors. But the legal form that many transactions take could simply not be explained were it not for tax considerations.

Discussion Questions

1. Why might two corporations wish to combine tax free? How could tax costs inhibit an otherwise efficient combination?

2. What is the step-transaction doctrine? Why is the step-transaction doctrine so important in the corporate restructuring arena?

3. Why might the IRS wish to consider cash (or other "boot") to be a dividend and not a repurchase of shares when a shareholder receives it in an otherwise tax-free reorganization? Does it make any difference to individual taxpayers after the 1986 Tax Act?

4. Why might an acquirer want to maintain a target company as a separate legal entity and not merge the target into one of its own subsidiaries or buy the target's assets?

5. What are the tax benefits and tax and nontax costs of using a Section 351 transfer of property to a controlled corporation? In what ways is it superior to a Section 368 reorganization? Why might there be more use of such transfer-of-control transactions after the 1986 Tax Act than previously? How has the 1989 Tax Act affected the attractiveness of Section 351 transactions?

6. Given the IRS concern about circumvention of the spirit of the repeal of the General Utilities doctrine, do you believe that Section 351 transactions and Section 355 spin-offs will continue to thrive? Does Section 355

dominate Section 351 as a way to rid the corporation of unwanted subsidiaries?

7. Why might you expect a cash merger to fetch a higher price for the target's shares than one in which the purchaser's stock is exchanged for the target's stock?

8. Can you think of any tax or nontax reasons why merger premia as conventionally measured (price paid in the merger less the value of the company before the merger announcement as determined by secondary market prices) mismeasures the *real* premium paid by the buyer?

Problem

C Corporation owns three subsidiaries. It wishes to dispose of one of them. If the subsidiary is sold, substantial recapture taxes and capital gains taxes will be incurred. C would like to use the proceeds of the sale to make investments or to pay down debt. P Corporation wishes to acquire the C subsidiary. It is willing to pay cash, its own stock (or that of a newly formed subsidiary that is capitalized with cash contributed by P), its own preferred stock (or that of a newly formed subsidiary that is capitalized with cash contributed by P), its own debt (or that of a newly formed subsidiary that is capitalized with cash contributed by P), or some combination of the above.

Required:

1. What are the differences among the alternatives in the degree to which C severs its economic interest in its subsidiary?

2. How do the alternatives differ in their tax consequences to C?

3. How do the alternatives differ in the tax and nontax costs to C of securing cash for investment or financial restructuring purposes?

CHAPTER 26
Preservation of Tax Attributes in Reorganizations

For many years, the U.S. Congress has sought to limit "trafficking" in corporate tax attributes such as net operating loss (NOLs) and tax credit carryforwards. It has apparently been viewed as inefficient or inequitable to allow NOLs to shelter the taxable income of parties that were not responsible for generating them in the first place. This has given rise to the passage of legislation that restricts the value of a target's tax attributes following changes in corporate ownership. The rules are far less restrictive with respect to *internal* reorganization strategies that may involve clientele-based arbitrage. In this and other respects, the tax law discriminates in favor of reorganizing the firm internally. We take up this theme in this chapter.

To the extent tax attributes are reduced in value following mergers and acquisitions, the tax law impedes changes in corporate control of firm resources. Moreover, restraints on free transferability of corporate tax attributes makes the corporate tax more progressive than it otherwise would be in that the marginal tax rate on income earned when the firm generates net operating losses can be much lower than when the firm is profitable. This in turn encourages corporations to undertake investment and financing strategies that reduce the riskiness of their taxable income streams, as we argued in Chapter Seven. Such risk-reducing strategies include making diversifying acquisitions of other profitable firms even when there may be pretax diseconomies from doing so. Or it may encourage the firm to broaden the scope of its operations through project selection, merely to reduce the chance of generating tax losses that it cannot use effectively. Similarly, it discourages debt financing, although other provisions of the tax law may encourage it as we have discussed elsewhere.

There are many possible motivations for restricting the free transferability of tax attributes. One is that it may create arbitrage opportunities and excessive risk-taking, especially when gains are taxed at favorable tax rates. For example, suppose a firm were to invest in plant and equipment with borrowed money. If the investment were profitable, the firm could sell it and be taxed, in part, at capital gains tax rates (possibly deferred) on the gain. If the investment were unsuccessful and gave rise to NOLs that were freely transferable to another taxpayer, such NOLs would fetch a market price equal to the marginal tax rate times the magnitude of the losses. The investor would receive a tax rebate for the losses. So, with good results, the firm pays a reduced rate of tax, and with bad results, it receives an immediate tax rebate. This could encourage more risk taking than is deemed to be sociably desirable, especially given other subsidies to risk-taking that already exist in the tax law.

Note, however, that firms with taxable profits from other projects *do* enjoy the full subsidy from tax rates on losses being lower than those on gains. That is, profitable firms *do* get immediate rebates on losses from projects that generate losses. So the playing field is not entirely level for all firms. This points to another possible motivation for restricting the transferability of corporate tax attributes: it is not always easy to determine whether tax losses are real rather than artificially generated through non-arm's-length pricing policies.

For example, suppose a corporation sells consumer goods and services at "excellent prices" to customers. Customers are required to be shareholders. If prices are set low enough so that the corporation generates losses that can be sold to other firms, customers effectively generate a partial tax rebate on their purchase of otherwise nondeductible consumer goods and services. Restricting the sale of NOLs reduces the scope for such arbitrage activity.[1]

A more serious problem would arise if a multinational corporation set prices such that its domestic (high-tax-rate) subsidiary generated large losses, while its low-tax-rate foreign subsidiaries generated artificially high profits. Note that it might pay a corporation to sell a small amount of goods or services on unprofitable terms to an *unrelated* party to establish an "arm's-length-price" that could be used as a basis for transferring similar goods and services between subsidiaries subject to different tax rates.

Congress feels so strongly about trafficking in NOLs that Section 269 gives the IRS broad powers to eliminate a target's NOLs if a purchaser buys 50% or more of a target company's stock and "the principal purpose" of the acquisition is to avoid tax by garnering the target's NOLs. Of course, "the principal purpose" test is far from objective. Was the buyer's purpose to acquire and operate the target's business, or was it to secure the target's NOLs? The taxing authority might rely on the parties' intentions. What notes, memos, and analyses were generated prior to the acquisition? What did the buyer do with the target's business units soon after the acquisition? If, for example, the buyer paid a large price for the acquired firm in relation to the latter's future operating prospects, this might signal that the buyer was interested primarily in acquiring the target's tax attributes.[2]

---

[1] Note, however, that if shareholders contribute more cash to the corporation than is required to run the business, interest income can be earned largely tax-free, so the scope for abuse is not eliminated by restricting the sale of NOLs.

[2] As we demonstrate below, the purchaser would not pay a large price for the target's NOLs subsequent to the 1986 Tax Act.

Chapter 26   Preservation of Tax Attributes in Reorganizations

Another factor that plays a role is whether the buyer moves unrelated business activities into the acquired firm to use up the latter's NOLs more quickly. Since, as we discuss below, the target's NOLs can only offset taxable income generated by the target after the acquisition, it would pay for the buyer to move profitable assets into the target company. For many acquisitions, the subjective definition of "the principal purpose" will make it difficult to gauge whether the firms reorganized to secure tax benefits or to improve the efficiency of the combined firm. This subjectivity might inhibit some firms from improving operations or from even undertaking an acquisition.

We believe that most mergers and acquisitions are motivated primarily by nontax considerations. In many cases, the targets have substantial amounts of NOL carryforwards, tax credit carryforwards (such as foreign tax credits, research and development credits, alternative minimum tax credits), capital loss carryforwards, and so called "built-in" (or unrealized) loss carryforwards (where the assets' current market value is below their tax basis). An acquiring firm obtains the direct or indirect use of a target's tax attributes if (1) assets or stock are acquired in a tax-free reorganization or (2) stock is acquired and the buyer does not make a Section 338 election. In a Section 338 election, where stock is acquired in a taxable transaction and an election is made to change the basis in the target's assets, all of the target's tax attributes are lost. Similarly, if the target company sells its assets and then liquidates, there is no carryover of its tax attributes.

In this chapter, we consider the extent to which pre-acquisition NOLs and other tax attributes continue to be available following acquisitions. We consider both situations in which purchasers and targets have pre-acquisition NOLs. We also explore how the tax rule restrictions on free transferability of tax attributes can be exploited by incumbent managers to impede hostile takeovers.

26.1   Use of a Target's Net Operating Losses and Other Tax Attributes

In Chapter 24, we indicated that a target company's tax attributes survive in some circumstances and disappear in others. Even when the attributes survive, however, they may be limited significantly, as discussed below. Figure 26.1 provides an overview of the treatment of tax attributes of target companies depending on how an ownership interest in the target is transferred to a buyer.

Section 382 imposes limitations on the use of NOLs, and Section 383 imposes limitations on the use of carryovers of other attributes such as foreign tax credits, R&D credits, and capital loss carryovers. Pre-acquisition NOLs and other attributes of target companies generally continue to be usable following an acquisition by the parties that "earned" them (that is, the target companies), as long as the tax basis in their assets are not stepped up or down to fair market value.

On the other hand, a target's carryforwards are *not* directly usable by the purchaser or its affiliates because of the separate return limitation year ("SRLY") rules of the consolidated return regulations. Generally, affiliated firms in the same corporation *can* use the income of one affiliate to offset the losses of another affiliate (by filing consolidated returns). But when an NOL firm is acquired, the

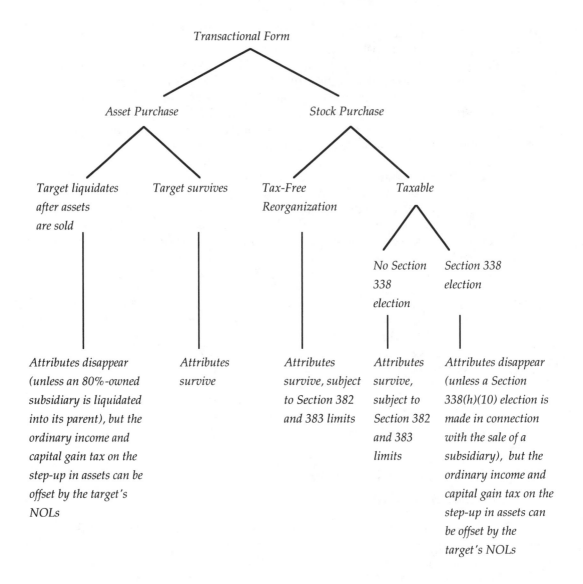

FIGURE 26.1   What Happens to a Target Company's Tax Attributes
Following an Ownership Shift in a Corporate Acquisition?

SRLY rules restrict the buyer's (and its other affiliates') use of a target's pre-acquisition NOLs. Only the post-acquisition losses of the NOL affiliate can be used to offset the income of other affiliates. The target's accumulated NOLs prior to the acquisition can only be used to offset its own future income. Table 26.1 illustrates the effect of the SRLY rules following acquisitions in which tax attributes survive.

Buyers can attempt to circumvent the SRLY rules and use up a target's pre-acquisition NOLs indirectly by diverting income-producing activities (or assets) from elsewhere in the organization to the target company. But there are potential

Chapter 26   Preservation of Tax Attributes in Reorganizations

Table 26.1 Illustration of the Consequences of the Separate Return Limitation Year Rules Following a Corporate Acquisition in which Tax Attributes Survive.

	Pre-Acquisition Profits		Post-Acquisiton Profits	
	Target	Purchaser	Target	Purchaser
Case 1	-100	1,000	50	1,000

50 of Target's pre-acquisition NOLs offset target's post-acquisition profits, subject to Section 382 limits.

Case 2	100	0	150	-200

Purchaser's 200 NOL offsets 150 of Target's post-acquisition profits. The remaining NOLs of 50 cannot be carried back to offset Target's past profits, so they must be carried forward.

Case 3	150	500	-200	1,000

Target's NOLs offset 200 of Purchaser's post-acquisition income.

Case 4	150	1,000	-200	0

Target's NOLs can be carried back only to its own pre-acquisiton earnings. As a result, 150 is carried back and the remaining 50 is carried forward.

tax and nontax costs associated with these transfers. The tax costs relate to potential difficulties under Section 269. Counter-balancing these costs, however, is the possibility that such transfers will improve the operating efficiency of the organization.

Fully taxable investments attract NOL firms as clients. By issuing equity to its new parent (which a target can presumably do at lower deadweight cost than it would have been able to achieve on its own, when unaffiliated), the target can use the proceeds to acquire fully taxable investments to speed up the use of its NOLs. Although the SRLY rules prevent the target from selling its accumulated NOLs to a buyer to offset the buyer's fully taxable income, they allow the target to acquire tax-disfavored investments that generate lots of taxable income to use up it's NOLs.

For example, a purchaser can transfer high income-producing activities to the affiliate, such as "cash cows" with few, if any, depreciable assets. Service businesses, such as consulting and investment banking, are good candidates here, as are mature-product businesses that require little research and development. The purchaser might also be able to negotiate sale and leaseback transactions or the transfer of property more efficiently than the target was able to accomplish as a stand-alone corporation.

To use up a target's NOLs more quickly, a purchaser and its affiliates can initiate partnerships and joint ventures with the target. For example, a profitable affiliate could bear the costs of experimentation for research and development activities (to generate early deductions) while the NOL affiliate contributes capital to the venture. The NOL affiliate, however, could realize a disproportionate share of future income on the success of the project. A risk here, however, is that the taxing authority will reallocate income to the affiliates in a way that is deemed to reflect arm's length pricing (under Section 482).

Since the SRLY rules restrict the use of pre-acquisition losses of a target company by its purchaser in an acquisition, but the SRLY rules do not apply to the target's post-acquisition losses, the tax rules encourage targets to merge in anticipation of generating future NOLs. An important factor here is that there are few restrictions on a purchaser's use of a target's NOLs if the target generates them as an affiliate of the purchaser.

Note that the SRLY rules encourage a degree of centralization in organizations to promote the use of pre-acquisition NOLs and other carryforwards of acquired companies. And this can exact significant nontax costs. Some firms establish decentralized organizational structures for incentive reasons. Each affiliate runs its own business, competing fiercely not only with outside corporations but also with its own affiliated brother and sister corporations. It might be very costly to force "cooperation" among these affiliates to speed up the use of a target's accumulated NOLs. It could destroy the incentive structure within the organization. Once again, this illustrates the potential conflict between tax and incentive considerations in structuring the organization.[3]

If a target company experiences NOLs as a result of the acquisition, it can use these NOLs to offset its taxable income in the three years prior to the acquisition. The company recomputes its taxable income for those years using the NOLs generated because of the acquisition to offset any taxable income, and if it paid taxes in those years, it files for a refund. Acquisition-related items that might generate NOLs include severance pay, acceleration of other compensation payments, plant closings, acceleration of interest expense or other costs related to debt repurchases, and certain reorganization costs.

26.2   Ownership Change Under Section 382

Prior to the 1986 Tax Act, a target's NOLs could be lost even in a tax-free reorganization under Section 368 (such as a statutory merger). Under old Section 382(b), if a target's shareholders retained less than 20% of the stock of the combined companies, the combination resulted in a loss of its NOL carryforwards at the rate of 5% for each 1% below this amount. For example, a 5% retained interest by target shareholders in the surviving company would preserve 25% (5/20) of the NOLs; and 75 cents of each of the NOLs would be lost in the reorganization. This restriction was relatively easy to circumvent, however, by merging the target into a subsidiary of a purchaser with modest assets. The target's shareholders would receive the purchaser's stock that would represent more than 20% of the subsidiary. Of course there was still the cost of having to operate the target's historical business to effect a tax-free combination.

To retain a target's NOLs in a taxable purchase of stock and forgoing a Section 338 election prior to the 1986 Tax Act, it was only necessary to continue operating the business of the newly acquired firm. So there were trade-offs

---

[3]We visited this issue earlier in the chapters on multinational tax planning (Chapters Thirteen and Fourteen).

Chapter 26   Preservation of Tax Attributes in Reorganizations

between the use of a taxable stock purchase and a tax-free reorganization to retain a target's NOLs.

Section 382 Rules Subsequent to the 1986 Tax Act

Following the 1986 Tax Act, new Section 382 rules limit the use of a target's NOLs (including built-in losses). Section 383 rules limit the use of such carryover credits as business, research and development, and foreign taxes and capital loss carryforwards, in much the same manner as Section 382 restricts the use of NOLs.

The new approach introduced several new definitions and limitations. They can be summarized as follows:

1. A 50% ownership change causes a limitation to be invoked.
2. If a 50% ownership change *does* occur, the amount of a target's future income that can be used to offset its pre-acquisition NOLs is severely restricted. The annual NOL-deduction limitation is calculated by multiplying the value of the stock of the acquired firm on the acquisition date by the (published) applicable federal long-term tax-exempt interest rate at that time.
3. Only the income of the loss affiliate can be offset by the annual limitation.
4. Failure to operate the acquired firm's historical business for at least two years after the acquisition results in the loss of *all* of its NOLs and other tax attributes. A buyer might find this to be a very costly constraint if it wishes to reorganize the acquired firm's activities.
5. The SRLY restrictions of the consolidated return rules are retained: only the target's post-acquisition NOLs can offset income of the acquirer or its other affiliates.
6. The built-in losses and gains (net unrealized loss or gain on assets) at the time of an ownership change are carried over for the year of a change and for the four succeeding years if they exceed the lesser of (a) 15% of the fair market value of the target's assets at the time of the acquisition and (b) $10 million. (Just prior to the 1989 Tax Act the threshold was 25% of the value of the target's assets.) If assets are sold in this time period, the built-in losses at the time of the merger are treated as if they were realized prior to the merger, and deductibility of the losses is restricted just as with NOLs. On the other hand, the NOL deduction limitation is *increased* by the built-in gains on assets at the time of the merger. This provides an incentive to overestimate built-in gains and underestimate built-in losses.

   If the purchaser had substantial NOLs, it could acquire the target, selling the latter's assets to step up their tax basis, and the purchaser could use its own NOLs to reduce the recapture and capital gains tax on the taxable sale of the target's assets. Under Section 384, enacted in 1987, the purchaser cannot use its NOLs to offset the target's built-in gains for a five-year period following the acquisition. This restriction is only effective if the target's built-in gains exceed 15% (or $10 million, whichever is less) of the value of its assets at the time of the acquisition.

Ownership Change

An "ownership change" under Section 382 occurs after certain "owner shifts" or "equity structure shifts." An owner shift arises under a taxable stock purchase followed by a failure to elect asset acquisition treatment under Section 338. An equity structure shift arises under Section 368 reorganizations.

More specifically, an owner shift occurs if a shareholder who holds 5% or more of a target company's stock changes the proportion of the stock held. If immediately after the shift, one or more 5% shareholders have increased their holdings of the target's stock by more than 50 percentage points, in the aggregate, over the lowest amount that they held in the previous 3 years (or at the date of incorporation if less then 3 years from the date of the owner shift), this causes an ownership change. For example, an ownership change would occur if a purchaser, which held no target company shares prior to the acquisition, buys more than 50% of the target's stock in a taxable or tax-free transaction. As explained below, it also occurs when a purchaser buys all of a target's assets in a tax-free acquisition if the target's shareholders own less than 50% of the purchaser's stock after the asset sale.

All of the target's shareholders who own less than 5% of the target's stock are considered collectively to be one 5% shareholder. So the sale of the target's stock among small shareholders does not cause an owner shift. On the other hand, a sale of stock by a small (less than 5%) shareholder to a large (5% or greater) shareholder *does* cause an owner shift that enters the calculus of whether, in the aggregate, an ownership change has occurred.[4]

An equity structure shift (or reorganization change) occurs with a 50 percentage point change in the ownership of the NOL corporation. For example, suppose that prior to an acquisition, there are no 5% shareholders, but a target with NOLs agrees to combine with a purchaser in a tax-free reorganization under Section 368. The target ends up with 30% of the combined company. There has been an ownership change because the purchasing company's old shareholders own 70% of the new company (increasing its ownership by more than 50 percentage points).

Examples of transactions in which Section 382 has operated to reduce the value of NOLs include CJI Industries' acquisition of Triangle Industries and the financial restructuring of Banks of Mid-America. In the CJI transaction, a proxy statement disclosed that about $100 million of past losses "may be wiped out and, at best, probably won't exceed $2 million a year."[5]

---

[4] The 5% aggregation rule is in place to prevent a random triggering of an ownership change, and, as a result, a severe limitation on a target's use of its NOLs, following secondary market trading by small shareholders. Without the 5% rule, 51% of the stock could be sold by a bunch of small shareholders in a 3-year period and this would trigger an ownership change. For example, 51 holders, each owning 1%, could sell their stock to 200 other shareholders and, without the 5% rule, would trigger an ownership change if the 51% turnover occurred within a 3-year period.

[5] "Plan to Merge CJI and Triangle Industries May Spell Demise of Sizable Tax-Loss Shelter," *Wall Street Journal* (April 14, 1988).

Chapter 26   Preservation of Tax Attributes in Reorganizations

In the case of Banks of Mid-America, the Section 382 limitations were triggered by a financial restructuring involving the exchange of debt and preferred stock for common stock, as well as the issuance of $75 million of new common stock.[6] The company had $24 million of NOLs at year-end 1987 and generated similar amounts of loss in 1988.

The Effect of NOL Limitations on Venture Capital Companies

Since many new ventures and start-up companies experience NOLs, the ownership change rule has important planning implications. For example, if a 5% shareholder changes his proportional holdings of a start-up's stock because he does not participate proportionally in a new stock issue, this would cause an owner shift. If there had been some stock sales (including the exercise of options) in the previous 3 years, the lowest percentage of stock held by all 5% holders in this period might be quite low. So outsiders who buy the new stock issue could easily trigger an ownership shift. That is, they could increase their holdings by at least 50 percentage points.

Under these circumstances, if the start-up desires additional capital, it might be forced to wait longer than it would like to raise it so that it can reduce the effect of an ownership change by, for example, generating more income. Alternately, it may be "forced" to issue debt when it would really prefer to issue equity. On the other hand, if the start-up company anticipates the potential adverse effects of Section 382, it might find it desirable to raise more capital when it begins operations than it would otherwise find optimal. The additional capital should generate extra taxable income to reduce the magnitude of anticipated NOLs, thereby making an ownership change less costly.

Each of these approaches, however, has nontax costs. Deferring development might prove to be costly, even fatal. And it might be very difficult for a small start-up firm to raise large amounts of equity capital in anticipation of future needs, because investors might fear that management would spend the money foolishly or in a self-interested fashion. Moreover, an attempt on the part of the founders to dilute their ownership by raising large amounts of external equity might signal a lack of confidence in the firm's prospects, causing the shares to be issued at "too low" a price.

26.3 Valuation of Companies with NOLs That Face Deduction Limitations

Following an ownership change under Section 382, the annual limitation on NOL deductions is given by the following relation:[7]

$$L = V \times R_e$$

---

[6] Shareholder proxy of Banks of Mid-America (September 9, 1988).

[7] If an ownership change occurs and the target's tax attributes survive subject to the limitations of Sections 382 and 383, then the surviving tax credits are converted into an equivalent amount of deductions, and the sum of NOLs, credits, and capital losses are subjected to the single limitation amount specified under Section 382.

where L   is the annual limitation amount,

V   is the value of the stock of the NOL corporation immediately before the ownership change, and

R_e is the long-term federal tax-exempt interest rate.

Suppose that a target firm T has an asset that will generate taxable cash flows, C, of $100 per year forever. T also has huge NOL carryforwards. Assume for the moment that NOLs can be carried forward forever (rather than only 15 years) to make it easier to illustrate the main components of the valuation analysis. What would a purchasing company P pay for T, assuming that to take control of T, P will cause an ownership change to occur that will restrict the availability of T's NOLs?

Assume that R_e is 5% and that t_c, the statutory corporate tax rate, is 40%. What is the value, V, of the NOL firm?

Since we assumed that C is a perpetuity, the value of the NOL firm is equal to the annual after-tax cash flow, divided by the after-tax discount rate. If we take the after-tax discount rate for this (hypothetically) riskless stream of cash flows to coincide with the long-term federal tax-exempt interest rate, R_e, then the value of T is equal to

$$V = \frac{[C - t_c(C - R_e V)]}{R_e}.$$

That is, T's NOLs can offset only $R_e V$ of its taxable income each year. As a result, an amount equal to only $R_e V$ of the NOLs is deductible against T's income before tax.

Rearranging terms, we find

$$V = \frac{C(1 - t_c)}{R_e(1 - t_c)} = \frac{C}{R_e}.$$

So P will pay only C/R_e for T. Since T will generate taxable income of $100 forever, P would pay $2,000 (or $100/.05). This is $800 more than a firm without any NOL carryforwards. That is, if T lost all of its NOLs and generated $100 a year forever, its after-tax cash flows would be $60 (or $100(1 - .40)). The present value of a $60 perpetuity, at a discount rate of 5%, is $1,200. As a result, P pays $800 for T's NOLs.

How much more would P pay for an extra $1 of T's NOLs? Not even a fraction of a cent. Why? Because the extra NOLs would yield no extra *tax shield* due to the limitations under Section 382.

As a corollary to the example above, how much would P pay for a firm that carries forward huge sums of NOLs, but lacks any earning assets whatsoever (a so-called "shell" corporation), assuming the firm is to be acquired in a transaction that triggers an "ownership change"? Nothing! Although the shell corporation has NOL carryforwards, it has no value to P, as we demonstrate below.

Suppose that P pays $500 for the net operating losses of a shell corporation and transfers assets into the shell in the hopes that the annual NOL deduction allowed will offset the taxable income earned from these assets. The annual limitation on the utilization of the NOLs would be $25 a year (or $500 × .05). Up

Chapter 26   Preservation of Tax Attributes in Reorganizations

to $25 of NOLs could offset any taxable income earned by the shell. If the shell generates sufficient taxable income, the annual limitation is worth $10 a year (or 40% of $25).

The present value of $10 a year forever is only $200 (or $10/.05), and this is only 40% of the purchase price of the shell company. So "stuffing" the shell with earning assets is not profitable. The reason that the shell corporation is worth only 40% of the investment is that the government rebates only 40%, not 100%, of each $1 of net operating loss that is used up. So it no longer pays, as it once did, to advertise in the financial press to sell companies with two "assets": cash and substantial sums of NOLs. In fact, such companies are effectively precluded from being acquired for such reasons.

As an example, MLX (which emerged out of the McLouth Steel bankruptcy restructuring in 1984) had $285 million in NOLs at year-end 1988. This was seven times the market value of the entire company! While MLX is hardly an attractive target, not surprisingly, it has been pursuing a strategy of buying up profitable companies.

In the preceding analysis, we assumed for convenience that NOLs could be carried forward forever. In actuality, however, they expire in the U.S. if not used up within 15 years of their creation. This means that the value of NOLs is even less than in the calculations above. For example, the value of the firm with unlimited amounts of NOLs with assets that generate $100 of taxable cash flow per year for n years is:

$$V = \frac{C(1 - t_c)}{R_e} + t_c R_e V \cdot PVAN\ (n, R_e),$$

where PVAN (n, r) denotes the present value of an annuity for n periods at a discount rate of r per period.

In the earlier analysis, we assumed the NOL-rebate annuity lasted forever, in which case the value of the annuity was $t_c R_e V / R_e$ or simply $t_c V$. Here, with $n = 15, r = R_e = 5\%$, and $t_c = 40\%$, the annuity is worth only .208V rather than .4V. This reduces the value of the firm to only $1,515 (versus $1,200 in the absence of NOLs and $2,000 when NOLs could be carried forward forever). So here the NOLs have a value of only $315 (or $1,515 - $1,200).

After the 1986 Tax Act, several NOL target firms attempted to use up their NOLs very quickly prior to an anticipated ownership change. For example, T might have purchased P's bonds with extremely large front-end interest charges or loan fees. That is, the bond might carry a 50% rate of interest for the first year, and then a 10% rate of interest for a number of years thereafter. T would use up some of its NOLs by offsetting the taxable income from the bonds. P, however, would deduct the large interest payments in that year. In effect, T was selling its NOLs to P. In 1989, the U.S. taxing authority ruled that P had to accrue the interest deduction over the life of the bond rather than expense the interest in the year that it was paid.

A similar result was achieved by some firms that had floated noncallable fixed-rate debt at a time when interest rates were high. These firms entered into interest-rate swaps with their targets for the targets' variable-rate debt obligations, paying the targets lump-sum up-front tax-deductible payments to compensate for the high interest rate on the purchasers' debt. As with the previous tax-planning strategy, however, such transactions are no longer granted favorable tax treatment under the law.

The tax rules also prevent capital contributions ("stuffing") in the two years preceding an ownership change from increasing the annual limitation on NOL utilization under Section 382.[8] P can obtain a foothold (less than an ownership change) in T and then add capital to T. This would be a good strategy if P waits for three years before causing an ownership change. If P contributes earning assets to T in return for less than 50% of T's stock, P can use T's NOLs to offset the income on those assets. Moreover, it allows P to use more of T's NOLs in a later acquisition.

It may be possible for P to gain control of T without effecting an ownership change. Once P has control of T, it must be careful that an ownership change does not occur within the three-year period, something that may be difficult for P to ensure. This procedure, while effective from a tax standpoint, has its own information problems that are likely to be more severe the less control P has over T's operations.

As an example, consider the case of Allis-Chalmers Corporation. At year-end 1989, Allis-Chalmers had very substantial carryforwards:

Carryforward Type	Amount ($ millions)	Years Expiring
NOL	500	1988-2004
Capital Loss	111	1990-1992
Investment Tax Credit	7	1997-2001
Foreign Tax Credit	2	1990-1991

In May of 1989, 40% of Allis-Chalmers stock was sold to a limited partnership for only $3.75 million. On page 2 of the 1989 Annual Report of Allis-Chalmers, the chairman and CEO (who is also the lead partner in the limited partnership that acquired 40% of Allis-Chalmers stock) stated:

> Overall, we continue to pursue a strategy that is designed to generate earnings and cash flow and that utilize the Company's substantial net operating loss and other tax credit carryforwards.

How could the chairman ensure that another 10% of the shares of Allis-Chalmers wouldn't be traded, by shareholders owning 5% or more of the stock, within 3 years, thereby triggering on ownership shift and a virtual elimination of carryforwards? Page 23 of the 1989 Financial Statements provides the fascinating answer:

> All Common Stock issued pursuant to the Plan has been deposited into an escrow maintained pursuant to the terms of a Stock Sales Escrow Agreement. The Stock Sales Escrow Agreement requires that certain restrictions be placed on the transfer of the Common Stock. The objective

---

[8] It may pay to postpone dividend declarations (even if cash flow is adequate) to increase the value of the firm in a manner that does not constitute a "capital contribution." Similarly, it may pay to default temporarily on preferred stock dividends. Of course, the nontax costs of these strategies may overwhelm the tax benefits. Other strategies that may relax the NOL utilization limitation are discussed in Section 26.6.

Chapter 26   Preservation of Tax Attributes in Reorganizations

of such restrictions is to maximize the likelihood of preserving the Company's net operating and other tax loss carryforwards. While such stock is held in the Stock Sales Escrow, neither the stock nor beneficial interests therein will be transferable, except as permitted by the Stock Sales Escrow Agreement. ... The shares of Common Stock will be released from the Stock Sales Escrow over a period not to exceed six years.

26.4 Sale of Assets

If P buys T's assets, rather than its stock, T retains its NOLs and other tax attributes (unless T subsequently is liquidated) and can use them to offset any recapture tax and capital gains tax on the sale without any limitation. Note that offsetting T's NOLs with recapture income and capital gains is not necessarily efficient tax planning, however, unless T has NOLs that are about to expire or its future income will be insufficient to use up these NOLs even after making capital structure adjustments. On the other hand, T's marginal tax rate *could* be far below the statutory marginal tax rate, as we argued in Chapter Eight. And where T's assets have appreciated in value, relative to their tax basis, a sale of assets will permit P to secure additional tax deductions from depreciation, cost of goods sold, etc.

For example, in 1986, Penn Central, armed with huge amounts of NOLs, contributed some of its assets (Buckeye Development and Buckeye Pipeline) to a master limited partnership in a transaction that ultimately triggered $450 in taxable gain to Penn Central. The transaction used up a fraction of Penn Central's NOLs and allowed other investors, who could use the write-offs more effectively, to garner depreciation deductions based on a stepped-up tax basis in the assets.

Firms with large NOLs often have further built-in losses rather than unrealized gains. In that case, the sale of T's assets only adds "insult to injury." T's assets get stepped *down* in value to P, and T is left with a still-larger NOL that may expire unused.

If P buys T's stock and makes a Section 338 election, T's NOLs will be available to offset T's recapture and capital gains taxes on the liquidation. If there are any excess NOLs, they survive only where T is a subsidiary of another company, and P and T's parent make a Section 338(h)(10) election to treat the transaction as if T had sold its assets to P and liquidated tax-free into its parent under Section 332.[9] As a result, T's parent inherits T's remaining NOLs, while P changes the basis in T's assets to their fair market value.

26.5 Use of P's Tax Attributes After an Acquisition

If P has NOLs, acquires at least 80% of T's stock, and files a consolidated tax return, P can use T's income to offset its NOLs. As mentioned previously,

---

[9] While the Tax Act of 1986 repealed the General Utilities doctrine, and therefore corporate liquidations are no longer exempted from capital gains tax at the corporate level, an exception is provided for subsidiaries, owned 80% or more by their parents, that are liquidated into their parents.

however, Section 384 limits the use of P's accumulated NOLs to offset T's built-in gains at the time of the acquisition. The limitation lasts for the 5 years following the acquisition and then only if the built-in gains exceed the lesser of $10 million and 15% of the value of T at the point of acquisition.

Moreover, when P acquires T's stock (or T's assets in a tax-free reorganization), Section 269 may prohibit the use of P's tax attributes to offset T's income. The IRS can claim that P's principal purpose was to acquire T to accelerate the use of its own NOL carryforwards.

Also, P's acquisition of T could cause an ownership change in P's stock. That is, more than 50% of P's stock could change hands in the acquisition. If this should occur, the Sections 382 and 383 limitations could severely restrict P's use of its own NOLs and other tax attributes.

Many large firms with NOLs acquire smaller profitable companies without causing an ownership change. The future income of such target companies (but not their pre-acquisition income) can be used to offset P's NOLs. For example, Penn Central,[10] U.S. Steel, and Wickes Corp.[11] acquired many other companies to use up their own NOL carryforwards.

As an example, at year-end 1983, Danaher Corporation had $121 million of NOLs and $4.3 million of capital loss carryforwards. The magnitude of the NOLs was roughly one-and-one-half times as large as Danaher's *aggregate revenues over the previous four years*. Over the next couple of years, Danaher spent hundreds of millions of dollars to acquire profitable companies. In discussing their acquisitions, the 1984 annual report indicated that "the considerations behind an acquisition strategy are particularly significant here because of the Company's tax-loss carryforward, which on a present value basis is worth far more if utilized expeditiously."

The value of companies that generate large sums of taxable income is greater to a large NOL firm than to other firms since taxes on profits can be shielded with the buyer's NOLs. Small NOL companies, on the other hand, have more difficulty in using stock acquisitions to buy the desired taxable cash flow to use up their own NOLs (and other tax attributes) because of capital constraints and the large fixed costs associated with effecting mergers. Moreover, they are more likely to experience an ownership shift that would restrict their ability to use NOLs against targets' profits.

On the other hand, even large NOL firms must worry about hidden information problems and related costs when contemplating the purchase of a business. Moreover, if cash cows are relatively scarce, large NOL firms might have to pay a premium (an implicit tax) to acquire them. It might be less costly for large NOL firms simply to undertake clientele-based arbitrage strategies through

---

[10] In 1978, Penn Central had $1.9 billion in NOLs. Over the next 5 years, it spent $1.3 billion to buy up what it expected would be profitable companies (Williams Energy, Marathon Manufacturing, GK Technologies, Gulf Energy Development Co., and Northern Propane Gas). By 1984, its NOLs were $1.4 billion.

[11] Wickes emerged from bankruptcy in 1985 with $493 million of NOLs. At the annual shareholders' meeting for 1985, the chairman of Wickes (Sanford Sigiloff) stated as a primary goal "to make major acquisitions which would enhance earnings, strengthen our balance sheet and *accelerate utilization of our net operating loss carryforwards*." (emphasis added)

Chapter 26   Preservation of Tax Attributes in Reorganizations

internal reorganization of their own asset and capital structures rather than to acquire other businesses. Companies like Chrysler, which reported $1.8 billion of NOLs and $240 million of investment tax credit carryforwards at year-end 1982, concentrated on internal restructuring strategies (like leasing assets, exchanging preferred stock for debt, issuing common stock, and postponing pension plan contributions) to use up their tax attributes.

A number of unprofitable companies, notably thrifts, have created subsidiaries capitalized with nonvoting (adjustable-rate) preferred stock, to generate taxable income that uses up consolidated NOLs. There were two motivations for setting up the subsidiary. First, unless the dividends on preferred stock are paid out of "accumulated earnings and profits," they are ineligible for the corporate dividend-received deduction. Many NOL firms have no accumulated earnings and profits, but by forming a new subsidiary and investing in ordinary interest-bearing securities, the requisite profits are earned by the party declaring the dividends.

A second motivation for forming the subsidiary was to segment the assets that stand behind the preferred stocks. It reduces the monitoring costs for the preferred stock investors. On the other hand, there is always a question as to whether the "corporate veil" of the subsidiary can be pierced in the event the parent company declares bankruptcy. This is an area of some ambiguity in the law.

In any event, following the 1989 Tax Act, if subsidiary preferred stock is to be issued to use up consolidated NOLs, such stock will have to include voting rights. The 1989 Act has restricted the issuance of nonvoting preferred stock by a profitable subsidiary of a consolidated group that has a consolidated NOL. The Act prohibits the use of the group's NOLs to offset the taxable profits of the profitable subsidiary to the extent of dividends on nonvoting preferred stock paid to minority shareholders.

Some NOL firms also enter into partnership arrangements with highly taxable investors to allocate the partnership's investment income in the early years to the NOL firm and the income in later years to the fully taxable partners.

26.6 Defensive Strategies

Because of limits on the use of target firm NOLs and other tax attributes under Sections 382 and 383, firms with large amounts of tax-attribute carryforwards may not be good acquisition candidates. Such firms might be better served employing internal capital restructurings to use up their tax attributes.

For those firms with limited NOLs relative to the potential future cash flows that they can generate from their assets, the annual limitation rules under Section 382 have little effect. But if T has significant sums of NOLs, prospective buyers can only offer a merger premium if they can restructure the target profitably to use up T's NOLs at a faster rate than could T's incumbent management.

The annual limitation rules of Section 382 allow T's management to undertake actions that reduce the value of T's NOLs to P. They can drive a wedge between the value of the NOLs to themselves as ongoing managers and the value of the NOLs to an outsider. This can come at the expense of T's stockholders. And like so many other defensive strategies, it is difficult to determine whether the actions are being taken for reasons that are in shareholders' best interests or simply in management's. In the discussion that follows, we consider tactics that can deter P from initiating a hostile takeover. These tactics include T's use, in the presence of large NOLs, of (1) leverage, (2) investments in non-business assets, and (3) the issuance of preferred stock that must be redeemed upon an "ownership change."

Leverage

If T has debt in its capital structure, P will be unable to use as large a fraction of T's NOLs as it might have if T had no debt. This is because the NOL limitations are based on T's *stock* value rather than on asset value. To illustrate the effect of leverage on the value of T's NOLs, let's compute the value of T's equity with leverage. We will assume that T will earn taxable cash flows of C per year in perpetuity on its operating assets and that T issues perpetual debt at interest rate R_b and repurchases common shares with the proceeds. The value of the debt is D and annual interest payments are $R_b D$. The value of the equity at the time of the ownership change is E. E is given from the following relation:

$$E = \frac{(C - R_b D)(1 - t_c)}{R_e} + t_c E,$$

where $t_c E$ is the present value of future NOL deductions of $R_e E$ per year under the annual limitation rules (and assuming that the NOLs can be carried forward forever).[12]

Solving for E, the value of the equity at the time of the ownership change, assuming that $R_e = R_b(1 - t_c)$, we find that

$$E = \frac{C}{R_e} - \frac{D}{(1 - t_c)}.$$

Since the annual limitation is based on the market value of T's stock at the time of an ownership change, debt in T's capital structure reduces the amount that P can pay for T's stock more than dollar for dollar. For example, if T has debt, D, of $100, P would pay $166.67 less (or $100/(1 - .4)) for T's equity than if T had no debt. P must reduce its bid by $66.67 for T's cash flows from operations (in addition to the $100 value of T's debt).

To maximize the value of its NOLs requires that T reduce its leverage prior to an ownership change. But Section 382 requires that if equity is issued for debt within two years prior to an acquisition, the new equity must be treated as if it were debt in computing the annual limitation. However, this does not restrict the firm's employees from taking equity for their accumulated deferred compensation loans. Moreover, convertible debt could be converted into equity to mitigate the limitation.

An NOL firm in this circumstance might regret having used debt to finance its activities. After all, NOL firms are the wrong clientele for fully tax-deductible borrowing.

---

[12] As we demonstrated earlier, it is straightforward to factor in the fact that NOLs can only be carried forward for 15 years, but the notation is messier and is more cumbersome to discuss.

Chapter 26   Preservation of Tax Attributes in Reorganizations

As the analysis above suggests, T could issue debt to defend against a potential takeover. Of course, there are high tax costs to such a strategy. The firm will not only limit its value to outsiders, but will also generate redundant interest deductions. On the other hand, T can mitigate the cost of redundant interest deductions (and still impede a hostile takeover) by subsequently issuing equity and repurchasing debt. As indicated above, such an equity increase will *not* increase the NOL limitation to buyers of T if T is acquired within two years of the equity increase.

Following the 1988 Tax Act, acquisition indebtedness might limit the use of T's NOLs. For example, if, in a management buyout, T's assets are used to secure debt issued by the management to take T private, this acquisition indebtedness must be subtracted from the stock value that was paid for the NOL firm in computing the annual limitation. For example, if management paid $100 for T's stock and used T's assets to borrow $95 to pay for the stock, then after the acquisition indebtedness is subtracted from T's value in determining the annual NOL deduction limitation, the annual limitation would be only $5 multiplied by the long-term tax-exempt rate. Similarly, if P uses T's assets to back its loan to acquire T's stock, it too must subtract the amount of the loan from the amount it paid for T's stock in computing the annual limitation.

Non-Business Assets

The Section 382 annual limitation rules also require that adjustments be made if non-business assets exceed one-third of the value of the firm at the time of an ownership change. Non-business assets include portfolio assets, such as government bonds, or other marketable securities.

Disagreements can arise as to what precisely constitutes portfolio assets. But the effects of an over-abundance of portfolio assets is clear. Holding such assets will reduce the value of the NOLs to outsiders.

The trade-off here is more interesting than it is for the case of issuing debt to ward off hostile attacks. Here the NOL firm is the correct tax clientele for the purchase of portfolio assets that generate generous amounts of taxable income, assuming that there will *not* be a change in corporate control. Such assets help to use up the firm's NOLs that are present. In contrast, the NOL firm is the wrong tax clientele for issuing debt (unless it is issued in conjunction with special supplier-contracting arrangements as discussed in Chapter Fifteen).

To illustrate the effect of "excess" portfolio assets on the value of NOLs to a bidder, assume that T has business assets that produce annual pretax cash flows (C) of $30. Also assume that T has large amounts of NOLs. What amount of portfolio assets (PA) can T own without violating the one-third rule? If T has portfolio assets that are less than a third of its value (V), then if T's NOLs could be carried forward forever, and if the portfolio assets yield taxable income at rate R_b per period, then P can pay up to

$$V = \frac{C}{R_b(1 - t_c)} + \frac{R_b PA}{R_b(1 - t_c)}$$

for T.

Note that after-tax cash flows are discounted at rate $R_b(1 - t_c)$. This is the same as discounting at rate R_e, but as seen below, the longer expression is algebraically more convenient for the present discussion.

For T's portfolio assets to be less than $V/3$ implies that

$$PA < \frac{1}{3}\left[\frac{C}{R_b(1 - t_c)} + \frac{R_bPA}{R_b(1 - t_c)}\right],$$

and after simplifying that

$$PA < \frac{C}{R_b(2 - 3t_c)}.$$

If before-tax cash flows, C, are $30, and R_b is 8.33% (or 5%/(1 - .4)), this implies that portfolio assets must be less than $450 at the time of an ownership change (or $30/[.08333 \times (2 - 3 \times 0.4)]$).[13] If PA > $450, the annual limitation would be given by

$$L = (V - PA)R_e.$$

If PA = V/3, the value of the firm is

$$V = \frac{\$30}{.05} + \frac{.0833 \times \$450}{.05}$$

$$= \$600 + \$750$$

$$= \$1350.$$

Portfolio assets of $450 represents one-third of $1350. So, if PA were $450 or less, all of T's portfolio assets could be used in computing the annual limitation. As a result, T's annual limitation would be $67.50 per year (or $1350 × .05). T's before-tax cash flows would also be $67.50 (or $30 + .0833 × $450), so T can use $67.50 of its accumulated NOLs to offset its before-tax cash flow. As a result, its taxable income is zero. The $450 worth of T's portfolio assets are worth $750 to P, because the bonds produce cash flows that are not taxable. In effect, P is paying T's shareholders for their NOLs.

On the other hand, if T's portfolio assets exceed one-third of V, P must subtract these portfolio assets from V before computing the annual limitation on the use of T's accumulated NOLs.[14] This would prevent P from using T's NOLs to offset the taxable income on T's portfolio assets. As a consequence, P would bid less for T by an amount equal to the present value of the tax on the income from the portfolio assets. This is equal to

$$\frac{t_cR_bPA}{R_b(1 - t_c)}$$

or

$$\frac{PAt_c}{(1 - t_c)}.$$

---

[13] If the NOLs are assumed to expire after 15 years, portfolio assets would have to be less than $261 to avoid the one-third rule.

[14] More precisely, V is reduced by the value of the nonbusiness assets less a prorated portion of T's indebtedness.

Chapter 26   Preservation of Tax Attributes in Reorganizations

In our example, P will bid $300 less for T's stock (or $450 × .4/.6) for a total of only $1050 (or $1350 - $300). If we assume that T has portfolio assets of $450.01 the annual limitation would be

$$L = (\$1050 - \$450) \times .05 = \$30.$$

Notice that the $30 annual limitation on the use of T's NOLs is the same limitation that P would have faced if T's cash flows resulted only from its operations. P would pay only $450 for T's portfolio assets.

This restriction reduces the value of the NOL firm to an outside bidder. But it is still worthwhile for the NOL firm to add portfolio assets prior to an ownership shift. If management wants an "offensive strategy" (to sell the firm to outsiders for the highest price), they would

1. issue new equity (common or preferred) and purchase assets that yield generous amounts of taxable income,
2. restrict portfolio assets to no more than one-third of the value of the firm,
3. reduce dividends to stockholders (another form of equity issuance), and
4. compensate employees with stock rather than cash.

As always, the tax benefits of each of these strategies must be balanced against information and other nontax costs.

For a target's management that is interested in "defensive strategies" (anti-takeover defenses), issuing debt and stocking up on non-business assets can cause potential bidders to back away from the firm. These defensive strategies are like poison pills. When used they may kill off a potential bidder.

For example, assume that T's stock was trading for $100 million. Assume that without the defensive strategies, P would be willing to pay $120 million for T, whereas with the defensive strategies in place, P is willing to pay only $95 million. As a result of the defensive strategies T is worth more under the status quo than with a change in corporate control. Presumably, management would undertake these strategies if the value to them of incumbency exceeds the value of the direct payoffs that they could receive from their stockholders from increasing the value of the firm to $120 million. But shareholders would be better off if T had not employed such defensive tactics. Although the tax rules have been put into place to prevent "stuffing" the firm with passive, income-generating assets to beef up the value of the NOL firm to a prospective buyer, the Section 382 rules can create perverse incentives.

Redeemable Preferred Stock

If stock is redeemed in connection with an ownership change, it is treated as if redeemed *prior to* the ownership change for purposes of calculating the annual NOL utilization limit. If the NOL firm issues preferred stock that *requires* redemption upon a substantial change in ownership, this reduces the NOL limit available to new buyers under Section 382. So the issuance of such stock makes the value of the NOLs greater to current owners than to prospective owners.

Our earlier analysis assumed that the corporate discount rate and the long-term riskless tax-exempt rate are the same. But in reality, a target firm's cash flows are risky, so the appropriate discount rate exceeds the riskless rate. This reduces the value of a target's NOLs even further than we indicated above. Far from being neutral (or promoting economic efficiency), this is but another way in which the tax rules discourage acquisitions and help to entrench incumbent managers.

26.7 Limitations on Interest Carrybacks in Debt-Financed Acquisitions

This chapter has concentrated on post-acquisition utilization of tax attributes. Due to a concern that many leveraged buyouts undertaken in the 1980s gave rise to *post*-acquisition NOLs that triggered refunds of taxes paid during pre-acquisition years, the 1989 Tax Act limited carrybacks in certain debt-financed transactions. In particular, the portion of NOLs attributable to interest created in so-called "corporate equity reduction transactions" (CERT) cannot be carried back from the year of, and the two years following, the CERT. Instead, the losses must be carried forward.

A CERT is a substantially above-average interest distribution (more than one-and-one-half times the average over the preceding three years) or a large stock acquisition (half or more of the stock in terms of votes or value). The amount of interest that must be carried forward is the lesser of (1) the interest resulting from the CERT and (2) the excess of the firm's interest expense in the year of the CERT over its average during the preceding three years. Once again, taxes inhibit hostile takeovers.

26.8 Strategic Uses of Bankruptcy Reorganizations

There is great potential for loss of NOLs where debt is restructured following a default. Equity is often swapped for debt in such circumstances, and this *may* give rise to a tax-free (E) reorganization under Section 368. This will only occur, however, if the debt exchanged is long-term and therefore constitutes "securities" for Section 368 purposes. In the event of a tax-free reorganization, the decline in the value of the debt, which can be considerable, does not yield a deductible loss to the debtholder; nor does the reduction in the debt obligation trigger taxable income to the creditor.

Firms with troubled debt outstanding often experience NOL carryforwards. If enough equity is issued for the debt in the restructuring agreement, an ownership shift will be triggered, and NOLs will be severely restricted, especially since equity values are often *very* low in such circumstances.

The problem can be mitigated in a couple of ways:

1. If warrants are issued for the debt rather than common stock, an ownership shift will not result. Moreover, the debtholder is allowed to

claim a loss deduction without having to sell the equity (which may have been difficult to market under the circumstances).[15] This will also trigger income to the borrower, but the income may be offset by NOLs.

2. Even if the transaction is tax-free, the debtholder who receives stock can sell the stock for a loss, just as the debt could have been sold at a loss.

3. Chapter 11 of the Bankruptcy Code may be chosen strategically as a tax-advantageous way to preserve NOLs in a restructuring.[16] In a Chapter 11 restructuring, the value of the "target's" equity, for purposes of calculating the annual limitation under Section 382, is defined as the value of target equity *after* the ownership change rather than before it.

As an example, consider the Republic Health Corporation exchange offers (November 1989) involving $750 million of outstanding debt. As of August 31, 1988, Republic had $131 million of NOL and $3 million of ITC carryforwards. In addition, Republic reported a $45 million loss for the 9 months ended May 31, 1989, so the total stock of NOLs amounted to $176 million on that date.

A prospectus dated November 10, 1989 describes two alternative recapitalization plans. One involves a restructuring outside of bankruptcy, and the other involves a restructuring under Chapter 11 of the Bankruptcy Code. Both recapitalization plans involve substantial amounts of stock to be issued in exchange for debt. On page 146 of the Prospectus, there appears a section entitled "Future Use of Net Operating Losses," where the following statement is made:

"If the Non-Bankruptcy Recapitalization is implemented, no pre-transaction net operating losses will be available for use by the Company to offset any taxable income earned by the Company and its subsidiaries in subsequent taxable years or during that portion of the current year beginning on the day after the Exchange is completed. However, if the Bankruptcy Recapitalization is implemented, any pre-transaction net operating losses might be available for use by the Company to offset taxable income earned by the Company and its subsidiaries in subsequent taxable years as well as during that portion of the current year beginning on the day after the Exchange Offers are completed. Under Section 382 of the Code, net operating losses are limited following a change in control (which would occur as a result of the Merger and Exchange Offers) to a fixed amount of taxable income equal to the fair market value of the loss company's stock times the federal tax exempt rate in effect for the month in which the change in control occurs. Normally, the fair market value of the loss company is determined immediately before an ownership change (which, in the case of the Company, results in a very small limitation, if any). However, subject to terms and conditions to be set forth in regulations not yet published,

---

[15] Note that this arrangement is not advantageous for tax-exempt bondholders.

[16] It should be kept in mind, however, that Section 269 could be invoked by the IRS to disallow the preservation of NOLs if the sole objective of the bankruptcy declaration were tax avoidance.

26.8   Strategic Uses of Bankruptcy Reorganizations

in the case of an exchange of stock for indebtedness in a bankruptcy case (such as the Bankruptcy Recapitalization), an election may be made to have the fair market value of loss company stock be determined immediately after the ownership change. Thus, if the Bankruptcy Recapitalization is implemented, and provided the terms and conditions of subsequently issued regulations are satisfied, the Company may be entitled to make an election that will permit a much larger amount of taxable income to be reduced by pre-transaction net operating losses of REPH and the Company."

Following the 1990 Tax Act, a restructuring under Chapter 11 of the Bankruptcy Code has another potential benefit: it allows a company that wishes to restructure its debt on more favorable terms (at the mutual consent of the lender) to avoid recognizing taxable income on so-called cancellation of indebtedness income.

Summary of Key Points

1. In most tax jurisdictions around the world, tax rule restrictions are in place that seek to prevent free transferability of tax attributes, such as net operating loss and tax credit carryforwards.

2. In the U.S., "trafficking" in NOLs is restrained by the broad coverage of Section 269 and the more specific restraints of Sections 381-384.

3. The costliness of transferring tax attributes from the taxpayer that "earned" them to other taxpayers: (a) discourages mergers; (b) encourages internal reorganization (clientele-based arbitrage strategies) to secure maximum benefit from the tax attributes; (c) encourages diversification to prevent wasting valuable tax attributes; and (d) adds a degree of progressivity to the corporate tax structure.

4. Where mergers *do* occur, the tax law may distort post-acquisition investment strategies of the combined entities (such as encouraging the retention of unprofitable businesses) to preserve tax benefits.

5. The "SRLY" rules operate to prevent the pre-acquisition NOLs of a target firm from offsetting post-acquisition taxable income of any member of its consolidated group *other than* the target. So the target must earn its own way out of its NOLs. This creates incentives to endow the target with profitable projects. Post-acquisition losses of the target, however, can offset the taxable income of members of its consolidated group.

6. The SRLY rules encourage centralization of the consolidated group's resource management to maximize the value of a target's tax attributes. This can exact significant nontax costs.

7. Several U.S. tax acts in the 1980s have limited considerably the ability to use a target's tax attributes following significant changes in corporate capital structure involving changes in equity ownership (including

Chapter 26   Preservation of Tax Attributes in Reorganizations

corporate combinations). These rules can hit venture capital start-ups particularly hard.

8. Limitations on net operating loss deductions following corporate acquisitions in the U.S. may render the value of NOLs very low, even when they survive the transaction.

9. The rules governing limitations on the availability of tax attributes following a corporate acquisition provide incumbent managers of target companies ample scope for driving a large wedge between the value of the company to current owners and the value of the company to outsiders. By choosing investments and capital structure strategically, incumbents can exploit the tax rules to defend against hostile takeovers. That is, incumbents can adopt poison tax pills.

10. A Chapter 11 Bankruptcy restructuring can be used to preserve NOLs. Since Chapter 11 may be elected for a host of nontax reasons as well, it can be difficult for an outsider to determine the motivation for choosing this form of restructuring.

Discussion Questions

1. Why might Congress wish to prevent trafficking in NOLs?

2. Under Section 269, the taxing authority can eliminate all of T's (or P's) surviving NOL carryforwards if it can show that the "principal purpose" of the transaction was to use T's (or P's) NOLs. What problems arise because of this restriction for firms that want to reorganize? What might the taxing authority look at, and how can firms plan for the possibility of a challenge?

3. What restrictions do the consolidated return rules place on P's use of the NOLs of an affiliate? What restrictions do these rules place on P's use of T's NOLs after an acquisition? What actions could T and P take to reduce the effect of these rules? What are the potential costs of reducing the effect of these rules?

4. What is an "ownership change" for purposes of determining whether restrictions on the availability of NOLs are to be applied? Why might start-up ventures be particularly vulnerable to the effects of an ownership change?

5. What is the annual limitation on NOLs and other tax attributes following an ownership change or an equity structure change? How does it affect the value of target companies? Does it pay for an acquirer to buy some of T's stock to gain control and then to stuff T with earning assets to use up the NOLs before an acquisition? Why? What about after an acquisition?

6. How does T's leverage policy affect the value of its NOLs to outsiders? How can T mitigate the effects of its leverage policy on its value?

7. How does holding portfolio assets affect the value of T's NOLs? Should NOL firms' portfolio assets be set above or below one-third of their business assets? Why? What are the tax and nontax costs of holding portfolio assets?

8. What problems result from the use of the long-term tax-exempt bond rate in the annual limitation calculation? Does the use of this rate help or hurt NOL firms?

9. A tax attribute that disappears in taxable mergers is a target's "accumulated earnings and profits." Why can this be undesirable from a tax standpoint? Can it ever be an advantage?

Problem

T, a U.S. corporation, has $90 million of net operating loss carryforwards that are due to expire in three years. Its balance sheet, ignoring the market value of its net operating losses, is as follows:

	Tax Basis (in $ millions)	Market Value (in $ millions)
Nonbusiness (passive) assets	$80	$80
Tangible business assets	50	100
Debt	60	60
Intangible business assets	0	20
Equity	70	140

The business has finally turned the corner and has become profitable. It is expected to generate taxable income of $16 million per year over the foreseeable future. The corporate tax rate for profitable companies is 40% on both ordinary income and realized capital gains, and the long-term federal tax-exempt interest rate is 7%.

a. If P Corporation were to purchase all the shares of T for $140 million, at what rate would the new owners be permitted to use up T's net operating losses?

b. How would your answer to (a) differ if half of T's nonbusiness assets were instead business assets?

c. Suppose that if P were to acquire T's stock and elect, under Section 338, to step up the basis in T's assets to market value, T's assets would yield additional tax deductions of $10 million per year for 5 years. The 338 election would also give rise to $20 million of nonamortizable goodwill.

1. If P discounts after-tax cash flows at a rate of 8%, how much better or worse off would P be if it stepped up assets under Section 338 relative to not doing so (under the assumptions given in part (a))? You may assume that the goodwill will remain on the books forever.

2. How does the answer change if the $20 million of goodwill is expected to be sold or liquidated, along with the rest of the business, in 10 years? in 20 years?

d. Suppose T decides not to sell the firm to P. Would it be desirable for tax purposes for T to sell its *business assets* to P for $100 million in cash, thereby enabling P to secure additional deductions (relative to T) of $10 million per year for 5 years? You may assume that T will invest the proceeds of the sale to earn the same level of pretax income as it would have generated absent the sale.

e. How does your answer to (d) change if T's net operating losses were scheduled to expire in 6 years rather than 3 and a $4 million after-tax transaction cost must be incurred to complete the transaction?

f. Assuming once again that T's net operating loss carryforwards of $90 million were to expire in 3 years, what would you advise T management to do?

Chapter 27
Estate and Gift Tax Planning

Suppose you, a relative, or a client have accumulated a substantial amount of wealth. You would like to ensure that family members, friends, and favorite causes are the beneficiaries of your good fortune: the taxing authority is not a desired beneficiary. Once you decide to transfer wealth, however, whether by gift or bequest, several forms of taxation can arise: gift taxes on the value of the assets given away, income taxes on the earnings generated by the transferred assets, and estate taxes on your death. Moreover, generation skipping transfer taxes might await you if you make transfers, whether through gift or bequest, that skip over one or more successive generations of beneficiaries.

Family tax planning for estate and gifts is not independent of family income-tax planning. A reduction in estate and gift taxes for one family member could lead to the family paying higher income taxes. For example, the transfer of assets from a parent to a child facing a higher income tax rate might reduce the estate tax but increase income taxes for the family.

Like other tax planning problems, estate and gift tax planning involves a repackaging of assets among taxpayers, and many of the same issues arise here as we discussed in Chapters Twenty and Twenty-One. Efficient tax planning trades off tax and nontax considerations among transferors and transferees of accumulated wealth. Nontax considerations loom large when parents give away assets to children: parents do not always have complete trust that their children will employ the assets in the desired way, and this makes certain tax-planning strategies costly. Many issues in estate and gift tax planning arise when parents "give" away assets to relatives and to charity to reduce the size of their estate, yet try to retain control over the use of these assets.

This chapter begins with a description of the general structure of estate and gift tax rules. We then discuss the substantial incentives provided by the tax law to effect charitable giving. We show that such incentives are even larger than is commonly believed, and that it generally pays to transfer wealth while alive rather than through the estate at death. We then demonstrate that taxpayers have similar incentives to make noncharitable gifts early to "freeze" the accumulation of wealth that is taxed in the estate. We present a model that considers both tax and nontax factors, which often conflict, to assess the tradeoffs between gifting now and making a bequest. The tax factors include the relative tax rates of the donor and donee, the estate tax rate, and the capital gains tax that the donor or the donee might incur because of the transfer of assets prior to bequest (due to the loss of an income-tax-free step-up in the basis of appreciated assets at death). We investigate a multitude of nontax factors such as the value of retaining control of the transferred assets as well as differences in before-tax rates of return on investment available to the donor and donee. At the end of the chapter, we discuss a variety of different forms through which the taxable size of an estate can be "frozen," as well as ways in which taxpayers can exploit differences in tax rates between the donor and donees.

27.1 Preliminaries: Illustration of Estate and Gift Tax Rules Circa 1990

Estate and gift tax rates in the U.S. can be as high as 60%. The tax rate reaches 55% at a $3 million estate and 60% on an estate of over $10 million but less than $21 million, and then returns to 55% for estates over $21 million. The 5% tax surcharge for estates between $10 and $21 million phases out the advantages of the progressivity of the estate tax below $3 million: large estates (those above $21 million) become taxable at a flat 55% rate.

Since the 1976 Tax Act, estate and gift taxes have been integrated in the U.S. The donor pays a gift tax on gifts exceeding $10,000 per donee per year ($20,000 if a spouse joins in the gift giving). Although a gift tax is paid as gifts are made (other than to qualified charities), the value of any taxable gifts is added back into the taxable estate at death, and any gift taxes paid during the decedent's lifetime is credited against the estate tax liability. The value of the gifts are not indexed for inflation, and the estate and gift tax schedule that is in effect at the date of death is used to compute the tax credit for previously taxed gifts.

Moreover, donors can give $600,000 in taxable gifts before paying any gift tax. The tax law provides for a $192,800 unified gift and estate tax credit, the tax on a $600,000 taxable estate. The marginal estate tax rate on the first dollar of taxable estate is 18%, and the marginal tax rate just above $600,000 is 37%!

An example of how the estate tax operates is shown in Table 27.1. The gross estate ($2,500,000 in the example) is determined by adding up the value of all of the decedent's assets at death. All taxable gifts above the $10,000 per donee per year exemption amount, made during the decedent's lifetime, are added back. This amounts to $800,000 in our example. The liabilities of the estate, as well as expenses, such as funeral and administration expenses ($200,000 in the example), reduce the value of the estate, as do gifts to charity ($100,000 in the example) and gifts to a spouse ($1,700,000 in the example), which can be made in unlimited amounts. The estate owes a tentative estate tax on the net taxable estate (of

$469,800 from the estate tax-rate schedule), from which it deducts both the gift tax on past taxable gifts and the unified credit. Many tax-planning strategies involve deciding on both the timing and the amounts to give to various categories of donees. Although you can avoid estate taxes completely by giving all of your assets away to charity or to your spouse, this, as we discuss below, is not necessarily the best tax-planning strategy. Neither is it typically the best strategy for nontax reasons.

Table 27.1   Illustration of How the Estate Tax Operates

Add up the value of all estate assets at death	$2,500,000
Add up all gifts above the $10,000 per donee per year exemption amount made during decedent's lifetime	800,000
Less estate liabilities and expenses	(200,000)
Less gifts to charity	(100,000)
Less gifts to spouse	(1,700,000)
Taxable estate	$1,300,000
Tentative tax from tax rate schedule	469,800[a]
Less credit for past gift taxes paid	(75,000)[b]
Less unified credit	(192,800)
Estate tax due (if positive)	$202,000

[a]$448,300 (estate tax on $1.25 million of taxable estate) + .43 ($1,300,000 - $1,250,000)

[b]First $600,000 of gifts are exempt. Tax on the remaining $200,000 of taxable gifts is $55,500 (tax on the first $150,000) + .39 ($200,000 - $150,000).

27.2   The Tax Subsidy to Charitable Giving

The tax law encourages charitable giving, and the subsidy is generally greater the earlier is the gift. Gifts to qualified charities are exempt from estate and gift taxes, whether made while living or at death. Beyond this, however, there are two important tax advantages to charitable giving over one's lifetime: (1) unlike bequests, gifts made to qualified charities, while alive, yield income tax deductions, and (2) charities, because they are tax exempt, can, in principle, invest funds at a higher after-tax rate of return than the donor can.

To illustrate how the tax rules encourage charitable giving, suppose that you are considering whether to make a gift to your daughter or to a charity. If you are in a 30% marginal tax bracket (or t_p = 30%), each $1 gift to charity costs you only $.70. Ignoring interest for the moment, you must decide then between a $1 gift to charity or increasing the size of your taxable estate by $.70. If the estate tax, t_e, is 60%, $.70 added to your estate will give rise to $.42 of estate tax, leaving only

$.28 to be passed on to your daughter. So each $1 of gift to charity reduces your daughter's bequest by $1(1 - t_p)(1 - t_e) or only $.28. This is an impressive difference. You must value leaving an extra dollar to your daughter more than three and one-half times as much as a dollar to charity. The income and estate tax rules create a very significant incentive to make charitable gifts.

If the charity is going to use the gift in n years, charitable giving has further tax advantages because charities are tax exempt and can earn at a higher rate than can the benefactor. Moreover, giving early yields an income tax deduction while bequests do not. The benefit of making a $1 after-tax gift now versus setting aside $1 to leave as a bequest in n years, depends on whether:

$$\frac{1}{1 - t_{po}} (1 + R_{ch})^n \text{ is greater than } (1 + R_p(1 - t_{pn}))^n$$

where t_{po} and t_{pn} are the donor's marginal tax rates now and in the future (on average over the n years), respectively, R_{ch} is the before-tax return earned by the charity, and R_p is the before-tax return earned on personal account by the donor.

Suppose current and future income tax rates are 30% (that is, $t_{po} = t_{pn} = .3$), that both the charity and the taxpayer can earn 10% before tax (that is, $R_{ch} = R_p = 10\%$), and that the future bequest will be made in 15 years (n = 15), when the estate tax rate is 60%. One dollar set aside now for a bequest in 15 years grows to $2.76 (given an *after-tax* rate of return of 7%), and after the estate tax, leaves $1.10 for your daughter.

A tax deductible gift of $1.4286 today to a charity has an after-tax cost of $1 (that is, $1.4286(1 - .3) = $1). It accumulates to $5.97 (or $1.4286(1 + .1)^{15}$) in 15 years, or 5.4 times the value of a gift to your daughter.

Moreover, giving to charity now versus at death yields a 116% advantage ($5.97 versus $2.76). Why is this so? If you give at death, you lose the income tax deduction and the opportunity to accumulate at the before-tax rate.

Future tax rates would have to increase dramatically to justify deferral of the charitable gift. Moreover, with increases in tax rates, the investment return advantage of the tax-exempt charity over the donor would likely increase.

There are, of course, nontax factors to consider as well. Perhaps you will want to change your mind between now and the date of your death as to which charity should be your beneficiary. Alternatively, your tastes or economic circumstances could change over the coming years, such that you decide you would prefer to have the resources for your own consumption.

To the extent the concern is over which charity you wish to support, rather than whether you wish to make a gift, this can be dealt with by establishing a philanthropic trust. Instead of the gifts being made directly to a charity, they can be made to the tax-exempt trust, and each year the trustee of the trust decides whether, and to what charities, to disburse funds. But the donor cannot reverse the decision to contribute funds to the trust.

To the extent the donor can invest the funds more efficiently than the charity, the advantage of giving early is reduced. You might gain nonpecuniary enjoyment, however, from making a gift today rather than later in life. You might also influence how the gift is invested or how the gift proceeds and income are spent. You cannot have too much control over the use of gift by the charity, however, or else you could lose your income tax deduction for the gift.

By reducing marginal tax rates, the 1986 Tax Act diminished the incentive to make lifetime charitable gifts. As a result, many taxpayers loaded up on charitable contributions in the last quarter of 1986 when marginal tax rates were still at 50% and taxpayers anticipated that they would be facing lower tax rates starting in 1987. One particularly effective planning strategy was to establish a large charitable trust in 1986 to fund future charitable contributions. An irrevocable contribution into the trust fund in 1986 was tax deductible at a 50% marginal tax rate, and disbursements from the fund could be made in future years, when donors resolved the uncertainty as to which charities they wished to support.

Small donors would find the costs prohibitive to establish a philanthropic trust on their own and to comply with the reporting rules. Consequently, many charitable foundations have established what are, in effect, group philanthropic trusts for relatively small donors. All donations are pooled into a common fund. The donors, however, do not control directly either the trust investments or the charities to which future disbursements are made. The trusts generally have approved lists of charities and seek recommendations from donors as to which charity should receive donations and in what amounts. Smart donors select a trust that is likely to be sympathetic with their views on appropriate charities. The tax rules require that the trust's realized investment returns be contributed to charity each year. Scholes and Wolfson both established a family philanthropic fund in 1986 to fund about 10 years of charitable contributions: the trusts' funds accumulate income free of tax, and it is possible to add new charitable contributions to the trusts at any time (which is especially desirable when tax rates are believed to be high).

For the reasons just discussed, the 1986 Tax Act should have stimulated charitable giving in the fourth quarter of 1986. In this regard, it is interesting to note that based on insider trading reports required to be filed with the Securities and Exchange Commission (SEC), 11,430 gift transactions were made in 1986 by corporate insiders, while only 8,225 such transactions were made in 1985 and only 7,893 were made in 1987.[1] Stanford University reported that at year-end 1985 it received 990 gifts of stock, worth $16.8 million; at year-end 1986 its receipts jumped, as expected, to 1,892 gifts of stock worth $46.8 million; at year-end 1987 it received only 780 gifts of stock worth $13 million; and at year-end 1988 it received 622 gifts of stock worth $20.7 million. The IRS also reported a dramatic fall-off in charitable contributions subsequent to the 1986 Tax Act.[2] For example, taxpayers reporting $500 thousand to $1 million of taxable income took charitable deductions of $33,000 in 1986, $21,000 in 1987, and $16,000 in 1988, on average, when marginal tax rates were 50%, 38.5%, and 28%, respectively.

Donors can take a tax deduction equal to the fair market value of securities contributed to charity. Moreover, they do not pay a capital gains tax on the appreciation in the value of assets contributed. Donating towards year-end

---

[1]*Chronicle of Philanthropy* (February 1990).

[2]*Wall Street Journal* (January 2, 1991), p. 1.

allows taxpayers to determine whether their tax rates are high, giving them an option to contribute, and to select stocks that have appreciated in value. There is substantial evidence of tax planning here in that 50% of all gifts of stock made by insiders, as reported in SEC reports, are made in the last quarter of the year, and over 35% of these gifts are made in December.[3]

There are limits to the tax subsidy available to charitable contributors. First, U.S. taxpayers' deductions for charitable contributions cannot exceed 50% of their adjusted gross income in any tax year (the limit is 20% or 30% of adjusted gross income for certain types of contributions): the excess, however, may be carried forward for five tax years. Second, the alternative minimum tax limits the benefit of donating appreciated securities to charity, as described more fully in a later section.

Charitable Giving Through Charitable Lead and Remainder Trusts

Investors often use trusts as a vehicle to effect charitable contributions. In a charitable lead or income trust, the charity retains the income from trust assets and the donor receives the assets back at the end of a set term or at death. When market rates of interest are above the rate used by the treasury to value the income flows, the lead trust becomes very popular. The reason for this is that the use of a below-market interest rate to discount cash flows overstates the value of the promised lead payments to a charity. This means that a charitable contribution deduction can be taken in an amount that exceeds the value of the gift made. Charitable lead trusts were particularly popular in the U.S. in the early 1980s when interest rates were very high and the IRS allowed taxpayers to use a low rate of interest (6%) to discount cash flows.

Charitable remainder trusts are mirror images of charitable lead trusts. Here the donor takes a lead annuity from a charitable trust, and the charity receives a remainder interest in the assets at a specified future date or upon the death of the donor.[4] With the elimination of many opportunities to reduce capital gains taxes from disposition of appreciated assets (such as installment sales of publicly traded securities)[5] and with the increase in capital gains tax rates that resulted from the passage of the 1986 Tax Act, charitable remainder trusts have become popular as a tool to reduce the cost of capital gains taxes.

To illustrate why the charitable remainder trust has become so popular, suppose you have a client that was successful in launching a new business venture. You recommend that she contribute $50 million worth of stock, for which she originally paid $3 million, to a tax-qualified (Section 501(c)(3)) univer-

---

[3]*Chronicle of Philanthropy, op. cit.*

[4]To qualify as a charitable remainder trust, the trust must either take the form of a charitable remainder annuity trust or a charitable remainder unitrust. A charitable remainder annuity trust pays the grantor a certain amount each period. The amount paid out each year can be stated as a fixed dollar amount or a fixed percentage of the initial value of the fund (but, in any case, the annual payment must be at least 5% of the initial market value of the property contributed to the fund). A charitable remainder unitrust is one where a fixed percentage, not less than 5% of the net market value of the contributed assets, valued annually, is paid at least annually.

[5]Recall that at a 7% after-tax discount rate, a 10-year interest only installment note reduces the capital gains tax by half.

Chapter 27   Estate and Gift Tax Planning

sity through a charitable remainder trust. You negotiate with the university to make payments to your client (or her beneficiaries) of $4 million per year for a period of 50 years. Suppose this has a present value to her of $45 million and that this coincides with the value the IRS places on the annuity. Then your client will be entitled to a $5 million charitable contribution deduction (worth $1.5 million if deductible at her marginal tax rate of 30% on income and capital gains). If, instead, she were to sell the stock, the $47 million capital gain would attract a tax of $14.1 million.

With the trust arrangement, the tax on the entire $47 million of capital gains is forgiven, and given the value of the annuity and the charitable deduction, the donor retains 93% of the value of the gift (($45 million + $1.5 million)/$50 million). It is as if she paid tax at a rate of 7% to sell her stock, which is far superior to the 28.2% rate (or $14.1 million/$50 million) she would pay if she sold her stock outright. Moreover, she has made a $5 million charitable contribution to her favorite charity, which she may value. Clearly, donating to charity is far superior to a sale of stock.

For example, in an advertisement from the office of development at the Graduate School of Business at Stanford University, we found the following quote from a donor:

> "I made my gift as an expression of my appreciation to the Business School. ... Giving a life income gift, rather than an outright gift, makes it possible to give much more without reducing my standard of living. ... If your portfolio is overloaded with equities you have held for many years, you may want to convert all or some of them into a more conservative fund yielding greater income. Instead of selling the stocks, paying the capital gains tax, and finding the right investments, you can save yourself the trouble and make a gift to the School at the same time."[6]

There are nontax factors, however, that can reduce the desirability of donating stock to the charity. Although the trust can sell the stock and use the proceeds to buy other securities, the funds are irrevocably tied up in the trust. What if your client comes upon a new venture or needs the funds for other purposes? She can only get her hands on 8% ($4 million) of the value of the trust each year. Alternatively, she could borrow using the annual income from the trust as security. But conversations we have had with experts suggest that banks appear willing to provide loans equal to only one or two years worth of future distributions.

Who bears the cost of these arrangements? Taxpayers do. Rather than collecting $14.1 million in capital gains taxes, society actually pays $1.5 million for a $5 million charitable contribution. Some might argue that this is going too far.[7] IRS statistics indicate that there was $2.5 billion tied up in charitable remainder

---

[6]From *Stanford Business School Magazine*, June 1990.

[7]An article entitled "Tax Dodges Begin at Home" (*Forbes*, November 26, 1990) begins with the following statement: "Here's an attractive proposition: You give a piece of appreciated real estate or shares of stock to charity and end up better off financially than if you'd sold your property and kept the proceeds. As a bonus you get a warm glow from giving to charity instead of the IRS. The loophole involves a charitable remainder trust."

27.2   The Tax Subsidy to Charitable Giving

trusts as of 1989. Moreover, many firms have been gearing up to mass market these trusts, and brokers have even been earning a fee for marrying donors with charities.[8] From time to time, there have been legislative proposals to tax the currently untaxed gain on an asset that is donated to charity. Congress has tried to reduce the benefits of charitable giving (and other deductions), to some extent, by introducing the alternative minimum tax (AMT) that taxes part of the untaxed portion of capital gains under certain circumstances.

The Alternative Minimum Tax and Charitable Giving

When appreciated shares are used to make charitable gifts, the untaxed capital gains that are exempt from ordinary income tax are subject to the AMT.[9] Taxable AMT income is calculated by adding to ordinary taxable income, under the regular tax, (1) deductions for state and local taxes, consumer interest, and miscellaneous deductions, and (2) certain tax preference items such as the appreciated element of charitable gifts, accelerated depreciation on depreciable property, incentive stock option benefits (the difference between the market value and exercise value of an incentive stock option when exercised), some passive investment losses, and the interest on certain private activity municipal bonds issued after 1986.

For individual taxpayers, the most important add-back is the state and local tax deduction for residents of such high-tax states as California, New York, and Massachusetts, and the most important preference item is the untaxed capital gains portion of charitable gifts. Some preference items, like accelerated depreciation, give rise to an AMT credit that may be used in the future to reduce regular taxes.

To explore the significance of the AMT, it will be convenient to introduce some notation:

t_{amt} = AMT tax rate

t_p = personal tax rate on regular taxable income

Y = regular taxable income

A = AMT preferences and disallowed deductions[10]

C = market value of assets contributed to charity

B = tax basis of assets contributed to charity[11]

If there are no deferral preferences on which a credit might be available to reduce future taxes, then a taxpayer's tax bill is equal to

$$\text{Maximum } ((Y + A)t_{amt}, Yt_p).$$

---

[8] *Ibid.*

[9] The full capital gain of $45 million in our illustration of the charitable remainder trust is *not* subject to the AMT. Only the amount equal to the charitable contribution deduction ($5 million in the example) is subject to the AMT. As we will see, this *could* mean an effective loss of the $5 million charitable contribution deduction.

[10] Note that AMT Taxable Income = Y + A.

[11] Note that C - B is the gain on appreciated assets that *would* be taxed if sold rather than contributed to charity.

In other words, the tax due is equal to the greater of the regular tax and the alternative minimum tax.

The AMT affects the value and timing of charitable giving of appreciated securities. Charitable contributions of appreciated securities are less valuable to a donor who is in an AMT tax position. Consider the case of a donor with stock that has a basis equal to zero. This is a good approximation for the founders of many successful companies.

If t_p = 40% and the AMT does not apply, $1.67 of stock can be donated for each $1 of after-tax cost. If the stock were to be sold, and cash (rather than stock) were donated, only $1 could be transferred to charity at an after-tax cost of $1 to the donor. Each dollar of stock sold triggers a $.40 capital gains tax, exactly equal to the tax refund from contributing $1 to charity.

On the other hand, if the AMT already *does* apply, even prior to making the charitable gift, and if t_{amt} is equal to 25%, then even if the appreciated stock is donated, only $1 worth of stock can be transferred per dollar of after-tax cost. The charitable contribution deduction is exactly offset by a corresponding increase in AMT preference items, so the total alternative minimum taxable income is unaffected. It is as if the stock had been sold and the proceeds donated to charity. If, on the other hand, the stock's basis, B, is 30% of its fair market value (rather than zero), the taxpayer could give *more* than $1 of stock to charity per dollar of after-tax cost. In general, the amount that can be contributed, C, to yield an after-tax cost of $1 satisfies the following condition:

$$- C + t_{amt} C - t_{amt} (C - B) = - 1.$$

The second term above represents the value of the charitable contribution deduction, and the third term represents the tax cost of the capital gain, which is a preference item for AMT purposes. For t_{amt} = 25% and B = .3C, as in our example, C = $1.0811. That is, $1.0811 worth of stock can be contributed to the charity and the after-tax cost of the gift will be one dollar. In effect, when the AMT exceeds the regular tax, the net tax benefit from donating stock is equal to the tax basis in the stock multiplied by the AMT tax rate ($1.0811 × .3 × .25 or $.0811 per $1.0811 worth of stock in the example). But once again, when the AMT applies, there is no advantage to donating appreciated stock to charity. The same after-tax cost would result if the stock were sold and $1.0811 in cash were donated to charity.

It is quite common for the AMT *not* to apply prior to making a major gift of appreciated stock, but *to apply* following the gift due to the creation of AMT tax preferences. In this case, it is advantageous to donate stock up until the point that the AMT equals the regular tax, and it is tax-neutral thereafter.

As indicated in footnote 9, the impact of the AMT on the tax benefits to donating appreciated stock can be mitigated considerably through the use of a charitable remainder trust. The reason is that the AMT preference amount for the untaxed capital gain is limited to the amount of the charitable contribution deduction. But in a charitable remainder trust, the forgiven capital gain can far exceed the value of the remainder interest left to charity (and it is the value of the remainder interest that is equal to the charitable contribution deduction).

Finally, we note that the effect of the AMT on the tax subsidy to donating appreciated securities can be mitigated by spreading the gift over several years. Planned carefully, this strategy results in the regular tax exceeding the AMT in each year, rather than the AMT exceeding the regular tax by a large amount in one year and falling well short of the regular tax in other years.

27.3   Non-Charitable Giving: Freezing an Estate

A Model of the Tradeoffs Between Gifting Now versus by Bequest

Giving away assets during one's lifetime, even to noncharitable entities, can be tax-advantageous. How? First, there is the annual $10,000 gift exemption per donee ($20,000 with spousal consent). Each dollar given this way removes *more* than a dollar, tax free, from the estate. Why is this so? Because it also removes the appreciation from the estate: it "freezes" the estate. That is, the estate is reduced by $(1 + r)^n$, where r is the after-tax rate of return earned on the assets and n is the number of years until bequest. The same logic applies to gifts of up to the unified estate and gift tax exemption amount of $600,000.

For gifts above the annual plus overall exemption amounts, the benefactor pays a gift tax now, and will receive a tax credit later (without interest), for the tax paid. The advantage of the gift here is that the benefactor keeps the appreciation on the assets given away out of the estate. In special cases, this turns out to be equivalent to obtaining an estate tax deduction for the gift tax paid plus interest on the gift tax. As a result, in a wide variety of circumstances, there are tax advantages to giving early. Let us take a closer look.

Suppose a $1 current gift triggers a gift tax today of t_0^e. The marginal estate tax rate, in n years, at death is t_n^e. Let R^K and R^P denote the before-tax rates of return on investments for the children and their parents, respectively. Let t^K and t^P denote the income tax rates of the children and their parents, respectively.

Notice that a $1 gift requires a present outlay of $1 + t_0^e$, dollars since it triggers a gift tax of t_0^e. So a comparison of the after-tax accumulations of a current gift and a future bequest requires that, for bequests, $1 + t_0^e$ dollars be set aside currently, for each dollar of current gift.[12]

Gift: $[1 + R^K(1 - t^K)]^n - (t_n^e - t_0^{e'})$

Bequest: $(1 + t_0^e)[(1 + R^P(1 - t^P))]^n(1 - t_n^e))$.

Since the gift tax credit is based on the schedule in place at death, $t_0^{e'}$ might differ from t_0^e. The term $(t_n^e - t_0^{e'})$ represents the difference between the estate tax at time n on $1 of additional taxable gifts that were added back to the estate and the gift tax that can be used as a credit against this tax. If the tax rate schedule is the same at time n as it was at the time of the gift, then $t_0^{e'}$ is equal to the actual tax that was paid on the gift initially, t_0^e. To simplify the analysis, we assume in what follows that the tax rate schedule remains unchanged.

To illustrate how the integration of the estate and gift tax could increase the benefits of early gifting, assume that the parent and child invest in assets that earn

---

[12] There are striking similarities between this analysis and the current-versus-future repatriation decision of multinational firms with respect to the income of their foreign subsidiaries. See Chapters Thirteen and Fourteen for details.

the same after-tax rate, r, and that the gift tax rate and the estate tax rate are the same, t^e, which is the case for large gifts and estates. In this case,

Gift now: $(1 + r)^n$ (27.1)

Bequest: $(1 + t^e)(1 + r)^n(1 - t^e) = (1 - t^{e2})(1 + r)^n$ (27.2)

So the family is better off with a current gift by $t^{e2}(1 + r)^n$. Alternatively stated,

$$\frac{\text{gift now}}{\text{bequest}} = \frac{1}{1 - t^{e2}}.$$

If, for example, $t^e = 50\%$, then

$$\frac{\text{gift now}}{\text{bequest}} = 1.333;$$

that is, the family is 33% better off with a current gift than a bequest. What is going on here? The family effectively achieves not only a tax credit for the gift tax paid earlier but also an estate tax deduction for the gift tax paid earlier with interest. That is, the size of the taxable estate is reduced by the gift taxes paid, plus any income that would have been earned from investing the additional funds.

Suppose a benefactor gave a $1 million gift to a relative and paid the $.5 million tax due on the gift the day before she died. Although the estate includes the value of the gift, $1 million, it does not include the $.5 million gift tax. At a 50% tax rate, this saves $250,000 in tax. Recognizing the tax-planning incentive to make deathbed gifts, the tax law requires that the gift tax paid be added back to the estate if the gift is made within three years of death.

In addition, because fewer appreciating assets are in an estate when a gift is made early, t_n^e may well be less when a gift is made than when a bequest is made. This further favors gifting of assets. For example, if the average estate tax rate on the additional bequest of $1.5 million, plus reinvested earnings, amounted to 55%, rather than 50%, the advantage of a current gift over a bequest would increase to $1/[(1 + t_0^e) (1 - t_n^e)] = 1.482$. The advantage of the gift is 11% greater than when the estate tax rate was 50%. As noted earlier, if the estate tax rate is expected to fall, however, this may favor postponing the gift.

The Tradeoffs Between Freezing an Estate and Losing the Step-up in Basis on Bequests

We next expand the model to account for the fact that many assets transferred from a donor to a donee may have a built-in capital gain and/or may produce one in the future. This feature favors bequests because of the tax-free step-up in the basis of the assets transferred by bequest. Beneficiaries retain their benefactor's original basis in assets that are gifted prior to death.[13] There is a trade off, then, between obtaining a step up in the basis of assets on a bequest (an *income* tax benefit) versus the *estate* tax benefits of early gifts.

---

[13] For assets that would be sold anyway prior to the death of a benefactor, the situation is quite different. Gifting early in this case can be particularly advantageous if the donee faces a lower capital gains tax rate than the donor.

Assume that a parent has owned a business for m years. The initial basis in the business was b dollars, the initial value of the business was V dollars,[14] and the business has been increasing in value at after-tax rate r^P per year. The parent is now contemplating a gift of the business to his children. There are n - m years left until his death. Each year, the business pays out a dividend, d_s. For simplicity, assume the dividend paid is that amount which leaves the income tax basis unchanged at amount b. The excess of r^P over d, then, represents the appreciation rate on the value of the business that is not subjected *currently* to the income gain. A sale of the business, however, would trigger a capital gains tax. If control of the business is transferred to the children, we assume that the parent receives the same compensation and "dividends" that would have been received had control *not* been transferred. Similarly, the children's compensation is assumed to be the same as if control had *not* been transferred. To make the model simple, we assume a constant rate of return through time, but we allow for the possibility that the parent and children do not operate the business with equal efficiency. In other words, we allow r^P to differ from r^K. We also assume a constant dividend yield, d, each year. At the date of the potential gift, the value of the business is

$$A = V(1 + r^P - d)^m,$$

which would attract a gift tax of At_m^e. At death, the estate must pay the differential estate tax on the gift, or $A(t_n^e - t_m^e)$. If a gift is made, we assume that the business is sold when the parent dies. The children must then pay income tax at a rate of t_n^I on the total appreciation of the business in excess of its basis of b. The children retain

$$A(1 + r^K - d)^{m-n} - A(t_n^e - t_m^e) - t_n^I [A(1 + r^K - d)^{m-n} - b], \qquad (27.3)$$

which simplifies to

$$A(1 + r^K - d)^{m-n}(1 - t_n^I) - A(t_n^e - t_m^e) + t_n^I[b]. \qquad (27.4)$$

Comparing this to the parent's decision to retain the business until death, a bequest would yield

$$A(1 + t_m^e)(1 + r^P - d)^n (1 - t_n^e).$$

If we assume $r^K - d = r^P - d = r$; $t_m^e = t_n^e = t^e$; and b = 0 and d = 0 (which most favors a bequest), we find

Gift: $A(1 + r)^n(1 - t_n^I)$

Bequest: $A(1 + r)^n(1 - t^{e2})$.

For example, if $t_n^I = 30\%$ and $t^e = 50\%$, which implies that $t^{e2} = 25\%$, then a bequest is superior to a gift by 75/70 or 7.1%. If, on the other hand, the appreciated asset will be retained by the donee beyond the death of the donor, so that the effective capital gains tax rate is lower (say, 20%), then the *gift* is better by 80/75 = 6.1%.

The higher is b, the more favorable is the gift. If assets yield "dividends," thereby reducing the capital gains, this, too, favors a gift. For the special case of b = V and d = r^P (that is, there is no appreciation on the asset to

---

[14] The initial value of the business can differ from the initial basis in the business because of the value of ideas brought into the business with a tax basis equal to zero.

Chapter 27   Estate and Gift Tax Planning

be taxed to the donee on the sale) then, per dollar of initial value of the business, the accumulations given by 27.3 and 27.4 simplify to those given by 27.1 and 27.2, respectively, our earlier cases.

Beyond these tax considerations, there are nontax costs to freezing an estate by gifting early that must be considered. To succeed in freezing the estate through gift giving requires relinquishing at least some control of the assets. A benefactor might not be willing to do so for personal reasons. Children have been known to squander their new-found wealth, or they might turn against their benefactors (the King Lear Syndrome).[15] To the extent freezing the estate by way of gift entails transferring assets to children who are less skillful in managing them, this, too, exacts a cost. Moreover, it is not uncommon for donors to *claim* that their donees are doing a poor job in managing the transferred assets, whether this is true or not. Such tensions can be painful for both parties. Finally, many parents resist transferring wealth to their children out of fear of removing incentives for them to succeed on their own.

Freezing an Estate and Maintaining Control of Assets Through the Use of Preferred Stock Recapitalizations

Over the years, the interaction of tax and nontax considerations in estate planning has given rise to many legal arrangements designed to freeze the benefactor's estate without losing control of the family business, and to preserve deferral (or elimination) of part of the capital gains tax on the transfer of the business. Preferred stock recapitalizations were a very common tax-planning strategy employed in family businesses prior to 1987 in the U.S. Parents would exchange their common stock for voting preferred stock with a fixed dividend rate and give their children nonvoting common stock. Consequently, they would retain complete control of the firm, but all appreciation in the value of the firm after the date of the gift would stay out of their estate and would inure to the children. Moreover, the exchange of preferred stock for common stock can often be structured as a tax-free exchange. This means that the preferred stock would be assigned a tax basis equal to that on the common stock, and upon the parents' death, the children could then still achieve a tax-free step-up in the basis of the preferred stock. The children's common stock shares are *not* stepped up on the death of their parents (as they would be if they had been retained by their parents), but the increase in their value since the date of gift is also not included in the parents' estate. On the initial exchange, the preferred stock represents most of the value of the firm, so the gift attracts very little gift tax.

Congress disallowed the benefits of these arrangements. The 1987 Tax Act requires that the benefactor include not only the basis of the preferred stock but also any appreciation in the value of the company as an estate asset unless the preferred stock is sold at least three years prior to the benefactor's death or voting control is relinquished. Even if benefactors were privy to the date of their death,

---

[15] In a *Wall Street Journal* article (July 16, 1990) entitled "U-Haul's Patriarch Now Battles Offspring in Bitterest of Feuds," we find the following quote from Mr. Shoen, who was engaged in a painful conflict with his children over the management of the company he founded, after having given shares in his company to them: "No man should give away his wealth or power until he dies. No way. No way."

27.3   Non-Charitable Giving: Freezing an Estate

and were to sell their preferred stock three years prior to their death, they would face the added tax cost of losing the tax-free step-up in the basis of the frozen part of their preferred-stock gain.

Prior to the 1987 Tax Act, many firms let the preferred dividends accumulate in the firm (in arrears, without interest or an intention to pay out these dividends) to avoid the double taxation of dividends. When the parent died, no accumulated dividends were paid on the preferred. Also, many of the prior freezes attached "bells and whistles" to the preferred stock, such as the right to receive income or the right to convert a noncumulative preferred stock into a cumulative preferred. Such rights increased the value of the preferred stock and reduced the value of the gift of common stock. In actuality, however, parents never intended to exercise these rights. Moreover, the common stock in many preferred stock recapitalization transactions was undervalued (thereby understating the taxable gift). The common stock represented a valuable call option (or warrant) on the company's assets, an option that was typically undervalued on the transfer. The April 30, 1990 edition of *Tax Notes* reported that Assistant Treasury Secretary Gideon estimated that allowing estates to be frozen through preferred stock recapitalizations would result in a loss of $1 billion in estate tax revenue from 1991 through 1995.

Bowing to intense lobbying efforts, however, to reinstate the estate freeze opportunity,[16] Congress, in the 1990 Tax Act, put new rules into place that resurrected the old freeze rules, but the legislation required that recapitalized firms pay out reasonable dividends on the preferred stock or else the 1987 tax rules would prevail. These dividend restrictions are quite onerous. Consequently, we expect to see far fewer recapitalizations in the 1990s than prior to the 1987 Tax Act.

To show what the estate tax freeze can accomplish, assume that a business is worth $10 million. The parents give $1 million in (nonvoting) common to the children and retain $9 million in (voting) preferred stock in a recapitalization. By the date of death, the value of the business has increased to $30 million. The value of the common would be $21 million, and the value of the preferred would still be $9 million. The estate would include the $1 million gift plus the $9 million preferred stock issue, less the value of any gift taxes that were paid earlier on the $1 million stock transfer to the children.

Actually, the IRS allows lower valuations on the transfer of nontraded assets and minority interests than on liquid assets. The values of these assets are given what are called "haircuts." These haircuts reduce the value of the loss of the step-up in basis at the time of death. Because the $1 million gift above was a nonvoting interest, and a minority interest, the IRS and the courts allow substantial haircuts (often 40% or more) on the valuation of the assets for gift tax purposes. On death, the parents' preferred stock could also be given a large haircut since it, too, is a non-traded asset. These same haircuts apply to minority interests in the stock of nontraded companies and in real estate. It is interesting

---

[16] A letter from a leading accounting firm (KPMG Peat Marwick) to a venture capitalist in 1989 illustrates the mechanics of organizing the lobbying effort: "Congress enacted legislation in 1987 aimed at the elimination of the estate freeze. We are currently coordinating a legislative effort for our closely-held clients who are interested in further discussion and exploration of an effort to repeal or modify the provisions."

to note that the Japanese allow estates to reduce the value of real estate by 50% in estimating its value for estate tax purposes. Some have argued that part of the value of land in Japan can be attributed to this estate-tax advantage.

In our example, the $20 million appreciation in the value of the stock was kept out of the estate. At a 50% estate tax rate, this saved $10 million in estate taxes. Of course the gift tax had to be paid on the gift of stock to the children. Suppose the gift tax was $.5 million, and it would have grown to $1.5 million by the time of death, leaving $.75 million more after estate tax (or .5 × $1.5 million). But the $.5 million gift tax can be credited against the estate tax. Paying the gift tax, then, results in a loss of $.25 million, leaving a net estate tax saving of $9.75 million. The basis in the $20 million appreciation in the stock, however, would have been stepped-up to market value if the stock were bequeathed and not gifted to the children. If the present value of the incremental capital gains tax to the children is 15% of the $20 million capital gain, this costs an additional $3 million. The net savings are $6.75 million. The net savings might actually be greater if the estate had to come up with $9.75 million to pay the estate tax. Without the freeze, the children might have had to sell the business, perhaps at a large discount due to information problems regarding the value of the business, or they may have had to lever up the business at high interest rates because of similar considerations.

As we noted, a cost of the preferred stock freeze is that the parents receive dividend income on their preferred stock. Such dividends are nondeductible for corporations and fully taxable to the parents, and this is tax disadvantageous relative to debt. This eats into part of the $9.75 million estate tax saving. The parent retains control but at the cost of receiving taxable dividends. This results from the fact that to retain voting control, the parent must retain stock. Note that preferred stock freezes can *not* be effected for S-corporations, since they can only have one class of stock. The common stock can be split into class A and class B shares with different dividend and voting rights, but it is difficult to freeze the appreciation of one class of shares.

LBOs as Alternatives to Preferred Stock Recapitalizations

The requirement that preferred stock pay out periodic dividends to validate the preferred stock recapitalizations (1990 Tax Act) gave a boost to leveraged buyouts (LBOs) as an estate planning device. LBOs allow the required payments to the parents to be tax-deductible to the corporation. The disadvantages of LBO freezes include: (1) the difficulty of designing debt covenants that allow parents to retain control over the operations of the business, and (2) loss of the step-up in basis of the business at the time of death. The parents, however, could receive installment notes for the stock of their company which would defer the payment of the capital gains tax otherwise due upon completion of the LBO. This reduces the disadvantage of losing the step-up in basis in the stock at death. Under Section 306, however, the payment of installment notes for the stock might be taxed as a dividend (up to the retained earnings of the firm). Under Section 302, the payment would *not* be considered a dividend if all the stock is redeemed and the parent does not participate in the operations of the company for 10 years, but this is a high price to pay for a parent who wishes to retain operating control of the business.

Following the LBO, the children would be free to convert to S-Corporation status to avoid double taxation of the corporation's profits. This is a nontaxable event except for the recapture of LIFO reserves on inventories. In addition, any assets sold within 10 years of an S-Corporation election trigger corporate-level capital gains taxes to the extent of the built-in gains on the firm's assets at the time of the election. Otherwise, the shareholders in an S-Corporation pay only one level of taxation, as in a partnership.

Swap Arrangements as Alternatives to Preferred Stock Recapitalizations

A simple structure that parents could employ to freeze the size of the business would be to swap, with their children, the returns on their common stock for the returns on some bond index. The parent thereby freezes the appreciation in the stock *and* retains control of the voting shares of the company. Moreover, the swap arrangement could be quite valuable if an LBO structure triggers an ownership shift, and the corporation becomes severely restricted in its use of tax attributes such as its NOLs or FTCs (as discussed in Chapter Twenty-Six). The swap contract can further provide that the swap payments only be payable at the termination of the swap contract. While this precludes children from deducting the appreciation on the deferred bond index (the interest payments) until the swap contract is settled for cash, the parents also do not realize interest income until the swap contract is settled. The children can also build into the swap agreement the right to cancel the swap on their parents' death. At that time, their parents' stock realizes a step-up in basis to fair market value.

For example, assume a swap contract is written on a notional $10 million when the stock of the company is worth $10 million, and by the time of death, the stock has appreciated to $30 million. The stock is worth $30 million in the estate, but the parent owes $20 million on the swap. The estate asset is frozen at $10 million.

But the parents have contracted to receive the deferred returns on some bond index, such as Libor. To offset this increment to the value of the estate, the parents can borrow enough money each year to meet consumption needs by using the $10 million stock, plus the appreciation in the bond index, as collateral against the loans. These loans, then, become liabilities of the estate. Therefore, any payment that the estate receives on the bond index will be offset by the amount of the liability on the debt.[17]

---

[17] The corporation can mitigate the effects of not being able to deduct the interest it owes on the bond index currently by entering into a swap on a notional $10 million with a tax exempt entity to receive the returns on some non-dividend paying asset such as gold for the returns on the bond index. The corporation can then borrow $10 million to buy gold to hedge the terms of the swap agreement. The interest on the $10 million loan to buy the gold is currently deductible to the corporation. Of course, transaction and information costs reduce the advantage of this series of transactions. This swap structure, if put into place, can be superior to both the preferred stock recapitalization and the LBO structure.

As noted in Chapter Twenty, it may be difficult to achieve a favorable advance ruling from the IRS for structures such as these. This reduces the attractiveness of the arrangements.

Chapter 27   Estate and Gift Tax Planning

Transferring the Family Business to Reduce the Tax on Bequest but at the Expense of a Potentially Higher Capital Gains Tax for the Beneficiaries

Gift of Minority Interests: Another strategy that is commonly employed to reduce the estate tax is to give away or bequeath a minority interest in the family business to several children. Either way, the courts allow the shares to be valued at a healthy discount relative to a majority interest in the company due to the lack of control. The courts have permitted valuation discounts of between 25% and 40% for minority interests. This device was used by the founder of Hallmark Cards to save more than $200 million in estate taxes. It was also used by newspaper magnate Samuel Newhouse, Sr., who built the largest privately held newspaper fortune in the U.S. His plan saved over half a billion dollars in estate taxes. It was litigated by the IRS, the largest estate tax case ever, and was found in the Newhouse's favor in March, 1990. These discounts reduce the estate tax, but transfer a built-in capital gain to the children.

Generous Compensation: Another way to avoid estate or gift taxes is to compensate beneficiaries very generously for services performed. These payments are deductible to the donor and taxable to the donee. When the donor's tax rate exceeds that of the donee, the net income tax cost is actually negative, and the assets are removed from the estate without any transfer taxes. Although tax rules prevent paying employees excessive compensation, it is very expensive for the IRS to monitor compensation levels. Moreover, the IRS allows an estate to determine the value of a closely held company for estate tax purposes by capitalizing its earnings over the five years prior to the parent's death. Paying large salaries during these years reduces earnings and the valuation of the business for estate tax purposes, but once again at the cost of passing on a low tax basis to the next generation. With low income tax rates relative to estate tax rates subsequent to the 1986 Tax Act, these types of tax-planning strategies have become particularly important.

Companion Businesses: Similar opportunities arise where the donee sets up a business that supplies or purchases goods or services from the donor's business. Judicious transfer pricing policies can shift wealth, free of the transfer tax, from the donor to the donee.

New Company Start-ups: With start-up companies, it is not uncommon for one parent to retain the voting common and give non-voting common to children if there are tax advantages to splitting off the assets of the estate. A start-up business would have a low valuation for gift-tax purposes. To secure S-Corporation status requires that the dividend rights and liquidation preferences for each share of stock be equal, although the stock *can* be broken into pieces with different voting rights. Family partnerships can achieve the same result: the parent becomes the general partner, and the children become the limited partners. The cost of these strategies, however, is that if the business were to fail, the capital losses on the business venture would be borne, in part, by the children, who may not be able to use the capital loss deductions as efficiently.

Special Provisions that Reduce the Estate Tax on Disposition of Family Businesses

It is difficult to value an interest in a closely held corporation on the death of an owner. Companies often employ stock redemption plans, which establish an acceptable value for estate tax purposes.[18] The plan must require that the principal shareholders' stock be acquired during their lifetimes or at their death at a specified or determinable price using an accepted formula such as net worth or capitalized earnings. If the parent allows children to buy stock at its formula value, the value of the company could be deemed to be quite low for estate tax purposes, especially if the children have been receiving generous compensation prior to the date of redemption. As we have noted several times before, a disadvantage of this low valuation is that the stock attracts a higher capital gains tax in the future. But for estates whose primary asset is the stock of a closely held company, the dead-weight costs of borrowing to pay the extra estate tax could outweigh the benefits of achieving a greater step-up in the basis of the stock. Perhaps more important, estate tax rates are potentially far greater than deferred capital gains tax rates, and there is a dollar-for-dollar tradeoff between the size of the taxable estate and the amount of deferred capital gain.[19]

Many corporate or partnership buy-out plans are funded with life insurance owned by the corporation on the life of a key executive. Although the corporation can not deduct the annual cost of the insurance on the executive's life, the insurance proceeds are ignored in valuing the company for estate tax purposes. Neither estate tax nor income tax is paid on the life-insurance proceeds.

Furthermore, these buy-sell and insurance agreements reduce the negotiation and audit costs of dealing with the IRS, as well as the incidence of litigation among owners. The liquid proceeds ensure that the decedents can pay the estate tax.

Under Section 306, redemption of the stock of a closely held corporation is treated as a dividend, and not as capital gain, up to the retained earnings in the corporation. An exception arises, however, if the stock redemption is for the purpose of paying gift taxes, where the closely held stock represents more than 35% of the benefactor's assets.

Also, if a major asset, such as a small business or a farm, represents more than 35% of the value of an estate, the estate can defer paying the estate tax on these assets for 5 years. After that, the IRS allows for a 10-year installment note (starting in the sixth year) payable at the applicable federal rate. This is in effect, a below-market interest-rate loan. In addition, annual interest of only 4% is charged on deferred tax of up to $1,000,000.

These rules lead to interesting planning considerations for those with assets slightly below the 35% estate value cut-off. If the nontax costs are not too great,

---

[18] As discussed in Chapter Twelve, Employee Stock Ownership Plans offer special tax planning opportunities here.

[19] The 1990 Tax Act provides that a buy-sell arrangement entered into or substantially modified after October 8, 1990, will not be recognized unless (1) it is a bona fide business arrangement, (2) it it not a device to transfer property to family members for less than full consideration, and (3) its terms are comparable to similar arrangements entered into by persons in an arm's length transaction. *Tax Topics Advisory* (Coopers & Lybrand), November 1990.

Chapter 27 Estate and Gift Tax Planning

it might pay to give away assets to increase the relative value of particular assets to above the 35% cut-off. It also can pay to consolidate assets into a single investment.

Other Forms of Estate Freezes

Generation Skipping Transfer Tax (GSTT): If grandparents could make gifts to grandchildren directly, this would be an excellent way to freeze both the estate of the grandparents as well as that of their children. The tax rules, however, restrict this strategy. Prior to the 1986 Tax Act, a trust that benefited both children and grandchildren was called a generation skipping trust. Such trusts often took the form that trust assets would support children for their lives, and upon their deaths, all trust assets and income would go to the grandchildren. Distributions to grandchildren from such trusts attracted a tax. There was an estate tax exclusion of $250,000 per grandchild. Moreover, the tax could be avoided by setting up trusts that provided for "direct skips" to grandchildren (giving nothing to the children in specific trusts).

The tax paid on transfers greater than $250,000 was the estate tax that would be paid by the skipped generation (the grantor's children) if *they* had made the gifts to the grandchildren.[20] The rules were intended to require that the estate tax be paid as if the money had been received by each successive generation. The rules were very difficult to administer because the grandparents paid the tax, and, to do so, they had to ascertain the estate tax rate of the skipped generation.

The 1986 Tax Act changed the rules both to simplify them as well as to impede taxpayers' ability to freeze an estate through generation-skipping techniques. In brief, the 1986 GSTT rules include (1) an exemption for generation-skipping transfers aggregating up to $1 million ($2 million with spousal consent), (2) a flat GSTT rate equal to the maximum rate under the estate and gift tax rate schedule (55% currently) on transfers in excess of the GSTT and gift tax exemptions, (3) a tax on both income and corpus, and (4) a tax on direct skips (but there was a $2 million exemption per grandchild for each direct skip made prior to 1990).

The grantor pays the GSTT. For example, if $4 million is transferred, and the GSTT rate is 55%, the GSTT is $2.2 million. For gift tax purposes, the transferor is deemed to have made a gift equal to the *sum* of the net transfer and the GSTT, or $6.2 million.

Despite this steep tax, it still pays to freeze an estate by making generation-skipping transfers. This is particularly so when two or more generations are skipped (as when a gift is made directly to a great grandchild), since the donor pays only one GSTT. In addition, the $1 million exemption is valuable.

To see this, let us compare a generation-skipping gift to a bequest. Suppose that a grandparent, whose GSTT and gift tax exclusions have already been used up, makes a gift of $2 million in trust to grandchildren on his deathbed. The transfer for gift tax purposes is $3 million, the GSTT is $1 million (assuming for case of illustration a GSTT rate of only 50%), and the gift tax is $1.5 million

---

[20] Note that this made it desirable to "skip" the poorest relative since the estate tax rate would be lowest for such a person. From an equity standpoint, this was a frustrating incentive.

(assuming a 50% estate tax on the $3 million gift). To make a net gift of $2 million requires the donor to transfer $4.5 million.

To make a net transfer of $2 million through an estate, however, requires $6 million. The GSTT of $1 million and an estate tax of $3 million is paid. The total tax rate is a whopping 67%! In general, the following accumulations result.

Gift Skip: $\quad (1 + r)^n - 1/[(1 + t_0^{gs}) (1 + t^g)] (t^e - t^g)$ $\qquad$ (27.5)

Bequest Skip: $\quad (1 + t_0^{gs}) (1 + t^g) (1 + r)^n (1 - t^e)/(1 + t_n^{gs})$ $\qquad$ (27.6)

where t^e, t^g, t_0^{gs}, and t_n^{gs} are the marginal estate tax, gift tax, and current and future GSTT rates, respectively. To understand how 27.6 is derived, note that each dollar of generation skipping gift *not* made allows $(1 + t_0^{gs}) (1 + t^g)$ to be invested for n periods. The total accumulation is then taxed at rate t^e. What is left is split between the GSTT and the net transfer to the beneficiary. That is, the net transfer, multiplied by $(1 + t_n^{gs})$, is equal to the estate net assets less the estate tax. So the net transfer to the beneficiary is equal to the estate net assets, less the estate tax, all divided by $(1 + t_n^{gs})$.

If all of these rates are equal (denoted by t below), as they are for large transfers, the choice comes down to a comparison of

Gift: $\qquad (1 + r)^n$

versus

Bequest: $\qquad (1 - t)^2 (1 + r)^n$

Note that these are the *same conditions* as the ones that compare a gift to a bequest in the absence of a generation skipping transfer (27.1 and 27.2). This means that waiting to bequeath is always worse than making a generation skipping gift prior to death if the after-tax returns are the same. The reason, as before, is the effective deductibility of the gift tax for estate tax purposes. Note that there is no advantage to having paid the generation skipping transfer tax prior to death, since the payment of this tax is deemed to be a gift and, therefore, is added back to the taxable estate.

Moreover, it always pays to skip generations (if the tax rates are constant) than to pay two levels of estate tax. That is,

Gift Skip: $\qquad (1 + r)^n$

versus

Two Bequests: $\qquad (1 + t)^2 (1 + r)^n (1 - t)^2$

If t is equal to .5, bequeathing twice produces 56% of the benefits of a gift to the skipped generation; if t is equal to .4, bequeathing twice produces 71% of the benefits. Skipping more than one generation produces even greater benefits.

Marital Deduction: A benefactor can avoid all estate taxes by bequeathing all assets to the spouse. This is another form of estate freeze. The marital deduction is unlimited. And if the spouse remarries, leaving all remaining assets to the new spouse, estate taxes are once again avoided.

How much of the marital deduction to use is an important estate-tax planning problem. The decision is often a difficult one. The first spouse might worry about the surviving spouse squandering the assets thereby preventing the children from getting a desired share of the estate assets.

Chapter 27 Estate and Gift Tax Planning

For many small estates, the unified credit (currently $192,800) is all that is necessary to reduce the estate tax to zero. In using the marital deduction, larger estates must trade off paying a lower estate tax now against a potentially larger estate tax in the future when the surviving spouse dies. Since estate tax rates are very progressive, it might pay to equalize estates and pay some estate tax at the first death. This would be particularly tax advantageous if the surviving spouse is expected to generate additional wealth beyond consumption needs.

Paying estate tax at the first death, however, has both tax and nontax costs. The surviving spouse's need for assets depends on a variety of factors that are uncertain at the time of the decedent's death, including future income, length of life, and health. If the surviving spouse anticipates depleting the assets in the estate, it would be tax advantageous to use the full marital deduction. More often than not, because of the uncertainty of future income needs, more assets are transferred to the surviving spouse than would be optimal in a world of certainty. The result is greater estate tax being paid on the death of the surviving spouse.

If there are plans to transfer assets to children, there are tax incentives to bequeath enough assets to them upon the death of the first spouse so that the unified credit can be used by both spouses. If direct bequests or gifts are made to the children, however, the surviving spouse could end up with insufficient funds on which to live. Many couples fail to trust their children to support them if all of the parents' assets are transferred to the children. Moreover, one spouse might not trust the surviving spouse or succeeding spouses to provide adequately for the children.

These problems can be mitigated by establishing trusts that control how resources are disbursed over time. Trusts can also protect a surviving spouse from the demands for resources by the children, and vice versa.

A trust that is not a grantor trust is taxed (as a single person) on income that is not required to be distributed currently. A grantor trust is one that is under the control of the grantor, and all income earned in such trusts is taxed directly to the grantor. Multiple trusts are often established on the death of a family member to hold the assets of the estate. One trust, for example, might hold only the marital deduction portion of the estate. It is common to set-up so-called "Qualified Terminable Interest Property" trusts. Not only does such a trust give the executor flexibility to decide the best marital deduction strategy at the time of death, but it offers the grantor some control over the corpus of the estate. The spouse might receive the income from the trust assets for life, with the remainder distributed to designated beneficiaries on the surviving spouse's death. The trustee generally controls the assets of both the surviving spouse and the children.

Trust law and estate tax law is rather accommodating to the many frictions that can develop among family members. They attempt to deal flexibly with the needs of family planning.

Insurance Policies: Insurance plays an important role in many estate plans. If the insured does not own the life insurance policy, the proceeds from the policy on the death of the insured are neither estate assets nor income to the decedent. The beneficiary must pay the insurance policy premiums. The insured, however, can transfer resources each year to the beneficiary, subject to the gift tax, to pay the premium. The insured cannot control the policy in any way; for example, the insured cannot retain the right to change the designation of the beneficiary nor to cancel the policy. This could become a little bit dicey in a divorce situation, or if a child, who is the policy owner, becomes a member of a militant organization.

To mitigate such problems, benefactors often establish life insurance trusts. The insured sets up a trust and transfers ownership of the insurance policies to the trust. The premiums are paid by the insured as gifts each year to the trust. The trustee, not the grantor, can change the designation of beneficiaries. Such arrangements allow the insurance proceeds to be controlled indirectly, and prevent young beneficiaries from obtaining the insurance proceeds too early, that is, when the grantor deems that they are financially immature.

Many financial consultants claim that insurance policies are the best way to reduce estate taxes.[21] If you buy an insurance policy, your estate will have the money to pay the estate taxes. Although insurance proceeds do provide liquidity for the estate, the insurance policy has a cost. If the implicit tax (the difference between the return on fully taxable bonds and the earnings rate in the policy) is high enough, buying single premium deferred annuities (with far less implicit tax) might be a superior strategy. This is especially so for insureds who expect to live longer than the insurance company assumes. On average, insurance premiums must cover insurance costs, including mortality costs, insurance company costs, and regulatory costs. The insurance premiums could eat up the tax benefits of the insurance.

Transfers of Property Rights at Below Market Prices: Dual ownership arrangements are common ways to freeze the estate tax. They apply in situations where the parent conducts research and development and makes a gift of the acquired knowledge. For example, the parent might inform the child, free of charge, of a good investment opportunity. In effect, this is a nontaxed gift. The IRS cannot tax this activity effectively. Another example is book royalties: it is common for an author to assign the rights or partial rights to a book to a beneficiary just prior to the publisher's acceptance of the book. Before any royalties are earned, the book is given a low value for gift tax purposes. The same type of transfer is effected for venture capital undertakings, or for investment knowledge. It is difficult to tax the advice that parents give to children as a gift, even though it could be extremely valuable advice. It is hard to assess a gift tax on the value of baby-sitting services provided by grandparents to their children. Parents provide for the college education of their children; they co-sign notes for mortgages and business ventures; they provide shelter and other services, all of which transfer wealth to their children. These arrangements freeze an estate and transfer income to the children.

---

[21] For example, see Barry Kaye, *Save A Fortune on Your Estate Taxes*, Longman Group USA Inc. (1990). In the book (and in advertisements in business magazines) it is claimed that life insurance can reduce your estate tax up to 90%, increase your annual $10,000 tax-free gift to $1,000,000, and increase your charitable donations at no additional cost. The analysis fails to take account of differences in the tax rates of children and parents, as well as the implicit tax one pays in owning life insurance policies. Buying life insurance with the proceeds of the annual $10,000 gift can be inferior to a variety of alternatives, particularly if the children's tax rates are below those of their parents and the pretax return available from the life insurance policy is below some less tax-favored alternatives. For example, the children could be better off with gifts and purchasing single premium deferred annuities (or even taxable bonds) with the proceeds.

Chapter 27   Estate and Gift Tax Planning

A famous example of the transfer of investment knowledge from parents to children is one involving oil drilling. The parent, P, buys lease rights to land and subdivides the land into parcels. The parent gives the parcels marked C, in Figure 27.1, to the children and then proceeds to drill for oil on the parcels marked P. As a result, children learn about the possibility of oil on their plots, C, without incurring the costs of the exploratory drilling. Moreover, since no oil had been discovered prior to the exploratory drilling, the plots are transferred to the children at a low value for gift tax purposes.

P	C	P
C	P	C
P	C	P

FIGURE 27.1

Another example of the transfer of investment knowledge to children is the experience of Scholes and Wolfson, who discovered the advantages of buying stock directly from companies at discounts through dividend reinvestment and stock purchase plans (for example, a 5% discount from market price on a $10,000 investment each month).[22] We passed on these discoveries to our respective children. By acquiring shares in 20 to 30 companies at discounted prices in the names of our children, we were able to secure virtually certain profits for them. The only real cost was that of our time, for which we did not charge the children. As an added bonus, this activity took place prior to 1986, so all income was taxed to the children at their lower income tax rate. This was a very effective way to set aside funds for their college educations.

At times, children reduce the size of their estates by making transfers to help parents. Unfortunately, this pertains to neither the children of Scholes nor Wolfson. Many children establish trusts to fund their parents' needs (freezing the appreciation in assets used to fund the trust). Children sometimes hire their parents at above market wages to render services. Children also rent property to parents at below-market rates. These are but a few of the many ways transfers, sometimes in large amounts, escape the gift tax.

A common device for parents to transfer assets to children is for parents and children to buy assets together, such as family vacation property or a family living

---

[22] For details, see Myron S. Scholes and Mark A. Wolfson, "Decentralized Investment Banking: The Case of Discount Dividend Reinvestment and Stock Purchase Plans," *Journal of Financial Economics* (September 1989), pp. 7-35.

27.3   Non-Charitable Giving: Freezing an Estate

complex. Here the parent buys a life interest (or a fixed-term interest), and the children buy a remainder interest in the property. The parent provides the improvements and maintenance on the property while alive, and any appreciation inures to the children free of estate tax. If the appreciation rate in the property is deemed to be low while the discount rate is deemed to be high, and the parents' life expectancy is generous (according to the IRS tables), the children's interest in the property would represent a small fraction of the value of the property. For example, assume that the expected appreciation rate on the property is 5%, the discount rate is 12%, and the life expectancy of the donor is 20 years. The remainder interest is worth only 27.5% of the value of the property.

Taxpayers have also used personal annuities to reduce estate taxes. For example, a parent can buy a life annuity from her children. To illustrate the possibilities, if the actuarial tables indicate an expected life of 15 years for the average arms-length annuity buyer, and the applicable federal interest rate is 9%, the children could promise to pay their parent $200,000 a year for life for a current payment to them of $1.61 million. If the sickly parent's life expectancy is really 5 years, the value of the annuity is $.778 million, and $.832 million is transferred to the children without gift or estate tax. In the early 1980s, taxpayers could use below-market rates of interest to value the annuities they promised to pay and thereby transfer staggering amounts of wealth estate tax-free. Of course, even the best-laid plans can backfire. A famous case in point involves the DuPont family. It is said that when Pierre DuPont was in his mid-60s, and rather sickly, he gave his entire wealth to his children in return for a personal annuity. He expected to die soon, and this would avoid the estate tax. As it turned out, he lived to age 95, and this almost bankrupted his children.

27.4 Tradeoffs Between Freezing the Estate and Paying Estate Taxes at a Discount

For many years the U.S. government issued long-term bonds that could be used as script to pay estate taxes. These securities came to be known as "flower bonds." The coupon rate on these bonds was typically well below the market rate of interest, so the bonds would sell at significant discounts. In valuing their estate, however, the bonds were also valued at par. The government stopped issuing these flower bonds many years ago, and only a few of these low coupon issues remain (the 3%s of 1995 and the 3.5%s of 1998).

Clientele-based arbitrage opportunities exist if flower bonds are in ample supply and the bonds sell at large discounts. Because the supply is limited, however, they sell at a high price (approximately 94–96% of par) to yield far below ordinary treasury bonds (approximately 4%). It appears that many taxpayers use these bonds solely for estate tax purposes. The proper clientele for these bonds is, in fact, those who expect to die soon. They bid up the prices of these bonds. Moreover, the rules do not restrict taxpayers from buying flower bonds on their deathbed. A famous case involves Thomas Watson, who built the I.B.M. corporation to prominence. He had granted the power of attorney to his lawyers, and they bought flower bonds for him when he was in a coma from which he never awoke. The tax courts upheld this transaction. Because of the low yield on these

Chapter 27   Estate and Gift Tax Planning

bonds, the longer the taxpayer holds them, the less valuable the arbitrage.[23] Note that holding the flower bonds, then, is a form of life insurance.

27.5 Exploiting Differences in Tax Rates Between Donors and Donees

Gifts from family members with high marginal income tax rates to those with lower marginal tax rates reduce the income tax paid by the family. The 1986 Tax Act, however, diminished the tax advantage here in two ways: (1) it reduced income tax rates and hence the advantage to shifting income to low-taxed relatives, and (2) it required that the unearned income of children under 14 years of age be integrated with that of their parents and be taxed at their parent's marginal tax rate (except for a small exclusion).

How should parents, with children under the age of 14, invest their children's funds in a tax-advantageous way, say to save for a college education? One investment choice is non-dividend paying common stock. It can be sold when a child reaches age 14 to exploit the child's lower tax rate at that time. For example, assume that the returns on a capital gains-yielding security that grows in value by 10% per year will be realized in 10 years, when a child is 14 years old. The child's marginal tax rate at that time will be 15% and the parent's marginal tax rate is 30%. The parent can either undertake the investment and make a later gift or make a current gift of the funds to the child, who in turn invests the funds. The following accumulations per $1 of after-tax investment result:

Child Invests: $(1.1)^{10}(1 - .15) + .15 = \$2.355$

Parent Invests: $(1.1)^{10}(1 - .3) + .3 = \$2.116$

The child would be able to accumulate 11.3% more after tax than the parent would be able to accumulate.

An ideal investment for the young child is one that provides deferral of income until the child reaches 14 years of age and does not bear high implicit taxes. Deferred swap contracts, as discussed in Chapter Twenty, might be ideal. Single premium deferred annuities would seem appropriate, but the child would have to incur a 15% excise tax on surrender of the policy unless the funds were withdrawn very slowly (as a life annuity). Although the inside buildup of life insurance policies on a child's life can also be used to accumulate funds, these policies bear implicit taxes if the child does not have any need for life insurance. Still another sensible investment is U.S. Savings Bonds, the interest on which can be deferred until they are cashed, although they do bear some implicit tax in that their yield is somewhat lower than on other securities issued by the U.S. government.

---

[23] We have been told that certain sophisticated traders capitalized on these low-yielding bonds. They borrowed flower bonds from their holders, and shorted them (sold them) in the market, using the proceeds to buy regular bonds. The traders paid a fee to the initial flower bond holders to borrow their bonds, still leaving a sizeable profit due to the yield spread between regular bonds and flower bonds. When the original owner died, the bonds were reacquired by the borrower in the market and returned to the owner to be used to pay estate taxes. This is a nifty tale, because it illustrates how more than one taxpayer could be covered by the same flower bond in the case either died unexpectedly.

Some universities offer deferred tuition contracts to students. The child buys a tuition contract from the university that is used to pay the student's tuition at that university some time in the future, say 10 years. The university, as a tax-exempt entity, earns the before-tax rate of return on the invested funds. In effect, it creates a tax-exempt account for its prospective students. These students must worry, however, that when the time comes, they might prefer attending a different university and that the IRS might require that the income on the tuition contract be taxable currently. A sophisticated university might agree to provide a forward contract for future education in return for a current donation to the university. Students or their parents make a donation to a university that enters into a implicit forward contract agreeing to provide the child with future educational services. This arrangement would fail to pass muster if made explicit. But certain parents do make donations to universities in anticipation of securing a spot for their child. (Such practices would not be observed at such institutions as Stanford University, of course).

Short-Term Trusts as Income Splitters

Prior to the 1986 Tax Acts, the two most common types of trusts that were established were Crummey Trusts and Clifford Trusts. These names arise from the taxpayers who initially received favorable letter rulings after establishing such trusts. They were used to transfer income to children without losing control of the assets in the trust. With a Crown Trust, the grantor often establishes a trust and funds it with a small amount of money. The grantor then makes a large loan to the trust at a low rate of interest. The Crowns, the founders of General Dynamics, established a trust for their children and lent money to the trust at a zero percent interest rate. Prior to the 1984 Tax Act, parents did not have to charge interest to their children on intra-family loans. In fact, the tax court upheld the Crown's trust arrangement. As a result, the Crowns retained control of the assets through the demand loan, and they could transfer enormous sums of income to their children without triggering estate and gift taxes. Now this arrangement produces a taxable gift and taxable income to the transferor.

Clifford Trusts have also been used to shift income to children. The grantor loses control of the assets and the income generated from the assets for the life of the trust, which must be for more than 10 years. On termination of the trust, the assets in the trust are returned to the grantor. With the 1986 Tax Act, the investment income of children under 14 years of age is integrated with that of their parents, regardless of whether the investment assets are held in trust or otherwise. But such arrangements are still effective in reducing taxes for beneficiaries 14 years of age and older.

To value the gift in a Clifford Trust, the grantor must use the applicable federal rate (generally an intermediate term government bond rate), to discount the promised payments. If the grantor contributes $32,549 into a Clifford trust for 10 years, the present value of the income flows to the income beneficiary is $20,000 if the discount rate is 10%, and the discounted value of the remainder is $12,549. The lower the rate of interest that is used to value the remainder interest, relative to current interest rates in the market, the larger is the value of the actual gift that

Chapter 27 Estate and Gift Tax Planning

can be made to a child without triggering gift taxes. (Recall that parents can make tax-free gifts of $20,000 per year to each child.)

These trusts were also used to provide benefits to parents or grandparents during their lifetimes. The trusts were set up by children or grandchildren who had become relatively well off. The 1986 Act taxes most Clifford Trusts as "grantor trusts": income of the trust is taxed directly to the grantor.

Crummey Trusts are also popular among parents who wish to make tax-free gifts (of up to $20,000 per year per donee) to their children while still maintaining control over the assets. To ensure that the transfer of assets into the trust is treated as a current gift to secure the annual $20,000 exemption, rather than as a gift of future interest, which is *not* eligible for the annual exemption, the children are given a period of time (say, 30 days) to withdraw funds from the trust at their discretion. Smart children know that if they exercise their option, against their parents' wishes, they might never see another gift in the future.

Grantor Retained Interest Trusts

Another planning device that is extremely important is the grantor retained interest trust (GRIT). This is a vehicle commonly used to transfer estate assets, including S-corporation stock, family businesses, and homes, to persons other than a spouse. The grantor retains the income from the property but loses working control over the assets, and the grantor's beneficiaries (usually children) receive the remainder interest in the property at the end of a specified period of time (which could coincide with the grantor's death). Prior to 1989, the gift of the remainder interest was deemed to have been made at the date the trust was established. Any appreciation in the value of the assets was *not* included in the grantor's estate. GRITs established after June 21, 1989, however, require that if the grantor dies during the term of the trust, the appreciation in value of the trust assets must be included in the grantor's estate.[24]

Statutory GRITs must invest in a restricted set of assets: cash, marketable securities, and income-producing real estate. Investing in other assets taints the GRIT (such trusts are called "outlaw GRITs"), and appreciation in the value of the assets in such trusts is included in the grantor's estate regardless of whether the grantor survives the term of the trust.[25] Statutory GRITs also impose a minimum annual distribution requirement to the income beneficiary, which limits the amount of assets that can be transferred tax-free to the remainder beneficiary.

Since these are gifts of future enjoyment, they do not qualify for the annual $10,000 exclusion. The discount rate used to value the gift is 120% of the applicable mid-term federal interest rate. Assume a single parent wishes to transfer $1.5 million to her children. If a 10-year qualified GRIT is established when the applicable federal rate is 8% (so 120% of the rate is 9.6%), and $1.5 million is transferred to the GRIT, the present value of the gift is $600,000. This

---

[24] To qualify for a statutory GRIT, the trust's life can no longer exceed 10 years; the grantor (or spouse) can no longer be trustees; and only a person who transferred property to the trust can receive income from it.

[25] More specifically, in an outlaw GRIT, a second gift to the beneficiary is deemed to have been made when the trust terminates. The value of the gift is equal to the amount distributed to the beneficiary, less the value of the initial gift.

27.5 Exploiting Differences in Tax Rates Between Donors and Donees

uses up the full estate and gift tax credit, and a current gift tax is avoided. If the parent survives the life of the trust, the appreciated value of the assets are transferred to the children free of estate and gift tax.

For example, at a 6% per year appreciation factor, the assets in the trust would grow in value to $2.69 million. Since the gift was initially valued at only $.6 million, this means that $2.09 million has been removed from the estate. At an estate tax rate of 55%, this saves $1.15 million in estate tax. On the other hand, the $2.69 million worth of assets have an income tax basis in the hands of the beneficiaries of only $600,000, so there is a deferred capital gain of $2.09 million which could have been avoided if the assets were transferred by bequest rather than by gift through the GRIT. If the effective capital gains tax rate is, say, 20% (given opportunities to defer further the payment of the capital gains tax), this reduces the tax savings by $.418 million, which is a bit more than one-third of the estate tax savings.

Note further that these benefits are only achieved if the grantor outlives the life of the qualified GRIT. A compensating benefit, however, is that on the grantor's premature death, the basis in the assets in the trust would be stepped up, income tax free, to fair market value as long as the GRIT provides that the assets revert to the grantor upon an early death. Moreover, such a provision reduces the actuarial value of the gift, and, therefore the gift tax. Actuarial tables provided by the IRS show that a 65 year old, for example, has a life expectancy of 16 years, and a .737 probability of surviving 10 years. For such a grantor, the gift would be valued at only 74% of the present value of a *certain* transfer.

The longer the life of the GRIT, the larger the amount of assets that can be transferred. Grantors can establish a series of GRITs, say one for four years, another for eight years, etc., to hedge against the possibility of early death.

27.6 Estate Taxation of Foreigners

One area that is particularly nettling is the estate taxation of the property of foreigners who may or may not be residents for tax purposes. For example, Canadians who own property in the U.S. are subject to U.S. estate taxes. With the 1988 Tax Act, a favorable tax rate schedule applying to foreigners was removed, and foreigners began to pay estate taxes at the same rates as U.S. persons. What is worse, foreigners only receive a credit for the tax on the first $60,000 of U.S. estate assets: they are not eligible for the $600,000 unified credit. And unless a surviving spouse is a U.S. citizen (regardless of whether they are a tax resident in the U.S.), the marital deduction is not available. This provision was put into the 1988 Tax Act to prevent non-U.S. citizen surviving spouses from receiving the estate assets free of tax under the spousal deduction, and then leaving the country, thereby escaping any U.S. estate taxation on their death. Because of the outcry over this provision, the 1990 Tax Act allows these non-U.S. citizens to establish a so-called "Qualifying Domestic Trust" (QDT). The estate tax is deferred if the assets that would be transferred to the surviving spouse are transferred to the QDT. A U.S. trustee is necessary to administer the trust assets, and the estate tax is due on the death of the beneficiary.

Although Canadian taxpayers pay no death taxes in Canada, 75% of the unrealized appreciation in most assets (other than a personal residence) is taxed at income tax rates at death or, if the assets are given away prior to death, at the time of the gift.[26] Canadians can establish spousal trusts to defer paying these taxes until the death of the surviving spouse. Canadians, with property in the U.S., face two levels of taxation: a U.S. estate tax and a Canadian income tax. The U.S. does recognize the Canadian income tax due on the transfer of U.S. property as a debt of the U.S. estate. The combination of these two taxes could lead to extremely high marginal tax rates for Canadians owning U.S. property with a low basis (a 35% income tax, followed by a 55% estate tax on the remaining value of the assets).

As a result of these taxes, many Canadian investors hold U.S. property in corporations incorporated outside of the U.S. For example, Olympia and York, a non-U.S. corporation owned by the Reichman family of Canada, is a big investor in U.S. real estate. Shares of non-U.S. corporations are not property that is considered to be in the U.S. for estate tax purposes. But holding real estate in corporate, rather than partnership, form can increase the income tax in Canada considerably on cash flows and on the sale of the assets. Also, the transfer of U.S. property to a non-U.S. corporation might trigger income tax.

U.S. citizens who reside in Canada and who hold Canadian assets are subject to the same Canadian income tax rules on their death as Canadians: there is a deemed sale at death. They can exclude shares in publicly traded companies if less than 25% owned. U.S. residents who hold Canadian assets are exempt from Canadian deemed sale rules under the U.S.-Canadian treaty on all assets other than real property such as vacation homes. Although U.S. persons receive an estate tax credit for estate taxes paid to foreign governments, they cannot use the Canadian deemed sale income taxes as a credit against U.S. estate taxes. U.S. taxpayers can avoid the Canadian tax on appreciated Canadian real property by holding it in a non-Canadian corporation. If the property is transferred after it has appreciated, however, it would result in a deemed sale for Canadian tax purposes.

We have discussed Canada in some detail because of the unique relation of the U.S. and Canada. Canadians and Americans are the largest holders of each other's assets.

Summary of Key Points

1. There is sometimes conflict between income tax planning and estate and gift tax planning. Most estate plans have important income tax consequences as well. There are also substantial conflicts between the tax and the nontax aspects of estate and gift tax planning.

---

[26] The U.S. allows non-resident taxpayers to make gifts of intangible property (such as shares of stock) to others free of the gift tax, and allows tax-free intraspousal transfers of $100,000 annually on any other property. Such transfers, however, could trigger additional Canadian income taxes.

2. The marginal estate and gift tax in the U.S can be quite high, reaching 55% on estates over $3 million. Gift and estate taxes are integrated in the U.S. The value of all gifts are added back to the estate at death, and any gift taxes paid are credited against the estate tax. Estates are allowed unlimited charitable and spousal deductions from the taxable estate, thereby encouraging these types of transfers.

3. Making charitable gifts during one's lifetime has two important tax advantages: (1) unlike bequests, gifts to charity over one's lifetime provide income tax deductions; and (2) the earnings on the assets given to the charity are tax exempt.

4. Donating appreciated securities to charity exempts the appreciation from ordinary income taxation. The alternative minimum tax, however, could result in some income tax being imposed.

5. A charitable remainder trust is particularly tax advantageous for a grantor who owns an asset that has appreciated substantially in value. No capital gains tax is paid when the asset is transferred to the trust, and the grantor earns income for the life of the trust. Moreover, the grantor receives a current deduction for the value of the remainder interest in the asset that will be transferred to a charitable beneficiary at a future date. Establishing a charitable *lead* trust results in a charitable gift of the *income* generated by the trust assets and a return of the remaining value of the trust assets to the grantor at the end of a specified period.

6. The alternative minimum tax (AMT) is a tax that is paid if it is higher than the regular tax. In the U.S., the AMT rate for individuals is 24%, and the alternative minimum taxable income is found by adding to regular taxable income such tax preference items as the untaxed appreciation in securities donated to charity and state and local taxes paid.

7. Charitable donations of appreciated securities are less valuable to a donor in an AMT tax position. While a taxpayer in a regular tax position receives a tax benefit equal to the marginal ordinary income tax rate times the value of the gift, a taxpayer in an AMT position receives a tax benefit equal to the AMT tax rate times the *basis* in the security.

8. Giving away assets during one's lifetime freezes an estate. Under U.S. tax laws, gifts can be made tax-free in the amount of $10,000 per donee, per year, and an additional $600,000 in gifts can be made tax-free over each donor's lifetime. Each dollar of exemption used removes more than a dollar, tax free, from the estate: it also removes the income that can be earned on these assets from the estate.

9. By gifting early, the family achieves an estate tax deduction (plus interest) for the gift tax paid at the time the gift was made. A nontax cost of early giving, however, is the donor's loss of control over the assets.

10. It might pay to bequeath rather than make a current gift of capital assets that have appreciated in value. On death, the beneficiary receives the assets with an income-tax-free step up in basis to fair market value. If received as a gift, on the other hand, the beneficiary retains the original basis of the donor. Gifting early removes the assets from the estate and

reduces the estate tax. The greater the basis in the assets and the more liberal the dividend policy (and therefore the lower is the future appreciation), the more likely it is that gifting the asset dominates bequeathing the asset.

11. Gifting assets such as a family business to children might give rise to significant nontax costs. The children might squander the assets or run the business less efficiently than the parents.

12. Preferred stock recapitalizations are but one example of the myriad devices that have been used over the years to freeze an estate. Preferred stock is received by the "donors" in exchange for common stock, and a small amount of common stock is given to donees. The preferred stock receives dividends (if actually paid) and a promised final redemption value that is typically approximately equal to the current value of the firm. The basis in the preferred stock is the same as the basis in the common stock that was exchanged. All future appreciation in the stock inures to the donors' decedents. Moreover, the donors achieve a step up in the basis of the preferred stock holdings on death and retain voting control of the business during their lifetimes.

13. With the 1987 Tax Act, the advantages of using this form of recapitalization was severely limited: not only was the market value of the equity that was given to the children subjected to the gift tax but also all of the appreciation of the business subsequent to the date of the gift must be included in the estate. The 1990 Tax Act reinstated the benefits, but requires that substantial dividends actually be paid on the preferred stock, or if not, added to the value of the preferred stock for estate tax purposes.

14. There are many ways to reduce estate taxes for family-run businesses. For example, buy-sell agreements at favorable prices provide partners with valuable options that are not taxed as gifts. In addition, special compensation arrangements and transfer pricing strategies are often employed to mitigate the tax. It is also difficult for the taxing authority to tax transfers of wealth in the form of valuable investment advice.

15. The Generation Skipping Transfer Tax was put into place to mitigate the effect of taxpayers making gifts to successive generations and avoiding at least one level of estate taxation. Generation-skipping gifts allow taxpayers to freeze not only their own estates, but also those of their children. Although such gifts attract a generation-skipping tax at a steep tax rate, such gifts are still quite tax-advantaged for wealthy families.

16. The marital deduction allows taxpayers to bequeath their entire estate to surviving spouses free of the gift and estate tax. With progressive estate tax rates, and the goal to pass wealth on to successive generations, paying more estate tax on the death of the first spouse and less on the death of the second spouse is often tax efficient. With uncertainties as to life expectancies and future demands on resources, however, this is a difficult planning exercise.

17. Family tax planning opportunities were reduced with the 1986 Tax Act, because income tax rates were lowered and new rules required the income of children under 14 years of age be taxed at their parents' marginal rates.

18. Trusts have been used to transfer larger amounts to successive generations than outright gifts. The grantor can control the assets in trusts more easily than the assets in an outright gift, and because of discounting rules, the valuation placed on gifts in trust can be lower than for outright gifts.

19. The Grantor Retained Interest Trust has become a popular vehicle to transfer large amounts of property to children and to reduce estate and gift taxes. The parent retains the income from the trust and transfers the property after a specified period of time, not to exceed 10 years, to the children. The longer the deferral period, the lower is the present value of the gift, and the lower the gift tax. This vehicle freezes the assets in the estate to the extent the value of the assets in the trust grow over time.

20. Foreigners are also subject to U.S. taxation on assets held in the U.S. They face the same marginal tax rates as U.S. persons, but they enjoy a smaller exemption ($60,000 versus $600,000). Citizens of some countries, like Canada, face double taxation, because the U.S. estate tax is not creditable against their home country's taxes. Canada has no estate tax, but has deemed sales rules: all assets (other than personal homes) are deemed to be sold at death, and income tax is paid on the deemed gain. The tax on the gain can be deferred, however, until the death of a surviving spouse.

21. The marital deduction is unavailable for surviving spouses who are not citizens of the U.S. Surviving spouses are eligible for deferral of the U.S. estate tax, however, if they establish a Qualifying Domestic Trust, with at least one U.S. citizen as trustee. This assures that on the death of the non-citizen spouse, the U.S. taxing authority can collect its share of U.S. estate tax.

Discussion Questions

1. Under what circumstances is it more tax advantageous to give to charity during your lifetime rather than on bequest? What are the nontax factors that might influence your decision?

2. What is a philanthropic fund? What are the tax and nontax costs and benefits of establishing such a fund?

3. What is the alternative minimum tax (AMT)? How does it affect the value of giving appreciated securities to charity?

4. How should parents invest the assets of their young children? What effect does implicit taxes have on the decision?

5. What are the advantages of gifting rather than bequeathing assets? What are the nontax costs of doing so?

6. If the basis in an asset is low relative to its current market value, bequeathing the asset might be more efficient than giving it as a gift. Why might this be so? Under what conditions will the gift route be preferred?

7. What nontax factors come into play when a parent considers gifting the family business to children? What alternative routes have parents taken to reduce the import of these nontax factors? What tax and nontax costs are associated with these devices?

8. Why might a parent want to use a preferred stock recapitalization to freeze the value of the family business for estate tax purposes? What are the tax costs of using such a structure? Why has Congress changed the rules that apply to such transactions?

9. Describe some ways in which taxpayers can reduce estate and gift taxes. What are the tax and nontax costs of these strategies?

10. While estate tax rates are very high, very little estate taxes seems to be collected. Why do you think that this is the case? Because of the various tightenings of the estate tax rules in recent years, do you think that tax collections from gift and estate taxes will increase in the future?

11. Apart from the $600,000 exclusion, should tax planners recommend that all estate assets be transferred to the surviving spouse, if the goal is to transfer resources to successive generations? What nontax issues arise in the planning problem?

12. When and why is it tax advantageous to give generation skipping gifts, even in light of the generation skipping tax?

13. What is a Clifford Trust? What advantages does this trust have over an outright gift to a child or a parent?

14. If a taxpayer has appreciated property to donate to charity, how can the use of a charitable remainder trust be more efficient than an outright gift? Consider gift and estate tax, income tax, and alternative minimum tax consequences.

Problems

1. A risk neutral taxpayer has $2 million of assets that will not be consumed during his lifetime. He invests only in fully taxable bonds that yield an annual return of 10% before tax. He is a widower, and he plans to leave his entire estate to his two children. His life expectancy is 10 years. His income tax rate is 30%, as are his children's. Suppose the *marginal* estate tax rate schedule is as follows:

$0 - $0.5 million	0%
$0.5 - $1 million	25%
$1 million - $2 million	40%
above $2 million	50%

a. What is the present value of (1) giving his children the $2 million now versus (2) giving the children half a million dollars now and the rest on death versus (3) waiting until death to distribute all of his assets? Why do the present values differ among the alternatives?

b. How would your answers in (a) change if the life expectancy of the donor was 20 years?

c. How do your answers to (a) change if the breakpoints in the estate tax schedule (that is, $0.5 million, $1.0 million, and $2.0 million) were increased each year by the after-tax rate of interest?

d. How would your answers to (a) change if the marginal income tax rates of the children were 40% (as compared to the 30% marginal income tax rate of the parent)? Why? What if the children's tax rates were 20%?

2. a. Suppose a taxpayer sets aside $5,000 at the beginning of each year for 25 years and invests the funds in bonds yielding 10% per year. The taxpayer's income tax rate is 40%, and the marginal estate tax rate, given other gifts already made and other estate assets, is 50%. How much would remain in the account, after all taxes, if the taxpayer died at the end of 25 years?

b. Suppose, instead, the taxpayer made a tax-free gift of $5,000 each year, and the donee invested the funds in bonds yielding 10% per year before tax and faced an income tax rate of 40%. How much would the beneficiary have accumulated upon the donor's death in 25 years? What nontax differences are there between this strategy and the one described in part (a)?

c. Suppose, as an alternative, our taxpayer sets aside $5,000 each year in a life insurance trust. The trust earns a tax-free return of 10% per year, and by giving up the right to change beneficiaries and all other incidents of ownership, the taxpayer avoids all estate taxes on the insurance proceeds as well. How much can be transferred to beneficiaries on the taxpayer's death in 25 years? What nontax differences are there between this strategy and the ones described in parts (a) and (b)?

d. How would your answers to (a) and (b) change if the funds were invested in single premium deferred annuities that earned a before-tax return of 9.5%?

e. How would your answer to (c) change if the life insurance trust generated a return of only 7% per year?

f. Ignoring nontax factors, and restricting attention to bonds, single premium deferred annuities, and life insurance policies, are there other strategies available that beat any of those described in parts (a) through (e)? How would the optimal tax planning strategy change if income tax rates of the donee/beneficiary were reduced to 35%? to 25%?

Index

Symbols

M

N

O

P

Y

Z

Table 3.1, which will be useful to you throughout the book, is reproduced here for your convenience.

Table 3.1 Six Different Legal Organizational Forms Through Which Investors Can Hold Riskless Bonds

Savings Vehicle (Example)	Is the Investment Tax Deductible?	Frequency that Earnings are Taxed	Rate at which Earnings are Taxed	After-tax Accumulation Per After-Tax Dollar Invested
I (Money market fund)	No	Annually	Ordinary	$[1 + R(1-t)]^n$
II (Single premium deferred annuity)	No	Deferred	Ordinary	$(1 + R)^n(1-t) + t$
III (Mutual fund)	No	Annually	Capital Gains	$[1 + R(1-gt)]^n$
IV (Foreign corporation)	No	Deferred	Capital Gains	$(1 + R)^n(1-gt) + gt$
V (Insurance policy)	No	Never	Exempt	$(1 + R)^n$
VI (Pension)	Yes	Deferred	Ordinary	$\dfrac{1}{1-t}(1 + R)^n(1-t)$ or $(1 + R)^n$

where:
R = before-tax rate of return
n = number of time periods
t = ordinary tax rate
g = percentage of capital gain taxed as ordinary income when the capital gain becomes taxable